Exploring
Judicial Politics

EXPLORING JUDICIAL POLITICS

Mark C. Miller

Clark University

New York   Oxford
OXFORD UNIVERSITY PRESS
2009

Oxford University Press, Inc., publishes works that further Oxford University's
objective of excellence in research, scholarship, and education.

Oxford New York
Auckland Cape Town Dar es Salaam Hong Kong Karachi
Kuala Lumpur Madrid Melbourne Mexico City Nairobi
New Delhi Shanghai Taipei Toronto

With offices in
Argentina Austria Brazil Chile Czech Republic France Greece
Guatemala Hungary Italy Japan Poland Portugal Singapore
South Korea Switzerland Thailand Turkey Ukraine Vietnam

Published by Oxford University Press, Inc.
198 Madison Avenue, New York, New York 10016
http://www.oup.com

Oxford is a registered trademark of Oxford University Press

Library of Congress Cataloging-in-Publication Data

Miller, Mark C. (Mark Carlton), 1958–
Exploring judicial politics / Mark Miller.
    p. cm.
Includes bibliographical references and index.
ISBN 978-0-19-534307-6
1. Judicial process—United States.   2. Judicial power—United States.
3. Political questions and judicial power—United States.   4. Courts—
United States.   5. Courts of last resort—United States.   6. Appellate Courts—
United States.   7. Justice, Administration of—United States.   8. Law—Political
aspects—United States.   I. Title.
  KF8775.M55 2009
  347.73'1—dc22   2008002471

Printing number: 9 8 7 6 5 4 3 2 1

Printed in the United States of America
on acid-free paper.

CONTENTS

TABLES AND FIGURES

Tables

Figures

ACKNOWLEDGMENTS

This project has an interesting history. I was first approached by a publisher several years ago who wanted to publish new and stimulating books in the field of judicial politics. I suggested an edited volume of original essays on the subject. He agreed, and I went about the task of finding chapter authors on a variety of topics in the field. Through various twists and turns, including the sale of the original publishing house to Oxford University Press, this volume has finally come to fruition.

There are many individuals and groups who have provided help and assistance along the way. I would first like to thank Jennifer Carpenter at Oxford University Press for shepherding this project to its completion. I certainly appreciate all her efforts.

I would also like to thank various individuals at Clark University in Worcester, Massachusetts for their assistance. Cynthia Fenner, the assistant in the Department of Government at Clark, was always helpful in every possible way. Two Clark students (we call our students Clarkies), Bethany Williard and Brian Burns, provided a great deal of assistance in finding bibliographic details and other information for me. All of the professional staff at the Goddard Library at Clark have also been quite willing to help me track down crucial sources and other information. I called upon their expertise quite often. My colleagues in the Law & Society Program and in the Government Department provided encouragement at various times in the process. A variety of Clarkies and other former students helped me gain interviews with key individuals in Washington, D.C. and elsewhere for my sabbatical research project, on which my own individual chapter in this volume is partly based. Thank you for sharing those connections and contacts with me.

Much of the final work on this project was completed while I was a Visiting Scholar at the Centennial Center for Political Science and Public Policy in Washington, D.C., affiliated with the American Political Science Association. The APSA's Centennial Center provided me with a home base in Washington for my sabbatical, giving me much needed office space and computer access in a prime location in the Nation's Capital. The staff at the APSA were always friendly and encouraging, making my stay most pleasant and productive. I would like especially to thank the other Visiting Scholars whom I met during the 2006–2007 year at the Centennial Center. Some were there for a short period, while others were there for the entire academic year. Although all of them were quite busy with their own projects, they always took the time to listen to my stories about getting this volume completed. I feel very lucky to have met them.

Finally, I must thank all the chapter authors for all their hard work during this process. All of them were quite professional in their approach to this project, as well as being quite patient. I certainly do appreciate all of their efforts, and I expect that the readers will gain a great deal from their insights.

Mark C. Miller
Washington, D.C.
June 2007

CONTRIBUTORS

JUDITH A. BAER is a professor of political science at Texas A&M University. Among her many works are *The Chains of Protection: The Judicial Response to Women's Labor Legislation*; *Women in American Law: The Struggle Toward Equality from the New Deal to the Present*; and she is the coauthor of *The Constitutional and Legal Rights of Women: Cases in Law and Social Change*. Her book, *Our Lives Before the Law: Constructing a Feminist Jurisprudence* won the American Political Science Association's Victoria Schuck Award for the best book on women and politics published in 1999.

JEB BARNES is an assistant professor and Director of Graduate Studies in the political science department at the University of Southern California. He is the author of *Overruled: Legislative Overrides, Pluralism, and Contemporary Court-Congress Relations* as well as the coeditor of *Making Policy, Making Law: An Interbranch Perspective*. In 2004–2005, he was a Robert Wood Johnson Health Policy Scholar at UC-Berkeley's School of Public Health.

LAUREN COHEN BELL is associate professor of political science at Randolph-Macon College, in Ashland, Virginia. She is the author of *Warring Factions: Interest Groups, Money, and the New Politics of Senate Confirmation* and *The U.S. Congress: A Simulation for Students* as well as single- and coauthored articles in *The Journal of Politics, Political Research Quarterly,* the *Journal of Legislative Studies*, and *Judicature*. During the 2006–2007 academic year, she was the Supreme Court Judicial Fellow at the U.S. Sentencing Commission. Previously, she has served as a Congressional Fellow with the Senate Judiciary Committee.

ROBERT G. BOATRIGHT is an assistant professor of government at Clark University. His PhD is from the University of Chicago. He is the author of *Expressive Politics: The Issue Strategies of Congressional Challengers* and *Improving Citizen Response to Jury Summonses*. Previously, he has worked for the Campaign Finance Institute and for the American Judicature Society. He has also served as a Congressional Fellow.

RICHARD A. BRISBIN, JR., is an associate professor of political science at West Virginia University. He is the author of *A Strike Like No Other Strike: Law and Resistance During the Pittston Coal Strike of 1989–1990* and *Justice Antonin Scalia and the Conservative Revival*. West Virginia University has named him as a Benedum Distinguished Scholar, its highest research award.

MICHAEL COMISKEY is associate professor of political science at the Penn State Fayette Campus and the author of *Seeking Justices: The Judging of Supreme Court Nominees*. He earned his PhD from Princeton University.

LOUIS FISHER is a specialist in constitutional law at the law library of the Library of Congress. He worked for the Congressional Research Service as a specialist in separation of powers from 1970–2005. Among his many books are *Constitutional Dialogues: Interpretation as Political Process*; *American Constitutional Law; Religious Liberty in America: Political Safeguards*; *Presidential War Powers*; *Military Tribunals and Presidential Power*; and his latest book, *In the Name of National Security: Unchecked Presidential Power and the Reynolds Case*. The views expressed by Louis Fisher in this volume are personal and do not reflect the views of the Library of Congress.

LAURA LANGER is an associate professor and Director of Graduate Studies in the Department of Political Science at the University of Arizona. She received her PhD from Florida State University. She is the author of *Judicial Review in State Supreme Courts: A Comparative Study* and has published articles in peer-reviewed journals, including *American Journal of Political Science* and *Journal of Politics*. Her current research projects evaluate the relationships among justices on state courts of last resort, legislators, and governors and were funded by a National Science Foundation Career Development Grant.

CHRISTINE LUDOWISE is an assistant professor of political science and the Director of the Justice Studies Program at Georgia Southern University. She received her PhD from the University of Tennessee, Knoxville. Her research includes the public agency accountability, criminal justice and juvenile justice administration, and constitutional and public law. She has published articles in *Administrative Change* and the *Journal of Health and Human Services Administration*. She is the author of several reports to community and state organizations as well as a coauthor for textbook chapters in corrections and on the courts. She was awarded the College of Liberal Arts and Social Sciences Award for Excellence in 2002 and was nominated for the Georgia Board of Regents excellence in instruction award in 2006.

BRYAN W. MARSHALL is assistant professor of political science at Miami University of Ohio. He received his PhD while a fellow with the Political Institutions and Public Choice (PIPC) program at Michigan State University. His areas of specialization include Congress, congressional-executive relations, and quantitative methods. Professor Marshall is the author of *Rules for War* and has published articles in *American Politics Research, American Review of Politics, Political Research Quarterly, Legislative Studies Quarterly*, and *Social Science Quarterly*.

WENDY L. MARTINEK is an associate professor of political science at Binghamton University (SUNY). She earned her PhD from Michigan State University. She is the coauthor of *Judging on a Collegial Court: Influences on Federal Appellate Decision Making*.

LYNN MATHER is a professor of law and political science, University at Buffalo Law School, the State University of New York. She is the coauthor of *Divorce Lawyers at Work: Varieties of Professionalism in Practice*, which received the C. Herman Pritchett Award from the American Political Science Association for the best book in the field of law and courts. When she was the Nelson A. Rockefeller Professor of Government at Dartmouth College, she was awarded the Distinguished Teaching Award.

NANCY MAVEETY is professor and former chair of political science at Tulane University. She received her PhD from The Johns Hopkins University. She is the author of *Representation Rights and the Burger Years* and *Justice Sandra Day O'Connor: Strategist on the Supreme*

Court, and the editor of *Pioneers of Judicial Behavior*. She was a Fellow of the Program in Law and Public Affairs at Princeton's Woodrow Wilson School during the fall of 2005. In 2001 she was a Fulbright lecturer at Tartu University in Estonia, and in 2007–2008 was a Fulbright lecturer at Shandong University in Jinan, China.

AMAN L. McLEOD is an assistant professor of political science and law at Rutgers University-Camden. He received his PhD from the University of Michigan, where he also earned his law degree. He is the author of the article "If at First You Don't Succeed: A Critical Evaluation of Judicial Selection Reform Efforts," published in the *West Virginia University Law Review*. He has also published articles in such journals as the *Fordham Urban Law Journal*.

MARK C. MILLER is associate professor and former chair of the Department of Government and International Relations at Clark University. He is also the Director of the Law and Society Program there. He received his PhD from the Ohio State University and his law degree from George Washington University. He served as the Supreme Court Judicial Fellow at the Supreme Court of the United States from 1999–2000, and he was a Congressional Fellow in the Office of U.S. Senator Paul Wellstone in 1995. He is author of *The High Priests of American Politics: The Role of Lawyers in American Political Institutions* and the coeditor of *Making Policy, Making Law: An Interbranch Perspective*. He has been named Teacher of the Year and Advisor of the Year at Clark University. During 2006–2007, he was a Visiting Scholar at the Centennial Center for Public Policy of the American Political Science Association. During the spring of 2008, he was the Thomas Jefferson Distinguished Chair, a Fulbright scholar to Leiden University in the Netherlands.

BRIAN J. OSTROM is a Principal Court Research Consultant at the National Center for State Courts in Williamsburg, Virginia. He is coauthor of *Trial Courts as Organizations*.

RICHARD L. PACELLE, JR., is professor and chair of the Department of Political Science at Georgia Southern University. He received his PhD from the Ohio State University. He is the author of a number of articles and chapters, as well as three books: *The Transformation of the Supreme Court's Agenda: From the New Deal to the Reagan Administration*, *The Supreme Court in American Politics: The Least Dangerous Branch of Government?* (winner of 2002 Choice Outstanding Titles Award), and *Between Law and Politics: The Solicitor General and the Structuring of Race, Gender and Reproductive Rights Policy*. Professor Pacelle is the recipient of the 2000 Chancellor's Award for Excellence in Teaching, the 2000–2001 Governor's Award for Excellence in Teaching, and the 2006–2007 CLASS Award for Distinction in Scholarship.

BARBARA A. PERRY is the Carter Glass Professor of Government and Executive Director of the Center for Civic Renewal at Sweet Briar College in Virginia. She is the author of many books, including *The Michigan Affirmative Action Cases*; *The Priestly Tribe: The Supreme Court's Image in the American Mind*; *Jacqueline Kennedy: First Lady of the New Frontier*; *Freedom and the Court: Civil Rights and Liberties in the United States* (with Henry J. Abraham); and *A "Representative" Supreme Court? The Impact of Race, Religion, and Gender on Appointments*.

SHAUNA M. STRICKLAND is a Court Research Analyst at the National Center for State Courts in Williamsburg, Virginia. She contributes to the annual publications *Examining the Work of State Courts* and *State Court Caseload Statistics*. She also coauthored "Examining

Trial Trends in State Courts: 1975–2002" and authored "Beyond the Vanishing Trial: A Look at the Composition of State Court Dispositions."

PETER N. UBERTACCIO III is the Director of the Joseph Martin Institute for Law and Society and an associate professor of political science at Stonehill College in Massachusetts. He is the author of *Learned in the Law and Politics: The Office of the Solicitor General*. He received his PhD from Brandeis University.

ARTEMUS WARD is assistant professor of political science at Northern Illinois University. He received his PhD from the Maxwell School at Syracuse University and was awarded the Hughes-Gossett Prize by the Supreme Court Historical Society for an article published in the Journal of Supreme Court History. During the 108th Congress, he served as a Congressional fellow on the House Judiciary Committee and in the summer of 2004 was a Visiting Scholar at the Centennial Center for Political Science & Public Affairs of the American Political Science Association. He is the author of *Deciding to Leave: The Politics of Retirement from the United States Supreme Court* and coauthor of *Sorcerers' Apprentices: Law Clerks at the United States Supreme Court*.

NICOLE L. WATERS is a Senior Court Research Associate in the Research Division at the National Center for State Courts in Williamsburg, Virginia. She authored numerous articles evaluating issues of civil justice at both the trial court and appellate court levels including "Standing Guard at the Jury's Gate: Daubert's Impact on the State Courts," "Efficient and Successful ADR in Appellate Courts: What Matters Most?" and "What's Half a Lung Worth? Civil Jurors' Accounts of Their Award Decision-Making." She is the recipient of a grant, 2005 Civil Justice Survey of State Courts, which compiles data on civil trials in 160 courts across the nation. She earned her PhD from the University of Delaware.

TEENA WILHELM is an assistant professor of political science at the University of Georgia. She received her PhD from the University of Arizona. Her teaching and research interests include political institutions, judicial politics and process, and state politics. Her research focuses on the policy-making consequences of inter-branch relations, as well as the interactions between state supreme courts and the U.S. Supreme Court. She has published in *Judicature* and *Legislative Studies Quarterly*.

EXPLORING
JUDICIAL POLITICS

1

INTRODUCTION

The Study of Judicial Politics

Mark C. Miller

Why study courts in the United States? And why study them from a political point of view? Courts are clearly part of the American system of government, but they are quite different from the other governmental institutions. Courts in the United States settle disputes, punish criminals, interpret various sources of law including the U.S. Constitution, protect the rights of political minorities, and make public policy. Judges in the United States are chosen through political selection processes, yet they make decisions based on concepts such as impartiality, precedent, and adherence to the rule of law. Thus courts are both legal institutions and political institutions at the same time in the United States. Political scientists who study the judiciary tend to emphasize the fact that the courts lie at the intersection of law and politics, and they use a variety of methods to try to get a better understanding of how these institutions function in both the legal and political worlds.

The study of judicial politics involves many different questions and many different issues. Clearly there are currently many law-related courses in the undergraduate curriculum (see, e.g., Sarat 2004). Those courses labeled as judicial politics, judicial process, judicial behavior or other courses on the courts generally involve studying the courts from a political science point of view. Even though I teach in a department of government, I am clearly a political scientist in my training and my socialization. I am also trained and socialized as a lawyer, but unlike

many law professors I tend to study the law from the view of politics. Almost all of the chapter authors in this book are political scientists, although some of them are law professors and lawyers as well. They all share a notion that the study of law and courts involves understanding the political aspects of these institutions.

LAW AND POLITICS

One of the core themes of this book is the study of the intersection of law and politics. For some, thinking of law and politics in the same sentence is difficult; especially those who are more familiar with the Continental European approach to law and courts (see, e.g., Jacob et al. 1996; Russell and O'Brien 2001). Even the British courts are seen as nonpolitical in many academic circles (see, e.g., Kritzer 1996). However, political scientists who study the courts and law in the United States will readily admit that our system has always merged and intertwined these two concepts. The authors in this book all feel that students need to understand how law and politics interact in the courts to gain an appreciation of how the courts actually function in our society. We want our students to be better consumers of political information about the law and the courts. For political scientists, it is the political aspects of the law and courts that excite us and our students.

From a legal perspective, the law has its own rules of logic and language. Law schools teach students to "think like lawyers" because "thinking like a lawyer" is the only way to understand the law in this country (see Vandevelde 1996). Even nonlawyers who serve in our legislative bodies must eventually learn to "think like lawyers" to understand an institutional culture and discourse that is dominated by lawyerly thinking, lawyerly language, and a lawyerly approach to decision making (see Miller 1995). Judges and lawyers share a common analytical approach to problem solving and a common vocabulary. For many law students, learning to "think like a lawyer" feels like learning a new language plus learning a new logical approach to problem solving. Courts are where lawyers and judges "produce justice" in accordance with legal rules and legal norms. The law treats all equally, at least in theory. In some ways, the legal perspective is quite different from the political perspective.

Politics, however, is generally the study of the distribution of power in society. It is also, "The process by which policy decisions are made" (O'Connor and Sabato 2006, 4). Politics involves notions of governmental institutions, political parties, interest groups, voters, the media, and political ideologies all struggling for power in the United States' highly pluralistic policy-making process. A classic definition of politics, and of political science, is the study of "who gets what, when, where, and how." Real world politics are often rough and tumble, far from the orderliness and formalism that Tocqueville said was the province of lawyers and judges in the United States (Tocqueville 1969, 266).

So where do the courts fit into this scheme? The courts are the critical third branch of both our federal government in the United States and of our state governments. Thus the courts are both legal and political institutions. As Donald Kommers noted, "From the nation's founding until today, courts have been a mainstay of American democracy. They settle legal conflicts between private parties, protect the legal rights of citizens generally, and supervise the administration of ordinary law. . . . [However], a threshold question needs to be addressed: What is democracy and where do the courts fit into the structure of government in an age of democracy?" (Kommers 2005,

200–201). Lawrence Baum partially answered this question when he wrote, "Courts in the United States have much in common with the other branches of government. Yet in some respects they are distinctive institutions: they differ from the legislative and executive branches in what they do and how they do it, and they are partially detached from the mainstream of government and politics. Because they are distinctive, courts and their judges carry out a special function in American democracy, operating as a counterbalance to the other branches and thereby changing the political system" (Baum 2005, 517).

Law and politics have long been intertwined in the American system of government. In the 1830s, the French philosopher Tocqueville visited the United States and wrote about the American government and court system. His famous book, *Democracy in America,* was the product of his visits to the United States and his keen ability to compare government and politics in the United States with those in Europe at the time. For our purposes, his most famous pronouncement was that in the United States every political question eventually becomes a legal one and vice versa. He also observed that lawyers were the natural political class in the United States. Tocqueville's view of the interactions of law and politics in the United States came early in our history, before the courts evolved into the powerful political decision-makers that they can often be today.

One of the most important political powers that the courts have in the United States is the power of judicial review, that is, the power to declare the actions of other governmental actors such as Congress, the President, or the states to be unconstitutional. Thus, judges in the United States can be powerful political as well as legal actors, especially when they exercise their power of judicial review. As Tocqueville also wrote, "The judicial organization of the United States is the hardest thing there for a foreigner to understand. . . . The Americans have given their judges the right to base their decisions on the *Constitution* rather than on the *laws.* In other words, they allow them not to apply laws which they consider unconstitutional. . . . In practice few laws can long escape the searching analysis of the judges, for there are very few that do not injure some private interest and which advocates cannot or should not question before the courts. . . . So then, the Americans have given their courts immense political power" (Tocqueville 1969, 99–102). The courts took for themselves this amazing power of judicial review in the famous case, *Marbury v. Madison* (1803). Tocqueville concluded his discussion of judicial review by declaring, "Restricted within its limits, the power granted to American courts to pronounce on the constitutionality of laws is yet one of the most powerful barriers ever erected against the tyranny of political assemblies" (Tocqueville 1969, 103–104).

For many reasons, but with their use of the power of judicial review clearly at the top of the list, American courts are probably the most powerful and the most activist in the world (see, e.g., Shapiro 1995, 44). As Doris Marie Provine argued, "The United States stands out from the rest of the world in its reliance on lawyers, courts, and litigation" (Provine 2005, 313). Herbert Jacob was one of the first political scientists to think about comparing courts in the United States with courts around the world. He described the connection between law and politics in the United States in this way, "Law and courts in the United States have direct and powerful links to the political arena. The habit of bringing social conflict into the legal arena is deeply embedded in American political culture. Law's roots extend into the political arena, where political coalitions in legislative bodies and partisan adherents in the executive branch formulate much of the law that governs the United States" (Jacob 1996, 16). Today, there are still many debates about the political role of the courts in our society and if the courts go too far in their policy-making powers. Students of the courts tend to spend a great deal of time trying to sort out how law and politics intersect and intertwine in our society.

HOW DO POLITICAL SCIENTISTS STUDY THE COURTS?

Most of the authors in this book are political scientists, and more specifically scholars of judicial politics. Thus this volume examines the courts and judicial politics from a distinct disciplinary point of view. The discipline of political science is quite diverse,

encompassing many different types of scholars who ask very different questions and use many different methodologies to help find answers to these questions. To understand the courts, students must also have some understanding of how judicial scholars approach the research puzzle. To understand something, it is important to understand how scholars go about studying that thing. Because different scholars ask different research questions, they will often get different answers. These approaches or methods are important for students to understand because students need the tools to help make sense of the current political debates surrounding the courts and judges in our society. Politicians, interest group representatives, and even judges talk a lot about the role of courts in our world. To evaluate these political messages, students need to understand what scholars already know about the courts and what we don't know. Because the political conversations about courts in our society almost always assume that law and politics are merged in the United States, to participate in these debates and evaluate them critically, students need insights into how scholars go about studying the courts. Thus understanding how scholars study an entity gives us greater insights into the essence of the entity itself. Again, because almost all the authors in this book are political scientists, students need to understand how scholars in this discipline approach their research questions to begin to understand the contemporary debates about law and courts in our society.

The discipline of political science is so multi-faceted that periodically the American Political Science Association publishes books with titles like *Political Science: The State of the Discipline* (Finister 1983) and *Political Science: The State of the Discipline II* (Finister 1993). Gabriel A. Almond (1990) entitled his collection of essays on political science, *A Discipline Divided: Schools and Sects in Political Science*. Mansfield and Sisson described the discipline in this way, "Political science commenced and continues as an 'interdisciplinary' and complex field of study, the subject of which is both fundamentally important and ever changing. Its chief aims have been to develop a body of verifiable political knowledge and to enhance the quality of both public and private life" (Mansfield and Sisson 2004, 1). Katznelson and Milner, in the

latest in the series of State of the Discipline books produced by the American Political Science Association,
gave this read on the condition of political science,
"*State of the Discipline* implies a discipline, yet even
this much about political science cannot be taken for
granted. As an organized profession, political science
has existed for nearly a century. However, it has been
a capacious, often cacophonous, undertaking. Political
scientists possess sharply divergent views about their
research and pedagogy. They disagree not only about
what they should study and what constitutes a persuasive argument and evidence, but also about how
to understand the discipline's past" (Katznelson and
Milner 2002, 1).

Just as the discipline of political science is a diverse
field that uses many different approaches to the study
of politics, the subfield of judicial politics also attracts
a variety of scholars using a variety of methodological
approaches. Thus the second theme of this book is an
examination of how political scientists are re-examin-
ing the study of judicial politics. The chapter authors
use a variety of methods to study law and the courts.
As Slotnick described the subfield of judicial politics
in the early 1990s, "The subfield of judicial politics
is, perhaps, the most schizophrenic of the recognized
sub-areas within our discipline. If that overstates my
premise, few, I think, would dispute the fact that we
have the earmarks of multiple personalities and that
the internal tensions abounding in the field in which
we labor are more sustained than in those areas mined
by our colleagues. Our roots are multidisciplinary,
and we owe a great deal to fields as diverse as history,
psychology, statistics, literature, philosophy, anthro-
pology, economics, sociology, and others" (Slotnick
1991, 67).

THE HISTORY OF THE STUDY
OF JUDICIAL POLITICS

It would now be useful to give the reader a sense of the
history of the subfield of judicial politics. Judicial politics scholars have always used the tools of other dis-
ciplines to help them understand how courts actually
work. As Nancy Maveety explained, "Public law, as
the field was originally known, began as the synthesis

of law, history, and philosophy, but a synthesis determined to engage the subject of politics and government
empirically. The empiricism of early public law—
and thus, early political science—was a descriptive
enterprise, emphasizing nineteenth-century physical
science's desire to collect, categorize, and comment"
(Maveety 2003, 1). The earliest political scientists thus
described and categorized the institutional structures
of courts and the law. They spent a great deal of time
analyzing court doctrines and decisions. In the early
1900s, the legal realism school became the dominant
way of thinking in the law schools, and thus as well
among political scientists who studied the courts. The
legal realists rebelled against a mechanical model of
courts and judges, arguing instead that legal decisions
were "a mixture of law, politics, and policy" (Maveety
2003, 3) and that judges' decisions were influenced by
their backgrounds, training, personality and ideology
(see Maveety 2003, 3). The legal realists in political
science cared about judicial behavior and judicial decision making, not just about legal structures and doctrine. They therefore "emphasized the creativity found
in judging" (Clayton 1999, 16). The legal realists thus
argued that judges did not just *find* the law, but they
made law. Thus the legal realists emphasized the fact
that law and politics tend to merge in our society.

Beginning around World War II, political scientists
began to become preoccupied with predicting the
behavior of individual political actors. This was an
outgrowth of the science of politics movement of the
1920s. By the 1960s, a Behavioral Revolution had taken
over political science and the study of judicial politics.
Instead of just studying constitutions, laws, and institutions; political scientists wanted to understand better
how individual political actors behave in our political
system. And they wanted to approach this discovery
scientifically, with a heavy emphasis on predicting
future political behavior. Maveety described the tenets
of Behavioralism in this way, "The scientific community's search would be for grand or general theories; . . . individuals and their political interactions with
other persons were to be a principal focus of research;
and research was to be theory guided, rigorous, empirical, and whenever possible quantitative as well as
value-free, detached, and objective" (Maveety 2003,
9–10). In theory, substance, and methodology, the new

behavioralists were distinguishing themselves from the old traditionalists and old institutionalists who "used informal historical and interpretative methods to study relatively formal or tangible subjects like statutes and judicial doctrines" (Clayton 1999, 28). Thus behavioralism became the dominant paradigm in both political science in general and in the specific study of judicial politics. The level of analysis centered on the individual decision-maker, and in the case of the courts that meant studying the political behavior of individual judges.

Behaviorists studied judicial decisions, often using quantitative methods to answer their research questions. As Baum described the approach, "Research on judicial behavior most often is framed as an effort to identify the determinants of judges' choices" (Baum 1997, 10). The focus of study for the behavioralists was clearly on the judicial behavior of individual justices and on their ideologies. Some early behavioralist works examined whether there were liberal and conservative blocs on the U.S. Supreme Court in a variety of issue areas. Other works looked at whether newer justices on the Court were less predictable in their behavior than justices who had served for longer periods. As Baum continued his explanation, "Analyses of votes on case outcomes in the Supreme Court typically have rested on the assumption that the justices' policy preferences are expressed directly in their votes" (Baum 1997, 93). Clayton and Gillman (1999, 1) described the focus of the behavioralist approach in this way, "This level of inquiry tends to focus on the backgrounds, attitudes, and ideological preferences of individual justices rather than on the nature of the Court as an institution and its significance for the political system." Or as these two authors wrote in another work, "For quite some time political scientists studying the Supreme Court treated this institution as little more than a collection of individuals who were pursuing their personal policy preferences" (Gillman and Clayton 1999, 1).

As the careful reader has quickly already realized, much of the early work on judicial politics centered on the study of the Supreme Court of the United States. Today, the majority of work in the judicial politics field still centers on the U.S. Supreme Court, and a quick glance at the table of contents of this book will show that many of the chapters in this volume focus on research questions that involve the Supreme Court of the United States. However, by studying the U.S. Supreme Court, today political scientists hope that their findings will also apply to other courts in other settings as well.

Slowly, the field of judicial politics expanded and started to reach beyond this one single court. Judicial scholars began to study lower appellate courts such as the U.S. Courts of Appeals and the state supreme courts. Then scholars discovered that trial courts in both the federal system and in the state systems could be policymakers as well. Eventually scholars began to study components of the court systems and other players beyond the judges, including prosecutors, defense lawyers, the police, lawyers in civil cases, juries, law clerks for appellate courts, and the solicitor general (the lawyer for the federal executive branch at the U.S. Supreme Court). Judicial scholars who started their careers studying American courts also discovered that we could learn a great deal about courts in the United States by comparing them to courts in other countries. Then some scholars began to examine courts in other countries in their own right. Eventually scholars began to examine international courts such as the European Union's European Court of Justice and the recently created International Criminal Court. The field of judicial politics was expanding greatly.

THE NEW INSTITUTIONALISM AND OTHER POSTBEHAVORIALIST APPROACHES TO THE STUDY OF THE COURTS

All the chapters in this book are influenced by behavioralism and its techniques. Thus all of the chapters look at empirical questions and use a scientific approach to help answer those questions. However all of these chapters are also influenced by some of the "postbehavioralist" approaches to the study of the courts and especially the new institutionalist approaches. By the 1990s, the study of judicial politics took on a variety of postbehavioralist approaches. All of these approaches attempt to combine the traditionalist scholar's interest in understanding governmental institutions with the behavioralist's emphasis on empirical, individual-level research (see, e.g., Epstein, Walker, and Dixon 1989). The postbehavioralist scholars wanted to look beyond the decision making of individual justices on the U.S. Supreme Court. Instead, they were interested in understanding how institutional structures, arrangements, and relationships affect the work of courts and their judges. The new institutionalist approaches therefore combine a variety of factors into examining how institutional constraints affect the decisions of judges. Most of the authors in this book who use a new institutionalist approach are utilizing what has become known as the historical institutionalist method (see Hall and Taylor 1996; Gillman and Clayton 1999; Pierson and Skocpol 2001). As Gillman and Clayton (1999, 5) described the approach, "Like traditional, pre-behavioral legal studies, much of the new work takes seriously the effects of judicial norms and legal traditions, and attempts to situate the Court in the larger political context." Thus the new institutionalist approach says that the study of courts is more complex than merely studying the ideology of individual judges. The new institutionalist scholars are not only interested in studying the ideology of judges, but also how the legal approach constrains the actions and decisions of judges. New institutionalist approaches want students to understand better how law and politics merge in the United States, as well as how institutional structures, norms, and cultures affect political decision making. Thus these approaches acknowledge that the work of judges is much richer and more complicated than merely making ideological choices.

The new institutionalist approach also allows the researcher to move from one level of analysis to another. The behavioralists were focused almost exclusively on the individual level of analysis. They studied individual Members of Congress, individual voters, or individual judges. The new institutionalist approaches, however, allowed the researcher to shift from one level of analysis to another. Thus some new institutionalist scholars studied the institution as a whole, looking for example, at the interactions between courts and Congress or courts and the executive branch. Other new institutionalist scholars examined an intermediate level of analysis, looking for example, at how the typical three judge panels function on the U.S. Courts of Appeals. Thus shifting levels of analysis allow the student to see the richness and complexity of judicial decision making.

MODELS OF JUDICIAL DECISION MAKING

In addition to taking institutions seriously, many of the chapters in this book utilize a variety of scholarly models to help us understand judicial politics. The current models or approaches present in many of the chapters in this book include the legal model, the attitudinal model, the strategic model, and various types of new institutionalist models. The *legal model* argues that judges are constrained in their behavior by such principles as precedent and adherence to the rules and norms of legal analysis. The *attitudinal model* suggests that the decisions of courts can be explained almost entirely by the ideologies of the judges making the decisions. The *strategic model* says that judges anticipate the reactions of other actors (such as the Congress and the president) or other justices on the Court before making their decisions. There are several models that use the *new institutionalist approaches.* The new institutionalism is a very broad umbrella term that incorporates many different strands or streams of research, but all of them share a willingness to move beyond examining only the decision making of individual judges. As Maveety states in chapter 17 of this volume, "a definition of the new institutionalist approach to the study of courts is that political institutions and the framework of rules, norms, and ideas that constitute them create an incentive structure for political actors, facilitating some behaviors and discouraging others."

A CHAPTER-BY-CHAPTER ROADMAP FOR THIS VOLUME

Thus the two main themes of this book are the intersection of law and politics, and the variety of approaches political scientists use to study this phenomenon. The chapters are a mixture of original research and review pieces that give an overview of a specific topic.

Generally the chapters are paired or on occasion three chapters approach similar topics. The organization of the chapters follows closely the organizational scheme found in most major textbooks on judicial politics, although instructors are free to assign the chapters in any order they see fit. Almost all textbooks in judicial politics begin with the organization of the courts in the United States, in part because we are unique around the world in having two separate courts systems (state and federal) sharing the same geographical space but with overlapping jurisdictions. Because both the state and federal courts systems are vitally important in our country, and because political scientists tend to specialize in either the state courts or in the federal courts, the early chapters of this volume will usually alternate chapters on the state courts with chapters that focus on the federal courts. Some instructors and some readers might prefer to assign or read all the chapters on state courts together, and then read the chapters on the federal courts. However most textbooks on judicial politics do not organize themselves in that way, preferring instead to examine the courts in a hierarchical fashion starting with trial courts in both systems and then moving to intermediate appeals courts, before turning to the highest court that hears cases from both the state and federal court systems, the U.S. Supreme Court.

The book begins with the selection of judges because judges are of course critical to understanding the courts, and because most judicial politics textbooks discuss the selection of judges right after they introduce the two separate court systems present in our country. The book then turns to several other important actors in the lower level trial courts, including lawyers and juries. Thus the book begins with the three key actors in the trial courts: judges, lawyers, and juries. Most textbooks then examine the decision-making role of judges in the hierarchy of courts. Therefore, this book will then turn to chapters that explore decision making in the trial courts, then to chapters that look at decision making on the intermediate appeals courts including the supreme courts of the states, and finally to chapters that focus almost exclusively on the U.S. Supreme Court.

The U.S. Supreme Court is unique in many ways, including the fact that certain actors such as the U.S. Solicitor General and the law clerks at the Supreme Court only exist at that level. Historically, the U.S. Supreme Court has received an enormous amount of attention from judicial politics scholars. Because most political science studies have traditionally focused on the U.S. Supreme Court, and because even today that trend continues in judicial scholarship, the reader will find a variety of chapters on that specific court in this volume. Judicial scholars often start with the U.S. Supreme Court, and then see whether their findings can apply to other courts. After spending some time on the U.S. Supreme Court, the book then turns to broader questions of judicial policy making. These chapters include an examination of how the courts fit into the broader field of political theory, as well as looking at the policy outputs of the courts. Finally, the book ends with two chapters that look beyond the U.S. judiciary, focusing on interactions between the courts and other institutions and on courts outside the United States, respectively. All of these chapters explore how law and politics interact, plus they explore how political scientists approach the study of that phenomenon.

The next section of this chapter will provide a more specific outline of the chapters in this volume. The book thus begins with two chapters that explore various issues surrounding the selection of judges. Chapter 2 by Aman L. McLeod provides a historical analysis of state judicial selection systems, and the issues raised in the ongoing struggle between the principles of judicial independence and judicial accountability. The choice of judicial selection system is not a neutral choice, always involving a tension between law and politics. Chapter 3 by Lauren Cohen Bell looks at how the issues of law and politics surround the selection and confirmation process for federal judges. Her specific focus is on the role of interest groups in these judicial confirmation events.

The book then turns to two chapters that examine key actors in the trial courts who are not judges: lawyers and juries. Traditionally these actors have not received the attention from political scientists that they deserve, and these chapters add greatly to the unique approach of this volume. Lynn Mather's chapter examines how lawyers make both legal and political decisions. She uses a new institutionalist approach to discuss the crucial role that the legal profession plays in judicial decision making. Robert G. Boatright's chapter then explores the legal and political issues surrounding the question of jury reform. This chapter looks at the jury as a political institution. It also looks at how various states have considered specific ways to improve the functioning of juries.

The next pair of chapters examines the policy-making roles of trial court judges in civil cases. Chapter 6 by Nicole L. Waters, Shauna M. Strickland, and Brian J. Ostrom examines the role of state judges in the civil litigation process. This chapter examines the structures of the state courts, the steps in the civil litigation process in state courts, and asks whether the state courts can accomplish all their varied missions. Chapter 7 by Jeb Barnes compares a general model of policy-making in the United States with the policy-making role of federal trial judges, using asbestos cases as an example.

Next the book turns to a pair of chapters that explores the policy-making roles of appellate courts below the level of the U.S. Supreme Court. This is a relatively new area of study for many political scientists, but the literature in this field is steadily growing. Using a strategic model, chapter 8 by Laura Langer and Teena Wilhelm explores the interactions between the policy-making role of state supreme courts and the selection system used for judges in that state. This chapter also looks at the relationship between the state supreme courts and the state legislatures. Chapter 9 by Wendy L. Martinek examines the policy-making roles of the U.S. Courts of Appeals as well as various approaches used to study these mid-level appellate courts.

The next section of the book focuses mostly on the U.S. Supreme Court and some noncourt actors that can affect the workings of that court. Most judicial politics textbooks do not spend much time on these actors, but studying them can make important contributions to understanding how law and politics intertwine in the United States. Chapter 10 by Peter N. Ubertaccio III examines the role of the U.S. Solicitor General, who is the president's chief lawyer before the U.S. Supreme Court. By statute and by necessity, the solicitor general must be learned in law and in politics. Chapter 11 by Artemus Ward looks at the legal and political aspects of those who assist the justices with their research and

opinion writing tasks: the law clerks. Drawing heavily on the papers of former justices, Ward traces the evolution of the job of the law clerks at the U.S. Supreme Court.

Following this look at noncourt actors, the next pair of chapters looks at decision making on the U.S. Supreme Court. Chapter 12 by Richard L. Pacelle, Jr., looks at how the Supreme Court makes policy. He uses a new institutionalist approach in his analysis, presenting a model of Supreme Court decision making. Chapter 13 by Bryan W. Marshall, Richard L. Pacelle, Jr., and Christine Ludowise presents a new institutionalist approach for understanding whether the courts use a legal model, an attitudinal model, or a strategic model in their decision making. They conclude that, "The Court operates in a political and legal context that imposes norms and duties on the institution." They clearly see the Supreme Court as both a legal and a political institution.

The book then turns to several important broader questions from democratic theory. These topics also often do not receive adequate attention in the major textbooks. The first question is what is the proper role of unelected federal judges in a democracy? The second question is when and why some individuals and groups refuse to follow court pronouncements? Chapter 14 by Michael Comiskey looks at whether the Supreme Court decisions generally go against the view of the majority in the United States or whether it generally supports the majoritarian position. Chapter 15 by Richard A. Brisbin, Jr., takes a very interesting look at resistance to the courts and to the policies courts pronounce. Combining a strategic and new institutionalist analysis, Brisbin concludes that the courts must anticipate that not everyone in society will follow the rulings of the courts.

The book then turns to three chapters that examine some of the actual policies produced by the U.S. Supreme Court. One of the unique aspects of this volume is these three chapters on the policy outputs of the courts and the effects that the courts have had in shaping public policy in these areas. Most judicial politics textbooks talk about court made policies in the abstract, but this volume explores in some detail three critical areas of court made policies that are part of the current political debate about the law in our country. All of these issues are currently in the news, with the legal and political debates becoming sometimes heated over these issues. Chapter 16 by Barbara Perry examines the pronouncements of the Supreme Court in the area of race, including the conflicts over affirmative action, while chapter 17 by Judith A. Baer looks at how the Supreme Court has decided sex discrimination cases. Both chapters use a legal model to emphasize the importance of precedents and legal tests for the Supreme Court. Chapter 18 by Louis Fisher looks at the policies the Supreme Court has produced regarding the issue of terrorism. The chapter examines how the federal courts have approached a new question, terrorism, but through the lens of earlier precedents on this issue. This chapter also explores how the Supreme Court handles separation of powers questions. All of these chapters provide in-depth analysis of specific policy areas and the way the Supreme Court has treated these policy questions. These chapters give us wonderful insights into the courts as policy makers and into the output of the judicial system.

The final pair of chapters takes us beyond the study of the courts alone to two new areas of judicial scholarship. Chapter 19 by Mark C. Miller examines the interactions between the federal courts and the other institutions of the federal government. He concludes that the relationship between the courts and the other branches is complex and often strained. Using a new institutionalist approach, he finds that we are currently in a high-conflict era, and that the interactions between the Congress and the courts especially are framed by highly ideological and partisan battles. Chapter 20 by Nancy Maveety takes us beyond the borders of the United States, helping us understand how the study of judicial politics in the United States can inform us about the workings of courts around the world. Maveety explores how the various models used by the other chapter authors can help us understand courts abroad.

Thus this book explores the relationship between law and politics, and the methods that judicial scholars use to try to solve the research puzzles that intrigue us. In my many years of teaching, I have discovered that students are often fascinated with the research puzzles that scholars ponder, as well as with the approaches that scholars use to try to understand these puzzles. Each chapter includes an introduction to that piece written by the editor to help students and instructors understand how we go about exploring judicial politics. Just as Tocqueville studied the political debates and legal debates surrounding American courts in the early 1800s, these chapters should help students better understand the contemporary debates surrounding the courts. We hope that these chapters will enable students to be better consumers of political information concerning the role of law, courts, and judges in our society.

2

DIFFERENCES IN STATE JUDICIAL SELECTION

Aman L. McLeod

In the United States, all judges are selected through political processes of some kind. Some of these processes stress the principle of judicial independence while others stress the principle of judicial accountability to the people. All Article III federal judges who sit on the U.S. District Courts, the U.S. Courts of Appeals, and the U.S. Supreme Court are appointed by the president and are confirmed by the U.S. Senate for life terms. Having a judge serve for life supports the concept of judicial independence.

State judges, however, are selected by a variety of methods. Many of these procedures favor the concept of judicial accountability, often through the mechanism of selecting or retaining state judges through some type of election process. This chapter examines the historical development of state judicial selection procedures, categorizing these processes into three broad types. These types include processes where state judges are appointed by the Governor, appointed by the state legislature, elected in partisan elections, elected in nonpartisan elections, and the so-called Missouri Plan or merit-selection processes. Because judges are selected through political processes, judicial selection is a key starting point for understanding how law and politics intertwine in the United States.

Today, states use a variety of methods to select the judges who preside over their courts. The fact that states use different methods to choose their judges reflects the lack of consensus that exists among the states about the relative importance of *judicial accountability* versus *judicial independence*, and about how best to promote public respect for the judiciary and its rulings. Some states use selection methods that are designed to insulate judges from influence by the legislative and executive branches of the government, and from the people. Providing the judiciary with such insulation reflects a belief in the idea that respect for the judiciary and its rulings is promoted by providing judges with a relatively high degree of institutional independence. On the other hand, some states have adopted judicial selection methods that more easily allow the people, or the other branches of government, to hold judges accountable for unpopular decisions by removing them from office. States that have adopted these methods of selecting their judges use systems that embody the principle that judges must be made to answer for decisions that do not reflect the values and policy preferences of the communities that they serve, and that respect for the judiciary is enhanced by a mandate from the people or their elected representatives.

In this chapter I discuss the methods that states currently use for selecting their judges. I also discuss the history of these selection methods, and the ideas that each of these methods reflect about the proper balance between judicial accountability and independence. Table 2.1 illustrates the methods currently used to select judges for the states' appellate courts and courts of general jurisdiction. This discussion of state judicial selection systems will highlight two major points: The first point is that since the early 1800s, the evolution of judicial selection methods has reflected changing ideas about judicial independence, accountability, and legitimacy; the second point is that political factors, such as judges' and judicial candidates' ideology, policy preferences, and personal connections, play an important role in every judicial selection system.

Table 2.1 Judicial Selection in the States: Appellate and General Jurisdiction Courts Initial Selection, Retention, and Term Length

State and Court	Merit Selection Through Nominating Commission	Gubernatorial (G) or Legislative Appointment (L) Without Nominating Convention	Nonpartisan Election	Partisan Election	Initial Term of Office (Years)	Method of Retention
ALABAMA						
Supreme Court				X	Six	Re-election (six-year term)
Court of Civil Appeals				X	Six	
Court of Criminal Appeals				X	Six	
Circuit Court				X	Six	
ALASKA						
Supreme Court	X				Three	Retention election (ten-year term)
Court of Appeals	X				Three	Retention election (eight-year term)
Superior Court	X				Three	Retention election (six-year term)
ARIZONA						
Supreme Court	X				Two	Retention election (six-year term)
Court of Appeals	X				Two	Retention election (six-year term)
Superior Court (county w/ pop. > 250,000)	X				Two	Retention election (six-year term)
Superior Court (county w/ pop. < 250,000)			X		Four	

continued

Table 2.1 *Continued*

State and Court	Merit Selection Through Nominating Commission	Gubernatorial (G) or Legislative Appointment (L) Without Nominating Convention	Nonpartisan Election	Partisan Election	Initial Term of Office (Years)	Method of Retention
ARKANSAS						
Supreme Court			X		Eight	
Court of Appeals			X		Eight	Re-election for additional terms
Circuit Court			X		Six	
CALIFORNIA						
Supreme Court		X(G)			Twelve	Retention election (twelve-year term)
Court of Appeal		X(G)			Twelve	Retention election (twelve-year term)
Superior Court[a]			X		Six	Nonpartisan election (six-year term)[b]
COLORADO						
Supreme Court	X				Two	Retention election (ten-year term)
Court of Appeals	X				Two	Retention election (eight-year term)
District Court	X				Two	Retention election (six-year term)
CONNECTICUT						
Supreme Court	X				Eight	Commission reviews the incumbent's performance on a noncompetitive basis; governor renominates and legislature confirms.
Appellate Court	X				Eight	
Superior Court	X				Eight	
DELAWARE						
Supreme Court	X				Twelve	Incumbent reapplies to the nominating commission along with other applicants. The governor may appoint the incumbent or another nominee, subject to senate approval.
Court of Chancery	X				Twelve	
Superior Court	X				Twelve	
DISTRICT OF COLUMBIA						
Court of Appeals	X				Fifteen	Reappointment by judicial tenure commission[c]
Superior Court	X				Fifteen	

Table 2.1 *Continued*

State and Court	Merit Selection Through Nominating Commission	Gubernatorial (G) or Legislative Appointment (L) Without Nominating Convention	Nonpartisan Election	Partisan Election	Initial Term of Office (Years)	Method of Retention
FLORIDA						
Supreme Court	X				One	Retention election (six-year term)
District Court of Appeal	X				One	Retention election (six-year term)
Superior Court			X		Six	Re-election to additional terms
GEORGIA						
Supreme Court			X		Six	Re-election to additional terms
Court of Appeals			X		Six	
Superior Court			X		Four	
HAWAII						
Supreme Court	X				Ten	Reappointed to subsequent terms by the judicial selection commission (ten-year term)
Intermediate Court of Appeals	X				Ten	
Circuit Court and Family Court	X				Ten	
IDAHO						
Supreme Court			X		Six	Re-election to additional terms
Court of Appeals			X		Six	
District Court			X		Four	
ILLINOIS						
Supreme Court				X	Ten	Retention election (ten-year term)
Court of Appeals				X	Ten	Retention election (ten-year term)
District Court				X	Six	Retention election (six-year term)
INDIANA						
Supreme Court	X				Two	Retention election (ten-year term)
Court of Appeals	X				Two	Retention election (ten-year term)
Circuit Court				X	Six	Re-election for additional terms

continued

Table 2.1 *Continued*

State and Court	Merit Selection Through Nominating Commission	Gubernatorial (G) or Legislative Appointment (L) Without Nominating Convention	Nonpartisan Election	Partisan Election	Initial Term of Office (Years)	Method of Retention
Circuit Court (Vanderburgh County)			X		Six	Re-election for additional terms
Superior Court				X	Six	Re-election for additional terms
Superior Court (Allen County)			X		Six	Re-election for additional terms
Superior Court (Lake County)	X[d]				Two	Retention election (six-year term)
Superior Court (St. Joseph County)	X				Two	Retention election (six-year term)
Superior Court (Vanderburgh County)			X		Six	Re-election for addition terms
IOWA						
Supreme Court	X				One	Retention election (eight-year term)
Court of Appeals	X				One	Retention election (six-year term)
District Court	X				One	Retention election (six-year term)
KANSAS						
Supreme Court	X				One	Retention election (six-year term)
Court of Appeals	X				One	Retention election (six-year term)
District Court (seventeen districts)	X				One	Retention election (six-year term)
District Court (fourteen Districts)				X	Four	Re-election for additional terms
KENTUCKY						
Supreme Court			X		Eight	Re-election for additional terms
Court of Appeals			X		Eight	
Circuit Court			X		Eight	
LOUISIANA						
Supreme Court				X[e]	Ten	Re-election for additional terms
Court of Appeals				X[e]	Ten	
District Court				X[e]	Six	

Table 2.1 *Continued*

State and Court	Merit Selection Through Nominating Commission	Gubernatorial (G) or Legislative Appointment (L) Without Nominating Convention	Nonpartisan Election	Partisan Election	Initial Term of Office (Years)	Method of Retention
MAINE						
Supreme Court		X(G)			Seven	Reappointment by the Governor subject to legislative confirmation
Superior Court		X(G)			Seven	
MARYLAND						
Court of Appeals	X				Until the first general election following the expiration of one year from the date of the occurrence of the vacancy	Retention election (ten-year term)
Court of Special Appeals	X					Retention election (ten-year term)
Circuit Court	X					Nonpartisan election (fifteen-year term)
MASSACHUSETTS						
Supreme Judicial Court	X				To age seventy	
Appeals Court	X					
Trial Court of Mass.	X					
MICHIGAN						
Supreme Court				X[f]	Eight	Re-election to additional terms
Court of Appeals			X		Six	
Circuit Court			X		Six	
MINNESOTA						
Supreme Court			X		Six	Re-election to additional terms
Court of Appeals			X		Six	
District Court			X		Six	

continued

Table 2.1 *Continued*

State and Court	Merit Selection Through Nominating Commission	Gubernatorial (G) or Legislative Appointment (L) Without Nominating Convention	Nonpartisan Election	Partisan Election	Initial Term of Office (Years)	Method of Retention
MISSISSIPPI						
Supreme Court			X		Eight	Re-election to additional terms
Court of Appeals			X		Eight	
Chancery Court			X		Four	
Circuit Court			X		Four	
MISSOURI						
Supreme Court	X				One	Retention election (twelve-year term)
Court of Appeals	X				One	Retention election (twelve-year term)
Circuit Court				X	Six	Re-election to additional terms
Circuit Court (Jackson, Platte, St. Louis counties)	X				One	Retention election (twelve-year term)
MONTANA						
Supreme Court			X		Eight	Re-election[g] to additional terms
District Court			X		Six	
NEBRASKA						
Supreme Court	X				Three	Retention election (six-year term)
Court of Appeals	X				Three	
District Court	X				Three	
NEVADA						
Supreme Court			X		Six	Re-election to additional terms
District Court			X		Six	
NEW HAMPSHIRE						
Supreme Court	X[h]				Until age seventy	
Superior Court	X					
NEW JERSEY						
Supreme Court		X(G)			Seven	Reappointment by Governor (until age seventy) subject to Senate confirmation
Appellate Superior Court Division of		X(G)			Seven	
Superior Court		X(G)			Seven	

Table 2.1 *Continued*

State and Court	Merit Selection Through Nominating Commission	Gubernatorial (G) or Legislative Appointment (L) Without Nominating Convention	Nonpartisan Election	Partisan Election	Initial Term of Office (Years)	Method of Retention
NEW MEXICO						
Supreme Court	X				Until the next general election	Partisan election for eight-year term for appellate judges, six-year term for district court judges; winners run in retention elections thereafter
Court of Appeals	X					
District Court	X					
NEW YORK						
Court of Appeals	X				Fourteen	See bottom of page
Appellate Division of the Supreme Court	X				Five	Commission reviews and recommends for/against reappointment by the governor
Supreme Court				X	Fourteen	Re-election for additional terms
County Court				X	Ten	Re-election for additional terms
NORTH CAROLINA						
Supreme Court			X		Eight	Re-election for additional terms
Court of Appeals			X		Eight	
Superior Court			X		Eight	
NORTH DAKOTA						
Supreme Court			X		Ten	Re-election for additional terms
District Court			X		Six	
OHIO						
Supreme Court				X[i]	Six	Re-election for additional terms
Court of Appeals				X[i]	Six	
Court of Common Pleas				X[i]	Six	
OKLAHOMA						
Supreme Court	X				One	Retention election (six-year term)
Court of Criminal Appeals	X				One	Retention election (six-year term)
Court of Appeals	X				One	Retention election (six-year term)
District Court			X		Four	Re-election for additional terms

continued

Table 2.1 *Continued*

State and Court	Merit Selection Through Nominating Commission	Gubernatorial (G) or Legislative Appointment (L) Without Nominating Convention	Nonpartisan Election	Partisan Election	Initial Term of Office (Years)	Method of Retention
OREGON						
Supreme Court			X		Six	Re-election for additional terms
Court of Appeals			X		Six	
Circuit Court			X		Six	
Tax Court			X		Six	
PENNSYLVANIA						
Supreme Court				X	Ten	Retention election (ten-year term)
Superior Court				X	Ten	
Commonwealth Court				X	Ten	
Court of Common Pleas				X	Ten	
RHODE ISLAND						
Supreme Court	X				Life	
Superior Court	X				Life	
Worker's Compensation Court	X				Life	
SOUTH CAROLINA						
Supreme Court	X				Ten	Reappointment by the legislature
Court of Appeals	X				Six	
Circuit Court	X				Six	
SOUTH DAKOTA						
Supreme Court	X				Three	Retention election (eight-year term)
Circuit Court			X		Eight	Re-election for additional terms
TENNESSEE						
Supreme Court	X				Until next general election	Retention election (eight-year term)
Court of Appeals	X				Until next general election	Retention election (eight-year term)
Court of Criminal Appeals	X				Until next general election	Retention election (eight-year term)

Table 2.1 *Continued*

State and Court	Merit Selection Through Nominating Commission	Gubernatorial (G) or Legislative Appointment (L) Without Nominating Convention	Nonpartisan Election	Partisan Election	Initial Term of Office (Years)	Method of Retention
Chancery Court				X	Eight	Re-election for additional terms
Criminal Court				X	Eight	
Circuit Court				X	Eight	
TEXAS						
Supreme Court				X	Six	Re-election for additional terms
Court of Criminal Appeals				X	Six	
Court of Appeals				X	Six	
District Court				X	Four	
UTAH						
Supreme Court	X					Retention election (ten-year term)
Court of Appeals	X				First general election after three years on the bench	Retention election (six-year term)
District Court	X					Retention election (six-year term)
Juvenile Court	X					Retention election (six-year term)
VERMONT						
Supreme Court	X				Six	Retained by vote of the legislature (six-year term)
Superior Court	X				Six	
District Court	X				Six	
VIRGINIA						
Supreme Court		X(L)			Twelve	Reappointment by the legislature
Court of Appeals		X(L)			Eight	
Circuit Court		X(L)			Eight	
WASHINGTON						
Supreme Court			X		Six	Re-election for additional terms
Court of Appeals			X		Six	
Superior Court			X		Four	

continued

Table 2.1 *Continued*

State and Court	Merit Selection Through Nominating Commission	Gubernatorial (G) or Legislative Appointment (L) Without Nominating Convention	Nonpartisan Election	Partisan Election	Initial Term of Office (Years)	Method of Retention
WEST VIRGINIA						
Supreme Court				X	Twelve	Re-election for additional terms
Circuit Court				X	Eight	
WISCONSIN						
Supreme Court			X			Re-election for additional terms
Court of Appeals			X			
Circuit Court			X			
WYOMING						
Supreme Court	X				One	Retention election (eight-year term)
District Court	X				One	Retention election (six-year term)

Note. Based on American Judicature Society (2003b).

ªCalifornia. The state constitution allows counties to choose gubernatorial appointment instead of nonpartisan election as a method of selecting superior court judges. To date, no counties had opted for gubernatorial appointment.

ᵇCalifornia. If the race is not contested, the incumbent's name does not appear on the ballot.

ᶜDistrict of Columbia. The initial appointment is made by the President of the United States, subject to confirmation by the US Senate. Six months prior to the expiration of the judge's term, the tenure commission reviews the judge's performance. Those found "well qualified" are automatically reappointed. If the judge is found to be "qualified," the President may reappoint the judge for an additional term, subject to Senate confirmation. If the President does not choose to reappoint the judge, the commission compiles a new list of candidates.

ᵈIndiana (Lake County). Three judges run in partisan elections for six-year terms then have to be re-elected for additional terms.

ᵉLouisiana. Judicial elections are formally partisan given that the judge's party affiliation is stated on the ballot. However, two factors tend to give these elections a somewhat non-partisan character: (1) primary elections are open to all candidates and (2) judicial candidates generally do not solicit party support for their campaigns.

ᶠMichigan. Although the candidates party affiliations do not appear on the ballot, the candidates are nominated at party conventions.

ᵍMontana. Unopposed judges run in a retention election.

ʰNew Hampshire. The governor's nomination is subject to the approval of a five-member executive council.

ⁱOhio. Although party affiliations for judicial candidates are not listed on the general election ballot, candidates are nominated in partisan primary elections.

Before discussing the various systems that are currently used to select judges, it is important to understand that the task of categorizing judicial selection systems is complicated by the fact that a state's selection system can display traits that justify its placement in more than one category. For example, in Table 2.1, Massachusetts is categorized as a state that uses merit selection. However, although Massachusetts uses a commission to vet candidates for judicial office, all of the commission members are appointed by the governor, who may decline to make an appointment until the commission recommends a candidate that the governor favors. State judges in Massachusetts also serve life terms until the mandatory retirement age of 70. The seemingly contradictory aspects of the Massachusetts system, plus the fact that the appointments need only be approved by the elected Governor's Council,[1] supports an argument that the Massachusetts judicial selection system should be categorized with those of New Hampshire and California, which do not use a nominating commission. Despite the difficulty of categorizing states' judicial selection systems, the following discussion separates states into three broad categories.

MERIT SELECTION

Merit selection is the most widely used system for initially selecting judges on the state level. The system takes its name from the fact that it is aimed at insuring that judges are selected on the basis of professional and personal merit, and to prevent political considerations from entering into the selection process. Today, thirty-three states and the District of Columbia use some form of merit-selection systems to select judges for their appellate courts or courts of general jurisdiction (American Judicature Society 2003b). All states that have merit-selection systems use commissions to select candidates for interim appointments to the bench when judges die or leave the bench before the expiration of their terms, and some states also use commissions to select candidates for a full term on the bench (which is known as initial selection). A specific subset of merit-selection states use the so-called Missouri Plan of nominating commissions plus retention elections for judges, as discussed in more detail later.

The central feature of the merit-selection system is the judicial nominating commission. Although the composition of these commissions varies from state to state, most are composed of lawyers, nonlawyers, and judges, and range in size from as many as twenty-one members to as few as five. Depending on the state, the commission members are usually chosen by some combination of the following: members of the state's legal bar, sitting judges, members of the state legislature, and the governor (American Judicature Society 2003a).[2] Furthermore, different states vary greatly in the number of commissions that they use to select judges for different courts. For example, Idaho uses a single commission to vet candidates for

vacancies in all of its appellate and general jurisdiction courts, whereas New Mexico has one commission for its appellate courts, one commission for each of its thirteen district courts, and one commission that is used only for selecting metropolitan judges for its most populous county (American Judicature Society 2003a).

Under all merit-selection plans, the nominating commission receives and reviews applications from lawyers who wish to be considered for a vacancy on the bench. After reviewing the applicants' professional and educational credentials and conducting interviews, the commissions send a list of candidates (typically with two to three names) to the governor. Under most merit-selection systems, the governor must select one of the candidates on the list to fill the vacant seat on the bench. It is difficult to overstate the power and influence of the nominating commissions in shaping the judiciary of a given state or municipality. This power is indicated by the fact that very few merit-selection systems allow the governor to appoint someone to the bench who has not been approved by the commission, or even to ask the commission to submit a new list of candidates. Furthermore, in most states, the candidate selected by the governor need not be confirmed by the state legislature or any other body, which enhances the power of the nominating commissions, because, in such situations, the commissions are the only bodies with the power and resources to vet judicial candidates (American Judicature Society 2003a).

Although most of the merit-selection plans that states use today have many features in common, these same states use a variety of methods to determine whether a judge should remain on the bench after his/her term has expired and have prescribed widely varying judicial terms of office. As Table 2.1 indicates, most states that use merit selection for initial selection to the bench mandate that judges face the voters in retention elections at the conclusion of each term of office. This specific system of nominating commissions plus retention elections is often referred to as the Missouri Plan, named for the first state to adopt this judicial selection system.

In retention elections, the incumbent judge appears on the ballot unopposed and without party identification, and the public is simply asked to vote yes or no as to whether the judge should be retained for another term. If a majority of the voters vote yes, the judge serves another term; if a majority of the voters vote no, the judge is removed from office, and a vacancy is created on the bench that the governor and the merit-selection commission must fill. In some states that use retention elections, newly appointed judges serve a short term (typically one to two years) before facing the voters to win the right to serve for a full term (typically six to eight years). Other states allow judges to serve a full term before facing the voters. Some states that use merit selection, however, do not use retention elections. For example, in Hawaii, the judicial selection commission is responsible for deciding whether judges should be retained at the conclusion of their terms in office. In other states, after initial selection to the bench under a merit system, judges serve for life (e.g., Rhode Island) or until reaching a mandatory retirement age (e.g., Massachusetts). Finally, in most states, the work of the commissions is confidential, so the public has no opportunity to scrutinize their work or to comment on the candidates who have been selected before the list of candidates goes to the appointing authority (American Judicature Society 2003a).

The idea of choosing judges using commissions composed primarily of lawyers and judges grew out of a movement for political and social reform in the early twentieth century, which is popularly known as the Progressive Movement (Krivosha 1990). Progressives believed that the answer to many of the country's political problems lay in promoting greater efficiency in the administration of government. Progressives also tended to dislike partisan politics, which many of them viewed as the source of most of the inefficiencies that plague government. They thought that government should be run like a business, that is, with singleness of purpose and discipline. Accordingly, during the second and third decades of the twentieth century, a number of prominent legal scholars with Progressive sympathies began to consider ways in which partisan politics could be removed from the judiciary at their point of greatest impact: the judicial selection process (Krivosha 1990). Efforts by proponents of merit-based judicial selection to see the system implemented on the state level initially met with failure, most notably

in California in 1936, when that state's voters rejected a merit-based system in a referendum (Krivosha 1990). However, supporters of the merit system would score their first victory four years later in Missouri, when voters there embraced a plan that called for the governor to select most of the state's judges from a list submitted by a judicial selection commission, and for incumbent judges to run in retention elections after twelve years in office. Today, merit selection is the most widely used system of judicial selection, having been adopted by more states for use with more courts than any other selection system.

Supporters of merit selection claim that it is superior to other methods for selecting judges because merit selection takes political considerations out of the selection process (Anderson 2004). To supporters of merit selection, the need for an impartial judiciary dictates the need for a judicial selection process that focuses on candidates' professional qualifications, without considering their political views or connections (Anderson 2004). Proponents also claim that merit selection encourages a more diverse judiciary because it leads to the appointment of more minorities and women to the bench (Webster 1995). In answer to critics who claim that merit selection is elitist and undemocratic, supporters point out that merit-selection systems can be (and usually are) combined with retention elections that give the public opportunity to remove a judge whose performance has been unsatisfactory (Maute 2000).

However, research by a number of scholars over the last three decades has cast doubt on some of the claims that have been made in support of merit selection. Regarding the claim that merit selection promotes gender and racial diversity on the bench, Hurwitz and Lanier (2001) found that the proportion of female and minority appellate judges in states that use merit selection was no greater than the proportion of female and minority appellate judges in states that did not use merit systems in 1999.

Furthermore, the results of research on the workings of judicial nominating commissions also casts doubt on the central claim of the proponents of merit selection, which is that merit selection removes politics from the judicial selection process. For example, Ashman and Alfini (1974) found that 33 percent of the merit-selection commission members that they studied reported that political considerations had entered into their deliberations and had at least some influence on the outcome, while Henschen et al. (1990) found that one-third of the commissioners that they studied had served in a political party office, and that one-fourth of the commissioners had held public office before joining the commission.[3]

It is also worth noting that retention elections, like partisan and nonpartisan elections, also require judges to raise money to fund their campaigns (see, e.g., Reid 1999), which can open judges to charges that they are beholden to those who have given them financial support. Retention elections can display the same sort of sensational campaigning that marks other varieties of judicial elections, whenever interest groups campaign for a judge's removal (Reid 1999). Furthermore, there is evidence that despite the very low probability of losing in retention elections[4] (M. G. Hall 2001), judges' rulings can still be influenced by the desire to ward off defeat (Huber and Gordon 2004).

CONTESTED ELECTIONS

Contested elections are the second most widely used method of judicial selection and retention among the states. Contested elections differ from retention elections in that multiple candidates are permitted to compete for a seat on the bench, and the public is permitted to choose between them. Contested elections also differ from retention elections in that they are also used to initially select as well as to retain judges. At present, thirty states hold contested elections to select and retain the judges of some or all of their courts (see Table 2.1).

Today, the states use two different types of contested elections to select their judges: partisan elections and nonpartisan elections. Partisan judicial elections resemble elections for nonjudicial offices because the candidates run as representatives of a party and their party affiliations are listed next to their names on the ballot. Furthermore, in partisan election systems, parties select judicial candidates in the same way that parties choose candidates for other offices, which is usually through a primary election or at a

party convention. Nonpartisan judicial elections differ from partisan judicial elections because candidates are generally not permitted to associate themselves publicly with or endorse a party or its candidates for other offices, and the candidates' partisan affiliations do not appear on the ballot. Candidates in nonpartisan judicial elections are usually selected in nonpartisan primaries in which the two candidates who received the most votes go on to the general election. However, the election systems that some states use for selecting their judges defy easy categorization. For example, in both Michigan and Ohio, supreme court candidates' party affiliations are omitted from the ballot in the general election, but in Michigan, the candidates for the general election are selected at party conventions, while in Ohio, the candidates for the general election are selected in partisan primaries (American Judicature Society 2005).

In the view of the reformers who championed the movement for an elected judiciary in the mid-1800s, allowing the people to choose their judges directly was in keeping with the belief that governmental power could only be legitimately exercised when sanctioned by a popular mandate (K. L. Hall 1983). In addition to being anti-elitist, these reformers were also motivated by a dislike for judicial activism (see Miller this volume, chapter 19). In that era when state judges were almost entirely appointed by either the governor or the state legislature, proponents of judicial elections believed that many judges had become "little aristocrats," who "legislated judicially despite the wishes of the people" (K. L. Hall 1983, 348). In their view, appointed judges often ruled against the interests of the poor and dispossessed, because, reformers said, the courts were dominated by "local elites and men of wealth and power who perpetuated their economic interests and social positions through the administration of justice" (K. L. Hall 1983, 348).

The reformers claimed that forcing judges to seek the endorsement of their constituents would reduce their propensity to protect their own class and economic interests at the expense of the other members of the community by forcing them to be more responsive to popular notions of justice. Furthermore, the reformers also believed that popular elections would diminish the propensity of judges to overrule the will of state legislatures by making them accountable to the state's voters. For most of the 1800s those who argued in favor of judicial elections and supported greater judicial accountability clearly won the political argument, as is evidenced by the fact that every state that entered the Union between 1848 and 1912 opted to choose their judges in either partisan or nonpartisan elections, and many of the older states that had chosen their judges through gubernatorial or legislative appointment decided to switch to elections (Hanssen 2004).

In making the choice to abandon executive or legislative appointment in favor of popular elections as a means of judicial selection, many American states embarked on an effort that few other countries have attempted (Croley 1995).[5] Thus many of the American states attempted to create a judicial institution that is, on the one hand, impartial, but on the other hand, accountable to the people. In a sense, the widespread adoption of judicial elections in America is very much in keeping with the country's long tradition of public participation in the justice system, which is evidenced by the fact that the right to a jury trial is guaranteed by the Constitution. Supporters of judicial elections have claimed that elections enhance judicial independence and legitimacy (Starcher 2001), that elections discourage judicial activism (DeBow et. al. 2002), and that they are an efficient means of removing judges from office who have been accused of unethical conduct (Larkin, 2001). Some also claim that judicial elections encourage the selection of people to the bench who are attuned to their community's values (Starcher, 2001). Finally, there are those who claim that judicial elections actually enhance judicial independence by providing incumbent judges an opportunity to educate the public about the importance of an independent judiciary that is not present in systems that do not use elections of any sort (Abrahamson 2001).

However, the use of elections to select judges has never been without controversy. For example, in the political debates of the nineteenth century that surrounded the adoption of elections as a means of judicial selection, a chorus of opponents spoke out against this reform. These opponents of judicial elections feared that the political independence of the judiciary would be compromised by forcing judges to run in elections, because judges would then have a strong incentive to

tailor their rulings to suit the opinions of their constituents, party leaders, and others who had influence in securing their election, rather than simply following the law (K. L. Hall 1983). Other opponents feared that judicial elections would turn the judiciary into a weapon that the poor would use against the wealthy in society (K. L. Hall 1983). Also, critics of judicial elections believed that forcing judges to stand for election would inevitably increase the incidence of partisanship in the judicial process, and generally bring the judiciary into disrepute (K. L. Hall 1983). Finally, some of the original opponents of judicial elections made arguments against electing judges that were based on the concept of legal formalism. To the formalists, judges were, ideally, technicians who "scientifically" arrived at their rulings through analytical and dispassionate application of the law (Cox 2003). As one conservative formalist argued, judges are the "professors" of the "science of law," and that neither "their will" nor the "will of the people" should interfere with the performance of their duties (K. L. Hall 1983, 349).

In many ways, judicial elections resemble elections that are held to fill other government offices, in that judicial candidates campaign for votes, raise money to support their campaign activities, and seek endorsements from local and national notables. What makes judicial elections different from elections from other state and local offices is that states have placed important restrictions on the political and campaign activities of judicial candidates in an effort to preserve the judiciary's reputation for impartiality. For example, although judicial candidates[6] are permitted to discuss their views on divisive political issues, such as whether they support or oppose abortion rights, the vast majority of state judicial ethics codes (which, for the most part, are closely based on the Model Code of Judicial Conduct produced by the American Bar Association) prohibit judicial candidates from making any promises relating to cases, controversies, or issues that are likely to come before the courts, or statements that are "inconsistent with the impartial performance of the adjudicative duties of the office." (See, e.g., American Bar Association [ABA] 2004, Rule 5A(2)(d)(i)).

Furthermore, most ethics codes also prohibit judicial candidates from, among other things, leading or holding offices in political parties (ABA 2004, Rule

5A(1)(a); from personally soliciting or accepting campaign contributions Rule 5C(2)); and from knowingly misrepresenting information about another candidate for a judicial office, Rule 5A(3)(d)(ii)).

Ethics rules tend to differ by state depending on the type of election that the state employs to select its judges. For example, in most states that use partisan elections, judicial candidates are permitted to publicly identify themselves as members of a political party, to endorse a party's candidates, and to participate in meetings and events sponsored by a political party, while candidates for judicial office who are running in nonpartisan or retention elections are prohibited from engaging in these activities and are often also prohibited from endorsing or opposing political parties (ABA 2004, Rule 5C(1)(a)(ii)).[7] Also, most state judicial ethics codes require judges to resign from the bench if he/she becomes a candidate for election to any other public office (ABA 2004, Rule 5A(2)).[8]

An important result of these restrictions on judicial candidates' political and campaign activities is that judicial elections tend to be low profile elections in which the public gets little information about the candidates on which to base their votes. For example, a nationwide survey found that only 13 percent of respondents reported that they had a "great deal" of information about the candidates, while 49 percent reported that they had only a little information or none at all (Justice at Stake Campaign 2001). The fact that the public appears to be woefully ill-informed about judicial contests has prompted the criticism that judicial elections create a situation in which the electorate is forced to choose among candidates on the basis of even less information than they usually have available to them in elections for other offices, given the restraints on judicial speech (American Judicature Society 2003c).

Still, despite the reluctance of many judicial candidates to engage in debates on contentious policy issues, the evidence indicates that contested judicial elections tend to look like legislative elections in terms of the factors that determine their outcomes. For example, research indicates that the presence of a quality challenger, candidate expenditures, and the ideological match between a judicial candidate and his/her constituency, are all significant factors in determining

the outcome of contested judicial elections (Bonneau 2005). A judicial candidate's political party affiliation is also an important cue for voters in judicial contests. For example, a survey of states with partisan judicial elections revealed that there was a high correlation (.84) between the percentage of the vote received by the gubernatorial candidate and the supreme court candidate of the same party on the county level (Dubois 1980). (A 1.0 correlation is considered evidence of a perfect correlation between two items).

Furthermore, a study of voting behavior in Ohio Supreme Court races suggested that individuals were more likely to support candidates who shared their party affiliation than those who did not (Klein and Baum, 2001). In states with nonpartisan judicial elections, it has been suggested that the public also depends on cues apart from the ballot to discover a candidate's political allegiance, such as whether a judicial candidate had been a candidate for a nonjudicial office in the past, or on whether a candidate's family name is heavily associated with a political party in the state (Dubois 1980).

The fact that the public appears to rely so heavily on party affiliation and candidate ideology when deciding which candidates to support in judicial elections suggests that many voters treat judicial elections as yet another avenue for affecting public policy, like gubernatorial or legislative elections. Also, research on how judges respond to the possibility of defeat at elections[9] suggests that at least some judges allow their decisions to be influenced by their perceptions of their own electoral vulnerability. For example, one study tested the hypothesis that in criminal appeals cases, elected judges respond to what they perceive to be their constituents' policy preferences by examining the voting patterns of the justices of the supreme courts of Kentucky, Louisiana, North Carolina, and of the Texas Court of Criminal Appeals (M. G. Hall 1992).[10] Public opinion polls in all of these states indicated that their citizens strongly supported the death penalty, which, in turn, suggested that the justices who supported the defense in such cases were acting contrary to the wishes of their constituents. Specifically, the study investigated whether the "liberal" justices of these supreme courts, that is, those justices who tended to side with defendants in criminal appeals, were seeking to blunt charges that they were "soft" on criminals by avoiding dissents in capital punishment cases. The findings confirmed the hypothesis that liberal justices in conservative states often seek to protect themselves from political criticism by siding with the majority in death penalty cases against the interests of the accused. The study's results also indicated that the liberal justices' voting behavior was influenced by other variables related to elections. Specifically, the results showed that the likelihood of these liberal justices joining the majority against the accused in a capital case rose (1) if they were elected from a district, as opposed to being elected statewide; (2) if the justice was in the last two years of his/her term; or (3) if the justice had held elective office prior to serving on the supreme court. The study also indicated that liberal justices who won their last elections by smaller margins and that justices who had run for re-election to the court at least once were more likely to vote with the conservative majority in death penalty cases than were justices who had won by larger margins or who had not yet sought re-election to the court.

These findings indicate that on at least the high profile issue of capital punishment, some elected judges behave in a manner similar to that of legislators, in that they are responsive to what they perceive to be their constituents' policy preferences. Furthermore, these findings about the sensitivity of judges to electoral concerns in death penalty cases were confirmed in a larger study published three years later (Brace and Hall 1995). That study included supreme court justices from eight states with different judicial selection systems,[11] and controlled for the influence of important state legislation, case facts, and the level of competition between the two major parties in the state. Its results indicated that justices from states with contested elections were significantly more likely than those from states with retention elections or without elections to favor the state in death penalty appeals.

Furthermore, the importance of money in winning judicial elections raises questions about the negative effects that the need to raise money for campaigns has on the independence of the judiciary. The importance of money to winning judicial elections is suggested in research by Bonneau (2005) and Bonneau and Hall

(2006) showing that spending by incumbents and challengers in state supreme court races can affect the outcomes of those races. The importance of money in judicial elections is further exemplified by the attitude of one judge who stated that the keys to winning his race were "(1) *Money*; (2) Organization; (3) An early start; (4) *Money*; (5) An excellent candidate; (6) A weak opponent; (7) Excellent public relations and use of media advice; (8) *Money*; (9) Luck"(Banner 1988, 457), and has been echoed by other judges (see, e.g., Phillips 1999; Hanes 2003). To illustrate the amount of money flowing into the hands of judges and judicial candidates, just under $47 million was contributed to state supreme court judges and to other candidates for state judicial offices in 2004 (Goldberg et al. 2005, vii). Two candidates for an open seat on the Illinois Supreme Court that year topped the list of recipients, with the candidates raising over $9.3 million combined in campaign contributions (Goldberg et al. 2005, 18). Another major source of the concern about the effect of campaign contributions on the judiciary is that no state has a rule preventing contributors, be they lawyers[12] or litigants, from having a case adjudicated by a judge to whom they have contributed (Alfini and Brooks 1989).

Some proponents of judicial elections see nothing wrong with judicial candidates receiving large contributions because, in their view, the more money the candidates have available to spend, the more information will reach the public about the candidates and the issues (Tarr 2003), whereas others claim that, "a judge's independence declines in direct proportion to a judge's dependence on others for financial support and other assistance needed to gain and retain the judicial office" (Barnhizer 2001, 370). Studies of the effects of campaign contributions on judicial decision making have indicated that there might be some reason to believe that campaign contributions might bias the judges who receive them to rule in favor of contributors who appear before them. For example, Texans for Public Justice (TPJ), a advocacy group opposed to judicial elections, researched the effects of campaign contributions on the certiorari decisions of the Texas Supreme Court between 1994 and 1998 (Texans for Public Justice 2001).[13] TPJ found that the court accepted 20 percent of the petitions filed by contributors, but accepted just 5.5 percent of petitions filed by noncontributors. Moreover, the results of the study showed that the probability that a petition would be accepted increased as the amount contributed to the court increased. Specifically, the TPJ found that, on average, a petition involving a contributor that gave the justices of the court $100,000 over the period was seven and a half times more likely to have its petition accepted than was a petitioner who did not contribute during the period, and that, on average, petitions from contributors that gave $250,000 or more were ten times more likely to be accepted than were petitions from those who did not contribute.

Other studies of the effect that contributions have on judges' voting habits also found a relationship between the campaign contributions and judges' decision making. For example, Waltenburg and Lopeman (2000) studied decisions in tort cases from the supreme courts of Alabama, Kentucky, and Ohio and found that proplaintiff contributions from attorneys and a justice's partisan affiliation were significant predictors of a justice casting a vote that favored the plaintiff in a decision. Later, McCall (2003) examined a group of cases decided by the Texas Supreme Court between 1994 and 1997 and found that conservative justices (i.e., justices not expected to favor plaintiffs in the cases that she studied) were more likely to vote for plaintiffs in cases concerning procedural issues if these plaintiffs or their lawyers had made contributions to those justices during the most recent election cycle.

Given the incentive that elections create for judicial candidates to curry favor with the public and with contributors, the existence of evidence that judges' decisions can be influenced by electoral considerations and by contributions is not surprising. However, the incentives that elections create for judicial candidates and other interested groups to generate attention and to sway public opinion encourage other behaviors that have equally troubling consequences for the judiciary's reputation for dignity, honesty, and impartiality. For example, although judicial candidates often confine themselves to speaking about noncontroversial topics, some do not. In some campaigns, candidates have been known to misrepresent their own or their opponents' past actions, or have criticized their opponents for failing to take actions that were beyond the

authority of the judiciary (Mathias 1990). Although these charges might constitute violations of various state judicial codes of ethics, most states lack a quick and effective mechanism for investigating, trying, and punishing judicial candidates whose behavior arguably violates those codes in elections (Reed and Schotland 2001).

More frequently, groups interested in influencing the outcome of judicial elections (e.g., political parties, issue advocacy groups, professional organizations, business interests, etc.) are responsible for making the most sensational charges about the candidates because these groups are legally permitted to make any statements that they wish about the candidates. For example, a group that opposed the retention of three justices of the California Supreme Court because of what the group viewed as the justices' procriminal defendant voting records, ran a television advertisement that depicted a woman weeping as she complained about the fact that her child's murderer had not been executed (Mathias 1990), while in Michigan, the state Republican Party accused a candidate for a state supreme court seat of letting an accused child molester off with a "slap-on-the-wrist" (Irwin 2000).[14] Another tactic used by pressure groups is to create advertisements that question the integrity and impartiality of judicial candidates they oppose by suggesting that these candidates are controlled by their major financial backers (Champagne 2001).

GUBERNATORIAL APPOINTMENT WITHOUT A NOMINATING COMMISSION AND LEGISLATIVE APPOINTMENT

As Table 2.1 indicates, in a number of states the governor or the state legislature is responsible for making appointments to the bench without the use of a nominating commission. These are the two oldest methods of judicial selection, and are the only systems that were in use among the states until the mid-1800s, when many of the new states joining the Union adopted partisan elections and some of the older states began to switch from gubernatorial and legislative appointment to partisan elections (Hanssen 2004). This is reflected in the fact that, with the exception of California, the only states that still use these selection methods are among the original states that ratified the Constitution.

In most states where the governor appoints judges to the bench, the appointment must be confirmed by either the entire state legislature, or by the state senate. In some states, such as California and New Hampshire, the governor's judicial nominees must be confirmed by bodies other than the state legislature. For example, in California, all appointments to its supreme court and its courts of appeal must be approved by a commission on judicial appointments. When the nomination is for a seat on the court of appeals, the commission is composed of the chief justice of the supreme court, the attorney general, and the senior presiding justice of the appellate court of the affected district. When a supreme court appointee is being considered, the senior presiding justice of the state's courts of appeal sits on the commission, instead of the chief justice of the supreme court. In New Hampshire, the governor's judicial appointments must be approved by the state's executive council, whose five members are directly elected by the people of the state in partisan elections.

Only Virginia vests unfettered authority in its legislature to elect and reelect judges.[15] In that state, a judicial candidate must be elected by majorities in both houses of the state legislature initially and at the end of each term of office. However, the leadership of the state legislature has recently established a citizens' advisory panel to interview and evaluate candidates for vacancies on the state supreme court and court of appeals (Long 2002). The advisory panel has fourteen members and is composed of lawyers and nonlawyers, but unlike other judicial selection commissions, it must be considered informal because its members are not paid for their services, and the legislature is not bound to elect anyone whom the panel has vetted.

Charges that the judicial selection in gubernatorial and legislative appointment systems is subject to political cronyism are nothing new, having been made in the mid-nineteenth century (K. L. Hall 1983) and by more recent observers (Federalist Society 2002). Indeed, accounts of legislative leaders using their influence to see that their friends are appointed to the bench (Jenkins 2005), of unelected party power brokers influencing the appointment process (Associated Press 2005), or of governors refusing to reappoint judges for ideological reasons (Hoffman, 1997) are evidence that political considerations play as important a role in these selection systems as in every judicial selection system.

THE FUTURE OF JUDICIAL SELECTION

Former New Jersey Supreme Court Chief Justice Arthur Vanderbilt once said that "judicial reform is no sport for the short-winded" (quoted in Armitage 2002, 626). Certainly this has been true historically regarding judicial selection, as many states have modified their method of selecting judges several times throughout their history, with the aim of most of the twentieth-century modifications being the removal of political considerations from the selection process to the greatest extent possible. Despite that, as we have seen, politics remains an inexorable part of the judicial selection and retention process in every state.

Even today, efforts aimed at changing judicial selection systems to remedy perceived faults and biases continue. Some recent successful examples include Tennessee, which switched in 1994 from contested elections to a system of merit-selection and retention elections for its supreme court, and Rhode Island, which also in 1994, switched from a system where the governor appointed judges for life with the consent of the state senate, to a merit-selection system, although one without retention elections (American Judicature Society 2005). However, not all efforts at reforming judicial-selection systems have been successful. For example, in 1987, Ohio voters defeated a ballot initiative that would have instituted a merit-selection system for choosing the state's judges (American Judicature Society 2003b). The measure lost by a 2 to 1 margin, and was supported by the state's chamber of commerce, the Ohio Bar Association, and by insurance companies, but it was strongly opposed by the state's two major political parties, by organized labor, and by the state's trial lawyers (American Judicature Society 2003b). Also in 2000, Florida voters in every county overwhelmingly rejected switching from nonpartisan elections to merit selection for choosing local trial court judges (American Judicature Society 2003b). In fact, despite all of the complaints about judicial elections, no state has completely abandoned elections in the judicial selection process after having once used them, since Virginia did so in 1869, which illustrates how difficult a task it is to persuade people that the public should not be allowed to choose a state's judges (Long 2002).

However, changing the formal rules for selecting judges is not the only way to reform the judicial selection process. For example, although North Carolina and Wisconsin continue to select their judges in contested elections, both states have attempted to reduce judicial candidates' dependence on contributions by making public funds available to judicial candidates[16] who agree to limit the amount of funds that they raise from private sources and to limit their spending during the campaign (McLeod 2005). Other jurisdictions have experimented with encouraging voluntary fair reporting compacts among media outlets, soliciting voluntary candidate speech codes, and with creating blind trust funds for distributing contributions to judicial candidates, but it is questionable whether any of these reforms will significantly eliminate the fundamental incompatibility between judicial elections and judicial independence (McLeod 2005). In fact, the American Bar Association Commission on the 21st Century Judiciary (2003) recommended that all states move away from elections, and all other forms of judicial reselection, in favor of having judges serve until a mandatory retirement age, or for single, nonrenewable terms. In the short term, moves aimed at changing how state judges are selected will continue, but it seems beyond doubt that states will continue to reform their judicial selection procedures as ideas about the proper balance between judicial accountability and independence continue to evolve.

Notes

1. The Governor's Council is a constitutionally ordained body that exercises certain advisory and confirmatory functions within the executive branch. The council is composed of eight members, each elected from a different district in the state, and the Lt. Governor who serves ex-officio. The eight councilors serve two-year terms.

2. The one exception to this general rule is South Carolina, which has a commission that is composed of members of state legislators and nonstate legislators.

3. One way to prevent the politicization of the selection process might be to require partisan balance on nominating commissions. This conclusion is suggested by the research of Ashman and Alfini (1974), which indicated that the number of commissioners who felt that politics plays a role in their deliberations and decisions was much lower in states where the law requires the commission to have an equal number of Republicans and Democrats, than in states where partisan balance is not required.

4. For example, Hall found that between 1980 and 1995, only 1.7 percent of all state supreme court judges who ran in retention elections were defeated.

5. At present, only Japan and Switzerland select judges through elections. In Japan, members of its Supreme Court must run in uncontested elections to continue in office at the conclusion of their terms, while in Switzerland, some lay judges in its cantonal courts are elected.

6. The term *judicial candidates* is used here to refer to all those running for a judicial office in an election, including incumbents and challengers.

7. A recent federal court of appeals decision has thrown the constitutionality of state rules prohibiting judicial candidates from identifying themselves as members of a political party, from participating in partisan political activities, and from personally soliciting and accepting campaign contributions into doubt. See *Republican Party of Minnesota v. White* (8th Cir. 2005), cert. denied sub nom. *Dimick v. Republican Party of Minnesota* (2006).

8. Similar rules of judicial conduct apply to the conduct of judicial candidates in states that use retention elections.

9. A few studies have shed light on the level of competition in state judicial elections. For example, M. G. Hall (2001) found that between 1980 and 1994, 1.7 percent of incumbent state supreme court judges who ran for reelection in retention elections were defeated, with the rate of incumbent defeat being 8.6 percent in nonpartisan elections and 18.8 percent in partisan elections. She also found that incumbents who retained their seats in contested elections regularly won by much larger margins, on average, than did challengers who defeated incumbents or winners of open seats. Furthermore, in a study that looked at partisan and nonpartisan judicial elections between 1996 and 1998, Abbe and Herrnson (2002) found that 41.5 percent of trial court races and 68.2 percent of appellate court races were competitive, which they defined as a race in which the winning candidate received between 40 percent and 60 percent of the vote.

10. The Texas Court of Criminal Appeals is the court of last resort for criminal cases in Texas. The Texas Supreme Court serves this function for all other types of cases.

11. These states are as follows: California, Illinois, Kentucky, Louisiana, New Jersey, North Carolina, Ohio, and Texas.

12. For example, in 2004, attorneys and law firms contributed almost nine million dollars to supreme court judges and candidates (Goldberg et al. 2005).

13. The Texas Supreme Court has nine justices and requires at least four justices to vote in favor of granting a petition for the court to decide the case. The justices' votes and their deliberations about the petitions are strictly confidential, and the justices are not required to explain why they granted or rejected a given petition.

14. Some television stations refused to broadcast this advertisement because it was considered too misleading (Irwin 2000).

15. South Carolina also vests its legislature with the power to elect the state's judges, but the legislature is limited to electing candidates who have been nominated for the vacancy by the state's judicial nominating commission.

16. In North Carolina, public funding is available for candidates for the state court of appeals and the supreme court, while in Wisconsin, public funding is available only for supreme court candidates.

3

IN THEIR OWN INTEREST

Pressure Groups in the Federal Judicial Selection Process

Lauren Cohen Bell

The Constitution creates a fairly simple process for the selection of federal judges at all three levels of the federal judiciary. So-called Article III judges who serve on the U.S. District Courts, the U.S. Courts of Appeals, and the U.S. Supreme Court are nominated by the president and then confirmed by the U.S. Senate for life terms. Although this process seems straightforward enough, in reality the federal judicial selection process has become quite complex. Some presidents value certain things in their judicial nominees while other presidents value other things. For example, President Reagan was far more concerned about the ideological views of his appointees to the lower federal courts than was President Clinton. President Carter even used nominating commissions similar to the merit commissions used in many states to help him choose his nominees to the lower federal courts. Nominations to the U.S. Supreme Court always receive a great deal of attention from the media and from interest groups, especially when the Supreme Court is divided 5 to 4 on many highly controversial issues.

At times the U.S. Senate confirms the presidential nominees to the bench with little controversy, while some nominees face fierce opposition in both the Senate Judiciary Committee and in the full Senate. One aspect that has complicated the federal judicial selection procedure is the increasing role that interest groups play in this process. This chapter explores how interest groups are becoming more and more important players in the federal judicial selection process, not just for nominees to the U.S. Supreme Court but also for appointees to the lower federal courts as well. Because political interest groups care deeply about the selection process for federal judges, this chapter illustrates the intersection of law and politics in our country.

I deeply regret that confirmation as a Federal Judge is becoming more like a political campaign for these nominees. They are being required to gather letters of support and urge their friends, colleagues and clients to support their candidacy or risk being mischaracterized by those who do not know them.

—*U.S. Senator Patrick Leahy, February 11, 1998*

The judicial selection process is crucial to providing the federal courts with a full complement of qualified jurists. Yet over the last decade and a half, the process has changed. What was once a straightforward process that could be completed in a matter of months, now is frequently subject to years-long delays and convoluted parliamentary maneuvers. These changes to the confirmation process can in large part be attributed to the interest groups that proliferate along the political spectrum. Hoping to shape judicial outcomes, interest groups have, in the words of one former senator, "turned the confirmation process into something that's not much different than passing a bill."[1] In this chapter I focus attention on the federal judicial appointment process generally, with special attention to the role that organized interests have played in transforming it over the last several decades.

THE APPOINTMENT PROCESS

Although it has varied somewhat throughout the course of history, the appointment process has always consisted of two distinct phases—the *nomination phase*, in which the president selects his nominee, and the *confirmation phase*, in which the U.S. Senate reviews the president's choice and acts (or fails to act) to confirm him or her. These processes are specified in Article III of the U.S. Constitution, which created the U.S. Supreme Court and "such inferior courts as the Congress shall from time to time ordain and establish." The courts created under Article III (U.S. District Courts, U.S. Courts of Appeals, and the U.S. Supreme Court) are the backbone of the federal judicial branch. Judges on these so-called Article III courts serve for terms of "good behavior," which means that barring the commission of an impeachable

offense, they have lifetime tenure from the moment of their appointment.

The Nominating Phase

The judges on Article III courts are selected according to the process specified in Article II, which established the presidency. Section II of that article gives the president the power to nominate and "by and with the advice and consent of the Senate" to appoint the judges required to staff the Supreme Court and the lower federal courts created by Congress in accordance with the provisions of Article III. All justices and judges that currently sit on the U.S. Supreme Court, U.S. Courts of Appeals, and U.S. District Courts were appointed through this process, although a handful first assumed the bench as recess appointees that were later confirmed by the Senate.

The process varies somewhat for individual nominees, and different presidents have used differing processes to select their nominees, but in general, when a vacancy or potential vacancy is identified, the White House Office of Presidential Personnel receives recommendations, checks references, conducts thorough background investigations of potential nominees, and, ultimately, makes a recommendation to the president. The Constitution offers the president little guidance in the selection of federal judges; Article II provides no list of qualifications for the office. Scholars have noted that when appointing Supreme Court justices, presidents consider such factors as whether the nomination will help to secure reelection votes, whether the nomination will affect the ideological balance on the Court, whether the prospective nominee has demonstrated loyalty to the president, and whether a particular judicial outcome is likely if a nomination is made (Langhauser 2006). Almost always presidents nominate someone from their own political party for federal judgeships (see, e.g., Baum 2004, 41).[2]

During the early period of American history, presidents virtually always selected nominees whom they knew personally or who had been recommended by powerful congressional allies. In the 1950s, under President Dwight D. Eisenhower, the process of selecting judicial nominees was routinized, as the president put into place a staff bureaucracy within the

White House that allowed him to be removed from all but the most important nominations. In 1977, President Jimmy Carter further reduced the role of the president in the selection process when he issued Executive Order 11972 creating nominating commissions designed to select judges for the U.S. Courts of Appeals (also sometimes known as the U.S. Circuit Courts; see Martinek this volume, chapter 9). The role of the commissions was to narrow the list of candidates for federal judgeships to five, from which the president would select his nominee. A year later, President Carter issued Executive Order 12059, which explicitly encouraged the recruitment of qualified women and minority candidates to serve as federal circuit court judges and that was designed to increase the diversity of the federal judiciary, where few women or minority judges were serving in the late 1970s. (These commissions were similar to the merit commissions used to select many state judges, as described in more detail in McLeod this volume, chapter 2.)

Table 3.1 provides a demographic overview of the current federal judiciary. It indicates how many current sitting judges were appointed by each of the five most recent U.S. presidents. In addition, Table 3.1 summarizes the gender and racial backgrounds of each active federal judge both overall and by appointing president. Several previous studies have found that the race and/or gender of a judicial nominee can affect how rapidly—and even whether—he or she is confirmed (see, e.g., MacClean 2006; Martinek, Kemper, and Van Winkle 2002; Bell 2002b). In addition, there

is evidence that a judge's descriptive characteristics, including race, ethnicity, and gender, can effect the way in which he or she makes judicial decisions (see, e.g., Milligan 2006). Presidential attentiveness to nominees' descriptive characteristics might also result from an interest "in diversifying the composition of the federal courts or satisfying underrepresented segments of society. Moreover, nominees' ages have been very important to some Presidents who wanted to ensure that their appointees could continue to serve as judges and Justices long after they left office" (Gerhardt 2005, 1208).

Regardless of where a nomination originates—from among the president's inner circle, from a home-state senator, or from a nominating commission—being nominated by the president is only the first step. Once the president announces the nomination, he formally submits it to the Senate for its consideration through the Office of Executive Clerk of the Senate.

The Confirmation Phase

Once a nomination has been received by the Senate, nominees to the federal courts are referred to the Senate Judiciary Committee, where they are investigated again by the Senate Judiciary Committee's majority and minority party staffers. If the investigators, who hold high-level security clearances, determine that there is nothing in a nominee's past that will embarrass him or her—or embarrass the members of the Senate—then the nomination will be sent forward to the chair of the

Table 3.1 Demographic Breakdown of the Federal Judiciary

Appointing President	Total Judges Serving	Female	African American	Hispanic	Other Minority
George W. Bush (R)	253	51	18	26	2
Bill Clinton (D)	341	97	60	21	5
George H. W. Bush (R)	113	30	8	6	1
Ronald Reagan (R)	97	10	3	5	1
Jimmy Carter (D)	25	9	4	1	0
Total	829[a]	197	93	59	9

Note. From Alliance for Justice (http://www.allianceforjustice.org/judicial/judicial_selection_resources/selection_database/activeJudges.asp) and the United States Department of Justice (http://www.usdoj.gov/olp/judicialnominations.htm). Data as of December 2006. R = Republican; D = Democrat.

[a] Number represents the total number of sitting judges in the federal judiciary as of December 1, 2006. Does not include the 51 vacant judgeships as of that date.

Senate Judiciary Committee, who will set a date for a hearing and a vote of the Committee. If a majority of members of the Senate Judiciary Committee vote to send the nomination forward to the full Senate, the nominee will be placed onto the Senate's Executive Calendar, which is used for the purpose of scheduling votes on presidential nominations and treaties awaiting Senate ratification. Nominees must receive a majority vote of the full Senate to be confirmed to the bench.

CHANGES TO THE FEDERAL JUDICIAL SELECTION PROCESS

Federal judicial selection has evolved in ways closely related to evolution of the role of the federal courts in the American government. Early in American history, the federal judiciary was small, its powers were not well-defined, and even early Supreme Court justices sometimes saw little reason to attend all the hearings before the Court. Despite the possibility of serving lifetime terms, judges' tenures were often relatively short, as they left office to pursue other positions in government that were considered to have more prestige or that offered steadier work. Indeed, the U.S. Supreme Court did not hear its first substantive case until 1793, when it heard *Chisholm v. Georgia* (1793), and its decision was promptly overturned by Congress and the states through passage and ratification of the Eleventh Amendment to the Constitution. Moreover, the Court was held in such low esteem that when the Court heard arguments in *Marbury v. Madison* (1803), no one from President Jefferson's administration showed up to argue Madison's side of the case.

During this period, judicial selection was relatively simple. Presidents would select their nominees from among their friends or political allies (there was no real presidential staff so the decision was the president's alone), and the Senate routinely acted quickly. For example, when President Washington submitted his first judicial nominees to the Senate for its approval, it took only a day for the Senate to act. Although President Washington did not always get his way when it came to appointing judges and other federal officials, the Senate did act quickly to determine the fate of his nominees. During the Washington Administration,

the norm of *senatorial courtesy* also was established. This is the practice of presidential consultation with, and the Senate's collective deference to, the senators from the state in which a judicial vacancy exists. In practice, what this means is that presidents will consult home-state senators when judicial vacancies within their states occur, especially when the president and home-state senators are from the same political party. In many cases, the president simply defers to the home-state senators, permitting them the *de facto* choice of nominee for vacancies in the federal district courts. The Senate rarely confirms nominees that are not approved by the home-state senators.

Although senatorial courtesy helped to make the confirmation of most district court nominees noncontroversial, over the course of U.S. history, the confirmation of appellate court nominees tended to be more conflictual because these nominees serve on federal courts with multistate jurisdictions. Without a specific Senate "champion" to promote their candidacies, appeals court nominees found that their waits for confirmation could be lengthy (Bell 2002a). Nevertheless, through the 1970s, the confirmation process operated relatively smoothly; in fact, a 1977 report by the public-interest group Common Cause lambasted "the Senate Rubber Stamp Machine" in a report by the same name (Common Cause 1977).

Although federal judicial selection was largely noncontroversial throughout most of the nation's history, in the modern era this has changed somewhat. Table 3.2 summarizes the trend toward lengthier processing times for confirmation of the president's nominees over the last few decades. It demonstrates that nominees generally wait far longer for confirmation during periods of divided government, where one party controls the presidency and the other party controls at least one house of Congress. Moreover, the table shows that with the exception of the 98th and 106th Congresses, judicial nominees wait longer for confirmation in Congresses preceding presidential elections than they do in those preceding midterm elections.

As Table 3.2 demonstrates, selecting and appointing judges is no longer the rapid process it once was. One of the primary reasons for this is the increasing participation of interest groups, although their participation is symptomatic of a multiplicity of other changes

Table 3.2 Average Number of Days, Nomination to Confirmation/Adjournment

Congress (Years)	President	Party of President	Majority Party in Senate	Average Number of Days
79th (1945–46)	Truman	D	D	17.7
80th (1947–48)[a]	Truman	D	R	47.0
81st (1949–50)	Truman	D	D	49.5
82nd (1951–52)	Truman	D	D	34.3
83rd (1953–54)	Eisenhower	R	R	25.3
84th (1955–56)[a]	Eisenhower	R	D	46.2
85th (1957–58)[a]	Eisenhower	R	D	50.5
86th (1959–60)[a]	Eisenhower	R	D	94.9
87th (1961–62)	Kennedy	D	D	32.8
88th (1963–64)	Kennedy/Johnson	D	D	43.7
89th (1965–66)	Johnson	D	D	25.7
90th (1967–68)	Johnson	D	D	34.1
91st (1969–70)[a]	Nixon	R	D	29.3
92nd (1971–72)[a]	Nixon	R	D	23.9
93rd (1973–74)[a]	Nixon/Ford	R	D	25.6
94th (1975–76)[a]	Ford	R	D	34.1
95th (1977–78)	Carter	D	D	35.4
96th (1979–80)	Carter	D	D	88.6
97th (1981–82)	Reagan	R	R	32.2
98th (1983–84)	Reagan	R	R	35.7
99th (1985–86)	Reagan	R	R	44.2
100th (1987–88)[a]	Reagan	R	D	144.8
101st (1989–90)[a]	Bush	R	D	78.2
102nd (1991–92)[a]	Bush	R	D	137.7
103rd (1993–94)	Clinton	D	D	80.9
104th (1995–96)[a]	Clinton	D	R	157.6
105th (1997–98)[a]	Clinton	D	R	203.5
106th (1999–2000)[a]	Clinton	D	R	224.6
107th (2001–02)	Bush	R	R/D	160.2[b]
108th (2003–04)	Bush	R	R	146.5
109th (2005–06)	Bush	R	R	133.9

Note. Data for the 98th through 106th Congresses compiled from Rutkus and Sollenberger, "Judicial Nomination Statistics: U.S. District and Circuit Courts 1977–2003." CRS Report for Congress, 2004. Data for the 107th through 109th Congresses compiled from the United States Department of Justice (http://www.usdoj.gov/olp/judicialnominations.htm).

[a] Periods of divided government.

[b] For individuals nominated prior to Senator Jim Jeffords' departure from the Republican party, in August 2001, the average number of days from nomination to confirmation or Senate adjournment was 194.95; for those individuals nominated after the switch, the average number of days was 150.64.

to the process over the past several years. Interest groups have participated in the judicial appointment process for three quarters of a century, first engaging in appointment politics at the Supreme Court level when President Herbert Hoover nominated John J. Parker to a seat on the U.S. Supreme Court in 1930.

Parker's nomination was opposed by several interest groups, including the National Association for the Advancement of Colored Persons (NAACP) and the American Federation of Labor (AFL). Parker was ultimately rejected by the Senate by a one-vote margin (O'Brien 1993).

As the federal courts generally, and the U.S. Supreme Court specifically, became important to the success of President Roosevelt's New Deal reforms, and as the appointment process for all federal positions became more routine, the opportunities for interest groups to participate increased. The American Bar Association (ABA) in 1948 began rating all judicial nominees and, in some cases, potential and presumptive nominees (Goldman 1997, 86); the purpose of their ratings was to convey to both the president and the Senate the level of esteem within which candidates were held by the legal profession. An ABA committee would generally evaluate the judicial nominees as "well qualified," "qualified," or "not qualified" (see Baum 2004, 30–31). By the late 1970s, representatives of the ABA and other interest groups were routinely invited to participate in confirmation hearings for nominees to the federal bench (Bell 2002a).[3]

Yet no nominations were considered as important to the groups as were (and continue to be) nominations to fill vacancies on the U.S. Supreme Court. One of the most important modern confirmation fights was over President Johnson's 1968 nomination of Associate Justice Abe Fortas to the chief justice's chair following the retirement of Chief Justice Earl Warren. During the committee hearings on the nomination, conservatives attempted to blame Fortas for all the evils they saw in the activism of the Warren Court era (see Silverstein 1994, 22–28). Seeing the election of President Nixon as being imminent, Republicans and conservative southern Democrats then filibustered the Fortas nomination on the floor of the Senate (see Epstein and Segal 2005, 98; Maltese 1995, 71). Because Senate rules allow an individual senator to debate any issue without time limits, senators may attempt to "talk a bill" to death or delay a nomination indefinitely through what is known as a filibuster. Today, it takes sixty votes in the Senate to invoke cloture and end a filibuster. Filibusters have been rare when it comes to judicial nominations, but following the disputed 2000 presidential election Democrats used the filibuster to stop several lower federal court nominations made by President George W. Bush, described in more detail later (see Epstein and Segal 2005, 98–99). After the filibuster of his nomination to be chief justice, eventually Justice Fortas resigned from the Supreme Court,

and President Nixon nominated Warren Burger to be the next chief justice.[4]

In 1987, interest groups demonstrated just how significant they believed seats on the U.S. Supreme Court to be when they waged an extraordinary campaign against Robert Bork, President Ronald Reagan's nominee to replace retiring Justice Lewis Powell. According to O'Brien (1993), more than eighty organizations opposed Bork's nomination; these groups included the American Civil Liberties Union (ACLU), the American Federation of Labor–Congress of Industrial Organizations (AFL–CIO), and the National Organization for Women (NOW). Four ABA committee members gave Bork a "not qualified" rating; even though he was a prestigious legal scholar and judge (see Baum 2004, 31).

It was not merely the presence of so many groups in this confirmation fight that was so remarkable; it was also their tactics. The groups waged an unprecedented battle to influence public opinion that included grassroots lobbying efforts and even featured television advertisements in which Academy Award–winning actor Gregory Peck encouraged viewers to articulate to their senators their opposition to Bork, whom he claimed would roll back civil rights. It was not a coincidence either that Peck's Oscar had been awarded to him for his portrayal of southern lawyer Atticus Finch in the screen version of Harper Lee's *To Kill a Mockingbird* or that Peck's character's role was to defend an innocent African American man in the Jim Crow–era South. Ultimately, Bork was rejected by the Senate, and the interest groups realized that through the same tactics they regularly employed in the legislative process, they could affect the outcomes of the judicial appointment process. This realization led to the formation or restructuring of several groups for them to wield even more influence over judicial appointments.

Coming soon after the failed nomination of Judge Bork to the Supreme Court, the 1991 nomination of Clarence Thomas to the Supreme Court by the first President Bush also proved quite contentious, although Thomas was eventually confirmed by a narrow vote in the full Senate. The ABA gave Thomas a merely qualified rating, which Savage described as "lukewarm" (Savage 1993, 432). Two members of the ABA committee even gave Thomas a not qualified rating (see Baum 2004, 31). When law professor Anita Hill testified that Clarence Thomas had sexually harassed her when she had worked for him at the Equal Employment Opportunity Commission, Thomas's confirmation hearings became a TV spectacle because "millions of viewers were gripped by the dramatic clash between the judge and the professor" (Savage 1993, 441). Interest groups lined up, both in support and in opposition to the Thomas nomination. Conservative groups such as the U.S. Chamber of Commerce and the Young Americans for Freedom wanted to see Clarence Thomas confirmed to the U.S. Supreme Court (see Baum 2004, 33). Opponents of the Thomas nomination included liberal groups such as the Leadership Conference on Civil Rights, the Alliance for Justice, and a coalition of 185 other civil rights and civil liberties groups. The National Abortion Rights Action League and the AFL–CIO also got involved in the confirmation process by opposing the Thomas nomination. As Baum concluded, "The opposition groups were unable to achieve the same kind of massive campaign against Thomas that they had launched against Bork. But their opposition helped to create concern about Thomas among liberal senators and thereby contributed to the decisions by most Democratic senators to vote against Thomas's confirmation" (Baum 2004, 33).[5] Clarence Thomas was confirmed by a highly partisan vote of 52 to 48 in the full Senate.

Although interest groups played a lesser role in the confirmations of Ruth Bader Ginsburg in 1993 and Stephen Breyer in 1994 (see Baum 2004, 33), they did attempt to weigh in on the nominations of Chief Justice John Roberts in 2005 and of Samuel Alito in 2005–2006. Although many liberal interest groups eventually opposed the Roberts nomination as chief justice, they withheld announcing their opposition until just before the Senate Judiciary Committee began his confirmation hearings (see, e.g., Becker 2005, A3). Roberts was confirmed as chief justice by a vote of 78 to 22. Interest groups took a much different strategy for the Alito nomination. Both conservative groups in favor of the nomination and liberal groups opposed to the nomination spent a great deal of money on television advertising well before the Judiciary Committee hearings in an attempt to sway uncommitted senators from both parties. Groups opposing the Alito nomination

included the nation's largest civil rights coalition, the Leadership Conference on Civil Rights; NARAL Pre-Choice America; MoveOn.org; the Human Rights Campaign; many environmental and labor groups, and the People for the American Way. Conservatives bought air time in support of Alito through a coalition called the Committee for Justice and another called the Judicial Confirmation Network (see Becker 2005, A3). Other conservative groups such as Progress for America and the Family Research Council bought TV ads and used phone and e-mail campaigns, to support the Alito nomination (Kiely and Memmott 2006, 7A).

On January 31, 2006, Justice Alito was confirmed by a vote of 58 to 42, with only 4 Democrats voting in favor of his nomination and 1 liberal Republican senator voting against the nomination (Stern and Perine 2006, 340–1). In fact, the confirmation vote for now Justice Alito was the most partisan in history. The only justice confirmed to sit on the Supreme Court who received more negative votes than Justice Alito was Justice Clarence Thomas. The interest group fight over the Alito nomination makes it clear that Supreme Court confirmations have become quite partisan and highly ideological events (Wittes 2006, 5–6).

The battles over Supreme Court nominations provide the context for understanding the fights over lower federal court nominations during the presidency of George W. Bush. For lower federal court nominations, throughout history on average about 80 percent of presidential nominations have been confirmed by the Senate (Epstein and Segal 2005, 99–100). During the Clinton presidency, the Republicans in the Senate slowed down as many Clinton nominees for the lower federal bench as they could because their conservative base still was quite angry over what they perceived as continued liberal judicial activism on the federal courts (see Miller this volume, chapter 19). When George W. Bush won the disputed 2000 presidential election, the Democrats decided to do what they could to prevent the most conservative Bush appointees from gaining federal judgeships. Several nominations were filibustered on the Senate floor, and the Republicans could not gather the necessary 41 votes to invoke cloture and end the filibusters. The Republicans responded by attempting to eliminate the filibuster option for all judicial appointments, which became known as the so-called nuclear option. If the majority Republicans had eliminated the filibuster as an option for the minority party, it is likely that the Democrats would have used every parliamentary weapon available to them to prevent the Senate from conducting any business (see Stolberg 2006). A group of fourteen moderate senators from both parties prevented further filibusters, but they also prevented conservatives from eliminating the filibuster entirely for judicial nominees (see Nather 2005). President Bush renominated each of the four contentious nominees at the outset of the 108th Congress, as will be discussed in more detail later.

Conventional wisdom suggests that it was the success of interest group opposition to Bork that led to their omnipresence in confirmation politics over the last two decades. However, it is an oversimplification to credit the liberal groups' successful opposition to Robert Bork with bringing about the widespread participation of interest groups in the appointment process for all levels of the federal judiciary. In fact, since 1987, the year that the Senate rejected Bork for the Supreme Court, interest groups have become less likely to participate in the public aspects of the confirmation process (such as Senate hearings), choosing instead to focus their efforts behind the scenes and at the grassroots level in the hope of influencing confirmation outcomes (Bell 2002a).

The widespread presence of interest groups in the appointment process can be accounted for by the convergence of several factors including: an increase in the number of interest groups since the middle of the twentieth century; changes to the role of the federal courts during this same time period, along with interest groups' concomitant recognition that the federal courts were likely to be responsible for driving change to the social, economic, and political issues they cared most about; and, finally, changes to the Senate confirmation phase of the appointment process. Each of these is discussed next.

INCREASING NUMBERS OF INTEREST GROUPS

The 2005 edition of *Washington Representatives*, the annual directory of registered interest groups

and lobbyists that is a reference for academics and congressional staffers alike, lists more than 11,000 organizations and more than 18,000 lobbyists that are registered under the guidelines of the Lobbying Disclosure Act of 1995 (Public Law 104–65, 1995). Organizations must register under the Lobbying Disclosure Act if they spend more than $49,000 per year on lobbying activities; individuals spending more than 20 percent of their professional time engaged in lobbying likewise must register. Section 3(8)(iv) of the Lobbying Disclosure Act applies the provisions of the law directly to the appointment process by mandating that organizations must report activities concerning, "the nomination or confirmation of a person for a position subject to confirmation by the Senate" (Public Law 104–65, 1995).

The numbers of organizations and lobbyists reported above reflect dramatic increases over time and are consistent with extant research. Lipset (1995) using different data noted that between 1974 and 1994, the number of lobbyists doubled from roughly 3,500 to more than 7,000. Berry (1997, 22) further illustrated the growth in pressure groups' efforts to influence electoral and legislative outcomes by comparing the number of Political Action Committees (PACs) in operation in 1974—608—with the number in operation in 1994—roughly 4,000.

As these data indicate, the number of organizations engaged in lobbying activities has grown dramatically over time. With more groups seeking to accomplish the policy goals of their members, the effect of the increasing number of groups is that policy makers find that they are being pulled in multiple directions simultaneously. In the judicial appointment process, this also means that no matter who is nominated, there are groups on both sides of the nomination seeking to influence whether the nominee ever takes a seat on the federal bench.

INTEREST GROUPS AND THE "DEMOCRATIZATION" OF THE APPOINTMENT PROCESS

A second reason for the proliferation of interest groups in the appointment process is that the federal courts today are thought of very differently than they were during the eighteenth and early nineteenth centuries. Public opinion polls routinely reveal that the public holds the judicial branch in higher esteem than it holds either the legislative or the executive branches of government. Since the early 1950s, substantial gains in civil and political rights for women, racial minorities, and other underrepresented groups have been precipitated by decisions made by the federal courts. In addition, many contentious and divisive political issues have been addressed by the federal courts, including prayer in schools, flag burning, gay marriage, abortion, and criminal defendants' rights, with the judicial branch at the forefront of policy changes in all of these areas. Emboldened by the success of civil rights organizations like the NAACP during the 1950s and 1960s, other political interests began to see the courts as viable alternatives to traditional mechanisms for bringing about policy changes (Glendon 1991). As Mark Silverstein (1994, 62) explained in *Judicious Choices*:

> With the coming of the Burger Court in the early 1970s, an assortment of…interests—for example, environmentalists, feminists, consumer groups, political reformers—found in the judiciary an attractive alternative to the other branches.…[I]n the modern era…increased access to the courts has combined with the new tools of judicial power to make the judiciary an attractive ally for a host of powerful constituent groups.

Berry (1997, 176) echoed these sentiments noting, "Interest groups not only use the courts as an appeals process for adverse decisions by other branches, but they also litigate when they feel that their lack of popular support makes it fruitless for them to lobby Congress or the executive branch."

The changing role for the federal courts increased tension between appointed federal judges and elected policy makers in the Congress and in state legislatures (see also Miller this volume, chapter 19). Two factors exacerbated these tensions. First, many of the decisions being made by the federal courts had the effect of overturning acts of Congress or the state legislatures. Indeed, when the courts strike down acts of Congress,

there is generally a direct effect on the confirmation process. For example, between 1995 and 2000, the U.S. Supreme Court struck down three federal laws in whole or in part—the Gun Free Schools Act, the Religious Freedom Restoration Act, and the Violence Against Women Act in *United States v. Lopez* (1995), *City of Boerne v. Flores* (1997), and *United States v. Morrison* (2000), respectively. In the confirmation hearings held for lower federal court nominees following each of these decisions, senators who supported the original legislation sought nominees' views on the appropriateness of striking down acts of Congress. In the case of the *Boerne* decision, conservative senators sought to determine whether President Bill Clinton's nominees were "judicial activists" by asking nominees to comment specifically on what they would have done if they had been on the Supreme Court and had heard the case. The politically astute nominees knew better than to answer these loaded questions.

In addition, interest group success before the courts begat additional efforts to secure policy changes through the judicial branch. Berry (1997) noted that interest groups have increased their use of litigation strategies over the last several decades, and Caldeira and Wright (1988) elsewhere determined that U.S. Supreme Court justices vote in favor of granting *certiorari* more frequently than their average rate in cases in which multiple, outside-interest groups file briefs *amicus curiae*. This is especially true when the groups filing briefs are "repeat players," meaning that they have long-established relationships with the Court through decades of litigation and brief filing. Thus, interest groups have incentives to participate before the courts at high rates. Other studies of repeat players before the federal judiciary have likewise found that when the solicitor general (see Ubertaccio this volume, chapter 10) or other prominent repeat players appear before the Court as litigants, their likelihood of gaining a judicial outcome favorable to their position increases (see, e.g., Salokar 1992; Bailey, Kamoie, and Maltzman 2005; Johnson 2004).

In combination, interest groups' increasing use of and success before the courts to dismantle acts of Congress and the state legislatures has led to significant tensions between the courts and Congress (see Miller this volume, chapter 19). In his "2004 Year End

Report on the Federal Judiciary," the late Chief Justice of the United States William Rehnquist highlighted the consequences of several of these tensions, including efforts to limit or reduce the salaries of federal judges, efforts to impeach judges, and efforts to reduce the jurisdiction of the federal courts (Rehnquist 2004). When tensions between the two institutions are running high, the confirmation process becomes an opportunity for Congress to attempt to reign in the federal courts. Recognizing that they are generally powerless to prevent the courts from overturning legislation, some members of Congress—not only in the Senate, but in the House of Representatives, too—believe that influencing who is confirmed is of paramount importance to public policy outcomes.

CHANGES TO THE U.S. SENATE

The third factor that has contributed to the changed nature of the appointment process is change within the Senate that has led to greater opportunity for the articulation and satisfaction of particularistic interests. Throughout much of the twentieth century, the judicial confirmation process usually was closed to interest group participation. Prior to the 1960s, the confirmation process was not yet a political process, and there was no room for interest group participation at all. Senators, following the age-old norms of the Senate, typically acquiesced to the president or to the Senate leadership. Further, the Senate's confirmation process for most nominees was *ad hoc*, with few committees requiring confirmation hearings and none requiring detailed personal or financial disclosures. The lack of standardized procedures combined with internal Senate norms of reciprocity and collegiality to make interest group participation a rare event. As Flemming, Macleod, and Talbert (1998, 620) noted, "Before Nixon's election, groups testified infrequently [at judicial confirmation hearings]."

During the 1960s and 1970s, as the once insular Senate moved away from being an institution in which senior members of the body made decisions that junior colleagues were expected to support toward a more open chamber of relative equals (Silverstein 1994), interest groups began to find additional opportunities to wield influence in the judicial confirmation process. Newly-enhanced, formalized screening procedures at the committee level created a greater number of veto points on nominations within the Senate. Additional reforms to the legislative process, such as the 1976 Government in the Sunshine Act (Public Law 94–409, 1976), clarified and reinforced the necessity of openness in public proceedings generally, and this new openness had predictable effects on the appointment process. Interest groups were able to get information ahead of time concerning when confirmation hearings would be held and thus were able to get themselves on the hearing panels or to stage public demonstrations of support or opposition.

With the launch in 1986 of C-SPAN2 (the cable public affairs network dedicated to gavel-to-gavel coverage of the U.S. Senate), members of the Senate had a broader audience for their floor speeches and committee activities. Recognizing that the network reached potentially thousands of their constituents each day, senators' incentive structures shifted. No longer could they control the way in which their constituents learned about their activities in Washington—constituents were able to monitor the legislative activities of their senators themselves. With this increased level of accountability, senators no longer could treat some votes, such as those on presidential nominations, as generally lacking in political consequence.

While this increased openness was largely perceived as good democratic practice, it also meant that the messages that interest groups were transmitting to senators at televised hearings or in rallies on the Capitol steps were subject to scrutiny from the media and the public. Such scrutiny left both the groups and members of the Senate vulnerable to criticism and made it increasingly necessary for senators to have to explain their votes on judicial nominees. Interest groups also recognized that they could use grassroots tactics, honed from decades of use in the legislative process, to influence senators' judicial confirmation decisions, and many senators found their votes on nominees being used against them during reelection campaigns. As a result, the Senate took steps to reduce the openness of the judicial confirmation process.

The changing role for the ABA between 1996 and 2001 provides a good example of changes to the

Senate's internal processes that had implications for the appointment of federal judges. In one of his first official acts of the 105th Congress, Senate Judiciary Committee Chairman Orrin Hatch in February of 1997 eliminated a formal role for the ABA in the confirmation process. Hatch's office issued a press release on February 18, 1997 that stated, "Sen. Hatch...has concluded that, while individual senators are free to weigh the input of any group how they see fit, the ABA should not play an official role." Hatch's rationale echoed that of the House Republican Policy Committee, which had issued a policy statement that read in part: "The ABA...has no right to a formal role in the process of judicial selection or confirmation" (House Republican Policy Committee 1996, 1).

Because of the ABA's low ratings for Supreme Court nominees Bork and Thomas, many conservatives had come to believe that the ABA had acquired a liberal bias in its assessment of judicial appointees (see Baum 2004, 30–31). The concern among conservatives was that the ABA's perceived liberal bias affected the organization's ratings of judicial nominees. In 2001, President George W. Bush likewise ended a formal role for the ABA in the judicial selection process (see, e.g., Baum 2004, 31). Although the organization continues to evaluate and distribute its ratings of all nominees to the federal courts, their influence over either the nomination or confirmation stages of the appointment process has been substantially reduced from what it was prior to 1997.

Hatch's actions with regard to the ABA sent a clear message that interest groups were not welcome to participate formally in judicial confirmations. In fact, interest groups were told that they would not be able to participate in confirmation hearings beginning in 1997. According to one Republican senator, who agreed to be interviewed on the condition of anonymity: "Senator Hatch says, and I agree, that interest groups shouldn't have a formal role in a confirmation hearing" (quoted in Bell 2002a, 76). The senator's next statement summed up the change in interest group participation in judicial appointments: "What's the use of hauling a bunch of them in to testify, when you can meet with them outside the hearing room?" (quoted in Bell 2002a, 76). The result was to reduce the number of interest groups offering testimony in favor

or against a judicial nominee to zero beginning in the late 1990s. To the extent that materials supporting or opposing specific nominees became part of the hearing record for judicial nominations hearings, it was because the materials were introduced into the record by a member of the Senate Judiciary Committee, and not because the groups had been permitted a formal role in the process.

CHANGING INTEREST GROUP TACTICS AND STRATEGIES

Interest groups' strategies for promoting judicial nominees they like and for working to keep those nominees they dislike off the federal bench have evolved since interest groups first began to participate in the confirmation hearings for Supreme Court nominees in the 1930s. The groups today pursue both public and private, behind-the-scenes strategies. Interest groups borrow extensively from their legislative strategies in their attempts to influence appointment outcomes through both the formal and informal channels that are available to them. When lobbying the administration or senators on behalf of, or in opposition to, a potential or named candidate to fill a vacancy, interest groups write letters, make phone calls, lobby face-to-face, hold press conferences, stage demonstrations, organize petition drives, gather information, or try to mobilize the grassroots membership of their organizations to apply external pressure. These activities can be divided into two broad categories: public efforts and private ones. Each category is discussed more fully next.

Public Strategies

As the Bork confirmation proceedings in 1987 demonstrated, interest groups' activities in the appointment process were largely public activities. From testifying at his confirmation hearings to running television advertisements opposing his nomination, there was little doubt where interest groups on both sides of the nomination stood. This is consistent with the ways in which interest groups participated in the appointment process for positions at all levels of the federal judiciary because the groups' ability to influence the process was increased in the late 1970s.

Beginning in the late 1970s and continuing until the mid-1990s, interest groups devoted substantial energies to exercising influence over the public aspects of the appointment process, most notably through their participation in confirmation hearings. The Senate Judiciary Committee generally welcomed the testimony of interest groups, both in person and through submissions for the record, and through the hearing process, interest groups were able to make their preferences known. Senators, likewise, were able to tease out the origins of the groups' opinions and were able to pursue questions about nominees' records with the groups on the record. In addition to testifying at hearings, the groups also participated in public demonstrations designed to urge the confirmation of nominees they supported.

Today, interest groups frequently find that their ability to wield influence in the appointment process is limited to taking action behind the scenes, with one important exception. The interest groups that have proliferated in the confirmation process have begun to link senators' confirmation decisions with their bids for reelection through the use of such things as voter guides and legislative scorecards. It is not uncommon to see confirmation votes among the list of votes used to rate members of Congress by groups such as the ACLU, the American Conservative Union, and the National Right to Life Foundation.

Private Strategies

Starting in the late 1990s, interest groups began to find that senators preferred closed-door tactics to more public, formal avenues of participation in the confirmation process. Shut out of the formal mechanisms of the judicial appointment process, interest groups' strategies shifted during the late 1990s to take advantage of their relationships with officials in the executive and legislative branches. Rather than focusing their energies on preparing testimony to be delivered at confirmation hearings, the groups worked behind the scenes to lobby their allies and encourage confirmation or rejection.

Interest groups' private strategies are, of course, more difficult to document. While confirmation hearings and press conferences are public events open to the scrutiny of the media and other political elites, much of what interest groups now do takes place away from the formal decision points of the appointment process. Many of the groups have cultivated long-standing relationships with offices or individuals in the executive branch or specific members of the Senate, and the groups' leaders work closely with these individuals to craft strategies for promoting candidates they support and for keeping individuals they oppose off the federal bench. Yet they do this almost entirely without being called to account for their actions because it is generally difficult to assess the accuracy or completeness of their claims. Often, when interest groups' private activities are discovered, it becomes clear that they are behaving in less than fully truthful or honest ways.

Two significant behind-the-scenes campaigns demonstrate the nature of interest group participation in the confirmation process. First, beginning in 1995, the Judicial Selection Monitoring Project adopted a private strategy and led a coalition of conservative interest groups, grassroots organizations, radio stations, and educators against then-President Bill Clinton's judicial nominees. The centerpiece of the group's private strategy was the group's "Hatch Pledge." Taken from a speech made by Senator Orrin Hatch to the Federalist Society, a membership society dedicated to promoting conservative constitutional principles, the so-called Hatch Pledge was a promise by willing senators not to vote for confirmation for any judicial nominee that was, or would be, a judicial activist. Although it was unclear what qualified a nominee as an activist, when the Judicial Selection Monitoring Project identified a nominee as a judicial activist, it strongly urged the senators who had signed onto the Hatch Pledge (there were eleven in all) to oppose the nominee. Ironically, Senator Hatch was not one of them.

Anecdotal and descriptive analyses of the district court nominees who were held up between 1995 and 2000 indicate that the senators who signed on to the Hatch pledge were the ones fighting against the Clinton nominees the Judicial Selection Monitoring Project opposed (Bell 2002a). For example, Steigerwalt (2004) reported that Senators Robert Smith (R–NH) and Jeff Sessions (R–AL) placed a hold—a request to the majority leader not to bring a measure or nominee up for debate—on the nominations of Clinton appointees Marsha Berzon and Richard Paez as a result of ideological disagreements with the nominees. Smith's objection—that the two nominees were judicial activists—was a claim originally made by the Judicial Selection Monitoring Project. The group alleged that all of Clinton's nominees were judicial activists who would inappropriately interpret the Constitution.

In addition, Senators Smith and Sessions were two of four sitting Republican senators who appeared in a videotape touting the Judicial Selection Monitoring Project's activities as part of a $1.4 million fundraising campaign for the organization. On September 9, 1997, contributors to the Free Congress Foundation, the "parent" organization for the Judicial Selection Monitoring Project, received a letter from Robert Bork that asked: "Can we afford to give President Clinton a free ride with his judicial appointments over the next three and a half years?" Indicating that the correct answer was no, Bork continued, "That is why I am taking the unusual step of sending you the enclosed video from the Free Congress Foundation's 'Judicial Selection Monitoring Project.'" The videotape featured testimony from prominent conservatives—in addition to Senators Smith and Sessions, Republican Senators James Inhofe (R–OK) and Phil Gramm (R–TX) actually appear in the video. All praise highly the work of the Judicial Selection Monitoring Project. Among the Republican senators, comments included: (from Senator Gramm): "The Judicial Selection Monitoring Project has the resources to get the facts, to provide information to provide information to people like me who are willing to use it." And, from Senator Sessions: "The Judicial Selection Monitoring Project is important because [it] shares information that senators may not have known and wouldn't have had time to consider." Three additional Republican senators—Kay Bailey Hutchison (R–TX), John Ashcroft (R–MO), and Christopher (Kit) Bond (R–MO)—lent written testimonials to the videotape's producers, and these were posted on the screen while the narrator pointed out to viewers how much support the organization had from members of the Senate ("Judge the Judges," 1997).

Included with the videotape was a fundraising pledge sheet, which promised that in recognition of gifts of $10,000 or more, donors would receive "invitations to attend periodic briefings and intimate dinners in Washington with Paul Weyrich [director of the Free Congress Foundation], JSMP [Judicial Selection Monitoring Project] Director Tom Jipping, and leading conservative elected and public figures closely involved with the judicial confirmation process" (Weyrich 1997).

The video and the letters from Paul Weyrich and Robert Bork came to light only because they were sent, likely unwittingly, to a relative of an embattled Clinton nominee to a seat on the U.S. District Court for the Northern District of Texas. The recipient turned the materials over to his relative, who on seeing them promptly made copies of all of them (the video was not copyrighted) and sent them to all other Clinton judicial nominees whose nominations were held up in the Senate with a note stating that the materials would make it clear why their nominations had languished for so long.

To be sure, the conservative interest groups are not the only groups wielding influence in the contemporary Senate confirmation process. The "memogate" scandal, which came to light in 2004, illustrates the extent to which liberal interest groups have also worked closely with their senatorial allies to shape the dynamics of the judicial confirmation process. In the fall of 2003, *The New York Times* revealed that Republican staff members on the United States Senate Committee on the Judiciary had surreptitiously obtained thousands of pages of Democratic Committee staff memoranda detailing the Democrats' strategies for processing President George W. Bush's nominees to the federal courts during the 2001–2002 period when Democrats briefly controlled the U.S. Senate. The Republicans again took control of the Senate following the 2002 elections.

Among those documents were several memos that documented meetings and strategy sessions between Democratic senators and their interest group allies beginning in Fall 2001, after Vermont Senator Jim Jeffords' departure from the Republican Party put control of the Senate into the Democrats' hands. These memos illustrate the ways in which interest groups and senators now work together to determine who gets appointed to the federal judiciary. The memos also offer a "who's who" of liberal interest group leaders involved in coordinating Senate Democrats' strategy in the confirmation process. For example, a June 5, 2002, memo to Senator Richard Durbin (D–IL), reads in part:

> Senator Kennedy has invited you and Senator Schumer to attend a meeting with civil rights leaders to discuss their priorities as the Judiciary Committee considers judicial nominees in the coming months.... This meeting is intended to follow-up your meetings in Senator Kennedy's office last fall. The guest list will be the same: Kate Michelman (NARAL), Nan Aron (Alliance for Justice), Wade Henderson (Leadership Conference on Civil Rights), Ralph Neas (People for the American Way), Nancy Zirkin (American Association of University Women), Marcia Greenberger (National Women's Law Center), and Judy Lichtman (National Partnership) (Durban Staff Memo 2002).

Two months earlier, an April 17th memo to Senator Kennedy from a member of his staff informed him that:

> Elaine Jones of the NAACP Legal Defense Fund (LDF) tried to call you today to ask that the Judiciary Committee consider scheduling Julia Scott Gibbons, the uncontroversial nominee to the 6th Circuit, at a later date, rather than at a hearing next Thursday, April 25th.... Elaine would like the Committee to hold off on any 6th Circuit nominees until the University of Michigan case regarding the constitutionality of affirmative action in higher education is decided by the *en banc* 6th Circuit. This case is considered the affirmative action case most likely to go to the Supreme Court (Kennedy Staff Memo 2002).

In light of these facts, Kennedy's staff member stated, "We recommend that Gibbons be scheduled for a later hearing" (Kennedy Staff Memo 2002). Ironically, the conservative interest group Coalition for a Fair Judiciary filed a grievance against Elaine Jones with the State Bar of Virginia on the basis of these memos, alleging that she inappropriately attempted to influence the outcome of a pending federal case (Coalition

for a Fair Judiciary 2003). Jones resigned her position as head of the NAACP's Legal Defense and Education Fund as a result ("Elaine Jones Resigns" 2004).

In addition to identifying those interest groups and leaders working closely with the Democrats, the poached memos very clearly articulated the groups' goals and strategies for achieving them. A November 7, 2001 memo to Senator Durbin from a member of his staff is particularly illustrative of this point. It stated,

> Due to the floor activity last night, you missed a meeting with Senator Kennedy and representatives of various civil rights groups. This was intended to follow up a meeting in Senator Kennedy's office in mid-October.... Yesterday's meeting accomplished two objectives. First, the groups advocated for some procedural ground rules. These include (1) only one hearing per month; (2) no more than three judges per hearing; (3) giving Committee Democrats and the public more advance notice of scheduled nominees; (4) no recess hearings; and (5) a commitment that nominees voted down in Committee will not get a floor vote. Earlier yesterday, Senator Leahy's staff committed to the third item in principle (Durbin Staff Memo 2001).

The Durbin memo also detailed his staff's assessment of the nominees the groups were most concerned about. The second part of the memo noted,

> Second, yesterday's meeting focused on identifying the most controversial and/or vulnerable judicial nominees, and a strategy for targeting them. The groups singled out three—Jeffrey Sutton (6th Circuit); Priscilla Owen (5th Circuit); and Caroline Kuhl (9th Circuit)—as a potential nominee for a contentious hearing early next year, with a [sic] eye to voting him or her down in Committee. They also identified Miguel Estrada (D.C. Circuit) as especially dangerous, because he has a minimal paper trail, he is Latino, and the White House seems to be grooming him for a Supreme Court appointment. They want to hold Estrada off as long as possible (Durbin Staff Memo 2001).

As this memo to Senator Durbin demonstrated, several liberal interest groups were working together to coordinate a strategy for Senate Democrats.

However, most interesting, the memo indicated that the Democratic leadership was receptive to their demands. Indeed, the four nominees identified in November 2001 as especially problematic all were subject to difficult confirmation processes. None of the four were confirmed and all were returned to the president at the end of the 107th Congress. Owen's nomination was never put to a full Senate vote because the Senate Judiciary Committee narrowly failed to vote her out of the committee on a 10 to 9 party line vote in September 2002.

President Bush renominated each of the four contentious nominees at the outset of the 108th Congress. Sutton was confirmed in April 2003, but Estrada withdrew from consideration in September 2003, and Kuhl withdrew her name in December 2003 after repeated Democratic filibusters on their nominations. Only Owen agreed to be renominated (for a third time) at the start of the 109th Congress in 2005. In May 2005, Owen was confirmed after seven moderate Democrats in the Senate agreed to vote to invoke cloture on a filibuster of her nomination as part of the compromise with moderate Republicans, who promised not to support Majority Leader Bill Frist's proposed "nuclear option." A group of fourteen moderate Senators from both parties prevented further filibusters, but they also prevented conservatives from eliminating the filibuster entirely for judicial nominees (see Nather 2005). Frist's nuclear option proposal would have allowed filibusters on judicial nominations to be ended on a parliamentary point of order (which would require only a majority vote to sustain) rather than through the usual cloture process, which currently requires sixty votes to end a filibuster.[6]

Both the Democrats' memogate activities and the Judicial Selection Monitoring Project's promise of access to "elected and public figures closely involved with the judicial confirmation process," demonstrate that interest groups and senators are willing to go to great lengths to wield influence in the judicial appointment process. Moreover, these two examples demonstrate a convergence of confirmation politics, interest groups, money, and senators that is unprecedented in its scope. In both cases, had it not been for the actions of interested third parties, the public would never have learned about the lengths to which interest groups and

their allies now go. The shift from public strategies to private ones, while likely done in good faith to attempt to reduce the influence of interest groups in the appointment process, seems to have had the opposite effect.

As this discussion has demonstrated, interest groups' activities in the appointment process are not limited to providing presidents and senators with advice or counsel about potential nominees. Instead, interest groups bring an arsenal of strategies and tactics with them when they enter the judicial appointment process to represent the opinions of their members. These techniques range from traditional tools of the lobbying trade—like letters and phone calls to members of the Senate—to more insidious efforts to wield influence, such as coordinating with senators behind closed doors to delay or deny confirmation to a judicial nominee. As the examples of beleaguered nominees earlier demonstrate, interest group participation in the appointment process can have a real effect on who ultimately is appointed to the federal bench. Although it is impossible to say that the interest groups' hostility to the nominees discussed earlier *caused* the difficulties they faced in the Senate, several recent studies of interest group participation in the confirmation process have reached the same conclusion: When interest groups target a specific nominee, his or her chances of being confirmed quickly are reduced (Bell 2002a; Nixon and Goss 2001; Shogan 1996).

CONCLUSIONS

Over the last decade, conditions in the judicial nomination and confirmation processes have generally worsened. Delays in both the nomination and confirmation stages have increased, interest group scrutiny of nominees has intensified, and there is some evidence that fewer and fewer individuals are willing to stand for appointment (Bell 2002a). In each of his year-end reports on the federal judiciary during the period 1997 to 2004, the late Chief Justice William Rehnquist highlighted aspects of the contentious relationship between Congress and the courts, noting in his last report in 2004 that attacks on the judicial branch's decisions and calls to impeach federal judges over the decisions they make violate established traditions and principles about the role of the judicial and legislative branches in American political life (Rehnquist 2004). Changed beliefs among legislators, interest group leaders, and the mass public about the roles for judges and courts have combined to make the appointment process a flash point for conflict.

Over the last sixty years, the nation's courts have become the arenas in which many of the country's most significant public policy battles are waged and are won or lost. As the federal courts have become central policy actors, the effects have been witnessed in the appointment process generally, but in the Senate's confirmation process most noticeably. Rather than being a routine process that simply places judges of the highest professional caliber in office, today the appointment of federal judges is perceived by a plethora of political actors to be central to the quality and direction of U.S. national policy. Add to the extensive list of issues the courts address the fact that the judges that sit on these courts are insulated electorally and generally serve lengthy terms, and it is clear why political interests up and down the ideological spectrum are so interested in being a part of determining who sits on the federal bench.

Once described as a "rubber stamp machine" for its tendency to endorse with little question presidential nominees to the federal courts, today the confirmation process captures the attention of political activists across the political spectrum who seek to shape the outcome of federal judicial proceedings. Among the most important of these political actors—and among those central to the changed nature of the confirmation process—are interest groups.

Notes

1. Interview by author, October 1997.

2. The percentages of presidential appointees to the U.S. Supreme Court who are from the president's party are even higher than for lower federal judges. As Baum described the situation, "About 90% of all nominees to the Supreme Court—and all those chosen since 1975—have been members of the president's party. One reason is that lawyers who share the president's policy views are more likely to come from the same party, but there is also a widespread feeling that such an attractive prize should to one of the party faithful" (Baum 2004, 41).

3. The Senate Judiciary Committee ended the formal role for the ABA at confirmation hearings in 1997. In 2001, President George W. Bush likewise ended a formal role for the ABA in the selection process (see, e.g., Baum 2004, 31). Although the organization continues to evaluate and distribute its ratings of all nominees to the federal courts, their influence over either the nomination or confirmation stages of the appointment process has been substantially reduced from what it was prior to 1997.

4. Thus there were several fights over Supreme Court nominations that have greatly affected the current state of interactions between the federal courts and the other branches (see Miller this volume, chapter 19). Following the Fortas resignation, President Nixon had a great deal of trouble in filling the seat. The Senate rejected two of Nixon's nominees for the Supreme Court, Clement F. Haynsworth and G. Harold Carswell, in part because they were not seen as qualified to sit on the nation's highest court (see Maltese 1995). In retaliation for the failure of the Senate to confirm the two Nixon appointees, conservatives in the House then convinced House Minority Leader Gerald Ford in 1970 to consider impeachment efforts against Justice William O. Douglas, an outspoken liberal on the Court (see Canellos 2006b). Those efforts failed after the successful nomination of Harry Blackmun to be an associate justice (see O'Brien 2003, 100–104).

5. Although they filibustered the nomination of Abe Fortas to be chief justice, conservatives took great offense at the nomination fights over Bork and Thomas, two Republican nominees to the U.S. Supreme Court. As one journalist described the situation, "In the 1980's and 90's, liberal attacks on conservative Supreme Court nominees like Robert Bork and Clarence Thomas spawned a new era of political hostility" (Rosenberg 2005, 24). Conservatives made the courts a large focus of their political efforts. Former Attorney General Meese stated the conservative view quite bluntly, "The Senate should use its confirmation authority to block the appointment of activist federal judges" (Meese and DeHart 1997, 181).

6. It should be noted, however, that although the Democrat-controlled Senate failed to act on these four lower court nominations during the 107th Congress, these nominees had originally been nominated in April 2001, several months prior to Senator Jeffords' decision to leave the Republican Party. Thus, these nominees were likely selected, at least in part, to be acceptable to a Republican majority, not a Democratic majority, in the Senate. When Jeffords' surprising party defection occurred, it gave Democrats majority party status in the Senate for a short time, and Democrats refused to act on many of President Bush's nominees whose names had been submitted prior to the Democrats gaining control. The Republicans then regained control of the Senate following the 2002 elections.

4

BRINGING THE LAWYERS BACK IN

Lynn Mather

Having examined the processes for the selection of judges, this next section turns to other key actors in the legal system. Lawyers are key players at almost all phases of both criminal and civil cases. Judicial politics scholars have begun to examine the political and professional role of lawyers in our legal system. This chapter begins by looking at the various tasks that lawyers perform in a variety of settings. The focus at the beginning of the chapter is on individual lawyers and their work. A central question is what *do* lawyers do? The chapter concludes with an examination of the legal profession as a whole. Has the legal profession become more open to women and minorities? How do the communities of practice within the legal profession affect the way in which lawyers perceive their duties? The entire chapter is framed around the lessons and truths that we can find by analyzing jokes about lawyers and the legal profession, although the chapter is quite serious in explaining the role that lawyers play in the American legal system.

What role do lawyers play in American courts and society? How do lawyers contribute to U.S. judicial processes? Public depictions of lawyers are mixed. For every cinematic portrayal of lawyers fighting racism, battling industrial polluters, or working to free an innocent defendant, we also see lawyers who cut ethical corners, charge outrageous fees, or exacerbate conflict by filing frivolous litigation. What *do* lawyers do?

One view of lawyers resides in popular jokes. Marc Galanter opens his masterful survey of lawyer jokes and legal culture with the following:

> "Question: How many lawyer jokes are there?
> Answer: Only three. The balance are documented case histories" (Galanter 2005, 3).[1]

Galanter demonstrated that lawyer jokes succeed with their humor because they tap into the public's deep ambivalence about lawyers. From the country's earliest days, lawyers played two roles. They were exalted as "America's aristocracy," in the words of the French philosopher Alexis de Tocqueville in the 1830s when he wrote his masterpiece entitled *Democracy in America*, comparing democracy in the United States with democracy in Europe. But lawyers were also reviled as troublemakers, hired guns for the mercantile elites, or simply beyond the reach of the common person. These dueling images of lawyers, as savior or scum, continue to contend for popular support.

Certain lawyer jokes have been told for centuries and were common in England as well. Galanter calls these jokes "the enduring core" and most of them focus on "what lawyers do" (Galanter 2005, 17). Consider three different clusters of jokes, each of which pokes fun at a different aspect of lawyers' behavior. Lawyers earn their living through their words, but their legal jargon and complicated discourse can obfuscate the truth and defy common sense. Thus, one category of jokes centers on *lawyers' command over language.*

"How can you tell if a lawyer is lying?"
"His lips are moving" (Galanter 2005, 31).

Or consider the drunken lawyer in England who mistakenly argued for the wrong side in trial and, when corrected, calmly continued, "Such, my lord, is the statement you will probably hear from my brother on the opposite side of the case. I shall now show your lordship how utterly untenable are the principles and how distorted are the facts upon which this very specious statement has proceeded" (Galanter 2005, 41).

Another category of jokes focuses on the lawyer as *economic predator,* who charges exorbitant fees but does little to earn it:

"Why do you want a new trial?"
"On the grounds of newly discovered evidence, your Honor."
"What's the nature of it?"
"My client dug up $400 that I didn't know he had" (Galanter 2005, 69).

During my research in the Los Angeles criminal courts, I often heard a similar joke whispered by court personnel when a private defense lawyer moved for a continuance for a client who had not yet paid the lawyer's fee: "Oh, he's just waiting for Witness Green to appear" (Mather 1979). Galanter traces a joke about the eighteenth century English judge, Lord Mansfield, which reappeared in a twentieth century version: "When President Theodore Roosevelt was trying to persuade his son to become a lawyer, he used the following argument: 'A man who never graduated from school might steal from a freight car. But a man who attends college and graduates as a lawyer might steal the whole railroad'" (Galanter 2005, 72). Jokes about lawyers' greed and pursuit of economic gain underscore the dissatisfaction people feel about the fact that they must pay someone to achieve justice. Why shouldn't access to the law and to courts be free? Why should money enter into the equation of legal rights and wrongs? (Galanter 2005, 94–96).

Because lawyers represent people in conflict and are supposed to advocate zealously for their clients' interests, it is not surprising that lawyers appear in numerous jokes as *creators of conflict* or "fomenters of strife" (Galanter 2005, 114). In one *New Yorker* cartoon, a small child looks up to her mother and says, "When will I be old enough to start suing people?" (Galanter 2005, 131). Do lawyers manufacture conflicts and construct their clients' injuries? The next joke taps into that pervasive belief:

"Are you badly injured?"
"Can't tell till I see my lawyer" (Galanter 2005, 119).

There is also the old joke about the sole lawyer in a small town whose business was suffering but then a second lawyer moved to town and they both thrived (Galanter 2005, 118).

What I like about these jokes—besides the fact that they lighten up my introduction—is that they underscore the complex and equivocal nature of lawyers' work. The first cluster of jokes points to the power and influence that lawyers have from their command over legal language, that is, their ability to frame and argue cases in many different ways. The second joke cluster points to the tension between lawyers' pursuit of private gain and their role as officers of the court, as members of a public profession. This tension underscores the interests, including financial self-interest, which lawyers may have, that are distinct from those of their clients. Finally, what role do lawyers play in creating or dampening conflicts? This is an enormous area for lawyers' discretion and is central to current debates over civil justice, tort reform, plea bargaining, and public interest litigation.

Lawyer jokes call attention to the *independent* influence of lawyers. That is, lawyers are not simple conduits for client interests, faithfully translating preconceived goals into legal language and shepherding clients through the legal process. Rather, lawyers frequently add their own goals, ideas, and values to clients' problems and conflicts. In class action, social reform, or government litigation, the identity of the "client" is unclear, giving lawyers considerable independence over action. A growing body of empirical research focuses on the contributions of lawyers in litigation.[2]

Yet all too often judicial process textbooks report uncritically the legal profession's official and politically neutral view of lawyering. In this view, the work of lawyers consists of advising and counseling clients, representing clients before public bodies, drafting written documents, negotiating conflicts, and litigating cases in court.[3] These tasks sound straightforward and technical, dependent on skill, training, and specialized legal knowledge. The political, value-laden, or contested nature of lawyers' work is not immediately obvious. Lawyers seem to be highly trained technicians; yes, you need one to go through court, but the lawyer will not substantively alter the client's case. Yet the jokes reveal a more skeptical—and perhaps more accurate—view of what attorneys do. Lawyers translate client objectives into legal language, but they also transform them through the translation process (Cain 1979; Mather and Yngvesson 1981). And lawyers have their own incentive structure apart from that of their clients, such as the pursuit of a political cause, an interest in maintaining smooth relations with opposing attorneys, or a desire to maximize fees.

The political science literature recognizes the importance of legal representation for *access* to court, but sometimes ignores the contribution of lawyers in court. In many quantitative judicial process studies, cases are coded by different types of issues, by types of litigants such as individual, private organization, or government; by the number of interest groups in support; and by the judges' political party or ideology. However, only a few researchers have specifically investigated the impact of lawyers on case outcomes, and they found significant effects from variation in lawyers' experience and specialization (see, e.g., Haire, Lindquist, and Hartley 1999; Kritzer 1990, 1998; McGuire 1993, 1998, 1999).

In this chapter I explore the work of lawyers, especially trial lawyers. My chapter title borrows from Evans, Rueschemeyer, and Skocpol's well-known book, *Bringing the State Back In* (1985), which challenged a society-centered paradigm of inputs and outputs and instead presented governments as independent actors, varying in state autonomy, state capacity, and organizational structure to exert influence on

social and political outcomes.[4] Similarly, the judicial politics paradigm depicts clients directing cases as inputs into court with court decisions as outputs. But lawyers influence the entire litigation process from case filing through settlement negotiations, pretrial motions, trial, and appeal (see Barnes this volume, chapter 7; Waters et al. this volume, chapter 6). By including variation in lawyers' independence from clients, lawyers' capacity and resources, and the structure and social networks of the legal profession, we can develop a more complete understanding of the judicial process.

In the next section I summarize the argument for bringing the lawyers back in, by emphasizing the content and political impact of lawyers' work. Looking at the legal process from mobilization of law to settlement or trial underscores the crucial contributions lawyers make in shaping case outcomes and also in developing law and policy. Lawyers are not just agents of their clients, however, but are also members of a profession. The third section of this chapter describes the population of the legal profession, including its history of discrimination, its current demographics, and lawyer differences according to workplace contexts. While this section provides a macro, or aggregate, view of the profession, the fourth section explores several specialized communities of legal practice such as divorce lawyers, criminal defense and prosecutors, personal injury attorneys, public interest or cause lawyers, and corporate lawyers. Because who lawyers are and where they work shapes much of what they do, I suggest that we integrate our knowledge of legal profession with research on lawyers at work in different areas of law. This integration will help us in understanding the contribution of lawyers to individual case outcomes and to the production of law.

THE CONTENT AND IMPACT OF TRIAL LAWYERS' WORK

Lawyers' work goes far beyond a set of technical, predetermined responsibilities, and instead includes a range of choices, which are contingent and uncertain. The results of those decisions shape the caseloads of trial courts, the experiences and perceptions of litigants, the outcomes of cases, the meaning of legal rules, and the development of new law. Thus, as Christine Harrington put it, we should examine, "the ideological content and political significance of the work that lawyers do" (1994, 55). Taking the rather straightforward set of lawyer tasks described earlier, consider what these tasks really entail.

Advising and counseling clients involves helping them to see whether their conflict or problem constitutes a legal case. Lawyers *construct cases* by renaming problems in legal language. A prosecutor listens to a victim of racial violence and constructs a "hate crime"; a neighbor's bitter complaint over a borrowed lawnmower becomes a charge of "petty theft"; a fight becomes an "assault." Or, in civil law, an employer hitting on his employees becomes a "sexual harassment" claim; an auto accident from careless driving becomes a "tort"; or injury from a defective chain saw becomes a "products liability" case.

Advising also entails *educating individuals and organizations* about what the law is—the meaning of legal terms and rules, their application to specific facts, and how the legal process works. As Martin Shapiro wrote, "What if we began our study of law with the proposition that law is not what judges say in the reports but what the lawyers say—to one another and to clients—in their offices?" (Shapiro 1981b, 1201). What view of law and of the legal system do lawyers communicate when counseling clients? And how does this vary by the type of client and lawyer? "No, we can't take that legal action because it will just alienate the opposing side"; or "because the judge will never approve it"; or "because you don't have the funds to support it"; or "because I can help you settle your problem without it"; or "because you'll regret litigation in the long run"; or.... Lawyers have myriad reasons against filing lawsuits. Lawyers' advice on the limits or inapplicability of law may stem from their legal knowledge, their economic self-interest, their personal values, or a host of other factors. Client counseling then influences *popular legal consciousness*, that is, popular understandings of law and the legal system.

Despite the common perception that Americans and their lawyers are eager to define all problems as legal claims, the empirical evidence shows a far more complex pattern (for summary, see Haltom and McCann 2004; see also Miller and Sarat 1981). Some personal problems require legal action from a court—transfer of real estate, executing a will, adoption, and divorce come to mind. Increasingly, however, people are representing themselves in lawsuits, filling out forms from the Web, or locating specialists besides lawyers to provide help for these actions. Rates of *pro se* (self-representation) for example have increased dramatically in family law cases (Mather 2003a). Individuals who are defendants in civil actions are especially likely to lack lawyers (see Waters et al. this volume, chapter 6). In divorce cases, wives are twice as likely as husbands to have legal counsel due largely to the fact that husbands are more frequently the defendants (Mather 2003a, 149).

Many potential plaintiffs in civil cases never file legal claims because they cannot afford—or choose not—to go to a lawyer, or because a lawyer rejects their case. The hourly fees of private attorneys are often beyond the reach of many claimants. Because there is no constitutional right to an attorney in a civil case (as exists for criminal cases), those seeking to file civil claims must have the funds to pay for private counsel, be accepted by a contingency-fee attorney, or be eligible for free legal services. A contingency fee means the lawyer collects a fee only if the case is won. This type of fee is typically only used in certain kinds of cases (e.g., those with large financial awards), however, and contingency-fee attorneys accept only a relatively small portion of clients seeking their counsel. There are also limited free or reduced fee, legal services for civil claims available through federally funded or group funded legal services, law school clinics, or through private attorneys acting in a pro bono capacity. This patchwork of civil legal services means that advice and counsel depends on client finances and the nature or size of the claim. Consequently, the economics of legal practice influences the civil law caseloads. Lawyers also shape court caseloads by steering conflicts away from courts and into alternative dispute resolution proceedings or, conversely, by initiating legal cases to take advantage of newly passed statutes or judicial rulings. Private lawyers are thus the *gatekeepers of civil trial courts*, while prosecuting attorneys are key *gatekeepers of criminal trial courts.* [5] Whether lawyers decide to represent clients and claims, or not, depends on a host of resource and other factors. There is nothing automatic or fixed about the lawyer's task of representing clients before public bodies.

Prosecutors represent governments, bringing criminal charges against defendants in state and federal courts. Nearly all chief state prosecutors are elected officials, serving a county-based jurisdiction. Some state district attorneys work part-time and alone, while other chief prosecutors oversee hundreds of assistant attorneys. Because of the large number of rural counties, the median number of assistant prosecutors in 2005 was only 3, while in counties over 1 million in size, the median was 141 (S. W. Perry 2006). The nature of advice and counsel that prosecutors offer to victims is quite different in a small community than that in a large bureaucracy in an urban area. Most large, district attorney offices also have specialized units for domestic violence prosecution, which smaller offices do not. U.S. attorneys, the chief federal prosecutors, are appointed by the president for each federal district court. Although the method of selecting prosecutors differs between the state and federal systems, both have political accountability, while has the potential to influence decision making, especially in highly visible cases. Elected state prosecutors in some areas face severe resource constraints that sharply limit their ability to do adequate investigation and case preparation for the criminal cases in their jurisdictions.

Drafting documents involves setting out the pleadings and arguments in a civil case or the facts and rationale for charges in a criminal case. Through lawyers' writing and advice to clients, they use law, that is, they *implement statutory law or rulings of appellate courts.* Conflict between prosecuting and defense attorneys over the constitutionality of a police search that produced the cocaine as evidence, for example, defines the law of search and seizure for that particular court, at least until overturned on appeal.

Client advising and drafting documents may also lead lawyers to suggest or allow *new interpretations of law.* Lawyers for Enron—or, a decade earlier, lawyers for Lincoln Savings & Loan[6]—endorsed their corporate clients' creative new ways of organizing financial transactions. With the collapse of these companies, the novel legal interpretations were rejected (and the attorneys sanctioned), but how many other similar schemes continue in force undetected and unchallenged? President George W. Bush's then Legal Counsel Alberto Gonzales wrote memos that argued for a new interpretation of the international Convention Against Torture (which the United States has signed) to expand the range of techniques the U.S. military could legally use in interrogating detainees considered to be terrorists (see also Fisher this volume, chapter 18). Some consider these infamous "torture memos" to be a blatant violation of professional legal ethics, purely political, and unconstrained by law (Abel 2005). However, until the interpretation is adjudicated, Gonzales' interpretation remains in some sense "legal."

The notion of creative legal advising can also provide a euphemistic cover for unethical, unconstrained behavior of lawyers who do whatever their clients want. These examples call to mind a lawyer joke that I retold several times without realizing that it was, according to Galanter, the "single most prevalent of all current lawyer jokes" (Galanter 2005, 192–95).

> Why have research labs started using lawyers instead of white rats in their experiments? There are three reasons: first, there are more of them; second, the lab assistants don't get attached to them; and third, there are some things a white rat just won't do.

Lawyers are trained to argue zealously for their clients within the bounds of the law. Powerful clients who work regularly with the same lawyers can urge them to *push the bounds of the law to suit the client's objectives.* Lawyers whose jobs depend on one or a small number of clients, such as the president's counsel, in-house corporate counsel, or counsel to one or two firms, may find it difficult to resist client demands.

Another realm of creative legal interpretation in drafting documents results from explicitly political or cause lawyering (Sarat and Scheingold 1998; Scheingold and Sarat 2004). For these lawyers, the courts are used primarily to advance a group's political goals.[7] Lawyers with an agenda for social or political change may counsel clients to enter litigation designed to test the bounds of the law or to *formulate new legal claims.* Test case litigation has led to the development of new constitutional rights in numerous areas, from the earlier liberal rulings (e.g., school desegregation and gender equality; see also B. A. Perry this volume, chapter 16; Baer this volume, chapter 17) to the more recent conservative ones (e.g., property rights, anti-abortion). Attorneys sometimes even seek out clients for the lawsuits rather than the other way around. Political activists and cause lawyers recognize the advantages of having a sympathetic plaintiff as the poster child for a cause. Other cause lawyers developed their legal theories out of their work with clients. Feminist legal advocates, for example, constructed legal theories of sexual harassment (MacKinnon 1979; Marshall 2003, 2005), comparable worth (McCann 1994), and self-defense for battered women who killed their husbands (Schneider 2000) from their experiences advising female clients.

New legal formulations underscore lawyers' political power as revealed in the first cluster of lawyer jokes, which centered on lawyers' language. What is verbal idiocy to some constitutes creative lawmaking to others. The first legal claims to extend the benefits of marriage to gay couples were ridiculed for altering the meaning of the word "marriage," but some courts (and a small but increasing segment of the public) have since accepted those claims (see e.g., Miller 2006). *Lawmaking* in the judicial process results from lawyers' command over language, particularly in an adversarial, common-law system that depends on parties to initiate legal claims (Levi 1949; Kagan 2001). Lawyers use logic or metaphorical reasoning to expand (or narrow) legal categories to suit the facts of a client's case. When judges make decisions, they are then choosing between the legal formulations presented to them by the lawyers.

Representing clients before public bodies and drafting written documents require lawyers to *construct a narrative* on behalf of the client or else to match the client's narrative with a predetermined one. What does the client want to do with her land? How does the family want to set up the trust? Why is the organization seeking the permit? How does the company justify denying the claim? Why didn't the tenant pay the rent? Why did the defendant have a gun in his satchel? What happened after the fight was over? Does she have a medical reason to explain the marijuana growing

in the basement? Some legal problems require little discretion, and attorneys learn quickly how to slot the pegs into their proper holes to convince public agencies or to produce appropriate documents. Other problems require considerably more tailoring and choice, with lawyers juggling the story as told by the client with alternative legal versions. And what should a lawyer do when faced with competing narratives, or a disagreement between her recommendation and the client's? Which narrative should be privileged when the lawyer prepares the legal documents or presents the case to the court? What does it mean for a lawyer to "represent" a client—to do what the client wants (delegate) or to do what the lawyer thinks is best (trustee)? Add a systematic race and class difference between lawyer and client, and the lawyer's task as representative of the client becomes much more political and contested (White 1990; Cunningham 1989; Alfieri 2005).

Negotiation and *litigation* round out the list of lawyers' tasks. These two processes overlap and intersect with various stages in between settlement and trial and with decisions to settle shaped by consideration of the alternative of trial. Most civil cases settle before trial and plea bargains are quite common in criminal cases. Thus, trials in the United States (especially jury trials) are quite rare.[8] In the federal courts in 2005, only 1.4 percent of all civil cases were decided by a judge or jury, down by more than one half from a decade earlier. Only 4.4 percent of the federal criminal cases went to trial in 2005, also a significant decrease (Administrative Office of the U.S. Courts, 2005b; Galanter 2004). In the state trial courts of general jurisdiction in 2002 (based on almost half the states), 16 percent of all civil case dispositions were by trial (fewer than one fourth of those by jury trial), and just over 3 percent of all criminal case dispositions were decided by judge or jury trial (Ostrom, Strickland, and Hannaford-Agor 2004, 775–776).

What do lawyers contribute to the overwhelming majority of cases that settle? In ordinary litigation, they often *broker* transactions and agreements (Kritzer 1990). That is, they act as intermediaries between their clients and other parties or organizations such as the court. As justice brokers, they exact a fee for their work and they draw on their insider knowledge of people and informal processes to do their work.

Through such repeated interactions with others, lawyers *establish going rates* for criminal plea bargains and for settlements in civil cases and *create operational categories* for handling of cases to achieve what they consider to be appropriate results. In theory these rates reflect shared views of a likely judicial ruling, so that the settlements are bargained, "in the shadow of the law" (Mnookin and Kornhauser 1979, 950). In some areas of law, however, there are so few judicial rulings and so many lawyer-influenced settlements that the rates lack much judicial input. For example, when Congress required states to adopt new rules for child support, divorce lawyers in several states interpreted the new numbers as a fixed—not minimum—amount that noncustodial parents were required to pay in child support (Jacob 1992; Mather, McEwen, and Maiman 2001).

Parties who frequently use the legal system ("repeat players") exercise greater control over their lawyers than do parties who are infrequently in court ("one-shotters") and thus are more dependent on their lawyers' advice and counsel (Galanter 1974; Heinz and Laumann 1982; Heinz et al. 2005). Repeat players in the legal process include large organizations, such as corporations or governments, in contrast to one-shotters who are typically individuals. The epitome of the repeat player before the U.S. Supreme Court is the U.S. Solicitor General, as discussed in more detail in Ubertaccio (this volume, chapter 10).

Another key advantage of repeat players at trial rests on their ability to play the game for the long-term gain of the development of legal rules, or in other words, to settle those cases that might lead to unfavorable legal rules and to push for trial in cases where more favorable rules could be established (Galanter 1974). When experienced lawyers recommend settlement or trial to clients who regularly use the legal system, part of their settlement calculus involves the *strategic selection of cases for law-making opportunities*. Lawyers for one-shot clients typically seek maximal gain in the instant case whereas counsel for repeat players may prefer to trade off a single monetary loss for the longer-term advantage of a favorable legal precedent. For example, an individual employee suing her employer seeks to win her specific case, whereas the employer potentially facing many similar

claims will decide to settle or litigate according to the case's impact on the development of legal precedent. Catherine Albiston (2003) found strong support for this pattern in her study of employment cases under the Family and Medical Leave Act of 1993. Nearly half of the cases in federal court were won by defendants (employers) on motions of summary judgment in their favor, a procedure for avoiding trial. On appeal, the appellate courts overwhelmingly upheld the lower courts' judgments and thus weakened the power of the federal law to guarantee employees medical leave. In cases where plaintiffs (employees) won at jury trial or through a generous settlement, they were paradoxically "losing by winning" (Albiston 2003, 168). That is, because jury verdicts and settlements never reached the appellate courts, the successful employees did not establish a judicial determination of their rights under the statute. Similar research on eight years of litigation under the disability rights statute found that employee plaintiffs had a relatively high win rate in cases at trial but their overall win rate was only 13 percent due to large number of adverse summary judgments (Colker 2005, 78–79).

Knowledge of the different stages of negotiation and litigation requires more than identifying the procedural steps or filing technical motions. It requires understanding the long-term consequences of actions and legal arguments, making choices about when to settle and when to appeal (see also, Barnes this volume, chapter 7; Waters et al. this volume, chapter 6). Lawyers' effectiveness in negotiation and litigation has been linked to their reputation (Kritzer 1998, 2004) and their reliability (McGuire 1993, 1999). Exaggeration or misrepresentation of claims for one client can backfire for a lawyer's other clients. Conversely, experienced lawyers who provide judges with high-quality and trustworthy information bring added advantage to their clients (McGuire 1999). Interestingly, one study found lawyer expertise to be a dichotomous rather than continuous variable in terms of its effect on judicial voting (Haire et al. 1999, 683). That is, lawyers were either experts or nonexperts within a particular court and area of law. Other research has similarly found a crucial dichotomy between "insider" and "outsider" criminal lawyers according to their familiarity and expertise within a local court (Mather 1979) and between "reasonable" and "unreasonable" divorce lawyers in their approach to negotiations (Sarat and Felstiner 1995; Mather et al. 2001).

Lawyers also draw on their substantive knowledge of where the law is, has been, and might be going as they craft arguments and create analogies for judges or juries. Lawyers have won or lost cases not only because of the judges' political ideologies but because the lawyers selected the wrong legal arguments, as Epstein and Kobylka (1992) detailed in their analysis of capital punishment and abortion cases before the Supreme Court. In litigation, lawyers *marshal expertise* and *construct arguments for particular audiences* (Wahlbeck 1997; Mather 1998). Judges constitute only one of the many audiences for legal argument; others include jurors, potential litigants, other lawyers, interest groups, specialists in the area, or the mass media. Depending on a lawyer's strategy, her arguments may be aimed narrowly within the courtroom or more broadly to newspapers, CNN, Fox News, and other media outlets.

Stuart Scheingold and Austin Sarat (2004) distinguished between cause lawyers, who explicitly use their legal skills to pursue political or social ideals, and conventional lawyers who simply pursue their clients' objectives. They acknowledged some convergence and overlap between the two in legal practice, but argued that "cause and conventional lawyers are marching to distinctly different ethical drummers" (Scheingold and Sarat 2004, 10). Cause lawyers, they noted, typically work as salaried employees for advocacy organizations, in small firms devoted to particular goals, or on pro bono cases in medium or large firms. However, in contrast to the richly drawn picture of cause lawyers from various studies, their image of conventional lawyers comes from official pronouncements of the bar in which lawyers are indifferent to the values of their clients, zealously advocate for them, and would have no "qualms about switching sides" (Scheingold and Sarat 2004, 7). How accurate is this picture of conventional lawyers? Research discussed below on specialization in the legal profession, social networks among lawyers, and shared values reinforced in daily practice suggests the need for a more nuanced understanding. Lawyers who do not wear their political values on

their sleeves may still be deeply engaged in promoting certain values and ideals through their client service. I question the usefulness of the distinction between cause lawyers and conventional lawyers[9] and would encourage more study on a wide variety of different types of lawyers to explore the role of commitment in legal work.

In sum, how does a focus on lawyers help in understanding judicial politics? If one seeks to explain *case outcomes* at any stage in court, then, as described above, there is good reason to believe that lawyers could exert some independent effect. The effect could come from a lawyer's political commitment, fee, expertise, experience, skill, reputation, or myriad other factors. Besides the substantive outcome (e.g., win or lose? size of award or length of sentence?) there is the type of disposition (e.g., dismissal, pretrial settlement, summary judgment, judicial decision, or jury verdict). Litigants' perceptions of *case disposition processes* are also important, although they tend to be studied more by sociologists and psychologists than by political scientists (e.g., How did claimants and defendants experience the legal process? Were they treated equally and with respect? Did they perceive court procedures to be open and fair? Did they think their lawyer helped them?)[10] Perceptions of case processing contribute to popular knowledge of law as well as to compliance and the legitimacy of courts.

Besides the outcomes and processes of individual cases, what about lawmaking through litigation? If one seeks to explain *how law changes*—not just why cases settle, how judges or juries make choices, or how clients perceive the legal process—then knowledge about lawyers and their political goals becomes even more important. In addition to consideration of lawyers' expertise, workplace, and relationship to clients, one might add lawyers' own values, experiences, political commitments, and relations with other lawyers. To what extent do lawyers trade off cases against one another, settling some, but aggressively pursuing others to take strategic advantage of opportunities in the legal environment? When new laws are passed (such as the Family and Medical Leave Act or the Americans with Disabilities Act) or when the potential for new case groupings of similar injuries arise (e.g., from asbestos, Bendectin, Vioxx), then early verdicts send crucial signals about how the law is developing (see also Mather 1998; Barnes this volume, chapter 7). A favorable verdict or judicial ruling may influence other legal decision makers, and simultaneously encourage others to pursue similar claims (and perhaps become clients of the lawyers engaged in the litigation). How do lawyers' own business strategies for building a successful practice, or their political principles, interact with their interest in legal change?

In complex litigation such as mass torts, plaintiff lawyers are fighting each other for clients, yet they may also coordinate efforts against what they define as a common adversary, the corporate defendant. The Master Settlement Agreement of 1998 between the major tobacco companies and attorneys general for forty-six states illustrates the need for coordination as well as the independence of government lawyers in making this new law (Mather 1998; Derthick 2002; Schmeling 2003). Lawyers working on political litigation, such as tobacco control, civil rights, gay marriage, or antiabortion campaigns, face problems of coordinating strategy for broader legal change while also effectively representing clients in individual cases. The fact that lawyers work in an economic world of competition for clients and a social world of cooperation to resolve conflicts may lead to cross-cutting ties that impact their legal strategy. In other words, some lawyers may worry more about their long-term relationships with other lawyers and judges than they do about the individual client in any given case.[11] In the United States, lawyers also work in a federal system, which means that variation in state politics provides a huge range of lawmaking opportunities through state litigation in addition to the federal courts.

THE LEGAL PROFESSION

Bringing lawyers back into judicial politics requires more than studying them as individuals who vary in ability, expertise, background, commitment, and so forth. Most important, lawyers are not randomly distributed across different kinds of cases. Indeed, individual attorney differences and patterns of client representation across legal specialties reflect the fundamental structure of the American legal profession.

With the number of lawyers tripling since 1971 (Carson 2004, 1) and with change in the market for legal services, that structure has undergone significant transformation. The bar's historic pattern of discrimination against women and minorities also affects their recruitment and career choices. Let us consider several key features of the legal profession today.

To begin, the legal profession is highly stratified by income and prestige. In no other profession is the gap between the highest and lowest paid practitioner as large as it is in the legal profession. The average annual income in 1995 of the top quartile of Chicago lawyers was *ten times* the average income of lawyers in the bottom quartile, a gap that had widened considerably in the past two decades (Heinz et al. 2005, 317). Who earns the top salaries and who are their clients? Although 8 percent of the nation's lawyers work for government (with about half of those in public defender or prosecutor's offices), it is the private practitioners who have the highest incomes.

Lawyers' income is also associated with firm size (Heinz et al. 2005). In 2000, 28 percent of all firm practitioners in the country worked in firms of over 100 lawyers (Carson 2004, 8). Law partners in "The Am Law 100," the nation's highest grossing law firms according to *The American Lawyer* magazine, averaged over a million dollars each in 2005, and they worked in law firms with 500 or more attorneys (Jones 2007). In contrast, one study of small franchise law firms found that staff attorneys on average barely made more than their legal secretaries (Van Hoy 1995, 711). In other words, lawyers working in solo practice or in small firms typically earn a pittance compared to those working at enormous national or global law firms.

Both income and firm size are associated with the nature of lawyers' clienteles. Lawyers in large firms generally serve corporate clients while those in smaller firms or solo practices serve individuals and small businesses. These two hemispheres of the legal profession, first described by Heinz and Laumann (1982), continue to divide lawyers according to the clients they represent. The amount of time lawyers devote to the corporate legal sector has grown. Corporate law work consumed 64 percent of lawyers' time in 1995 compared to 29 percent of lawyers' time in the personal services/small business sector and 7 percent in other fields (Heinz et al. 2005, 43). Furthermore, the educational backgrounds and social characteristics of lawyers working in these two hemispheres differ, with graduates of elite law schools and higher-class backgrounds typically working in the large corporate law firms. Graduates of local law schools, and those with middle-class backgrounds, are more likely to work as solo practitioners or in small offices serving individual clients.

Lawyers increasingly specialize in specific legal fields (e.g., antitrust, criminal defense, divorce, environment, banking, patents, civil rights) rather than handling a broad range of legal work as general practitioners. In response to a list of forty-two legal areas, one-third of Chicago attorneys said that they practiced in only *one* of them, a significant rise in lawyers' specialization (Heinz et al. 2005, 37). And even within specialized areas of law, lawyers specialize further by concentrating on different types of clients or issues. Thus there are pecking orders within law specialties as well as across them. Attorneys working in solo practices (who are more likely to work in a variety of fields) are also finding that they need to develop some special expertise as a way to attract clients (Seron 1996).

Historically the legal profession was comprised of white males, and many state laws prohibited women from becoming lawyers (see also, Baer this volume, chapter 17). In 1873 the U.S. Supreme Court upheld a typical Illinois statute prohibiting women from practicing law against a constitutional challenge (*Bradwell v. State* 1872). By the twentieth century states had changed their laws, but informal discrimination against women lawyers continued. Harvard Law School, for example, did not admit women until 1950, and many schools discriminated in admissions on grounds of sex, race, or ethnicity until the change in federal law in the 1970s. Women lawyers constituted only 3 percent of the bar in 1971, but made up 29.4 percent of the profession in 2005 (American Bar Association 2005). Racial and ethnic minorities have also dramatically increased in the legal profession, after years of systematic discrimination by the American Bar Association and law school admissions committees. Beginning in the 1960s, with civil rights

laws and affirmative action, the percentage of lawyers who are African American, Asian, or Hispanic rose to over 10 percent in 2005 (Bureau of Labor Statistics 2005).

Although patterns of recruitment and promotion in large corporate law firms are now more favorable to women and minorities than in earlier decades, partnership in large law firms remains difficult to attain. According to 2006 figures, women comprised 18 percent of partners in the nation's major law firms, whereas minorities were 5 percent; minority women constituted only 1.5 percent of partners in large firms (NALP 2006). Women are more likely to work in certain fields such as family law and criminal prosecution, and slightly more likely than male lawyers to work for government or in solo private practice, rather than in private firms (Carson 2004). For new law graduates, women were almost twice as likely to choose work in public interest positions than men (American Bar Association 2005).

How, if at all, do these macrostructural characteristics of the legal profession influence the behavior of lawyers in ways that could affect case outcomes or the creation of law? The answer, I believe, can be found through a focus on communities of practice. Through such communities, lawyers articulate and share informal norms that guide them in their work. Lawyers do not practice simply as individuals. Even when they work as sole practitioners—as did almost half of all private lawyers in 2000 (Carson 2004, 7)—they typically have ongoing relationships with others in a local community (banks, insurance companies, real estate brokers, women's shelters, political groups, etc.) depending on the nature of their practice. For private practitioners working in firms, their workplace creates an institutional environment that may affect their practice through the social bonds of work groups, the economic ties of billing practices, or the firm's organizational culture. And specialists in certain fields of law dealing with similar cases on a daily basis, perhaps encountering the same attorneys in negotiations, share informal understandings about how to approach work. Government lawyers such as prosecutors or legal services lawyers similarly develop work routines around shared political goals, resource constraints, and their personal backgrounds and ideologies.

The next section explains the concept of communities of practice through a detailed look at the divorce bar, followed by an overview of several other communities of law practice.

COMMUNITIES OF PRACTICE

In our research on divorce attorneys, we found that "divorce lawyers understand and make choices at work through *communities of practice*—groups of lawyers with whom practitioners interact and to whom they compare themselves and look for common expectations and standards" (Mather et al. 2001, 6). These communities were fluid and overlapping, reflecting differences in types of practice, income of clients, gender of lawyer, and geographic areas. Nevertheless, members of the overall divorce lawyer community shared an understanding of informal norms governing the process and substance of handling divorce.[12] Most saw themselves as reasonable lawyers who might differ in their evaluation of particular facts but who approached cases with a similar framework and common expectations of likely outcomes. Advocacy for one's client, for example, meant negotiating to achieve an equitable settlement, but also being willing to go to trial if necessary. Advising involved educating clients about what to expect in their cases, and teaching them realistic expectations about case outcomes, knowing that there was no such thing as a "win" in a divorce. Divorce lawyers who regularly worked with one another hated facing outsider lawyers who occasionally did a divorce case but who "haven't a clue as to what's been happening in the practice of family law" (Mather et al. 2001, 51).

Within the general divorce bar lay more particularized norms. Divisions existed between specialists whose practices were heavily concentrated in divorce and those who handled divorce as part of a more general practice. Specialists tended to use more formal discovery techniques; spent more time negotiating settlements or litigating; and had an expansive notion of legal expertise to include family dynamics, pensions, and tax law. Divorce specialists were disproportionately women, and they represented more affluent clients. Thus, the collegial control that emerged from

different communities of divorce practice reflected the intersection of lawyers' specialization, gender, and class of clientele.

As an example, compare the views of two lawyers, a male general practitioner and a female divorce specialist. Both noted the increased complexity and formality in divorce but differed in their assessment of the change. The general practitioner explained:

> It becomes very difficult now to deal in divorce cases because there has I think developed in New Hampshire a cadre of attorneys who specialize in divorce work, and they make it very difficult to settle a lot of divorce cases that I find frankly are nickel and dime divorce cases and that normally ten years ago or five years ago were able to be settled. And you simply can't settle them. They always end up going to trial with lots of pretrial discovery and interrogatories. In the old days—I am old enough to say "in the old days"—we would get letters from attorneys and telephone calls and you get: "This is what my client has." And now you get interrogatories (Mather et al. 2001, 53).

However, in contrast to the generalist's desire for the speedier informal settlements, the following specialist preferred to work with attorneys who shared *her* ideas about practice:

> I tend to call this group, with some exception, the ham and eggers. By and large I don't like to see them on the other side of a case. A lot of these people do not work a file the way a divorce file should be worked. They resist a legitimate request by the other attorney because they're time-consuming. I'll have ongoing problems with discovery from these types of attorneys. They will not respond to legitimate and reasonable request for information, which means you have to either file a motion, get them in court and tell the judge that they have to do it, or they've got to find some alternate means to get the information. I prefer working with [divorce specialists]. I prefer it because I know what I'm dealing with. I know that as far as the broad rules that they'll be supplied with that there's an air of professional courtesy that will exist between myself and the other attorney and that makes the thing go smoother and probably result in a better outcome for both parties (Mather et al. 2001, 54).

The general practitioner preferred the "old days" in part because informal sharing of information saved time and money for his less affluent clientele. But gender dynamics were also at work. Those informal exchanges took place within a "good old boys" network, and some women attorneys, as newcomers to the community, felt they had been excluded from the conversations or were not taken seriously in negotiations. The formal techniques of discovery preferred by the specialist were an attempt to equalize the playing field and also allowed her to enact her feminist ideals on behalf of her (mostly) female clients.

Collegial norms developed within different communities of practice influence lawyers in those communities concerning how they represent clients, approach opposing counsel, and think about their work. These norms reflect broader shifts in the legal and social environment and in the organization of practice. Changes such as the increased specialization in divorce law, increased complexity of divorce procedures and the introduction of divorce mediation, the entry of women into the divorce bar, greater differentiation of clients by income, feminist consciousness, and the decline of solo practice could all be seen as important forces affecting collegial control of lawyers. Therefore:

> Collegial control thus is a microlevel concept, insofar as it identifies the influences on crucial work decisions in day-to-day practice...at the same time these microlevel processes are embedded in much larger social and institutional developments that can profoundly affect the nature of collegial control of legal work (Mather et al. 2001, 81).

A focus on the communities of practice allows us to explore linkages between the macrostructure of the legal profession described earlier and the decisions of individual lawyers. The conceptual lens of collegial control may not fit all communities of practice. In some fields of law the image of a lawyer acting alone and unconstrained by colleagues may be more apt. Nevertheless, a significant body of research on lawyers outside of the divorce bar supports the concept. For example, variation in local legal cultures was observed through lawyers working in different cities who each followed informal norms about what constitutes inappropriate delay in civil courts (Church 1985). Also, a major study of three different law firms found that each developed its own style for dealing with clients and colleagues and standards for success and creating meaning in work; organizational culture explained these differences (Kelly 1994). Other examples of communities of practice include: the informal procedures and standards created by business lawyers in Silicon Valley to facilitate dispute resolution outside of courts (Suchman and Cahill 1996); the lawyer/client and lawyer/lawyer interactions of attorneys on both sides of the "OSHA bar," the community of lawyers in regulatory politics around the Occupational Safety and Health Act (OSHA; Schmidt 2005); and the fields of criminal law and personal injury law.

Criminal law attorneys resemble divorce lawyers in that both are typically low in prestige and income, their practices center around local trial courts, they work repeatedly with attorneys on the other side, negotiation is common, cases depend heavily on facts rather than legal complexity, and clients are often one-shot litigants (although there are undoubtedly more repeaters among criminal defendants than those getting divorced). Criminal court practitioners operate in workgroups, seek predictability of outcomes that leads to an aversion to trial, develop patterns of plea bargaining ("going rates") to settle cases, know "what a case is worth" in bargaining and also know which cases should be tried (see, e.g., Eisenstein and Jacob 1977; Heumann 1978; Mather 1979). Criminal court communities share legal cultures but also have more particularized sets of views for judges, prosecuting attorneys, public defenders, and private defense counsel. The private defense bar divides further into low-cost attorneys who represent many clients and the more high-end lawyers who specialize in drug cases or white-collar crime. Thinking about criminal courts as communities helps to integrate findings from individual, organizational, and environmental approaches to trial courts (Eisenstein, Flemming, and Nardulli 1988).

Personal injury plaintiff lawyers also organize themselves and their work through social networks (Parikh 2001). These networks range from the boutique specialist attorneys handling a few big cases such as class actions or toxic torts, to the mass-market firms with large number of clients injured in auto accidents or with slip and fall claims. Kritzer (1998) showed the importance of reputation for contingency-fee attorneys and suggested that the concept of professional reputation functions to constrain lawyers' greed. Maintaining a good reputation helps in getting clients and also bolsters their credibility in negotiations with insurance adjustors and other counsel.

Attorneys doing plaintiff work in personal injury law rarely switch to the defense side. The political divisions between the sides are too strong. Personal injury defense lawyers work with insurance companies, hospitals, and corporations. Their social networks involve chambers of commerce, business, and political organizations that lobby for tort reform (Haltom and McCann 2004). Thus, the political ideology of tort lawyers (on both sides) is embedded in their daily practice, not only in their representation of clients but also in their contributions to judicial campaigns and their political associations now that tort reform has become a partisan issue. Moreover, tort lawyers contribute directly to the production of law, according to research by economists showing the influence of the tort bar on modern products liability legal doctrine (Rubin and Bailey 1994; and see Cross 1996).

This brief survey of different lawyer communities begins to provide the answer to the question posed earlier about the how the macrocharacteristics of the legal profession help to explain the work of lawyers in the judicial process. That is, how do we link aggregate social structure of the profession to individual choices of lawyers? First, we see lawyers embedded in professional communities that shape their values and influence their decisions. In these communities, lawyers *do* "take sides" in the work that they do. Contrary to the romantic nineteenth century image of the legal professional who goes briefcase in hand to represent whoever hires him, the twenty-first century lawyer specializes in certain areas of law and certain clienteles as well. Personal injury lawyers do not switch sides, nor do corporate lawyers ever change places with lawyers handling individual problems (except to do an occasional divorce for a corporate client). An important new survey of the political values of lawyers revealed enormous differences—between the liberalism of the labor lawyer, environmental, or antitrust plaintiff lawyer versus the conservatism of lawyers for management, environmental, or antitrust defense. Similarly lawyers' political views were associated with the type of organization where they worked—with the most liberal working solo or for government and the most conservative working in large firms (Heinz et al. 2005).

Second, where do these political value differences come from? On the one hand, law school graduates self-select into different kinds of firms and different areas of practice. Gender differences can be seen here as well as differences from substantive interests and personality (e.g., the high risk, more extroverted toward litigation or the quieter, more conservative toward tax or banking). The most ambitious law grads may seek out the highest paying and most prestigious positions. The selection process runs two ways, however, and firms choose as well. The major corporate law firms only select top students from the elite law schools so that career path is rarely open to graduates of regional or local law schools. The hierarchy of law schools plays a major role in shaping the job opportunities available to new graduates and in producing the stratification of the profession. At the individual level, then, there is an initial sorting process at work through which law school graduates select, and are channeled to, different kinds of firms and practice.

On the other hand, there is a second level of sorting that involves the collegial and client influences on lawyers after they are on the job. Young lawyers work for a few years in a position to get experience or pay off loans, and then decide the field or firm is not for them. Personal satisfaction is lowest for lawyers working in large law firms, leading some to decide that quality of life matters more than money (Heinz et al. 2005). Selective attrition and lawyer mobility thus help attorneys to find their niche in the profession. As Ronit Dinovitzer and Bryant Garth (2007) demonstrated, lawyers' job satisfaction provides a powerful lens for understanding the structure of legal careers.

For lawyers who stay for years in the same firm, they may come to adopt the values and ideals of their clients. As Karl Llewellyn said in 1933, "the practice of corporation law not only works for business men toward business ends, but develops within itself a business point of view...toward the way in which to do the work" (quoted in Heinz et al. 2005, 310). Hence, some of lawyers' political values might be learned on the job. The relative power of clients over lawyers illustrates a third way to think about connections between communities of practice and lawyers as political actors. Tenets of professionalism require attorneys to advocate zealously for their clients but also to exercise independent judgment. When facing a choice between what a client wants and what the professional thinks is right, lawyers listen to the norms of their communities of practice. The organizational context explains some of the differences across communities. In large firms, Nelson (1985) found that attorneys closely identified with their clients and rarely saw a conflict between their own personal values and what they were asked to do. Lawyers in large firms also had the least autonomy to design their own work strategies or refuse clients or work assignments, in comparison to attorneys in smaller firms or solo practice (Heinz et al. 2005). In certain specialized fields of practice such as divorce, criminal defense, and personal injury (plaintiff), lawyers are more independent from their clients and more likely to be "in charge" of decisions (Rosenthal 1974; see Southworth 1996; Mather 2003b, for a summary of this literature).

Finally, formal professional controls can augment the informal collegial control to further reinforce differences in lawyers across fields of specialization and across sides in conflict. Some legal specialties have adopted guides for conduct that recognize the particular nature of their field. The American Academy of Matrimonial Lawyers publishes its own standards to define and reinforce the special features of divorce law practice. And patent law goes the farthest by administering its own special exam for admission to certain kinds of patent law practice (Graham 2005).

Another type of professional control lies in the ethical prohibition against representing clients where there is a conflict of interest. Many firms have interpreted this expansively to mean that they will avoid "positional conflicts," those in which the sides are opposed but there is no direct conflict between the parties. Thus, lawyers representing banks will not allow their firms to represent debtors in bankruptcy; and others say they "represent either the insurer or the insured.

And it's very hard to do both" (Shapiro 2002, 150). Declining to represent certain interests out of loyalty to their clients also has significant consequences for lawmaking, as suggested by one large firm lawyer:

> We will not try to advance certain theories in a tax court, because we know that there will be adverse reaction—I mean adverse impact—on lots of clients....In the antitrust area...we wouldn't, probably, like to challenge too many mergers, because we do a lot of mergers and acquisitions. We might not like to go in and try to make new law in the antitrust area to expand the reaches of the antitrust laws, because it would impact, probably, a lot more clients than the one that we're helping. The same way in the securities law. You wouldn't want to necessarily try to make new law that would be adverse to, quote, "corporate America" (Shapiro 2002, 148).

These different mechanisms allow, and indeed encourage, lawyers to reflect their political and moral values in choices about where to practice and about what kind of legal work to do.

CONCLUSIONS

As I reflect back on lawyer jokes and the themes of this chapter, I recall the three points of comparison between lawyers and laboratory rats (too many of them; not likeable; and there are some things a rat just won't do). The large number of lawyers in the United States is obvious; but how many is too many, and what is the standard for comparison? The number of lawyers per capita in the United States is high but it is not the highest in the world. Moreover, given our governmental structure in which power is decentralized through federalism and dispersed among three branches, Americans have historically been suspicious of centralized regulation and relied more on legal claims as forms of political participation and lawsuits to call attention to problems and assert legal rights (Kagan 2001).

Second, lab assistants *do* get attached to lawyers—they marry them, hire them to resolve conflicts, support litigation campaigns for their favorite causes, and vote for them as public officials entrusting them to make law. In fact, there are many lawyers in all three branches of government (see Miller 1995). Lawyers' choices, along with stratification in the profession and informal norms in different communities of practice, produce very different kinds of lawyering behavior. Third, and as a consequence of this variation, lawyers differ in their likelihood to refuse client demands to do certain things. Some lawyers are beholden to their clients and act as hired guns for them, while others because of the context of their work show more independence.

We might think of the structure of the legal profession as creating and reinforcing a kind of selective breeding for different types of lawyers. Each sector or community of practice has its own collegial controls and rewards. Those who succeed in a community become its leaders, articulating its values and norms, and attracting more likeminded types. However, the rejected or unhappy lawyers migrate to other specialized fields or organizational settings and attract more likeminded ones there. This sorting process within the profession has political impact as well as its obvious economic and social consequences.

The three clusters of lawyer jokes described at the outset emphasize and speak to different communities in the profession. Command over language includes the verbal skills needed especially for litigation, appellate work, and lawmaking. Lawyers' greed is rewarded in the highest echelons of corporate law work in the largest firms. And conflict escalation could point either to lawyers' self-interest in manufacturing conflicts to generate fees, or to lawyers' public-regarding interest in constructing legal claims to fight for a cause.

Notes

Many thanks to Jesika Gonzalez for her helpful research and editorial assistance.

1. The jokes discussed in this section are drawn from Galanter (2005). Galanter organized his collection of lawyer jokes into eleven clusters or categories, three of which I address here.

2. During the 1970s, political science studies of lawyers flourished as attention was focused on issues such as poverty law, criminal justice, citizen participation, and social reform litigation. See, for example, Casper (1972), Heumann (1978), Mather (1979), Rosenthal (1974), and Olson (1984). More recent research includes McCann (1994), Harrington (1994), Kritzer (1990, 1998), Sarat and Felstiner (1995), Mather et al. (2001), Sarat and Scheingold (1998), and Scheingold and Sarat (2004).

3. These descriptions from popular judicial process texts (Neubauer and Meinhold 2004, 153–56; Baum 2001, 55–56) closely resemble those found in law school texts on clinical legal practice. Elsewhere in these judicial process texts, the authors do explore important aspects of lawyers' behavior and of the legal profession.

4. See also Abel and Lewis (1995) who argued for "Putting Law Back into the Sociology of Lawyers." I realized after completing this chapter that I am also borrowing its title from my coauthors on an earlier project; see McEwen et al. (1995), "Bring in the Lawyers: Challenging the Dominant Approaches to Ensuring Fairness in Divorce Mediation."

5. In civil cases litigants who represent themselves (*pro se*) play the gatekeeper role, while in criminal cases police play this role as well.

6. See Simon (1998) on the role of lawyers and professional ethics in the context of the Lincoln Savings & Loan debacle. On Enron, see the comprehensive edited collection of commentary and analysis by Rapoport and Dharan (2004).

7. According to Scheingold and Sarat, cause lawyers are defined by their moral and political commitment, that is, their "intent" to serve particular ideals. "Serving a cause by accident does not, in our judgment, qualify as cause lawyering" (Scheingold and Sarat 2004, 3).

8. The American Bar Association Section on Litigation recently sponsored a major research project on "The Vanishing Trial." Data and analysis from the project are found in fifteen articles published in Volume 1(3) of *Journal of Empirical Legal Studies* (2004). See, for example, Galanter (2004) and Ostrom et al. (2004).

9. Labeling behavior according to intent is a slippery definition, providing little guidance to researchers seeking to investigate cause lawyering. Further, if cause lawyers can have "mixed motives," as the authors acknowledge (Scheingold and Sarat 2004, 4), then why can't conventional lawyers as well? And if so, that supports the argument of this chapter that many so-called conventional lawyers are, like cause lawyers, "political actors whose work involves doing law" (Scheingold and Sarat 2004, 3).

10. See Casper (1972) for a classic survey of defendants' perceptions of the criminal process.

11. As Baum explained this phenomenon for criminal lawyers, "The people who make up the core of the courthouse work group—attorneys and judges—tend to develop close working relationships through their constant interaction and interdependence. Indeed, as one lawyer observed of public defenders and prosecutors, 'It's like prison guards and prisoners: they're all locked in together'" (Baum 2001, 175).

12. This profile of divorce lawyers at work is drawn from research by Mather et al. 2001, but the general picture is consistent with other studies of the divorce bar. See, for example, Sarat and Felstiner (1995); Gilson and Mnookin (1994); Erlanger, Chambliss, and Melli (1987); and Kressel (1985).

5

THE POLITICS OF JURY REFORM

Robert G. Boatright

Juries are very important aspects of the court system, but there has been surprisingly little research among judicial scholars about them. This chapter looks at jury reform proposals in a variety of states. These proposals mean that juries and their functions have become highly contested political issues in many places. In the United States, we want our juries to be representative of the general population but also to be impartial. Are these two goals incompatible? This chapter focuses on several aspects of jury reform. Are there representativeness issues in who actually shows up at the courthouse to serve on juries? Are there biases in the jury selection process? Do the rules for jury deliberations create unintended problems or biases? The chapter concludes with a discussion of jury nullification, where a jury refuses to convict a criminal defendant because they feel the underlying criminal law is unjust or the potential punishments are too harsh. Jury reform is another issue on which law and politics can collide.

The jury is often overlooked in political scientists' considerations of the American court system. In a way, this is logical—few jurors approach jury service with political objectives in mind, and the jury is generally held to be an antidote to politics in court decision making. Defendants should be tried, as the Sixth Amendment to the U.S. Constitution instructs us, by "an impartial jury." Yet throughout American history, achieving impartiality has been difficult. Although the Sixth Amendment does not elaborate on what makes for an impartial jury, it has traditionally been held that the best way to achieve an impartial jury is to try to achieve a representative jury, a randomly selected cross-section of the citizenry, a "jury of one's peers."

For the most part, these two goals are compatible with each other. At a minimum, it is easier to measure whether juries are representative than it is to measure whether they are impartial. To say that courts can measure how representative their juries are of the general population, however, is not to say that

courts have been able to seat juries that *are* representative of the population. In the past three decades, American courts have become more sensitive to the many sources of bias in the jury system, the many ways in which the procedures they use to summon jurors, select jurors, and conduct jury trials may affect the kinds of people who wind up serving and the decisions these people make.

Jury selection proceeds in several stages (listed in Table 5.1); during each of these stages, there is the potential for bias to be introduced. In this chapter I focus on three of these stages and hence, three sources of bias in the jury system, and the reforms that courts have adopted to address or compensate for these biases. First, I consider biases in who responds to jury summonses. Even if courts make a good-faith effort to summon a random cross-section of the eligible population for jury service, the *venire*, or group of citizens who arrive at the court for jury service, may not be representative of the population. Exemptions granted

Table 5.1 Stages of Jury Selection

Source lists acquired and duplicates removed

Lists of eligible jurors prepared

Jury questionnaires sent (some jurisdictions)

Summoned jurors selected and summonses sent

Summoned jurors eligible to request excuses or deferrals

Jurors appear in court

Jurors selected for voir dire

Voir dire

Challenges for cause exercised

Peremptory challenges exercised

Jurors selected

Jurors sit in case

to certain types of citizens may bring about a jury pool that does not reflect the composition of the population. The lists that courts maintain of eligible jurors may underrepresent particular groups within the population. Some citizens may wish to serve but find themselves unable to take the time off from work, to get to the courthouse, and so on. And some citizens may simply do whatever they can to avoid jury service. Few courts have the resources or the motivation to ensure that all citizens respond to their jury summonses.

Second, I consider biases in jury selection. Once the questioning of potential jurors has begun, attorneys on both sides are permitted an unlimited number of *challenges for cause*, to remove potential jurors who have unavoidable conflicts, believe themselves unable to deliberate impartially, or have had a personal experience that might influence their judgment. Attorneys are also generally permitted a limited number of *peremptory challenges*. Although the courts have gradually made it illegal to exercise peremptory challenges for the purpose of excluding women, African Americans, or Latinos, peremptory challenges often do have the effect of altering the composition of the jury to the point that it is unrepresentative of the population.

Third, I consider the rules governing jury deliberations. Even if one assumes the selection of an impartial jury, rules governing what jurors can do—for instance, whether they are permitted to take notes, ask questions of the witnesses, or discuss the case before the presentation of evidence has concluded—can

influence the quality of the jury's deliberations and the fairness of its verdict. These rules can, in turn, influence the legitimacy of the court's decision in the eyes of the public and create a feedback loop, in which those who receive summonses in the future evaluate their willingness to serve based on reasonably accurate expectations of the costs and benefits of serving.

Problems in each of these areas have fed an ongoing debate over whether the jury system is "broken"—whether American courts deliberately or accidentally exclude some citizens, whether they impede the abilities of jurors to deliberate fairly, and ultimately, whether they produce unfair or illegitimate verdicts. The number of civil and criminal jury trials has declined sharply over the past twenty years; at the state level, 0.6 percent of civil cases are tried before a jury, and at the federal level, a mere 1.2 percent are tried before a jury (National Center for State Courts 2005, 1). Some critics have applauded this reduction in the number of jury trials or have called for abandoning the goal of seeking a random cross-section of the population for jury service.

Although some of this decline can be attributed to an increasing willingness on the part of litigants to engage in mediated settlements, it is still of concern to those who see juries as an important aspect of democracy. The decline in jury trials has taken place at a time when American courts are in the middle of a broad "jury reform" (or as some within that community prefer to call it, "jury improvement") movement, spearheaded by individual courts and judges, by professional associations, and by advocacy groups. Many within the state and federal courts have sought to protect jury trials by improving their quality or by improving citizens' experience as jurors. In most states, there has been a consensus that piecemeal approaches, in which one of the above three issues is addressed, will not be as effective as comprehensive approaches that link these three areas of concern.

In this chapter I first address the state of the American jury and the groups that have a stake in jury reform. I then explore research, laws, and reforms that relate to the areas of concern noted above, and the politics behind these reforms. I close by revisiting the relationship between the twin goals of impartiality and representativeness.

THE REPRESENTATIVENESS
OF THE JURY

Although the jury trial has been a constant of American society since the founding, there are several notable landmarks in the development of contemporary jury practices. For much of American history, jurors have in practice been "self-selected." As Bowles (1980) noted, jurors have generally been people who were not resourceful enough to avoid service or were sufficiently interested in it to serve voluntarily. Until the 1960s, courts often sought to choose "blue ribbon" juries, in which high community standing was a sought-after trait. The Supreme Court has gradually asserted the rights of most citizens to serve on juries. Table 5.2 shows several of the landmark cases in establishing these rights. As the table shows, by the late twentieth century federal law had reached a point where it clearly upholds the rights of all classes of citizens (except minors and convicted criminals) to serve and to be summoned for jury duty (see Abramson 1994, 136).

These cases all concern purposeful attempts to discriminate in the selection of jurors. Researchers have established that many court practices, although not deliberately discriminatory, can affect the jury pool. To take one example, consider the lists of eligible jurors from which courts randomly draw individuals to summon for service. Throughout much of U.S. history, courts relied solely on lists of registered voters. The American Bar Association's (ABA) *Standards*

Relating to Juror Use and Management noted that such lists included only 64 percent of the voting-age population (American Bar Association 1992, 13–14) and recommend using other lists, including lists of licensed drivers, public utility customers, or even recipients of various forms of public assistance. Yet each of these lists contains its own biases, and acquiring such lists can be problematic for several reasons. First, courts must expend resources to acquire these lists and merge them into their master list, removing duplicates. Second, in instances where the name is the same but there are different addresses in different lists, how are courts to determine whether they are in fact looking at two different individuals, or at one individual with two addresses, one of which may be outdated? Third, courts may require legislative sanction to use some of these lists; lists of utility customers or state aid recipients may not be publicly available, and some citizens or legislators may oppose using such lists. Fourth, perhaps the most accurate list available, the list of taxpayers, is protected by statutes from use at both the federal level and, in nearly all states, at the state level. And fifth, some citizens may be unable to serve or may simply ignore their summons, and the court may lack the resources to confront this problem. To summarize, then, even if all citizens have the right to serve, the courts may be unable to construct a list of potential jurors that adequately represents the public.

Even these problems, however, tend at least to be measurable. Statistical analysis can determine whether the jury pool is representative of the public,

Table 5.2 Notable Decisions on the Right to Jury Service

Strauder v. West Virginia, 100 U.S. 303 (1880)	Established right of African Americans to serve on juries
Ballard v. United States, 329 U.S. 187 (1946)	Established right of women to serve on juries
Hernandez v. Texas, 347 U.S. 475 (1954)	Established right of Latinos to serve on juries
Batson v. Kentucky, 476 U.S. 86 (1986) *Powers v. Ohio*, 499 U.S. 400 (1991) *Edmonson v. Leesville Concrete Co.*, 500 U.S. 614 (1994) *Miller-El v. Dretke*, 545 U.S. 231 (2005)	Established that jurors cannot be struck from the jury because of race
J.E.B. v. Alabama ex rel. T.B., 511 U.S. 127 (1994)	Established that jurors cannot be struck from the jury on the basis of sex

and courts may conduct their own analyses to measure bias. Yet the simple laws of statistics dictate that one, twelve-person jury will not necessarily reflect the general population. If citizens or the press observe, for instance, an all-white jury deliberating over the fate of an African American defendant, they may conclude that bias exists in the system, even if other juries in the same jurisdiction are racially balanced, and even if the jury pool for that trial was balanced. The public, in other words, may draw its own conclusions about the jury system.

PUBLIC SUPPORT FOR JURIES AS INSTITUTIONS

What impact has the growing attention to inclusiveness and representation had on the jury system or on the public? There is no easy metric to measure the current state of the American jury system. This is so, in part, because one cannot be certain what factors to study. On the "outcome" end, one certainly cannot measure the quality of jury deliberations or verdicts. On the "input" end, one might draw conclusions about the representativeness of juries, but few courts keep detailed information on the characteristics of summoned or empanelled jurors, and there is no national database to measure any attributes of juries. It is

possible, however, to draw on public opinion surveys, surveys of summoned jurors, and juror exit surveys to measure some aspects of attitudes toward the jury system.

Virtually all surveys have found that large majorities of the public support the jury system and the courts in the abstract. A recent national survey by the National Center for State Courts (1999) found that a majority of the public expresses higher confidence in the courts than in other government institutions, and that respondents generally rated state courts (where the vast majority of jury trials take place) higher than federal courts. A four-jurisdiction 1998 survey by the American Judicature Society (AJS) asked more explicitly about jury service; as Table 5.3 shows, a majority of the citizens surveyed responded that they felt prepared for jury service and felt that juries in their jurisdiction were representative of the community (Boatright 1998, 63). This pattern existed among jurors, nonjurors, and those who have avoided jury service (although those who avoided jury service are somewhat more skeptical).

Yet the strongest determinant of public support for the jury is prior service as a juror. Several studies (Allen 1977; Pabst, Munsterman, and Mount 1976, 1977; Richert 1977a, 1977b; Shuman and Hamilton 1992) have concluded that citizens feel more favorably toward the courts and toward jury service after

Table 5.3 Citizen Attitudes Toward Jury Service

	PERCENTAGE ANSWERING "YES" AMONG CITIZENS WHO			
	Responded to Their Jury Summons	Did Not Respond to Their Jury Summons	Were Excused	Total (%)
Do you think that juries are representative of your community as a whole?	60.1	53.8	51.8	56.9
Do you feel that you know enough about how the legal system works to be a fair and impartial juror?	86.2	53.8	80.4	81.8
If you were to serve on a jury, do you think that the judge and other court personnel would treat you with respect?	94.6	69.2	96.4	93.3
If you were to serve on a jury, do you think that the lawyers arguing the case would treat you with respect?	82.8	69.2	87.4	83.2
N	203	26	112	341

Note. From Boatright 1998, 67–68.

they have served than they did before serving, and these findings have strongly influenced the movement toward changes in the deliberation process or in juror treatment. As a result, courts have sought to use former jurors as ambassadors for the jury system in their appeals to the public. The AJS study also found that citizens, whether they have served or not, are quite knowledgeable about many aspects of jury service, including the quality of the facilities, the expected wait time, juror compensation fees, and the quality of the jury experience itself (Boatright 1998, 63–64). In sum, citizens know a fair amount about jury service and tend to support the institution of the jury.

DO AVERAGE PEOPLE WANT TO SERVE ON JURIES?

An abstract support for juries, however, does not necessarily translate into public enthusiasm for jury service. It has been reported that in large cities such as Los Angeles or Washington, D.C., fewer than half of those summoned for jury service show up. Such low summons response rates make it more difficult to bring sufficient numbers of citizens into the courthouse, and again, can bias the composition of juries.

It is difficult to tell what the causes of these nonresponse rates are, but it is tempting to attribute them to a desire of citizens to "vote with their feet," or in other words to express their unhappiness with juries by declining to serve themselves. One of the goals of the AJS study was to demonstrate that willful nonresponse is generally caused by an inability to serve or a belief that one is unlikely to be seated on a jury (Boatright 1998, 68–73). As Table 5.4, drawn from the AJS study, shows there is little difference between citizens who serve and citizens who do not serve in beliefs about jury service. Yet other studies (Fukurai and Butler 1991; Fukurai, Butler, and Krooth 1991; Fukurai and Krooth 2003) have contended that some citizens, particularly racial minorities, believe court decisions are biased or that they will be treated poorly as jurors. And there was much discussion about the harmful effects on jury summons response rates after the O. J. Simpson trial, and the racial biases many perceived in that trial.

Most of the calls for reform have been based on frustrations jurors have expressed with particular aspects of jury service or on a desire by courts to improve the overall quality of their jury systems. The hope of reformers is that if citizens observe that courts are trying to be inclusive and to improve the

Table 5.4 Citizen Expectations About Jury Service

	PERCENTAGE ANSWERING "YES" AMONG CITIZENS WHO		
	Responded to Their Summons	Did Not Respond to Their Summons	Total
Do you believe that serving on a jury would be interesting?	86.8	88.9	87.6
Do you think that if you served on a jury you would have to spend too much time away from your daily routine?	49.1	50.0	49.5
Do you think it would be easy to get information from your local court about what jury service involves?	72.8	65.3	69.9
Do you think that your local court would pay you for jury service?	80.7	77.8	79.6
Do you think your local court gives you any training or orientation on how to be a juror?	63.2	69.4	65.6
Do you think the court excuses some people from jury service if they cannot serve?	94.7	90.3	93.0
N	114	72	186

Note. From Boatright 1998, 70.

experience of jurors, they will be more interested in serving. Many state courts have taken strong steps to alter radically the way in which they manage jurors. In 1979, Massachusetts instituted a comprehensive set of reforms, including an increase in juror pay, a revised deferral policy, shorter terms of service, and a requirement that employers pay jurors during the first three days of service (Amar 1995, 1184–85; Brown 1998; Office of the Jury Commissioner, State of Massachusetts 1997). In 1993, New York, a state that many felt had the nation's most problematic jury system, eliminated virtually all exemptions from service, improved the quality of its juror lists, streamlined the voir dire process, increased compensation from $15 to $40 per day, increased summons enforcement, and instituted a raft of reforms in in-court procedures (Jury Project 1996, 2001; McMahon and Kornblau 1995; Vikoren 1996). The Arizona courts have become national leaders in allowing researchers access to their courts to experiment with and evaluate changes in jury practices, and have also instituted a wide number of changes in jury deliberation procedures (Arizona Supreme Court Committee on More Effective Use of Juries 1994; Myers and Griller 1997). California and the District of Columbia are currently in the process of instituting major reforms. In each of these jurisdictions, courts have cited low summons response or public desire for change, yet in many, these are simply ideas that make sense on their own. In these states and others, courts have drawn on the research of social scientists and legal scholars to improve their jury systems.

WHAT IS AT STAKE IN JURY REFORM

Jury reform is not a partisan or left–right political issue, but it is an issue that has identifiable constituencies and interests. In some states or on some issues, these interests are relatively organized, while in others they are diffuse. These constituencies include the following:

- **Judges**: It is certainly in the interest of judges to have satisfied and capable jurors. On a personal level, almost all judges can be expected to take pride in ensuring that their trials bring about just verdicts. It is also, however, in the interest of judges to dispense with cases promptly, and the fact that many judicial dockets are overloaded today may restrain judges from expending effort to slow down the court system. Many elected state judges have also argued that reform is in their political interest.

- **Attorneys**: Attorneys certainly have incentives to try to shape the composition of juries to favor their case, and are directly affected by any reform that influences the composition of the jury pool or the ability of jurors to make decisions. In many states, attorneys' groups have been among the most visible proponents or opponents of changes in the jury system. The American Board of Trial Advocates (ABOTA), an organization of plaintiff's lawyers, has developed videos on the importance of jury service and has worked to develop sample curricula on the jury for students. At the same time, however, organized groups of both plaintiff's and defense lawyers have vigorously opposed reforms such as attempts to reduce the number of peremptory challenges.

- **Jury Commissioners and Court Administrators**: It goes without saying that jury commissioners and court administrators have an interest in jury improvements if they are serious about their work. Jury commissioners are often elected, so they have the same political concerns that elected judges do about ensuring that jurors leave the courthouse happy. Yet staffing and budgetary limitations and ensconced ways of doing things can lead court personnel to be reluctant to make changes in established procedures.

- **Employers and Businesses**: Jury service rarely is ranked among the top priorities of American businesses, yet businesses have much at stake on both ends of the jury system. The Chamber of Commerce and other large trade associations have long been concerned about "runaway juries" and costly punitive damages in civil cases.[1] And employers may object to losing vital employees on a regular basis due to jury service. In all states, employers are forbidden to penalize their employees for serving as jurors, but these laws do not mean that employers cannot make their views on jury service clear, and anecdotes abound of employees being punished for serving on juries. Some corporations have voluntarily cooperated with courts in matters such as reducing the time of service for jurors, but others have objected to reforms. Our nation's largest employer, the federal government, does compensate workers for time spent on juries, but only two states and the District of Columbia require companies to continue to pay their workers while they serve on juries.

- **The Media**: At its best, the media can serve as a watchdog of the courts, reporting on juror treatment and giving a platform for unhappy jurors. In some instances, media reports have prompted changes in court procedures (see Houser 2002). The media can also serve as a valuable ally of the courts in publicizing changes in the jury system or in reporting on "show cause" hearings, in which nonrespondents are required to appear before a judge to explain why they did not arrive at the court for jury service. The media can also pose problems for the courts in the areas of juror privacy or in sensational reporting on trials or verdicts. The natural impulse of those in the media to find compelling stories can either improve or harm the public's understanding of jury service.
- **Public Interest Groups**: Several interest groups exist to advocate for changes in the jury system. Many groups that are not primarily concerned with the courts, however, do have a vested interest in jury-related issues. Civil rights organizations, for instance, can be expected to play a role where summoning procedures or jury selection procedures threaten the racial balance of juries.
- **The Public, Jurors, and Potential Jurors**: Easily the largest latent group influenced by the jury system, however, is the public. In a few cases, former jurors have been inspired by their service to take a continuing interest in the jury system. Yet most former jurors certainly regard jury service as an obligation that, once completed, they need not worry about again for several years; in most states they will not be summoned again for

at least one to three years. Yet citizens are clearly the ones most influenced by all aspects of jury reform. Most of the larger jury reform proposals have included a public outreach directed toward the public at large or toward students, immigrants, or others who may be less familiar with jury service.

Each of these different players has had an influence in one or more areas of jury reform. Although in many instances changes to the jury have simply been matters of a small number of judges taking the initiative, in instances where reforms have garnered support or opposition these groups have at times been at odds. The issues discussed later show the shifting alliances between these players.

JURY SUMMONS RESPONSE AND PUBLIC OUTREACH

Perhaps the two most basic questions regarding jury service are whether courts are calling a representative sample of citizens to serve and whether those who are called show up for jury service. One of these questions is a technical one, while the other addresses citizens' attitudes. Yet the two are related because courts must produce an answer of "yes" to both if they are to have representative venires.

As noted earlier, summoning a representative sample of the public is generally a matter of drawing on as many source lists as possible. Although each list may contain some bias, aggregating lists can minimize biases. State practices in this area vary. New York abolished its "permanent qualified list" of jurors in 1996. Prior to that time, state lists had automatically excluded numerous occupations, such as pharmacists, doctors, judges, and others (Jury Project 2001, 7–9). New York added lists of registered drivers, and now updates its lists annually. As a result of this, Chief Judge Judith Kaye and Mayor Rudolph Giuliani were summoned in the late 1990s, and both spoke with the media about their experience. Since 2000, the District of Columbia has supplemented lists of registered voters and driver's license holders with income tax lists and public assistance lists. And Alaska supplements the traditional lists with names drawn from the state's list of fish and game licenses (American Judicature Society 1999). Other states, however, have been stymied in some of their efforts. Arizona has been prevented by the state legislature from using tax lists, and Florida has yet to receive authorization to abolish the fee for changing driver's license addresses, a proposal the courts argue would improve the quality of its lists (Florida Jury Innovations Committee 2001).

Ensuring that individuals who are summoned for jury service arrive in court is generally a matter of education and outreach, but it also is a function of understanding why citizens do not serve. At the most basic level, courts can work with state legislatures to institute a "Juror Appreciation Week" or a similar recognition program. This has been done in several states. The District of Columbia took matters one step further, commissioning a report on public health campaigns to learn from marketing professionals how it could best publicize jury service (Council for Court Excellence 1998). And several courts publish newsletters, present television shows, or maintain websites to communicate regularly with the public (see Munsterman, Hannaford, and Whitehead 1997, 26).

Courts have generally chosen the "carrot" of making jury service seem worthwhile rather than the "stick"—the enforcement of jury summonses—because it is so difficult and costly to force unwilling jurors to appear. Some courts have vigorous enforcement programs, others have rather haphazard ones in which a random sample of nonrespondents is called to the court, and many others have no enforcement at all.

When citizens have legitimate reasons not to serve, however, courts have had a somewhat more difficult time learning how to address citizen concerns. Juror compensation currently ranges from $5 to $50 per day, depending on the state and locality. In some instances, courts add reimbursement for mileage, use of public transportation, or parking. Several states also provide child care (or child care reimbursement) for jurors. And several states that provide low levels of compensation will increase fees if jurors are able to demonstrate that their employers are not paying them while on jury duty.

There is little evidence that juror fees influence whether citizens are willing to serve on juries (Munsterman, Munsterman, Lynch, and Penrod 1991), although jurors may be pleased to have at least their out-of-pocket expenses covered. And there are several arguments that tend to be raised against increased compensation. Some have argued that requiring businesses to pay their workers while serving on juries places an undue burden on businesses, and it has also been argued that citizens should not be paid for fulfilling a basic civic obligation. When New York increased compensation from $15 to $40, it was only able to do so because the courts sought to find offsetting savings in their own budget (Jury Project 2001, 13–14). The Massachusetts increases in juror fees were only accepted by the legislature and the business community because they were accompanied by the establishment of a one-day/one-trial system—jurors would be paid more but would serve less (Boatright 1998, 21–22). A reform commission established in New Hampshire criticized the Massachusetts compensation system for its complexity and for the fact that, in the eyes of the commission, it treated different citizens differently (New Hampshire Superior Court Jury Reform Study Committee 1997). And the California reform commission ultimately abandoned efforts to substantially increase juror fees, opting instead to work with the state legislature on a plan to offer tax credits to employers who pay their employees' salary while they are serving as jurors (Blue Ribbon Commission on Jury System Improvement 1996, 41–46).

A related reform proposal is changing the summoning process itself. A jury summons can be an imposing document, and summonses are often designed in a manner that can prevent citizens from understanding what to do if they have concerns about their ability to serve. Massachusetts, New York, and the District of Columbia have all redesigned their jury summonses in the past decade to make jurors' options clearer and to make jury service appear more attractive (Boatright 1998). In New York, for instance, summonses to serve at the court in midtown Manhattan include a list of local restaurants and sample walking tours of the area (Jury Project 2001, 23). Some critics of these changes have argued that such changes can lead jurors to consider their summonses, or their jury service, too casually, but such changes are not costly for the courts, nor do they require outside approval.

A growing number of researchers have also begun to question the traditional random sampling method of summoning jurors. Some researchers have pointed to variation in summons response rates that correspond to the racial makeup or income level of different areas of courts' jurisdictions, and have proposed that courts adopt a stratified sampling method, in which courts adjust the number of summonses sent to different neighborhoods according to the neighborhoods' racial or ethnic composition and summons response rate. As King and Munsterman (1996) noted, such an approach is legal, but critics have claimed that this approach does away with the benefits of random selection of the jury pool (see also Alschuler and Deiss 1994; Fukurai et al. 1991). Currently, some states employ this method on a limited, race-neutral basis—Connecticut, for instance, employs a stratified sampling method to balance out representation by county in multicounty jurisdictions—but no states have yet adopted this method to achieve racial balance.

Although there is a broad consensus that everyone should have a right to serve as a juror, there is no consensus about how far courts must go to help jurors with their service. If some citizens are reluctant to purchase their own meals while they are serving, drive downtown, ride the bus, find a babysitter, or take a day off work, are these truly the types of people one would want as jurors? On one level, such questions return to the issue of bias—if the jury pool is not dramatically different from the general population in its racial or socioeconomic composition, does it matter that large numbers of citizens are not serving? On another, though, it seems that this is at least partially an issue of opportunity—some citizens may avoid jury service simply because they do not want to serve, but if some citizens have needs that prevent them from serving, it would seem that these citizens represent an important segment of the population even if they do not fall into a well-defined category of race, gender, or income.

JURY SELECTION

Because of the potential for racial or gender biases to influence challenges to jurors, jury selection has been one of the most controversial areas of jury reform.

On the one hand, *Batson v. Kentucky* (1986) and its successors established the illegality of striking jurors on the basis of race or gender, and efforts to extend the Batson coverages to other characteristics continue in the lower courts. On the other hand, peremptory challenges are one of the most jealously guarded prerogatives of attorneys, and the question of whether a juror is truly being struck on account of race or gender is a subjective decision on the part of the judge. In the *Batson* decision, the court declined to mandate a particular procedure for adjudicating Batson charges.[2] In practice, then, much is left at the discretion of the judge, and it has been argued by some that attorneys merely substitute "silly" reasons to justify what are really race-based challenges (Melilli 1996). As Rose (1999) demonstrated, in practice this restriction may have diminished the tendency of prosecutors to strike prospective jurors of the same race as the defendant, but it has by no means eliminated them.

Voir dire is the process by which the trial judge and the lawyers question potential jurors to discover if the individual has any biases that could influence their decision making if selected for the jury. Once voir dire for a case has begun, jurors can be removed from the panel for one of three reasons. First, jurors who truly are *unable to serve* because of personal circumstances (generally because of economic hardship) are excused at the discretion of the judge. Second, jurors can be *struck for cause*—because they appear to the judge to be unable to deliberate impartially. For instance, a juror who has been the victim of a crime similar to that alleged to have been committed by the defendant may be struck if the judge determines that that juror would be unable to put his or her own personal experiences aside. Third, attorneys may exercise one of their *peremptory challenges* to strike a juror. Attorneys can be challenged to explain their reasoning, but as long as their reasoning is not based on race or gender, the peremptory challenge is allowed.

The number of peremptory challenges permitted varies across states, and occasionally across jurisdictions (Jury Project 1994, 64). ABA Standards recommend that for twelve-person juries the number of peremptory challenges allowed be limited to no more than three for civil cases, and to between three and ten in criminal cases, depending on the severity of the crime (American Bar Association 1992, xv–xvi). Because of these limits, as Rose (1999, 698) noted, attorneys prefer to strike jurors they find objectionable for cause, and exercise their peremptories if challenges for cause are denied. Rose's study concluded that it is rare for peremptories to be used systematically by both sides in a case to strike minority jurors or women, but that they are often used by one side in a case (that is, an attorney representing an African American litigant may seek to keep African Americans on the jury while the opposing attorney may seek to strike them).

Organizations representing plaintiffs' attorneys and defense attorneys have vigorously defended peremptory challenges on the grounds that an attorney may have a "gut feeling" that an individual will not be able to deliberate impartially. In *Swain v. Alabama* (1965), the Supreme Court articulated several reasons for peremptory challenges, mostly dealing with the importance of assuring impartiality and the appearance of justice. Although many reform plans have advocated limiting the number of peremptories, few have argued for eliminating them.[3] Many legal scholars, however, have argued that the potential for racial bias is large enough and the *Batson* safeguards insufficient enough that peremptories should be eliminated (see Amar 1995, 1169; Bader 1996; Hoffman 1997), and some judges have sympathized. Eliminating peremptories entirely may be too radical a step to expect of reform commissions composed largely of those who have some stake in the current system.

Another proposal, which stops short of eliminating peremptories, is to ensure that juries are balanced along lines of race and gender even if individuals can still be removed. If a *venire* (the jury pool) is racially representative, one might assume that if peremptories are limited, juries in the aggregate will be representative as well. This is, however, no panacea if a small number of racially freighted cases wind up with unrepresentative juries. Fukurai and Krooth (2003) explored the feasibility of what they called "affirmative action in the jury box" (Fukurai and Krooth 2003, 19), juries in which a certain number of seats are reserved for racial minorities. They justified their proposals in part by emphasizing the importance of representativeness, but they go even further than this. Fukurai and Krooth drew on literature on jury deliberation and

small-group decision making to argue that a "quarter-jury," in which at least three jurors are minorities, will ensure that the minority jurors will be sufficient in number to withstand pressure from other jurors in their deliberation.

Existing reform plans have generally recommended that peremptories should be limited not abolished. The reform proposal in Washington, D.C. advocates reducing peremptories while simultaneously expanding the information gathered about jurors before voir dire and encouraging more detailed questioning by attorneys. This increase in information would compensate for the reduced number of peremptories by increasing the probability that jurors who should be struck for cause are identified and removed (Council for Court Excellence 1998, 34–35). The New York, Arizona, and California reforms have all reduced the number of peremptories and have sought to standardize the number permitted in different jurisdiction in accordance with the ABA Standards (Arizona Supreme Court Committee on More Effective Use of Juries 1994, 68–71; Blue Ribbon Commission on Jury System Improvement 1996, 55; Jury Project 1994, 65).

Another common thread in recent jury reforms, suggested by the approach of the Washington, D.C. reform panel, has been to streamline the voir dire process. While the Washington, D.C. plan explicitly links increasing information provided by jurors to the reduction of peremptories, other courts have emphasized the need for efficiency and for ensuring that jurors who are removed understand and support the voir dire process. In addition to expanding the use and length of juror questionnaires, the major reforms have sought to have the attorneys give "mini-opening statements" before voir dire so that those in the venire better understand the issues at stake (Arizona Supreme Court Committee on More Effective Use of Juries 1994, 59–60); to protect juror privacy during voir dire, by allowing the judge to prohibit questions by the attorneys he or she does not believe are relevant to jury selection, by referring to jurors by number rather than name, and by allowing jurors to discuss sensitive personal information in chambers rather than in an open courtroom (Arizona Supreme Court Committee on More Effective Use of Juries 1994, 67–68); and to impose time limits and limit venires to the minimum size that will ensure that a jury can be selected (Jury Project 1994, 58, 81).

At times, however, the voir dire process can become problematic precisely because of steps such as these. Although expanded use of questionnaires can be vital to ensuring a fair and efficient voir dire process, in several notorious cases the jury questionnaire itself has had a harmful effect on public perceptions of trials. The 302-question, 75-page jury questionnaire in the O. J. Simpson case was deemed by some to be excessively long, to be invasive of juror privacy, and to include questions with little relevance to the case or to jury selection (see Toobin 1994). Even a casual perusal of the questionnaire[4] reveals many questions that seem to have only the most tenuous connection to the case, while others seem almost insulting to the jurors. Perhaps in response to this, the jury questionnaire in the Michael Jackson case[5] was limited to eight pages, and of its forty-one questions only five are obviously linked to the high publicity surrounding the case. The brief questionnaire may have influenced the relatively quick selection process and shielded jury selection from the sensational media atmosphere that surrounded the case. Jury selection proceeded much more quickly in the case than most experts predicted (Chawkins 2005a, 2005b). As Hans and Jehle (2003) noted, reforms of the type noted above appear to improve the quality of the jury (by increasing the probability that jurors who will exercise bias will be noted) as well as increasing public satisfaction and racial fairness.

JURY BEHAVIOR AND DECISION MAKING

One of the most frequently studied pieces of the jury reform puzzle is the issue of aiding jurors in the deliberations. Among the alterations most frequently mentioned in reform proposals are allowing jurors to take notes during the trial; providing jurors with notebooks listing the witnesses and various elements of their testimony; allowing jurors to ask questions, through the judge, of the attorneys or witnesses; providing jurors with preliminary and interim instructions during the trial; providing jurors with instructions written in

"plain English" before their deliberations; directing attorneys to provide jurors with interim summations of their case; allowing jurors to discuss the evidence before deliberations have begun; and providing written guidebooks on ways to structure deliberations. All of these reforms are summed up by former Arizona Judge B. Michael Dann as a movement from the "judicial" or "legal" model of the jury toward an "educational" or "behavioral" model (Dann 1993). Dann compared the jury to students in a classroom, and he even developed a video illustrating how poorly traditional models of jury behavior corresponded to our understanding of how students learn. Imagine, he argued, that students entered a classroom and were told that they were not permitted to take notes, to ask questions of the instructor, to compare ideas with each other, or to use any sort of study aids, and were then given an exam that used terms they did not fully understand. This, Dann claimed, is essentially how jurors are treated.

The Arizona courts, during Dann's tenure on the bench and beyond, have opened themselves up to social scientists to experiment with new methods of juror use. The biggest obstacle to acting on these researchers' recommendations, according to some in the Arizona courts, has been the reluctance of some judges and attorneys to adopt new, unproven methods—out of concern that the ruling in the case would be overturned or that there would be harm to one of the litigants (Dann and Logan 1996; Myers and Griller 1997). However, as Brody and Neiswander (2000) noted, many skeptics have been won over after seeing these changes in practice. Researchers have found that in addition to potentially assisting in bringing about fair verdicts, these reforms improved juror satisfaction (Diamond 1993), and have the potential to prompt jurors to tell others that jury service is useful and satisfying. And some have even argued that there is a cost-saving element to some of these reforms—if juries make decisions more efficiently, courts can conduct trials faster (Schuck 1993).

Many of these reforms have now been accepted across the country. According to Kistler and Nealon (2002), forty-eight states now allow some form of juror note taking. Although some early critics argued that allowing note taking can distract jurors or give more literate and diligent jurors an advantage (Moore

1973, 106), most contemporary studies have found few downsides to allowing note taking (see Heuer and Penrod 1994; 1996). Current ABA Standards recommend that courts should ordinarily permit jurors to take notes, although a Brookings Institution (1992, 18–19) task force on the jury emphasized the importance of directing jurors to take notes sparingly.

It is more difficult to measure the adoption of many of the other reforms noted above. Some courts permit jurors to submit questions to the judge, but in many cases this matter is at the judge's discretion. As Table 5.5 shows, Boatright (1998, 51) estimated that 39 percent of state court judges allow juror questions. Only one state (Georgia) explicitly prohibits juror questions (Curry and Krugler 1999). The Brookings task force and the ABA Standards both recommend allowing juror questions, again, with some restrictions. The same pattern is true of preliminary or interim instructions, interim summations, and providing written instructions to jurors at the beginning of deliberations. Few courts expressly prohibit them and several task forces have endorsed them, but their use is scattered (Munsterman et al. 1997, 151–53, 155, 174–75). And although there have been efforts in many states to educate judges on how to present instructions to jurors in nontechnical language (Tiersma 1993), it is again difficult to measure the quality of the instructions that have resulted. Among the most noteworthy changes in this area has been the adoption in California and other states of standard jury instructions for civil and criminal cases (Schwartz 1981, 732–37). Boatright (1998, 51) estimated that 21 percent of state courts have implemented some sort of "plain English" guidelines for instructions; many courts or judges also provide guidebooks to jurors that explain common legal terms, inform jurors when they may ask questions of the judge, and provide suggestions on deliberation that draw on social scientists' research on small group decision making (Boatright and Murphy 1999a, 1999b).

Perhaps the most controversial change in jury behavior advocated over the past decade is allowing jurors to discuss the evidence before deliberations have formally begun. Many of the above changes retain some element of judicial control. A judge will ultimately determine the content of jury instructions or juror notebooks, and a judge can decline to ask questions submitted by jurors if he or she deems them prejudicial or irrelevant. Yet jurors themselves are in charge of their discussion, and it can violate the established principle of the impartial juror if jurors are discussing the case and drawing conclusions together before all evidence has been presented.

Studies have shown, however, that a substantial number of jurors do discuss evidence informally even when not allowed to or directed to by judges (Loftus and Leber 1986). And although jurors are often told not to discuss the case with their spouses or others, surely some jurors ignore this admonition as well. Researchers have argued, then, that allowing predeliberation discussions, with the requirement that

Table 5.5 Implementation of Selected Jury Reforms as of 1998

Reform	Percentage of Courts That Have Implemented Reform	Median Implementation Date
Exit questionnaires for jurors	59	1992
Limiting juror reporting dates	51	1992
Increased summons enforcement and follow-up	51	1995
Expanded source lists	49	1992
Increased juror compensation	46	1994
One-step qualification and summons	44	1995
Permitting juror questions	39	1990
One day/one trial	36	1993
"Plain English" jury instructions	21	1993

Note. From Boatright, 1998, 51.

all jurors be present and that jurors limit their discussions to their recollection of the evidence, can actually help jurors once deliberations have begun (Hannaford, Hans, and Munsterman 1999; Hans, Hannaford, and Munsterman 2000). Although critics have argued that these discussions might lead jurors to make premature judgments or to establish harmful patterns of dialogue and persuasion (Uebelein 1999), few studies have borne out these criticisms. Most reform plans have limited themselves to allowing such discussions at the discretion of the judge.

All of these reforms exhibit a different type of politics from the reforms in jury summoning or selection. Whereas those reforms often featured civil rights advocates, different segments of the bar, or even different factions within state legislatures, most of the conflict over changes in juror use have been a contest of different personality types—those willing to experiment and draw on social scientific research against those who take a more conservative view of the function of juries. As such, the personality of the judge in each case may determine the latitude jurors are given.

IMPARTIALITY AND REPRESENTATIVENESS REVISITED

Virtually all of the reforms discussed earlier have been implemented in at least a few state courts. This is because these reforms are not inconsistent with the twin goals of impartiality and representativeness. For the most part, the different views that judges, attorneys, or legal scholars have had about each of these reforms match the priority they place on these goals or their understanding of how these reforms would further these goals. Is improving representation in the jury pool, for instance, sufficiently important that courts should expend additional resources seeking to improve the representation of minority groups? Is improving representation on juries of sufficient importance that peremptory challenges should be abandoned? Would juror impartiality and competence be improved by allowing jurors to take notes, ask questions, take notes, or confer among themselves during the trial?

There are, however, several proposals that are premised on questioning whether courts should, in fact, move beyond these traditional emphases or expand the definition of these emphases in unconventional ways. A randomly selected jury is not necessarily an impartial jury, although random selection may increase the chance of arriving at an impartial jury. And an impartial jury need not be representative of the population or randomly selected. The Fukurai and Krooth (2003) argument for "affirmative action" for juries is one such proposal and stratified sampling is another. Other such proposals include altering the size of juries or qualifications of jurors; doing away with jury trials entirely in some instances; and allowing jurors to nullify charges or conduct their own inquiries.

Many of these proposals have been advanced by those who have reservations about the fact-finding abilities or the competence of juries in complex cases. Several states have experimented with changes in jury size for particular types of trials or with changing unanimity rules. Proponents of smaller juries have argued that smaller juries are less likely to be hung, are likely to deliberate more efficiently, or to arrive at correct decisions (see Fedderson and Pesendorfer 1998; Hastie, Penrod, and Pennington 1983; McCord 2005). Opponents of such changes have contended that smaller juries will, by definition, be less diverse and hence more likely to exclude minorities (Kerr and McCoun 1987; Landsman 2005; Nemeth 1987; Zeisel and Diamond 1987). As Munsterman and Hannaford (1997, 7) recount, many courts that have moved toward smaller juries initially did so as a cost-cutting measure but have begun to reconsider these decisions.

A related issue, one that has bearing both on the efficiency of the courts and the quality of decisions, is tinkering with the unanimity rule in criminal cases. An estimated 5 percent of juries fail to reach a decision (Kalven and Zeisel 1966, 461); whether this number is too high or not depends on one's point of view. Only two states currently allow for nonunanimous criminal verdicts, and in some states unanimous verdicts are required by the state constitution (Blue Ribbon Commission on Jury System Improvement 1996, 71). In the states where nonunanimous verdicts are permitted, a substantial majority—generally ten to two—is required. Some critics have argued that allowing such verdicts defeats the purpose of ensuring a diverse, representative jury insofar as, for instance, a jury of ten whites and two African Americans could still vote to convict or acquit on race-based lines. In the Supreme Court's *Johnson v. Louisiana* (1972) and *Apodaca v. Oregon* (1972) decisions, which established the permissibility of nonunanimous verdicts, the court concluded that the participation of all jurors would not be diminished because juries would still be required to thoroughly discuss all issues in the case (Blue Ribbon Commission on Jury System Improvement 1996, 71). This remains a controversial claim; the most compelling empirical argument for nonunanimous decisions has been that hung juries tend to feature only one or two recalcitrant, at times irrational jurors, and that a ten to two decision rule would decrease hung juries by approximately 40 percent (Kalven and Zeisel 1966, 461).

Some have also questioned the traditional emphasis on excluding jurors who might have special knowledge pertinent to the trial. Two instances here are relevant. First, consider again the Michael Jackson or O. J. Simpson cases. The jury questionnaire in each case sought to identify and exclude jurors who had followed the development of these cases and had some knowledge of the evidence in these cases. Given that a substantial number of citizens did follow the events leading up to these trials, critics argued, how could one say that citizens who had failed to read about them in the newspaper truly be deemed representative of the population? A second instance is that of the juror who has specialized knowledge germane to the case. In a medical malpractice suit, for instance, would not a doctor bring special expertise to the jury? In other words, are there not some advantages in returning to the "blue ribbon jury" model? Few courts have been willing in recent years to actively seek out such citizens, but many courts have sought to combat the perception that such individuals will be deliberately excluded from juries. Accompanying New York's abolition of the lengthy list of occupations exempt from jury service has been an effort by some within the judiciary to advocate for allowing the judge and jury commissioner greater discretion in determining whether, to take the instances above, jurors who did have knowledge relevant to the case are to be believed if they still contend that they can be impartial (Jury Project 1994, 31–37).

Another proposal that would substantially alter the function of the jury entirely is simply to limit the number of jury trials—or at least of jury trials in civil cases. Three related arguments have been made in this regard. First, Priest (1993) contended that the rules governing the decision-making process for jurors in tort cases and other types of civil jury trials impeded the ability of jurors to arrive at just decisions. The complexity of the law in many cases rendered jury decisions somewhat inconsistent, and tended to overwhelm the capacities of many court systems. For Priest, there were simply too many civil trials for courts to handle, and in many instances a judge could more efficiently and fairly dispense justice. Second, some argued that civil trial jurors have so much latitude in granting punitive damages that their decisions were inconsistent and took irrelevant factors into account—for instance, by taking the wealth of the defendant into account in assessing damages (Kahneman, Schkade, and Sunstein 2002; Priest 2002). And third, some within the courts have argued that litigants capitalize on the unpredictability of the civil jury to use the jury as a "club"—to set a trial date and use the trial as a bargaining tool in negotiating a settlement. In many such cases, jurors are called and cases are brought to trial before settling, wasting the resources of the courts and the time of jurors. Although advocates for the jury have argued that, in principle, sharply curtailing jury trials is antidemocratic (see Galanter 1993), many of these same advocates concede the main points noted earlier. They merely put the burden of improving trials on the courts, in the form of better jury instructions and greater efforts by judges to order settlements, instead of calling for fewer jury trials. Galanter (1993) argued that juries serve an important social function in such cases and that judges will be no more impartial than juries.

JURY NULLIFICATION

Perhaps the least popular proposal (in the eyes of the courts) for altering the function of the jury, however, comes not from those who would limit the role of the jury, but from those who would dramatically expand it. Many of the jury decision-making reforms have been premised on the notion that jurors should have wider latitude in making their decisions. All of these reforms stop short, however, of permitting jurors to pass judgment on the nature of the charge itself. Jurors may, for instance, find a defendant guilty of violating the law, but they may also believe that the law itself is unjust. In many instances, voir dire is designed to weed out such jurors—to exclude death penalty opponents from juries that will deliberate over a death penalty charge, or to exclude those who believe "three strikes" laws are unfair from trials in which the defendant faces the possibility of a third strike. Jurors are also sternly admonished in almost all cases not to question the fairness of the law itself. To do so—to find a defendant not guilty on the grounds that a law is unjust—is known as *jury nullification.*

Nullification likely happens in a significant number of cases. Anecdotal reports often surface of hung juries in which at least one member balks at convicting a defendant because of the overly harsh sentence they believe he or she will receive. The Fully Informed Jury Association (FIJA) was formed in 1989 to advocate for protecting the right of jury nullification. As Abramson (1994, 59) recounts, FIJA's membership includes gun rights advocates, environmentalists, drug law reformers, tax protesters, and abortion opponents. These groups all share at least the potential for advocacy for practices that tend to run afoul of the law. Yet one can argue for allowing nullification even without referring to such practices. If we truly do believe that jurors serve as the voice of a community, one might argue that they should be able to set the law aside in certain cases. Juries generally are not required to provide a reason for their decisions, so it is always possible for a jury to nullify a law, but courts have almost unanimously sought to avoid telling jurors that they can nullify.

Fukurai and Krooth (2003, 199) contended that there are three different kinds of jury nullification—merciful acquittals, in which the jury believes the defendant did violate the law but that the penalty is too harsh; vengeful convictions, when the jury convicts despite dubious evidence because of the severity of the crime; and racial acquittals, in which the defendant appears guilty but jurors of the defendant's race refuse to convict. According to Fukurai and Krooth, the first of these types of nullification is of higher moral standing than the second and third. That is, if courts are seeking to limit jurors' ability to nullify, they should be aware of the different reasons why jurors nullify and should be less concerned with the first of these reasons. Determining reasons for nullification, however, can only be done after the fact, by interviewing jurors or acquiring a record of jury deliberations. Jurors themselves may be unaware that they are engaging in jury nullification. In one instance, a CBS News team filming jury deliberations captured arguments made by jurors in a drug smuggling case that clearly count as nullification—in this case, one holdout juror argued that although the defendant appeared to be guilty, the required punishment was far too severe, and the jury should therefore acquit (Fallahay and Schneider 1997, 30–31). Such arguments are surely common in jury deliberations; in this case, another juror admonished the holdout that these considerations were not relevant to the jury's decision to convict or acquit, but a plausible case can be made that they were, in fact, relevant.

In each of these instances, the reforms proposed go far beyond the myriad changes that have been made over the past three decades. In each of these instances, normative beliefs about the competence of the jury are called into question, and the traditional correspondence of the representative jury and the impartial jury is also called into question. Some supporters of curtailing jury trials have pointed to inconsistencies in jury verdicts as evidence of incompetence, but given that no two cases are exactly alike, the fact that a jury finds differently in one case from another jury in a similar case falls short of proof. These cases may have slightly different types of evidence, they may be argued in a different fashion, or there may have had different juror use procedures. This is not to say that all juries are equally competent, but absent the ability to fully understand the deliberations in particular cases, it is impossible to provide scientific evidence on this point. The benchmark study of juror competence, Kalven and Zeisel's *The American Jury* (1966), used a somewhat simpler measure, the percentage of times jury and judge agreed about the proper verdict. Kalven and Zeisel found a high degree of agreement, but experts disagree on what the outcome of such a study would be today.

THE POLITICS OF JURY REFORM

The careful reader will note that the same handful of states has appeared throughout this study on the list of courts that have implemented or advocated various reforms. Table 5.6 summarizes some of the better-known state reform packages. The politics behind reforms in each of the areas noted earlier do not necessarily correspond with a traditional liberal/conservative framework, and the states that have implemented jury reforms also do not share similar political cultures. Yet there are several common themes that arise when one considers the politics behind reforms

in states such as Arizona, New York, California, and Colorado as well as in the District of Columbia.

First, many of these state court systems have opened themselves up to academic researchers and have sought to educate judges about the goals of such researchers and the legal standing of their research procedures. In Arizona, many of the in-court reforms listed earlier were first implemented as pilot studies, so that any initial resistance might be worn down simply by the results of these studies. In Massachusetts, an early leader in jury reform, reform advocates in the state courts have worked closely with the state's law schools to present research on juries to those who

Table 5.6 Selected State Jury Reform Efforts

State	Date of Initial Report	Selected Reforms
Arizona	1994	Enforced time limits for trials Increase juror privacy Allow juror notebooks and note taking Allow jurors to ask questions Allow juror discussions of evidence during the trial Encourage juror questions during deliberations Increase efforts to detect and treat juror stress
California	1996	Increase summons enforcement Increase juror fees Adopt one day/one trial system Rewrite jury instructions in "plain English"
Colorado	1997	Expand juror source lists Limit exemptions from jury service Allow jurors to ask questions Allow juror discussions of evidence during the trial Encourage juror questions during deliberations
District of Columbia	1998	Require employers to pay jurors while serving Expand source lists Reduce terms of service Allow juror notebooks and note taking Allow jurors to ask questions Hold regular meetings to educate the public about jury service
New York	1996	Expand source lists Limit exemptions from jury service Standardize deferral policies Increase summons enforcement Reduce number of peremptory challenges Increase juror privacy Increase juror fees

Note. Adapted from American Judicature Society 1999.

might later join the bar or the judiciary. And the New York courts have hosted national conferences aimed at bringing together researchers and court personnel.

Second, courts that have been successful in bringing about changes have sought to work in tandem with the business community and with legislators. Massachusetts, New York, and California have all worked to estimate the consequences of changes in the summoning process on their overall budget and to present legislators with offsetting cuts in the court budgets. Massachusetts was able to require employer compensation of jurors because it paired this requirement with a reduction in the terms of service for jurors. Similarly, the District of Columbia was able to require employer compensation after promising businesses that it would seek to limit the number of times citizens received summonses. And New York developed a plan for gradual juror compensation increases that would begin at the end of each fiscal year, thus spreading out the budgetary impact.

Third, many of these states had centralized court systems that could mandate changes or provide resources for all courts in the state. Massachusetts and New York, states with unified court systems, are the foremost example of this. In a unified court system, all of the state's courts are organized hierarchically under a single administrative body, and rules can be enacted and enforced across all courts. Reforms endorsed by a state's chief judge or supreme court thus may also carry more weight with judges around the state than would similar reforms in a decentralized system.

Fourth, many of these state courts had a precipitating crisis that could be used as evidence that changes were necessary. New York, Los Angeles, and the District of Columbia all are cities that have traditionally had very poor summons response rates, and in many of these cities, citizens' complaints about jury service are common. In New York, there was a wide consensus that the jury system functioned poorly—that jurors were subject to long wait times, unpleasant conditions, frequent summonses, and an unpleasant voir dire process. Reform in New York thus could be framed in a manner that appealed to citizens. The District of Columbia had similar problems, compounded by a perception that the courts were overloaded with cases. And in California, notorious trials such as those of

Rodney King and O. J. Simpson focused attention on the courts and may have increased citizens' interest in the jury system.

Finally, many of these changes may simply be attributed to the force of personality. These states are clearly not the only ones that, for instance, have poor summons response rates, have hosted notorious trials, or have a centralized leadership. Many other states have implemented some reforms, and all states clearly have some advocates for jury reform. Yet not all states have had a chief judge who has made jury reform a priority, as have prominent judges in New York, Arizona, and California. In some cases, these states have also had the benefit of having a governor, a mayor, or even a prominent celebrity who has worked to publicize reforms. For instance, Richard Dysart, who played a lawyer on the long-running television series *L. A. Law*, served as a prominent advocate for jury reform since his retirement. These reforms run the gamut in terms of their cost and their potential to inspire heated opposition. Many of these changes, particularly those regarding jury decision making, do not even require any sort of approval from the state judiciary or the legislature—they simply require judges to take an interest in the jury and in research on the jury.

THE FEEDBACK LOOP

As noted at the beginning of this chapter, it is difficult to mobilize members of the public to advocate for changes in the jury. Although jury service is the only form of political participation that is both a right and an obligation in American society, it comes with a guarantee that one will not be required to serve again for one, two, or even three years. As a consequence, even those who have served may not feel inspired to present their thoughts on their experience to judges or politicians. These same citizens, however, surely are likely to offer their thoughts to friends and neighbors. A striking feature of public opinion surveys on jury service is that even citizens who have never served acquire an accurate understanding of many details of jury service soon after they receive their summonses.

The accuracy of this information may be demonstrated by the fact that Americans tend to be fascinated by courtroom dramas, fictional television judges, and high-profile criminal cases, yet most citizens do not expect that their own experience will resemble these trials. The fact that citizens draw much of their knowledge about jury service from others who have served illustrates both the opportunities and the limits of change in the American jury. On the one hand, researchers have shown that most jurors leave the courtroom with a more positive impression than they had when they entered. And changes in the actual experience of jurors may spill over to the expectations of those who receive summonses. That is, giving jurors an impression that voir dire is conducted fairly, or giving jurors greater control over their deliberations by allowing them to take notes or ask questions, may leave jurors feeling more satisfied and more likely to tell others that their experience was an important one. Some of those with whom they speak may, in turn, receive a summons and decide to approach jury service with enthusiasm. This, at least, is the hope of reformers. On the other hand, if courts discuss the importance of jury service but do not tailor it to the needs of jurors, no amount of rhetoric about civic duty is likely to leave jurors feeling favorably disposed toward service.

Within the community of jury commissioners, court administrators, jury researchers, and judges who have taken a special interest in jury procedures, there are few who have framed the jury reform movement in political terms. In a few cases, such as the discussions of how best to increase minority representation on juries, the language used is not that different from language used in reference to other issues of civil rights or affirmative action. Yet in other instances, the lines are not as neatly drawn. In the case of some reforms, the conflict is between state legislators and the courts regarding budgetary policy. In others, it is a debate among judges—between those who value experimentation or drawing on psychological research and those who value traditional jury practices. On several diverse issues, the conflict is between courts and businesses, regarding businesses policies toward employees serving on juries or the decisions made by juries on civil issues. Some of the conflicts over reforms have antagonized particular sections of the bar, who have worried about the consequences of some in-court changes on the fortunes of plaintiffs or defendants, or have simply wished to guard established prerogatives. And in several instances the courts have sought to frame media coverage of cases—to control access to jurors, or simply to get their message out about reforms.

Such a diversity of conflicts may be inevitable given that those interested in the jury cannot even agree on how to measure change. Is the jury "broken"? According to some, it is, but according to others, it works well. Do enough citizens respond to jury summonses? Are juries sufficiently representative of their communities? Do juries tend to reach impartial, accurate decisions? It is difficult to answer such questions. Yet when one considers all of the evidence covered in this chapter, it seems evident that the American jury is not only one of our most resilient institutions—it is one of the few political institutions that would be easily recognizable to Americans of two centuries ago—but it is also undergoing a period of change that, reformers hope, will leave it better equipped to reflect the ideals of twenty-first century America.[6]

Notes

1. See the Chamber's tort reform website, http://www.legalreformnow.com, for more detail on this issue. For a compendium of research on this issue, see Sunstein et al. 2002.

2. Justice Powell held that, "In deciding whether the defendant has made the requisite showing, the trial court should consider all relevant circumstances.... Though this requirement imposes a limitation on some cases on the full peremptory character of the historic challenge, we emphasize that the prosecutor's explanation need not rise to the level justifying exercise of a challenge for cause" *Batson v. Kentucky* 476 U.S. 79 at 96 (1986). Powell went on to hold that

"the prosecutor must articulate a neutral explanation related to the particular case to be tried" (476 U.S. at 98).

3. The Washington, D.C. reform plan is an exception; see Council for Court Excellence 1998, 30–31.

4. Available at http://www.vortex.com/privacy/simpson-jq.

5. Available at http://www.courttv.com/trials/jackson/docs/juror.pdf.

6. This research was drawn in part from reports prepared for Pennsylvanians for Modern Courts and the New York State Unified Court System's *Jury 2001* conference. I thank Lynn Marks, Julia Hoke, and Elissa Krauss for comments on these earlier reports, and David McCord for comments on this chapter.

6

STATE TRIAL COURTS

Achieving Justice in Civil Litigation

Nicole L. Waters, Shauna M. Strickland, and Brian J. Ostrom

The United States has an extremely complex system of state courts. Each state can decide how to structure its own court system, including how many levels of courts the system will have and which courts will have the jurisdiction to hear what types of specific cases. Because the state court systems vary so greatly from state to state, it is difficult for scholars to study these courts effectively. State courts handle the vast majority of both civil and criminal cases in this country, leaving a much smaller number of cases to the federal court system. If an individual has any personal contact with a court, it is highly likely that that court will be a state trial court of some type. This chapter focuses on civil litigation in the state trial courts. The National Center for State Courts was established to help scholars and practioners better the workings of the state courts. The three coauthors of this chapter all work for that organization.

This chapter serves a variety of purposes. First, it underscores the importance of the state courts in our highly complicated legal system. Second, the chapter examines the general structure of state courts, including explaining the differences between the functions of state trial courts and state appellate courts. Third, the chapter outlines the steps in the civil litigation process and explains why so few civil disputes actually end in full trials. Finally, the chapter asks whether the state courts can accomplish their mission of resolving disputes through fair, accessible, impartial, and efficient processes in the administration of justice.

The American judicial system is not, in actuality, a single system. Instead, it comprises both the federal and state judiciaries, and students are typically introduced to it through a discussion of the federal courts. The appeal of the federal court system is its simplicity—it has a unified structure and a standardized system of procedures, known as the Federal Rules of Procedure, to which all federal courts must adhere (see, e.g., Baum 2001, 20–39). By focusing on the federal court system, textbooks can explain how American courts function without having to delve into the endless variations that make up the structure and procedures of the individual state courts. However, omitting a discussion of state courts overlooks the forum in which most people interact with the justice system.

According to the Court Statistics Project of the National Center for State Courts, state courts handle approximately 98 percent of all court filings in the United States and process approximately 100 million cases a year across more than 16,000 courts. They employ more than 30,000 judicial officers (i.e., justices, judges, magistrates, commissioners, etc.) and support innumerable court personnel. State courts are where most citizens, either as jurors or as litigants, experience justice in action (Court Statistics Project 2005).

Amidst all this activity, state courts have a mission to serve the community by resolving disputes through the fair, accessible, impartial, and efficient administration of justice and to be held accountable by the people whom they serve. The role of the court thus becomes more than simply resolving individual disputes. Court leaders (judges, administrators, and managers) must also be cognizant of the policy implications of their decisions. Court procedures must, for example, instill in the public a trust and confidence in the court's ability to fulfill its mission while simultaneously serving the needs of the litigants involved in a particular case. A court system's need to meet the expectations of its community is the basis for the different structures and procedures seen in the state courts. However, it is also this varied landscape that offers an array of options for court leaders to consider, evaluate, and implement in their quest to achieve justice.

In this chapter we focus on the civil justice system in state courts for civil lawsuits of many types. Civil litigation involves wrongs among individuals broadly defined (as will be discussed in more detail later), while criminal cases involve wrongs against society. General civil cases comprise just over one-third of all civil filings in the state courts (Schauffler et al. 2006). Our focus on civil litigation is not meant to detract from the other important areas of law that are handled by the courts. We duly note that state courts are responsible for hearing criminal, domestic relations, juvenile, and traffic cases, in addition to civil litigation, and that each area of law has its own set of participants, procedures, and policy implications. We have chosen to focus only on one area of law to provide a continuity of ideas throughout the chapter and to show how courts, through their handling of civil cases, do and do not fulfill their mission. In Section 1 of the chapter, we outline the structure of state courts and introduce the reader to the participants in civil litigation. In Section 2, we walk the reader through the steps that civil disputes take from beginning to end and provide a historical framework of the civil litigation trends in state courts. Finally, in Section 3, we evaluate the civil justice system as a whole and discuss several salient policy implications that have arisen, again taking note of how well state courts are implementing their mission.

STATE COURT STRUCTURE

When we think of state courts, we are actually thinking of the combination of the courts of the fifty states, the District of Columbia, the Commonwealth of Puerto Rico, and the American territories. Each of these entities, called states in this chapter for the purpose of simplicity, varies in terms of how its courts are organized and administered. Despite these differences, some generalizations can, and should, be made to understand the basic structure and function of the state judicial system.

Jurisdictional Structure

There are two basic structural components common to all state court systems. These are the concepts of court levels and court tiers.

There are always two *levels of court*—the appellate level and the trial level. The appellate courts act, in part, as the reviewers of the decisions made by the trial courts (see also Langer and Wilhelm this volume, chapter 8). The trial courts, on the other hand, are the initial arbiters of disputes. Trial court judges, sometimes with the aid of a jury (see Boatright this volume, chapter 5), decide cases based on the facts before them and the law that applies to those facts. That each case is (1) decided on its own merits and (2) has the opportunity to receive appellate review helps to ensure that the judicial system is both fair and impartial.

Within each court level there are *tiers of courts*. The appellate court level may be divided into courts of last resort (often generically called state supreme courts) and intermediate appellate courts, while the trial court level may be divided into general jurisdiction courts and limited jurisdiction courts. Each state will have at least one court of last resort and one general jurisdiction court. Some states have one court at each tier (Florida, Hawaii, and Kansas are examples). Still others have more than one court at each tier (examples include Oklahoma, which has two courts of last resort; Tennessee, which has two intermediate appellate courts; Michigan with two courts of general jurisdiction; and Washington, which has two courts of limited jurisdiction). How a state organizes its courts can speak to both the accessibility and the efficiency of the justice system in that state.

The American Bar Association (ABA 1990) has promulgated standards of court organization and recommends that, "the structure of the court system should be simple, consisting of a trial court and an appellate court, each having divisions and departments as needed"[1] with a provision for the introduction of an intermediate appellate court "where the volume of appeals is such that the state's highest court cannot satisfactorily perform [its] functions."[2] As of 2004, only one state, the District of Columbia, met the ABA's recommendation to maintain only a trial court and an appellate court. Five additional states (California, Illinois, Iowa, Minnesota, and Puerto Rico) also maintain a single trial court, but have added an intermediate appellate court to their appellate tier. All other states, as evidenced by the examples above, utilize varying numbers of courts within each tier (see McLeod this volume, chapter 2). It is important to keep in mind, though, that court structure merely provides the foundation on which court leaders can work to meet the mission of the court and that no one structure meets the needs of every state. It is the combination of court structure, judicial and managerial leadership, and the relationship that the judicial branch has with the other branches of government that enable courts to resolve disputes through the fair, accessible, impartial, and efficient administration of justice (see also Langer and Wilhelm this volume, chapter 8).

Appellate Courts

Each state has a court of last resort, usually called the state supreme court (although unfortunately in New York and Maryland the highest court is known as the court of appeals). This court is at the apex of each state's judicial system, and, unless litigants choose to appeal their case to the United States Supreme Court, it is the final arbiter of all disputes within a state's court system (see also Langer and Wilhelm this volume, chapter 8). The primary role of an appellate court is to review the decisions made by the trial courts. More precisely, appellate courts review the findings of law made by the trial courts to determine if those findings match the facts presented in each case. This is their *appellate jurisdiction*, and such review applies to the findings of administrative agencies as well. In exercising their appellate jurisdiction, courts help to ensure the fairness of the judicial system. They check for and correct any harmful error that is found. In this role, they also legitimize the decisions made by the trial courts. By affirming the decisions of trial courts, appellate courts reinforce the idea that the trial courts applied the law accurately, thus improving both the litigant's and the public's perception of the courts as fair and impartial decision makers.

Appellate courts also hear cases for the first time. These cases often involve such issues as judicial and attorney discipline, certified questions, advisory opinions, and writ applications. In these proceedings appellate courts are exercising their *original jurisdiction*.

Whether exercising original or appellate jurisdiction, appellate courts contribute to the development of statutory, constitutional, and common law. Through their opinions, they help to direct the interpretation of the law, and, in this role, appellate courts are said to be involved in institutional review or lawmaking. It is also in this role that appellate courts are seen as policy makers. Their decisions affect public opinion and are intended to be followed as precedent by the judges in lower courts. The idea of judges as law or policy makers is a contentious one. However, this role is just as important to the public's overall perception of the court system as being a fair and impartial body as is the role it plays when reviewing lower court decisions for error.

Many appellate courts have the ability to decide which appeals or original proceedings they will consider. This ability is referred to as *discretionary jurisdiction*. In contrast, an appellate court's *mandatory jurisdiction* includes appeals and original proceedings that a court must hear. Whether a court has mandatory or discretionary jurisdiction, and to what cases each type of jurisdiction applies, is determined by the state constitution, state statutes, or court rules and varies greatly from state to state. Although most courts have both mandatory and discretionary jurisdiction, there are some instances in which a court must hear all of the cases that come before it. This occurrence is more common in intermediate appellate courts: fourteen intermediate appellate courts employ only mandatory jurisdiction while two courts of last resort have the same requirement.

All but eleven states have an intermediate appellate court. These courts are usually called the court of appeals, and it is often the case that in states with two tiers of appellate courts the intermediate court of appeals is expected to hear the majority of the appeals arising out of the trial level. This arrangement enables the court of last resort to focus on cases it deems to be of the most legal importance to the greatest number of people. This type of relationship between the appellate courts determines the role that each court plays in the judicial system, with the intermediate appellate court generally acting as an error corrector and the court of last resort generally acting as a law and policy maker.

Appeals are transferred to the appellate courts from the trial courts in one of two ways. The most common is for all appeals to be first filed with the intermediate appellate court with an additional review conducted by the court of last resort only if that court grants such review. The alternative route of appeal, with all cases first filed with the court of last resort, which then assigns the case to the intermediate appellate court, is only utilized by five states. Although cases from general jurisdiction courts must be appealed to the appellate level, general jurisdiction courts in states with two tiers of trial level courts can, themselves, act as appellate courts. In these instances, cases that originate in the limited jurisdiction tier would pass through the general jurisdiction tier prior to an appeal at the appellate level.

Trial Courts

Each state operates at least one general jurisdiction trial court. These courts serve as the upper tier courts within the trial level and typically hold the authority to hear all types of cases: civil, domestic relations, criminal, juvenile, and traffic. Indeed, in the six states with only a single general jurisdiction court, it is in this court that all cases originate.

In states with two-tiered trial courts, cases may be filed in either the general or limited jurisdiction court depending on the authority vested in each court. This authority may be provided by a state's constitution, statute, or court rule. For our purposes, we will explore the trial courts' civil jurisdiction.

Civil cases can be classified as general civil (i.e., tort, contract, and real property), small claims, probate/estate, civil appeals, or as other civil cases (e.g., habeas corpus petitions, name change petitions, nondomestic relations restraining orders, etc.). In most states, general and limited jurisdiction courts hold *concurrent jurisdiction* over civil cases. This means that civil complaints can initiate in either tier. For general civil cases a dollar amount limitation may determine which court will hear the case. The dollar amount limitation varies widely among states, ranging from no minimum dollar amount requirement up to, for example, a $25,000 minimum requirement for cases to be heard in Michigan's general jurisdiction court.

Small claims cases are those claims in which a certain dollar amount (usually $5,000 or less) is at stake, and they are typically heard in limited jurisdiction courts that may not allow legal counsel to represent the parties. Probate/estate claims are mainly guardianships, conservatorships, wills, and estate management, and, in thirteen states, these cases are heard in their own court, twelve of which are classified as limited jurisdiction. Most states with two-tiered trial courts have bestowed on their general jurisdiction court the authority to hear civil appeals from the limited jurisdiction courts. Three states (Delaware, Mississippi, and Texas) have designated this authority to one of their limited jurisdiction courts as well.

In the next section we walk the reader through the steps of civil litigation. Most of those steps, from the filing of the initial complaint through the filing of a notice of appeal, will take place in a trial court. A trial is the most time and resource intensive of those steps for it is during trial that evidence is presented and witnesses are called to testify. All courts, whether general or limited jurisdiction, hold *bench trials* (also called court trials). In bench trials, the judge alone is responsible for reviewing the facts presented in the case and applying the law to those facts because there is no jury in a bench trial. In *jury trials*, it is the jury—usually a group of six or twelve citizens—that review the facts of the case and, with guidance from the judge, apply the law to those facts. In about half of the states jury trials are reserved for the general jurisdiction court, while in the other half, jury trials may be held in both general and limited jurisdiction courts (see also Boatright this volume, chapter 5).

The differences in state court structure are most obvious at the trial court level, with as many variances in state court jurisdictional structure as there are states. Despite these differences, each state has a responsibility to provide access to its justice system. Whether that access is best gained by maintaining one trial and one appellate court or through a combination of courts at each tier is best decided by the citizens in each state as it is the citizens of each state to whom the courts are accountable.

THE STEPS IN CIVIL LAWSUITS AND LITIGATION

Civil litigation at the trial court level involves the following participants: *litigants*, or the parties to a dispute; *litigators*, the attorneys who work for the litigants (see Mather this volume, chapter 4); *jurors*, citizens who may be the arbiters of the dispute (see Boatright this volume, chapter 5); and a *judge*, who oversees all aspects of the dispute as it goes through the appropriate procedural steps and in bench trials, also acts as the fact finder (see McLeod this volume, chapter 2).

The litigants in a civil case are called the *plaintiff*, the person who brings a claim to the court, and the *defendant*, the person who defends against the claim. In many civil cases the plaintiff is requesting a monetary award, but there are also instances, such as in equity cases, in which the plaintiff is asking the court to either force the defendant to, or prohibit the defendant from, acting in a particular way.

Litigants may or may not be represented by attorneys. Litigants who are not represented by attorneys are referred to as *pro se* (or pro per) litigants. The reasons for not retaining an attorney are often financial in nature, but some litigants may simply feel that they can successfully navigate the civil process on their own. Other litigants, however, do not have a choice but to represent themselves. This occurs in small claims cases

where, in eleven states, attorneys are prohibited from representing the litigants. When attorneys are involved in civil litigation, it is their job to counsel their litigants on the best course of action for their particular case (see also Mather this volume, chapter 4).

Civil litigation may or may not involve juries. Litigants may either waive their right to a jury trial or, per statute, may not have a right to a jury trial in the first place. Again, in small claims cases there are thirty-six states that do not afford litigants the right to a jury trial. When juries are utilized, though, it is their job to review the facts presented to them and apply the law to those facts, ultimately reaching a decision that resolves the particular dispute before them.

With few exceptions, civil juries consist of six to twelve citizens chosen randomly from the court's community. Courts often use voter registration and/or Department of Motor Vehicles (DMV) records to create a source list of citizens from which to choose a jury. Qualified citizens summoned to the courthouse comprise the pool of citizens who are subject to *voir dire*, or questioning, by the court to determine their ability to serve as a fair and impartial arbiter to the trial proceedings. Although juries are encouraged to reach an agreement about their decision in a case, their decision is not always required to be unanimous. In fact, over half of the states allow for verdict decisions that are less than unanimous, using the rationale that unanimity is not a prerequisite for a fair and impartial decision (see also Boatright this volume, chapter 5).

Given the intricacies of today's legal environment, judges are required to be licensed attorneys (with only a few exceptions in some courts of limited jurisdiction). In some states, attorneys must also have been in practice for a certain number of years, usually ranging from five to ten, prior to being eligible to become a judge. Once eligible, there are three common routes through which an attorney can become a judge: by appointment of the executive, by nomination of the executive with confirmation by the legislature, or by election (either partisan or nonpartisan; see McLeod this volume, chapter 2). Once on the bench, state judges serve terms that range from as short as two to four years to as long as ten years, depending on the state in which they serve and, in a few states, judges are appointed for life.

Traditionally, judges approach civil cases as observers, leaving it to the parties and their attorneys to set the pace of litigation. Increasingly, though, judges are taking a more active role in the processing of civil litigation through such caseflow management techniques as early and continuous court involvement (i.e., the monitoring of a case as it progresses through the pretrial phase), case settlement conferences, and differentiated case management (e.g., the selection of cases that are deemed appropriate for expedited procedures or the classification of a case as "complex"). A very large percentage of civil cases never go to trial because they settle before that step in the process (see Baum 2001, 218–19). Regardless of the role that an individual judge takes in the processing of cases, all judges are ultimately responsible for the fair and impartial resolution of the cases that come before them.

Civil litigation at the appellate court level also involves the litigants, now called *appellants*, and a panel of judges. There are no juries at the appellate court level and no trial proceedings. Appellate courts, as will be explained further in the next section, review the documents of the trial court to ensure that not only was the law appropriately applied, but that proper procedure was followed as well.

COURT PROCEDURES

In this section, we describe how a civil case proceeds through the state courts, how the purpose of courts has changed over time, and how this trend impacts the current adversarial system. It is important, at this point, to underscore the fact that most civil disputes are not resolved by trial. Although popular media images would suggest otherwise, most claims are actually settled by mutual agreement of the parties, and many potential disputes are never brought to the attention of the courts. In the early 1980s, Richard E. Miller and Austin Sarat (1981) proposed the "dispute pyramid," a model to explain common disputes and the frequency with which they resulted in civil tort litigation.

Although this model specifically addresses tort litigation, the filtering concept that they described applies across a range of civil actions. The dispute pyramid models tort litigation as beginning with a set of events in which someone is injured. At this stage, the injured party must decide how to proceed. One possible course is that the individual does not perceive the injury as an event requiring legal action. This may be due to considerations about the cost of litigation, lack of knowledge of how to file a formal claim with the court, lack of accessibility to the courts, or simply the belief that the injury is too minor to pursue compensation. Alternatively, individuals may attribute the cause of the injury to the negligence of another party and initiate legal action to resolve the *grievance.*

If the injured party complains to the responsible party and seeks compensation, the model states that a *claim* of injury is made. If the party blamed for the injury declines responsibility, a lawyer will evaluate the claim to determine whether the injured party should file a formal complaint with the court. Such a formal complaint, or *court filing,* effectively initiates litigation between the parties by formally identifying the legal claim alleged by the injured party, the plaintiff, and notifying the blamed party, the defendant, of the stated allegations.

The dispute pyramid in Figure 6.1 most notably illustrates the attrition with which disputes reach the courthouse. Researchers estimate that only about one in every twenty grievances result in an actual court filing. This pattern of attrition persists throughout the court proceedings, with 96 percent of civil cases

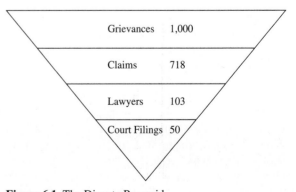

Figure 6.1 The Dispute Pyramid

resolved during the pretrial phase and only 4 percent of civil cases decided through a full trial.

Civil Litigation: Filing to Disposition

On filing, the plaintiff initiates a complaint with the court that includes his or her version of the facts along with the applicable legal claim. The plaintiff also requests compensation, typically money or other relief. The court notifies the named defendant that a lawsuit has been filed and informs the defendant of the allegations stated in the complaint. The defendant is then required to file an *answer* with the court in response to the complaint. The answer may offer alternative facts, plead an excuse, or contain a *counterclaim*, an allegation that the plaintiff has injured the defendant and should be ordered to compensate the defendant for that injury.

If the defendant does not respond in the allotted time frame, the court may award the plaintiff whatever compensation is requested in the complaint. In this situation, the court resolves the dispute in favor of the plaintiff through a *default judgment.* In absence of an answer, the defendant is assumed to agree with the complaint; thus, there is no matter of law or issue of fact in dispute. Courts resolve cases in this manner approximately one-third of the time.

After filing an answer, or in conjunction with the answer, the defendant may file additional *motions* that request action of the court. Some motions are considered to be dispositive (they may resolve the dispute), and are filed soon after the pleadings. For example, the defendant may file a motion to dismiss the case because it lacks merit. Or the defendant may file a motion for *summary judgment* claiming that there is no dispute of the material facts and asking the court to determine a question of law. If the only matter in dispute is a question of law, the judge may rule on the issue without holding a trial.

The next phase in litigation is when the parties prepare for trial. This is called the pretrial phase and both sides begin a well-documented discussion as per the rules of procedure to compile evidence about the dispute. This process is aptly called *discovery*. During discovery, parties will learn what evidence or testimony will be proffered by the opposing party at trial.

The discovery phase is often strategic in the same way as a game of cards. Each player must assess his hand, his opponent's hand, and act accordingly.

After all the playing cards are disclosed, the parties begin to negotiate. One of the parties in the case may offer to settle for a particular dollar amount. A benefit of settlement realized by the defendant is that the settlement is typically not of public record, as it would be in a court file, and does not require the defendant to admit responsibility.

In a civil dispute, settlements are desirable for parties concerned about preserving a reputation. For example, a business or large corporation is subject to possible media coverage and a finding of liability against it that appears in the court records, both of which may tarnish its reputation and deter potential future business. Similarly, a medical doctor named in a malpractice suit and found liable may harm not only her own business, but also that of the entire practice or hospital in which she works.

Courts and individual judges also take steps to resolve cases prior to trial. Gaining in popularity among courts is to refer cases to court-annexed *alternative dispute resolution* (ADR). ADR encompasses arbitration, mediation, and other alternative methods aimed at encouraging agreement among the parties. In ADR, parties present their case to a neutral, third-party, who then offers a proposed decision. In most forms of ADR the parties are not obligated to follow the proposed decision, so the dissatisfied parties can usually return to the traditional path and present their case in front of a judge or jury.[3] Even if a case is not completely resolved through ADR proceedings, the parties benefit from presenting their case and refining the contested issues.

Some judges encourage the parties to settle their dispute, or particular claims within a case, by emphasizing case management techniques such as status or pretrial settlement conferences. By using these techniques, the judge is better able to manage a case by anticipating what issues remain contested among the parties and thus can continue to drive the case forward, and by estimating if, and when, the case is ready for trial. These conferences thus bring more focus to the actual dispute at hand and remove issues from the case on which both sides can agree. From a court's perspective, the impetus for encouraging parties to settle a case is to save the court time and money (e.g., by reducing the costs of calling citizens to serve on a jury). However, time and cost savings resulting from settlement are also realized by the parties. Litigation is costly; attorney fees and witness fees, along with the cost incurred through a prolonged delay in compensation, will influence a party's decision to proceed to trial. Of course, parties also factor the chances of winning into their decision to play their odds at trial.

Savings of money, time, and the risk of publicity are only a few of the issues parties contemplate when navigating their path toward resolution. Litigation may alter relationships, exacerbate conflicts, and be emotionally damaging. With so much at stake, very few cases proceed to trial.

TRENDS IN CIVIL LITIGATION

National data tracked by the National Center for State Courts reports that approximately seventeen million new civil cases are filed in state courts each year (Schauffler et al. 2005). Using a population-adjusted statistic, this translates into about 5,000 civil filings for every 100,000 people per state. Of these claims, less than 4 percent are resolved through a jury or a bench trial. Though relatively small in number, jury and bench trial outcomes can garner significant attention outside the courthouse.

A common "poster-child" of the civil legal system portrayed by the media stars a plaintiff who names a large corporation in a tort claim and wins an astronomical money damage award. In the 1980s, Stella Liebeck did just this. She was an elderly woman who spilled hot coffee from McDonald's drive-thru on her lap, resulting in severe, third-degree burns. A jury awarded her $2.9 million dollars for her injuries (Berliner 1994). She was awarded both *compensatory* damages, which compensate for the injury (e.g., medical expenses) and *punitive* damages, which punish the wrongdoer for intentional, negligent actions. In a more recent example, Vioxx litigation has resulted in a $250 million award ($229 million were punitive damages) against Merck (see, e.g., Adams 2005). Although such awards create eye-catching headlines, the full story,

including the reduction of award amounts on appeal, does not emerge in the brief media reports of the cases that most people see. Regardless, the image of a litigious society is a message often delivered to the general public. Thus, the media and many politicians complain about a litigation explosion in the United States.

Actual court statistics on civil filings and dispositions provide a more accurate picture of our society's litigation habits. As stated previously, civil cases can be classified as general civil (i.e., tort, contract, and real property), small claims, probate/estate, civil appeals, or into an "other" civil case category. For the purposes of this chapter, we will confine our discussions to general civil cases, which comprise just over one-third of all civil filings in the state courts (Schauffler et al. 2006).

Disputes between litigants arising out of a contractual agreement (contract cases), comprise the majority of general civil filings. Contract disputes arise from unsatisfied parties in a business agreement, such as buyer or seller disputes, allegations of fraud, or violations of a lease agreement. Real property claims are relatively small in number and most often involve *eminent domain*, when the government offers to purchase private property for public use or title disputes. Due to the nature of the claims, judges, rather than juries, most often decide contract and real property disputes. Conversely, parties in a tort case more often opt for a jury over a judge.

Tort claims encompass injuries to an individual or damage to personal property, and account for approximately one-fifth of the general civil caseload (Schauffler et al. 2006). Although courts' caseloads vary by jurisdiction, typically *automobile torts*, injuries as a result of an automobile accident, comprise 60 to 70 percent of all tort filings in state courts. Nevertheless, claims for *premises liability* (injuries from a slip and fall), *product liability* (injury resulting from faulty or dangerous products such as Vioxx), and *medical malpractice* (negligence by a medical practitioner) usually get the most attention from the media and from the public. Combined, nonauto torts comprise only one-third of tort filings in state courts (Schauffler et al. 2006).

In the last two decades, the number of civil filings has increased across the nation by 15 percent.

Courts have similarly reported an upward trend in civil dispositions. Despite the growth in filings and dispositions, the trend of civil jury trial rates over the last three decades has declined by approximately one-third (Ostrom, Strickland, & Hannaford-Agor 2004). As a result of declining trial rates, courts are shifting resources, such as personnel, from trial activities to nontrial activities, and the changing nature of dispute resolution means that judges and court staff now focus more on the pretrial activities of motions, hearings, and pretrial conferences. New courthouse designs also are beginning to reflect and better accommodate changing facility demands.

The court community has been attuned to the decline of trials, namely jury trials, and the phenomenon has been dubbed by legal scholars as the "vanishing trial" (see generally special issue in *Journal of Empirical Legal Studies,* vol. 1, 2004). Although the complete reason for the decline remains unclear, fewer trials mean the body of publicly accessible law will decline. One result is that litigants will face greater uncertainty about the parameters of acceptable settlement offers and just compensation (for a discussion of how communities of practice among lawyers help determine the "going rate" for settling civil cases before they go to trial, see Mather this volume, chapter 4).

Perhaps the most detrimental impact of the vanishing jury trial is the reduction of community involvement in the civil justice system. Authors of the Constitution of the United States, in the Seventh Amendment, guaranteed the right to a jury trial in civil suits. This right was bestowed on the community to protect the people from arbitrary power by the government. Furthermore, the jury system provides opportunities for the public to participate in dispensing justice, which through these decisions, represents community values. All public institutions must have the support of the community they serve, and juror participation bolsters the public's trust and confidence in the court system as a fair and impartial body (see also Boatright this volume, chapter 5).

Currently state courts handle approximately 164,000 jury trials a year from which approximately 31.9 million potential jurors are summonsed to appear for jury duty (Hannaford-Agor, Waters, & Wait 2007). Although one frequently hears neighbors, family,

and friends impart tips on how to avoid jury duty, citizens who serve on juries frequently leave the court empowered by their civic duty and find the experience rewarding. Whereas television shows and movies portray eloquent lawyers presenting a story that unfolds in front of a jury, the real jury system employs fewer theatrics, but nevertheless provides an important element of transparency in how civil justice is dispensed. This transparency, or lack thereof, is a public policy concern if jury trial rates continue on the current declining trend.

CIVIL LITIGATION: POSTTRIAL

The resolution of a civil dispute does not necessarily end after the jury renders a verdict or the judge issues a final judgment. In fact, posttrial motions to amend the outcome of the trial or a notice of appeal requesting review by a higher court may be filed by a party who can articulate that a legally substantiated error may have occurred during trial. An appeal cannot simply be filed by a party who is dissatisfied with the result of the trial. Instead, the appellant must offer a written brief that presents a justification for the alleged errors and requests the appellate court to adjust or reverse the decision of the trial court.

Dispositive judgments or jury verdicts rendered after trial in general civil cases are appealed by a litigant approximately 15 percent of the time (Cohen 2006). As with decisions to file a claim or pursue the claim to trial, the dispute pyramid model similarly applies to the appeal process. In nearly half of general civil appeals from a trial, courts dismiss the appeal (e.g., for procedural error or lack of jurisdiction), appellants withdraw the appeal prior to an appellate court decision on the merits, or the court transfers the appeal to another court (Cohen 2006).

In state appellate courts of last resort (usually called state supreme courts), justices hear appeals *en banc*, meaning that the full bench participates (to compare the practice at the U.S. Courts of Appeals, see Martinek this volume, chapter 9). At the intermediate state appellate courts, judges typically sit in panels, comprising a portion of the full bench. If after a review of the written briefs, and if applicable, oral arguments, the appellate court finds that the trial court erred, the court will reverse or modify the outcome or remand the case back to the trial court for a new trial to correct the error. For example, if evidence presented at trial was erroneously admitted and thereby prejudiced the jury in its verdict, the appellate court will order the trial court to retry the case to a new jury without the prejudicial evidence. Appellate court decisions may be explained in a written opinion or order, which carries *precedence*. If a case "sets precedent" it means that subsequent cases covered by the court's jurisdiction must adhere to the decision.

The purpose of the appellate courts is to provide the litigants with a procedure with which to question the actions of the trial court. This step in the process reinforces the notion of a fair court, again fulfilling a component of the court's mission to its community.

POLICY IMPLICATIONS

Recall that the mission of state courts is *to serve the community by resolving disputes through the fair, accessible, impartial, and efficient administration of justice*. Per this mission, state courts are accountable to their constituents in crafting a just system in which to resolve disputes. In this final section, we discuss each element of the mission statement and describe how it contributes to important policy issues.

Our civil justice system is based on an *adversary system* in which parties are required to argue in a manner that is most persuasive to his or her best interests. In such a system, litigants direct the presentation of evidence and decide how the "story" is told. Of course, formal legal procedures limit the scope of possible actions, but the parties maintain control while they present a case to a judge and/or to a jury (the adjudicator). The adjudicator, in an adversary model, passively absorbs the evidence presented and imparts a decision, fulfilling its fact-finding role. Rules of evidence dissuade fact finders from independent investigations or out-of-court inquiries, except when, for example, judges consult experts in cases covering unusually complicated topics.

The adversarial system is based on hundreds of years of tradition. During that time, though, the court community has experimented with alternative truth-seeking models such as the inquisitorial system, as used in most Western European countries and Latin America. The inquisitorial system of justice encourages such innovations as those proposed by retired judge, B. Michael Dann (Dann 1993). Judge Dann proposed the educational model for juries in which he emphasized that jurors are akin to students in a classroom—they learn more about the case and better process the information provided when in a participatory environment. Innovations to jury trials that incorporate the educational model shift juror participation away from that of a passive listener toward more active engagement in the trial process. As an example, jurors may take notes during trial, and in some states, ask witnesses for clarification of testimony (see also Boatright this volume, chapter 5).

Fairness

Whichever truth-seeking model the court adopts gains legitimacy if it is accepted as a fair process by those it serves. In fact, social scientists have found that people's perspective that the process is fair and impartial, also known as *procedural justice*, is ultimately the most important component of any justice system and even surpasses the importance of who wins and loses (Thibault and Walker 1975; Tyler 1988). Therefore, only through a procedurally just system is the court's mission fulfilled.

Undoubtedly, trial outcomes influence policy decisions through an exchange of dialogue between the court and the community it serves. Trial outcomes directly affect businesses by dictating norms of acceptable business practice (see also Barnes this volume, chapter 7). For example, court decisions indirectly set safety standards for products and require the disclosure of terms prior to a party's consent to a contractual agreement. Court judgments or jury verdicts provide assessments of what is reasonable compensation for parties engaged in settlement offers or negotiations. Even when citizens called for jury duty object to the time wasted in the assembly room, attorneys and judges report that juror presence in the courthouse is the impetus for settlements that occur "in the shadow of the jury."

It remains an open debate among legal scholars as to the fairness of current trends to divert disputes out of the courtroom and instead into ADR proceedings. Although ADR proceedings benefit overburdened courts by reducing caseloads and potentially allow litigants to resolve their dispute faster and cheaper, critics have expressed skepticism about whether the proceedings are fair to the parties. From a business model perspective, judges are applauded for judicial management techniques that encourage settlements or successfully resolve a case through court-annexed ADR. However, ADR may also have a downside. Arbitration clauses, which require parties to consent to private out-of-court arbitration, raise questions of fairness when they occur between parties of disproportionate power. Marc Galanter clarified and persuasively presented questions of fairness in his seminal piece on the "haves and have nots" (Galanter 1974). He underscored the implications a power differential has on the parties and, more broadly, our culture. The "haves" understand the rules of the game and have the resources and knowledge to fully develop and pursue their cases. With such advantages, the "haves" typically come out ahead, and that challenges the fairness element of the court's mission.

Accessibility

The second element in the mission statement is *accessibility*. As we discussed in the last section, parties lacking financial resources may be inhibited in their ability to bring their disputes to court. Litigants incur hardships due to costs such as filing fees, attorney fees, and legislative caps on damage awards or due to personal costs such as day care, transportation, or use of vacation time to handle court meetings, and so forth. Accessibility also applies to physical disabilities such as whether the courthouse accommodates citizens confined to a wheelchair or those with a hearing or sight impairment. Language barriers for non-English-speaking citizens or illiterate individuals will similarly impact accessibility. Parties are also required to know where to file a claim. At first this decision appears simple, but with court structure nuances and complexities, easily locating the right court or division for any given dispute is often not easy.

In addition, access to public records is not necessarily straightforward. Access implies that court files contain all of the pertinent documents and that the archival procedure for retaining and retrieving older court files is maintained. A current trend is for court records to be published online, so ready public access to computers and the Internet become an issue courts must consider.

Impartiality

Political pressures experienced by decision makers lead to our third element in the mission statement. Courts must maintain an image of *impartiality*. As such, judges and jurors must have decisional independence, or be independent of political influence, and the court system must have institutional independence, or be independent from other branches of government (see also McLeod this volume, chapter 2). Institutional independence is complicated when the legislature controls the purse strings, dictating whether funding for programs or resources is available to the courts (see also Langer and Wilhelm this volume, chapter 8).

Debates about whether judges "legislate" from the bench and become judicial activists are common (see Miller this volume, chapter 19). Judges must resolve cases that come before them and some of their decisions will be controversial. In particular, judicial decisions that strike down legislation or decisions of other branches of government are often the source for cries of misused judicial activism (see also Langer and Wilhelm this volume, chapter 8). Recent trends in which special interest groups seek to politicize the judiciary are threatening the safeguards that allow the judiciary to provide the checks and balances that are fundamental to the justice system.

Most state court judges decide cases that are governed by clear precedent, so the opportunity to legislate from the bench on political or social controversies is rare. At the appellate level, tempered by what cases are brought in front of the court, judicial policy making takes place in the form of appellate opinions (see also Martinek this volume, chapter 9). In preparing the opinion, which may include additional concurring and dissenting opinions by individual judges, bargaining and debate between judges within a panel is common. Although the ideal is a judiciary free from political or social pressures, some observers assert these pressures too often intrude in judicial decisions. What political persuasion or party with which a judge or justice aligns receives a great deal of attention from legal scholars and news agencies. As a case in point, justices of the U.S. Supreme Court are constantly in the political limelight while legal analysts attempt to predict their propensity for one side of an issue.

Juries, unlike trial judges, provide impartiality as a group. A jury sits on only one case, and, thus, is not held accountable for controversial decisions. Furthermore, juries are not required to justify reasons for their decision. In essence, the jury provides protection from the "tyranny of the majority" (see Tocqueville 1990). A jury provides a check against government intimidation or a biased judge by speaking for the community and representing its values. Through its ability to nullify or refuse to follow the law in favor of its own perception of justice, the jury has been a source of protection of community values. Nullification permits a jury to vote with its conscience, conveying a message, popular or not, from the community (see also Boatright this volume, chapter 5).

Periodically, proposals to limit the use or power of a jury arise. Reducing the size of a jury will undoubtedly require fewer citizens to serve and will cut costs to the parties as well as the court. Other jury reforms, such as placing a maximum cap on the punitive or noneconomic damages a jury can award, limit the discretion of the jury. Courts also have altered decision rules, eliminating a requirement of unanimity, which weakens the minority group's viewpoint and decreases the chance of a hung jury. Proponents of such reform efforts must exercise caution not to encroach on the powers bestowed on juries, lest their democratic function be threatened.

Efficiency

Up to now, we have discussed the court's mission for administering justice. What must be balanced with that effort is the final concept pledged in the mission statement—to *efficiently* resolve disputes. Certainly, processing cases efficiently lends itself to the administration of justice, so much so that court administrators and judges implement techniques to simplify court

procedures and overcome bottlenecks. In fact, case-flow management is such an important function of the courts that leadership organizations in the court community have set time standards for processing cases (Dodge and Pankey 2003; Steelman et al. 2000).

To help ensure the timely resolution of cases, courts have adopted separate processing rules to more efficiently handle specific disputes arising in a case. For example, a court may assign cases to an expedited track when the dispute is either time sensitive (e.g., civil protective orders) or when the issues are straightforward (e.g., small claims). In addition, courts may screen cases for their amenability to ADR, assuming that some cases may come to a faster resolution through ADR than would be possible through traditional court processing.

Efficiency is accomplished through clearly understood and administered processes, and that is one underlying force behind a trend toward specialized courts. Specialization enhances familiarity and knowledge of relevant issues among the judges on the court, and offers the possibility to resolve specific types of cases in both a fair and timely fashion. Many courts devote considerable staff and resources to a particular type of case, such as family court, drug court, or tax court. Specialized courts hold the promise of better serving their litigants through a deeper understanding of the social, psychological, and economical contexts in which such disputes arise and by learning how best to resolve them.

Specialization is also achieved through the use of a select judge who coordinates and manages the litigation. Various case management techniques have been developed to expedite complex civil litigation, such as mass torts or class action lawsuits. The purpose for courts to certify a dispute as a class action is to consolidate litigation for a group of plaintiffs and reduce unnecessary or duplicative court activity. Consolidation and other organizational techniques reduce the time and resources that would be required to process the litigation as separate filings.

SUMMARY AND CONCLUSIONS

As we have seen, understanding and negotiating state court structure and jurisdiction requires care. Each state has established various levels and types of courts, and two or more courts in a jurisdiction may share the authority to decide a particular type of case. Thus, in many states, both a general jurisdiction court and a limited jurisdiction court may hear complaints in torts or contracts below a set maximum-dollar amount. In some courts, jurisdiction is restricted to specific proceedings such as small claims.

The lack of uniformity in court structure and jurisdiction among the states even extends to the names given to the courts at various levels. The supreme court in most states is the court of last resort, the appellate court with final jurisdiction over all appeals within the state. In New York, however, the title "supreme court" denotes the main general jurisdiction trial court while the highest court in the state is known as the Court of Appeals. In Maryland, the highest court is also known as the Court of Appeals. A knowledge of court structure and jurisdiction is necessary before one can determine whether like is being compared to like.

Given that state courts resolve nearly 100 million cases a year, understanding their operations is clearly valuable, and court leaders should take the lead in communicating whether the court is meeting its goals. The other branches of government, the media, and the public at large all have a stake in our court system, and their awareness and understanding of court operations are essential if they are to be knowledgeable in their relations with the courts. Legislatures and executive agencies initiate and plan structural and procedural changes that affect the courts. The state legislature might want to know, for example, how proposed changes to speedy trial rules, amendments to the rules of civil procedure, or the implementation of specialized mental health courts requiring expanded judicial intervention will likely affect the functioning of the court. Participating effectively in the reform process requires courts to provide information on how well

they are meeting their mission to serve the public. At the very least, the information compiled should make it possible for the legislature, the executive, and the public to hold courts accountable and assess their efficiency. Only in this way can the courts expect to receive the public support they need.

The past hundred years has witnessed considerable development in how state courts can best organize themselves to provide high levels of service and to be responsive to the changing needs of society. Beginning with Roscoe Pound's 1906 speech to the American Bar Association that "kindled the white flame of progress" in judicial administration (quoted in Wigmore 1937), courts have focused on addressing problems through innovations in their structure and their processes. A key assumption has been that a causal link exists between structures, resources and processes, and court effectiveness. For example, many hold the belief that court unification—the consolidation and simplification of court structure—has a direct impact on court performance. Yet, this remains a largely untested assumption. Successfully meeting the court's mission statement of fair, accessible, impartial, and efficient service requires courts to investigate more deeply the relationship between court organization and the outcomes actually achieved.

CourTools, a project of the National Center for State Courts, begun in 2003, represent a milestone in the development of concepts, techniques, and strategies to examine the performance of courts and the justice system (Ostrom & Hall 2005). *CourTools* provide a direct means for courts to evaluate how well they are meeting their mission statement and broaden court performance measurement from one of identifying structural and jurisdictional reforms to one of critical review and evaluation of actual implementation. It is through such resources and tools of accountability and continued dialogue with the community that the civil justice system will ultimately succeed.

Notes

1. American Bar Association, Standards of Judicial Administration, Volume 1: Standards Relating to Court Organization, Section 1.10—Unified Court System: General Principle (1990).

2. American Bar Association, Standards of Judicial Administration, Volume 1: Standards Relating to Court Organization, Section 1.13—Appellate Court (1990).

3. In arbitration, the parties agree in advance to be bound by the decision of the third-party arbitrator. For example, most contract disputes regarding professional athletes are resolved through arbitration. Mediation, on the other hand, means that the third party merely suggests a solution to the dispute, but the parties are not bound by that suggestion. (For more details on the wide variety of ADR mechanisms available today, see, e.g., Baum 2001, 221–24).

7

U.S. DISTRICT COURTS, LITIGATION, AND THE POLICY-MAKING PROCESS

Jeb Barnes

Trial courts, including the U.S. District Courts, have generally received less attention from scholars than have appellate courts. Because trial courts deal with the facts of the specific cases before them, some have argued that the trial courts don't really have a policy-making role in our society. Others argue that collectively the trial courts are very important policy makers. This chapter examines the federal trial courts and their collective policy-making abilities. The chapter begins by presenting a general model of policy making. During each stage of the model, the chapter compares policy making in the courts with policy making in Congress. The chapter concludes by examining the role of the U.S. District Courts in the policy-making process, using the asbestos issue to illustrate the collective policy making found in the federal trial courts. Clearly these federal trial judges are making decisions with important political and legal ramifications.

INTRODUCTION

When we think of the federal judiciary, we tend to think of the U.S. Supreme Court. However, the U.S. District Courts, which are primarily responsible for conducting trials and managing the enormous federal caseload on a daily basis, do most of the work. In 2004, the Supreme Court disposed of 7,542 cases. Of that total, 87 cases were decided after oral argument, an average of 7.25 decisions a month. The district courts, by contrast, terminated 241,864 cases, which is almost one case every two minutes of every day. Meanwhile, 60,505 district court cases were appealed to the U.S. Courts of Appeals, which in turn, terminated 56,243 cases (see Martinek this volume, chapter 9). Using these numbers, over 180,000 cases were resolved in the district courts in 2004, more than three times the

total in the U.S. Courts of Appeal, and over 23 times the number in the Supreme Court (Administrative Office of the U.S. Courts 2005b, Tables A-1, C, B).

Given their relative output, one might expect scholars to focus on district courts first, U.S. Courts of Appeal next, and the Supreme Court last. However, scholars have tended to do just the opposite. They have concentrated on the Supreme Court and have asked whether the law or "nonlegal" factors, such as political ideology, primarily motivate justices' decisions. Over time, this approach has yielded an elegant model of judicial behavior, known as the *attitudinal model*, which holds, "judges decide disputes in light of the facts of the case vis-à-vis their sincere ideological attitudes and values" (Segal 1997, 28; see also Pritchett 1948; Schubert 1960, 1965; Segal and Cover 1989; Segal and Spaeth 1993, 2002).

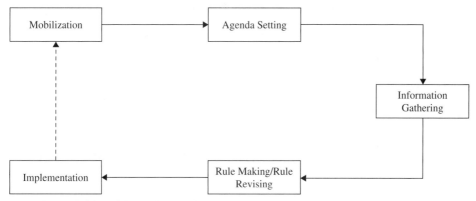

Figure 7.1 A Working Definition of the Policy-Making Process

Although understanding what motivates Supreme Court decision making is clearly important, this narrow focus has at least two disadvantages. First, it draws our attention away from the front lines of the federal judiciary. Second, focusing on the determinants of judicial behavior and the internal workings of the Supreme Court obscures how courts serve broader policy-making processes (Shapiro 1993; Barnes 2007a). This is particularly problematic in the context of the United States, where lower federal courts have shaped issues ranging from contested constitutional matters, such as the right to abortion, to the interpretation of far-reaching statutes, such as the tax code, the Clean Air and Water Acts, the Americans with Disabilities Act, and others.

Instead of concentrating on judicial behavior and the Supreme Court, this chapter explores how litigation at the district court level constitutes a distinct mode of policy making. To examine this issue on a preliminary basis—a comprehensive account would require whole volumes—this chapter begins by offering a working definition of the policy-making process. It next describes civil litigation in terms of this definition, contrasting judicial policy making with its more familiar congressional counterpart.[1] With this conceptual framework in place, it then discusses some of the policy trade-offs associated with judicial policy making and briefly considers the normative debate over its proper role in American democracy. Along the way, it is hoped that students will gain a better understanding of the litigation process and how seemingly arcane

legal proceedings relate to the everyday practice of policy making.

A WORKING DEFINITION OF THE POLICY-MAKING PROCESS

For purposes of this chapter, we can divide the generic policy-making process into five analytic stages: *mobilization, agenda setting, information gathering, rulemaking,* and *implementation* (see generally Kingdon 1995; Feeley and Rubin 1998). Each stage, in turn, represents a discrete process. Mobilization involves organizing claimants for making demands on official decision makers. Agenda setting entails placing demands on the list of issues governmental decision makers are taking seriously at any given moment. Information gathering assembles facts and expert opinions about the underlying issues, including their scope, underlying causes, and alternative solutions. Rulemaking produces authoritative choices about the official response—or lack of response—to the issues. Implementation applies general rules to specific cases. During implementation, concerns may arise that trigger the entire process anew, resulting in the revision of policies.

This framework is admittedly a gross oversimplification. Any attempt to impose a single definition on the "barroom brawl" of American policy making (Wilson 1989, 299–300) will inevitably fail to capture its interactive, contingent, and ad hoc nature and its variability across issue areas and over time (see Lindblom 1959,

1979; Lowi 1972; Barnes 2004b; Barnes and Miller 2004a; 2004b). In addition, policy making does not always proceed from agenda setting to implementation in linear fashion. In some cases, policy makers have solutions ready-made and seek to find problems and political opportunities to implement them (March and Olson 1989). Nevertheless, even an imperfect working definition can be analytically useful. It can provide temporary scaffolding to organize thoughts about a very complicated subject and offer a touchstone for comparing core policy-making functions across institutional settings.

AN OVERVIEW OF LITIGATION AS A POLICY-MAKING PROCESS

This simplified framework represents a useful first step, but understanding litigation as a policy-making process remains daunting because litigation in the trial courts unfolds according to detailed, technical rules and specialized professional norms. So, when lawyers talk about litigation, they are likely to use an array of unfamiliar terms, such as *contingency fees*, the *rules of justiciability, interrogatories*, and so on (see also Mather this volume, chapter 4). This is not a criticism—every profession has its own language that serves as convenient and necessary shorthand for

practitioners. However, this jargon creates a barrier to recognizing how litigation constitutes a policy-making process that involves the same analytic stages that unfold in Congress or elsewhere.

The implication is *not* that judicial policy making is the same as policy making in other institutional settings. To the contrary, the civil litigation process structures each stage of policy making differently than other institutions. The point is that viewing civil litigation in terms of general policy-making stages reveals functions that are routinely missed when courts and litigation are examined through the narrow prisms of law and judicial behavior. Thus, as discussed later, a policy-making perspective envisages the legal claiming process as a form of mobilization; the filing of a lawsuit as a type of agenda setting; "discovery" as a method of information gathering; judicial decision making as a mode of rulemaking; and postjudgment enforcement orders, consent decrees, and injunctions as tools of implementation.

A CLOSER LOOK

Litigation and Mobilization

Public policy does not just happen. Some one or some group must organize for action. In the context

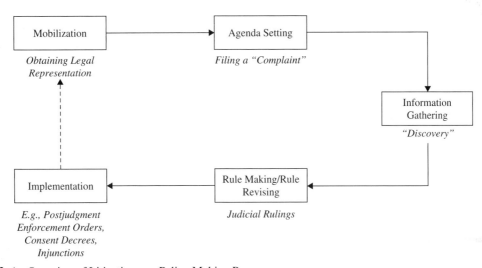

Figure 7.2 An Overview of Litigation as a Policy-Making Process

of congressional action, individual citizens, interest groups, lobbyists, elected officials, and their staffs all can play a role in mobilization. In the classic formulation, citizens with common interests band together in response to a problem and organize at the grassroots level (Madison 1788; Truman 1951; Dahl 1961). Others stress how well-established interests use their organizational advantages, extensive networks, and resources to mobilize for action through insider channels (Mills 1956; Olsen 1971; Easterbrook 1983, 1984). In addition, policy entrepreneurs, such as Ralph Nader, can use sophisticated media campaigns to drum up public interest and pressure elected officials (Wilson 1980). Inside government, elected officials can mobilize interests from the top down by "going public" (Kernell 1993) or from the bottom up by sponsoring the formation of groups (Walker 1991; Knott and Miller 1989).

With respect to litigation, mobilization typically involves finding a lawyer who can translate an injury into a legal claim. Structurally, the American legal system facilitates mobilization in a number of ways. In contrast to other countries, the United States permits lawyers to work on contingency fees, which allow them to represent clients in exchange for a percentage of any eventual verdict or settlement. Fueled by the prospect of recovering 30 to 40 percent of large verdicts and aided by the easing of restrictions on the advertising of legal services (*Bates v. State Bar* 1977), a highly competitive litigation industry has emerged (Kagan 2001, 133–34). As a result, entrepreneurial lawyers now routinely hold press conferences at the sites of accidents, deploy representatives to screen potential clients, and market themselves on television, radio, bus stops, and billboards. The American Trial Lawyers Association (ATLA), the Center for Automotive Safety, Public Citizen Health Research Group, and others have created litigation databases, standing lists of experts, and strategy kits to help lawyers find new clients and sue for injuries allegedly caused by specific automobiles, medical products, lead paint, silicone breast implants, and the list goes on (Rabin 1993; Stipp 1993; Kolata 1995; see also Seager 1991).

At first blush, these legal practices may seem far removed from policy making, but they have significant policy and political implications. Through the lens of mobilization, contingency fees not only fund litigation, they create a class of policy entrepreneurs. Legal advertising and media strategies not only offer lawyers a method to sign up new clients but also provide lawyers-as-policy-entrepreneurs a means of going public, educating the public of their rights, and energizing interests.

This is not an exhaustive list. Consider another example: *class-action lawsuits.* From a narrow legal viewpoint, class actions are a procedural mechanism for combining similar individual claims into a single lawsuit (Federal Rules of Civil Procedure [hereinafter "FRCP"], Rule 23). From the vantage of mobilization, however, they offer lawyers-as-policy-entrepreneurs a tool for organizing diffuse individual interests into a potent group of claimants and thus overcome a potential collective action problem—the inherent difficulty of mobilizing diffuse interests, especially when the expected individual rewards for taking action on behalf of the group are relatively small (Olsen 1971). Pushing this logic further, recent federal legislation aimed at reining in the filing of class actions in state courts is not merely a technical adjustment of legal procedures. It is an attempt to limit access to a key policy-making forum—the courts—by curtailing a potentially potent method for mobilizing diffuse interests (Barnes 2007a).

The argument is not that legal mobilization is easy in the United States or that Americans are litigation crazy. Contrary to popular perception, most injuries do not produce litigation (see generally Tarr 2006, 219–22). Studies show that only ten of every one hundred Americans hurt in accidents file any type of claim, and only two of one hundred file lawsuits (Hensler et al. 1991, 121). Only five of every one hundred Americans who believe that another's illegal conduct cost them over $1,000 file lawsuits (Trubek et al. 1983, summary 19, Figure 2). Even in the area of medical malpractice—a supposed hotbed of litigation—a leading study shows that only one of every eight patients seriously injured by doctors' negligence file lawsuits (Weiler et al. 1993). Thus, like any form of mobilization, legal mobilization is not automatic and may be better suited for some types of claims than others (Rosenberg 1991).

At the same time, litigation undoubtedly represents a significant channel for mobilization in the United

States, one that is supported by an active network of entrepreneurial lawyers. Given this network, there is no shortage of legal activity or lawsuits in the district court in absolute terms. According to the U.S. Statistical Abstract, Americans spent $149.7 billion on legal services in 2003 alone. By comparison, Americans spent $27.9 billion on agricultural services, $34.6 billion on the making of movies and sound recordings, and $30.6 billion on the manufacture of furniture and related products. And although many injuries never produce a lawsuit, Americans still managed to file an average of 261,763 civil lawsuits *per year* in the district courts from 1995 to 2005 (Administrative Office of the U.S. Courts 2005a, Table S-7; 2003a, Table S-7; 1997, Table S-7).

Litigation and Agenda Setting

Once mobilized, advocates must place their demands on the "to do" list of governmental decision makers. In Congress, agenda setting is highly politicized and subject to many factors outside of the control of claimants (Kingdon 1995; Hacker 1997). An unexpected crisis or sudden shift in media attention can push items off Congress' radar screen. Budgetary constraints or a negative cost assessment from the Congressional Budgeting Office can derail a proposal. A popular issue can be joined with less popular ones and be robbed of momentum.

By contrast, an individual claimant or "plaintiff" has greater control over agenda setting in the district courts. Specifically, a plaintiff places an issue on a district court's agenda or "docket" by filing a *complaint* (the first step in a lawsuit), which must satisfy a number of substantive and procedure requirements (FRCP, Rules 3–6). Substantively, it must (a) allege at least one valid *cause of action* that asserts that the target of the lawsuit, the "defendant," has violated the law and caused the plaintiff harm; and (b) set forth a "demand for judgment" that seeks a *remedy* for the alleged harm. This remedy might be money damages, an injunction, clarification of legal rights, or other such judicial actions. Procedurally, civil complaints must establish *jurisdiction* and *venue*, meaning that the district court is authorized to address the issues in the complaint and that the case is filed in the proper location (see 28

U.S.C. § 1331–1355, 1391). They must also satisfy the *rules of justiciability*. These rules include the doctrine of standing, which lays out when a claimant has a sufficient stake in a controversy to sue; the doctrines of ripeness and mootness, which determine whether the underlying controversy is either too premature or settled for adjudication; and the political question doctrine, which holds that some controversies are better left to the other branches. There are other requirements as well, such as rules governing the notification of interested parties and "statutes of limitation" that set time limits for bringing specific types of claims.

These requirements may seem onerous in the abstract but typically are not in practice. The rules of jurisdiction and venue are reasonably flexible, allowing some plaintiffs to engage in "forum shopping"— choosing a court that is most likely to be sympathetic to their claims. Similarly, the rules of justiciability are relatively open, allowing a wide range of claimants to bring a broad spectrum of controversies. In addition, the federal rules of civil procedure allow plaintiffs in most cases to make broad allegations that can be amended as the case proceeds (FRCP, Rule 8(a)). This is called *notice pleading*, which means that the complaint will be allowed as long as it gives the defendant fair warning of the underlying grievance and relief sought.[2]

Again, it is easy to become lost in the technical ins-and-outs of these rules and lose sight of the fact that these rules related to core policy-making functions. They govern a distinctive mode of agenda setting, one that sharply differs from congressional agenda setting and has been central to groups fighting for civil rights, woman's equality, environmental protection, states' rights, abortion rights, and many others.

Litigation and Information Gathering

Once on the agenda, the next step is information gathering. Members of Congress have an elaborate tool kit for collecting background material and expert opinions on policy issues (Fisher 2002). They have staffs on Capitol Hill and their home districts. The Congressional Research Service, Government Accounting Office, Congressional Budget Office, and many others are available to answer congressional inquiries and provide analysis of legislation and governmental programs. Members of Congress also serve on committees, which have their own staffs and hold hearings. As part of the hearing process, members and their staffs can subpoena witnesses and documents. And members of Congress can—and do—turn to an army of lobbyists, pollsters, interest groups, and think tanks, which are more than willing to lend their expertise to a policy debate.

Civil litigation also features tools for information gathering. Once a complaint is filed (and the defendant answers), litigation moves to a new stage called *discovery* (see FRCP, Rules 26–37). During discovery, lawyers on each side independently investigate the facts of the case by, among other things, (a) filing *interrogatories*, which are written questions (FRCP, Rule 33); (b) taking *depositions*, which are interviews recorded by a court stenographer (FRCP, Rules 30, 31); and (c) *subpoenaing documents* (FRCP, Rule 34). As a general matter, each side enjoys considerable latitude in deciding what information to pursue and have the right to investigate broadly.

During discovery, district court judges mainly serve as referees, determining whether each side is entitled to certain types of information, ruling on whether information can be used at trial, and facilitating negotiations through a variety of mechanisms, such as pretrial conferences. It should be added that, although lawyers dominate discovery, district judges have their own staffs, including law clerks from top law schools, which can help gather information, especially about the relevant law.

Perhaps not surprisingly, discovery can be very costly, as each side engages in parallel and often redundant investigations and seeks to leave no stone unturned prior to "all-at-once" trials (Kagan 2001; Langbein 1985).[3] In high profile cases, such as the battle over the fortune of Seward Johnson, the heir to the Johnson & Johnson fortune, discovery can cost millions of dollars (Langbein 1994). Even in routine cases, the costs of litigation are striking. In auto accident cases, lawyers' fees consume more than 40 percent of insurance settlements (Hensler et al. 1985, 27–28). A systematic study of 1,649 federal and state lawsuits similarly found that, in cases where plaintiffs recovered less than $10,000, the median plaintiff's

legal costs totaled 35 percent when lawyers worked on contingency fees and 46 percent when the lawyers were paid on an hourly basis (Trubeck et al. 1983, 111). Defendants' legal costs were similar, suggesting legal fees accounted for more than half of the total recovery in relatively small stakes cases.

Studies of specific types of lawsuits reinforce these findings. A 1993 survey found that corporations paid law firms an average of $967,000 per case in defending their officers and directors in stockholders' securities fraud claims, which includes the "less expensive" cases where the responding company won without paying a settlement (Lambert 1995, B16). The American Intellectual Property Law Association (AIPLA) found that the median cost per party of a patent case with $1 to $25 million at risk was almost $1.5 million in 2001 and $2 million in 2003. As the stakes increased, so did the costs. In cases with more than $25 million at stake, these costs were $3 million in 2001 and $4 million in 2003 (AIPLA 2001, 84–85, 2003, 93).

When viewed from the perspective of the legal system, the costliness of litigation can distort the process (Kagan 2001). Sometimes plaintiffs use the threat of litigation to coerce defendants to settle questionable claims—called *strike suits*—because it is cheaper for defendants to pay a few thousand dollars and settle a claim quickly than spend thousands on protracted litigation. In other cases, defendants use the cost of litigation to their advantage, burying plaintiffs under an avalanche of requests and depositions. Faced with such an onslaught, plaintiffs may agree to settle cheaply or even walk away from a small but meritorious claim.

Yet discovery can advance the pubic interest. In the case of asbestos litigation, discussed later, it uncovered sometimes egregious corporate conduct that concealed significant health risks (Brodeur 1986). This information, in turn, has become part of the public record. The central point is that discovery is a powerful—albeit often costly—means for gathering information that not only shapes the resolution of specific lawsuits but also can shape broader public discourse on policy issues.

Litigation and Rulemaking

Once information is gathered, officials can make rules designed to address the underlying issues. Congress makes rules by passing legislation. The legislative process begins when an individual member of Congress or a group of members sponsor a bill. Before becoming a law, a bill must run a gauntlet of subcommittee and committee hearings and mark-up sessions, floor debates, and majority votes in both chambers of Congress. If differences exist between the House and Senate versions of a bill, a final compromise must be hammered out in conference committees and a majority in both chambers must approve it. Once it passes Congress, the bill goes to the president, who can veto the bill and send it back to Congress, which can override a veto with a two-thirds vote (see, e.g., Davidson and Oleszek 2004).

Under these circumstances, congressional rulemaking power can be seen as collective and broad. It is collective in that, although individual members can initiate a bill, only a majority may pass a law. It is broad in that, if individual members can build stable majority coalitions that withstand the multiple-veto points in the rulemaking process, Congress passes statutes that are nationally binding, provided that the laws are constitutional.

In a sense, the district court's formal rulemaking power is the mirror opposite; it is individual and limited. Throughout the litigation process, individual district court judges can make authoritative decisions. Prior to trial, judges may rule on the admissibility of evidence; the validity of claims; and the proper jurisdiction, venue, and justiciability of a claim. During trial, judges make decisions on the proper scope of testimony, the appropriateness of evidence, and, if there is a jury, the wording of the jury instructions. After trial, district courts issue decisions with findings of fact and rulings of law and may become involved in enforcing their orders.

At the same time, when compared to Congress' lawmaking power, the scope of district court judges' rulemaking power is formally limited. As a legal matter, the doctrine of *stare decisis* provides that district court judges' decisions only formally bind the parties to the specific litigation and not other courts. In addition, district court judges must adhere to the decisions of higher courts within their circuit. From a policy-making perspective, *stare decisis* is not only a formal limitation on judicial power but also a distinct norm

of judicial rulemaking, which requires judges to use specialized modes of legal reasoning to convince other judges to adopt their decisions and arguably promotes incrementalism (Feeley and Rubin 1998, 242).

Despite these limitations, district court decisions can pack significant policy-making punch. Although not binding, district court decisions are often cited as persuasive precedents. Moreover, federal legislation and legal precedents are often vague or distinguishable on the facts, which leave district court judges considerable room to maneuver in shaping the law. Indeed, district court judges often must engage in "interstitial legislation," filling gaps that inevitably appear when general legal rules are applied to particular cases (Cardozo 1921). Filling gaps in the law can require leaps in policy. The Americans with Disabilities Act, for example, was vague with respect to whether a disability for purposes of the statute should be assessed in its treated or untreated state. Resolving this ambiguity in the statute literally affected millions of Americans and tens of thousands of businesses (Barnes 2004a).

Litigation and Implementation

Making rules is one thing; implementing them is quite another. *Implementation* means actually putting the specific policy into practice. In general, Congress delegates the difficult and often contentious task of implementation to agencies, which have the power to promulgate specific regulations for enforcing general federal laws. Congress then can engage in "fire alarm" oversight (McCubbins and Schwartz 1984), addressing issues raised by disgruntled groups who appeal to Congress for assistance in dealing with agencies.

Unlike Congress, district courts are often directly engaged in enforcing their own decisions. For instance, if the defendant refuses to pay a judgment for damages, the plaintiff can return to court and seek an order that places a lien on the defendant's assets or garnish the defendant's wages. In law school, these orders fall under the broad headings of *remedy law* and *postenforcement judgments*. From a policy-making vantage, these actions represent a form of judicial implementation.

District court judges also implement decisions using their injunctive powers, which enable them to order specific conduct, and shaping consent decrees, which are agreements among the litigants enforced by the courts. For example, courts have—with mixed results—used these powers to reform schools, public housing, mental health institutions, police practices, and prisons (Sabel and Simon 1999; Feeley and Rubin 1998; Sandler and Schoenbrod 2004; see also Chayes 1976; Fuller 1978). These cases, in turn, have produced diverse styles of judicial implementation, which underscore the flexibility of the courts' implementation powers.

Compare efforts to reform mental health institutions in Alabama and the District of Columbia. In Alabama, the court adopted a top-down, fixed rule approach to reforming mental health institutions (*Wyatt v. Stickney* 1972), mandating at least ten square feet of space per patient in the dining room, an air temperature between 68°F and 83°F, hot water at 110°, one toilet for every eight patients, no more than six patients per room, and specific patient–staff ratios for thirty-five job categories. In the District of Columbia, the court rejected the command and control model of *Wyatt* and fostered an "experimentalist" approach, which set forth broad goals, such as "appropriate individualized" treatment in the "least restrictive, most integrated, and least restrictive setting" and required the individualized service plans for treatment to be updated at least annually (Sabel and Simon 1999, 18).

Of course, judicial implementation of court decisions and consent decrees barely scratches the surface of the district courts' role in implementing federal policy (Melnick 2004; Kagan 2001; Shapiro 1988). Shifts in the structure of legislative programs have greatly extended the district courts' influence over administrative procedures and rulemaking. To elaborate briefly, beginning in the late 1960s, Congress passed laws that sought to address widespread social problems, such as discrimination, consumer safety, and environment degradation. To implement this ambitious agenda, Congress created an alphabet soup of new, often overlapping federal agencies. At the same time, Congress feared that industries would eventually dominate the very agencies designed to regulate their conduct. To inoculate agencies from industry capture, Congress created a host of procedural mechanisms, such as "private attorneys general" provisions, which allow public interest groups to participate in administrative rulemaking and haul agencies into court for failure to meet their obligations.[4]

During the same period, federal judges created new legal doctrines that extended their role in reviewing agency decisions. For example, the landmark Supreme Court decision of *Goldberg v. Kelly* (1970) required hearings for those facing the loss of welfare benefits and triggered the creation of myriad administrative hearings subject to district court review. Meanwhile, federal judges relaxed the rules of justiciability, such as the standing doctrine, which facilitated public interest group litigation against agencies (Stewart and Sunstein 1982).

This pincer movement by Congress and the courts has had a predictable and profound effect judicial power in the United States. Today, district court judges not only serve their traditional role of resolving politically important legal cases and enforcing their decisions, but also play a significant role in overseeing federal agencies and deciding regulatory disputes under the "hard look" doctrine, which can serve as a doctrine of judicial second guessing (Melnick 2004).[5] In this dual role, district court judges have shaped polices far beyond the reach of judges in other industrialized democracies, including coal mine safety, nursing home care, corporate insolvency, educational opportunity, labor relations, the introduction of new drugs, air pollution, the use of polyvinyl chlorides, and others (Kagan 2001, Table 8, collecting authority).

THE COSTS AND BENEFITS OF JUDICIAL POLICY MAKING: THE ASBESTOS LITIGATION EXAMPLE

Once litigation is seen as a distinctive type of policy making, it is natural to ask: What are its costs and benefits? General cost-benefit assessments of any form of policy making—legislative, administrative, or judicial—are always problematic. The effectiveness, fairness, and efficiency of any process are highly context specific, depending less on the form of policy making than how the process is used by the particular parties (Rubin 1996; Komesar 1994). However, a large body of comparative literature associates some characteristic trade-offs with American-style judicial policy making or *adversarial legalism* (Kagan 2001, 9). Adversarial legalism describes the American style of policy making and implementation where various groups often take their policy disputes to the courts at almost any stage of the policy-making process (see Kagan 2004). In other countries, many disputes that are handled by the courts in the United States are instead handled exclusively by executive or legislative branch decisions. Collectively, this literature suggests that adversarial legalism in the United States is a double-edged sword—it can be flexible and innovative but also costly and unpredictable.

This chapter will now turn to an example of the policy-making role of trial courts, using asbestos litigation as an example. Asbestos litigation is an extreme case of adversarial legalism, which can be used as a kind of an engineer's stress test to illustrate these strengths and weaknesses when pushed the system is pushed to its limits (see Kagan 2001, 126–27). This litigation traces its roots to the confluence of two factors in the mid-1960s (Brodeur 1986; see also Barnes 2007b). One was medical. In October 1964, a team of doctors and epidemiologists led by Dr. Irving Selikoff presented a detailed study of mortality rates among asbestos-insulation workers, which provided scientific support for workers' claims that asbestos had caused their illnesses (Selikoff et al. 1965). The other was legal. In the spring of 1965, the American Law Institute published the second edition of its *Restatement of the Law of Torts*, a comprehensive redefinition of tort law by a leading group of law professors, judges, and lawyers. Section 402A of the *Restatement* set forth a new theory of product liability, which holds that, if manufacturers fail to warn users of a product's dangers, they are strictly liable for resulting harms, even if the product is unavoidably unsafe.

Armed with these findings and Section 402A, entrepreneurial plaintiff lawyers working on contingency fees began suing companies that allegedly failed to provide adequate warnings about their asbestos-laden products. The first major legal breakthrough occurred in the early 1970s, when a district court in Texas recognized that third-party suppliers of asbestos products to the workplace could be strictly liable under Section 402A, and the Fifth Circuit for the U.S.

Courts of Appeal affirmed (*Borel v. Fibreboard Paper Products Corporation* 1973). Other circuits followed suit (see, e.g., *Karjala v. Johns-Manville Products Corporation* 1975; *Moran v. Johns-Manville Sales Corporation* 1982).

These cases eventually unleashed a tidal wave of litigation. RAND estimates that over 730,000 individual claims for asbestos-related injuries had been filed as of 2002 and that the number of annual claims is rising (Carroll 2005, xxiv). Over 8,400 firms have been sued, including at least one company in 75 of 83 categories of economic activity in the Standard Industrial Classification (Carroll 2005, xxv). In 2002, *Barron's* named forty publicly traded companies with significant—and growing—asbestos liability exposure (often through the acquisition of firms that once produced asbestos products; Abelson 2002). The list reads like a corporate *Who's Who*, including Dow Chemical, Daimler Chrysler, Ford, IBM, Kaiser Aluminum, Pfizer, Sears, Viacom, and even Disney.

At the outset, asbestos litigation served important—even heroic—policy functions (Brodeur 1986; see generally Frymer 2003; Bogus 2001; Mather 1998). Working within a flexible common law tradition, courts provided asbestos workers a forum to raise their concerns when other branches and levels of government did not. Once established, asbestos litigation provided asbestos workers a means to supplement often meager state workers' compensation programs; it raised awareness about the dangers of asbestos; and uncovered decades of corporate malfeasance.

As asbestos litigation spread, however, careful policy studies questioned its efficiency and fairness as a means of compensation. A 1983 RAND study showed that asbestos plaintiffs received only thirty-seven cents of every dollar spent to resolve asbestos claims, which is significantly less than ordinary tort claims (Kakalik et al. 1983). Recent follow-up studies show that transaction costs continue to consume more than half of total spending on claims and may go up as new plaintiffs and defendants sue each other (Hensler et al. 2001; Carroll 2005; see also White 2002).

The Black Lung Program, which has been criticized as a poorly run administrative compensation program (Nelson 1985), offers an instructive contrast. Similar to asbestos litigation, this program aimed to compensate workers suffering from exposure to toxic materials that caused diseases with long latency periods. From 1992 to 2001, annual administrative costs accounted for 4.5 percent to 5.8 percent of the program's total obligations and 9.5 percent to 13.1 percent of total benefits (Office of Workers Compensation Programs [OWCP] Annual Report 2001, Table B-4). As part of the benefits package, successful claimants are entitled to attorneys' fees, which averaged around $7,600 per claim and represented less than two-tenths of one percent of all benefits paid that year (OWCP Annual Report 2001, 16). These costs are not trivial—the program's administrative costs topped $52 million for fiscal year 2001 alone—but they are dwarfed by the expense of private-asbestos litigation.

The costs of asbestos litigation might be bearable if litigation produced fair and consistent decisions, but it has been erratic. In Texas, five juries in a multi-plaintiff trial heard exactly the same evidence and ruled differently on specific liability and causation issues (Bell and O'Connell 1997, 22). Jury damage awards also have varied case to case and jurisdiction to jurisdiction, providing similarly situated plaintiffs different compensation and those with harder to prove claims nothing at all (Sugarman 1989, 46; Carroll 2002, 63).

Some may counter that unpredictability enhances the effectiveness of tort law as a deterrent, forcing companies to become extra vigilant. However, even under the best circumstances, tort law's deterrent value is uncertain. As Sugarman (1989) argued, manufacturers are subject to other pressures to act with care, including market forces that provide strong financial incentives to avoid widely publicized problems. Moreover, as asbestos litigation has increasingly focused on defendants who played a relatively minor role in exposing workers to asbestos and covering up its dangers, the deterrence value of these suits has become even more attenuated. A recent RAND report made the point as follows: "If business leaders believe that tort outcomes have little to do with their own behavior, then there is no reason for them to shape their behavior so as to minimize tort exposure" (Carroll 2005, 129).

Others may stress that asbestos litigation promises individualized treatment of asbestos claims, which is essential to perceptions of procedural fairness and trust in the legal system (Tyler 1990). However, as early as the mid-1980s, many asbestos claimants did not enjoy their day in court. After six or more years of asbestos litigation, the state court in San Francisco had completed only 11 percent of their asbestos cases. In Massachusetts, the news was worse—the state court had resolved only 10 of 2,141 claims or less than 1 percent (Hensler et al. 1985, 84–85). Today, leading asbestos litigation attorneys have massive portfolios of claims, called "inventories," which are often settled *en masse* or tried in groups. The upshot, according to RAND, is that "individualized process is a myth" in asbestos litigation (Carroll 2005, 129). In addition, serious concerns have emerged about fraudulent claiming practices in asbestos litigation (*Mealey's Litigation Report: Asbestos Bankruptcy* 2005), which hardly bolster perceptions of fairness or trust in the litigation process.

It must be re-emphasized that asbestos litigation is not typical (for comparisons to tobacco litigation, see, e.g., Mather 1998). It is a dramatic example of the potential costs and benefits of using the courts to address widespread, complex, and contested policy issues. It suggests that judicial policy making has the capacity to respond to new claims and issues that the other branches will not. However, adversarial legalism is often an inefficient and inconsistent decision-making process that can be manipulated by lawyers on both sides.

There is no simple formula for balancing these costs and benefits across-the-board. In specific cases, the assessment turns on at least two inherently contested factors: (a) the urgency of the underlying policy issue and (b) the political feasibility of action in other branches (see Rubin and Feeley 2003; Frymer 2003; Sabel and Simon 1999). If one believes that the policy issues are urgent and courts seem the only feasible forum, then judicial policy making may be acceptable even if the policy response is less than optimal, the administrative costs are high, and the results are somewhat inconsistent. If not, the relative cost and unpredictability of judicial policy making are harder to accept, especially if litigation does not act as a catalyst for efforts to build consensus and political coalitions within a policy community for further action.

IS JUDICIAL POLICY MAKING DEMOCRATIC?

Putting aside its policy trade-offs, judicial policy making raises fundamental normative questions about the role of courts in American democracy. This brief chapter cannot adequately address these questions. It can, however, offer some thoughts on the broad contours of the debate. Although it is difficult to generalize, the debate often invokes two competing definitions of democracy: participatory versus Madisonian democracy (see e.g. Barnes 2004a, 42–43, 46–47). In general, advocates of *participatory democracy* are distrustful of judicial policy making, preferring that elected officials take the policy-making lead. Advocates of *Madisonian democracy* tend to be more open to judicial policy making, which they see as part of an ongoing dialogue among overlapping and diversely representative policy forums, none of which has the final say on the meaning of the law.

The Least Dangerous Branch (Bickel 1962) provides a classic statement of the participatory view (see also Derthick 2005). It argued that majority rule lies at the heart of American democracy. Accordingly, elected officials represent the principal lawmakers and should make all major policy decisions. By contrast, unelected officials, such as federal judges and civil servants, should serve as agents for elected officials and faithfully apply the law as written as long as it is constitutional.

The Least Dangerous Branch conceded that this ideal division of labor cannot be fully realized in practice. Elected officials simply lack the time and resources to make every decision or micromanage the courts or agencies. Consequently, Congress inevitably delegates some decisions to judges and/or civil servants, who enjoy significant opportunities to make policy under the guise of statutory interpretation and implementation.

Because delegation provides courts and agencies significant policy-making opportunities, it can lead to the "counter-majoritarian difficulty": decisions by unelected officials that are contrary to the will of the majority (Bickel 1962, 16–23; see also Comiskey this volume, chapter 14). Such counter-majoritarian decision making is objectionable on at least two grounds:

it violates the core value of majority rule and it erodes the courts' institutional legitimacy as a neutral arbiter of disputes. The point is not that the courts should never make policy, but rather judicial policy making should be limited to protecting core constitutional rights. When in doubt, the federal courts should defer to the elected branches.

The Madisonian view sharply differs (Perretti 1999; Sunstein 1993). It rejects that the framers' primary concern was promoting majority rule and legislative supremacy. It was preventing the "mischief of faction": the natural tendency of individual citizens to form groups—either majority or minority groups—that pursue narrow self-interests at the expense of others (Madison 1788, Federalist Paper No. 10). Given this definition of the problem, the challenge was to design political institutions that would curb minority and majority tyranny without unduly restricting popular sovereignty or individual liberties.

With respect to the threat of minority tyranny, the framers' solution was straightforward. They provided regular elections so that popular majorities would have ample opportunities to remove corrupt or biased representatives. The threat of majority tyranny, however, posed a thornier problem because a majority faction, by definition, cannot be voted out of office. As a result, the framers had to look beyond elections and majority rule.

Specifically, to curtail the risks of majority tyranny, the Constitution employs a series of complementary institutional strategies, which are designed to reduce the likelihood that any single faction will control the policy-making process. Most obviously, the framers fragmented policy-making power. They divided legislative power between the Senate and House of Representations, which they viewed as the most susceptible to majority faction, and adopted federalism, separation of powers, and an elaborate system of checks and balances. This dispersal of power ensures that policy-making power is shared: Congress is given the primary power to draft laws, subject to the president's veto and judicial review; the Executive Branch is given the primary power to implement laws, subject to congressional oversight and judicial review; and the courts have the primary power to interpret laws, subject to a variety of legislative and executive checks, including the passage of overrides. Consequently, even if a tyrannical majority seizes one branch of government, it cannot unilaterally impose its will on the other branches. Instead, the faction must persuade other branches to endorse its preferences.

Fragmenting lawmaking power offers only an imperfect safeguard against majority tyranny, because dividing power does not prevent a faction from monopolizing *all* branches of government. Accordingly, the framers buttressed fragmented authority in two ways. First, they designed each branch of government to respond to different constituencies. Thus, members of the House of Representatives are elected by voters in local congressional districts; members of the Senate originally were elected by state representatives (and now are elected by voters in statewide elections); the president is selected by majority of Electoral College votes following a nationwide election; and federal judges are insulated from electoral pressures as political appointees with lifetime tenure and salary protection. By making the branches diversely representative, the framers built political tension into the American policy-making process, which decreases the likelihood that any single constituency will control all the branches of government simultaneously. Second, the framers staggered the terms of the Senate, House, and president, and provided that the Senate would be a continuing body, in that only one-third of its members run for re-election at a time. This system of staggered terms requires majority coalitions to persist over multiple-election cycles, which decreases the likelihood that a temporary surge in popular sentiment will sweep a tyrannical majority into office.

According to the Madisonian view, this complex system of checks and balances serves both negative and positive functions. The negative function is familiar; checks and balances limit any single branch of government or faction from unilaterally implementing self-serving laws. The positive function is that fragmented and open policy-making structures should promote continuing policy discourse among separate institutions sharing power. Such policy discourse, in turn, should engender interbranch feedback, revision of vague or outmoded laws, and, over time, policy consensus and legal certainty.

From this vantage, courts should not shrink from the policy-making process. They should actively participate in it, lending their (slightly different) voice to an ongoing dialogue. Thus, for a Madisonian, the issue is not whether judicial decisions encroach on the policy-making prerogatives of the other branches because policy-making power is dispersed among all branches of government. Instead, the central issue is whether judges use their policy-making power to advance important democratic values, especially broad participation in governmental processes.

CONCLUSIONS

This chapter has provided a general overview of litigation as a form of policy making. This topic is vast and by necessity the discussion has been impressionistic, sketching a framework for conceptualizing litigation as a policy-making process and reviewing some policy trade-offs and normative debates associated with judicial policy making in the literature. The central lesson is straight forward. Whether we like it or not, district court judges are policy makers and litigation is a mode of policy making (see also Mather 1991, 1995). Even seemingly technical aspects of litigation have significant political and policy dimensions. Contingency fees create a class of policy entrepreneurs. Class-action lawsuits mobilize diffuse consumer interests. Jurisdiction, venue, and the rules of justiciability shape a distinct type of agenda setting. Discovery gathers information. Judicial decisions represent a form of rulemaking. Postjudgment orders, consent decrees, and injunctions are tools of policy implementation. Re-conceptualizing legal practices along these lines naturally draws our attention away from standard questions about the determinants of judicial behavior and forces consideration of the instrumental value of courts and litigation to American policy making and democracy. Although these questions are often messy, they place district courts and litigation where they belong—at the center of national politics and policy making (Barnes 2007a).

Notes

1. This chapter focuses on civil not criminal litigation. Criminal law establishes which acts constitute offenses against society and prescribes punishments for such conduct. Examples of crimes include murder, theft, kidnapping, and fraud. Civil law is everything else. Thus, civil litigation includes lawsuits involving tax law, environmental law, antidiscrimination statutes, free speech, voting rights, and so on.

2. There are some exceptions to this rule. For example, allegations of fraud must be pleaded with specificity (FRCP, Rule 9(b)).

3. In Europe, there are often "episodic" trials, which allow the discovery process to focus on threshold issues first and thus potentially save the cost of investigating secondary issues (Kagan 2001; Langbein 1985).

4. Such provisions are common in environmental statutes, such as the Clean Air Act, the 1986 Superfund Act, the Endangered Species Act, and others (Melnick 1983).

5. Circuit Judge Harold Leventhal coined this phrase in *Greater Boston Television Corp. v. FCC* (1970).

8

STATE SUPREME COURTS AS POLICYMAKERS

Are They Loved?

Laura Langer and Teena Wilhelm

State supreme courts are the last word on matters of purely state law. In some ways, these state supreme courts can be thought of as policy-making bodies, just like the U.S. Supreme Court. Although the U.S. Supreme Court can overturn a state supreme court decision as a matter of federal law, the state supreme courts remain the court of last resort for purely state law issues. State supreme courts can hand down highly controversial decisions, such as the one in Massachusetts that declared that same-sex couples have the right to marry in that state. Other controversial state supreme court decisions in a variety of states have involved changes to the school funding system in the state.

Judges who sit on state supreme courts are selected in a variety of ways, as discussed in more detail in chapter 2 of this volume. Some of these state selection systems promote the notion of judicial independence from political pressures, while other methods favor more judicial accountability to the people. In addition, state supreme courts do not exist in a vacuum, but must make their decisions in the context of the institutional wills of the executive and legislative branches in their states.

This chapter looks at the policy-making role of state supreme courts with two key questions in mind: (1) Do differences in state judicial selection systems affect the policy-making role of state supreme courts? (2) How does the relationship between the state supreme court and the state legislature affect policy making by courts? This chapter uses a new institutionalist approach to these issues. These questions are in part answered through a series of elite interviews with a large number of state legislators and state supreme court justices. The chapter examines state supreme courts as both legal and political bodies.

A perennial issue in political science is the question of whether courts should serve as policy-making institutions. Central to this debate is the relationship between the traditional policy-making institutions (i.e., the legislative body) and the judicial branch (see also Miller this volume, chapter 19). At the state level, extraordinary tensions have ensued between state courts of last resort and state legislatures, which can have alarming consequences on the policy-making process.[1] Not surprisingly, the role of state supreme courts in policy making has become a fundamental issue for scholars, political pundits, and citizens across the American states. On one hand, some suggest that the issue of rights should be addressed by these courts, whereas others argue that policy-making authority resides with the legislative branch. Those in the latter camp argue that, when courts make policy, they usurp power from the other branches and become legislators in robes (for a further discussion of judicial activism, see Miller this volume, chapter 19).

Tension between the legislative and judicial branch across the states has intensified as the federal government devolves more responsibility to state governments and citizens turn to state courts to make policy (e.g., Tarr 2003; Langer 2002; National Center for State Courts 1999). As a result, judges on these courts increasingly resolve issues that have far-reaching implications for both policy and constitutionality. The issue is only further complicated by the variance of institutional rules in state political systems. Thus, as state supreme court justices are selected or retained in different ways, policy-making roles of state courts also vary (for a more specific discussion of differences in state judicial selection methods, see McLeod this volume, chapter 2).

Decisions by these courts have made them the focal point of much scrutiny. A recent decision by the Massachusetts Supreme Judicial Court that made gay marriage constitutional, *Goodridge v. Department of Public Health* (2003), has not only prompted adverse responses from both the Massachusetts Legislature and Governor (see Miller 2006), but has galvanized the issue across the country.[2] The heightened importance of legislative–judicial relationships is also marked by the increased propensity of state supreme courts to decide budgetary matters on behalf of state legislatures. For example, education funding has sparked some heated debates between the Texas and New York Legislatures and their state's court of last resort. In Kansas the conflict between these two branches reached an impasse when the Kansas Supreme Court demanded that the Legislature provide $143 million more toward education in the next school year. The range of issues resolved by state supreme courts is by no means limited to education. Washington State prosecutors, for example, asked

the Washington Supreme Court to rewrite the state's criminal sentencing guidelines in case that state's lawmakers failed to devise a solution to a political dispute over the guidelines. In Louisiana, state supreme court justices were asked to rewrite the state's policy on cock-fighting. The power struggle between the Ohio Supreme Court and Ohio Legislature has ensued for decades and has covered a myriad of issues. The increasingly broad range of policy decided by these courts has ignited discussions about judicial activism and raised questions about the separation of powers in the American states.

In many ways, state supreme courts have become the scapegoat for governmental problems. These courts of last resort are easy targets because debate over judicial selection and retention in the American states continues, and the shortcomings of each method remain the foci of political discussion (e.g., Hall 2001). Intense public and political scrutiny of justices on state supreme courts, as well as the method by which they attain office, will continue as long as these courts resolve controversial policy issues. Policy wars between state supreme courts and legislatures can ensue, which makes the process more contentious. Of course policy clashes between state courts of last resort and the legislature are not new, and a certain amount of friction is inherent. However, the extent to which state legislatures view these courts as inappropriate and manipulative policy makers has obvious implications for public policy. As legislatures approve more of the policy-making role of courts, there is more accord and less political volatility. Alternatively, as disapproval (and consequently, discord) increases, policy making becomes more contentious and the focus shifts from policy output to power sharing. Separation of powers is premised (in part) on legislative–judicial relations and how each branch views the other. Ultimately, legislative perceptions about the role of the judiciary in the policy-making process influence state governance.

In this chapter, we explore these perceptions and provide information regarding how legislators view state supreme courts and their relationship with these courts. Given the controversy that continues over judicial selection, we also observe if perceptions vary across six states with different selection methods.

The states chosen reflect six common methods of selection and retention for state supreme court justices. We have not noted exactly which states are included in this study because we promised the judges whom we interviewed that we would not reveal their identities. Thus this chapter will not refer to the specific states we studied, but instead will discuss these states in terms of their being representative of a broader category of states with similar judicial selection systems.

Differences in state judicial selection systems might influence legislative perceptions of interbranch relations given the linkages that each system creates with both the public and other governmental actors. Like the proper role of courts in policy making, how justices on these courts should be selected and retained is a perennial question that is fundamentally tied to intergovernmental relations (see also McLeod this volume, chapter 2). Whose policy preferences will become and remain law is a direct function of the degree to which governmental branches are tied to one another. These bridges serve as a way to maintain intergovernmental policy oversight. Moreover, systems of checks and balances are intended to prevent one governmental branch from dominating policy preferences; presumably such oversight contributes to "better policy outcomes." Some obvious mechanisms for government oversight in the policy-making process include legislative budgetary responsibility, gubernatorial veto, judicial review, referendums, and elections. These institutional structures are meant to maintain an impartial, equitable democratic form of government. As a result, policy output should represent the majority rather than any one segment of society, political party, or governmental branch. This of course, precludes the notion of majority tyranny. Quite simply, the framers were deliberate in the creation of the systems of checks and balances and separation of powers. *Judicial review* is perhaps the most powerful policy tool available to courts in our system of checks and balances. How members of the legislative branch perceive judicial behavior is even more critical given that state supreme courts resolve a greater number of issues that place them in direct conflict with state legislatures (for a perspective on these issues at the federal level, see Miller this volume, chapter 19).

Judicial selection and retention ultimately are about who will control political power. The method of judicial selection and retention, as noted earlier, is also another mechanism of governmental oversight, which perpetuates the system of checks and balances. The main tenets of separation of powers are often not in dispute, yet the methods of judicial selection and retention remain very much at the forefront of political debate. This is especially true among legislators. When we asked legislators how they perceived overall relations with the state supreme court, 68 percent of the legislators interviewed raised concerns over judicial selection and retention methods—without prompting. The controversial attention given to this topic is in large part due to the power this mechanism affords to some actors and removes from other actors. When the legislative branch is concerned, judicial selection systems can create adversarial relations. Selection and retention of state judges defines the source and degree of policy oversight (Epstein, Knight, and Shvetsova 2002). Whose preferences get translated into public policy is linked, arguably, directly to the selection and retention of judges, which has implications for legislative–judicial relations. Yet, to date, scholars have not explored legislative perceptions of relations with state supreme courts and the extent to which their views across methods of judicial selection and retention.

The purpose of this chapter is to assess perceptions about legislative–judicial relations in six states that represent six different methods of judicial selection and retention in the American states.[3] We report our conclusions from 314 one-on-one interviews with state legislators and state supreme court justices. Our attention focuses on the responses from three questions asked of each interviewee: (1) Do you feel your state supreme court's role in the policy-making process has been appropriate or inappropriate? (2) How would you describe the relationship between the legislature and the state supreme court? and (3) How do you or your colleagues respond to an objectionable decision by the state supreme court?[4] When combined, these questions provide commentary on how legislators view these courts and whether their perceptions differ across judicial selection and retention methods.

LEGISLATIVE PERCEPTIONS ACROSS METHODS OF JUDICIAL SELECTION AND RETENTION

As discussed in chapter 2 in this volume, there are a variety of ways that states select and retain state supreme court justices. Despite the idiosyncrasies of each state's system, there are some important elements shared by certain systems. These commonalities allow us to identify six general types of judicial selection and retention systems: gubernatorial appointment; legislative appointment;[5] life appointment; partisan election; nonpartisan election;[6] and merit selection. Today most states employ some form of the merit-selection system for judicial selection and retention. Yet, the debate continues over which method of judicial selection and retention is best (see, e.g., Tarr 2003).[7] Political scientists are interested in this debate because presumably method of selection and retention make some justices more vulnerable to political pressures than other justices (see, e.g., Dubois 1980; Sheldon and Maule 1997; Hall 2001; Pinello 1995).

Drawing from our earlier discussion, we posit that the method for selecting and retaining state supreme court justices serves as a policy oversight mechanism; it is an institutional check on the other branches. A judiciary that is independent from the political pressures exerted by other governmental branches is likely to impose its preferences in the policy-making process with greater regularity, which should create a more hostile policy-making environment. An independent judiciary can also presumably have a more permanent policy impact because the checks from other branches are less threatening. Epstein et al. (2002) posit that selection and retention systems that are more independent from other governmental branches emerge in environments of high political uncertainty. Political actors who are uncertain about political outcomes choose the type of selection and retention system that create judicial independence from other branches. The result is an environment reflective of an on-going constitutional conflict among the three branches of government (Epstein et al. 2002, 215). If we apply this logic to interbranch relations, selection and retention systems that utilize elections should perpetuate combative relations between state supreme courts and

the other branches. Alternatively, selection and retention systems that minimize independence by affording the power of judicial retention to the legislative or executive branch should reflect more harmonious relations. In the former, an important mechanism through which the other branches can constrain the state supreme court is absent. Governmental oversight of the judiciary can be exerted via judicial retention in the latter. Figure 8.1 demonstrates the degree of independence afforded the states supreme court and the degree of conflict likely to emerge.

Research has demonstrated that judicial behavior varies across method of judicial selection and retention (see, e.g., Brace and Hall 1997; Hall 1992; Pinello 1995). For example, research has shown that justices who are selected and retained by the legislative branch shift behavior toward legislative preferences (see, e.g., Pinello 1995). Drawing from the earlier discussion, partisan and nonpartisan election systems should exhibit constitutional battles between the states supreme court and the other governmental branches. At the other end of the continuum, selection and retention systems that reduce judicial independence from government actors should exhibit the least amount of tension.

PERCEPTIONS OF INTERBRANCH RELATIONS

One implication from the earlier discussion is that interbranch relations are influenced by method of judicial selection and retention. A fundamental component of intergovernmental relations is the view that each branch has of one another's role in the policy-making process (see also Miller this volume, chapter 19). It is integral for a government designed with a built-in system of checks and balances. This raises an important question: Does the perception of courts as appropriate or inappropriate policy-making institutions vary across methods of judicial selection and retention? Extant literature demonstrates that state supreme courts play an important role in the policy-making process (see, e.g., Tarr and Porter 1988; Tarr 1998b, 2003; Glick 1991). Thus, we think it is important to ask if state supreme courts are perceived as appropriate policy-making institutions, and to assess whether these perceptions

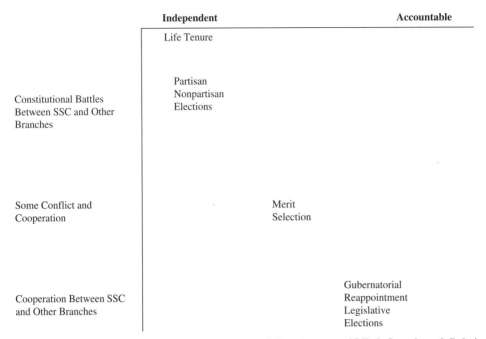

Figure 8.1 Degree of Judicial Accountability to Other Branches of Government and Likely Inter-branch Relations

are different in at least six ways justices attain and retain seats on these courts.

One general consideration is the notion of a "proper" role for the judicial branch in policy making. Simply, what constitutes "appropriate" versus "inappropriate" policy making by courts? Furthermore, is there a difference? The answer to this question, of course, varies as does the person being asked, which speaks to the importance of the interview data presented in this chapter. The conversation of an activist versus a restrained judiciary is as nearly old as the nation itself. Suffice to say, it is not the intent of the chapter to debate nor explain (both equally difficult tasks) the normative qualifications of activist or restrained courts. Instead, we focus on the idea that how this perception varies not only is fundamentally *affected by* the design of the political system, but also fundamentally *affects* the policy output of the system itself.

When state courts of last resort are viewed as policy makers, either generally or due to a specific decision, such perceptions can fundamentally change the nature of legislative–judicial relations. We investigate whether legislators view relations as adversarial

or consensual depending on method of judicial selection and retention. When state supreme court justices are elected, perceptions might suggest more strained relations between the state supreme court and legislators exist because justices presumably act more like legislators seeking reelection. Consequently, a heightened political environment might be imagined. Alternatively, when justices are selected and retained by the legislative branch, legislators might perceive cooperative legislative–judicial relations exist. Here legislators might feel that the court is less likely to stand against the legislature given the threat of legislative electoral retribution. Similarly, when the governor is responsible for selection and retention of state supreme court justices, perceptions about the court might be more friendly compared to election systems. Legislative perceptions about these courts might be neither extremely divisive nor perfectly cooperative in a state where the system splits selection and retention responsibility between one branch of government and voters (e.g., merit-selection systems).

We further explore how legislators perceive judicial behavior and how they react to such behavior.

Moreover, we investigate if these perceptions vary in the six states. If state supreme courts continue to play a more prominent role in the policy-making process, we might expect increased tension between these state governmental actors. As a result, legislators and justices are very likely to engage in strategic behavior. Strategic behavior is when an actor votes in a given way because of the anticipated response from another actor who has the power to penalize this actor for an objectionable decision. A liberal state supreme court justice, for example, might vote in a conservative direction for fear that the conservative legislature might otherwise punish the justice. The conservative legislature might use the budget as its sword against the court (e.g., Baum 2001; Douglas and Hartley 2003); override court decisions; or mobilize citizens to remove an elected justice (e.g., Culver and Wold 1986; Tarr 2003). In some systems, the legislature can directly remove a justice (or choose not to retain him/her).

OBSERVATIONS

The following discussion summarizes our findings during a series of elite interviews with state supreme court justices and state legislators. The interviews were conducted in six states with different methods of judicial selection and retention. More information about these interviews and the techniques employed in the data collection can be found in the Appendix. For now, it is important to note that every effort was made to select states that were most similar across important state characteristics. The primary difference in the states chosen was the method of judicial selection and retention.

Overall, the observations we make from the interviews suggest that legislative–judicial relations are seemingly linked to judicial selection and retention methods. At the very least, there is some important variation that warrants further study. For example, we found variation in elite responses across the six states, which vary in judicial selection method. Of course responses to some questions varied more than others. We begin with some observations about legislators' perceptions of the state supreme court's role in policy making. Here each interviewee was asked

if he/she thought his/her state supreme court played an active role in the policy-making process and if the active policy role was appropriate. Members on the state's supreme court were also asked if they believed their state supreme court's role in policy making was appropriate. Figure 8.2 presents responses from the state legislators and state supreme court justices.

The interviewees' perceptions of the state supreme court's policy-making role are displayed across the six states representing six different methods of judicial selection and retention. Across the board, the figure shows that the majority of state supreme court justices said it is *not inappropriate* for them to make policy or for the court of last resort to assume a policy-making role. Rather, most of the justices interviewed thought it was the court's responsibility to engage in the policy-making process. Some justices went so far as to describe the court's role in policy making as a duty that is *necessary* to keep check on legislative policy. Other justices explained that courts must be active participants in the policy-making process to protect minority rights. One justice commented, "We certainly can't expect the legislature to protect the minority."

Although most justices saw policy making as an appropriate and necessary role for state supreme courts, it is interesting to note that where justices are citizen-elected and thereby held accountable to the public, many more justices viewed policy making as inappropriate compared with justices retained by the legislative or executive branch. For example, in nonpartisan retention election states, four of the nine justices interviewed perceived an active role by the state supreme court as inappropriate. In partisan retention election, merit states, and states with life tenure, three of nine, three of seven, and three of seven justices interviewed in each state, respectively, perceived the states supreme court as an inappropriate player in the policy-making process.

Presumably, justices on these courts view the judiciary as another elected policy-making institution that is responsible to public needs. When elected, despite reservations, justices must respond to public needs and consequently engage in policy making to keep the seat on the bench. Responsiveness to the public is a necessity, but also a way in which courts seemingly create conflict with legislators and some segments of society.

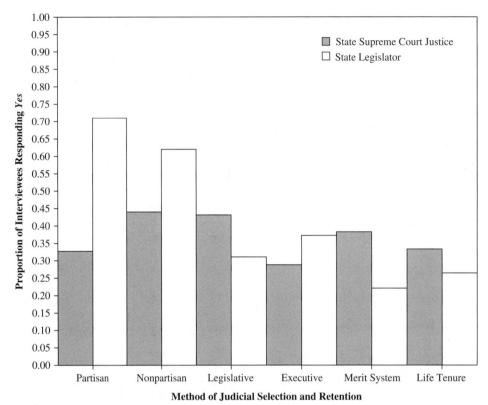

Figure 8.2 Does Your State Supreme Court Play an Inappropriate Role in Policy-making Process?

This conflict subsequently presents a double-edged sword. Perhaps it is these justices, those who are most overtly similar to the other democratic branches via the elected nature of their position, who have the most problems reconciling judicial policy making.

Turning to legislators' perceptions about the state supreme court's policy-making role, a majority of legislators viewed popularly elected justices as inappropriate policy makers. Specifically, thirty-five of the forty-nine legislators complained of an active court in the state where justices were selected in partisan elections. These legislators expressed discontent with members of their state supreme courts and specifically referred to their court as "out of line" and "over-stepping policy boundaries." Some legislators in various leadership positions commented that the state supreme court made more policy than the legislature. They referred to justices as "politicians legislating to

save their seats." Such behavior was viewed as "an outrageous abuse of power and a blatant violation of the separation of powers." However, legislators' perceptions of justices were somewhat different when the members of the state's high court were retained by the legislature. Similarly the role of the state supreme court in the policy-making process was viewed differently in one form of the merit-selection system and in the state where justices served for life.

Specifically, we found that when the legislative branch was responsible for judicial selection and retention, only fifteen of forty-eight legislators interviewed, about 30 percent, thought policy making by state supreme court justices was inappropriate. This pattern suggests that an overwhelming majority of legislators viewed justices as "some of their own" and thus deemed policy making by this court as permissible. Across the other three methods of selection and

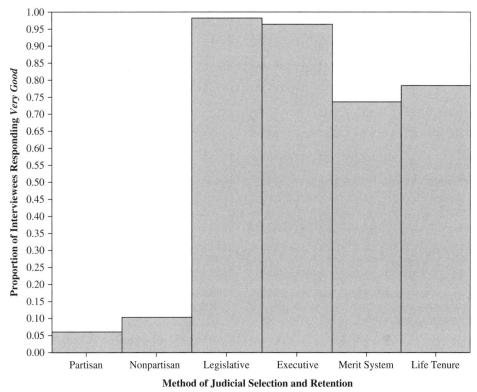

Figure 8.3 Would You (i.e., State Legislator) Describe Relations with the State Supreme Court as Very Good?

retention (i.e., merit selection and retention, guber-natorial appointment, and life appointment) a little less than two-thirds of the legislators interviewed expressed any discontent with policy roles by justices. In these states, legislators did not feel that policy making by the justices on their state supreme courts was improper. In fact, one leader in the legislature commented, "yes we have an activist court and yes I am very thankful for that." Only eleven of fifty-one legislators in the merit-selection state viewed state supreme court justices as inappropriate policy makers. Similarly, eleven of forty-two legislators found the state supreme court's policy role inappropriate in the state where justices served for life.

Perceptions about the proper role of courts in the policy arena are seemingly different across method of selection and retention; yet overall, legislators view justices as appropriate players in the policy game and justices view themselves as integral to the process.

We now turn to the responses from legislators about legislative–judicial relations. Here we asked how the legislator would describe relations with the state supreme court. We concluded this question with "If you were to categorize your perception of relations, would you say they were very good, very poor, or one of growing tension?" We present summary responses in Figures 8.3, 8.4, and 8.5. We turn first to those who described relations with the state supreme court as very good.

One immediate observation is that perceptions of relations with the state supreme court are very good when the legislative or executive branch is respon-sible for judicial selection and retention. Forty-six of forty-eight legislators viewed relations with the state supreme court as very good in the state in which jus-tices are retained by the legislative branch. Similarly, more than half of the legislators interviewed in the gubernatorial retention state perceived relations with

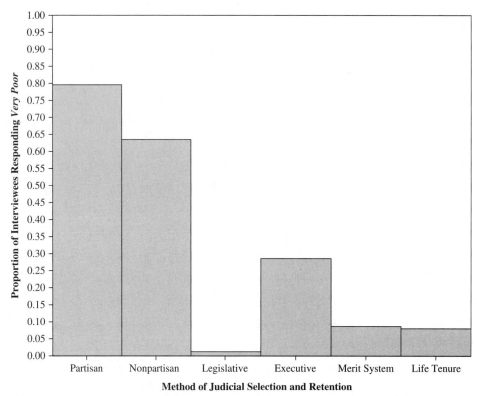

Figure 8.4 Would You (i.e., State Legislator) Describe Relations with the State Supreme Court as Very Poor?

the state supreme court as very good. Conversely, only three of the forty-nine legislators interviewed in the partisan election state described relations with the court as very good. In the nonpartisan election retention state, only four of the thirty-nine legislators interviewed perceived good relations with the court. The responses also show that most legislators perceive relations with the state supreme court as very good in the state in which justices are appointed for life and in the state where justices serve in a merit-selection system. Accordingly, Figure 8.4 shows that relations with the state supreme court were perceived predominantly as very poor in states with either partisan or nonpartisan elections. Few legislators in the other selection and retention systems viewed relations with the state supreme court as very poor.

Interestingly, Figure 8.5 shows that about one-quarter of legislators interviewed perceived growing tensions between the legislature and state supreme

court where justices are selected and retained in nonpartisan elections, by the hand of the governor, and where justices enjoy life tenure. This could be indicative of the trend for state supreme courts to be involved players in salient political issues of the day, including those issues discussed earlier such as gay marriage and education finance systems.

A certain amount of constitutional conflict and tension is inherent in our system of government; however, the extent to which the conflict is borne from retaliatory motives has important consequences for governmental relations, policy outcomes, and court decisions. If legislators perceive judicial behavior as deliberate attempts to punish the legislative branch for its policy decisions and vice versa, actors in both branches might engage in strategic behavior. Moreover, relations between the branches might suffer. We thus turn our attention to our last question: Do perceptions of retaliatory behavior exist and do

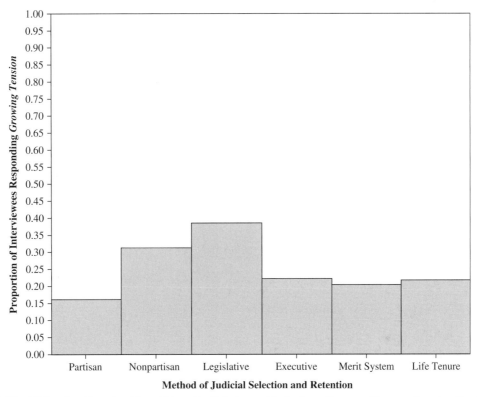

Figure 8.5 Would You (i.e., State Legislator) Describe Relations with the State Supreme Court as Growing Tension?

they vary in these six states? For example, we asked legislators if they perceived that state supreme court decisions were deliberate attempts to penalize the legislature for its behavior. Similarly, we asked the justices if they viewed legislative behavior as deliberate action to punish members on the court for judicial decisions. Figure 8.6 suggests that judicial perceptions of legislative retaliatory behavior are pervasive in all six states. Across the different methods of selection in these states, over 50 percent of the state supreme court justices and legislators said a "tit-for-tat" game ensues between the court and the legislature. Perceptions of retaliatory behavior were most prevalent in systems in which justices confront the electorate. Forty-seven of the forty-nine legislators interviewed in the state in which justices are retained in partisan elections perceived the actions of the state supreme court as retaliatory. In the state where justices were selected and retained in nonpartisan elections, thirty-four of

the thirty-nine legislators interviewed described state supreme court behavior as retaliatory.

Figure 8.7 also indicates that state supreme court justices, across all methods of selection/retention, believed legislators deliberately rewrote policy or took other actions to penalize justices for objectionable decisions. These perceptions were strongest in states where justices are elected. The merit-selection system also exhibited an overwhelming number of justices who perceived legislator behavior as retaliatory. Here six of the eight justices believed, for example, that legislators reduced the court's budget or engaged in various campaign tactics to punish them for objectionable decisions. Overall, perceptions of retaliatory behavior are highest when justices of the state's high court are elected. Conversely, very few legislators and justices view the actions of each other as retaliatory in the states in which justices are selected and retained by the legislative or executive branch.

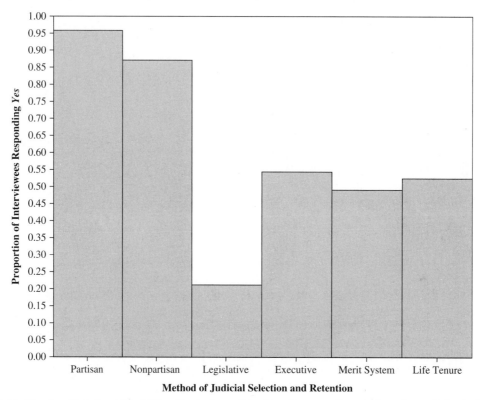

Figure 8.6 Do You (i.e., State Legislator) View the Actions of the State Supreme Court as Retaliatory Behavior?

Combined, the responses from these interviews provide support for the notion that members of the legislature and court make decisions or take actions that are meant to send a message to the other branch. Retribution by legislators and justices is not only a perception held by each branch about the other (especially the court), but a reality that is practiced. Clearly, political motivations for strategic behavior exist.

One interesting finding from the interviews is that although many of the interviewees admitted to engaging in retaliatory behavior, and most viewed the other branches as retaliatory, there were some who thought such behavior was professional. For example, if the legislative branch used its power to send a message to the court for an objectionable decision, there were some justices who thought this was simply a necessary function in systems of checks and balances. This suggests that, for some policy makers—both legislative

and judicial alike—the struggle as policy is made is simply indicative of how the game is played. In short, conflict is a part of constitutional design.

CONCLUSIONS

There are two primary observations from this endeavor that deserve emphasis. First, our interviews suggest that perceptions differ across judicial method of selection and retention. Second, and most important, although most legislators perceive the court as an appropriate actor in the policy-making process, they perceive judicial behavior as retaliatory. Moreover legislators admittedly engage in such behavior as well. A shared belief is that the other branch will respond to an objectionable decision with intent to undermine or overturn the decision. The tit-for-tat game played by these two branches of government seems to set the

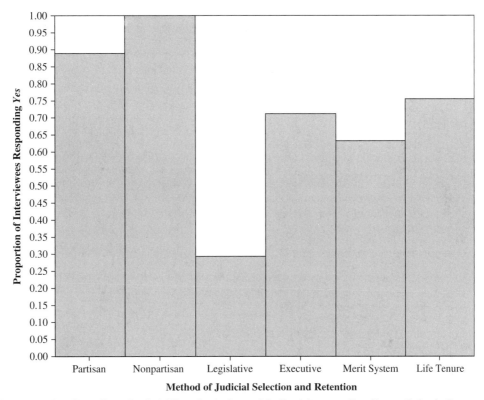

Figure 8.7 Do You (i.e., State Court Justice) View the Actions of the Legislature as Retaliatory Behavior?

stage for strategic behavior by legislators and justices. Strong perceptions about the existence of retaliatory behavior are especially significant given the amount of scholarly attention given to the question of whether justices vote strategically in response to anticipated legislative reaction (see, e.g., Segal 1997; Baum 1997; Epstein and Knight 1998, 2000). A common criticism of scholarly works about strategic behavior is that there are few quantifiable instances when legislatures penalize judges (see, e.g., Baum 1997, 1999). Much of what we know about strategic interplay between justices and legislatures, for example, is inferred from the existence of predictable shifts in behavior when we evaluate the votes of justices using statistical modeling (see, e.g., Spiller and Gely 1992; but see Segal 1997). One can easily recognize that as a judge's and legislator's perception of a threat becomes greater, efforts to quantify such threats become more difficult. As a result, the ability to make such inferences from statistical analysis is limited. We offer direct evidence from legislators and justices in six states that strategic behavior is expected.

Notes

1. State supreme courts and state courts of last resort are used interchangeably throughout this chapter.

2. The Florida Supreme Court's involvement in the 2000 presidential election also sparked state governmental tensions. According to a recent editorial in the *St. Petersburg Times*, the Florida

high court is under attack again with continuous proposals to strip power away from the court and give it to the state legislature (*St. Petersburg Times* 2004).

3. Most research describes five formal judicial selection and retention systems; however, in this chapter we treat systems in which state supreme court justices serve for life as a distinct method of selection and retention because the accountability mechanism is fundamentally different.

4. For questions two and three, we changed the wording according to which branch the interviewee belonged. For example, when we asked justices question two, the question posed was, "how would you describe the relationship between the court and the legislature?"

5. The "revolving door practice" of sitting legislators becoming state supreme court justices, however, has been recently changed in one state with the passage of a law that prohibits current members of the legislature from running for state supreme court. The law requires a two-year wait period before former legislators can run for a seat on the state supreme court.

6. In theory, these elections are meant to be competitive. See McLeod this volume, chapter 2.

7. Our purpose is not to weigh-in on the normative debate over method of judicial selection and retention, but rather to assess if perceptions about legislative–judicial relations vary across systems.

8. In every question, attention was directed to the state's court of last resort rather than the state's judicial branch of government.

APPENDIX

ELITE INTERVIEWS AND DATA COLLECTION

Data for this chapter were collected from personal interviews conducted in six states with different methods of judicial selection and retention. Elite interviews provide valuable information, especially because we can directly assess how legislators perceive interactions with the state supreme court, the extent to which they get along, as well as their motivations.

Setting Up Interviews

Letters requesting a thirty-minute person-to-person interview were sent to each member of the state legislature and state supreme court. Follow-up email messages and phone calls also were made to secure as many interviews as possible. Special efforts were made to get interviews with state legislators on important committees, such as the Judiciary Committee, the Appropriations Committee, and the Rules Committee. These members, for example, were phoned more frequently than other members and were pursued more aggressively at the state capitals. The rationale for these efforts was that members on these committees have more interactions with the state supreme court.

Confidentiality

The interviewer guaranteed our participants confidentiality so we are unable to reveal the names of the states in which interviews were conducted.

Most Similar Research Design

We employed most similar research design in choosing the six states. Thus, we made every effort to select states most similar across important state characteristics with the primary difference being method of judicial selection and retention. All interviews were conducted by

Table 8.1 State Profiles Across Six Methods of Judicial Selection and Retention

State Characteristics	State A: Partisan	State B: Nonpartisan	State C: Legislative Election	State D: Gubernatorial Appointment	State E: Merit Selection	State F: Life Tenure
Economic outlook	Strong	Strong	Strong	Strong	Strong	Strong
Population diversity	Diverse	Diverse	Diverse	Diverse	Diverse	Diverse
Population size	Large	Large	Medium	Medium	Large	Medium
Partisan makeup of government	Divided	Divided	Divided	Divided	Divided	Divided
Partisan makeup of SSC	Divided	Divided	Divided	Divided	Divided	Divided
Degree of legislative professionalism	High	High	High	High	High	High
Presence of advisory opinion	Yes	Yes	Yes	Yes	Yes	Yes
Presence of term limits	Yes	Yes	No	Yes	Yes	Yes
Presence of ballot initiative	Yes	Yes	Yes	Yes	Yes	No
Formalized communication between SSC and government	Yes	Yes	Yes	Yes	Yes	Yes
Chief justice controls opinion assignment	Yes	Yes	Yes	Yes	No	Yes
Top issue confronting government according to polls	Education	Education	Education	Education	Education	Education
States with selection/retention system	AL, IL, LA, PA, TX, WV	AR, GA, ID, KY, MI,[a] MN, MS, MT, NV, NC, ND, OH, OR, WA, WI	SC, VA	ME, NJ	CA,[b] K, AZ, CO, CT,[c] DE, FL, HI,[c] IN, IA, KS, MD, MO, NE, NM, NY,[c] OK, SD, TN, UT, VT,[d] WY	MA,[d] NH,[d] RI

Note. SSC = state supreme court.

[a]Both Michigan and Ohio justices are nominated at *partisan* primaries, but elected in *nonpartisan* elections.

[b]California State Supreme Court justices are subject to evaluation by the *State Bar of California's Commission on Judicial Nominees,* although the governor is not bound to this evaluation. Justices are then retained by unopposed elections.

[c]In these states, justices are chosen by Judicial Selection Commission and subject to reappointment by same commission, or legislative/ gubernatorial approval. In all other states with merit selection system, justices are retained in general elections.

[d]To age 70.

the same researcher. In addition, the interviewer went to great lengths to equalize the number of legislators interviewed from both political parties. Table 8.1 illustrates the similarities and differences, across these six states.

Generalizability

Interviews were conducted with 314 state level politicians in the same year across six methods of judicial selection and retention (i.e., six American states). Even though only six states are represented, we believe our observations can be generalized to other states.

A comparison of interviews across only six states also increases the validity of our data as additional states would have increased the duration of time over which the interviews could be conducted. A shorter time frame reduced the validity threats of time and history (for a discussion on single state studies, see, e.g., Nicholson-Crotty and Meier 2002).

Interview Questions

In every state, interviews were conducted with the leadership of the majority and minority party in both

Table 8.2 Number of Persons Interviewed Across Six States by Selection Method

Branch of Government	State A: Partisan	State B: Nonpartisan	State C: Legislative Election	State D: Gubernatorial Appointment	State E: Merit Selection	State F: Life Tenure	Totals
State supreme court	9 (100%)	9 (100%)	5 (100%)	7 (100%)	7 (100%)	7 (100%)	44 (100%)
Legislature	49 (27%)	39 (27%)	48 (28%)	41 (34%)	51 (43%)	42 (21%)	270 (29%)
Totals	58	48	53	48	59	49	314

Note. Interviews were conducted in eleven states total; however, access was limited in some states to court members and/or legislature. This did not allow for comparable comparisons. As a result, we include only interviews from six states to represent six common types of selection and retention methods. Percentage figure below number indicates percentage of total members interviewed.

legislative chambers. Also each of the six chief justices on the state's court of last resort was interviewed and with a few exceptions all associate justices. During the interviews, the researcher asked about the policy-making role of the state supreme court, retaliatory mechanisms employed to send signals to one another, and the overall nature of relations. More specifically, a series of questions was asked to ascertain whether legislators believed his/her state supreme court had overstepped its boundaries and whether his/her court played an appropriate or inappropriate role in the policy-making process. The interviewer also asked several questions to ascertain the extent to which legislators perceived the actions of the court as retaliatory in response to objectionable decisions. In every question, attention was directed to the state's court of last resort rather than the state's judicial branch of government. In addition, each legislator was asked to describe the relationship with the court. Because we promised confidentiality, and therefore did not record interviews, the interviewer was able to elicit very candid answers. We made every attempt to interview the same number of legislators across states. Table 8.2 provides the number of interviews conducted per state.

9

APPELLATE WORKHORSES OF THE FEDERAL JUDICIARY

The U.S. Courts of Appeals

Wendy L. Martinek

Judicial scholars have paid far less attention to the U.S. Courts of Appeals than they have to the U.S. Supreme Court. Because the U.S. Supreme Court hears so few cases each year, the second level courts in the federal court system, the U.S. Courts of Appeals (often known as the U.S. Circuit Courts), are the key courts in deciding appeals based on federal law. These courts correct errors made at the U.S. District Courts as well as make policy in many areas of federal law. Usually these appellate courts hear cases in randomly chosen three-judge panels, although the loser may request that the entire court rehear the case in an *en banc* proceeding. On the U.S. Supreme Court, all nine justices usually hear every case, making the Supreme Court easier to study in many ways. Decisions from the U.S. Courts of Appeals often make the news, such as the ones concerning the constitutionality of affirmative action programs or the ones that involve the question of whether school children can be required to say the Pledge of Allegiance when it includes the words "under God."

The methods judicial scholars use to study the behavior and decisions of the U.S. Supreme Court may or may not apply to the randomly chosen three-judge panels used in the U.S. Courts of Appeals. Small group theory would apply to the study of both courts. Also, the fact that the U.S. Supreme Court may choose to review the decisions of the U.S. Courts of Appeals also means that scholars may need to use different approaches such as the principal-agent theory to understand more fully the behavior and decisions of these federal appellate courts. Thus the U.S. Courts of Appeals are key political and legal actors in our federal court system.

An unhappy litigant may proclaim, "I'm going to take my case all the way to the Supreme Court!" The truth of the matter is that the U.S. Supreme Court hears but a few cases each year, cases chosen through the virtually unfettered discretion of the Court (Cameron, Segal, and Songer 2000; Pacelle 1995; Perry 1991). Instead, the vast majority of federal appeals are disposed of instead in the U.S. Courts of Appeals, the major intermediate appellate courts in the federal judiciary, which occupy a position in the federal judiciary hierarchy just below the U.S. Supreme Court and just above the U.S. District Courts. These courts are sometimes known as the U.S. Circuit Courts, as I discuss in more detail later. They have been dubbed "the vital center of the federal judicial system" by Chief Judge J. Edward Lumbard (1968, 29). Organized geographically, these courts are nonetheless intended to partake of and contribute to a coherent federal jurisprudence (Harrington and Ward 1995). The Courts of Appeals are "the de facto (if not the de jure) court of last resort in the overwhelming majority of [federal] appeals" (Hettinger, Lindquist, and Martinek 2006, 13). As a consequence, although it may not have the same rhetorical punch, a more realistic proclamation by a litigant dissatisfied with the outcome of a federal case would be: "I'm going to take my case all the way to the U.S. Courts of Appeals!"

These courts are clearly important to individual appellants and appellees because they render what are usually definitive final decisions affecting those litigants. In doing so, the U.S. Courts of Appeals also serve an important error correction function, a function central to any appellate system (Shavell 1995). However, they are arguably even more important because of the policy-making functions they perform in the larger legal and political systems. In resolving appeals that come before them, the U.S. Courts of Appeals make law. They make law primarily in the form of the opinions they render.[1] Those opinions articulate legal rules that, unless and until superseded by a ruling from the U.S. Supreme Court, are binding under the doctrine of *stare decisis* on the lower federal courts covered by the circuit issuing the ruling. *Stare decisis* is the principle that judges should abide by and apply past rulings to contemporary cases. Furthermore, the courts' decisions are often persuasive for other federal courts outside the circuit's geographic boundaries (Klein 2002).

Notwithstanding the important functions they perform, both in terms of correcting federal district court errors and making policy, "the courts of appeals exist at the very edge of the average American's consciousness if at all" (Songer, Sheehan, and Haire 2000, xiii). To be sure, the public has become much more aware of these courts due to the conflictual nature of the contemporary judicial confirmation process for all federal judges (Bell 2002a; Goldman 1997; Scherer 2005). Presidents, senators, and legal observers have participated in spirited and very public debate, each side charging the other variously with obstructionism,

pandering, deliberate ignorance, and various other nefarious behaviors (see Bell this volume, chapter 3). However, that public awareness is largely limited to the context of confirmation politics. The public knows these courts must be important because of the pitched battles that attend efforts to appoint individuals to them. It is doubtful the public understands what exactly it is they do any more than when J. Woodford Howard, Jr., wrote: "Beyond general impressions…knowledge of the functions and operations of circuit courts is largely intuitive and fragmentary" (Howard 1981, xvii).

Key to understanding these important appellate courts is appreciating their institutional structure, including the formal decision-making mechanisms by which they render decisions, especially the panel decision-making process and the en banc procedure that, though rarely employed, is nonetheless consequential. Likewise important is considering the nature of the cases they handle and the ways the courts of appeals have attempted to deal with their rapidly increasing workload. With an understanding of their organization, procedural rules, and workload in hand, we can then also assess theories of judicial decision making as they apply to the U.S. Courts of Appeals.

ORIGINS, ORGANIZATION, AND OPERATION

The U.S. Supreme Court, the only court whose existence is mandated in the Constitution,[2] has what amounts to an entirely discretionary docket (Pacelle 1995). In other words, the U.S. Supreme Court decides which cases to hear and it can refuse almost any case. In exercising its discretion, the U.S. Supreme Court has heard fewer than a hundred cases per term over the past decade (Epstein et al. 2003, Table 2–8). The U.S. Courts of Appeals, in contrast, have a mandatory docket, which means that they cannot refuse a request for them to hear an appeal. As a consequence, the U.S. Courts of Appeals hear a volume of cases that positively dwarfs that of the U.S. Supreme Court. For example, in the fiscal year ending September 1997, the U.S. Courts of Appeals decided over 50,000 appeals (Administrative Office of the United States Courts 1997, Table B). Seven years later, they decided over

56,000 appeals (Administrative Office of the United States Courts 2004, Table B). The workload of the courts of appeals reflects their role in providing the opportunity generally accorded each litigant for a review of an adverse decision (that is, each litigant has the right of appeal). Indeed, the inability of the U.S. Supreme Court to provide this opportunity effectively and expeditiously is what led to the establishment of the U.S. Courts of Appeals by the Judiciary Act of 1891, commonly known as the Evarts Act (Howard 1981, 3–6). The common law principle that every litigant should have the opportunity for at least one review means that many of the cases that come before the U.S. Courts of Appeals, although no doubt terribly important to the litigants in the case, are legally frivolous in the sense of raising no important issues of law, a marked difference from the situation at the U.S. Supreme Court.

When the U.S. Courts of Appeals were created in 1891 in their current institutional structure, the U.S. Circuit Courts of Appeals were already in existence. The U.S. Circuit Courts were originally composed of a combination of district court judges and U.S. Supreme Court justices sitting together. These courts originally also had both trial and (limited) appellate responsibilities. Later the composition of the U.S. Circuit Courts became primarily district court judges and specially appointed circuit court judges. Workload pressures, stemming from expansions in the jurisdiction of the federal courts, resulted in a situation in which the circuit courts of appeals could not adequately alleviate the U.S. Supreme Court's appellate burden. Hence, Congress created the U.S. Courts of Appeals with the principal responsibility for providing appellate review in the federal judicial system. The old circuit courts were ultimately abolished in 1911, although the name continues as a colloquial term for the modern U.S. Courts of Appeals.

There are eleven numbered courts of appeals plus the U.S. Court of Appeals for the District of Columbia. Each of these courts wields jurisdiction over a specified geographic area.[3] The geographic jurisdiction of the U.S. Court of Appeals for the District of Columbia is obviously the District of Columbia. Each of the other eleven circuits covers anywhere from three (the Second, Fifth, Seventh, and Eleventh) to nine (the Ninth) states. The Court of Appeals for the Ninth Circuit also includes

Guam and the Northern Mariana Islands. The Court of Appeals for the First Circuit includes Puerto Rico in addition to four states while the Court of Appeals for the Third Circuit includes the U.S. Virgin Islands in addition to three states. Each circuit exercises appellate jurisdiction over the federal district courts within its boundaries. The courts of appeals also have substantial responsibilities for the review of many contested administrative agency decisions.[4]

The number of court of appeals judges varies considerably by circuit and is statutorily determined by Congress. For example, while in 2006 the Court of Appeals for the First Circuit had 6 judges, the Court of Appeals for the Ninth Circuit had 28 judges. Collectively, there were 167 authorized judgeships for the courts of appeals as of 2006. As stipulated in the Constitution, individuals are nominated for a position on the appeals court bench by the president and must be confirmed by a majority vote in the Senate. Because these judges serve on Article III courts (that is, courts created by Congress under its authority under Article III),[5] they serve during good behavior, which essentially means they enjoy life tenure.

STAFFING THE COURTS OF APPEALS

For much of the nation's history, there was little public attention paid to the process of staffing the lower federal court bench (Bell 2002a; Goldman 1997). Presidents were accorded virtually complete deference by senators.[6] This norm of deference, however, began to decay in the late 1970s and early 1980s. Though scholars differ a bit as to the original cause of this change, there is general agreement that it was in response to changes in presidential strategies regarding the lower federal judiciary. President Nixon campaigned, in part, on a promise to appoint law-and-order judges (Hartley and Holmes 1997). President Carter took proactive steps to diversify the federal bench in terms of gender and race (Goldman 1997). President Reagan pledged to select judges for the appeals and district courts who reflected a conservative political philosophy (Scherer 2005). Collectively, as presidents became more publicly self-conscious about their approach to selecting individuals to nominate for the federal bench, senators began scrutinizing those nominees in a way they simply had not done before.

The contemporary nomination and confirmation process is characterized by rampant rancor and contention. Though changes in the rate at which presidential nominations are confirmed have remained relatively minor, there have been significant changes in the process (Citizens for Independent Courts 2000). In particular, the length of time presidents take to nominate individuals once vacancies arise and the length of time the Senate takes to process those nominations once they are made have skyrocketed (Bell 2002a; Martinek, Kemper, and Van Winkle 2002). The increased use of the "blue slip" procedure, the process by which senators make known their objection to permitting a nomination to go forward, and more extensive interest group involvement (Bell 2002a; Scherer 2005), especially, have made the senatorial confirmation process long, drawn out, and protracted.[7] The blue slip procedure is of special interest with regard to confirmation delay because it has become, over time, comparable to a senatorial veto of presidential nominations. The blue slip refers to the color of the paper sent to home-state senators by the chair of the Senate Judiciary Committee to indicate their support of or opposition to the president's nominee. In practice, the failure to return the blue slip stops the nomination from going forward. One of the consequences of increased delay in the confirmation process has been vacancies on the U.S. Courts of Appeals (as well as the U.S. District Courts) that go unfilled for lengthy periods of time, sometimes years.

Unlike at the U.S. Supreme Court, where cases are typically decided by the entire membership of the Court, at the U.S. Courts of Appeals most decisions are the product of three-judge panels (Howard 1981, 188–92; Songer et al. 2000, 8). Panel membership rotates among the judges of a circuit. Panels also may, and often do, include visiting judges (as well as retired judges serving on senior status). Visiting judges include active or senior judges from other circuits and district court judges sitting by designation. The chief judge of a circuit has the discretion to designate a district court judge from within the circuit to serve temporarily in an appellate capacity.[8] The practice of using designated district court judges serves two purposes. First, it facilitates the socialization of newly appointed district court judges into the circuit (Wasby 1980). Second, it aids the circuit in processing its workload (Saphire and Solimine 1995). The chief judge can also request the assistance of judges from other circuits.

Numerous close observers of the legal process have been concerned about the increased use of designated district court judges. The work of a district court judge is quite different from that of a circuit court judge. Carrington (1969), and more recently Saphire and Solimine (1995), suggested that those differences mean that the use of designated district court judges has consequences for the quality of the appellate review process. Others have focused on the potential for designated district court judges to compromise the consistency of the law (Green and Atkins 1978). Still others have questioned whether the use of designated district court judges might degrade the legitimacy of the courts of appeals (Alexander 1965). Recent empirical scholarship does support the notion that designated district court judges behave differently on the courts of appeals in that they are less likely to author majority opinions (Brudney and Ditslear 2001), and they are less likely to write separate opinions (Hettinger et al. 2006). Moreover, judges themselves have expressed some misgivings about this practice:

> We get some visiting judges who are absolutely first-class troops, and they pull their weight and it is no problem. If you pull off a sitting district judge, an active district judge with a busy calendar, and put them on a panel with us, they get no credit for sitting with us. So this kind of thing is really kind of a distraction to them. They have a helluva time getting their share of the work done, so that slows us down some. I never feel that we are really first on their plate (Cohen 2002, 197).

Senior judges, too, play a prominent role in decision making on the U.S. Courts of Appeals. Judges who meet certain requirements as to length of service and age have the option of taking senior status.[9] Such judges have come to be seen as playing an essential role in processing the workload of the circuits (Watson 1989; Van Duch 1996). When a judge takes senior status, his position on the bench officially becomes vacant, giving the president the opportunity to nominate another individual to fill that seat. However, a senior judge continues to draw his full salary and participate in cases, albeit at a much reduced workload. Senior judges have

Table 9.1 Case Participations in Cases Disposed of On the Merits, Fiscal Years 1996–2003

Fiscal Year	Percentage of Resident Senior Circuit Judges	Percentage of Visiting Judges	Percentage of Senior and Visiting Judges
1996	15.4	6.2	21.5
1997	16.2	6.7	22.8
1998	14.5	6.5	21.0
1999	17.1	6.0	23.1
2000	15.2	5.8	21.0
2001	16.5	6.4	22.9
2002	16.4	5.7	22.0
2003	17.0	5.1	22.0

Note. From Administrative Office of the United States Courts, Judicial Business of the U.S. Courts, various years, Table S-2. A case participation refers to the participation of a judge in a given case. Typically a three-judge panel decision yields three case participants.

Table 9.2 Number of Case Participations by Visiting Judges in Cases Disposed of On the Merits, Fiscal Years 1996 to 2003

Fiscal Year	Active Appeals Court Judges	Senior Appeals Court Judges	Designated District Court Judges
1996	182 (9 judges)	1,273 (75 judges)	3,659 (323 judges)
1997	241 (11 judges)	1,433 (80 judges)	3,873 (303 judges)
1998	218 (16 judges)	1,343 (73 judges)	3,881 (319 judges)
1999	162 (11 judges)	1,286 (74 judges)	3,844 (295 judges)
2000	328 (15 judges)	1,191 (79 judges)	4,065 (301 judges)
2001	178 (12 judges)	1,359 (92 judges)	4,232 (306 judges)
2002	201 (13 judges)	1,099 (82 judges)	3,678 (268 judges)
2003	116 (14 judges)	1,041 (78 judges)	3,284 (250 judges)

Note. From Administrative Office of the United States Courts, Judicial Business of the U.S. Courts, various years, Table V-2. A case participation refers to the participation of a judge in a given case. Typically a three-judge panel decision yields three case participants.

been characterized as "very experienced members of the court...[who with]...their accumulated insight and wisdom...are a valuable national resource" (Feinberg 1990, 412). As with the use of designated district court judges, however, some have expressed misgivings regarding the extensive use of senior judges on court of appeals panels. They may not be representative of the regularly serving judges on the circuit in terms of their outlook on the contemporary meaning of the law (Carrington 1969). Furthermore, they may be too sensitive to their desire to leave a judicial legacy and, hence, seek to distinguish themselves through writing superfluous separate opinions.

Although the majority of case participations on the courts of appeals panels[10] are by the regularly sitting, active duty appeals court judges in a circuit, as reported in Table 9.1, between one in six and one in seven case participations has been by judges on senior status in recent years, with another 5 or 6 percent being by visitors (circuit or district court judges) from outside the circuit. Collectively, slightly more than one of every five case participations on courts of appeals panels has been by a judge other than a regularly sitting, active duty appeals court judge in the past decade. In absolute terms, district court judges serving by designation provide the greatest volume of service, with anywhere from 250 to 323 designated district court judges serving in any given year, providing anywhere from 3,284 to 4,232 case participations, in the past decade (see Table 9.2).

Although the chief judge of each circuit is responsible for determining the composition of panels, in practice panels are determined on a random basis by the circuit clerk (Hettinger, Lindquist, and Martinek 2003a; Wasby 2003a).[11] Given the variation in the number of judges per circuit, coupled with the expansive geographic coverage of most circuits, many judges have limited interaction with some of their circuit colleagues, typically only when they serve together on a three-judge panel (Cohen 2002, 153–60). Panel-based decision making serves the important institutional objective of processing large numbers of appeals while simultaneously providing the collective review that is thought to enhance the quality of the appellate process. Notwithstanding the fact that panel decisions are, by definition, the product of the collective deliberations of less than the entire membership of a circuit, they are considered the decision of the circuit unless they are reviewed by the circuit en banc.

WHEN THE U.S. COURTS OF APPEALS HEAR CASES EN BANC

En banc proceedings involve review of a panel decision by the full set of appeals court judges in a circuit or, in the case of the extremely large Court of Appeals for the Ninth Circuit, fifteen judges (including the chief judge;

Hellman 2000; Solimine 2006; Wasby 2002). Such proceedings are quite rare, historically representing less than 1 percent of courts of appeals cases (George 1999; Solimine 1988; see Table 9.3.) Although there is variation in the rate of en banc proceedings across circuits, over the 2000–2004 fiscal year period the percentage of case dispositions via en banc proceedings never exceeded one half of one percent of the total number of dispositions (see Table 9.4). This is consistent with the Federal Rules of Appellate Procedure as well as the internal operating procedures adopted by

Table 9.3 En Banc Proceedings, Fiscal Years 1997 to 2005

Fiscal Year	Number	Percentage of Dispositions
1997	80	0.31
1998	83	0.33
1999	94	0.35
2000	73	0.27
2001	81	0.28
2002	77	0.28
2003	68	0.25
2004	59	0.22
2005	56	0.19

Note. Calculated from Administrative Office of the United States Courts, Judicial Business of the U.S. Courts, various years, Table S-1.

Table 9.4 En Banc Proceedings by Circuit, Fiscal Years 2000 to 2004

Circuit	Number	Percentage of Dispositions
1st	10	0.26
2nd	5	0.05
3rd	17	0.17
4th	24	0.19
5th	45	0.24
6th	31	0.24
7th	14	0.19
8th	38	0.39
9th	93	0.34
10th	26	0.36
11th	29	0.17
D.C.	9	0.34

Note. Calculated from Administrative Office of the United States Courts, Judicial Business of the U.S. Courts, various years, Table S-1.

the various circuits, both of which discourage en banc review in the absence of exceptional circumstances. En banc review typically can only occur when a losing litigant is unsuccessful in convincing the original panel to rehear the case and a member of the original panel supports rehearing by the entire circuit. A majority of the active judges in the circuit must vote to grant the en banc rehearing (McFeeley 1987).

Recent analysis of the en banc procedure by Giles and colleagues (Giles, Walker, and Zorn 2006) suggests that the decision to grant en banc review is a multistage process driven, first, by the goals of litigants and, subsequently, by the goals of the judges. In particular, Giles, Walker, and Zorn found that litigants—or, more precisely, litigants' attorneys—factor in the likelihood of ultimately prevailing if an en banc hearing is granted as well as how high the stakes are for the litigant in deciding whether to seek en banc review at all. The court of appeals judges who are deciding whether to grant en banc review, on the other hand, focus on uncertainty or inconsistency in the law (e.g., circuit conflict, disagreement between the district court and appellate court judges).

The U.S. Courts of Appeals were born of the necessity to ameliorate the intense appellate workload pressures faced by the U.S. Supreme Court. Organized on a geographic basis, judges on the courts of appeals are nonetheless expected to behave as members of the federal judiciary and are active participants in making national law. As presidents and senators have become more cognizant of the important policy-making role these courts perform, the process of staffing the U.S. Courts of Appeals bench has become ever more conflictual. This has led to lengthy vacancies on the courts

of appeals, with a resulting increase in the use of senior and visiting judges. With the aid of these judges, the courts of appeals process a high volume of cases that cover a broad array of subjects.

THE WORK OF THE U.S. COURTS OF APPEALS

Most of the cases dealt with by the U.S. Courts of Appeals involve appeals from the federal district courts, with anywhere from 72 to 85 percent of their work since 2000 coming from the major trial courts at the federal level (see Table 9-5). In recent years, however, anywhere from one in five to one in ten cases has come from administrative agencies, including the National Labor Relations Board, the Environmental Protection Agency, and the Immigration and Naturalization Service. The Court of Appeals for the District of Columbia shoulders a disproportionate share of agency appeals, with more than one in three of its cases involving appeal from an agency decision (Administrative Office of the United States Courts 2004, Table B-3). This is a function of its geographic jurisdiction because many federal agencies are located in the District of Columbia.

In terms of the substance of the cases with which the courts deal, approximately one-third has dealt with criminal issues in recent years. This represents a marked change in that only one in ten or one in eleven cases involved criminal appeals from 1925 until about 1945 (Songer et al. 2000, Table 3.1). This increase, especially during the 1960s, corresponds with changes in both federal jurisdiction and legal doctrine; in

Table 9.5 Sources of United States Courts of Appeals Caseload, 2000 to 2004

Fiscal Year	U.S. District Courts	Administrative Agencies	Bankruptcy	Original Proceedings
2000	85.0%	5.9%	1.8%	7.3%
2001	82.4%	5.7%	1.7%	10.2%
2002	81.8%	10.1%	1.5%	6.7%
2003	76.2%	16.4%	1.5%	5.9%
2004	72.6%	19.5%	1.4%	6.5%

Note. Calculated from Administrative Office of the United States Courts, Judicial Business of the U.S. Courts, various years, Table B-3. May not sum to 100% due to rounding.

particular, the application of most of the Bill of Rights by the Supreme Court to state action during the Warren Court era. The rate of growth in criminal cases does appear to have stabilized, however (Davis and Songer 1989; Songer et al. 2000). Economic issues (such as contract disputes, debt collection, and economic regulation) remain a staple on the agenda of the courts of appeals, although they constitute a much smaller proportion of the courts' docket in the past few decades than they did in the 1920s and 1930s. Private economic issues (i.e., those not involving the federal government as a litigant) once made up almost half of the courts of appeals' workload. Now they comprise about one-quarter of their workload (Songer et al. 2000, Table 3.1). Public economic interests comprise another quarter

(Songer et al. 2000, Table 3.1). The remaining cases are those dealing with the interpretation of constitutional protections for individual freedoms (e.g., free speech, religious freedom), what are generally termed civil liberties, and those dealing with issues relating to discrimination (e.g., the application of the Equal Protection Clause in the context of affirmative action programs), which are generally termed civil rights.

The most dramatic change in the work of the U.S. Courts of Appeals since their inception has been the burgeoning volume of cases. A recent study documents an almost 50 percent increase in the number of cases filed from fiscal year 1925 (2,525 filings) to fiscal year 1960 (3,765 filings), with an almost nine-fold increase between 1960 and 1985 (33,360 filings; Songer et al.

Table 9.6 United States Courts of Appeals Caseload, 1981 to 2004

Fiscal Year	Number of Filings	Annual Percentage of Change in Filings	Number of Dispositions	Annual Percentage of Change in Dispositions
1981	26,362	—	25,066	—
1982	27,946	6.0	27,984	11.6
1983	29,630	6.0	28,660	2.4
1984	31,490	6.3	31,185	8.8
1985	33,360	5.9	31,387	0.6
1986	34,292	2.8	33,774	7.6
1987	35,176	2.6	34,444	2.0
1988	37,524	6.7	35,888	4.2
1989	39,900	6.3	37,509	4.5
1990	40,858	2.4	38,790	3.4
1991	43,027	5.3	41,640	7.3
1992	47,013	9.3	44,373	6.6
1993	50,224	6.8	47,790	7.7
1994	48,322	−3.8	48,184	0.8
1995	50,072	3.6	49,805	3.4
1996	51,991	3.8	50,413	1.2
1997	52,319	0.6	51,194	1.5
1998	53,805	2.8	52,002	1.6
1999	54,693	1.7	54,088	4.0
2000	54,697	0.0	56,512	4.5
2001	57,464	5.1	57,422	1.6
2002	57,555	0.2	56,586	−1.5
2003	60,847	5.7	56,396	−0.3
2004	62,762	3.1	56,381	0.0

Note. From Administrative Office of the United States Courts, Judicial Business of the U.S. Courts, various years, Table B.

2000, Table 2.1). As reported in Table 9.5, the annual number of filings passed the 50,000 mark for the first time in 1993, with 50,224 total filings. Although the number of filings dipped below 50,000 in 1994, it exceeded the 50,000 mark again in 1994 and every year since, hitting almost 63,000 case filings in fiscal year 2003. Table 9.6 also reports the number of cases disposed of, which has been over 50,000 annually in the past decade, hovering in the 56,000-range for the past five years.

The U.S. Courts of Appeals are not the only courts facing a mushrooming workload (Posner 1985). However, as Judge Richard Posner observed, "The increase in cases filed in the district courts, however dramatic,...[has been]...dwarfed by the increase in cases filed in the courts of appeals" (Posner 1996, 59). The caseload "crisis" has been decried by a host of scholars, judges, and legal observers (Baker 1994; Rehnquist 1996; Starr 1991; Tobias 1996). These concerns have resulted in a plethora of reform suggestions, including increasing the number of authorized judgeships (Carpenter 1999) and fundamentally restructuring the federal judiciary (Dragich 1996).

The circuits themselves have responded by developing a host of coping strategies in the circuits, including an increased reliance on senior and visiting judges, as already discussed. Another strategy is more extensive use of law clerks and staff attorneys in the screening process that sorts cases into those that will receive full review and those that will be disposed of without full review. Yet another is the reduction in the use of oral argument. When oral argument is granted, each side is generally allotted 30 minutes, although it may be much less (Songer et al. 2000, 10). In recent years, the percentage of cases disposed of on the merits after oral argument has been roughly 30 percent, down from more than 60 percent in the early 1980s (see Table 9.7), but there is considerable variation across circuits. For example, in fiscal year 2003, almost six of every ten cases disposed of on the merits in the Court of Appeals for the Second Circuit received oral argument but less than one of every five cases disposed of on the merits in the Courts of Appeals for the Fourth Circuit and the Fifth Circuit received oral argument (Administrative Office of the United States Courts 2004, Table S-1).

An additional tool the circuits have increasingly taken advantage of is unpublished decisions. Each

Table 9.7 Appeals Disposed of On the Merits After Oral Argument

Fiscal Year	Percentage
1981	62.9
1982	69.2
1983	66.9
1984	60.8
1985	56.3
1986	53.8
1987	50.7
1988	51.2
1989	48.4
1990	45.1
1991	44.4
1992	43.9
1993	39.7
1994	40.6
1995	39.9
1996	40.1
1997	41.0
1998	37.1
1999	35.4
2000	32.3
2001	32.9
2002	32.5
2003	31.5

Note. From Administrative Office of the United States Courts, Judicial Business of the U.S. Courts, various years, Table S-1.

circuit has its own rules regarding the publication of rulings (cf. Wasby 2004); however, the common theme is that publication is reserved for "decisions that will make a contribution to the body of law of the circuit—that is, only those decisions that create new precedent or modify existing precedent" (Songer et al. 2000, 10). Publication has steadily declined over the past two decades, as reported in Table 9.8. Currently only one in five opinions, on average, is published. Unpublished opinions are typically brief and routine, generally requiring the expenditure of less time and effort in their construction (Wasby 2004). There is, however, some evidence to suggest that nonpublication is not merely a tool to enhance efficiency (Gulati and McCauliff 1998).

Table 9.8 Appeals Disposed of
On the Merits Without Publication

Fiscal Year	Percentage
1990	68.0
1991	69.3
1992	70.3
1993	73.8
1994	74.2
1995	75.9
1996	76.0
1997	76.5
1998	74.9
1999	78.1
2000	79.8
2001	80.5
2002	79.9
2003	81.0

Note. From Administrative Office of the United States Courts, Judicial Business of the U.S. Courts, various years, Table S-3.

The distinction between published and unpublished opinions is quite important because only published opinions may be cited as supporting authority. In practice, however, many "unpublished" opinions have been available through online legal research tools such as LexisNexis and Westlaw, leaving attorneys at a loss when they identify unpublished opinions online that are on point in a future case (Cohen 2002, 79). This situation has prompted a proposed rule change to the Federal Rules of Appellate Procedure, which would require circuits to permit citation to any unpublished opinion (Coyle 2004).

The composition of the U.S. Courts of Appeals docket has changed both in terms of substance and volume over the course of their history. The majority of the courts' workload comes from the U.S. District Courts and is dominated by criminal matters and economic issues. The dramatic increase in caseload—whether measured by appeals filed or cases disposed of—has prompted the courts of appeals to adopt a variety of strategies for managing their work, including a reduction in the use of oral argument and an increase in the issuance of unpublished decisions. What remain unexplored are the

factors that influence the decision making of judges on the courts of appeals.

MODELS OF JUDICIAL BEHAVIOR ON THE U.S. COURTS OF APPEALS

This chapter will now turn to an examination of the models that political scientists use to study the unique aspects of the U.S. Courts of Appeals. Some of the models used to study the U.S. Supreme Court are relevant to the study of other appellate courts (see Marshall, Pacelle, and Ludowise this volume, chapter 13), while other models have been developed because of the unique setting of the U.S. Courts of Appeals. Thus students of the courts have developed a variety of models to explain the behavior of judges. Models are intended to capture the most critical factors that account for whatever phenomenon we are trying to understand; for example, a judge's vote in a case, a judge's decision to file a concurring or dissenting opinion. "A model is a simplified representation of reality; it does not constitute reality itself" (Segal, Songer, and Cameron 1995, 229). Models, then, focus our attention on what matters most, ignoring "idiosyncratic factors" to separate the wheat from the chaff (Segal et al. 1995, 229). Three models, in particular, have prima facie relevance in the context of the U.S. Courts of Appeals: the attitudinal model, the hierarchical model, and the small group model.

The Attitudinal Model

The *attitudinal model* has its intellectual roots in the legal realism of the early twentieth century. Legal realists, such as Jerome Frank and Karl Llewellyn, saw judicial decision making as a function of more than merely the rote application of law. In fact, they were skeptical that there could be such a thing as the rote application of law. Rather, judging was a process imbued with the exercise of discretion by judges, whether consciously or not. Using legal realism as a springboard, scholars like C. Herman Pritchett (1948, 1954), and more recently Segal and Spaeth (1993, 2002), developed the attitudinal model, which simply "holds that the Supreme Court decides disputes in light of the facts of the case vis-à-vis the ideological attitudes and values of the justices" (Segal and Spaeth 2002, 86). The attitudinal model basically says that individual judges further their ideological policy goals. In short, liberal justices vote liberally and conservative judges vote conservatively.

Segal and Spaeth (1993, 2002) amassed a voluminous body of evidence as to the utility of the attitudinal model for understanding the behavior of Supreme Court justices. The attitudinal model is not, however, without its critics. For example, scholars such as Maltzman, Spriggs, and Wahlbeck (2000) have taken issue with the singular focus of the attitudinal model on liberal versus conservative outcomes with little regard for the content of opinions and the strategic bargaining that gives birth to majority opinions (see also Epstein and Knight 1998; Hammond, Bonneau, and Sheehan 2005). Others have chided Segal and Spaeth for stacking the cards in favor of finding evidence in support of the attitudinal model by comparing it to oversimplified versions of legal models of decision making (see, e.g., Brisbin 1996; see also Gillman 2003; Kritzer 2003b). Nevertheless, the attitudinal model remains key for understanding decisions at the U.S. Supreme Court.

There is also considerable research demonstrating the influence of the attitudes of courts of appeals judges on the decision making of those judges. For example, in their examination of obscenity case decision making in the U.S. Courts of Appeals, Songer and Haire (1992) found partisanship, a surrogate for judge ideology, to matter for the votes of judges. Likewise, Songer and Davis (1990) uncovered the influence of the preferences of courts of appeals judges (also measured in part by partisanship) on voting behavior in several other areas of law. Segal and his coauthors examined the effect of judicial attitudes, again using partisanship to tap into judge preferences, on the voting behavior of appeals court jurists in search and seizure cases and found attitudes an important component in the explanation of decision making in that area of law (Segal et al. 1995).

Evidence consistent with the attitudinal model is also apparent in research on other kinds of judicial behavior. Hettinger et al. (2003b), for example, found the ideology of appeals court judges to be quite important for understanding the decisions of judges to file separate opinions (i.e., a concurrence or dissent). In particular, Hettinger and colleagues found that the greater the ideological disagreement between a judge and the majority opinion writer, the greater the likelihood the judge would file a separate opinion. In other work, Hettinger et al. (2006) also found that ideological disagreement mattered, although in an indirect way, for understanding the decision of a court of appeals panel to reverse a lower court decision. The greater the ideological disagreement among court of appeals judges, the more likely separate opinions are and, hence, the more fractured and ambiguous circuit policy is. As a consequence, lower court judges find it harder to "get it right" and are more likely to be reversed.

Although it might not conform to idealized notions of judging, the idea that the attitudes of courts of appeals judges matter in their decision making should not be surprising. Clearly, presidents, senators, and interest groups believe that judges' attitudes matter for the decisions they make, as evidenced by the intense political skirmishes over selecting and confirming nominees to the U.S. Courts of Appeals bench. The attitudinal model was developed originally in the context of the U.S. Supreme Court. However, as Segal and Spaeth also noted, the autonomous control the Supreme Court exercises over its docket, coupled with the fact that the justices lack any serious threat to their continuance in office and are not subject to review by a higher court, provides considerable latitude for the policy preferences of the justices to influence their decision making (Segal and Spaeth 1993, 2002). The situation is different, however, for the judges serving on the U.S. Courts of Appeals.

The Hierarchical Model

It is true that, like their brethren on the Supreme Court, courts of appeals jurists do not face any real threats to their continued tenure in office. Impeachment is constitutionally possible but exceedingly unlikely. And, although appeals court judges would most likely find a seat on the U.S. Supreme Court a dream come true, it is also probably true that they understand this is an unlikely event and see their present jobs as prestigious enough to keep them on the appeals bench for the rest of their professional lives.

An important difference between the U.S. Courts of Appeals and the U.S. Supreme Court is the difference in their respective locations in the judicial hierarchy.

Although the Supreme Court is not subject to review by a higher court (because it is the highest court in the American judiciary), the courts of appeals are subject to review by the U.S. Supreme Court. Several scholars have suggested that this relationship is best captured by the *theory of principal and agent* (Benesh 2002; Songer, Segal, and Cameron 1994). This theory suggests that the U.S. Courts of Appeals serve as agents for the U.S. Supreme Court, the principal. The preferences of judges on the courts of appeals may or may not comport with those of the Supreme Court justices, but they are formally obligated to abide by the decisions of their judicial superior. In other words, the judges on the courts of appeals are bound to apply the precedents articulated by the U.S. Supreme Court.

Several scholars have empirically investigated the hierarchical model concerning the relationship between the U.S. Supreme Court and the U.S. Courts of Appeals. For example, Songer and Reid (1989) explored decision making by the courts of appeals in First Amendment cases and substantive due process cases after changes in Supreme Court doctrine, finding courts of appeals decision making sensitive to those changes. In addition, Songer and his coauthors (1994) examined decision making by courts of appeals jurists in the area of search and seizure law and found that, although the attitudes of the judges mattered, so, too, did the preferences of the U.S. Supreme Court (see also Segal et al. 1995). Furthermore, Benesh (2002) examined decision making on the U.S. Courts of Appeals in confession cases and found similar evidence that the U.S. Supreme Court influenced the decisions of circuit court judges. And, although Reddick (1997) had a slightly different substantive focus (the treatment of U.S. Supreme Court precedent by the appeals courts), she, too, found evidence supportive of the hierarchical model.

The hierarchical model as an explanation of decision making on the courts of appeals is attractive because it fits nicely with the formal structure of the federal judiciary as well as traditional legal norms that require subordinate courts to be faithful to superior courts. However, despite the evidence supportive of this model, there is reason to be skeptical that it constitutes an entirely adequate model of judicial decision making on the U.S. Courts of Appeals. The principal agency theory that underlies the hierarchical model assumes that principals (like the U.S. Supreme Court) will have to monitor (as in grant review) the behavior of their agents (like the U.S. Courts of Appeals) and impose sanctions when the agents do not follow the dictates of the principals (as in overturning errant lower court decisions). As the respective workloads of the two courts makes clear, there is very little monitoring of the decisions of the U.S. Courts of Appeals that the U.S. Supreme Court can do or is doing.[12]

The Small Group Model

Neither the attitudinal nor the hierarchical model takes explicit account of either the three-judge panel decision-making mechanism by which the U.S. Courts of Appeals dispose of the overwhelming majority of their caseload or the potential impact of the identities of the individuals who serve on those panels. The attitudinal model views a judge as an entirely individual actor. However:

> The most salient organizational characteristic that distinguishes the federal appellate courts...is that the judges...make their decisions in groups of three or more, which suggests that the interaction among the members of those groups has some impact on the judicial process. Highly individualist...approaches virtually ignore that key characteristic. Adding the study of the interaction among judges to the individualist approach suggests a model of the court that views the appellate process as the functioning of a small group of individual judges interacting with one another (Cohen 2002, 25).

The hierarchical model treats the three-judge panel as a unitary actor, disregarding the identities of the individuals who make up any given panel. The *small group model*, on the other hand, recognizes the importance of both the three-judge panel and the identities of the judges serving on them.

Ulmer (1971) was one of the earliest students of the courts to apply the small group approach to decision making by collegial courts. "Small-group theory holds that group variables influence the individual participant to behave differently from the way he would act alone toward the same task" (Ulmer 1971, 1). This implies that key to understanding the behavior of a judge serving on a three-judge panel is understanding not only who that judge is but also the identities of her fellow judges on that panel. To illustrate, consider work done by Walker (1973) on special three-judge district courts. Congress created these special three-judge courts to handle challenges to the constitutionality of state and federal statutes in an effort to avoid having a single district court judge exercise the authority to invalidate such statutes under the Constitution. These panels were typically composed of two district court judges plus one court of appeals judge. Walker explored whether the court of appeals judge (as the judge with the "highest" status on the panel) would enjoy, among other things, greater levels of support from his colleagues (e.g., fewer separate opinions when he wrote the majority opinion). Walker did, in fact, find that to be the case, thus providing support for the small group approach. Parenthetically in 1976, Congress greatly restricted the grounds on which a case could be heard before a three-judge district court panel, and these three-judge district panels are used quite rarely today (Baum 2001, 29–30).

More recently, work by Hettinger and her colleagues (2006) examined both whether the chief judge's role shaped his own behavior and whether the chief judge's presence on a panel influenced the behavior of other judges on that panel. Chief judges have unique institutional responsibilities. They are the administrative heads of their respective circuits. As such, they are responsible for the smooth operation of their circuits and the expeditious processing of their circuit's caseload. Given these institutional responsibilities, Hettinger and her coauthors examined whether chief judges were less likely to file separate opinions based on the following logic: "Given such a position of institutional authority, the chief may feel particularly responsible for ensuring collegial relations among judges in the circuit and, hence, be less likely to file dissenting opinions" (Hettinger et al. 2006, 38). What they found is that chief judges did file separate opinions less often but that their presence on the panel (whether as the majority opinion writer or simply as a fellow panelist) did not alter the behavior of other members of the panel.

Of greater relevance in light of the increasing use of designated district court judges and senior judges,

Hettinger et al. (2003a) found that the former are less likely to file separate opinions and their presence depresses the likelihood that other panel members will, although senior judges are more likely to file a separate opinion (though when they write the majority opinion their fellow panelists are no more or less likely to file separate opinions).

The small group model does not eschew the influence of the attitudes and preferences of judges. Recent work by Revesz (1997), for example, suggested that a court of appeals judge's attitudes matter but so do those of the judges with whom he or she is serving. Nor does the small group model exclude the influence of the U.S. Supreme Court. For example, it may well be that courts of appeals judges with certain kinds of prior experience or legal training are more attentive to the requirements of stare decisis. Although the body of work that applies the small group model to decision making on the U.S. Courts of Appeals is small relative to that which applies the attitudinal or the hierarchical model, the research that has been conducted thus far suggests the small group model is very promising in terms of its ability to help us understand appeals court judge behavior. Perhaps the biggest challenge for scholars applying this model will be in distinguishing between situations in which judges behave differently because they are being strategic and situations in which judges behave differently because they are desirous of felicitous relations with their colleagues. It is a challenge, however, that is likely to yield a host of profitable insights if met.

CONCLUSIONS

The U.S. Courts of Appeals are major policy makers despite their subordinate position in the federal judicial hierarchy. The controversial nomination and confirmation processes give testament to that. As does the fact that they have become, for all intents and purposes, the first and last stop in the federal appellate process for most unhappy litigants. While the Supreme Court picks and chooses the cases it wants to hear, ultimately granting review to less than a 100 cases a year, the courts of appeals process 50,000 cases or more each year. Truly, they are the appellate workhorses of the federal judiciary. As the nature of their caseload has changed, both in terms of substance and volume, so, too, have the institutional practices they rely on to accomplish their work. Greater use of senior and visiting judges, reduced oral argument, and increased rates of nonpublication have all facilitated the courts of appeals' efforts to stay abreast of their work, although these practices are not without their critics. Those who study the U.S. Courts of Appeals have found evidence that both the attitudes of the judges and the intermediate position of the courts of appeals are important for understanding decision making on these courts. Future work would do well to continue exploring how the unique three-judge panel decision-making process, coupled with the roles and identities of panel members, combine to influence decision making as well.

Notes

1. Courts, including the U.S. Courts of Appeals, also make law through the pattern of outcomes that emerges when they issue rulings in a series of cases dealing with the same or closely related legal questions (Glick and Vines 1973).

2. Article III, Section 1 of the Constitution reads, in part: "The judicial Power of the United States, shall be vested in one supreme Court, and in such inferior Courts as the Congress may from time to time ordain and establish."

3. The Court of Appeals for the Federal Circuit, located in Washington, D.C., is a specialized appellate court that exercises subject matter rather than geographic jurisdiction. It was created by Congress in 1982 through the consolidation of the old Court of Customs Appeals and the old Court of Claims.

4. Depending on the federal agency involved, the courts of appeals may review an agency decision directly or after treatment by a federal district court.

5. Article I courts are created by Congress under authority granted it in Article I. As stipulated in Article I, Section 8: "The Congress shall have Power . . . To constitute Tribunals inferior to the supreme Court." Judges serving on such courts serve for fixed terms.

6. The one exception was the norm of senatorial courtesy. Presidents abiding by this norm paid particular attention to the preferences of home-state senators when making nominations for a district court judgeship (Bell 2002a; Goldman 1997). Senatorial courtesy applies most directly when the nomination is of an individual to fill a district court vacancy because the geographic boundaries of each district court do not cross state lines. However, because individual appeals court seats have traditionally been associated with particular states, senatorial courtesy is also at play when the nomination is of an individual to fill an appeals court vacancy (Chase 1972; Goldman 1967, 186–214; Hartley and Holmes 2002; Sheldon and Maule 1997, 184).

7. In the legislative process, delay can be an incredibly useful tool. In the context of confirmation politics, delay can result in the failure of a nominee to secure confirmation because nominations typically do not carry over from one congressional term to the next (Martinek et al. 2002).

8. Chief judges have this authority under 28 U.S.C. § 292.

9. Judges who have served for fifteen years and are at least sixty-five years of age may take senior status. With each additional year of age, a judge may take senior status with one less year of service.

10. A case participation refers to the participation of a judge in a given case. Typically a three-judge panel decision yields three case participations.

11. Though random assignment is typical, there is evidence to suggest that Chief Judge Elbert Tuttle of the Court of Appeals for the Fifth Circuit manipulated panel composition in cases involving race relations (Atkins and Zavoina 1974). There were also claims that Chief Judge Boyce Martin of the Court of Appeals for the Sixth Circuit manipulated the membership of the panel that heard the case about the affirmative action admissions programs at the University of Michigan, *Gratz v. Bollinger* (2003).

12. It should be noted, however, that although it is true that not all appeals court decisions can be reviewed, it is also true that not all appeals court decisions have the same likelihood of being reviewed. Some cases are more likely to be reviewed and at least some research suggests that evidence of shirking on the part of lower court judges enhances the likelihood of review by the Supreme Court (Caldeira, Wright, and Zorn 1999).

10

THE SOLICITOR GENERAL

Learned in the Law and Politics

Peter N. Ubertaccio III

The solicitor general of the United States is the only official to have an office at the U.S. Supreme Court who is not a justice or an employee of the Supreme Court. The solicitor general is the lawyer for the president and the executive branch before the Supreme Court. The solicitor general is appointed by the president, confirmed by the Senate, and can be fired by the president at any time. The office was created within the Department of Justice in 1870, and it was designed to relieve the attorney general of litigation responsibility. The solicitor general often has a close relationship with the president and the U.S. attorney general, although he must also maintain a good standing with the justices of the U.S. Supreme Court. Because the federal government litigates more cases before the Supreme Court than any other litigant, this office has received a great deal of recent attention from judicial politics scholars. The solicitor general can participate in oral arguments before the U.S. Supreme Court even when the U.S. Government is not a party to the case. There is a clear tension between having the solicitor general serve a solely legal function and having the solicitor general further the president's political agenda through his arguments before the Court. Given the solicitor general's unique role in the federal government, this individual must usually take positions on many of the most controversial issues of the day. This chapter examines the contemporary role of the Office of the Solicitor General as well as looking at the historical evolution of that office.

The solicitor general is the attorney for the United States of America, or more specifically for the executive branch of the federal government. The solicitor general serves as the president's lawyer before the U.S. Supreme Court, representing the views of the executive branch of the U.S. Government before the Court. The solicitor's office normally decides which cases the United States will appeal to the Supreme Court, submits the brief for the government to the Supreme Court, and addresses the justices during oral arguments even when the U.S. Government is not a party to the case.

The solicitor general's office also determines whether the U.S. Government will appeal any lower court decision. This is a rather straightforward job description. However, the Office of Solicitor General (OSG) is no ordinary law firm. It exists at the intersection of judicial and executive politics, law and partisanship, public policy, and jurisprudence. For government attorneys, it is the pinnacle of legal prominence. Francis Biddle, who served as Franklin Roosevelt's Solicitor General, commented that, "The Solicitor General has no master to serve except his country" (Biddle 1962, 97–98).

Archibald Cox, Solicitor General during the Kennedy years, once said, "[M]y whole life and career had trained me to look upon the Solicitor's office as second only to God" (quoted in Navasky 1971, 318).

Although perhaps not as celestial as these pronouncements might indicate, the office is, because of its unusual nexus, the gold standard of the legal field. Biddle and Cox described the OSG in such glowing terms, in part because the office is devoid of both significant administrative and overtly political activities. It is in theory a purely a legal office, concerned with crafting the legal position in the courts of the U.S. Government. As Seth Waxman, Solicitor General under Bill Clinton, noted to the Supreme Court Historical Association, "Ultimately, it is the responsibility of the Solicitor General to ensure that the United States speaks in court with a single voice—a voice that speaks on behalf of the rule of law" (Waxman 1998, 1). And that voice is often heard. In the U.S. Supreme Court's 2002 session, the government filed 23 petitions, responded to 349 others, delivered to the Court 27 amicus (friend of the court) briefs, received invitations to file 24 additional amicus briefs, and filed briefs at the merits stage in 70 cases. During the 2001 term the government participated either as a party or as an amicus in over 85 percent of the cases in which the Supreme Court heard arguments (Baum 2004, 88). The solicitor general's office also has a very high success rate at the Supreme Court, as will be discussed in more detail below. However, because the solicitor general must work with both the president and the Supreme Court, Richard Pacelle argued that the solicitor general must straddle the line "between law and politics" (Pacelle 2003).

Created in 1870 as part of the newly established Department of Justice, the solicitor general's office was designed to relieve the attorney general of litigation responsibility. As lawsuits involving the federal government grew rapidly after the Civil War, the attorney general needed support. Without enough attorneys to handle its litigation, the government was forced to rely on expensive private counsel. In this new OSG, the government gained a person who had specifically studied the law, or be "learned in the law" according to the language of the statute. This legal office would argue on behalf of the United States wherever it was

a party in legal action. In this role the solicitor represents the government before the Supreme Court and, in theory, all federal courts. Although still technically inferior to the attorney general and part of the Department of Justice, many solicitors general have developed independent relationships with the presidents for whom they serve. Standing at the epicenter of executive legal strategies and the development of the law provides the office with a rich history, an usual responsibility in our federal system, and a good deal of controversy (see, e.g., Ubertaccio 2005). This chapter will focus on the relationship between the solicitor general, the president, and the Supreme Court.

RESPONSIBILITIES AND ROLE

The solicitor general's duties in conjunction with the Supreme Court have developed over time into three general areas. First, and most significantly, the office decides which cases the government will appeal to the Supreme Court and to the U.S. Courts of Appeals (see Martinek this volume, chapter 9). Second, the OSG either presents or supervises the government's arguments before the Supreme Court. And third, the OSG represents the federal executive branch in amicus curiae (friend of the court) briefs, where the government has a substantial interest in a case to which it is not a party. The solicitor general is the epitome of the "repeat player" who appears before the U.S. Supreme Court (see, e.g., Salokar 1992, 31) because, "Of all the litigants in the Supreme Court, the federal government appears most frequently" (Baum 2004, 88; see also Mather this volume, chapter 4).

The solicitor general is aided in the duties of the office by an elite organization of government lawyers: four deputy solicitors, three of whom are career officials, and seventeen assistant solicitors. Only the principal deputy solicitor and the solicitor change positions with each new administration because they are political appointees who are appointed by the president and confirmed by the Senate. The president can fire these political appointees at any time. The relatively little turnover that occurs in the office also adds to its aura and professionalism. A great deal of institutional memory is retained in the office. As Paul Clement,

George W. Bush's second Solicitor General, noted in his confirmation hearings, "The lawyers and other public servants in the Office of the Solicitor General are quite literally the most talented group of people that you can imagine. Collectively, they represent decades of experience representing the interests of the United States before the Supreme Court" (Clement 2005, 5).

Next this chapter will explore some of these aspects that may influence the solicitor general's decision on whether to appeal a specific case. Whenever the government loses a case in federal Courts of Appeal, the appellate section of the Justice Department that handled the case recommends whether the decision should be appealed. If the initial recommendation is negative, the process usually ends at that point. If the recommendation is positive, the solicitor general makes an independent judgment. Then the solicitor general reviews both recommendations as well as the record of the case to make a final decision. When the solicitor general chooses to appeal the case, a lawyer from the OSG will prepare and argue the appeal. If the solicitor general decides not to pursue an appeal, the United States Code prohibits, with few exceptions, any government attorney other than the attorney general from pursuing an appeal in any court.

When litigation involving the departments and agencies of the executive branch works its way through the judicial process, the deputy solicitor general becomes involved only after a significant amount of paperwork has been produced by these agencies. Although the OSG authorizes appeals to the U.S. Courts of Appeals, it does not handle such matters itself, leaving litigation at this stage in the hands of one of the six divisions within the Department of Justice. These divisions all have their own trial staffs.[1] It is at the next level that the solicitor's role takes on the importance to which history has assigned it.

The decision to seek certiorari or to file an amicus brief at the U.S. Supreme Court rests with the solicitor general alone. Elaborate recommendations from the appropriate divisions within the Justice Department, the agency, or departmental counsel and the assistant and deputy solicitors then become part of the case file. It is this singular decision that thrusts the OSG into the public spotlight and highlights its unique role in crafting law. This role is so important that one of the first

books to study the OSG systematically was entitled, *The Tenth Justice: The Solicitor General and the Rule of Law* (Caplan 1987). There are several factors that weigh on the decision-making process as the OSG decides whether to seek certiorari review at the U.S. Supreme Court: Whether the case presents a single legal question based on noncontroversial facts, the prestige of the appellate court that wrote the opinion, the attitude of the Court toward the particular issue, whether there are disputes between Circuit Courts, the political issues involved, and the likelihood that another case will raise the same issue in the near future.

When the solicitor general does seek certiorari at the Supreme Court, either when the Government is a party to the case or when the solicitor general files an amicus brief at the certiorari stage, the solicitor general is unusually successful at convincing the Supreme Court to accept the case. In general, the U.S. Supreme Court grants certiorari in only about 1 to 2 percent of the cases it is requested to hear each year. The solicitor general's success rate, however, was well over 70 percent in the 1954 to 1985 period (see O'Brien 1993, 266). During the 2001 term, the solicitor general's success rate was an amazing 90 percent (Baum 2004, 100).

Some would argue that the solicitor general is so successful at the Supreme Court because the OSC serves a gateway function for the Supreme Court. The solicitor general refrains from recommending that the Court hear frivolous or unimportant cases. The solicitor general also has a large number of cases to choose from in making requests that the Supreme Court grant certiorari in any given case so that the solicitor general can only recommend that the Court hear a case with facts sympathetic to the government's position. As Baum noted, "The Solicitor General's office is far more selective in asking for hearings than are private litigants. This restraint allows the government generally to take only its strongest cases to the Court. One benefit is that the justices expect government petitions to be meritorious" (Baum 2001, 262). The solicitor general's repeat player status with the Supreme Court also gives the office a great deal of institutional knowledge about what kinds of cases the justices are likely to accept and what kinds they will refuse to hear. Given that the justices have come to expect that the solicitor general will only push for hearings in the most important cases, this relationship with the Court also provides an incentive for the solicitor general to continue to screen carefully his requests that the Supreme Court grant certiorari in any specific case.[2] Otherwise, the solicitor general could lose credibility with the Court.

Centralizing the legal representation of the United States in the OSG allows it great latitude in the development of American jurisprudence. Consider, for example, the George W. Bush Administration's decision to file an amicus brief urging the Supreme Court to overturn the University of Michigan's affirmative action plans for its law school and for its undergraduate college. Although it was widely expected that the solicitor general would submit an amicus brief asking the Court to take a strong stand against affirmative action in *Gratz v. Bollinger* (2003) and in *Grutter v. Bollinger* (2003), the two cases that sought to overturn the University of Michigan's affirmative action policies (at the undergraduate college and at the law school, respectively), the OSG took a different route. The brief submitted by Solicitor General Theodore Olson was substantially different than the hopes of many of the President's conservative supporters. The President publicly suggested that the administration would "file a brief with the Court arguing that the University of Michigan's admissions policies, which award students a significant number of extra points based solely on their race, and establishes numerical targets for incoming minority students, are unconstitutional" (Bush 2003, 1). Indeed, the brief submitted by Olson to the Court did make this claim but it also *informed* the Court that, "this case does not require this Court to break any new ground to hold that respondents' race-base admissions policy is unconstitutional" (*Grutter* brief, 2003). Thus did the OSG invite the type of opinion crafted by moderate Justice Sandra Day O'Connor in the law school case, where her majority opinion in *Grutter* held that, "the Equal Protection Clause [of the U.S. Constitution] does not prohibit the Law School's narrowly tailored use of race in admissions decisions to further a compelling interest in obtaining the educational benefits that flow from a diverse student body" (539 U.S. at 343).

The solicitor general's office enjoys substantial control over the process of filing amicus briefs with the Supreme Court. The Supreme Court often invites the submission of an amicus brief by the OSG, and such invitations are normally treated as orders. At other times, however, the solicitor general decides to file an amicus brief without an invitation. When the government files an uninvited brief, it clearly has greater freedom to do so than most other parties. Supreme Court Rule 37 requires that all amicus briefs obtain the consent of either the parties or the Court before filing. Any brief that the U.S. Government presents to the Court, however, is exempt from the party consent requirement. Although the solicitor general has been required since 1970 to state the government's interest in cases when it files an amicus brief, the solicitor is free to submit briefs in any case where he can articulate such an interest. It is very rare for the Supreme Court to refuse to accept an amicus brief from the solicitor general.

It is widely agreed that the modern OSG is the president's most powerful tool to influence the justices who sit on the U.S. Supreme Court. H. W. Perry believed the solicitor general to be "the most important person in the country, except for the justices themselves, in determining which cases are heard in the Supreme Court" (H. W. Perry 1991, 129). Furthermore, the solicitor general stands at the center of executive litigation strategies. Donald Horowitz noted that intergovernmental disagreements are resolved "in the office of either the Attorney General (or his deputy) or, more commonly, the Solicitor General, who has the authority to establish the litigating position of the United States" (Horowitz 1977, 10). Due to the extraordinary relationship the solicitor has with the Court, "he is not only a favored party in the cases the Supreme Court accepts for decision, but the dominant one as well," wrote Robert Scigliano (1971, 177). Both Scigliano and a more recent student of the office, Rebecca Mae Salokar, agreed that due to the unique position of the office, the solicitor general can influence both executive and judicial policies (see Salokar 1992, 7). As President George W. Bush's second Solicitor General Paul Clement noted in his 2005 confirmation hearings:

> The office quite literally sits at the crossroads of the separation of powers as the primary vehicle through which the Article II branch of Government speaks

to Article III. But, of course, the office also owes important responsibilities to the Article I branch, the Congress of the United States (Clement 2005, 6).

Because most major political issues become issues worthy of judicial resolution, the OSG has been thrust into the political debates over abortion, affirmative action, the establishment clause, the detention of enemy combatants, gay rights, and environmental regulation. Before he became solicitor general, Paul Clement served as the Principal Deputy in the OSG and argued on behalf of the United States in some of the key cases of the first four years of the George W. Bush Administration: *Cheney v. U.S. District Court for the District of Columbia* (2004) dealing with executive privilege; and *Rumsfeld v. Padilla* (2004) and *Hamdi v. Rumsfeld* (2004), both dealing with the rights of enemy combatants (see Fisher this volume, chapter 18). Since assuming his role in 2005, Clement argued cases dealing with military tribunals, the display of the Ten Commandments on public property, and the federal ban on partial birth abortion procedures.

Because of its centralized role in articulating the legal position of the government, the solicitor general's office can greatly influence the nation's jurisprudence in these politically divisive areas. It is the closest the modern office comes to overtly political duties and it is a far cry from the activities of early solicitors general. This chapter will now turn to an examination of the historical evolution of the OSG.

EARLY HISTORY

The cabinet level Department of Justice was not created by Congress until 1870. At that time, Congress also created the position of the solicitor general to handle litigation in which the federal government had an interest. This next section of this chapter will explore how the executive branch handled questions of law before the creation of the federal Department of Justice. In general, the government maintained a decentralized approach to the law until 1870.

By 1870, the attorney general clearly needed help. Despite the office's status as an original member of the Cabinet, the underlying legislation creating the office of the attorney general lacked specific grants of authority, and the failure to create a department in which to house the new office left the new attorney general the task of forming the contours of the office. The attorney general, unlike the secretaries of state and treasury and war, did not preside over an agency of government. The responsibility of early office was specifically to give legal advice to the president and members of the cabinet.

The multiple facets of the modern office of the attorney general are evident from this early attempt by Congress to create the nation's first government attorney. Although the attorney general had no department and was therefore not an administrator, the statutory language gave to the office two important jobs: litigator and legal advisor. Still, the language of the statute suggests the beginning of a dilemma regarding the attorney general's responsibilities regarding public versus political interests. Although the statute mandated that the attorney general would litigate all lawsuits of concern to the United States, the meaning of the word "concern" was not defined. The confusion within the federal government over the role of the attorney general was evident soon after the office was created. Without a legal staff and with very little federal litigation to attend to, the attorney general became a roving solicitor, and only achieved cabinet secretary status due to the prestige and determination of the first Attorney General, Edmund Randolph. A personal friend and lawyer to George Washington since the Revolutionary War, Randolph had long been a student of the law and administration and after much persuading accepted the position. Despite his stature, Randolph lacked a staff, was paid half the salary of other cabinet officers, and only regularly attended cabinet meetings after 1792.

As president, Washington used his cabinet as a collective decision-making enterprise. When in need of opinions and advice on matters constitutional, the president requested the input of all of his secretaries. Thus the legal and constitutional opinions and interpretations of the attorney general competed with those of other officials. Furthermore, problems of centralized administration appeared early. Federal district attorneys had been placed under the supervisory control of the secretary of state. Randolph wrote to the president that, "[M]any instances have occurred in which the heads of the Departments have requested that suits should be prosecuted in different States under my direction." However, the lack of formal supervisory controls over the legal officers of the government "has rendered it impossible for me to take charge of matters on which I was not authorized to give instructions" (quoted in White 1948, 167–68). Randolph pushed for more effective control over the U.S. District Attorneys and for a staff member to assist with his duties. Congress refused to act. Still, Leonard White claimed an important precedent was set during the tenure of the first attorney general: "As an administrative agency, the office was insignificant; but since its incumbent early won a place in the Cabinet, the Attorney General played a role of substantial importance in the general policy of the Federalist era" (White 1948, 172). Cornell Clayton noted that since Washington's appointment of Randolph, "Presidents have always sought to appoint a close personal friend or confidant as Attorney General and the office's conventional inclusion in the cabinet institutionalized its role as a political advisor" (1992, 17).

The duties of the attorney general's office, despite Randolph's stature, did not occupy much time and energy during the early years of the republic. Between 1800 and 1814 the attorney general did not live in the nation's capital. This situation ended only when the Judiciary Committee of the House of Representatives convinced the president to nominate an attorney general who would agree to at least live in the District of Columbia while Congress was in session. This was deemed necessary because Congress regularly asked the attorney general for legal advice and began to use the office as its legal counsel. Attorney General William Wirt ended this practice in 1820. In addition to establishing the practice of compiling and publishing the *Opinions of the Attorney General*, Wirt informed Congress that his office interpreted the attorney general's statutory duties to serve only the president.

Unbowed, Congress continued to refer cases to the attorney general's office and continued to solicit opinions through department heads. Attorney General Butler refused to answer any questions from the departments unrelated to their duties and also refused to answer any questions from the Congress unless they

related to the official duties of the president. Thus the attorney general's office was established as the legal office for the executive branch and by extension for the United States, although the legal functions of the federal government still suffered from decentralization.

Presidents and their attorneys general routinely suggested a centralization of legal functions, but Congress continued the decentralizing tendencies that had dominated the federal government since the Judiciary Act of 1789. The problem of decentralization was first noticed by the Congress under the Articles of Confederation. Though the Confederacy had no provisions for a national legal officer, Congress soon realized it needed such officials to prosecute on its behalf in the states and appointed an attorney to litigate in each state.

As presidents complained, and as the numbers of district attorneys and department lawyers grew, Congress responded in piecemeal fashion. In 1830, the post of Solicitor of the Treasury was created to assist in retrieving debts owed from the war of 1812. The new solicitor was also given authority to instruct district attorneys. However, the officeholder was an accountant, not a lawyer, and in any case was under the jurisdiction of the Secretary of the Treasury. Congress had not responded in the manner that the executive requested. Part of the problem stemmed from Senator Daniel Webster's fear of increasing the centralization of the executive branch as it existed under his political opponent Andrew Jackson.

Despite the political battles that prevented the creation of a federal law department, by the 1850's the office of attorney general (OAG) began to take on the types of duties that would require the creation of a Cabinet level department. Under Attorney General Caleb Cushing (1853 to 1857), the office took on new responsibilities that had formerly been handled by other political actors. From the State Department, the OAG was given the responsibility for advising the president on matters of pardons and judicial nominations. From the Interior Department, the OAG gained the responsibility for handling the accounts of the federal courts. During this time period the OAG also became responsible for writing all the legal correspondence for the federal government. Congress also added to the office's duties by giving the OAG supervisory power over treaty commissioners, government land titles, the adjudication of claims under Indian treaties, representation in the newly created Court of Claims, the granting of government patents, and compiling and publishing all federal laws. The push to create a Cabinet-level legal department in the executive branch did not gain steam until the aftermath of the Civil War and the rapid increase in governmental litigation that occurred in that period.

THE BIRTH OF THE DEPARTMENT OF JUSTICE AND THE OSG

Finally, in 1870 Congress created the Department of Justice and within it the OSG. The 1870 legislation creating a Department of Justice and the OSG was a step toward long-neglected centralization of law issues within a single department. The solicitor general was to become the preeminent lawyer for the United States. The congressional movement to create a Department of Justice and a solicitor general's office was one in a series of reform efforts during the post–Civil War era. The bill to create a Department of Justice was crafted by Representative Thomas A. Jenckes, a Republican of Rhode Island.

Jenckes was a noted reformer who also took up the cause of civil service and reform of the U.S. Patent Office. Leonard White maintained that Jenckes "is entitled to high recognition among a small band of reformers who against great odds finally secured enactment of civil service legislation" (White 1958, 279–80). A political supporter of Jenckes once commented that, "I am much pleased with your bill relating to a Department of Justice—I think it a fitting addition to your other great works: Bankruptcy Law, Civil Service, Patent Office. You deserve the hearty thanks of all good citizens for these measures so important and salutary. I really think your organizing power a great blessing to the whole country" (quoted in Jenckes 1870).

Despite being defeated for his reelection bid in 1870, Jenckes continued to push for governmental reforms, seeing the Department of Justice bill through to its final passage. His desire was to strengthen the ability of the United States to act in its own defense.

As Jenckes described the new office of the solicitor general, "We propose to have a man of sufficient learning, ability, and experience that he can be sent to New Orleans or to New York, or into any court wherever the Government has any interest in litigation, and there present the case of the United States as it should be presented" (*Congressional Globe* 1870, 3036). Jenckes lobbied the Senate to act on the bill by explaining,

> We have found that there has been a most unfortunate result from this separation of law powers. We find one interpretation of the laws in the United States in one Department and another interpretation in another Department....It is for the purpose of having a unity of decision, a unity of jurisprudence, if I may use that expression, in the executive law of the United States, that this bill proposes that all the law officers therein provided for shall be subordinated to one head (*Congressional Globe* 1870, 3036).

The early years of the OSG would prove frustrating because the first two officeholders, Bristow and Samuel Field Phillips, found themselves spending a significant amount of time on matters of patronage and administrative organization. Their advocacy of federal power in the area of civil rights met with a severe rebuke from local officials in the South and from the Supreme Court. Their immediate successors found themselves in a highly charged partisan atmosphere. Solicitor General Lawrence Maxwell was forced to resign for promoting a case Attorney General Richard Olney thought detrimental to the fortunes of the Democratic Party and Acting Solicitor General John Goode's nomination was defeated at the hands of the Republican Party in the aftermath of the highly contentious 1884 presidential race won by Democrat Grover Cleveland.

However, the competitive system of party competition and the loose organization of the newly established department succeeded in setting precedents that would free future solicitors. Bristow and Phillips argued strenuously for federal protection of black civil rights in the South at a time when neither the Court, local elected officials, and, increasingly, public opinion favored such a course of action. Bristow's advocacy and stellar reputation would advance him to the Treasury Department, and he became a leading presidential candidate following his resignation from the corrupted Grant administration in 1876. He later became a founding member and second president of the American Bar Association, an organization that would further advance the separation of law and politics.

Neither Bristow nor Phillips took complete control of government litigation. Both the attorney general and the assistant attorneys general handled cases before the Court, and would continue to do so into the early twentieth century. During the December 1870 term of the Court, Bristow presented oral arguments in thirteen cases—three alone, five together with Attorney General Ackerman, and five others with assistant attorneys general. Seven cases were argued that term by the attorney general and/or the assistant attorneys general without Bristow. The following year, the solicitor general argued twenty-seven Supreme Court cases—seven alone, five with the attorney general, and fifteen with the assistant attorneys general.

Samuel Field Phillips continued in that vein. During the 1873 term, Phillips' first full term as solicitor general, he argued eighteen cases before the Supreme Court—eleven alone and seven in conjunction with the attorney general. During Phillips' twelve-year tenure as solicitor general the number of cases argued by attorneys general declined. And Phillips's skill as an oral advocate set an important example to future solicitors. As a contemporary recalled:

> His habit was to discard the minor points of a case, and address himself to the great questions upon which [the Court's] decision ought to rest; and then he was so candid in stating the position of his opponents and the facts appearing in the record, and so lucid and strong in his argument, that he commanded the entire confidence, as well as the respect, of the Court (Battle 1904, 27).

In so doing, Phillips was again carrying on a tradition set by Bristow and one that will become a leading internal expectation of the OSG. A tract about Bristow's life in connection with his much-anticipated bid for the Republican presidential nomination in 1876 noted:

> One marked characteristic of Mr. Bristow's arguments was an absence of all attempt at display. He always thoroughly prepared himself, going over every case in which he did not make the brief, with as much care as if nothing had been done in its preparation, and making voluminous notes and memoranda. But when he came to speak he would never make any further use of these than the posture of the case demanded; and if he thought the case had been sufficiently argued by his associate, would add but a few remarks on one or two of the most vital points. The great judgment he thus showed in arguing the important questions and leaving the others alone, and never unnecessarily taking up the time of the overworked judges, was one reason why he was so great a favorite with them, and was always listened to with respectful attention (*Some Facts* 1876, 20–22).

President Grant put two leading advocates into the newly created office of solicitor general. Their commitment to an unpopular cause, their advocacy skills, and their desire to bring order to the organizational chaos of the early department would emerge as the leading internal characteristics of the office in the twentieth century. This chapter will now turn to an examination of the modern OSG.

THE BEGINNING OF THE MODERN ERA

During the early part of the twentieth century, changes were underway at the Department of Justice to narrow the scope of the workload for the solicitor general.[3] Attorney General George Wickersham created a dual track of responsibilities for the Department—the attorney general was to supervise litigation and administer the Department while the solicitor was to focus on casework. In 1919, Attorney General A. Mitchell Palmer created various divisions within the Department, each headed by an assistant attorney general: antitrust, criminal prosecutions, claims, tax, and internal revenue, and other miscellaneous matters. This division of responsibility still exists in the modern DOJ.

Solicitors at the turn of the century also represented a new trend in legal professionalism and were leaders in the emerging strength of the American Bar Association. The nation's top lawyers worked in the solicitor's office before advancing either to the top spot or in and out of other elite law firms, law schools, or legal organizations. Future Solicitors James Beck, James Crawford Biggs, and Erwin Griswold all worked in the OSG during the progressive era. President Taft, himself a former law professor, appointed Lloyd Wheaton Bowers to the post, the first solicitor to attend an elite law school, Columbia. Taft's second solicitor, Frederick Lehmann, was previously the President of the American Bar Association. The professionalization of legal studies and the narrowing of the office's responsibilities created a perfect storm of organizational identity—the office became the dream job of governmental attorneys who relished the role and the freedom it brought. And many of the nation's top lawyers held the prestigious post. And freed from most of its administrative duties, it became a leading component in the rise of executive power during the mid-twentieth century.

For the OSG during the New Deal era, the advocacy of legal and constitutional change affected the office's organizational strength. Franklin Roosevelt appointed five solicitors general during his tenure, but his first, James Crawford Biggs, was such a poor advocate for administration policy that the OSG lost its institutional footing. It was sidelined in administration deliberations regarding policy development and litigation strategies. The OSG became an outcast in an administration intent on changing constitutional norms—a process that would put it in direct conflict with the Supreme Court, an institution with which the OSG could have exercised much influence. Despite this setback, under the latter four solicitors the office emerged as an important institutional ally to the process of regime change instigated by Roosevelt because it served an important role in linking together other institutions and political actors necessary to effectuate such change. Organizational and hierarchical lines were clearly established, administrative duties were restricted, and litigation became the exclusive focus of the solicitor general's office. Interesting, FDR first approached Felix Frankfurter to serve as solicitor general, a request Frankfurter declined, preferring to advise the new president from other positions. The

choice of the lackluster Biggs to fill the post cost the administration dearly.

Scholarship on Franklin Roosevelt's "reconstruction" of American politics rarely focuses on the important role the OSG played in his transformational leadership. The solicitor general's office underwent significant development during the twelve years it served FDR. In its advocacy, the office served as the first line in Roosevelt's constitutional defense of the New Deal before the Supreme Court and the professional legal community—furthering FDR's vision of the Constitution articulated during his Commonwealth Club address of 1932. Later, when Roosevelt's constitutional vision became institutionalized, the solicitor general's office became an organizational center of legislative and public opinion strategy before and during the war years. By the end of Roosevelt's presidency, the office and its occupant would be viewed as the government's chief litigator and defender of the law, as its administrative and explicitly political duties lessened. The transformation from a figure that combined legal, political, and administrative duties into a purely legal officer was nearly complete.

The New Deal liberalism that pervaded the solicitor general's office in the 1930s and 1940s transformed the organizational identity of the office. However, the idea that there existed a standing rule of law untouchable by executive authority became a trend in the aftermath of the OSG's activities in the 1950s and 1960s. Although an important and crucial aspect of New Deal constitutionalism was deference to the executive, when the Supreme Court under Chief Justice Earl Warren became the only institution at the federal level to deal with the lingering issue of racial segregation, the OSG became a defender of a different conception of the rule of law. This view maximized the authority of the Supreme Court and the federal judiciary to intervene in areas of law heretofore delegated to the states or political branches. As the Court applied this logic to the cases it confronted during the Warren Court era, it found an ally in the OSG. The solicitor general's office became a protector of civil rights statutes and Court opinions during this period. Though the strength and independence of the office into the 1970s was unthinkable without the organizational reforms of the New Deal, those reforms also helped to ensure that a wall of separation between executive politics and litigation activities could be used by critics to ensure that future presidents' intent on constitutional change would face a much more difficult legal environment.

SHOULD THE SOLICITOR GENERAL BE A LEGAL OR A POLITICAL ACTOR?

Although largely unknown to the general public, the OSG became a hot political topic among academics and other court watchers. By the time Ronald Reagan became president, the former nonpolitical nature of the OSG would change dramatically (see Caplan 1987). In many ways, the solicitor general became a spokesperson in court for the so-called Reagan Revolution. Thus, President Reagan's Solicitor General Charles Fried had a clearly articulated political agenda. In her review of Fried's (1991) memoir, *Order and Law,* Harvard Law Professor and Reagan administration critic Lani Guinier took issue with the advocacy of Charles Fried as solicitor general and Fried's view of the Reagan agenda:

> The effect of the Administration agenda is clear. Assisted by a now ideologically compatible judiciary, the Republican President would rule majestically as the ultimate and most legitimate source of government. The "muscular" presidency, the heart of Fried's geometric theorem of constitutional law, would beat in the champers of young, ideologically committed judicial soldiers for years after the Revolution itself passed (Guinier 1994, 166).

According to Guinier, Fried's advocacy of the Reagan legal and constitutional agenda was nothing more than the advocacy of "piecemeal adjudications, Fried's own personal view of what is right, and an administration committed to its own perpetuity" (Guinier 1994, 167). It was, in short, the advocacy of politics over law. This mantra became the most public criticism of the OSG in its history. Nothing close to the type of politics versus law debate over the role of the OSG can be found previous to the election of Ronald Reagan in 1980, and it is a debate that continues to rage today.

It was into this environment that Ronald Reagan's solicitors general stepped. As the first truly conservative president in the post-New Deal era, Reagan's conception of the law and the strides made during the Warren Court era did not match the prevailing legal wisdom and precedent of the time. The administration made an early effort to promote conservative jurists for judicial posts and attempted to roll back the gains of liberal jurists. The Reagan Administration in part hoped to achieve these goals through the briefs written by the solicitor general.

Some would argue that the courts became as important politically during the Reagan Administration as they had been during the FDR years. After his study of judicial selection, Sheldon Goldman commented, "What struck me most was, the Reagan administration seems in many ways the mirror image of the Roosevelt administration.…Roosevelt recognized the courts were crucial to the fulfillment of many objectives and goals" (Coyle 1988, 22). The Reagan administration likewise understood the political role of the courts, but the legal and administrative paradigm it faced was far different from that which faced Roosevelt. The ability of the OSG to articulate a defense of the President's view of the Constitution was challenged as an unhealthy "politicization" of the office. Although the criticism itself was a form of political conflict, the charge affected the legal standing of the executive branch. According to the dictates of the charge, presidents ought to be free to enforce the law but not to interpret it.

In navigating this conception of executive power, the OSG is a crucial institutional actor but one that faces a distinct challenge. Reagan's first solicitor, Rex Lee offered a warning:

> There has been built up, over 115 years since this office was first created in 1870, a reservoir of credibility on which the incumbent Solicitor General may draw to his immediate adversarial advantage. But if he draws too deeply, too greedily, or too indiscriminately, then he jeopardizes not only that advantage in that particular case, but also an important institution of government (Lee 1986, 600).

Because the OSG is the lawyer for the United States, it occupies a crucial position in the scheme of separated power. Often called on to defend congressional statutes, at the Supreme Court it must also articulate an executive conception of the law. And because the

Court often defers to the expertise and judgment of the OSG, the office owes deference to the justices. "For centuries, lawyers and judges have viewed the separation of law from politics as a 'primary intellectual premise' of the legal profession," Ronald S. Chamberlein wrote in the beginning of his study of the OSG. "Under this view, law is immune to the whims of the masses." (Chamberlain 1987, 379) However, the president is also charged with the duty to enforce and interpret the laws, a balancing act that further complicates the relationship between the OSG and the Court.

In his review of the memoirs of Reagan's second Solicitor General Charles Fried, John O. McGinnis wrote,

> It is not the Solicitor General's responsibility to the President, however, but the President's responsibility to the Constitution that makes the Solicitor General a unique litigator before the Supreme Court. All Supreme Court advocates have clients who give general direction to the arguments presented in Court. The Solicitor General is no exception—his client is the President. However, as a matter of constitutional theory, the Solicitor General's role is different because his client has taken an oath to "preserve, protect and defend the Constitution of the United States," and because his client must "take Care that the Laws be faithfully executed." Thus, through his relationship with the President and by the terms of his own oath, the Solicitor General has an obligation that no private lawyer has: not simply to win cases, but to advance the President's interpretation of the Constitution and the laws made under it (McGinnis 1992, 804).

This dual responsibility was hampered during the Reagan administration due to strategic mistakes in advancing cases such as *Bob Jones University v. United States* (1983), in which the Court ruled that colleges and universities that discriminated according to race could be denied all federal funds, but also due to the misdirected criticisms of the politicization of the OSG. Whereas former solicitors general freely engaged in the overtly political acts of party and electoral campaigns, as well as offering advice to Presidents and executive officials, modern solicitors general have a confined constitutional space. Their sole function is litigation. Previous solicitors were free to further their advocacy

of a president's view of the Constitution in public and professional settings. Modern solicitors general no longer engage in that type of advocacy unless called before Congress, and even then their articulation of the executive's conception of the law is muted. The Reagan solicitors general advanced a novel conception of the law, one that was based in an earlier constitutionalism. In so doing they acted much like their New Deal predecessors. The space given to the executive to offer a view of the Constitution and standing law at odds with the prevailing paradigm had significantly narrowed. Although this chapter has attempted to demonstrate that the Reagan solicitors general were not more "political" than earlier occupants of the office, their ability to defend presidential prerogatives regarding the law and the Constitution had been hampered by the external expectations placed on their office.

The law versus politics debate continues today. During his confirmation hearings in the spring of 2001, Solicitor General–designate Theodore Olson encountered the same criticism as had his immediate predecessors in the Reagan, Bush, and Clinton Administrations. Senator Richard Durbin (D–IL) proclaimed that, "I can't find in history of anyone who was as actively involved in politics as you and went on to become solicitor general" (quoted in Caplan 2001, A19). The coverage of Olson's hearings was widespread. As an assistant attorney general during the Reagan Administration, Olson was the subject of an independent counsel investigation to determine whether he had withheld information from a congressional investigation. His refusal to cooperate with the investigation resulted in the landmark case *Morrison v. Olson* (1988), which upheld the constitutionality of the Ethics in Government Act of 1978, the statute that had created the independent counsel position. Olson went on to become a leading critic of the Clinton administration and had ties to the Arkansas Project, a conservative group committed to opposing Bill and Hillary Clinton. Finally, Olson was the lead attorney for the Bush campaign in *Bush v. Gore* (2000) in December of 2000, the Supreme Court case that resulted in the halting of recount efforts in the state of Florida following the irregularities during that year's presidential election. The decision effectively ensured the election of George W. Bush to the presidency. Olson's appointment as solicitor general furthered the politics versus law debate that is now a ritual in each successive appointment to the office.

In the twentieth century presidents have faced a greater responsibility to administer the law and have largely preferred to articulate emancipation from constitutional forms rather than formal constitutional change. The greatest such change occurred during the New Deal years. However, the New Deal is better appreciated as "quasi-constitutional" change: A commitment to ground the constitutional vision of the president into underlying traditions and judicial precedents. Roosevelt sought not to change the formal terms of the Constitution but, rather, argued that his reformist program was in line with existing constitutional norms. Whereas Lincoln changed the very form of constitutional government with the Thirteenth, Fourteenth, and Fifteenth Amendments, Roosevelt argued before the Supreme Court and public opinion that the New Deal was in line with constitutional precedent and ought to be accepted as such. When presidents attempt such an argument, the activities of the OSG are crucial not simply to their success or failure but also to retaining the executive prerogative power.

And the OSG had developed in such a way during the course of its history to allow it to become the articulator of quasi-constitutional change.

CONCLUSIONS

George W. Bush's second Solicitor General, Paul Clement, occupied an office relatively unchanged since Benjamin Bristow first gave definition and form to the nation's top lawyer. It is without question the premier legal institution in the United States and many of the nation's top lawyers, from Bristow and Phillips to John W. Davis, Robert Jackson, Archibald Cox, Thurgood Marshall, Robert Bork, and Ken Starr, have been called on to represent the United States. When they do so they address the Court in formal attire of striped pants, ascot, a waistcoat and morning coat. The solicitor general is the only participant in the process of hearing oral arguments before the justices who is so formally attired. This symbolic gesture of respect highlights the unusual role played by the solicitor general in the process of creating and defending the American system of law.

Notes

1. Congressional statutes have tended to confuse this centralization of authority only slightly. For example, the National Transportation Safety Board and the Federal Reserve Board have no litigation authority whatsoever. The Equal Employment Opportunity Commission has litigation authority up to the level of the federal appeals courts while the Federal Election Commission has litigation authority up to the Supreme Court (see Devins 1994). Despite these aberrations, the solicitor general remains the premier attorney in the federal government. The office enjoys substantial control over the process of filing amicus briefs.

2. This chapter uses the masculine adjective "his" to refer to the solicitor general because as of this writing in late 2006 the nation has never had a female solicitor general.

3. During the late nineteenth and early twentieth century, the solicitor general's nonlitigation duties were significantly reduced as the workload of the Supreme Court declined and narrowed. The 1891 Circuit Court of Appeals Act created an intermediate appellate level of federal courts and defined the concept of certiorari: both enactments reduced the number of cases the Court received and refined the quality of those cases that did emerge from the appellate process. Chief Justice Melville Fuller wrote a series of opinions between 1892 and 1910 that broadened the concept of certiorari to be discretionary. A "Judges Bill" was passed in 1925, at the behest of former Solicitor General and Chief Justice William Howard Taft that established statutory certiorari, further limiting the Court's obligatory jurisdiction.

11

SORCERERS' APPRENTICES

U.S. Supreme Court Law Clerks

Artemus Ward

The justices on the U.S. Supreme Court hire law clerks to assist them with their jobs. These clerks are generally young lawyers who have recently graduated from some of the best law schools in the country. Some estimates state that Harvard and Yale law schools account for roughly 40 percent of the recent clerks at the U.S. Supreme Court. Usually, these young lawyers have spent a year clerking for a lower court appellate judge before going to work at the U.S. Supreme Court. This chapter explores the historical evolution of the job of the Supreme Court law clerk, from what was in the beginning a mostly secretarial role to a crucial position that helps the justices with their most important work. The research for this chapter is based in large part on the official papers of past justices located in various archives around the country. Although today each justice is allowed a maximum of four law clerks, this small group of young attorneys can have a powerful impact on the workings of the Supreme Court, and especially on the process by which the Court decides which cases it will hear each year. Because the U.S. Supreme Court only accepts roughly 2 to 3 percent of the requests for it to hear a case, the importance of the law clerks has grown. This chapter is part of a relatively new line of research in judicial politics that looks at the role of actors who work for and with judges but who are not judges themselves. The chapter views law clerks as both legal and political actors.

U.S. Supreme Court law clerks do their work behind closed doors, largely invisible to public scrutiny. Yet they have come to play an integral role in the day-to-day functioning of the nation's highest court. Clerks are selected by and work for individual justices for one year. They come to the Court after having clerked the previous year for a prestigious judge on the U.S. Courts of Appeals and after graduating at the top of their classes from elite law schools such as Harvard, Yale, Chicago, Columbia, and Stanford. They do legal research, make recommendations on case outcomes, play a vital role in setting the Court's agenda, act as informal ambassadors across chambers in the negotiation and compromise of forming coalitions, and draft the opinions issued by the Court (see, e.g., Ward and Weiden 2006; Peppers 2006; Best 2002; Hutchinson and Garrow 2002; Lazarus 1998; Perry 1991). Yet in the first century of the Court's existence, there were no law clerks. To paraphrase Justice Louis Brandeis, the justices did their own work. What accounted for this extraordinary change?

This chapter will discuss the historical development of the institution of the law clerk from its genesis as an apprenticeship in learning the law to its modern incarnation as an indispensable and influential part of the Court's operation. Before formal legal education became commonplace, prospective attorneys trained with lawyers to learn the law. This apprentice model of legal education eventually gave rise to the phenomenon of the law clerk. Beginning with the first law clerk, Samuel Williston, who started clerking for Justice Horace Gray on the Supreme Court in 1882, the institution of the law clerk underwent successive transformations with clerks gaining increasing responsibility and influence. Changes in the way the justices conducted their work, as well as the number of law clerks allotted to the justices, caused one law clerk regime to be replaced by another. While there is some overlap and carryover from one regime to the next, each era of clerks had distinct characteristics that differentiated it in important ways from previous eras.

Table 11.1 shows the institutional development of the Supreme Court law clerk. The *recurrent structures*, such as research assistance and drafting opinions, reflect the most important routinized behaviors of clerks over time. These shared behaviors became more or less dominant at certain points because of the *emergent structures* that were imposed on the institution. On three occasions, the institution was transformed. Each time, Congress agreed with the Court's request to expand the number of clerks. The clerkship institution necessarily grew as the Court's workload increased and the justices struggled to keep up.

The first major transformation occurred in 1919. Clerks went from performing largely secretarial duties such as taking dictation and typing, to research assistance on cases. Clerks edited opinion drafts, added footnotes, and began reviewing certiorari (commonly referred to as cert.) petitions, still relatively few in number compared to recent years. In all, clerks performed these duties more for an advanced education in the law than because their justice needed the help.

The second major change took place in 1941. The number of clerks gradually doubled and they moved from research assistants to active decision makers. By this time, all of the justices and their clerks worked together in the new Supreme Court building. This gave rise to the clerk network with justices using their clerks to gain information across chambers to help in coalition formation. The number of cases petitioned to the Court, certiorari petitions, dramatically increased and each clerk was responsible for reviewing a larger number of prospective cases than ever before or since. It was also in this period that bench memos became the norm. Used in oral argument and conference, and often serving as the basis for written opinions, clerks analyzed cases and provided recommendations for their justices. When chief justices began assigning opinions equally rather than based on the speed of the author, clerks began drafting opinions with justices acting as editors.

Table 11.1 Regime Changes and Dominant Structures of Law Clerks in the U.S. Supreme Court

Years	Regime	Emergen Structures	Recurrent Structures
1882 to 1918	Secretaries	Clerks introduced Funded by justices Career appointments	Secretarial duties Learning the law
1919 to 1941	Research assistants	"Law clerk" established Funded by Congress	Research assistance
1942 to 1969	Junior justices	Clerks doubled in number Dead listing Opinion equalization Clerk network	Bench memos Certiorari memos Opinion drafting
1970 to present	Sorcerers' apprentices	Clerks doubled again Explosion of clerk applications Cert pool established	Pool memos Opinion writing

Once again, in 1970, the institution was transformed. Clerks went from largely being decision makers—making recommendations on cert. petitions and
in bench memos—to opinion writers. This was caused
by the addition of a third clerk, and later fourth, per
justice and the creation of the cert. pool. Each clerk
actually reviewed fewer petitions than in the previous
regime, and with more clerks per justice, they had
more time to devote to opinion writing. Clerk-written
opinions became the norm. Viewed through the lens
of historical development, the modern law clerk
bears little resemblance to its late-nineteenth-century
predecessor.

SECRETARIES: 1882 TO 1918

Initially, Congress appropriated funds for each justice to obtain the services of a single stenographer.
Some justices decided to pay for an additional clerk
themselves. Early clerks were commonly referred to
as "secretaries" because they performed clerical and
stenographical services for their justices and had little
authority or autonomy. Their duties included typing,
dictation, proofreading, and performing errands
such as paying the bills and even giving hair cuts!
(Newland 1961, 306). The tasks performed by early
clerks varied considerably, however, and some clerks
did perform legal tasks. Yet because early clerks had
relatively little responsibility, and because there were
very few applicants each year, ideology played no role
in clerk selection. Like the justices they served, every
one of the early clerks was a white male and nearly all
attended Harvard Law School.

An informal norm eventually developed with regard
to the tenure of law clerks. The career appointments
that were common in the early years of clerks soon
gave way to term appointments with tenure becoming
increasingly shorter until virtually every clerk worked
on the High Court for a single year. For example,
during this period, in the late-eighteenth and early-
nineteenth century, Clarence M. York and Frederick J.
Haig clerked for seventeen consecutive years—nearly
the entire tenures of the men for whom they clerked,
Chief Justice Melville Fuller and Justice David
Brewer. Yet since 1947, the last term of Justice Frank

Murphy's five-term clerk Eugene Gressman, only one
clerk served for three years on the High Court: John
W. Nields who clerked for Justice Byron White from
1974 through the 1976 term.[1]

Today, clerks have little desire to serve more than
one or two years for both financial and professional
reasons. Clerks have already served on a lower court
before coming to the Supreme Court. They often have
substantial student loans to pay back. Clerk salaries
are relatively low with the base pay for clerks with one
year of experience at $51,927 in 2005.[2] Because of
their academic success and clerking experience, they
are guaranteed a far more financially rewarding position when they leave public life. Clerks feel a strong
pull to leave their clerkships for private practice where
their salaries will immediately double or even triple.

Another hallmark of the early clerk was that, before
1935 and the creation of the present Supreme Court
building, the clerks typically performed their duties at
the private residences of the justices, and some clerks
even lived with their justices. Justice Charles Evans
Hughes discussed the role of early clerks, "My secretaries…were fine young men who had been admitted
to the bar, but as I kept them busy with dictation, hating
to write in longhand, they had little or no time to devote
to research and whatever was necessary in that line I
did myself. Occasionally, the question of providing law
clerks in addition to secretaries was raised, but nothing
was done. Some suggested that if we had experienced
law clerks, it might be thought that they were writing
our opinions" (quoted in Bickel 1964, 82).

RESEARCH ASSISTANTS: 1919 TO 1940

The year 1919 marked the first transformation of
the institution as law clerks became differentiated
from stenographic clerks. Also, long-standing career
appointments gave way to shorter, term appointments.
Clerkships continued to be the exclusive province
of white males and Harvard Law School continued
to provide more than half of Court's clerks with
Columbia and Yale beginning to make inroads. In
1919, Congress provided for a "stenographic clerk" at
an annual salary of $2,000 and a "law clerk" with a
salary of $3,600 per year (41 Stat. 209, July 19, 1919).

The justices responded by routinely employing two assistants with at least one largely acting as a research assistant. The clear division of labor firmly established the clerk's role as a legal researcher. For example, during the 1925 Term, Brandeis clerk James M. Landis did research for the Justice for the case of *Myers v. United States* (1926). Landis immersed himself in Senate publications regarding the Tenure of Office Act, calling his work "as thorough a piece of historical research as you would find in the Supreme Court Reports anywhere" (Baker 1984, 197).

Legal research also included drafting footnotes. Dean Acheson, who clerked during the 1919 term, described the division of labor between himself and Justice Brandeis as the justice writing the opinion, while he filled in the footnotes (Acheson 1957, 355). Even footnotes can be controversial. For example, 1953 Earl Warren clerk Richard Flynn inserted references in footnote eleven to seven different works of social scientists, including Gunnar Myrdal's sociological study of racism, in *Brown v. Board of Education*, 347 U.S. at 494, n.11 (1954). The references were essentially ignored by the members of the Court but hotly debated by the public.[3] Footnote four of *United States v. Carolene Products Co.*, 304 U.S. at 152 n.4 (1938), which sparked a transformation of equal protection jurisprudence, was largely written by Louis Lusky, clerk to Chief Justice Harlan Fiske Stone in 1937 (see Lusky 1982, 1993; Stone Papers, Box 67).[4] Herbert Wechsler, Stone's clerk from 1932, described Stone's penchant for footnotes as like "a squirrel storing nuts to be pulled out at some later time" (Stone Papers, Box 48).

As part of their apprenticeship early clerks were occasionally given the task of drafting an opinion. They soon found out that it was largely an exercise in learning the law and not for use by their justice. Acheson recalled Brandeis' practice, "When I finished my work on a draft which had been assigned to me or got as far as I could, I gave it to him. He tore it to pieces, sometimes using a little, sometimes none" (Abraham 1975, 238). It was reported that Justice Harlan Fiske Stone, who joined the Court in 1925, wrote the general outlines of his opinions on yellow legal pads, dictated facts and arguments to a stenographer, and then charged his clerk with writing the drafts (Pearson and Allen 1936, 109). Stone's secretary wrote:

In preparing opinions the Justice prepares a draft opinion in typewritten form. When he has gotten it into final shape, a carbon is given to the law clerk. The law clerk goes over the opinion....It will be the law clerk's responsibility to check the accuracy of all citations, both as to the name of the case and its citation, and as to its holding; to criticize the form of the opinions, so that so far as possible it may be expressed in terse, lucid English, accurately expressing the thought which is intended to be conveyed....and then he and the Justice go over it together (Undated and unsigned "office procedure" memorandum, Stone Papers, Box 81).

The clerks for Justice Holmes discussed cases with the justice, checked citations, and made editing suggestions for opinions. They worked at Holmes's house and frequently had time to themselves to read and study. Holmes once summoned a clerk, who was reading a novel in the next room, to discuss a case. When the clerk suggested the justice consider a particular precedent he had read while at Harvard, Holmes responded, "Do you think you might spare me a moment from your cultivated leisure to look out that citation?" (quoted in Bent 1932, 306). In *Danovitz v. United States* (1930), Holmes wrote, "The decisions under the revenue acts have little weight as against legislation under the afflatus of the Eighteenth Amendment" (281 U.S. at 389). One of his clerks questioned using the word "afflatus," noting that many people thought he purposely picked obscure words. Holmes replied, "Yes. I felt myself that it was rather a cabriole word" and left it in. When the same clerk objected to what he felt was an unclear paragraph in another opinion Holmes was writing, the Justice responded, "What the hell do you mean—not clear! Give it to me. Well, if you don't understand it, there may be some other damn fool who won't. So I would better change it." But on another occasion when a clerk suggested that a certain phrase the justice had included in an opinion would only be understood by one man in one thousand, Holmes answered, "I write for that man" (quoted in Bent 1932, 306).

During this era, clerks began writing memos on the cases petitioned to the Court. Initially, this was part of the clerks' apprenticeship and not a function performed for the benefit of the justice. John Knox, a clerk for Justice James McReynolds in 1936, recalled,

"Only gradually did it dawn upon me that the Justice regarded all of my work on these petitions as little more than a mental exercise to keep me busy and out of mischief. It was undeniably true that a great many petitions were without merit, and even without any of my summaries before him in conference McReynolds could have held his own with the other Justices"(Hutchinson and Garrow 2002, 86).

JUNIOR JUSTICES: 1941 TO 1969

Clerking was transformed again in 1941 when the number of clerks began to double to two per justice. Chief Justice Stone was the first to employ two formal law clerks expanding his staff to five including two secretaries and one messenger. Fred Vinson succeeded him as Chief in 1946. Vinson immediately added a third clerk when he joined the Court, prompting Judge Learned Hand to dub him "Vinson Incorporated." A former clerk thought that "Vinson Limited" was a more appropriate description.[5] With Vinson now using three clerks, most of his colleagues increased their allotments to two each. Justice William O. Douglas made a fleeting attempt to work with two clerks but he felt they had little to do. After a one-term experiment, he reverted back to his practice of a single clerk. In 1965, Douglas explained, "I tried two one year and discovered they spend about half their time writing memoranda to each other. I work pretty well with only one man. If he is married his wife ends up hating me because she never sees her husband" (William O. Douglas to Harry W. Jones, November 5, 1965, Douglas Papers, Box 1102).

It was during this period that the clerk-corps began to diversify—albeit slowly. While more than one-third of the clerks continued to come from Harvard Law School, The University of Chicago, Stanford, Virginia, and Michigan joined Yale and Columbia to form the stable "top-seven" accounting for three-fourths of the clerks during this period and into the next. While the first female clerk (Lucile Lomen) was hired by Justice Douglas in 1944, the second and third female clerks (Margaret J. Corcoran and Martha F. Alschuler) were not hired until 1966 and 1968 by Justices Hugo Black and Abe Fortas, respectively. The first African

American clerk (William T. Coleman) was selected by Justice Frankfurter in 1948. Chief Justice Warren selected the Court's second African American (Tyrone Brown) in 1967.

Agenda Setting: Dead Listing

The creation of the "dead list" under Chief Justice Hughes prompted the justices to rely more heavily on their clerks for certiorari memos—brief summaries of the case and a determination of whether the case should be accepted for review. Previously, every case petitioned to the Court was discussed in conference with the Chief Justice summarizing the facts and issues involved. When Hughes started circulating a "dead list" of cases he would not discuss in conference unless one of the other justices requested it, justices who had previously relied on the Chief's summaries to familiarize themselves with the cases now turned to their clerks for assistance. The practice expanded under Chief Justices Stone and Vinson as the number of cases placed on the dead list climbed.

Although some clerks continued to assist their justices with correspondence, the preparation of speeches, and other clerical tasks, dead listing resulted in most clerks becoming key players in the agenda-setting process. In 1950, Chief Justice Vinson stopped circulating the dead list (Provine 1980, 28–29). Since then, the justices have only worked from the "discuss list" with any justice able to place a case on the list at any time and as many times as he or she wishes. By the 1950s, justices who still did their own cert. work, like Justice Felix Frankfurter, were rare. Justice William Brennan also largely reviewed cert. petitions himself. Frankfurter and Brennan were somewhat unique during this period when many justices had two clerks and had to find something for them to do.

As dockets grew, and a greater number of cases failed to make the discuss list, the justices were forced to rely more heavily on their clerks. Chief Justice Earl Warren told one of his clerks, "I just read your memos and I don't think you need twenty pages to convince me that those are cert-worthy cases. I hope you can be more brief in the future, because I have to wade through an awful lot of these memos for each conference" (Schwartz and Lesher 1983, 32). In 1961, Justice

Douglas said, "My law clerk writes a memorandum on all the certioraris and appeals that come in—a very useful record. I make some notes on his memoranda and they are good reference material, particularly if the case comes up for argument or of it comes back for a rehearing."[6]

At this time, cert. memos written by clerks were only read by that clerk's justice and were not circulated to other chambers, as would later be the case. The exception, however, was the Miscellaneous Docket, which included capital cases in the form of *in forma pauperis* (IFP) petitions. One clerk described them as "that handwritten garbage" because they often came to the Court scrawled on scraps of paper, usually by prisoners claiming violations of their constitutional rights (Schwartz and Lesher 1983, 38–39). Beginning with the Chief Justiceship of Charles Evans Hughes, these petitions were only screened by the chief's clerks who wrote brief memos on each. Initially only Hughes reviewed the memos, but subsequent chief justices

circulated the memos to all the chambers for review. If the clerk felt the petition had merit, he included it with his memo for circulation, but this happened only rarely.

The petition in *Gideon v. Wainwright* (1963) came to the Court in this form and ultimately led to the landmark ruling that indigent defendants have a constitutional right to proper counsel. The unique IFP role performed by the chief justice's clerks gave them considerable discretion over the Court's Miscellaneous Docket and continued until the Court abolished the Miscellaneous Docket in 1971, placing all cases, including IFPs, on a single docket for review by every justice. Indeed, as Figure 11.1 shows, this rule change immediately eased the enormous burden the chief's clerks were under with the IFPs.

The clerk's role in the certiorari process transformed the institution during this era. As the number of petitions increased, clerk influence grew. Clerks now constituted a Court-within-a-Court as justices

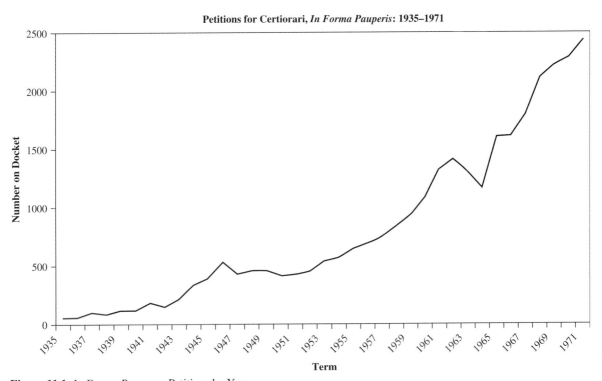

Figure 11.1 *In Forma Pauperus* Petitions by Year

increasingly relied on them. Growing dockets meant that justices were less able to read the petitions themselves as a check against their clerks. In most cases, the only check in place was that each chambers had at least one clerk reviewing each case for their justice. Litigants were assured that at least nine different clerks looked at their case. Of course with IFP petitions, only one clerk in the Chief's chambers reviewed each case.

By 1970 the Court was receiving over 4,000 petitions a year and the Court struggled to keep pace. Table 11.2 shows the number of cert. petitions reviewed by clerks of associate justices prior to the inception of the pool. The data for the 1940s are telling. On the surface, it appears that the single clerk that each justice annually employed for most of the decade was terribly burdened by cert. petitions. The reality, however, was that most of the justices helped their clerks in reviewing the cases, thereby reducing clerk workload. Justice Frankfurter, for example, handled all the cert. petitions himself. It was the rare justice who completely delegated the review of all the petitions to his clerk. Justice McReynolds followed this then-unusual practice. His clerk from 1936, John Knox, described his first day of work in late August, "The floor of the entire room was literally filled to a depth of more than a foot with hundreds of statements of fact, briefs, answers, etc.—all comprising what seemed to be countless petitions for certiorari. There were at the time approximately five hundred petitions piled on the floor of that room.[7] All of these would have to be read before the opening of Court in October, and a page referring to each petition would then have to be typed. I had five weeks and two days in which to do this work" (quoted in Hutchinson and Garrow 2002, 14).

However, by the late 1960s, clerks had largely taken over this task and with growing dockets, were overwhelmed with work. In 1965, each clerk reviewed 582 cert. petitions or more than 11 petitions each week. By 1970, the last term before the rule change, each justice had three clerks but the non-IFP docket had expanded to almost 2,000 cases. On average, each clerk reviewed 634 petitions for the 1970 term, or more than 12 per week. This left little time for anything else, including opinion writing, which was less pronounced, however, at this time.

As Table 11.3 shows, the chief justice's clerks were even more overworked as they had to review all the cert. petitions for the chief, as well as the petitions on the Court's Miscellaneous Docket, largely comprised of IFP petitions, for the entire Court. However, chief justices devised ways to lighten the burden of reviewing the IFP petitions. Warren was so stunned by the crushing workload that fell on his clerks that he sought additional help. Warren spoke to recently retired Justice Stanley Reed, and they devised a plan. Former clerk Arthur Rosett explained, "It was during this period that the miscellaneous docket was growing rapidly. And they hit upon the scheme of putting in an appropriation line item for a clerk for the retired justices who, at that time, were Reed and Burton" (Arthur Rosett Interview, Stanley Forman Reed Oral History Project, University of Kentucky) In 1959, Rosett was the first clerk ever selected for a retired justice. Reed and Warren came to an agreement whereby the chief

Table 11.2 Law Clerk Workload 1: Cert. Petitions and Associate Justices

Year	Number of Clerks Per Associate Justice	Total Number of Cert. Petitions[a]	Number of Cert. Petitions Reviewed by Each Clerk
1940	1	814	824
1945	1	774	774
1950	2	640	320
1955	2	842	421
1960	2	789	395
1965	2	1,164	582
1970	3	1,903	634

[a] Does not include *in forma pauperis* petitions, as they were reviewed exclusively by the chief justice's clerks.

Table 11.3 Law Clerk Workload 2: Cert. Petitions and Chief Justices

Year	Number of Chief Justice's Clerks	Total Number of Cert. Petitions[a]	Number of Cert. Petitions Reviewed by Each Clerk
1940	1	934	934
1945	2	1,167	834
1950	2	1,055	528
1955	3	1,487	496
1960	4[b]	1,874	469
1965	4[b]	2,774	694
1968	4[b]	3,376	844

[a] Includes *in forma pauperis* petitions, as they were reviewed exclusively by the chief justice's clerks.

[b] Includes clerks for retired justices used primarily by the chief justice.

would primarily use the new clerk. While the system may have worked well for Douglas and the other associate justices, in Chief Justice Warren's last year the four clerks reviewed nearly 850 petitions each, an average of over 16 per week.

Bench Memos

Another significant innovation in the era of junior justices was the introduction of bench memos. Justice Harold Burton and several other justices began requiring their clerks to prepare short summaries of the cases that were to be argued before the Court and discussed in conference. These memos outlined the relevant facts and issues of the case, suggested questions to be put forth during oral argument, and depending on the justice, occasionally made recommendations on the merits of the case (O'Brien 1990). In a note to Justice John Marshall Harlan, Justice Felix Frankfurter expressed his, concern over the justices who "have [their] mind[s] all made up on [the] basis of [their] law clerk's bench memos, as I see the C.J. reading those bench memos" (Schwartz 1996, 52).

Writing bench memos became a standard clerk function during this period and continued with nearly every justice into the next era. The forty-one-page bench memo prepared by one of Justice Harry Blackmun's 1971 clerks John T. Rich in the case of *Moose Lodge v. Irvis* (1972) was a typical example of the kind of detail Blackmun expected (John T. Rich to Harry A. Blackmun, February 19, 1972, Blackmun

Papers, Box 139). One former clerk commented that the clerks who "worked by some considerable measure the hardest" were those of Justices Harry Blackmun and Sandra Day O'Connor. The clerk continued, "Both had clerks writing fairly substantial memoranda on each case that was to be argued. I think from early September until May I had one day away from the office" (Gamarekian 1989, B7). Powell felt that his Chambers was so overburdened that he even sent some of his bench memo work to the staff clerks on the Fourth Circuit Court of Appeals! (see, e.g., Lewis F. Powell, Jr., to Larry G. Alexander, July 18, 1973, Powell Papers, Box 130b).

After reading the bench memos, it was not uncommon for justices to discuss the cases with their clerks prior to oral argument. Justice Anthony Kennedy explained that he liked, "to talk through the cases with my clerks" and modeled his interaction with them at this stage on the "discursive" exchanges between barristers and judges in England where informal oral argument can last days as the precedents are consulted and discussed (Taylor 1988, B7).

Similar to bench memos, clerks were sometimes directed to write lengthy memoranda on particular areas of the law. In 1954, Justice Frankfurter asked his clerk Alexander Bickel to write a memo on segregation. Bickel, who went on to become a highly respected and widely published law professor, produced a ninety-one-page analysis of the issue (O'Brien 1990, 162). Justice Robert Jackson asked his clerk, William H. Rehnquist, for a memo on the same topic. At the end of his analysis entitled, "A Random Thought on the Segregation Cases," Rehnquist concluded, "I realize that it is an unpopular and unhamanitarian position, but I think *Plessy v. Ferguson* was right and should be reaffirmed" (O'Brien 1990, 168).

With considerable influence in the cert. process and bench memos, clerks were treated with a new level of respect by their justices. Justice Frankfurter said, "They are, as it were, my junior partners—junior only in years. In the realm of the mind there is no hierarchy. I take them fully into my confidence so that the relation is free and easy. However, I am, they will tell you, a very exacting task-master; no nonsense, intellectually speaking, is tolerated, no short-cuts, no deference to position is permitted, no yes-sing, however much some of them in the beginning be awed" (Baker 1984, 415).

Equalizing Opinion Assignment: Clerk Opinion Drafting

As clerks demonstrated high levels of competence in the cert. process and in drafting bench memos, justices felt more comfortable allowing their clerks to draft opinions, sometimes rarely or occasionally as with Justices Black and Douglas, and sometimes regularly as was the case with Chief Justice Vinson and Justices Frankfurter, Murphy, and Burton. Burton codified his expectations in a memorandum to his clerks that he wanted them, "to feel a keen personal interest in our joint product," and expected, "the most complete possible exchange of views and the utmost freedom of expression of opinion on all matters to the end that the best possible product may result" (O'Brien 1990, 161).

Beginning with Fred Vinson's Chief Justiceship, and fully realized under Earl Warren, the opinion writing process changed dramatically, and with it the role of clerks. Justices who were accustomed to writing very few opinions each term under Chief Justices Taft, Hughes, and Stone, and in the early years of Vinson's tenure, were suddenly expected to greatly increase their opinion output, and they turned to their clerks for help. Clerks for justices who wrote their own opinions at a relatively quick pace like Black and Douglas were unaffected while clerks for more methodical writers like Frankfurter and Reed found themselves writing virtually all of their justice's opinions.[8]

The equality principle produced significant changes. Justice Douglas commented on the new system, "It has disadvantages to those of us who get out our work promptly because there is practically nothing to do from the first of May on. And judges who work more slowly are working long hours, Sundays, until the whole thing comes to a halt sometimes near the end of June."[9] In an attempt to cut down on these long hours, clerks took on an increased role. Judge Richard Posner, who clerked for Justice Brennan in 1962, said, "By 1959, a majority of the Supreme Court's opinions were being written by law clerks" (Posner 1995, 57).

Justice Douglas remarked on the increasing use of clerks in opinion writing, "As the years passed, it became more and more evident that the law clerks were drafting opinions. Brandeis, I think, was correct in believing that the totality of one decision should rest wholly on the Justice. That simply could not happen unless he was the architect, carpenter, mason, plumber, plasterer and roofer who put the whole structure together" (Douglas 1980, 173). Douglas wrote most of his own opinions and in general kept his clerks at arms length. In 1961, Douglas said, "I have written all my own opinions. I use my law clerk to do research for me. I often send him to the library to prepare a footnote to an opinion that I am writing, telling him the cases pro and con that I want him to collect. Sometimes I ask him to prepare a digest for me that I'll put in a footnote. My law clerk has the responsibility of approving all my opinions for accuracy."[10]

Some of Justice Felix Frankfurter's most famous opinions were almost entirely the handiwork of his clerks, like his dissent in *Baker v. Carr* (1962). Anthony G. Amsterdam clerked for Frankfurter in 1960 and often prepared opinions in which Frankfurter only made minor changes. After Amsterdam submitted a dissent in *Elkins v. United States* (1960) to the justice, Frankfurter returned it with the attached note, "If you approve of my revisions send to printer and duly circulate" (quoted in Schwartz and Lesher 1983, 38). Frankfurter himself, however, was keenly aware of the extent to which his colleagues used their clerks in opinion writing and thought that he had struck the proper balance. He remarked, "The problem with Stanley [Reed] is that he doesn't let his law clerks do enough of the work. The trouble with Murphy is that he lets them do too much."[11]

The Clerk Network: Coalition Formation

During the junior justice era clerks also took on a crucial role in coalition formation through the clerk network (see, e.g., Woodward and Armstrong 1979, 34–36). Clerks began to regularly talk to each other about their justices' as well as their own views and positions on cases and issues and then relay that information to their justices. Martha Minow, Harvard law professor and former clerk for Justice Thurgood Marshall during the 1980 term, explained, "It's almost an ambassadorial role, trying to pick up information behind the scenes" (quoted in Mauro 1998, 13A). Clerks informally mine the network during the coalition forming stage as votes are cast, opinions are joined, and requests for changes are made from chambers to chambers (See Maltzman, Spriggs, and Wahlbeck 2000).

The clerk network started to emerge after the Supreme Court building was completed in 1935. At first, only Chief Justice Charles Evans Hughes and Justice Owen Roberts regularly used their chambers while their colleagues preferred to continue doing their work at home (Hutchinson and Garrow 2002, 12). Hugo Black's appointment in 1937 started the practice of new justices choosing to work primarily at the Court. With the exception of Chief Justice Stone, by 1941, every member of the Court was regularly using his High Court chambers. The Court was fully occupied by all the justices and their staffs beginning in 1946 when Chief Justice Fred Vinson was appointed.

The result was that instead of working in the homes of their justices, geographically isolated from one another, every clerk worked in the same building, on the same floor, and in offices next to each other. The importance of this new working environment cannot be overstated. Clerks from different chambers saw each other on a daily basis: on the way to work, in the Court's parking garage, during lunch, at the Court's gym, and after work. Clerks began regularly lunching together and the discussions frequently involved the cases on which they were working. When the Court established a separate dining room for the clerks,

they saw even more of each other. For their part, the justices saw that they could benefit from the clerk network, and formally establishing a clerk's dining room was a way to foster it.

Clerks became an important resource to their justices as the least obtrusive means of obtaining information about the positions of their colleagues. Because clerks were already commenting on the memoranda and opinions from the other chambers, and making recommendations on whether to issue separate opinions, both clerks and justices recognized the benefits of obtaining further information. The clerk network continued to flourish into the next era as the doubling of clerks meant more opportunities for contacts in other chambers.

SORCERERS' APPRENTICES: 1970 TO PRESENT

In 1970, Congress once again increased the number of clerks to three and then to four in 1974. With their increasing responsibility, it might be thought that doubling the number of clerks would result in placing checks on and stemming the tide of clerk influence on the decision-making process. Instead, the power of clerks grew as the justices increasingly relied on them to conduct the business of the Court. Indeed, with continually rising dockets and generally increased workload, it was widely understood that the Court could not function without the clerks.

Nearly all the clerks continued to come from the top-seven clerk-producing schools with Harvard leading the pack by providing one-quarter of the clerks each term. Beginning in 1971 the Court always had at least one female clerk and two or more regularly since 1974. And while the number of female clerks increased through the period, by the inception of the Roberts' Court, they still comprised no more than 40 percent of the total clerking corps. The Court has never employed African American clerks with any kind of regularity. Through 1996, the justices had only selected seventeen African American clerks. The relative lack of female and African American clerks has not gone unnoticed, and there have been recent calls to further diversify the clerking corps (see, e.g.,

Mauro 2006b; Greenhouse 2006). In general, there is a high degree of ideological congruence between justices and clerks (Ward and Weiden 2006; Peppers 2006). Prior to the modern period, justices received very few applications and clerks were more selective to whom they applied, often excluding justices with whom they did not ideologically agree. However, in the modern period the number of applications the justices receive has exploded with prospective clerks now routinely applying to all nine justices. Justices are able to gauge the ideological persuasion of clerks through application cues such as membership in organizations like the conservative Federalist Society and their clerkships with Courts of Appeals judges. Indeed, the top "feeder-judges" that provide Supreme Court clerks have become an increasingly polarized group with more ideological extreme judges providing Supreme Court clerks in the modern era (Garrow 2006, 417).

Deciding to Decide: The Cert. Pool

The justices immediately took advantage of their new allotment of clerks in the 1970s. The cert. pool was created in 1972 and once again the institution of the law clerk was transformed. Up to this point, each chamber was responsible for separately reviewing each case petitioned to the Court. The two or three clerks in each chamber divided the petitions between them so that each justice had a memo on each case written by one of his own clerks. To reduce the growing workload caused by the increasing number of cases filed, Justice Powell suggested the Court pool its clerks to reduce the duplication of effort by the clerks in each justice's chambers. A number of justices agreed to participate in the "cert. pool" and over time, an increasing number of new justices joined. The idea was a simple one. Rather than have nine clerk-written memos on each case, the pool of clerks would divide up all the petitions and produce only one memo on each case for all the justices who chose to participate. After the retirement of Justice Thurgood Marshall in 1991, only Justice Stevens remained outside the pool, choosing to have his clerks review all the cert. petitions themselves, as was the practice before the creation of the cert. pool. One reason Stevens decided to remain outside the pool was to provide a check against what

he saw as a dangerous practice that ceded too much authority to a single clerk.

The law clerks are the initial gatekeepers for access to the Court in the cert. process. Justice Rehnquist explained, "As soon as I am confident that my new law clerks are reliable, I take their word and that of the pool memo writer as to the underlying facts and contentions of the parties in the various petitions, and with a large majority of the petitions it is not necessary to go any further than the pool memo. In cases that seem from the memo perhaps to warrant a vote to grant certiorari, I may ask my law clerk to further check out one of the issues, and may review the lower court opinion, the petition, and the response myself"(Rehnquist 2001, 233–34). Rehnquist's comments indicate an important caveat to the importance of the clerks in the certiorari process, though. In landmark or controversial cases, the justices are unlikely to rely on the clerk's recommendation much, if at all. In general then, the clerk's influence is likely to be greatest where the justice does not have a strong preference (Perry 1991; Sturley 1992).

The creation and expansion of the cert. pool has led to a number of unintended consequences. First, there has been a decline in candor as pool memos are now written for multiple justices. This has led to a rise in the discussion of more "neutral" factors of cert.-worthiness such as conflict among lower courts. Second, the cert. pool has fostered an increased emphasis on partisanship and strategy as clerks now have the ear of multiple chambers. Knowing this, clerks and justices read pool memos skeptically with an eye toward detecting partisan arguments or omissions from other chambers. Finally, the pool has had a significant effect on the workload of individual clerks. Each modern law clerk actually reviews far fewer petitions than their predecessors did giving them more time to devote to other tasks such as mining the clerk network and writing opinions. This chapter will now discuss each of these unforeseen cert.-pool effects in turn.

The Decline of Candor and the Rise of Circuit Conflict

Although clerk influence in the cert. process is not total, it is considerable, to say the least. The institutionalization of the law clerk has shaped the ways in which the cert. pool operates. First, there is a culture of high achievement and competence among the clerks, accompanied by a corresponding status competition. Former Blackmun clerk Dan Coenen noted, "Law clerks are, by and large, hard-driven high achievers who develop profound loyalties to their own Justices; to such persons, producing written work that brings disrepute upon themselves and their chambers is little less than a heart-stopping prospect" (Coenen 1993, 185). This culture of competitiveness, ability, and expertise is hardly surprising, given that the clerks are almost uniformly chosen from the elite law schools and are ranked at the top of their classes. Despite the tremendous workload that is imposed on them, the culture of the clerks that developed through the process of institutionalization ensured that they would expend a great deal of effort when preparing the pool memos, knowing that this signed memo would be widely distributed among other clerks and the justices.[12] Laura Ingraham, who clerked for Justice Clarence Thomas in 1992 explained, "You're in perpetual fear of making a mistake. The fear factor keeps the work product reliable" (quoted in Mauro 1998, 13A).

There is some evidence that clerks who wrote only for their own justice were more candid in the past, particularly with political analyses and recommendations, than are current clerks who write one memo for eight justices who occupy different ends of the ideological spectrum. Justice Powell wrote to his incoming clerks for the 1973 term:

> While every petition, including the IFP's, merits careful consideration, it will be obvious to you fairly quickly that a substantial percentage—especially of the criminal IFP's—are without merit or frivolous. When this is perfectly clear, do not devote a great deal of time to writing a long memorandum. When you are writing for the Pool, you have to be somewhat more careful to "lay out" the pros and cons of a meritless or frivolous petition than when you are writing solely for me (Lewis F. Powell, Jr., to John J. Buckley, John C. Jeffries, Jr., and Jack B. Owens, June 26, 1973, Powell Papers, Box 130b).

One example of candid analysis from long before the cert. pool began took place in November 1954, six months after the Court's decision in *Brown v. Board of Education* (1954). The Court was asked to consider the constitutionality of a state antimiscegenation law. In his cert. memo, Chief Justice Warren's clerk wrote, "If students cannot be segregated on the basis of race, what of spouses?...Perhaps someday the court will have to [rule] on these questions. But review at the present time could only seriously aggravate the tensions stimulated by last term's segregation decision" (Price 1997, 1E). Justice Harold Burton's clerk made a similar analysis, "because of the political repercussions of the segregation decision, it would not be feasible politically to take this case at this time" (Price 1997, 1E). In another case prior to the pool, a clerk for Justice Douglas wrote, "It will begin to look obvious if the case is not taken that the court is trying to run away from its obligation to decide the case" (Price 1997, 1E).

Some Justices like Hugo Black and Potter Stewart preferred short, candid cert. memos. Pool writers, however, generally take an opposite approach, attempting to incorporate every possible argument in an objective fashion. Although still a proponent of pooling clerks, Justice Blackmun explained the notable difference in the cert. memos he read after the first year of the cert. pool:

> I am all in favor of the cert pool and the accomplishment of its intended purpose to conserve the time of the clerks. It has the opposite effect for me personally for, because of the extra length of the memoranda, the system takes more of my time than if the memos were prepared in my own chambers. This is partly due, I suspect, to the fact that each memo-writer, while he may know his own Justice, wishes to be sure that he covers every possible point in which any of the other Justices might be interested (Harry A. Blackmun to Kenneth F. Ripple, September 25, 1973, Blackmun Papers, Box 1374).

Some pool memos do not even contain recommendations. Instead, they provide analysis of what the Court may want to do and how they could go about doing it. The decline of candid analyses in pool memos is no doubt one reason why justices ask their own clerks to mark up the pool memo and do further research if a pool memo piques their interest. The case of *Regents of the University of California v. Bakke* (1978) illustrates this. Powell clerk David A. Martin wrote his Justice,

"A clean grant.... This case presents with clarity an issue of great importance.... I recommend you assign one of us promptly to begin reading and thinking in preparation for this case" (David A. Martin to Lewis F. Powell, Jr., January 13, 1977, Powell Papers, Box 46).

It should be kept in mind that the clerks, although in possession of topnotch academic credentials, do not typically have a broad vision of the Court's jurisprudential trends or a great deal of legal experience (see, e.g., Crump 1986, 236). This point is underscored by a former clerk who noted that certain constitutional issues would not be given preference by the clerks, simply due to their lack of experience (Crump 1986, 236).[13] Given that the clerks wish to write a credible pool memo, they will naturally seek factors to justify their recommendations that are easily identifiable and defensible. The clerk culture has created an atmosphere in which clerks tend to emphasize the presence of a conflict between the circuit courts as a reason to recommend granting certiorari. To be sure, the presence of a circuit conflict has always been viewed as an important criterion in the decision to grant review. Commentators have noted the relevance of the role of the Court in assuring national uniformity of the law through the resolution of conflicts (see, e.g., Stern 1953, 465; Stern, Gressman, and Shapiro 1986). Previous research has shown that circuit conflict was the most significant predictor for certiorari decisions on the Vinson and Warren Courts (Ulmer 1984, 901). Thus, it is certainly not novel to comment on the importance of conflict in the certiorari process.

How important has circuit conflict been since the Warren Court and particularly since the cert. pool was created? The evidence suggests that clerks, lacking institutional memory and a broad outline of the Court's trends, focused on the observable features of cases that could be justified as being "cert.-worthy." With the creation of the cert. pool in 1972, clerks increasingly emphasized circuit conflict. Knowing that they were writing for all of the justices in the pool as well as other law clerks, pool clerks gravitated toward a criterion that was easily defensible and not subject to attack by other clerks.

In his book on the certiorari process, H. W. Perry (1991) reported that all sixty-four former clerks he interviewed noted that a conflict in the lower courts

was the factor that was most important to them when reviewing cert. petitions. In response to this development, Justice Byron White had an internal check against pool memos that cited circuit conflict. In 1983, White clerk Kevin Worthen said, "Clerks were not allowed to rely on the parties' assertion that the conflict existed. They were not even permitted to take the word of clerks from other chambers who may have prepared the cert memo. Clerks had to read the cases themselves and certify whether the conflict was real" (Worthen 1994, 355).

Partisanship and Strategy

Despite the incentives for pool clerks to write objectively, there is evidence that they behave in partisan and strategic ways. One way that clerks exercise influence in the cert. pool is through the substance and form of the cert. memos themselves. Sometimes, the line between objective analysis and advocacy is blurred as clerks are charged with making recommendations. For example, Michael Conley, a Blackmun clerk from 1990 said, "To the extent that you are looking at pool memos from clerks indicating that a case shouldn't be taken, very often that's a defensive posture. You realize that it is much better for a case not to be taken.... There is room for judgment on whether it is now the right time" (Murdoch and Price 2001, 17).

This suggests that some clerks may have crossed the line. For example, separate opinions from the lower court have often been omitted from pool memos. Indeed, Justice Blackmun made an annual plea to the chambers of his colleagues in the pool, "I have sensed... in the pool memos, a tendency to overlook dissents. I personally would appreciate it if clerks, in preparing the memoranda, would outline the position of dissenting judges. A dissent expresses judicial disagreement, and I, for one, want to know the opposing posture without having to dig back myself each time" (Harry A. Blackmun to Warren E. Burger, Byron R. White, Lewis F. Powell, and William H. Rehnquist, October 28, 1977, Blackmun Papers, Box 1374). Were these omissions calculated? Chief Justice Burger replied, "Some clerks are plainly 'sloppy' on this. Please each of you, tell your clerks that we will set up some 'Williamsburg stocks' in the courtyards to discipline those who err" (Warren E. Burger to the chambers of Byron R. White, Harry A. Blackmun, Lewis F. Powell, and William H. Rehnquist, August 3, 1978, Blackmun Papers, Box 1374).

Another common omission that Justice Blackmun was concerned about was the absence of the names of the judges participating in the case. Blackmun wrote, "I have noted a tendency this year (as in some prior years) to omit the names of the judges participating in the decision below and to use, instead, a phrase such as 'per curiam' or nothing at all. I like to know who the judges below were, even when the petition or jurisdictional statement comes from a state court" (Harry A. Blackmun to Jan Horbaly, September 18, 1984, Blackmun Papers, Box 1374). Whether pool clerks were behaving strategically or not, omitting the names of judges makes it more difficult to identify the ideological direction of the outcome, that is, whether it was liberal or conservative.

A similar problem exists with the labels that are placed after the names of the parties to the case. One problem is omission. Clerks were reminded, "When a case is styled 'SMITH v. DOE, et al.' and one of the parties is a senator, congressman, cabinet officer, judge, mayor, police officer, warden, school board member, inventor, husband or wife (in a divorce action), employer or employee (in a labor matter), etc., the party should be identified. For example, 'SMITH (Attorney General) v. DOE (taxpayer), et al.' This information is helpful to the Justices because it makes it easy to identify the party who lost in the Court of Appeals or the District Court" (Jan Horbaly to Law Clerks in the Cert. Pool, September 15, 1984, Blackmun Papers, Box 1374). The following is a list of examples of labels on a group of IFP cert memos chosen at random from 1983, "sex offender," "prisoner," "prison officials," "murderer," "convicted of murder," "schemer," "sibling bank robbers," "criminal deft," "criminal," "car thief," "Sec'y HHS," "former guardian *ad litem*," "alien smuggler," "Prison Superintendent," "warden," "defrauder," "convict," and "counterfeiter" (Certiorari Memoranda, *In Forma Pauperis*, 83–5809 to 83–5853, Blackmun Papers, Box 1021). Plainly, the labeling prerogative suggests the problem of "editorializing." For example, in the cross-burning case *R.A.V. v. St. Paul* (1992), Rehnquist clerk Jeffrey L. Bleich

labeled the petitioner, "R.A.V. (skinhead)" (Certiorari Memoranda, *In Forma Pauperis*, 83–5809 to 83–5853, Blackmun Papers, Box 1021).

There is also a danger that pool writers as well as the chief clerk may manipulate the timing of releasing pool memos to the justices before the conference vote. Of course it may also be that pool clerks and the chief clerk are simply behind in their work. The files of Justices Blackmun and Powell contain numerous complaints from pool justices over the lateness of pool memos.

Suspicions about partisan pool clerks have led the justices to place internal checks on pool memos to guard against outside influence. The mark-up memo is the most important formal check. In discussing the process of reviewing pool memos from other chambers, outgoing 1977 chief administrative clerk for Justice Powell, Sam Estreicher, wrote the incoming clerks, "You will quickly develop a mental list of the clerks who can be relied upon to write a fair, soundly reasoned memo. Where the cert. pool author recommends a 'grant' or a 'note,' I found it useful to go to the papers and at least read the opinion of the court below" (Samuel Estreicher to Paul B. Stephan, III, Eric G. Andersen, James Bruce Boisture, and David L. Westin, July 21, 1978, Powell Papers, Box 130b). In 1986, Justice Blackmun began to have his clerks add more information to the last name of the pool clerk appearing at the end of each pool memo. Blackmun's clerks added the first name, law school attended, the last name, and circuit or district of the lower court judge he or she clerked for, and then the name of the justice he or she was currently working for (see, e.g., Blackmun Papers, Box 1093). For example, "Dunnigan" became "Vaughn Dunnigan (SOC, Browning, Columbia)" (Blackmun Papers, Box 1289). Clearly such information would not be necessary if each pool clerk provided objective analyses.

Workload

However, even with the important developments of the decline of candor, the rise of the use of circuit conflict, and strategic behavior, the key effect of the cert. pool was the drastic reduction in the number of cases that pool clerks had to review. Table 11.4 shows the radical transformation in clerk workload that took place

Table 11.4 Law Clerk Workload 3: Cert. Petitions and Effect of Cert. Pool

Year	Number of Justices in Pool	Number of Clerks in Pool[a]	Total Number of Cert. Petitions	Number of Cert. Petitions Per Pool Clerk
1972	5	18	4,619	257
1975	5	18	4,747	264
1980	5	19	5,120	269
1985	5	22	5,148	234
1990	7	29	6,758	233
1995	8	34	7,554	222
2000	8	29	7,851	271

Note. From Epstein et al., *The Supreme Court Compendium*, 1997, 82–83; U.S. Supreme Court.
[a] Includes clerks for retired justices who participated in cert. pool.

beginning in 1972 with the creation of the cert. pool. Over time, rising dockets have been balanced by the combination of increases in law clerks and the growing number of justices, and therefore clerks, entering the pool. This has resulted in a relatively stable number of cert. petitions assigned to each pool clerk: roughly 250 each, or an average of 4 to 5 petitions per week. In essence, the pool clerk's workload has been cut in half—an astonishing feat given that the Court's docket has almost doubled at the same time.

Clerks are spending far less time now on cert. petitions than they did thirty years ago before the pool started. Former Stevens clerk Sean Donahue, who along with the other Stevens clerks did not participate in the pool, said, "I would estimate that cert petitions took up roughly a third of our work time. My guess is that this is more time than the average cert pool clerk spent on petitions, but only slightly more" (Donahue 1995, 79). With Stevens's clerks reviewing far more petitions than the pool clerks, but spending nearly the same amount of time on the process, it is likely that pool clerks are able to delve more deeply into each case, than clerks from the previous era. It can also be deduced that clerks from the late 1960s were probably spending about two-thirds of their time reviewing cert. petitions. This suggests that most of the additional time modern clerks gained by the creation of the cert. pool has been spent on opinion writing and is likely a contributing factor in the explosion in the number of separate concurring and dissenting opinions now issued by the Court (see, e.g., Best 2002).

Another implication of the increased use of clerks in the cert. process is that the Court has granted certiorari in, and subsequently decided, fewer cases. Figure 11.2 shows the shrinking number of cases that the Court has decided in recent years (see O'Brien 1997, 58). The most dramatic decreases during the Rehnquist Court (1986 to 2005) coincide with the increasing number of justices and clerks joining the cert. pool. While further research needs to be done on the link between the cert. process and the number of cases granted, there is some evidence to suggest that the cert. pool has had a chilling effect on the willingness of clerks to recommend grants.

It was initially thought by Justice Blackmun that the cert. pool would make pool clerks more likely to recommend granting the cases they reviewed. As a result, he urged the other justices for a modification in the procedure:

> I feel…there is some merit in going 'off' the Pool for three or four weeks during the summer. This enables the new clerks to get a heavy dose of certiorari applications and jurisdictional statements, something they do not have when they have only a one-fifth share. It gives them a feel for the business of the Court, and I think, makes them more appreciative and more selective when they pick up the Pool work (Harry A. Blackmun to Warren E. Burger, June 11, 1974, Blackmun Papers, Box 1374).

While the pool was "off" the first two summers, 1973 to 1974, it functioned year-round thereafter (see Lewis F. Powell to Warren E. Burger, June 24, 1975,

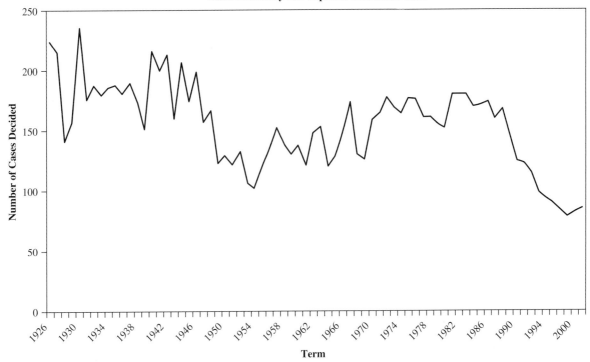

Figure 11.2 The Number of Cases Decided by the U.S. Supreme Court Annually

Blackmun Papers, Box 1374). Contrary to Blackmun's concern, pool clerks did not overzealously recommend grants. Instead, the opposite occurred. As the number of justices and clerks joining the pool and reviewing pool memos increased, clerks became more cautious. Justice Stevens recognized the decline in the number of cert. grants and suggested that it was directly related to the Court's increasing reliance on law clerks to make recommendations on which cases to take (Mauro 1998). Stevens explained, "You stick your neck out as a clerk when you recommend to grant a case. The risk-averse thing to do is to recommend not to take a case. I think it accounts for the lessening of the docket" (quoted in Mauro 1998, 13A). It has also been suggested by some like Kenneth Starr, a former federal judge and clerk to Chief Justice Warren Burger, that clerks fail to recommend seemingly uninteresting business cases (see Mauro 1998). Judge Richard Posner noted that, "there seems to be a bias in favor of non-commercial cases" (quoted in Mauro 1998, 13A)

The formation of the cert. pool, the addition of a third and fourth clerk, and the creation of the legal office in 1973, which is staffed with semipermanent lawyers who assist the justices and clerks with the cert. pool, have considerably lightened the workload of each clerk.[14] Except for the clerks who worked for justices not participating in the pool, clerks had more time to devote to other tasks—principally opinion writing. In the years since Chief Justices Vinson and Warren began equally assigning opinions, it became increasingly common for justices to delegate opinion writing to clerks and an institutional norm developed. After the cert. pool was created and expanded, the number of separate concurring and dissenting opinions issued by the justices exploded. I suggest that this was largely caused by the combination of the norm of clerk-written opinions that developed under Warren and the fact that modern clerks are spending less time on cert. petitions than clerks from the previous era. Because of the cert. pool, each clerk reviews fewer petitions than their counterparts did thirty years ago, leaving them more time to devote to other tasks— namely opinion writing.

Opinion Writing

The most prominent and certainly most controversial task that the modern law clerk performs is the drafting of judicial opinions. The degree to which the nonappointed and nonelected law clerks influence the final output of the Court has been the subject of periodic and intense debate (see, e.g., Rehnquist 1957; Newland 1961; Bickel 1965; Woodward and Armstrong 1979; Vining 1981, 248; Edwards 1981, 259; Rehnquist, 2001; Kozinski 1995, 55; Posner 1996). Whatever the merits of judicial delegation of opinion drafting to law clerks, it is plain that this is a crucial feature of the modern law clerk. Oakley stated that, "The drafting of opinions by law clerks is prevalent, and increasingly so, to the point where it is seen as something of a quaint idiosyncrasy when a judge attempts to draft his or her own opinions" (Oakley 1995, 86). Indeed, of the current members of the Supreme Court only Justice Stevens regularly drafts his own opinions, with Justices Scalia and Souter also doing some of their own drafting. It was during this modern era of the law clerk that it became standard practice for justices to delegate the drafting of opinions to their clerks. This was a marked change from previous eras where about half the justices wrote first drafts and clerks added footnotes and citations, edited, and suggested small changes, while opinion equalization forced the other half to delegate opinion writing to their clerks.

The modern law clerk is not only directly responsible for the dramatic increase in separate concurring and dissenting opinions now issued by the Court, but also the increased length and detail of the opinions. Indeed, in one instance when Chief Justice Burger's concerns were met by the writer of the majority opinion, he still issued the concurrence written by one of his law clerks because to withdraw it "would break [the] law clerk's heart" (O'Brien 1990, 322).

Modern justices now see themselves and their clerks as comprising an opinion writing team. In 1986 Justice Lewis F. Powell, Jr., wrote his clerks, "Apparently the Chief Justice does not like my law clerks, as again it seems to me that we have been 'short changed' on cases to write" (Lewis F. Powell, Jr., to C. Cabell Chinnis, Jr., Ann Marie Coughlin, William J. Stuntz, Robert Stack, and Michael W. Mosman, April 8, 1986, Powell Papers, Box 130b). In a 1979 speech, Justice William J. Brennan described his opinions as "opinions that came from the Brennan chambers over the past twenty-three years. I say from 'the Brennan chambers' because, as Bentham said, the 'Law is not the work of judge alone but of judge and company.' The company in this case consisted of the sixty-five law clerks who have been associated with me on the Court" (William J. Brennan, Dean's Day Address, New York University Law School 1979).

Justice Powell's chambers provides an example of how the process currently works. Justice Powell checked his clerk's draft opinions very carefully, not only editing throughout, but also suggesting substantive changes. For example, he wrote 1986 clerk Leslie S. Gielow regarding *Edwards v. Aguillard* (1987), "You also have done quite well in incorporating many of my views in Part II, as we have discussed. I think, however, that some additions—either in the text or in notes—would strengthen the discussion of what properly can be taught and why. I now identify possible ideas or facts that may be included in the revision of Part II" (Lewis F. Powell, Jr., to Leslie S. Gielow, March 10, 1987, Powell Papers, Box 135). After the clerk revised and sent Powell a second draft, he wrote, "This now reflects my views very well…let's move this through the Chambers normal process" (Powell notes from March 17, 1987, on "No. 85–1513, Edwards v. Aguillard, SECOND DRAFT," undated, Powell Papers, Box 135).

Chief Justice Rehnquist described in some detail the process by which he delegated the process of opinion drafting:

> The clerk is given, as best I can, a summary of the conference discussion, a description of the result reached by the majority in that discussion, and my views as to how a written opinion can best be prepared embodying that reasoning. The law clerk is not off on a frolic of his own, but is instead engaged in a highly structured task which has been largely mapped out for him by the conference discussion and my suggestions to him. This is

not to say that the clerk who prepares a first draft does not have considerable responsibility in the matter. The discussion in conference has been entirely oral…nine oral statements of position suffice to convey the broad outlines of the views of the justices but do not invariably settle exactly how the opinion will be reasoned through (Rehnquist 2001, 262–63).

What is perhaps most revealing about the above passage is the complete lack of coyness or reticence from a sitting chief justice regarding the degree of delegation to the law clerk in opinion writing. Indeed, Rehnquist has described the justices' chambers as "opinion writing bureaus."[15] "In my case," Rehnquist continued, "the clerks do the first draft of almost all cases to which I have been assigned to write the Court's opinion. When the caseload is heavy, [I] help by doing the first draft of a case myself. [This] practice…may undoubtedly…cause raised eyebrows. I think the practice is entirely proper: The Justice must retain for himself control not merely of the outcome of the case, but of the explanation of the outcome, and I do not believe this practice sacrifices either" (Schwartz 1996, 52). Contrast Rehnquist's remarks with Justice Charles Evans Hughes' earlier fear that "it might be thought that [the law clerks] were writing our opinions" and it is plain that the opinion writing process has been completely transformed from its earlier incarnation (Bickel 1964, 82).

CLERKS IN COMPARATIVE PERSPECTIVE

The preceding portrait of the development of the U.S. Supreme Court law clerk bears much resemblance to clerks on other American courts as well as clerks in other nations. Yet, there are also a number of important differences. Although research on clerks in general is relatively sparse, there is much less known about lower American court clerks than U.S. Supreme Court clerks and even less about clerks outside the United States. Still, it is possible to make some comparisons based on the little research that is available (see also Maveety this volume, chapter 20).

In some countries, such as the United Kingdom, judges do not employ law clerks. Clerkships in Canada largely follow the American apprentice model of short-term clerks working for individual judges. Other nations have followed the long-term staff model. In Germany, judges employ experienced lawyers as their clerks in a kind of hybrid of the staff attorneys and short-term clerks that work at the U.S. Supreme Court. Although French judges do not have law clerks, their highest court (the *Conseil d'Etat*) is composed of a large number of judges with a wide-range of experience. The more junior judges engage in apprentice-like work on the French High Court. Similarly, in Sweden short-term clerks act much like junior French judges as their apprenticeships quickly lead to actual judging and ultimately judgeships. For example, in Sweden's general courts, after six months of training clerks begin their apprenticeships by granting relatively simple matters such as marriages and adoptions. After one year, Swedish clerks are entrusted with deciding basic civil and criminal cases. After two years, Swedish clerks can formally apply to become full-fledged judges.

Sally Kenney's article on clerks, or *Referendaires*, on the European Union's European Court of Justice (ECJ) provided a uniquely detailed point of comparison with clerks on the U.S. Supreme Court (Kenney 2000). The ECJ serves as the highest court on the constitutional issues facing the member countries of the European Union (see, e.g., Miller 1999). There are a number of major differences between ECJ clerks and their American counterparts, largely because of the way the two courts are structured. One key difference is that ECJ clerks, while hired by individual judges, serve long tenures as opposed to the one-year-clerkship norm at the U.S. Supreme Court. This gives ECJ clerks considerable expertise and power. Because ECJ judges serve six-year renewable terms and only issue unanimous opinions, the most important role of ECJ clerks is to facilitate uniformity and continuity across chambers, among member-states, and over time. Furthermore, this role is heightened because the European Union is composed of very different countries with disparate legal systems. Kenney found that ECJ clerks provide legal and linguistic expertise—all opinions are issued in French, ease the workload of their members, participate in oral and written interactions between chambers, and provide continuity as judges rapidly change. While Kenney concluded that they have more power than their counterparts on the U.S. Supreme Court, ECJ clerks act as agents for their principals (judges) and are not the puppeteers that critics suggest.

Let's now compare clerks on the U.S. Supreme Court with clerks on lower courts in the U.S. Both short-term and long-term staff assist judges at all levels of American courts with permanent staff-attorneys generally more pronounced in state courts and at the appellate level (see, e.g., Stow and Spaeth 1992). This is largely because, in general, appeals courts have more discretion over their dockets than trial courts and because the duties performed by clerks are generally more suited to appeals than trials where judges spend much more time in the courtroom managing proceedings. For example, since the 1980s, California courts have almost completely moved from short-term clerks to permanent staff attorneys (Yakar 2006). Short-term clerks generally have more close interaction with their judges than permanent staff attorneys and federal clerks work more closely with their judges than do clerks at the state level (Oakley and Thompson 1980, 108–9). Pre-argument memoranda are prepared by clerks at all levels in the American context. However, at the federal level the relatively haphazard, often individualized nature of these memos—such as bench memos prepared within each chambers at the U.S. Supreme Court contrasted with pooled bench-memos in some circuits at the U.S. Courts of Appeals—lead to a higher degree of clerk-judge interaction than at state courts (Cohen 2002, 146). Unlike at the U.S. Supreme Court, at the U.S. Courts of Appeals post-argument conference memos are prepared by the clerks of the presiding judges after the three-judge panels take preliminary votes on the cases (Cohen 2002, 136–37). Conference memos summarize each judge's position and provide the basic layout for the clerk-drafted opinions that will ultimately follow (see also Martinek this volume, chapter 9). Clerks draft opinions in nearly all American courts, including trial courts at both the state and federal level (Oakley and Thompson 1980, 109).

Clerk interaction in America varies across courts and is largely due to the number of judges and clerks on a given court and geographic considerations. Clerks who regularly see each other are more likely to engage in the kind of negotiation and bargaining that takes place in the clerk network at the U.S. Supreme Court. Unlike at the U.S. Supreme Court, U.S. Courts of Appeals judges and their staffs do not have the same degree of regular interaction across chambers because of the nature of their working environment (see Martinek this volume, chapter 9). "Cybercollegiality" has become the norm because there are large numbers of federal appellate judges in each circuit; they sit in randomly-assigned panels, and travel throughout their circuit to hear cases. Therefore, while a clerk network exists within each Circuit Court of Appeals, both clerks and judges have much more limited interactions—particularly face-to-face interactions—than in smaller courts where all clerks and judges are physically in the same location. In short, numerical size and geographic dispersion hampers collegiality (Cohen 2002, 152–66).

In all, there are more similarities than differences between U.S. Supreme Court law clerks and those in lower American courts. Although little is presently known about clerks outside the American context, what we do know suggests a wide variety of models from a total absence of clerks to a true apprenticeship, judge-in-training model. Future research on a greater number of countries will be able to shed considerable light on whether the roles played American clerks are relatively common or somewhat unique.

CONCLUSIONS

When thinking about the role of U.S. Supreme Court law clerks, it is important to remember that for the first 100 years of the nation's history, the justices did their own work. Litigants knew that their petitions were examined by each of the justices rather than one pool clerk, oral argument questions were posed by the justices themselves not written down beforehand in bench memos by subordinates, justices negotiated face to face not through intermediaries in the clerk network, and justices composed the words contained in the opinions they issued rather than dictated the writing to their clerks. The institution of the law clerk has undergone such dramatic transformations that it barely resembles its earliest incarnation. A far cry from an advanced apprenticeship in the law, modern clerks play an indispensable role in the day-to-day functioning of the Court.

What the preceding account demonstrates is that three seemingly unrelated changes in the way the justices conducted their work, led to dramatic transformations in the role of the law clerk. When then Chief Justice Hughes created the dead list, rather than discuss each cert. petition in conference, justices began to rely on clerk-written memos for guidance in the agenda-setting process. When the justices and their clerks moved into their first permanent building and no longer worked at home, the clerk network was established. When Chief Justices Vinson and Warren started assigning opinions equally, rather than based on the speed at which their colleagues produced them, justices began to rely on their clerks to keep up with the demand. To be sure, clerks reviewed petitions and drafted some opinions before these developments. These activities were part of the clerk's apprenticeship in learning the law rather than substantive help for their justices. It is plain that institutional changes can have dramatic, unintended consequences.

As clerks have become integral to the Supreme Court, there has been increased concern over their power and influence on the law. In 1993, Kenneth Starr wrote, "Selecting 100 or so cases from the pool of 6,000 petitions is just too important to invest in very smart but brand-new lawyers" (Mauro 1998, 13A) With the current caseload approaching 10,000 cases and no end in sight, the process will almost certainly continue to come under increasing scrutiny. Currently, Justice Stevens is the only member of the Court outside the cert. pool. As a result, his chambers provides the only check against the sole clerk-written pool memo on each case petitioned to the Court. Chief Justice John Roberts, who participated in the pool as a clerk to then Associate Justice Rehnquist, has been critical of the pool and in a 1997 speech suggested that creating a second pool would provide an important check on the current process (Mauro 2005).

With opinions now almost entirely written by clerks, there is a real danger that opinions will lose authority. Indeed, it is only respect for the Court's legitimacy that gives its judgments weight with both the public and lower court judges who are expected to follow its mandates. Judge Posner commented, "The less that lawyers and especially other judges regard judicial opinions as authentic expressions of what the judges think, the less they will rely on judicial opinions for guidance and authority.... The more the thinking embodied in opinions is done by law clerks rather than by judges, the less authority opinions will have" (Posner 1985, 110). Pressuring justices to revert to writing their own opinions may be too much to ask. However, fully disclosing the role that clerks play may be a small step in the right direction. Is it too far-fetched to imagine a world where opinions are issue with the language: The Chambers of Chief Justice Roberts delivered the opinion of the Court?

In the 1779 poem by Johann Wolfgang von Goethe (reprinted in Zeydel 1955), the sorcerer's apprentice could not resist the temptation to put on the robes of the master and try his hand at sorcery:

> That old sorcerer has vanished
> And for once has gone away!
> Spirits called by him, now banished,
> My commands shall soon obey.
> Every step and saying
> That he used, I know,
> And with sprites obeying
> My arts I will show.

While the temptation may only be natural, and to some extent encouraged by the master, the apprentice has a responsibility to be true to his or her role. In the context of law clerks, that responsibility is a great one for it is only the judges who have the legitimate authority to discharge the duties of their offices. If both justices and clerks continue to blur the distinction between their very different commissions, not only will public confidence in the Court be jeopardized, but also like the apprentice in von Goethe's poem, the clerks may find themselves unable to quell increasing threats to the Court's legitimacy that their institution has fostered.

Notes

1. Nield's tenure was Justice White's response to Chief Justice Burger's 1974 proposal that each member of the Court have one permanent clerk. However, because a majority of the justices were strongly opposed, no institutional change took place (Abraham 1975, 241).

2. See the Federal Law Clerk Information System at www.uscourts.gov.

3. In 1971, seventeen years after the decision, Justice Clark said, "I questioned the Chief's going with Myrdal in that opinion. I told him—and Hugo Black did, too—that it wouldn't go down well in the South and he didn't need it." However, author Bernard Schwartz argued that the only reason Clark brought this footnote up was to change one of the citations from simply the last name "Clark" to "K. B. Clark" so that no one would confuse the justice with sociologist Kenneth Clark (Schwartz and Lesher 1983, 5–6, 46–47).

4. As part of the research for this project, I consulted the official papers of a variety of justices including Justices Black, Blackmun, Douglas, Thurgood Marshall, Rutledge and Chief Justices Stone and Warren, all of which are currently housed in the Madison Building at the Library of Congress. I also read the papers of Justices Powell at Washington and Lee University and Harlan II at Princeton University. Future references will be to the Papers of the specific justices and the appropriate box number.

5. Robert von Mehren Interview, Stanley Forman Reed Oral History Project, University of Kentucky.

6. Transcriptions of Conversations Between Justice William O. Douglas and Professor Walter F. Murphy, Cassette No.3: December 20, 1961, Princeton University Library 1981.

7. That term the Court's docket consisted of 809 petitions for certiorari, excluding the 60 *in forma pauperis* petitions handled solely by Chief Justice Hughes.

8. The data compiled by Palmer and Brenner illustrate this effect. After Vinson began equalizing opinion assignment, the Court's slowest opinion writers actually finished their opinions more quickly. Frankfurter went from 104 days to 77, Burton from 99 days to 73 and Vinson from 99 to 75. Though the authors argued that this was due to the criticism by Douglas that the process was taking too long, I suggest it is likely the result of the rise of equality in opinion assignment and the resultant increased role of law clerks in opinion writing by these justices (Palmer and Brenner 1988, 183).

9. Transcriptions of Conversations Between Justice William O. Douglas and Professor Walter F. Murphy, Cassette No.14: April 5, 1963, Princeton University Library, 1981. Douglas was so perturbed by the glacial pace of some of his colleagues that he proposed a rule change at the end of the 1948 term. Specifically, Douglas suggested that an opinion should be reassigned if the opinion writer did not complete his assignment within three months (Fine 1984, 254).

10. Transcriptions of Conversations Between Justice William O. Douglas and Professor Walter F. Murphy, Cassette No. 3: December 20, 1961, Princeton University Library, 1981.

11. F. Aley Allen Interview, Stanley Forman Reed Oral History Project, University of Kentucky.

12. This differs from David M. O'Brien's assertion, "Clerks' memos do not fully explore whether an alleged conflict is 'real,' 'tolerable,' or 'square' and must be decided. The workload usually precludes such an examination until a case has already been granted and set for oral argument," (O'Brien 1990, 216). While this may have been true in the late 1960s, the emergent structure of the cert. pool has drastically decreased the number of cases that each clerk reviews. This allows modern clerks not only more time for opinion writing and other tasks, but also additional time to explore cert. petitions more fully and make more thoughtful recommendations. Furthermore, based on my interviews with former clerks, I suggest that the institutionalization of the clerk culture has created an atmosphere in which the clerks will perform significant research when they identify a case that may present a conflict.

13. See Wasby, 2003b, for a discussion of how some clerks prefer subjects they studied in law school, including constitutional law.

14. The Supreme Court's decision to create permanent staff attorney units was modeled on the staff attorneys who worked at the U.S. Courts of Appeals and at state high courts. See, e.g., Oakley and Thompson 1980; Hellman 1980, 937; Sheldon 1981, 346, 1988, 45.

15. William H. Rehnquist, "Are the Old Times Dead?" Mac Swinford Lecture, University of Kentucky, September 23, 1983.

12

THE EMERGENCE AND EVOLUTION OF SUPREME COURT POLICY

Richard L. Pacelle, Jr.

Some cases decided by the U.S. Supreme Court are clearly more important than others. This chapter explores how the Supreme Court makes policy through these landmark opinions, but it also explores how that policy evolved over time as the Court issued later decisions that helped clarify and further defined its previous landmark opinions. This chapter argues that judicial doctrine and policy evolves through a series of decisions and a number of different stages because constitutional rights are neither self-defining nor absolute. The chapter also explores how landmark judicial decisions helped shape other important judicial policies and doctrines, sometimes in seemingly unrelated issue areas. Once a landmark decision is handed down by the Supreme Court, other political actors immediately bring additional lawsuits to the courts to clarify and further define that policy. Thus the creation and development of judicial doctrine demands multiple rounds of litigation. This chapter thus defines judicial policy making as a highly complicated and constantly changing process that evolves over time.

   The chapter thus presents a model of the evolution of the policy process, breaking down that process into five stages. The chapter then tests this model, using the evolution of the Supreme Court's line of cases in its free exercise of religion doctrine. The chapter explores how landmark cases handed down by the U.S. Supreme Court have both legal and political aspects.

On January 22, 1973, former President Lyndon B. Johnson died. It was front page news across the nation. Below the fold on many newspapers was a story that the United States Supreme Court issued a decision in a case called *Roe v. Wade* (1973). In that decision, the Court effectively struck down state laws that criminalized abortions. That landmark decision was the major Supreme Court pronouncement on the question of reproductive freedom. As such, it has been identified as the Court's "policy" on the issue. However, like most important court decisions, it did not answer every question about reproductive rights. For instance, could a state impose a waiting period on a woman seeking to have an abortion? Could a minor obtain an abortion without a parent's consent? What if the prospective father wanted to stop the abortion?

   Although *Roe* is the major decision that supporters and opponents both point to, it was hardly the last word on the Supreme Court's policy or doctrine in this area. For over three decades, the Court has been refining, modifying, advancing, and retreating in numerous cases that help define reproductive rights. As the membership of the Court has changed and presidents have come and gone, there have been predictions that the Court would overturn *Roe v. Wade*. Although *Roe* was more controversial than most Supreme Court decisions, the process that led up to *Roe* and what has happened since is not particularly unusual. In this chapter, I propose a model of Supreme Court policy evolution to explain how landmark cases emerge and what happens in their wake.

This chapter is a study of the origination and development of policies in the Supreme Court. The analysis attempts to identify the doctrinal and policy antecedents of major landmark decisions and the construction of doctrine that follows in the wake of a major judicial pronouncement. The initiation and development of judicial policy is considered within the context of a framework of policy evolution. The patterns of change are the result of the purposive intervention of major actors in the judicial system (Epstein and Knight 1998; Wahlbeck 1997; Galanter 1974; Baird 2004).

Constitutional rights are neither self-defining nor absolute. The creation and development of doctrine demands multiple rounds of litigation. The individual cases that reach the Court are not decided in isolation. Rather, doctrine is built over a period of time. A given policy is born of related issues and subsequently spawns other issues. As a result, decisions in one area will have ripple effects on other areas.[1]

Justices and litigants have a strong incentive to see their policy preferences reflected in the interpretation of the Constitution. They seek the opportunities to create favorable decisions. At the same time, they face a variety of constraints as doctrine evolves through the various stages. Policy evolves in predictable ways and follows basic patterns of development. At the initial stage, policy is unstable. Justices and litigants search for a niche for the new issue. Often it comes from a related area of law. The Court needs to stabilize doctrine to guide the lower courts and let citizens know the extent of their rights. Ultimately, the Court lays down the fundamental principle that guides the future development of doctrine. Once the central standard has been established, the Court applies it as the cases get more difficult. The issue may get attached to other issues, creating instability in doctrine and inconsistency in decision making.

The construction of judicial doctrine and Supreme Court policy has been compared to piecing together a giant mosaic. Public policy is normally associated with landmark Court decisions, like *Roe v. Wade, Mapp v. Ohio* (1961), or *Brown v. Board of Education* (1954),

or seminal legislation like the Civil Rights Act of 1964 or the Patriot Act of 2001, ignoring the processes that made such important pronouncements possible and the work necessary to flesh out the questions left in the wake of the landmarks (but see Baumgartner and Jones 1993; Kingdon 1995). Supreme Court decisions and Congressional legislation, no matter how significant, raise more questions than they answer. Such Court decisions also have important implications for related areas of law. Landmark decisions like *Brown, Roe,* and *Mapp* were far from the last words in their areas of law. In fact, each preceded an explosion of litigation and Court attention in the areas of school desegregation, reproductive rights, and search and seizure, respectively (Pacelle 1991). Thus, it is useful to view judicial doctrine and policy as evolving through a series of decisions and a number of stages.

EVOLUTION AS A METAPHOR FOR POLICY CHANGE

This chapter's model of issue evolution is concerned with the origin of new issues, how they develop over time, the impact of the environment on these issues, and how issues are related to each other. The process of doctrinal construction involves the emergence of a new issue, which is often the result of activity in a related issue area, periods of stability, increased issue complexity, the spawning of other new issues, and occasionally, a retreat to a previous stage of development.[2]

Notions of evolution conjure the image of gradual change and inexorable progress. However, some argue that gradual progress is not an accurate description of evolutionary change. Analyses of policy change and historical events, like retrospective reconstructions of development, tend to reflect a neater path of progression than the process that actually occurred. Judicial policy and doctrinal construction display ebbs and flows, advances and retreats rather than clear patterns of certain progression. For example, Stephen Jay Gould (1983, 14) advocated such a revised view of evolutionary change, rejecting traditional notions of gradualism in favor of "punctuated equilibrium." He argued that the pace of change is "jerky or episodic" rather than smooth and gradual (Gould 1983, 259). Some major events or environmental forces break a long period of *stasis* and cause significant changes.

Edward Carmines and James Stimson (1989, 13) used the notion of punctuated equilibrium as the basis of their "dynamic growth model" of political change. They argued that a dramatic pulse to the system interrupts the normal trend and alters the future context for that issue:

> It is dynamic because it presumes that at some point the system moves from a fairly stationary state to a fairly dramatic rapid change; that change is manifested by a "critical moment" in the time series—a point where change is large enough to be visible and, perhaps, the origin of a dynamic process. Significantly, however, the change—dynamic growth—does not end with the critical moment; instead it continues over an extended period, albeit at much slower pace. This continued growth after the initial shock defines the evolutionary character of the model (Carmines and Stimson 1989, 13).

Landmark decisions are the shocks represented in the punctuated equilibrium model by altering the process of doctrinal development. However, they are just a step rather than the end of the process.

THE DYNAMICS OF JUDICIAL POLICY MAKING

Traditionally, a case law focus or the *legal approach* overemphasizes the importance of landmark judicial decisions. Policy and policy change are not individual events or a single landmark decision, but a series of decisions. Landmark decisions interrupt the previous stationary pattern and initiate a new pattern of development. Thus, policy is better defined as the sum total of legislative or judicial initiatives in a given area. To be sure, seminal decisions alter the dynamics of policy making, affect the authoritative allocation of values, expand, narrow, or in some cases overturn previous policy. They are not, however, the last word in that substantive area of law. In fact, in most instances they create a flood of litigation in that area (Baird 2004). The changes in doctrine are visible and serve as the beginning or the acceleration of the dynamic process

that underlies the development of that issue (Kahn 1994; Kritzer and Richards 2003).

Studies of the Supreme Court typically offer generalizations that appear to govern every circumstance. In practice, the behavior of justices and litigants varies as a function of different conditions or situations (Richards and Kritzer 2002; Kobylka 1987; Epstein and Kobylka 1992; Pacelle 2003; Baird 2004). This chapter's framework considers the evolution of policy in the Supreme Court by examining the expected behavior of justices and repeat player litigants in different contextual settings. This perspective maintains that the Court's decisions are a function of the individual preferences of the justices as well as the institutional norms and rules that affect the Court's work.

To develop a framework or model for understanding how issues evolve, we need to consider how the Supreme Court operates. Rohde and Spaeth (1976) argued that judicial decisions result from the interaction of judges' goals, rules, and situations. Goals refer to the policy preferences of the justices, the most important determinant of decision making. Some analysts, using the *attitudinal model*, argue that the justices are free to decide cases on the basis of their policy preferences because they are not elected, have lifetime tenure, have reached the pinnacles of their careers, and are members of the court of last resort (Segal and Spaeth 1993). The evidence suggests that individual justices are very consistent in their decision making. So, for example, liberal justices tend to make liberal decisions. More likely, regardless of how liberal or conservative the Supreme Court is, it has to follow a set of norms and rules.

Rules involve formal institutional procedures and norms that structure decision making. For judges, *the judicial role* is the primary "rule" that influences decision making (see Miller this volume, chapter 19). This role orientation assimilates notions such as consistency in the law, attention to precedent, and a need to keep order in the judicial system (Pacelle 2002; Provine 1980). Richards and Kritzer (2002) have shown that justices are constrained by what they call *jurisprudential regimes*. A jurisprudential regime is defined as "a key precedent, or a set of related precedents, that structures the way in which the Supreme Court justices evaluate key elements of cases in arriving at decisions in a particular legal area" (Richards and Kritzer 2002,

308). Jurisprudential regimes highlight the relevant facts that justices consider when deciding cases.

There are also external forces that can also constrain the Supreme Court. The fact that the justices are not elected requires them to be careful in the scope of their decisions and creates a normative imperative: The Court should adopt restraint in its decision making. In addition, as Alexander Hamilton wrote in Federalist 78 (Hamilton, Madison, and Jay 1787/1788), the Court lacks the sword and the purse. The Court needs to rely on Congress and the president to support and implement its decisions. Thus, some analysts who advocate *the strategic approach* argue that the Court will act strategically and take into account the reactions of the elected branches of government and perhaps defer to them (Epstein and Knight 1998; Eskridge 1994).

Finally, the existence of certain situations or conditions can enhance or slow processes of policy making. Studies of public policy (Kingdon 1995; Walker 1977) acknowledge that policy emergence and change require favorable conditions. Both *legal factors* (precedent, the language of decisions, facts of the case) and *extralegal factors* (the policy preferences of the justices and external constraints) play significant roles in doctrinal construction (George and Epstein 1992). (See chapter 13 in this volume.)

Policy change does not occur randomly. Various political actors intentionally bring additional cases to the Court to clarify its past decisions. The overall process by which cases come to the Supreme Court and are decided by the Court is evolutionary in scope and pace (Baird 2004). The process by which cases are selected by the Court and decided are different parts of the same general decision-making process (Pacelle 1991, 1995).

Thus, to review: Justices on the Supreme Court have the incentive to tailor policy to reflect their sincere policy preferences. Justices are policy makers pursuing their own values or goals through the cases they accept (Pacelle 1991; Perry 1991; Ulmer 1972, 1978) and the decisions they make (Schubert 1965, 1974; Segal and Spaeth 1993, 2002). Studies demonstrate high levels of consistency in the behavior of individual justices within policy areas. At the same time, members of the High Court have institutional responsibilities to lower court judges and to those who must implement judicial decisions (Johnson and Canon 1999; Hansford and Spriggs 2006). This is manifested in the judicial role, part of the rules and norms of the institution (Baum 1997; Gibson 1978; Provine 1980). The responsibilities of being the court of last resort constrain the Supreme Court and its members (Hellman 1983). Thus, the behavior of the Court should reflect the policy preferences and the judicial role orientations of individual members. In addition, the Court may adapt its decisions to avoid retaliation from Congress or the president. For instance, the Burger Court, despite being rather conservative, issued a number of procivil rights decisions, including support for affirmative action, in part in deference to a liberal Congress. The Court also pays attention to the position of the president. Indeed, the president has an important repeat player, the solicitor general, who can argue the position of the administration or Congress before the justices (Pacelle 2003; Bailey, Kamoie, and Maltzman 2005; see also Ubertaccio this volume, chapter 10).

JUSTICES AND LITIGANTS:
POLICY ENTREPRENEURS

The work of organized litigants cannot be minimized because they bring the cases to the Supreme Court in the first place. The judicial process requires the assistance of interest groups and litigants who monitor the decisions of the Court and sponsor or join later cases. Thus, judicial policy making and doctrine building is a shared enterprise between two sets of policy entrepreneurs: justices and the organized litigants who bring cases to the Court. Policy entrepreneurs are defined as actors who attempt to influence political and legal change (Schneider and Teske 1992). Justices and litigants, particularly those who use the courts regularly (often called "repeat players," Galanter 1974; and "legal elites," McGuire 1993), are actors seeking to advance their notions of good public policy and legitimate constitutional interpretation.

There are many examples of interest groups who actively use the judicial branch to achieve their policy goals. The National Association for the Advancement of Colored People (NAACP) in race litigation and the

National Organization of Women (NOW) in gender litigation sponsor cases, react to the Court's decisions, and prepare their next round of cases based on these prior decisions. The Supreme Court is not a self-starter. It must wait for litigants to bring the appropriate cases to its attention. This highlights the role of "repeat players" who attempt to use litigation to pursue policy goals that cannot be achieved elsewhere, issues that are inappropriate for the other branches, or to protect gains earned elsewhere (Epstein 1985, 5–6). Litigation is a slow, incremental process in which issues are raised, addressed, percolate through the system, and beget further cases. This protracted process is a significant constraint imposed by institutional rules.

To activate groups to help in the process of constructing doctrine, the Court has three devices to signal litigants to bring more cases to the Court: extending or reducing the queuing process in case selection, the consistency of substantive decisions in related cases, and the language of its decisions. In granting the petitions of some groups and systematically excluding others, the Court sends a message regarding its priorities (Baird 2004; Pacelle 1991). During the Warren Court the justices were sympathetic to petitions in support of the accused in criminal procedure cases, and many groups brought additional such cases to the Court. During the Burger Court, however, the state was advantaged in seeking review from adverse lower court decisions in criminal cases (Hellman 1985). Prodefendant interest groups therefore brought fewer cases to the Supreme Court during that era. Decisions that consistently expand or narrow the rights of groups or individuals send relatively clear signals to future litigants. The language of the decisions as well as the tone of the dissenting and concurring opinions convey explicit testimony concerning the views of individual justices and the policy stance of the Court (Baird 2006).

The work of translating these cues and signals into an effective strategy for using the courts falls primarily to organized group litigants. Successful groups can sequence cases to help structure the evolution of policy and influence the nature of debate.[3] Groups lacking sufficient resources can enter pending cases through an *amicus curiae* or friend of the court brief (Caldeira and Wright 1990). Such briefs serve to inform the Court about the impact of a decision on a group that is not directly involved in the case. *Amicus* briefs can frame issues in a different context and suggest different alternatives for the Court to consider. In effect, such briefs serve to marshal specialized opinion, provide general and technical information, and provide an informal tally of public opinion for the Court (Schlozman and Tierney 1986, 290–301). The landmark affirmative action case *Regents of the University of California v. Bakke* (1978) directly affected the two parties, Allan Bakke and the University of California–Davis, but the Court's decision would have a decided impact on most colleges and universities, so many of them filed *amicus* briefs to provide the justices with their different perspectives.

The role of repeat player litigants cannot be stressed enough. Because the Court is not a self-starter, they play a vital role in bringing cases to help the courts with the long process of building coherent doctrine. Of course, that occurs once the Supreme Court has formally entered the issue area. It might be useful to step back a moment and ask how do new issues get to the Court's agenda and get the attention necessary to move through the evolutionary process.

THE PROPER CONDITIONS FOR POLICY CHANGE

The Supreme Court's agenda tends to be inhospitable to new issues. Wholly new ideas do not suddenly appear on the agenda; rather "new ideas" tend to be recombinations of old ideas.[4] Landmark decisions like *Miranda v. Arizona* (1966), *Reed v. Reed* (1971), and *Roe v. Wade* (1973) appear to establish a new area of law. And in a sense, they do, but those decisions have historical roots that can be traced to other areas of law. The existence of such connections to existing precedents is deliberate by the Court. The appropriate conditions must exist to allow the new issue to emerge. Thus, previous issues are often used to introduce new issues that are closely related or they may influence the development of other issues that are not derived from a common source.

Thus litigants and policy entrepreneurs often urge the Supreme Court to extend and further refine past decisions or constitutional principles. Justices with specific policy designs may also be involved in paving the way for new issues. This process, like the notion of a punctuated equilibrium, breaks a pattern of gradual change and accelerates issue evolution.

Casting new issues in terms that are already familiar to policy makers serves two purposes. First, it conserves precious resources because new issues take more time to resolve than existing issues. If justices and litigants can find analogues from previous cases, they have a frame of reference for the new issue. Second, the difficulty of getting attention for new issues can be overcome by recasting the new issue in terms of other issues that have already successfully navigated the policy process. If proponents of the "new" policy are successful, then the coalitions that passed the "old" issue can be reconstituted.[5]

The incremental nature of the process creates an inertia that resists new ideas. It is the role of the policy entrepreneur to break this cycle and create a favorable environment for the policy proposal (Kingdon 1995). Advocates must await the opportunities for action. A window for change may open as a result of an event in the political environment or because a problem reaches prominence. For instance, the events of September 11, 2001, created the conditions for the passage of the Patriot Act. Changes in the political environment for the Court might include membership change on the Court, different strategies by litigants, or the intervention of an external actor like the president or Congress. Problems may reach prominence due to increased attention to an issue by lower courts, specialized publics in the legal community, the media, the elected branches, or other governmental agencies. Thus, despite the goals of policy makers and policy entrepreneurs, the proper situational context must be present for the introduction of a new issue to the agenda.

When conditions reinforce the goals of members, the influence of institutional barriers can be overcome. The use of Constitutional provisions that have been used to address other issues may provide a ready solution to the newly recognized problem. For instance, decisions concerning the rights of the accused in criminal cases led to changes in administrative law doctrine, including administrative searches (Pritchett 1984, 185).

If proper conditions are not present, the new issue may not emerge at the Supreme Court. For instance, the Court's refusal for many years to attend to gay and lesbian rights is an example of an issue the Court avoided. Petitioners brought a variety of cases dealing with existing issues including criminal law, education, and public employment in the hope that the Court would tackle the gay and lesbian rights issue. Their claims invoked equal protection, privacy, due process, and the First Amendment (Hellman 1985, 1006–1007). However, the Supreme Court largely ignored them for years.

Once a new issue is recognized by the Supreme Court, it could remain on the Court's agenda for the foreseeable future (Pacelle 1991; Baird 2004). Perhaps more significantly, this success may serve as the impetus to deal with related issues (Kingdon 1995; Baumgartner and Jones 1993). For example, New Deal legislation that spread across a variety of issue areas created a classic spillover effect, enabling the Court to decide cases in a variety of issue areas (Brady and Stewart 1982, 352–57).

Justices thus begin work in one area and spread their attention to related issues. Once a breakthrough occurs in a new issue area, it typically leads to a surge of activity in related areas.[6] In general the rise of an issue may create recognition among justices and litigants that other areas merit attention. When an institution like the Supreme Court decides to consider an issue, it may, in effect, "commit itself to a whole chain of rationally related issues" (Crenson 1971, 172). Policy entrepreneurs flushed with success, rush to the next issue to take advantage of the momentum (Kingdon 1995).

Group litigation is an important component in the rise of new issues and the metamorphosis of existing issues. First, major groups are typically involved in a variety of issue areas. The solicitor general (Scigliano 1971; Salokar 1992), the ACLU (Donahue 1985; Walker 1990), the NAACP (Wasby, D'Amato, and Metrailer 1977), as well as conservative groups like the Washington Legal Foundation (Epstein 1985) litigate across a range of issues. These groups will try to adapt arguments and provisions that have been used elsewhere to new issues. Groups may bring cases or enter pre-existing cases through the use of *amicus* briefs. Groups attempt to emulate the successes of other litigants (O'Connor 1980; Epstein 1985). Equality litigation is a classic example as groups advocating the rights of the handicapped and the elderly, among others, used principles and strategies advanced by the NAACP in race litigation cases (Olson 1981). As a result, it is not surprising that new issues have antecedents in existing policies. Groups will operate aggressively when the environment is welcoming and seek to transplant favorable doctrine to other areas. However, when the environment changes and becomes unfavorable, groups must react defensively. Savvy groups may need to retreat to their core, "trimming their argumentative sails" to protect their previous gains (Kobylka 1995, 125).

Therefore the notion of policy evolution makes a great deal of sense. Supreme Court policy is doctrine woven from a number of cases over time. Litigants have the incentive to bring cases to further their litigation goals. Justices have the desire to see their constitutional visions put into the law. Justices have an institutional obligation to build doctrine in a coherent fashion. The Court's decisions settle individual disputes. Its doctrine develops policy, creates precedents, and guides lower courts and litigants in wide-ranging areas. The opinions help actors overcome uncertainty in their decision-making processes (Hansford and Spriggs 2006, 3).

THE EMERGENCE AND EVOLUTION OF ISSUES: A FRAMEWORK

Using the propositions about Supreme Court decision-making and judicial process, I now will construct a framework for analyzing policy emergence and evolution. Policy initiation and evolution in the Supreme Court can be conceptualized as a complicated multi-stage process. The framework or model includes four stages of a policy's evolution: the episodic stage, the emergent stage, the elaborative stage, and the complex stage. A fifth stage, the exit stage, is achieved if the Supreme Court decides to leave an issue area altogether. This is a rare phenomenon. Figure 12.1 traces the typical pattern of policy development for issue areas. A new issue results from a related existing area and takes on the color of that issue until it emerges in its own right. Once the new issue is evaluated on its own terms, it begins to move through its

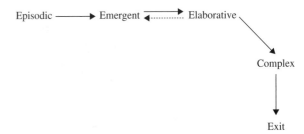

Figure 12.1 Supreme Court Policy Evolution: A Framework

own evolutionary cycle. Figure 12.2 shows the different expectations for each stage of policy evolution.

In some ways, this evolutionary policy process is similar to evolution among living species. As Gould argued: "New species...receive a complex genetic system and a set of developmental pathways for translating genetic products....These pathways do constrain the expression of genetic variation, they do channel it along certain lines" (Gould 1983, 142). So too, newly emergent issues carry the baggage of past related precedents and the existing interpretations of relevant constitutional provisions when they ultimately emerge. Their pattern of growth is constrained to a significant degree. For example, supporters of the right to an abortion lament the fact that the right is based on privacy and not the Fourteenth Amendment (Rubin 1987, 87), feeling that the former imposes constraints that might not exist if equal protection was the basis of *Roe*.

Let's now explore the details of each of these stages in the evolutionary policy process. The first stage of policy evolution in the Supreme Court is the *episodic stage*. The episodic phase is marked by infrequent, inconsistent appearance on the Court's agenda of the issue and by inconsistency in individual- and institutional-level decision making. Because the issue does not arise annually or with any predictability, the nature of doctrine in an episodic policy area is likely to be unstable. Compounding this problem is the fact that the new policy in question has probably been transplanted from another area that is at a later stage of policy development. The new issue typically results as a conscious effort on behalf of litigants or justices seeking to adapt success from other areas. At this stage, the new issue may be viewed in the context

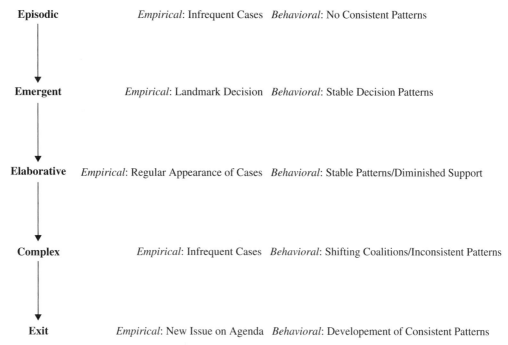

Episodic   *Empirical*: Infrequent Cases   *Behavioral*: No Consistent Patterns

Emergent   *Empirical*: Landmark Decision   *Behavioral*: Stable Decision Patterns

Elaborative   *Empirical*: Regular Appearance of Cases   *Behavioral*: Stable Patterns/Diminished Support

Complex   *Empirical*: Infrequent Cases   *Behavioral*: Shifting Coalitions/Inconsistent Patterns

Exit   *Empirical*: New Issue on Agenda   *Behavioral*: Developement of Consistent Patterns

Figure 12.2 Supreme Court Policy Evolution: Empirical and Behavioral Expectations

of the issue that spawned it. The novel area may take a while to develop its own doctrinal identity.

To reach the agenda and attract the Court's consciousness as a separate issue, a novel issue must surmount the typical barriers that all new issues face. Once the specific issue reaches the decision agenda, it may serve as the catalyst for introducing related items to the Court's agenda (see Kingdon 1995, 200–204). Once a breakthrough occurs in a new issue area it may lead to a surge of activity in other areas (Downs 1973, 40–45).

The emergence of a new issue is what I call an "organic extension" of an existing issue when the novel issue is structurally related to the issue from which it is derived. This occurs when the Court creates the new issue from the precedents that govern the existing area. This typically involves the use of the same constitutional provisions and principles for both issues. Often many of the same groups are involved in bringing litigation or providing support through *amicus* briefs. Interest groups, having attracted the Court's attention with a previous issue, would attempt to use similar principles to push new issues on to the

Court's agenda. For example, gender equality policy was an organic extension of race litigation, utilizing tools and doctrines the Court created under the Fourteenth Amendment's equal protection clause.

New issues can also emerge from policy areas that are not structurally related to each other. The new issue may have a logical relationship to the old issue, but instead it evolves from different sources and doctrinal bases. For example, the recognition of reproductive rights by the Supreme Court occurred about the same time as the Court's first real recognition of gender equality and appears to have sensitized some of the justices even though the constitutional foundations of the two rights are very different (Rubin 1987). As another example, the Court created freedom of association rights under the First Amendment specifically to protect African Americans and civil rights protestors (Belknap 2005). The source of the rights comes from very different constitutional provisions. I refer to this less prevalent occurrence as "collateral development."

To achieve its own status, the new policy area must advance to the second phase, the *emergent stage*.

During the emergent stage, the policy area makes a regular claim to be on the agenda. This signals the Court's recognition that additional doctrinal work is necessary and its intention to address the issue systematically. The ability to take a number of cases allows justices to isolate the issue from its predecessor and to treat the new issue on its own terms. To be sure, the emerging doctrine will bear resemblance to pre-existing areas, but it will increasingly develop its own focus. Litigants typically marshal an array of possible constitutional violations, giving the Court a choice of provisions. Alternatively, the justices, through issue expansion or suppression (Ulmer 1982; McGuire and Palmer 1995), adapt the petition to reflect the wishes of a majority on the Court.[7]

Substantively, emergent stage cases are first generation questions, the core concern of the policy area. The stage is normally marked by the development and initial application of a standard or test that will serve as the basis for evaluating future cases in this policy area. There is an expectation that the Court will come to evaluate these questions in a consistent manner. First, justices tend to be consistent ideologically in their decisions. Second, as members of the Court of last resort, justices have an institutional obligation to decide cases in a consistent manner so as to guide lower courts because of their judicial role. The impact of the jurisprudential regimes or precedents will structure their decisions in similar cases. Thus, justices' goals mediated by institutional rules and norms, that is their conceptions of the judicial role, affect the evolution of policy.

The emergent stage is often marked by the cases immediately preceding, including, and following the central landmark decision. Cases preceding the landmark opinion begin to shape the contours of the central issue before the Court, and thus limit or constrain the range of long-term choices available to the Court. The landmark opinion defines that question, and the cases immediately following define the scope of the seminal decision. As a result, this stage should not be especially long in duration. It does, however, create the shock to the system that begins the process of dynamic growth, thus serving as a punctuated equilibrium.[8]

The decisions that follow in subsequent cases are more fact intensive and thus narrower in applying the existing standard and are found in the *elaborative stage.* There is an expectation that at some point in the emergent stage, the Court should resolve first generation questions in a manner that will guide lower courts. Litigants attempt to induce the Court to expand its previous decisions. Having settled the core questions in the emergent stage, it is uncertain how much further the justices are willing to go. At that point, the issue is expected to progress to the elaborative stage. This phase is marked by the increased difficulty of the questions being litigated, but the Court applies the standard created in the emergent stage. There are individual and institutional level expectations that accompany this stage. Supreme Court support for the issue should decline as the facts in the cases get more difficult. For instance, after deciding that public officials had to meet a very high standard to win a libel judgment, the Court was flooded with cases asking it to define who was a public official.

Regardless of the stage of development of the issue, individual cases may be emergent, elaborative, or complex. Occasionally, an elaborative case arrives too early for the justices. Repeat players may misread the Court's signals and rush the next round of cases too quickly. Justices may narrow the issue in the petition and keep the issue at an early stage. The opposite process can occur as well: though the issue is at the elaborative stage, emergent cases may still arise. A lower court may misinterpret the Supreme Court's decision on the core issue or a conflict between lower courts ensues. For example, following *Brown,* Southern school boards constructed a number of barriers to racial desegregation and forced the Court to address emergent stage questions as cases involving labor relations and access to accommodations were pushing race litigation into the elaborative stage.

Given normal expectations and stable membership, the Court should impose consistency and stability on elaborative stage cases. Consistency in elaborative cases, however, is seldom established because of membership changes or the introduction of additional issues that arise from separate areas of law. Membership changes can have two effects depending on their nature and scope. First, marginal changes could upset the existing stability in individual decision patterns and send mixed or confusing signals to litigants and lower courts. Thus, policies remain in the elaborative stage for a long period of time as the Court assimilates new members and develops a new stability. Second, fundamental changes in the ideological composition of the Court can have profound effects on the evolution of policy. In particular, such changes can reverse the trend of policy development and lead the Court to revisit the landmark decision. The changes in the Court lead to frequent predictions that the Court will overturn *Roe v. Wade*.

A new Court that is antagonistic to its predecessor's precedents can begin to reverse decisions at the elaborative stage. The effect is to send clear signals to litigants interested in changing the original doctrine. If the new Supreme Court majority imposes consistency on elaborative stage cases, it may raise the question of whether the Court is willing to reconsider emergent precedents. Normally, the type of membership change required to achieve this policy retreat is extensive and involves wholesale changes in the ideological composition of the Court.

In the absence of significant ideological change in the Court's membership, policy is expected to evolve from the elaborative to the *complex stage.* During the complex stage, additional components are added to the basic issue. The specific issue may be attached to other, unrelated issues by litigants or by justices interested in pursuing certain policy goals. For instance, during the gestation of civil rights litigation, a number of cases arose involving the freedom of association rights of members of the NAACP (*NAACP v. Button* 1963; *Shelton v. Tucker* 1960). Some southern states attempted to expose membership in the NAACP, possibly to harass such members. As a result, these cases raised First Amendment issues in a context of equal protection, falling under the Fourteenth Amendment. Contrast that with cases during the same period involving the associational rights of alleged Communists that the Court did not protect (see Ball and Cooper 1992).

At the complex stage, the general behavioral impact is expected to be instability in individual and institutional decision making and coalitional patterns. Among litigants, traditional allies may find themselves on different sides (Kobylka 1995). Some members of the Court may decide the case on the basis of one issue, while their colleagues view a different issue as controlling. Thus, votes of individual members and decisions of the Court may appear to contradict votes and decisions found in the elaborative stage cases. The need for consistency in decisions may induce the Court to separate the issues and address them individually. If this represents a new issue, that issue is expected to form its own episodic or emergent stage, while the Court returns the original issue to the elaborative stage. Thus, the new issue is probably an organic extension (related issue) of the existing policy. Litigants attempt to reconstruct the coalition that passed the basic issue by casting the new issue in terms of the existing policy (Kingdon 1995). Litigants may attempt to utilize the process of collateral development (unrelated issue) to assist the process by highlighting parallels or connections between existing issues that are thriving and issues that are seeking recognition.

The emergence and evolution of judicial policies structure the scope and pace of agenda change. Venerable issues may directly or indirectly lead to the emergence of other issues. As noted, new issues may be related to existing issues. Less direct, work in one policy area may sensitize justices and litigants to proximate issues. When a new issue arises, it will begin to proceed through the various stages of development. As a result, the new issue will be a part of the Court's agenda for the foreseeable future.

THE EMERGENCE AND EVOLUTION OF FREE EXERCISE POLICY

To evaluate the model that I have presented, I will now use the evolution of free exercise of religion doctrine. The Court was not called on to deal with many of these free exercise of religion issues for the first century of its existence. In *Reynolds v. United States* (1878), the Court determined the constitutionality of a statute banning polygamy. In upholding the law against free exercise of religion challenges, the justices ruled that religious exercise must yield to a criminal law with a clear secular purpose (Long 2000). Figure 12.3 shows the emergence of free exercise policy.

One of the reasons that there were so few cases regarding the free exercise of religion is that most restrictions on religion would come from state

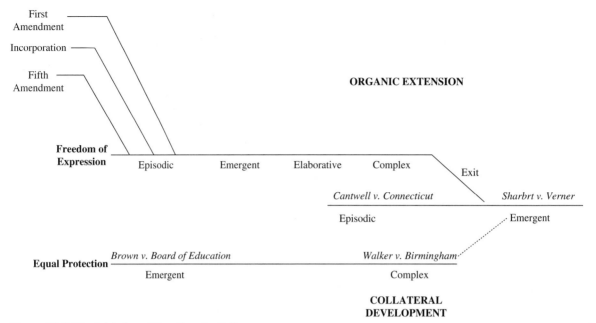

Figure 12.3 The Initiation of Free Exercise Policy

governments. Well into the early twentieth century, the First Amendment had not been incorporated (or applied) to the states; therefore, it only protected citizens from actions by the federal government. Without a policy window, protection against encroachments on free exercise would have to come from the states. However, two events changed that. First, the Court began the process of selective incorporation of the Bill of Rights against the states in *Gitlow v. New York* (1925). Although that solved one problem, there was a larger one looming. The existing Secular Regulation rule articulated in the *Reynolds* case was very deferential to the government. There were hints that would change when Justice Stone filed his famous footnote four in the *United States v. Carolene Products Company* (1938) case. In this footnote, Stone argued that civil liberties and the rights of insular minorities should be held in a preferred position. Thus, the Court should adopt a more rigorous standard of review that would not be deferential to the government. Quite to the contrary, it would ask the government to meet a very high standard before it could restrict a person's

individual liberties. The policy window had been thrown open and a number of groups tried to push their issues through it (Pacelle 1991).

Free exercise of religion policy evolved from a related issue area, freedom of expression, inheriting the basic structure from the two issues' common backgrounds. The connection between the early free exercise cases and free speech policy was not surprising or accidental considering the influence of the Jehovah's Witnesses. Given the proselytizing efforts of the religion, the free exercise questions raised by the Witnesses were inexorably interwoven with free speech concerns (see Konvitz 1966). In *Cantwell v. Connecticut* (1940), the Supreme Court incorporated the free exercise provision of the First Amendment (Cortner 1981), but ultimately focused on the free speech aspects of the case.

In *Cantwell*, attorneys for the Jehovah's Witnesses raised free exercise questions in their arguments, but the Supreme Court based its decision on the free speech doctrine that was at its emergent stage of development. Thus decisions that upheld freedom of speech rights

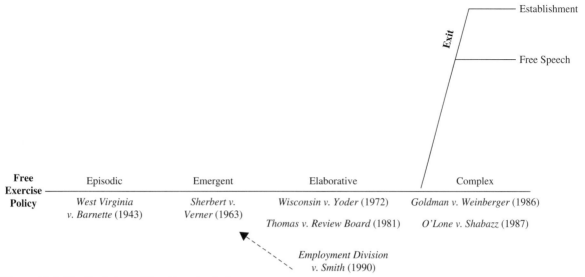

Figure 12.4 The Evolution of Free Exercise Policy

helped create a favorable environment for recognition of free exercise of religion rights.

The *Cantwell* case is part of the episodic stage of free exercise policy because the decision did not clearly define the standards for later exercise cases. The Court was searching for applicable tests for future cases. *Cantwell* had an important influence on the development of free expression policy. In his opinion, Justice Owen Roberts reiterated the differences between belief and action, but held that the latter was not without some First Amendment protection. This was the first time that the Court recognized the value of expressive action (Morgan 1972).[9]

The transition of free exercise policy from the episodic to the emergent stage was halting and painful for the Court. The cases, largely brought at the behest of the Jehovah's Witnesses, continued to involve a number of different issues and the Court was inconsistent in its treatment of the early cases. The legal arm of the Witnesses rushed a number of cases to the docket, which may have affected the Court's ability to process the multiple cases and build the new doctrine coherently. In addition, the environment was not favorable for an expansion of civil liberties. A variety of new issues were confronting justices with little experience,

turnover in the Court's membership was relatively high, and the looming war clouds were not conducive to the broad protection of liberties and rights (Pacelle 1991). Figure 12.4 shows the evolution of free exercise policy.

In the flag salute case, *Minersville School District v. Gobitis* (1940), Chief Justice Hughes worked hard at the conference on the case to suppress the religious question and keep it out of the Court's eventual opinion (Bartee 1984, 53–55). Given the mood of the country and rising patriotic fervor at that time, that was not difficult.[10] In a subsequent case involving the Jehovah's Witnesses, *Jones v. Opelika* (1942), four justices dissented and took the unusual step of admitting the error of their votes in *Minersville*. As noted, justices sometimes send cues to litigants, though they are seldom this clear. The religion cases and other early civil liberties issues caused the justices a great deal of difficulty. Justices like Douglas, Black, and Murphy increasingly felt comfortable on the Court and supportive of individual liberties (Ball and Cooper 1992, 236). With the appointment of Justice Wiley Rutledge, the Court had a narrow working majority in favor of civil liberties.

In a series of cases decided in 1943, the Court reversed its ruling in *Minersville* (*West Virginia State*

Board of Education v. Barnette 1943) and *Jones* (*Murdoch v. Pennsylvania* 1943). This shows the inconsistency of the Court and the justices as the new issue was taking shape. The Court was increasingly sympathetic to freedom of religion, but still no clear uniform standards resulted. Many of the elements expected at the emergent stage were becoming evident. The Court was increasingly isolating the religion question and making it the basis of decisions. Individual justices and the Court began to exhibit consistent behavior in deciding these cases. Such cases, due to the activity of the Jehovah's Witnesses, were becoming regular staples of the Court's annual agenda. The old, deferential Secular Regulation rule that the Court had been using had been eroded (Morgan 1972), but it stood nominally as the prevailing standard. As Figure 12-4 shows, *Barnette* is the transition to the emergent stage. For the first time, the Court's decision concentrated on freedom of religion. Once the Court defined religious issues as being distinct from similar cases involving nonreligious activity, the Court immediately confronted new issues, all the more challenging due to the fact that the Court lacked a coherent doctrine on which to structure its decisions.

The evolutionary development of free exercise doctrine was an organic extension of the more venerable free speech cases. As a relatively new issue, the presence of existing free speech precedents gave the Court a foundation on which to build free exercise doctrine. The cost, however, was that the development of religion policy was constrained by free speech standards. Developmental pathways channel and shape the evolution of the new issue and constrain the variation. The doctrine woven of free speech and free exercise cases was not clear, but it became the core of free exercise policy for decades.

During the 1943 to 1961 period, the Court decided few important free exercise of religion cases. As a result, free exercise doctrine remained in the emergent stage. During this period, the Court shifted its attention to no establishment of religion cases as well as a variety of other First Amendment and equal protection cases. In fact, the success of the Jehovah's Witnesses served as an impetus for the civil rights movement and its litigation strategies, which in turn were the models for subsequent groups (Peters 2000). The evolution of

equal protection doctrine was thus a collateral development of the emergence and evolution of the free speech and free exercise doctrines.

In its decisions on cases involving Sunday closing laws, the Supreme Court further refined and developed its test for free exercise of religion cases. The Sunday closing law cases represent emergent stage cases as the Court continued to tinker with the core question and formulate a standard for the evaluation of subsequent cases. In the decisions, most of the justices confined the issue to the single, free exercise issue. The Court's plurality opinions distinguished between direct and indirect effects on religion and added a least restrictive means component to the test, borrowed from free speech cases.

Just when the Court appeared to adopt a coherent standard, a majority refashioned the test for free exercise cases in another landmark case. In *Sherbert v. Verner* (1963), the Court ruled that South Carolina's denial of social service benefits to a woman fired because of her refusal to work on her Sabbath was a denial of her free exercise of religion. The essence of Justice Brennan's dissent in *Braunfeld v. Brown* (1961), one of the Sunday closing law cases, became the majority opinion in *Sherbert*. The new standard added an additional component to the existing standard: the state must have a "compelling interest" to regulate the exercise of religion. In so doing, Brennan reestablished the close connections between free exercise of religion and free speech doctrines (Morgan 1972). The decision had the effect of providing more protection for religious freedom (Eisler 1993). The *Sherbert* case thus marks the transition from the emergent stage to the elaborative stage of issue evolution.

The elaborative stage of development represents the increased difficulty of cases in the free exercise domain. Once a standard has been established, the fact situations in later cases present the Court with more difficult issues. Cases like *Wisconsin v. Yoder* (1972; involving the objections of the Amish to compulsory school attendance laws) and *Thomas v. Review Board* (1981; involving unemployment benefits for an individual who quit his job for religious purposes though there was a disagreement among practitioners as to whether the religion required it) are good examples of elaborative stage cases. The decisions in these cases represented high points for the protection of free exercise of religion.

Other issues also emerged at this stage of the policy-making model. After regulations that mandated that one seeking conscientious objection status be a member of a recognized pacifist religion were emasculated by the Court, the justices were forced to confront more gray areas. Conscientious objection cases tied to the Vietnam War like *United States v. Seeger* (1965), *Welsh v. United States* (1970), and *Gillette v. United States* (1971) are found at the elaborative stage as well. The cases no longer involved traditional religious beliefs, but personal moral codes and political, ideological, and philosophical beliefs that constituted justifications for refusal to partake in war.

Later free exercise cases faced a less hospitable environment brought about by the accumulation of membership changes on the Supreme Court. As the Court was handing down some of its most accommodating establishment clause decisions, it allowed restrictions on the free exercise of religion. As one would expect of elaborative cases, the cases raised more difficult questions. In *United States v. Lee* (1982), the Court did not allow an exemption from Social Security taxes for Amish employers. The majority found the need for uniformity in the Social Security tax system to be a compelling rationale for putting a restriction of free exercise (Ivers 1991).

Once policy areas reach the elaborative stage, there is an expectation that multi-issue complex stage cases will arise. Many of these cases involved religious expression (free speech) in a public forum and bore no small resemblance to the cases brought by Jehovah's Witnesses that opened the door to modern free exercise doctrine. Cases raising free exercise questions have allowed the Court to refine its policies regarding the definition, use, and limits of a public forum. *Board of Airport Commissioners v. Jews for Jesus* (1987) and *Lee v. International Society for Krishna Consciousness* (1992) involved proselytizing and solicitation efforts in airports. The groups consistently raised free exercise claims, but the Court confined its evaluation to free speech issues.

Cases like *Goldman v. Weinberger* (1986) and *O'Lone v. Estate of Shabazz* (1987) raised multiple-complex stage issues as well: military regulations and prison security, respectively. *Goldman* was a complex

stage case because military discipline could dictate the Air Force's dress code and deny an Orthodox Jew the right to wear a yarmulke.[11] *O'Lone* involved a similar need for discipline in a prison that permitted some restriction on the free exercise of religion.

Because of the multiple issues in these cases, a variety of groups were involved, complicating the work of the Court. Therefore the reader should note that the complex stage is marked by great instability. In some ways, this looks like the episodic stage, except that there is now mature doctrine, whereas there was no coherent precedent when the episodic cases were decided.

The trend of the elaborative and complex decisions was increasingly restrictive of free exercise rights. It is important to note, the evolution of doctrine is not necessarily an unbroken chain of advancement. The accumulation of membership changes gave the Court a more deferential attitude toward state regulations. These decisions seemed at odds with the core standard, coming from *Sherbert*, which was protective of free exercise. When such tensions exist, the Court may decide to reexamine the central core questions and return the issue to the emergent stage.

In *Employment Division, Department of Human Resources of Oregon v. Smith* (1990), the Court returned to the emergent stage by abandoning the compelling interest standard of *Sherbert v. Verner* (1963). Attorneys for Smith attempted to tie this case to *Sherbert* and *Thomas* because he was denied unemployment compensation after being fired for using peyote in a religious ceremony. Although the majority opinion could have reached the same result without tampering with the existing standard, given the state's compelling interest in halting the use of drugs, Justice Scalia's opinion gave the state much wider authority and appeared to revisit the Secular Regulation rule (Long 2000). The majority could have constructed this as a complex stage issue and confined its decision to the police power aspect, upholding criminal sanctions (as Justice O'Connor advocated). Instead, the opinion concentrated on free exercise and rejected *Sherbert* and the compelling interest standard.

Justice O'Connor, who concurred in the result, disagreed with the scope of Scalia's opinion: "In my view, today's holding dramatically departs from well-settled First Amendment jurisprudence, appears unnecessary to resolve the question presented, and is incompatible with our nation's fundamental commitment to individual religious liberty" (494 U.S. at 891). The effect of the decision was to move the issue back to the emergent stage of issue evolution, by reopening the standards of evaluation for free exercise of religion cases.

Given the notion of spillovers and policy windows, Scalia's opinion in *Smith* represented a situation for change that could spread across related issue domains. Establishment of religion doctrine is related (an organic extension) to free exercise of religion, and the prospects for change toward further accommodation between church and state are almost certain. Restricting the state's need to demonstrate a compelling interest could be transplanted to other areas of civil liberties, suggesting the process I have called collateral development. Indeed, such a process has been underway in a number of issue areas.[12]

In an unusual circumstance, however, the intervention into the policy environment by external actors tempered the movement back to the emergent stage. Congress passed the Religious Freedom Restoration Act of 1993, which required courts analyzing free exercise cases to use the compelling interest/least restrictive means standard that had been in force since the *Sherbert* decision (Ivers 1991, 88).

The Court rebuffed Congressional efforts in *City of Boerne v. Flores* (1997) by declaring that it had the authority to determine the appropriate standard for evaluating these claims. In doing so, the Court stayed with the more forgiving *Smith* standard. This has triggered a new round of elaborative litigation as states and communities restrict the religious freedom of different, often small, religious sects. It has led to decisions like *Church of Lukumi Babalu Aye v. Hialeah* (1993), involving municipal ordinances against animal sacrifice, a central tenet of the Santeria religion. The Court ruled that though *Smith* was the governing principle, Hialeah had gone too far with this ordinance

that singled out this particular religion for unequal treatment.

Viewed from the doctrinal perspective, free exercise policy fits the framework of issue emergence and evolution. Free speech doctrine and establishment of religion doctrine shaped the emergence of free exercise policy. The questions before the Court got more difficult as the stages progressed. A number of the more recent cases involve multiple issues and suggest instability in the Court's decision making. That instability was resolved by revisiting the emergent stage and changing the underlying precedent.

CONCLUSIONS

Because the policy goals of the justices are considered the most significant influence on decision making, research tends to concentrate on them to the exclusion of other factors. This framework of issue evolution suggests that institutional rules and norms also structure decision making and doctrinal construction. In addition, appropriate conditions are necessary for policy emergence.

Policy evolution is an independent variable that helps explain institutional decision making (see chapter 13 of this volume). The behavior of justices and litigants is a function of the relevant stage of that issue's development. The stage of evolution reflects a confluence of factors: the political environment, the composition of the Court, the activities and identity of the litigants, existing precedents in the relevant area of law, the nature of the political theory that underlies the construction of doctrine, and the evolution of issues in related areas of law. An examination of free exercise doctrine suggests that the behavior of justices and litigants varies under different conditions and by the stage in the evolutionary policy model.[13]

Notes

1. Landmark cases and their relevant areas of law often trace their doctrinal roots to other issue areas. In many instances, those areas of law are constitutionally proximate and derived from related areas. In other areas, however, the roots of a new issue area can

be traced to doctrine in policy areas that appear on the face to bear no resemblance to the emerging area. In addition, these landmark decisions have been used as a wedge to open or expand other areas of law (Pacelle 1991; Baird 2004). *Brown v. Board* (1954), for example, helped create the conditions for gender equality litigation in addition to creating desegregation policies.

2. The notion of policy evolution is implicit in many studies of the president (Light 1982; Skowronek 1997), Congress (Kingdon 1995; Sinclair 1989), and the bureaucracy (Wood and Waterman 1993, 1994; Ripley and Franklin 1982, 1990). Studies of the outputs of the elected branches (Smith 1993; Walker 1977) show how policy is built in stages. Analyses of specific areas of law (Richards and Kritzer 2002; Hoff 1991; Kahn 1994; Haiman 1981; Cortner 1981; Graber 1991; McCloskey 1960) demonstrate how current decisions are layered on existing precedents to flesh out the Court's policy.

The judicial behavior literature, most notably analyses of decision making by justices (Schubert 1965, 1974; Segal and Spaeth 2002) and analyses of the facts of cases (Kort 1957; Segal 1984, 1986; Ignagni 1993), lend credence to the processes by which issues evolve and become more complex over time (Baum 1988, 1992). These studies implicitly or explicitly demonstrate that differing fact or case situations have a significant impact on the decisions of individual justices and the Court as a whole (George and Epstein 1992).

3. Wasby (1984) maintained that it is more difficult to implement a strategy for purposive litigation given the proliferation of groups, costs of litigation, and that litigants must attend to a large number of diverse areas of law to protect their interests. Considering the wholesale changes in the ideology of the Court as a dominant environmental force, liberal groups have simply lost the support of the Court in many instances. Past successes created a broad terrain that needed to be defended from the increasing attacks by the Court. Groups like the ACLU and NAACP litigate across a variety of areas and need to protect their gains across those areas. In periods during which the Court is sympathetic, groups are encouraged to push the frontiers of litigation across boundaries. Yet, in times of negative change, the resources of these groups are too broadly spread out. With environmental pressures and increased litigation from opponents, the groups that had held an advantage prior to the dramatic change must retreat and protect the core of their concerns (Kobylka 1987, 1995; Wasby 1984).

4. Confronted with unprecedented issues, justices turned to well-honed solutions that had worked in other areas. Perspectives changed as the Court abandoned traditional economic issues, but extensive foundation building was needed to convert the agenda to civil liberties issues. Justices retained perceptual and intellectual baggage from economic issues. The scrutiny tests developed to resolve equal protection issues were borrowed directly from economic policies (Balkin 1985, 185).

5. The new issue for the courts typically results from a related issue as a conscious effort on behalf of litigants or justices seeking to adapt success in other areas to the new area. At this stage, the new issue may be viewed in the context of the issue that spawned it and takes on the color of that issue until it emerges in its own right. The novel area may take a while to develop its own doctrinal identity.

6. The incorporation of the preponderance of the Bill of Rights followed a two stage process involving such spillovers. The initial selective incorporation of the most fundamental provisions occurred in the 1940s and was followed by wholesale additions in the 1960s (Cortner 1981).

7. The usual pattern of issue expansion is that a case arrives in the normal course of litigation for another area or presents a narrow question. The Court then converts the issue to a landmark in a different issue area or expands the impact beyond the facts of the specific dispute. *Mapp v. Ohio*, 367 U.S. 643 (1961) is an example of issue expansion. The case reached the Supreme Court as a test of the legality of Ohio's obscenity law. On the basis of an *amicus* brief, the Court turned it into a major pronouncement on search and seizure and incorporation. *Gideon v. Wainwright*, 372 U.S. 335 (1963) is an example of an issue that was expanded within the same framework. The case raised the issue of the right to counsel for indigents (Ulmer 1982, 323). The Court instructed the attorneys to expand the case to address the issue of incorporation.

8. This is consistent with Sunstein's notion of width. Sunstein (1999, 16–19) argued that decisions have width if they set a clear standard, are applicable to other cases in the specific issue area, and are the governing principles for that area of law.

9. In speech cases, the Court draws lines between pure speech, which gets broad protection, and conduct, which has some value, but in the eyes of many justices diminished protection (Ball and Cooper 1992). In a similar fashion, the Court used these distinctions in its free exercise decisions, an organic extension of free speech. The right to hold any belief was absolute, the exercise of those rights, like conduct could be regulated under some circumstances. The speech/conduct connections drawn between speech and religion served to constrain the development of free exercise doctrine.

10. *Chaplinsky v. New Hampshire* (1942) and *Jones v. Opelika* (1942) were brought by the Jehovah's Witnesses, but the Court's pronouncements in those cases were largely concerned with free speech. The Court defined unprotected speech in *Chaplinsky* (Cord 1982) and focused on commercial speech in *Jones* (Pritchett 1984).

11. *Goldman* prompted a response from Congress, which resulted in a change in the military code creating exceptions to the ban on wearing religious apparel (Carter 1991, 24–25).

12. *Miranda* rights have been undermined with "public safety" exceptions, the "cat out of the bag," and the "inevitability of discovery" exception. *Mapp* has similarly had exceptions, like "good faith," which suggest that the core will be reevaluated (Pacelle 2004). *Roe* has been undermined by a plethora of regulations, but the central precedent remains on the books. Courts do not often overturn their decisions (Ball 1978); rather, through attrition or exception they undermine the emergent core issue. At some point, the Court may return to the emergent stage, but the existing precedent often lasts beyond its predicted demise.

13. In some ways, the past is prologue for free exercise litigation. The Court's more favorable approach to civil liberties issues since the famous footnote four in *United States v. Carolene Products Company* (1938) and the application of the free exercise clause to the states dramatically opened a policy window. Groups like the Jehovah's Witnesses, the American Civil Liberties Union, and the American Jewish Congress used the opportunity to pursue their policy goals. Significant changes in the membership of the Court then created a new policy window that has led to substantial change in recent free exercise of religion doctrine. Although massive

membership changes altered the sincere preferences of the Court, the process of dismantling doctrine is, like the process of creating it, lengthy. It is the nature of spillovers that the recent retreat that has marked free exercise doctrine is spreading to other areas of law. The slow nature of change is a function of the need to have stability and predictability in the law, but it is also the result of the purposive behavior of actors who want to protect the existing interpretation of the law. In that regard, as Kobylka (1995, 125) noted, "it demonstrates the capacity of the law to withstand politically directed efforts at change."

13

A COURT OF LAWS OR A
SUPER LEGISLATURE?

An Integrated Model of Supreme
Court Decision Making

Bryan W. Marshall, Richard L. Pacelle, Jr., and Christine Ludowise

Political scientists and other judicial scholars often use quantitative or statistical methods to test their hypotheses about judicial behavior. This chapter gives an example of a quantitative model to help sort out the question of whether the legal approach, the attitudinal approach, or the strategic approach is the best for predicting U.S. Supreme Court decisions. The statistical model used in this chapter uses a conservative or liberal outcome in civil rights and civil liberties cases to test the effects of a variety of independent variables, drawn from the legal, attitudinal, and strategic models. The chapter concludes that none of the three main approaches can explain every aspect of judicial decision making, but that scholars should combine these three approaches to get a fuller understanding of how the Supreme Court makes its decisions.

Ernesto Miranda's name is arguably the most famous in American constitutional law. If Linda Brown, the plaintiff from *Brown v. Board* (1954), is the smiling face of judicial activism and the symbol for the great decisions of the Warren Court, Ernesto Miranda is the poster boy for "handcuffing the police" and opposition to judicial policy making. One need not know the first thing about the Constitution to know of the "Miranda warnings" that carry his name. Television and movies frequently show police officers "Mirandizing" a suspect when making an arrest.

When the Supreme Court made its monumental decision in *Miranda v. Arizona* (1966), it was only one in a string of decisions such as *Mapp v. Ohio* (1961), *Malloy v. Hogan* (1964), and *Escobedo v. Illinois* (1964)

that launched the so-called due process revolution in American constitutional law. For example, *Mapp v. Ohio* (1961) declared that the exclusionary rule should apply to criminal proceedings in state courts. The exclusionary rule basically says that any evidence obtained illegally must be excluded from use in a criminal trial. Thus decisions like *Miranda* and *Mapp* were met with widespread opposition. Police and prosecutors objected to the decisions. The public strongly criticized the Warren Court for this and other sweeping decisions. Congress attacked the Court and tried a variety of measures in an attempt to overturn the decisions. In fact, in 1968 Congress passed a law to limit the impact of *Miranda*.[1] At the same time presidential candidate Richard Nixon made law and order the centerpiece of his campaign (Belknap 2005).

Nixon's appeal to law and order resonated with the public. The Republicans were able to control the White House for sixteen of the next twenty years. Maybe the most important consequence of this domination was the opportunity to pack the Supreme Court. By the end of George H.W. Bush's term in 1992, Republicans had appointed eight of the nine justices. Not long after the Warren Court became the Burger Court, a majority of the justices began chipping away at many of the due process protections. Indeed, some have claimed that the Burger Court appeared to be "stalking the exclusionary rule" and undermining the foundation of *Miranda* (Urofsky 1991, 167).

The Burger Court soon developed a number of exceptions to the exclusionary rule. In addition to these exceptions to the exclusionary rule the Court also created a number of exceptions to the *Miranda* warnings (Pacelle 2004). The Court adopted the public safety exception, the "cat out of the bag" exception, and the harmless error exception to *Miranda* (Haynie 2004). Was this a precursor to overturning the right to be informed of one's rights?

Many analysts and pundits predicted the end of *Miranda*. What was the basis of that prediction? This raises the question that is the subject of this chapter: How does the Supreme Court make its decisions? Analysts characterize the determinants of judicial decision making as either legal or extralegal. *Legal factors* are seen as legitimate and suggest that judges adhere to a distinctive set of norms and traditions in carrying out their responsibilities. Legal factors would include reliance on precedent and deference to the elected branches (Clayton 1999). To utilize legal factors would underline that the justices form a Court of Laws. In contrast, extra-legal considerations emphasize the Court as a political institution. *Extra-legal factors* include the attitudes of the justices, small group bargaining, and strategic decision making that would see the Court move from its ideal position to avoid retaliation by the other branches of government (Pacelle 2002). Although it may better reflect reality, there is something normatively disconcerting about thinking of the justices as legislators in robes and the Supreme Court as an unelected super legislature.

The question of whether the *Miranda* decision would be overturned came to the forefront in 2000 in the case of *Dickerson v. United States* (2000). Charles Thomas Dickerson was arrested for armed bank robbery. He moved to suppress his confession because he had not been properly Mirandized. The government argued that *Miranda* was not a constitutional decision and therefore the 1968 congressional law that attempted to overturn the decision was the controlling law. Members of Congress from both parties filed an *amicus curiae* or friend of the court brief urging the Supreme Court to uphold the law passed to reverse the *Miranda* requirements. Four former attorneys general filed *amicus* briefs in support of the government's position. Various victims' rights groups, police associations, and state governments also filed briefs in support of limiting or overturning *Miranda v. Arizona*.

How would the Court deal with this particular case? In *Dickerson v. United States*, the determinants of decision making sent decidedly mixed signals. Precedent favored retaining *Miranda*. Strategic decision making (i.e., moving toward the political positions of the other branches to avoid retaliation) favored overturning *Miranda*. The attitudes or policy preferences of the justices also seemed to signal the death knell for *Miranda*. Chief Justice William Rehnquist, and Justices Antonin Scalia and Clarence Thomas, as solid conservatives, were likely to support the state in criminal cases and to vote to overturn *Miranda*. The moderates, Sandra O'Connor, Anthony Kennedy, and David Souter, were not as consistent as their conservative brethren, but more often than not, they also decided in favor of the state. Even the three most liberal justices, John Paul Stevens, Ruth Bader Ginsburg, and Stephen Breyer, were as likely to support the state over the accused in criminal procedure cases. No nose count seemed to favor Dickerson.

A funny thing happened on the way to the demise of *Miranda*. Rehnquist, a long-time opponent of *Miranda*, wrote the opinion for a seven member majority upholding the landmark precedent and rebuffing congressional attempts to overturn the spirit of *Miranda*. Rehnquist wrote that, "*Miranda*, being a constitutional decision of this Court, may not be in effect overruled by an Act of Congress" (530 US at 412). Rehnquist went further to note that, "*Miranda* has become embedded in routine police practice to the point where such warnings have become a part of our national culture" (530 US at 443). He concluded the opinion by writing, "Following the rule of *stare decisis*, we decline to overrule *Miranda* ourselves" (530 US at 444).[2]

This case is but one of a hundred or so that the Supreme Court decides each term. In those cases, the justices have to make individual decisions as to how they will vote and why. They consult their personal preferences, weigh precedent, and consider the views of their colleagues. Presumably, they also take a step back and think about how the decision will affect the Court as an institution.

In studying judicial decision making, there has been a disconnection between individual and institutional levels of analysis. The individual level of analysis examines how and why specific justices voted as they did, while an institutional analysis looks at the Supreme Court as a whole. Perhaps that disconnection is best represented in considering the supposed independence of the Court and the justices. Lifetime tenure and the nomination process insulate individual justices and permit them to act on their own views. At the same time, the institution is hardly independent. The Court lacks the "sword and purse" and must rely on the other branches to fund or implement its directives (see Miller this volume, chapter 19). So although the justices are free to vote their individual attitudes, the Court needs to pay attention to its limitations as an institution (Pacelle 2002).

MODELS OF SUPREME COURT DECISION MAKING

The *Dickerson* decision offers an intriguing look at the three major models of judicial decision making: the legal model, the attitudinal model, and the strategic model. The majority opted to abide by precedent (the legal model) and put aside their individual values (the attitudinal model) and concerns with the reactions of the other two branches (the strategic model). This chapter examines these three models and their relative effects on Supreme Court decision making. To begin the analysis, we start by defining these three models of decision making.

In its purest form, the *legal model* stands for the notion that the justices carefully weigh existing precedents and relevant constitutional or statutory (laws of Congress) provisions when deciding cases. Justices look to decisions in similar cases and seek to discover the intent of the framers of the Constitution or the legislation in question. When they evaluate the Constitution, they should apply neutral principles. In a dispassionate manner, the justices are supposed to begin cases with no preconceptions or biases. Although this seems like a description that is oddly removed from reality, all nominees sit in front of the Judiciary Committee and publicly proclaim that they come to the Court with no preformed ideas about the issues that will come before them (Pacelle 2002). Despite changes that frequently alter the ideological balance of the Court, the evidence demonstrates that very few precedents are overturned (Epstein et al. 2003). However, as George and Epstein (1992) argued, the legal model suggests that if the Court is following precedent, doctrinal change is impossible.

The *attitudinal model* lies 180 degrees away from the legal model. In its purest form, it states that the justices are unencumbered in deciding cases. They are free to decide cases on the basis of their sincere policy preferences. Justices have lifetime tenure and have reached the pinnacle of their careers (Segal and Spaeth 2002). Thus, they are unconstrained in their behavior (Segal and Spaeth 1993). The evidence suggests that individual justices are ideologically very consistent in their decision making (Schubert 1965, 1974; Rohde and Spaeth 1976; but see Epstein et al. 1998). But as George and Epstein (1992) noted, the attitudinal model suggests that doctrinal change is expected to be constant and in the direction of the ideological changes on the Court. The fact that the Court, as an institution, overturns very few precedents suggests that the attitudinal model has some limitations.

The *strategic model* of decision making recognizes internal and external constraints on the Court. When the Court makes decisions, the strategic model maintains that it collectively will consider the position of the president who will have to implement the decision and the Congress that can overturn a decision with which it disagrees (Eskridge 1991a, 1991b; Spiller and Gely 1992). On an individual level, justices may act strategically, taking into account their colleagues on the Court (Murphy 1964; Maltzman, Spriggs, and Wahlbeck 2000). Epstein and Knight (1998) argued that justices would like to make decisions based on their sincere policy values. However, the Court faces important constraints, particularly in cases involving statutory interpretation, and the justices must respect those in making decisions (Fisher and Devins 2006). Congress can overturn statutory decisions by a simple majority so the Court may have to adjust its preferred outcome to get closer to a point Congress will find acceptable. Although in theory Congress can only use a constitutional amendment to overturn a constitutionally based decision from the Court, in reality Congress has attempted to use other means to overturn various constitutionally based judicial decisions (see, e.g., Bragaw and Miller 2004).

THE COURT AS AN INSTITUTION

This brief analysis of the three models of decision making mixes individual and institutional levels of decision making. Is it possible that many of the justices act on their sincere preferences, but the Court as an institution acts in a legal or strategic fashion? The Court is part of an institutional and political context that would be expected to influence, if not shape, its decisions (Gillman 1999). Let's return to the *Dickerson* decision for a moment. Some of the justices decided the case on the basis of their values and attitudes. Why did the majority resist the opportunity to overturn a decision they had criticized for years? Were they protecting the Court as an institution?

The Court faces a variety of constraints in its decision making. In statutory decisions, the constraints appear to be significant. A simple Congressional majority can reverse such decisions. The Court needs to react to the interpretation of the sitting Congress, which can overturn the decision, more than the Congress that passed the legislation in question (Eskridge 1991a, 1991b, 1994). In theory, these constraints could induce the Court to move from its collective sincere preferences (Epstein and Knight 1998). If *Miranda* was not a constitutional decision, Congressional pressure might have induced the Court to overturn it in the *Dickerson* decision.

In practical terms, however, such constraints are not always imposing. For much of the last fifty years, American politics has been dominated by divided government (Fiorina 1996; Peterson 1990). This may free the Court to a degree. If the Court makes a statutory interpretation decision that Congress finds objectionable, Congress can pass legislation to overturn it. During periods of divided government, the president can veto retaliatory legislation. If that occurs, then Congress needs to muster an extraordinary majority to override the veto and overturn the decision (Krehbiel 1998). On other occasions, the policy positions of Congress and the Court may be congruent. In either case, the Court has an ally to protect it.

Constitutional issues provide the justices with the freedom to pursue their sincere preferences; thus, they provide the strongest hypothetical support for the attitudinal model. Such decisions can only be reversed in theory by a constitutional amendment. This takes an extraordinary majority; thus, there appears to be little likelihood of reversing such a decision (but see Meernick and Ignagni 1997). Because *Miranda* was constitutional, Congress could not overturn it without an amendment to the Constitution.

Still, the executive and legislative branches have checks if they are unhappy with the Court's decision. If the Court bends its preferences to reflect those of the elected branches, is it because it is responsive to the pressures that can be brought by the elected branches, or a matter of agreement between the Supreme Court and the executive branch or Congress?

Robert Dahl (1957) noted that the Court cannot long hold out against majority sentiment to the contrary. One of the major reasons for that is that the president will eventually have the opportunity to appoint justices who will reflect his views, thus pulling the Court into alignment with at least one of the elected branches. The power to appoint justices allows the president to impress his philosophy on the Court. If a Court is closely divided, one or two judicial appointments can dramatically change the membership and potentially influence decisional trends (Abraham 1999; Smith 1993; Epstein and Segal 2005).

Any U.S. Supreme Court decision has to be enforced. However, the enforcement power is the province of the president and the executive branch. Thus, the Court is at the mercy of the executive branch. If the president does not like the decision, he does not have to enforce it (Johnson and Canon 1999). Indeed, history reports that Andrew Jackson, upset at the *Worcester v. Georgia* (1832) decision allegedly growled, "John Marshall made his decision, now let him enforce it." (see, e.g., Remini 1988, 70). (For other presidential reactions to Supreme Court decisions, see Miller this volume, chapter 19).

The president also has a check through the Justice Department and the point man for the executive branch in the Supreme Court, the solicitor general (SG). The president may try to use the SG to pursue his agenda through the Court. Because of the volume of litigation with which the government is involved, the SG plays a major role in helping the Court control its docket. In particular, analysts argue that the SG can use *amicus* briefs to advance the president's agenda (Salokar 1992; Segal 1988, 1990). (For more on the role of the solicitor general, see Ubertaccio this volume, chapter 10).

Congress has checks over the Court short of overturning its decisions. Congress can introduce blocking legislation to limit the impact of a decision it opposes. Not long after *Roe v. Wade,* 410 U.S. 113 (1973) was handed down by the Court, Congress, unable to muster the extraordinary majorities necessary for a constitutional amendment to overturn the decision, passed the Hyde Amendment to cut off federal funds for abortions. The decision did not overturn *Roe*, but it made the exercise of reproductive rights more difficult (Hoff 1991, 302–305).

The Constitution gives Congress authority to alter the Court's jurisdiction. Many of the successful attempts to alter jurisdiction have been done in a neutral fashion to assist the Court in handling its growing caseload.[3] In other circumstances, attempts to alter the Court's jurisdiction were not designed to help the Court. Often they involved a reaction to a Court decision that members of Congress opposed (Curry 2005). Supreme Court decisions in controversial cases are bound to provoke a response and have led members of Congress to introduce legislation to limit or deny jurisdiction (Katzmann 1997).[4] (See also Miller this volume, chapter 19).

Although these efforts typically do not succeed, they can have an impact. First, they create a precedent for attacking the Court when members of Congress oppose a particular decision. Second, they undermine respect for the judiciary as an institution. That respect and legitimacy are the Court's ultimate resources. On a few occasions, the Court has retreated in subsequent cases, thus giving Congress a short-term victory (Murphy 1962).

The Court may act strategically, not because of a specific perceived threat, but to blunt broad range opposition to the institution. An individual decision might not create a problem, but a long-term trend might endanger the Court. The Court may act strategically or retreat to allow itself to pursue its designs in other areas. If the Court oversteps its boundaries, it risks losing its legitimacy (Pacelle 2002).

If none of the three models describes all judicial decision making, then what are the factors that appear to make some cases amenable to the legal model, others to the attitudinal model, and a third set to the strategic model? Perhaps the most notable factor is the issue area. In their studies of case selection and the Court's agenda, Perry (1991), Ulmer (1972, 1978, 1984) and Pacelle (1991) argued that justices care more about some issues, and decisions in those areas are governed more by their values and attitudes. For other issues, the Court's role at the top of the judicial hierarchy takes precedent. The justices may decide a case to settle a lower court conflict. The substance of the decision is less important than the fact that the issue is settled. Constitutional decisions would appear to be more amenable to the attitudinal model, while statutory decisions might invoke a strategic response from the Court.

The remaining part of this chapter offers an empirical analysis to explain Supreme Court decision making on a subset of constitutional cases. We analyze Supreme Court decision making within the context of neo-institutional research (see Epstein, Walker, and Dixon 1989), which treats the Court as a single actor whose behavior can be explained systematically. This perspective maintains that institutional rules structure the aggregation of individual preferences within a decision-making body (see chapter 12 in this volume). Thus, decisions are not merely the collective expression of the individual preferences of its members, but are a function of the interaction of individual preferences and institutional structures and rules. Institutions thus shape the behavior of the actors in the legal system (Smith 1988).

We begin with the argument that no single model explains judicial decision making under all circumstances. The composition of the Court is the most important factor, but the Court is constrained by the need to impose doctrinal stability and to protect its legitimacy by seeing its decisions implemented and respected. What the Court does is the result of multiple-intertwined forces that operate in complicated ways to shape decisions (Baum 1997). Our study is designed to integrate the multiple factors related to the legal, attitudinal, and strategic perspectives.

By using constitutional cases, we consider conditions that are most favorable to the attitudinal model because the chances of a decision being overturned are minimal. In addition, we isolate civil liberties and civil rights cases[5] because they are more likely to be central to the policy designs of the justices. Since the Court announced its intention to treat individual liberties and the rights of insular minorities in 1938 in *United States v. Carolene Products Company* (1938), they have been the most important issues for the Court and litigants and the dominant issues on the Court's agenda (Pacelle 1991).

RESEARCH DESIGN

This analysis examines a portion of the Court's plenary docket: constitutional civil liberties and civil rights cases in the 1953 to 1998 period as determined by the Supreme Court data base. We use full decisions from orally argued cases. This yields a total of 1,392 decisions. The dependent variable (the variable we are hoping to explain) is the ideological direction of the Supreme Court's decision, coded the value (1) for pro–civil liberties or liberal decisions and (0) for conservative decisions that limit civil rights and liberties. So, the analysis seeks to explain why the Court sometimes makes liberal decisions while at other times making conservative decisions. Because the dependent variable has just two values (a liberal or conservative decision), we use a statistical technique called logistic regression for the empirical analysis (see Long 1997).

Logistic regression (also called logit) is a useful statistical tool because it allows us to examine the effects of legal, attitudinal, and strategic factors in explaining the Court's decisions. In other words, the logit model helps us determine which factors influence the Court's decisions—the substantive effect—and the relative strength of these factors—the statistical effect.[6]

The *attitudinal model*, taken to its logical conclusion, has a single independent variable: the values and attitudes of the justices. Those values and attitudes would explain judicial decisions. We argue that the factors contributing to decision making are more complicated than approaches that use the attitudinal model alone. Judicial decisions are a function of the attitudes of individual justices, precedent, institutional norms, the history of the issue, constitutional and statutory provisions, and the position of the elected branches and the agencies (Clayton 1999). The problem is to provide measurements for many of these explanatory factors.

Our analysis addresses this problem by incorporating measures related to each of these important factors. These measures represent the independent variables of the analysis—the factors used to explain variation in the Court's decision making. Thus, the analysis models Supreme Court decisions as a function of the Court's ideological composition, the evolution of the specific issue, existing precedent, and the policy position of the president and Congress. In this fashion, we incorporate variables from each of the legal, attitudinal, and strategic models.

To assess the potential role of factors related to the *legal model* perspective, we utilize a precedent variable. This variable codes the direction of the most important precedents cited in the syllabus of the case. This permits us to examine the decision in the particular case as a function of the direction of the precedent. If precedent is important, it should guide the Court's decision making.[7] The precedent variable is expected to be positively related to the decision. Thus, the Court is more likely to make a favorable civil rights decision when the precedent for the decision is favorable to civil rights. In addition, there may be some instances when the case before the Court is a direct reflection of a previous decision and there is a precedent directly on point. This often occurs just after the Court announces an important decision and then receives a series of cases that were percolating through the lower courts before the landmarks and raise very similar issues. To better assess the legal model perspective, the analysis utilizes an on-point variable designed to capture the relevance of this condition of precedent. When the precedent is on-point, the justices are constrained by the previous decision. The variable is expected to be strongly significant and positively related to the decision.[8] Thus the Court is expected to make a decision favoring civil rights and individual liberties when there is an on-point precedent in the case and it supports civil rights and liberties.

We also incorporate an additional variable called issue evolution to assess the importance of the legal perspective in explaining the Court's decision making. To examine issue evolution, we use a measure devised by Pacelle (1990, 2003) that traces the development of an issue from its emergence, through the creation of the landmark decision that defines the particular issue area, through second generation cases that raise more difficult questions, and finally through the "complex" stage when the specific issue may get tied to other issues (Ulmer 1982; see also chapter 12 in this volume). This measure combines aspects of legal change (Wahlbeck 1997), precedent, and the difficulty of the facts in the case. In this regard, it resembles Richards and Kritzer's (2002) conception of jurisprudential regimes.

Let's now walk though the stages of the issue evolution variable. In the first stage (episodic), doctrine is unstable, as the Court, having little experience with the new issue, tries to find a doctrinal home in an existing area of law. For instance, the Court treated the first free exercise of religion cases like free speech cases. The second stage (emergent) involves the cases that immediately precede and follow the landmark decision. In establishment litigation, the cases that led to *Lemon v. Kurtzman* (1971) and helped refine the Court-created so-called *Lemon* test would constitute this stage. In the third stage (elaborative), cases get more difficult, causing judicial support to decline. Aid to religious colleges and cases that forced the Court to balance more difficult forms of government assistance would fit this stage. The fourth stage (complex) is marked by multiple issues. In other words,

the original issue is joined to a separate issue (Wasby 1993, 202–203). Hate speech cases, raising both issues of free speech and civil rights, challenged the Court to find a doctrinal niche. We expect the issue evolution variable to be negatively related to the Court's liberal decisions on constitutional civil rights and civil liberties cases. Thus, as the facts of the case get more difficult, we predict that it will be more difficult for the Court to make a decision favorable to civil liberties or civil rights.

To assess the *attitudinal perspective*, the analysis incorporates a measure of the Supreme Court's policy attitudes or ideological position on a liberal–conservative continuum. The variable we use is the Segal–Cover score (1989) (updated in Segal et al. 1995), which uses newspaper editorials to determine how liberal or conservative a justice is. The scores are externally generated measures of the ideology of individual justices. For the analysis, we use an aggregate score for the Court as a single actor. The attitudinal perspective would predict a positive relationship between the Court's ideology and liberal decision making. That is, as the Court becomes more liberal the likelihood of liberal decisions should increase.

In a similar fashion, we measure the ideological position of the other branches of government on a liberal–conservative continuum to determine the relevance of *strategic factors* on Supreme Court decision making. To measure the policy position of the president, we utilize the Erikson, MacKuen, and Stimson (2002) measure of presidential liberalism on key issues. For the House and Senate, we use the Poole and Rosenthal (1997) "nominate" score medians, a common measure of Congressional ideology. These represent factors related to the strategic perspective and therefore will permit us to examine the influence of the ideological position of the other branches on the Court's decisions. Given the close connections between the executive and judicial branches, the strategic model would predict a positive relationship between presidential ideology and the likelihood of liberal Court decisions (Scigliano 1971; Pacelle 2003). Thus, as the president gets more liberal, the decisions of the Court should be more favorable to civil rights and liberties. However, Congress's ability to influence the Court's decisions on constitutional issues is far more remote.

So, the strategic model would expect that Congress's policy position would have no appreciable effect on the Court's decisions.

Finally, we include a variable that measures the ideological mood of public opinion. We use Stimson's measure of public mood to tap into the overall ideological direction of public opinion. Because the Court is a political institution, we utilize the public mood variable to assess whether the Court's decisions appear to respond to the public at large. The relationship between the Court and public opinion is uncertain. Some studies have found a relationship under some circumstances (Mishler and Sheehan 1993; McGuire and Stimson 2004).[9] One of the major arguments for having an independent Supreme Court is that it can protect insular minorities from tyranny of the majority. The public mood variable in the analysis allows us to determine whether the Court responds to such majoritarian tendencies in its decision making. Because we have isolated a set of cases that involve individual rights and liberties, we do not expect a strong positive relationship between the Court's decision and aggregate public opinion.

INTERPRETING THE RESULTS

Table 13.1 shows the results of the logistic regression that integrates the variables for precedent, on-point, issue evolution, public opinion, and the ideological position of the three branches of government. Remember, these independent variables are designed to assess the effects of the three models of judicial decision making: the legal, attitudinal, and strategic models. Instead of focusing on the values of the logit coefficients, what one needs to pay attention to is whether the independent variable has a statistically significant impact on the Supreme Court's decisions. If it is statistically significant, there will be an asterisk or two (* or **) following the coefficient. Based on the results in the table, one can see that at least one variable from each cluster is statistically significant.

However, let's take a closer look at the results for each variable and their substantive and statistical significance. The substantive effect will allow us to determine whether the variable has a real impact on

the Court's decisions. The statistical effect tells us how big the impact is relative to the impact of the other variables in our model. The magnitude of that effect is found in the last column (Change in the Probability).

We begin by looking at the attitudinal variable, generally considered the most important factor. The results in Table 13.1 show that the ideological predisposition of the Court plays a major role in explaining constitutional civil liberties and civil rights decisions. The substantive impact of the Court's ideology is very influential in explaining the decisions of the Court. As expected, the attitudinal variable, measured by the aggregate Segal and Cover scores, is positively related to civil rights and civil liberties decisions and strongly significant, controlling for the other variables. The results mean that as the Court becomes more liberal, the likelihood of liberal decisions increases significantly. The statistical effect, shown in the last column, is also quite strong suggesting that a one-unit change in the Court's ideology (in the liberal direction) increases the probability of a liberal decision by .11. The results demonstrate that the attitudinal variable helps explain institutional level decision making.

Next we consider the three variables related to the legal perspective. The legal model is often considered to be the antithesis of the attitudinal model. The impact of the legal model is confirmed, if muted. The on-point precedent and the issue evolution variables are both substantively important in explaining the Court's decisions. The results for the on-point variable suggest that the Court is significantly constrained in its decision making when the precedent is directly on point. Such precedents are specific to the case at hand. In other words, the instant case has very similar facts and therefore is governed by the precedent that is on point. Under such circumstances, the justices are constrained by the precedent. The results of the model confirm the impact of those constraints: the coefficient is strongly positive and statistically significant.

The on-point variable is so strong that it overwhelms the precedent variable throwing an important caveat into the results. Accordingly, the Court is only constrained by precedent when it is on point. So the effects of this legal variable are conditional, as it suggests that unless the instant case is very similar to the existing precedent, the justices are not overly

Table 13.1 An Integrated Model of Supreme Court Decision Making

	Independent Variables	Model 1 Logit Coefficient/*SE*	Change in Probability
Attitudinal variable	Supreme Court ideology	2.80** (.71)	.11
Legal variables	Precedent	.02 (.08)	.01
	On point	1.15** (.13)	.52
	Issue evolution	−.45** (.10)	−.11
Strategic variables	President ideology	1.41** (.50)	.06
	House ideology	.67 (.94)	.01
	Senate ideology	−.15 (1.05)	.00
	Public mood	−1.07 (.71)	−.01
Constant	Constant	−.11 (.48)	—
	Log likelihood = −821.9 *p* < .000 *N* = 1,392		

Note: Values in Column 3 represent the growth (or decline) in the probability of a pro-civil liberties or pro-civil rights decision for a one standard deviation change in the level of the independent variable, controlling for the other independent variables. *SE* = standard error.
*p < .05. **p < .01.[1]

constrained and can presumably fall back on their own values and attitudes. The statistical impact of the on-point variable is also relatively large. For instance, when an on-point precedent is in the liberal direction, it increases the probability of a pro-civil rights or civil liberties decision on a given case by .52, controlling for the other variables.

The substantive effects of the issue evolution variable are also interesting. In particular, the model results suggest that as issues get more complicated and cases get more difficult, the probability of a positive civil liberties and civil rights decreases. The statistical impact of this variable in the model is also sizable. The last column of the table shows that a one-unit change in the complexity of the case decreases the probability of a pro-civil liberties or civil rights decision by .11, controlling for the other variables.

In assessing factors related to the strategic perspective, we see some mixed results in the model from Table 13-1. The variable measuring the impact of presidential ideology is shown to be important while the variables measuring the ideology of the House and Senate are not. This also follows expectations in that the president has greater opportunity to influence the Court whereas congressional potential for such influence is often times far removed. The substantive interpretation of the results for the executive branch suggests that as the president's ideological position becomes more liberal, the likelihood of liberal decisions by the Court increases. The statistical effect of the president ideology variable is important, but smaller than some of the other variables in the model. The last column shows that a one-unit change of the president's ideology in the liberal direction increases the probability of a liberal Court decision by .06.

Why is the president so important? The president has the solicitor general (SG) and the appointment power to improve the chances of congruence between the two branches. Presidents appoint justices to the Supreme Court. Thus, with enough opportunities, a president can bring the ideology of the Court into line with his own. However, the opportunity to appoint new justices occurs infrequently. In the interim, the president has influence through the appointment of the SG who argues cases on behalf of the U.S. government and is sometimes referred to as the "tenth justice." The SG has the most success of any litigant in getting cases accepted and in winning on the merits. Indeed, the influence of the SG is probably the most significant. The SG serves as a link between the executive and judicial branches. This connection between the president and the Court is more direct than any linkages between the legislative and judicial branches (Pacelle 2003).

In constitutional cases involving civil rights and individual liberties, the analysis suggests that the impact of Congress is nonexistent. Why does Congress seem to lack influence on these decisions? Civil rights and liberties are often issues that pit majoritarian impulses against the protection of minority rights. Congress is probably a reflection of the former rather than the latter because the Congress reflects majoritarian views on most issues. The Court does not need to worry about Congress, as most of the issues are decided on constitutional grounds and thus it takes an extraordinary majority to overturn the Court's decision through the Constitutional amendment process.

The public mood variable is not related to the Court's decisions and is statistically significant, suggesting that the Supreme Court is willing to stand up to public opinion. This seems to contradict past findings that show that the Supreme Court does follow public opinion (Mishler and Sheehan 1993, 1996; McGuire and Stimson 2004). The lack of a relationship is a reflection of what some claim is the most important role of the Supreme Court to protect the rights and liberties of minorities despite majority opposition (Dahl 1957; Casper 1976). Indeed, one of the strongest normative arguments for the undemocratic nature of the Supreme Court is its protection of individual rights.

Overall, the results show that parts of each of the three main perspectives—*legal, attitudinal, and strategic*—play an important role in explaining Supreme Court decisions. The conditional impact of precedent does raise some interesting questions regarding the legal perspective as an explanation for Supreme Court decision making that merit further discussion. It is certainly true that the impact of legal considerations is difficult to discern because the law seldom lies conclusively on one side or the other. The legal ambiguity of such cases makes it difficult to follow precedents and frees the Court to rely on its collective preferences. Perhaps this result is not that surprising. Pacelle (1991) and Perry (1991) argued that civil liberties and civil rights are among the issues justices care the most about. Thus, justices are most interested in pursuing their sincere preferences in such cases.

The results raise the question of whether precedent is a viable factor in judicial decision making or merely a normative construct that shrouds the dominance of the attitudinal model (Brisbin 1996; Brenner and Spaeth 1995). The impact of precedent is difficult to gauge because the precedent is seldom clear, except when it is on point. The cases before the Supreme Court raise different questions than those settled in the precedents. The lower courts can take care of those cases that are just like the precedent. In addition, legal ambiguity frees justices to rely on their policy preferences (Baum 1997).

Before we dismiss the impact of precedent, we need to consider two possibilities. First, precedent may vary by issue area: It is likely that the Court will pay closer attention to precedent in areas that are less salient to the justices. Second, it may vary over time. We cannot test that proposition as we have examined only one set of issues: civil liberties and civil rights. However, we can examine the second. The Warren Court was certainly an activist court and initiated a constitutional revolution in which it defined, expanded, or created freedom of association, libel, civil rights, and privacy, among other rights. We can isolate the Warren Court era (1953 to 1969) to see if the effect of precedent is temporal. The results are interesting. Precedent is not statistically significant during the Warren Court, but it is during the Burger and Rehnquist Courts, even controlling for on-point precedents. The results should give pause before we reject the impact of precedent and the legal variables. Our results reflect many of the studies of the Courts of this period. The Warren Court was seen as launching a constitutional revolution built in no small part by overturning a number of existing precedents. The Burger Court and, to a lesser extent, the Rehnquist Court did not undertake a constitutional counter-revolution. Although these Courts limited the reach of precedents like *Brown*, *Mapp*, and *Miranda*, they never took the final step of overturning them.

There may be a hidden impact of precedent, related to issue evolution. Richards and Kritzer (2002) identified jurisprudential regimes as influences on decisions. A *jurisprudential regime* is defined as "a key precedent, or a set of related precedents, that structures the way in which the Supreme Court justices evaluate key elements of cases in arriving at decisions in a particular legal area" (Richards and Kritzer 2002, 308). Jurisprudential regimes highlight the relevant facts that justices consider when deciding a case.

The notion of issue evolution is related to the legal model. Issue evolution is a realistic reflection of the development of issues in the Supreme Court. Doctrine is built in stages with the Court trying to maximize its policy preferences while it attempts to stabilize the law. Litigants, often repeat players, assist the Court by bringing the next set of cases, usually progressively more difficult as they attempt to push the envelope in that particular issue area.

IMPLICATIONS

The results suggest that issue evolution and precedent play an important role in decision making and an integrated model is the best explanation for institutional behavior. Too often scholars have treated the Court as little more than the collection of nine individuals who were separately pursuing their personal policy preferences. The results of the analysis suggest that although the individual justices have a great deal of discretion, the Court does not have complete independence. The Court is often seen as the protector of individual rights and liberties and often makes countermajoritarian decisions.

The legal model deserves more attention. The Court pays attention to precedent and seeks to establish consistency in the law, particularly when the precedent is on point. Under those circumstances, the constraints are clear. However, the application of law is ambiguous. Often, there are competing related precedents that are analogous, but not controlling thus giving the Court discretion. The Court devises tests and tries to build doctrine in a coherent fashion. The impact of issue evolution supports that conclusion.

Robert Scigliano (1971, vii) argued that the framers designed the judicial and executive branches as "an informal and limited alliance against Congress." This analysis tends to confirm the existence of that relationship. Whatever the source of the congruence, the appointment power or the SG, the Court seems to be influenced by the president. The Court does not seem to react to changes in the House or the Senate. This is not surprising given the extraordinary majorities needed to overturn a constitutional decision.

The behavior of the Supreme Court is governed by the personal preferences of the justices, but that is tempered by the need to attend to precedent as well as the institution's sense of duty and obligation to the law and the Constitution. The Court needs to protect its legitimacy and that serves as a restraint on the institution. The results suggest that institutional contexts, norms, and rules matter. The Court is, as Justice Robert Jackson said, part of "a complex, interdependent scheme of government from which it cannot be severed" (Jackson 1955, 2).

In terms of democratic theory, the results do not seem to be encouraging at first blush. The elected branches and public opinion have little or no impact. That is partially understandable because we selected a subset of cases that are most conducive to judicial independence. The ultimate justification for the modern Court is its ability to stand up to public opinion and the elected branches and to protect the rights and liberties of unpopular minorities. In civil liberties and civil rights cases, until recently, the Court had been decidedly countermajoritarian since footnote four in the *United States v. Carolene Products Company* (1938) case.

CONCLUSIONS

Let's return to the questions that animated this research. How does our integrated model help us understand the

Dickerson decision? Chief Justice Rehnquist seemed to answer that question in his opinion. He outlined the development of the law governing the admissions of confessions. He emphasized that *Miranda* was a constitutional decision and thus could not be overruled by a statute or a lower court. Thus, the impact of the other branches was muted. Finally, Rehnquist wrote that "whether we would agree with Miranda's reasoning and result (attitudes) … the principles of *stare decisis* (precedent) weigh heavily against overruling it now" (530 U.S. at 445).

More significantly, how do we reconcile these results with individual level analyses that show the domination of the attitudinal model? If individual justices are consistent in their decision making and there are membership changes, why doesn't the Court change its policies to reflect those membership changes? Although the Court overturns few precedents, it does chip away at existing precedents, like *Miranda*, *Mapp v. Ohio* (1961), *Brown v. Board of Education* (1954), and *Roe v. Wade* (1973). Attitudes are the basis of decisions and are supposed to be stable over time. When membership changes threaten to tip the Court ideologically, it seems that one or more justices move in the opposite direction to counter the membership changes. Justices Blackmun, Powell, O'Connor, and Kennedy are all recent examples of this phenomenon. Someone migrates ideologically to protect the Court as an institution. This reflects the view that justices' decisions "are a function of what they prefer to do, tempered by what they think they ought to do, but constrained by what they perceive is feasible to do" (Gibson 1983, 9).

So, can we answer the question posed in the title: Is it a Court of Laws or a Super Legislature? We will hedge and say a little of both. Although the ideological composition of the Court is the most important factor, it is not simply a constitutional convention or a super legislature. The Court operates in a political and legal context that imposes norms and duties on the institution. The Court has been referred to as the "schoolmaster of the republic" (Franklin and Kosaki 1989). As a result, members of the Court are the modern political theorists of the polity. The Court carved a new role for itself in 1938 in declaring that civil liberties and civil rights would be held in a "preferred position," acting perhaps as a super legislature. In fulfilling that role and imposing some consistency on emerging doctrine, it once again assumed the role of a Court of Laws. Indeed, even after all the proponents of the preferred position doctrine had left the Court, the Court continued to uphold many of its precedents. Thus, even the Rehnquist Court, which was hostile to defendants' rights protected *Miranda* from being overturned in the *Dickerson* decision. It is true, though, that more recently, some have argued that the Court has acted like a super legislature in rejecting the preferred position and creating a new dominant philosophy (Pacelle 2002; Keck 2004). However, as a Court of Laws, the Supreme Court will be trying to impose stability on the new and emerging doctrine.

Notes

1. This Act of Congress was eventually declared unconstitutional in *Dickerson v. U.S.*, 530 U.S. 428 (2000), discussed later in the chapter.

2. Chief Justice Rehnquist's support for *Miranda* was probably more strategic than anything else. As long as the Chief Justice is in the majority, he gets to assign the opinion in the case. Thus, Rehnquist probably sided with the majority to retain the ability to assign the opinion (in this case to himself) rather than let the next most senior justice, Stevens, assign and possibly make the opinion of the Court more liberal.

3. In 1925, Congress created the discretionary writ of *certiorari*. Prior to that time, the Court had to hear every case properly brought. In 1988, Congress extended the writ of *certiorari* and limited the types of cases that were part of the mandatory, writ of appeals jurisdiction of the Court.

4. Attempts have been made to tamper with the Court's jurisdiction in areas like legislative redistricting, busing, abortion, freedom of religion, criminal procedure, and Congressional investigations in response to decisions that members of Congress opposed.

5. Civil rights and civil liberties cases include criminal procedure, First Amendment, reproductive rights, and all forms of equal protection cases. We used the Supreme Court data base to identify these cases.

6. Logistic regression or logit is used for dichotomous dependent variables, that is those dependent variables that only have two possible values. Because the dependent variable in this model only has a liberal or conservative possible result or value, logit is a highly appropriate statistical technique for this particular research puzzle.

7. There are a number of studies that demonstrate the impact of different fact situations on the justices individually (Segal 1984, 1986; George and Epstein 1992; Wahlbeck 1997) or on the Court (Baum 1988, 1992). More traditional doctrinal analyses show similar impacts (McCloskey 1960; Kahn 1994).

8. To create on point, a measure of how close the precedent is to the case at hand, we coded precedents that were directly relevant and created a directional variable by multiplying on point by precedent.

9. Mishler and Sheehan (1993, 1996) used a four-year lag on public opinion. There does not seem to be a good theoretical reason for such a long lag. We opted for a lag of two years because it appears to be the most consequential theoretically. There is no difference in using a one-, two-, three-, or four-year lag. None of them are statistically significant and positively related to Supreme Court decisions in civil rights and individual liberties.

14

IS THERE REALLY A
COUNTERMAJORITARIAN PROBLEM?

Michael Comiskey

Judicial review is the power of the courts to determine the constitutionality of the actions of other political actors, such as the Congress, the president, the bureaucracy, and the states. The U.S. Supreme Court took this power for itself in *Marbury v. Madison* (1803). Legal scholars and political theorists have long debated whether having unelected federal judges exercising the power of judicial review is compatible with the democratic notion of majority rule. Some scholars have argued that whenever the courts declare some governmental action to be unconstitutional, they are protecting the needs of the minority at the expense of the will of the majority. This view has been called the countermajoritarian dilemma. Is the power of judicial review congruent with a majoritarian democracy? This chapter uses a more normative approach to argue that the entire debate is overblown for a variety of reasons. Central to this chapter is the pivotal question of the proper role of the courts in a democracy.

For the past several decades, constitutional theorists have worried about the "countermajoritarian problem": the perceived incompatibility between democratic government and the American practice of judicial review (the power of unelected, life-tenured federal judges to strike down executive and legislative acts as unconstitutional). Statements of the importance of this problem are easy to find. In the 1980s, law professor Stephen Griffin (1989, 495) wrote that, "the central project of constitutional theory" over the previous fifty years was "reconciling judicial review with democratic government." More recently, law professor Barry Friedman wrote in an article titled, "The Birth of an Academic Obsession: The History of the Countermajoritarian Difficulty," that "Constitutional scholars are fixated on the legitimacy of constitutional courts. They cannot stop talking about the countermajoritarian difficulty" (Friedman 2002, 162–63).

Friedman offered several examples of recent scholarly works to prove his point. And as recently as 2004, law professor Larry Kramer could write that, "the question of judicial supremacy [the judiciary's power to nullify the acts of the other branches] has been at the heart of constitutional theory for more than two generations" (Kramer 2004, 1001).

This chapter defines the countermajoritarian thesis as the claim that the federal judiciary issues decisions that reverse the policies of political majorities as represented in the enactments of the democratically elected, representative branches of government at all levels—federal, state, and local—and that this countermajoritarianism is at odds with the principles of democracy. This chapter focuses on the U.S. Supreme Court as the most visible and powerful federal court, although much of the argument applies to the lower federal courts as noted throughout the chapter.

My argument is that the countermajoritarian "problem" as just stated rests on faulty factual and philosophical assumptions about the American political system. As a factual matter, many scholars have exaggerated the extent to which the Supreme Court dominates the process of constitutional interpretation and acts contrary to the wishes of elected majorities. The next section of this chapter begins by describing several ways in which the Supreme Court shares the power to interpret the Constitution with others in our country, such as the president, Congress, the state governments, and the public (see also Miller this volume, chapter 19). I then show that the decisions of the elected branches of the government do not always represent the views of a majority of Americans, and that the high-profile decisions of the Supreme Court usually do. So when the Court strikes down the acts of the elected branches, it does not necessarily act in a countermajoritarian fashion.

The subsequent section maintains that as a philosophical matter, to the extent that the Supreme Court is countermajoritarian, that countermajoritarianism poses few problems for the theory of constitutional democracy embodied in the U.S. Constitution. To put it briefly, our political system was not intended to be entirely majoritarian.

FACTUAL FLAWS IN THE COUNTERMAJORITARIAN THESIS

Nearly everyone agrees that the U.S. Supreme Court has a powerful voice in the process of constitutional interpretation. Even some scholars who stress the ways the Court shares in this process with others agree that, "Court decisions figure prominently in the shaping of constitutional values" (Devins and Fisher 2004, 9). However, many students of the Court exaggerate the Court's role and obsess about the "countermajoritarian difficulty."

The first problem with this obsession is that much if not most of American constitutional interpretation and development has taken place outside the judiciary. As various observers have pointed out, perhaps the most important constitutional interpretation in American history was authored by a president, Abraham Lincoln, who decided in the absence of any constitutional language on the question that a state may not leave the Union, and enforced that decision on the battlefields of the Civil War.

On many other matters, our constitutional system has been built by forces outside the judiciary. Among these matters are the rise of political parties (in which the courts played no part), the federal government's power to acquire new territories (decided by President Jefferson and Congress when they acquired the Louisiana Territories in 1803), and the creation of Cabinet departments and independent regulatory agencies by various presidents and Congresses over the past 200 years (Griffin 1996). Indeed, political scientist Keith Whittington (1999, 12) offered a list of some eighty constitutional "constructions" including such varied developments as creation of the civil service and the lower federal courts, Congress's specification of the size of the Supreme Court at nine justices, "fast track" authorization of treaties, executive agreements between the president and foreign governments, federal authority to regulate wages and prices and to bar racial discrimination by using the Constitution's Commerce Clause, use of the secret ballot in elections, open meeting requirements, specification of single-member U.S. House districts, setting the size of the U.S. House by legislation at 435, home rule for the District of Columbia, the development of the welfare state, and America's entry into international organizations such as the United Nations and NATO, among other developments. The federal courts later ratified some of these developments but did not initiate them. The other branches of the federal government or the state governments devised these policies and arrangements, which we might fairly call "constitutional" in a broad sense of that term.

A second, closely related flaw in the countermajoritarian framework is that when the Supreme Court speaks on constitutional issues it does so as part of a continuing "constitutional dialogue" with the other branches of the federal government, and with state governments, interest groups, the American public, and individual litigants (see, e.g., Miller and Barnes 2004). As political scientist Louis Fisher explained this concept, "Judicial decisions rest undisturbed only to the extent that Congress, the President, and the general public find the decisions convincing, reasonable, and acceptable. Otherwise, the debate on constitutional principles will continue" (Fisher 1988, 244; see also Griffin 1996).

In this ongoing dialogue, the Court may reverse itself in whole or in part, as it did in its about-face on the regulation of commerce in 1937. Prior to that year, the Supreme Court often used various constitutional doctrines to strike down state and federal regulations of economic activity, such as laws banning child labor and requiring minimum wages. When faced by the overwhelming popularity of Franklin Roosevelt's New Deal and its many economic regulations, the Court in 1937 suddenly abandoned these doctrines and adopted a policy of deferring to legislative decisions about regulating the economy.

A more recent and less dramatic example of constitutional dialogue is American policy on abortion. The Supreme Court in *Roe v. Wade* (1973) virtually eliminated the states' authority to restrict abortion in the first six months of pregnancy. Nearly twenty years later, the Court responded to continuing attempts by state and local governments to regulate abortions by downgrading the status of the abortion right and permitting greater state regulation of abortion—but still rejecting outright bans on abortion—in *Planned Parenthood of Southern Pennsylvania v. Casey* (1992) (see also Baer this volume, chapter 17).

A third example of this ongoing constitutional dialogue is the death penalty. In *Furman v. Georgia* (1972), a majority of the Supreme Court held that death sentences could not be imposed in an arbitrary manner. This ruling had the effect of nullifying the death penalty laws of the federal government and all of the states that had the death penalty at the time. In response, thirty-five states and the Congress enacted new death penalty laws, most of which specified factors for juries to weigh in capital sentencing. In *Gregg v. Georgia* (1976), seven justices upheld these laws. They justified their refusal to rule that the death penalty is *necessarily* unconstitutional by citing other participants in the constitutional dialogue: the actions of the thirty-five state legislatures and Congress, the juries that continued to issue death sentences, "society's moral outrage at particularly offensive conduct," and the pro-death penalty outcome of "the only statewide

referendum occurring since *Furman* [in California]" (*Gregg* at 179–80, 181–82, 183, 181).

Constitutional law has emerged from a constitutional dialogue on a wide variety of subjects in addition to those just cited. Among them are federalism, the separation of powers, the war power, the rights of gays, and the freedoms of speech and religion (Devins and Fisher 2004). On commercial regulation, abortion, and the death penalty, the elected branches of government have participated in the constitutional dialogue mainly by passing laws to which the Supreme Court has then reacted.

Worthy of special mention are two other ways the elected branches can speak in the constitutional dialogue: amending the Constitution and stripping the federal courts of authority to hear cases on certain subjects (see Miller this volume, chapter 19). The elected branches use these methods of speaking much less often than ordinary legislation, but they are especially powerful when used.

Congress and the states have collaborated to overturn Supreme Court rulings by constitutional amendment on four occasions. The amendments that overturned controversial Supreme Court rulings are the Eleventh Amendment (1798), which overturned *Chisholm v. Georgia* (1793), a decision permitting federal courts to hear suits against a state by citizens of another state; the Fourteenth Amendment (1868), which overturned the 1857 ruling in *Dred Scott v. Sandford* (1857), holding that a black person could never be a U.S. citizen; the Sixteenth Amendment (1913), which overturned the holding in *Pollock v. Farmers' Loan & Trust* (1895) that a federal income tax was unconstitutional; and the Twenty-Sixth Amendment, which effectively overturned the holding in *Oregon v. Mitchell* (1970) that Congress could not set a voting age of eighteen in state elections.

Because the courts can rule on disputes over the meaning of an amendment's terms, amendments do not always end the constitutional dialogue on the subjects they address. To cite just one example, the Supreme Court has decided many cases on the question of whether the Fourteenth Amendment's guarantee of equal protection for all persons allows affirmative action programs. However, constitutional amendments do often settle fundamental issues: no one can claim that African Americans lack equal citizenship or that the federal income tax is unconstitutional. And although four reversals by amendment is a small number, the possibility of constitutional amendment has probably deterred the justices in some larger number of cases from issuing a decision they might otherwise have made. One recent decision that may fit this description is *Elk Grove Unified School District v. Newdow* (2004), in which five justices overrode a federal appeals court ruling that Michael Newdow had standing under California law to challenge the daily recitation of the Pledge of Allegiance in his daughter's public school. The Court remained silent, however, on the lower court's decision that the inclusion of the words "under God" in the Pledge of Allegiance violated the First Amendment's ban on establishing a religion.

The second unusual but powerful way for the elected branches to speak on constitutional issues involves Congress's power to strip the federal courts of jurisdiction to hear certain types of cases, or cases on certain issues. Called "court-stripping," this power comes from provisions in Article III of the Constitution that give Congress the power to "ordain and establish" lower federal courts and to make "Regulations" and "Exceptions" to the Supreme Court's appellate jurisdiction.

In modern times, congressional attempts to curtail the jurisdiction of the federal courts have had a split history. On the one hand, Congress has repeatedly declined to use this "court-stripping" power to stymie the Supreme Court after it handed down unpopular rulings on several salient issues. In the 1950s and 1960s, Congress rejected some sixty attempts by conservatives to eliminate the Court's appellate jurisdiction over cases involving desegregation, criminal confessions, and suspected Communist subversives (Devins and Fisher 2004, 26). In the 1970s and 1980s, Congress rejected proposed curbs on the Court's jurisdiction in cases involving abortion, busing, and school prayer (Fisher and Devins 1996, 44–54).

On the other hand, Republican Congresses in the 1990s enacted legislation curtailing the federal courts' authority to hear successive *habeas corpus* appeals of state prison inmates. They also inserted a number of less visible "court-stripping" provisions into assorted

bills, including measures to block some class action suits brought by poor people and immigrants (both legal and illegal), and to prevent federal court review of rulings unfavorable to such groups (Greenhouse 1996). When attempts at court-stripping have succeeded, they have diminished the voice of the federal courts in the constitutional dialogue and amplified the voices of Congress, the president, and state and local governments.

Finally, the president and the Senate exert a powerful influence on the rulings of the federal courts by appointing all federal judges, including Supreme Court justices. (The president nominates them and the Senate confirms or rejects the president's nominees; see Bell this volume, chapter 3). When a group of justices has consistently ruled in a manner that upsets much of the country, the president and Senate may, when vacancies arise, appoint justices likely to rule differently. The best example of this phenomenon are the justices of the "Roosevelt Court," nominated by Franklin Roosevelt and confirmed by the Senate beginning in 1937, who upheld the federal government's authority to regulate the economy. A more recent although less dramatic example is the slow rightward swing of the Supreme Court since the 1960s due to Republican appointments made in reaction to the liberal decisions of the Warren Court in the 1950s and 1960s, and, to some extent, those of the Burger Court in the 1970s. Vacancies arise every year on the federal trial and appellate courts, and about once every two years, on the average, on the Supreme Court.[1] Although various factors complicate the efforts of presidents and senators to change the composition of the federal courts— including the fact that they frequently disagree over the desirable legal philosophy of new judges—their joint appointment of federal judges clearly constrains the federal judiciary over the long run.

The reality that federal judges are appointed by elected officials and share the power to interpret the Constitution with those officials and with the public should ease concerns about unelected, life-tenured federal judges riding roughshod over the views of a majority of Americans. So should the fact that the elected branches do not always follow the people's wishes while the Supreme Court usually does, at least in high-profile cases.

DEMOCRATIC ELECTIONS, UNDEMOCRATIC COURTS?

We tend to assume that judicial review is "undemocratic" when unelected judges who serve for life strike down the actions of democratically elected officials who must answer to the people at the next election. This view of things is often incorrect. Scholars in the "public choice" school have demonstrated theoretically that legislative elections do not guarantee the election of lawmakers who represent the views of most voters, and that "even if members of Congress are perfectly representative of their constituents, taking votes among elected members of Congress does not guarantee majoritarian legislation" (Barnes 2004a, 43).

Data from the real world of American politics provides support for these claims. At the national level, federal policies are consistent with the public's preferences about two-thirds of the time. Federal public policy violates the public's preferences about one-third of the time (Page and Shapiro 1992, 2). Observation of federal elections helps explain the imperfect connection between public opinion and public policy. Consider the common but dubious claim that when voters place Candidate A rather than Candidate B in the White House, voters issue a mandate. (That is, they endorse Candidate A's policies and command policy makers to enact them.)

In reality, mandates in presidential elections are rare. Think of the four presidential elections in 1992, 1996, 2000, and 2004. President Clinton won the 1992 and 1996 elections with 43 and 49 percent of the popular vote, respectively. President George W. Bush won the election of 2000 despite losing the popular vote to Democrat Al Gore. Bush won reelection in 2004 with just 51 percent of the popular vote. Voters clearly gave no mandate to the winners in these four consecutive elections. Indeed, political scientist Stanley Kelley, Jr., has shown that presidents may get no mandate even when they win by a landslide. Voters supporting a landslide winner may do so for widely divergent reasons, or voters may overwhelmingly agree that one candidate is just a little better than another or is just not as bad as another (Kelley 1983, 126–42).

The design of Congress and congressional elections also makes Congress members imperfect representatives of a majority of all Americans. Congressional incumbents are likely to win reelection due to the gerrymandering of House districts, the heavily Republican or Democratic character of some states, and the advantages in funding and name recognition that incumbents enjoy over challengers. And voters elect only one-third of the Senate every two years. These factors make the composition of Congress resistant, although certainly not immune, to swings in public opinion.

The equal representation of unequally populated states in the Senate can also make the Senate unrepresentative of the American people. In 2005/2006, for instance, the forty-five Democratic senators then serving represented some 148 million people, while the fifty-five Republicans represented 144 million people (Dionne 2005, A17).[2] And in the senatorial elections of 2004, the Republicans picked up four seats even though Democratic candidates outpolled Republican candidates nationwide by 42 million votes to 38 million.[3] This result can occur because Democrats can win many millions of votes while winning—or losing—Senate races in heavily populated states, while Republicans can win Senate seats in less populous states with a smaller number of votes.

Despite these obstacles, the decisions of Congress and the president (and state and local officials) usually agree with public opinion; however, the Supreme Court's high-profile decisions usually do, too (Marshall 1989; Mondak and Smithey 1997). This is true, for instance, of the "Rehnquist Court's" decisions on abortion, gay rights, and the rights of criminal suspects and defendants (Comiskey 2004, 178–79). It is also true that the Court usually affirms the legality of congressional legislation when it is challenged (Keith 2005). The evidence on this point is so strong that Larry Kramer could write in 2004 that "a sizeable body of empirical work supports the view that the judiciary is seldom far out-of-step with legislative majorities at the national level.…the data are numerous and consistent, and there is now a general consensus among social scientists that courts have not been a strong or consistent countermajoritarian force in American politics" (Kramer 2004, 970–71).[4]

We should also note that the Supreme Court can reinforce majoritarian democracy even when it strikes down a policy of the democratically elected branches. The most oft-cited example here is the line of "one-person-one-vote" decisions of the 1960s that required every U.S. House district and every state legislative district to be equal in population to every other such district within a state (*Wesberry v. Sanders* (1964); *Reynolds v. Sims* (1964)). Until the 1960s, many states had malapportioned congressional and state legislative districts of vastly unequal populations, effectively giving some of their citizens much more representation than others.

An important body of recent research identifies various other ways that judicial review may serve the purposes of political majorities. Mark Graber (1993) argued that elected officials have not only *accepted* policy making by judges, they have actively *encouraged* it on issues where they are unable or unwilling to make policy themselves. Such inaction by an elected majority may result because the majority's preferred policies on certain issues are controversial or unpopular. Or perhaps the majority party is split over an issue, as the majority Democrats were over civil rights from the 1940s to the 1960s. The majority party, or the leading faction of the party, may therefore invite the judicial branch to settle the issue and take the political "heat" for doing so.

Similarly, Keith Whittington (2005) has shown how judicial review can enable national majorities to triumph over minorities who sometimes thwart the majority's attempts to enact its program in a political system studded with obstacles to action. Michael Klarman (1996) and Lucas Powe (2000) likewise demonstrated how judges can use judicial review to help a popular majority to prevail over a recalcitrant minority or to uproot the "entrenched" policies of an earlier but now displaced majority. Their work shows how the Warren Court's liberal rulings in the 1950s and 1960s impacted primarily those states and political interests that resisted national social and political developments—such as Southern segregationists and the conservative rural interests that had long dominated the malapportioned state legislatures.

All of these authors portrayed the Supreme Court as an institution with considerable power to break political "logjams." However, this judicial power is not necessarily countermajoritarian. Graber emphasized the

Court's power to decide issues where there is no clear-cut national majority (Hence the title of his famous 1993 article: "The Nonmajoritarian Difficulty.") Whittington, Powe, and Klarman emphasized the ways the Court permits actual majorities to triumph over well dug-in minorities.

This is not to say that judicial review always serves majoritarian purposes. The Supreme Court will at least occasionally take stands that offend national majorities, such as banning nonsectarian prayers from public schools and protecting the right of protestors to burn the American flag (*Engel v. Vitale* (1962); *Texas v. Johnson* (1989)). And judicial review does not always uproot the policies of defunct majorities. Sometimes it entrenches them. Howard Gillman (2002) and Ran Hirschl (2004) have shown that fragile and lame-duck legislative majorities, contemplating their future loss of legislative power, sometimes expand the power of constitutional courts precisely to frustrate the ability of the incoming majority to govern. This strategy may achieve some success, as when late nineteenth-century Republicans favoring conservative economic policies strengthened and then packed the federal judiciary with economically conservative judges who struck down much Progressive regulatory legislation well into the twentieth century (Gillman 2002). Few people would applaud judicial review when it serves mainly to embalm the discretionary policy judgments of a dethroned majority.

So the point here is *not* that judicial review is always majoritarian. The point is simply that the policies of elected officials are not always majoritarian, and that the results of judicial review are not always countermajoritarian.

PHILOSOPHICAL OBJECTIONS TO THE COUNTERMAJORITARIAN COMPLAINT

The previous section demonstrated that worries about the supposedly undemocratic character of judicial review rest on an incomplete and distorted picture of the process of American constitutional interpretation. This section argues that the countermajoritarian thesis, in particular its assumption that countermajoritarianism violates appropriate principles of American democracy, is mistaken on normative or philosophical grounds.

The American constitutional system is a constitutional democracy that combines democratic elements, whose core principle is majority rule, with constitutionalism, or limits on what the majority may do. Judicial review is perhaps the best known example of an (at least occasionally) antimajoritarian practice in the Constitution as it operates today—though one might nominate the lack of a popularly elected chief executive, the chief executive's veto, or the equal representation of unequally populated states in the Senate for this distinction. Not surprisingly, the democratic and antidemocratic elements in the system coexist uneasily. This uneasy coexistence led Ruth Bader Ginsburg, while serving as a federal appellate judge, to speak of "the tension between judicial supremacy [or judicial review] and democratic theory" (Ginsburg 1988, 112). The inability or unwillingness of some students of American courts to recognize and accept this uneasy hybrid of constitutionalism and democracy—in addition to the failure to describe accurately the actual workings of the system, as detailed in the previous section—has produced an unwarranted obsession with the countermajoritarian difficulty.

Some legal scholars understand this dual nature of the American political system. Erwin Chemerinsky, for example, argued that the American system of government was not meant to be highly majoritarian (Chemerinsky 1988). Lawrence Sager (1990, 897) similarly concluded that, "Our constitutional tradition cannot possibly be squared with the absolutism of popular sovereignty [or popular rule], and we should abandon the effort." Hence the occasional countermajoritarianism of the U.S. Supreme Court is nothing to lament; it is part and parcel of the American system of constitutional democracy. The tension Judge Ginsburg spoke of is built into the system.

Officials in the elected branches of the federal government also seem to recognize and sometimes even protect the Supreme Court's occasional countermajoritarian actions. After the unsuccessful attempt to remove Justice Samuel Chase from office in 1803 because of his partisan rulings against Jeffersonian Republicans (Chase was a Federalist), the notion took

hold that Congress should not try to impeach justices simply because it disagrees with their rulings (see Rehnquist 1992). Another norm has evolved against changing the size of the Supreme Court, which the Constitution allows Congress to do by legislation. Congress has proved unwilling to change the Court's size even when such a change might undo High Court rulings obstructing the elected branches' responses to a national emergency. In the midst of the Great Depression, an overwhelmingly Democratic Senate by a vote of seventy to twenty rejected Democrat Franklin Roosevelt's attempt to enlarge the Court and reverse the Court's decisions striking down key parts of the New Deal economic recovery program (Burns 1956, 291–315). The Supreme Court, as we saw above, later gave in and upheld the New Deal's economic regulations. And Congress continues to fund the Supreme Court year after year with little or no complaint, regardless of congressional unhappiness with the Court's rulings.

Similarly, Congress has rejected attempts at Court-stripping even after highly controversial rulings mandating legal abortions, permitting the busing of schoolchildren for purposes of integration, and prohibiting prayers in public schools. Among the leading opponents of these liberal decisions was the father of modern American conservatism, Senator Barry Goldwater of Arizona, who also led opposition to the court-stripping efforts these decisions generated. Goldwater told the Senate that proposals to strip the federal courts of jurisdiction over these types of cases, aimed though they were at High Court rulings with which he disagreed, "would interfere with Federal court independence" and constituted a "frontal assault on the independence of the courts" and "a dangerous blow to the foundations of a free society" (Fisher and Devins 1996, 48–49).

The successful attempts at court-stripping described in the previous section demonstrate that principled opposition to court-stripping is not as profound as opposition to other court-curbing methods such as changing the Supreme Court's size and impeaching justices because of disagreement with their opinions. Many political leaders undoubtedly shared Goldwater's sentiments. Principled opposition to court-stripping is not insurmountable, but it does exist.

While all segments of American society are capable of disagreeing with particular Supreme Court rulings, it seems that deep-seated concern over the illegitimacy of judicial review itself is confined to a subset of American legal academicians.

CONCLUSIONS

Everyone agrees that the Supreme Court has a very important voice in defining the Constitution's terms. However, it is one voice among many in the constitutional dialogue. Fixation on the decisions of the Supreme Court slights this rich national conversation and tradition of shared Constitution making. And when the Court speaks, it is not as countermajoritarian as people commonly suppose. Nor is countermajoritarianism necessarily a problem in a constitutional system whose "whole design and spirit...was as much to control the excesses of popular majorities as to give the people a voice in government decision-making" (*The Economist* 1999, 43). Recognition that the countermajoritarian "problem" has been overstated directs our attention to the more useful if vexing question of *when* the courts should try to be countermajoritarian and *when* they should not.

Notes

1. This "every two years" figure is just an average. The Supreme Court went without a vacancy for eleven years from 1994 to 2005.

2. This calculation evenly divides the population of states with split Senate representation and counts among the Democrats Senator James Jeffords, Independent of Vermont, who caucused with and usually voted with the Democrats.

3. Chris Bowers. March 14, 2005. *Senate Democrats Have a Mandate to Oppose Bush.* Available at www.mydd.com/story/2005/3/14/124043/336.

4. The claim that the Supreme Court is by and large majoritarian was first advanced by Dahl (1957).

15

RESISTANCE TO THE JUDICIARY

The Boundaries of Judicial Power

Richard A. Brisbin, Jr.

Many Americans assume that the courts are legitimate governmental actors that punish criminals and settle disputes in our society. Americans tend to have great respect for courts and for their decisions. What happens when individuals and groups disagree with judicial decisions to the point that they do not see these decisions as being legitimate or as being too political in nature? What happens when various political actors and groups rebel against a court's decision?

This chapter explores various techniques and reasons for resistance to court decisions. This resistance can range from appealing an unfavorable court decision to a higher court, to ignoring a court order, to organizing massive protests against judicial policies like the Supreme Court's abortion ruling in *Roe v. Wade* (1973). This chapter also examines the broader consequences of such resistance to the decisions of the judiciary. The chapter clearly sees resistance to court decisions in both legal and political terms.

To secure the right of their children to attend racially desegregated schools, in 1974 African American parents sued the Boston School Committee (city school board). They asked a federal judge to require the School Committee to abide by a series of judicial decisions that held that intentional racial discrimination in the public schools violated the Constitution. The judge ordered the School Committee to undertake the reassignment and busing of pupils to desegregate the Boston public schools.

During a coal strike in 1989 by the United Mine Workers of America (UMWA) in western Virginia and West Virginia, the Pittston Coal Group lawyers went before a Virginia state judge and obtained an injunction to prevent striker blockades at mine entrances so their firm could continue to operate its mines.

Whether filed by "have not" black children or "have" corporations, these two cases suggest that Americans have great faith in lawyers and courts. Americans initiate lawsuits and employ law and rights because they assume the courts will declare them a victor. However, lawsuits are not always a way to find ready relief for injuries and abuses of liberties. The conflicts framed in a lawsuit can mutate so that they induce social, economic, or political changes, disorder, violence, or other transgressions that frustrate the initial victor. Using lawyers to resolve problems or trials to adjudicate cases thus poses a difficulty for even the victorious litigant. The difficulty is securing the *enforcement* of the judgment and remedy granted by a judge as well as the *implementation* of the broader policy communicated by the court's decision

(Baum 1977). It therefore is not uncommon that winning parties cannot collect money damages or secure the rights they thought they had won.

Instead, the victors in court find that the losing party, and often the allies of the losing party, have chosen to *resist* (oppose) the victor and in addition–in a few cases—to *transgress* (violate) the decisions of judges. For example, after an initial judgment in favor of the black children in Boston, the core of the judge's ruling did not take effect until years later. The implementation of the court decision was delayed because of years of additional litigation by the School Committee, political opposition from city and state leaders, limited official action to desegregate, and public transgressions such as disorderly demonstrations, beatings, and mob violence. However, after the desegregation ruling went into effect, within a decade many white parents removed their children from the public schools and left the city. Soon, the initial aim of the desegregation suit became impossible to fulfill because there were far fewer white pupils left in the Boston city schools (Buell 1982; Formisano 1991).

Resistance and transgressions also marked the Pittston coal strike. After the judge granted Pittston its injunction, camouflage-clad strikers, their families, and their allies conducted mass sit-ins to block coal shipments on the roads of Virginia. They occupied Pittston Coal headquarters and one of its coal processing plants. For months they slowed the movement of coal trucks by deploying hundreds of vehicles in slow-moving "convoys" or "caravans." When federal and state judges further enjoined their protests, rock throwing, the infliction of damage on vehicles by gunshots and jackrocks (spikes designed to puncture coal truck tires), assaults, and bombings became a daily event in the coalfields. Violations of injunctions on civil disobedience grounds and the anonymous lawbreaking resulted in the arrest of the national and local UMWA leadership, 212 felony warnings, 2,337 misdemeanor arrests, 549 traffic citations, 712 reported injuries to persons, and more than $64 million in fines against the union and its leaders for contempt of court for violations of injunctions of the protests (Brisbin 2002).

This chapter will explore how resistance to court decisions creates boundaries on judicial power. Especially it addresses four questions: Why does resistance to specific judicial decisions or settlements originate? How do people resist judicial decisions or legal agreements? When is resistance effective? What are the consequences of resistance to courts?

THE ORIGINS OF RESISTANCE

Why is there resistance to specific judicial decisions? Before proceeding to define when resistance to law occurs, it is important to understand the meaning of resistance in light of the American faith in the legitimacy and efficacy of the law. What makes law legitimate and efficacious? More than two decades ago Stuart Scheingold remarked that, "The law is real, but it also is a figment of our imaginations" (1974, 3). He described law as a way of thinking that, in the words of Austin Sarat and Thomas Kearns (1993), *constitutes* how we Americans imagine the world to be. Americans simply accept that law is a proper and ethically sufficient way to keep social peace and govern their community. Americans obey the law because they assume it is right and proper to do so. Law and judicial processes consequently share a psychological perception that they are the naturally fair way to address the world of disputes.

Law and courts have a transcendent value; they are not just instruments that a plaintiff can use to try to get something from a defendant. Hence, if a neighbor's stereo causes noise late at night, the dispute could be speedily resolved by cutting the electric line to her house with a hedge trimmer. However, most persons will call the police and hope that the neighbor is warned by police or is later fined by a judge. Although some religious groups and Native Americans might constitute their world differently (see, e.g., Greenhouse 1986; Espeland 1994; Gooding 1994; Richland 2005), most Americans simply cannot imagine the legitimacy of a nonlegal way of settling conflicts. For example, Americans no longer regard shaming, such as making adulterers wear a scarlet letter, and dueling as legitimate ways to deal with disputes.[1]

At the same time courts serve as an *instrument* for seeking certain personal or business interests. Individuals and corporations can try to induce the judiciary to deploy its power on their behalf. The Boston desegregation case and the Pittston coal strike litigation began when the plaintiffs (the parents of black students and the union, respectively) attempted to use the official power of the courts to serve their interests. Consequently, it is important to recognize that when people resist judicial decisions they have chosen to engage in a political act that opposes both the court and the parties who have successfully advanced their interests through the use of law.

After interviewing New Jersey residents about their experiences with courts and law, Patricia Ewick and Susan Silbey (1998, 223–50) concluded that a contradiction exists between these two dimensions of legality–*constitutive* and *instrumental*.[2] Instrumentalist views of law conceive of law as external to social practice, meaning that it is studied as an instrument or tool for effecting behavior (policy, etc.). This is a conventional view (i.e., pass a law to change some situation). By contrast, a constitutive view notes that laws shape society not only from the "outside" but also by providing the categories, meanings, and practices that make up social life in the first place. However, Ewick and Silbey found that people switch between these two dimensions of law when discussing legal experiences. For example, a man might say, "Judges are good because they are women of the law," then say, "The judge was biased against me at my trial because I was not rich." Ewick and Silbey argued that the incompatibility of these two perspectives sustains the legitimacy of law and courts and deters acts of resistance. With two perspectives to interpret judicial decisions and two kinds of knowledge about courts, people always have a way to make sense of what judges do. Even if a decision goes against their interests, litigants can assess courts as worthy institutions because they have constitutive faith in the majesty of the law.

The linkage of the constitutive and instrumental dimensions of American legality points to the need for certain conditions to appear if there is to be resistance to judicial actions. One set of conditions is an erosion of faith in the legitimacy and efficacy of judicial action. The erosion of faith in the constitutive authority of courts is "internal" or occurs through the psychological assessment of the fairness of personal experiences with the judiciary. Often this unfairness is linked to disadvantaged social status and social marginality.

The second set of conditions includes the political or instrumental outcomes of judicial decisions that disadvantage a person or group. The realization of a disadvantageous outcome is "external" or is the consequence of the actions of others through the courts on an individual's interests (see Ewick and Silbey 1998, 234–41). Let us examine these sources of resistance more fully.

PSYCHOLOGICAL PERCEPTIONS OF FAIRNESS AND ACTS OF RESISTANCE

Studies of *procedural justice* provide insights into the depth and limits of the constitutive faith of Americans in the legitimacy of the law. In one study, investigators interviewed convicted defendants in Connecticut. Despite losing their case and their liberty, they found that convicts with preexisting support for the legal system, often acquired when quite young and reinforced through social connections to their communities, retained faith in the system. In addition, despite the negative outcome, their sense that the disposition of their case was procedurally fair–they were treated politely with respect shown for their rights and the opportunity to speak to the judge or prosecutor—buttressed their allegiance to the legal system (Tyler, Casper, and Fisher 1988).

Studies of people's assessments of the work of courts and police in various other situations provide additional evidence that most people feel obligated to obey the law and the directives of judges and police. The obligation is the strongest when individuals have had experiences with law and courts and felt that the process was fair. For them fairness has two dimensions. It means the decision-making process is perceived to exhibit opportunity for representation, neutrality by the judge, honesty, and a clear and reasonable decision. Also, fairness means perceived attentive or personalized treatment by court personnel. Consequently, the stronger a loser's sense of procedural justice, the less antipathy they tend to hold toward courts and the more legitimate they regard legal processes. Conversely, the studies found that a lack of fair procedures and personal treatment undermined the legitimacy of the courts and police. Resistance to the law thus in part seems to be

EXPLORING JUDICIAL POLITICS

based on psychological assessments of unfairness and losses that work to undermine the constitutive faith in law and the legitimacy of judicial decisions held by many Americans (see Tyler 1990; Tyler and Huo 2002; Gibson, Caldiera, and Spence 2005).

UTILITY CALCULATIONS AND RESISTANCE

When he remarked that law is the command of the sovereign, the nineteenth century British scholar John Austin conceded that judicial decisions are also a coercive act external to individuals (see Campbell and Philip 1998). As coercive instruments, the political authority of the government backs law and judicial decisions. Therefore, a person might obey judicial decisions because of the threat of government penalization of his behavior. For example, because of the threat of arrest and jail, a divorced man might pay child support payments that he deems to be excessive—even if he senses a lack of fairness by the judge in awarding the payments. This example indicates that, although a sense of procedural justice can shape a person's acceptance of judicial actions, a sense of the legitimacy and morality of courts and law cannot offset assessments all experiences of unfavorable losses and penalties that a judge might impose. The outcomes of a lawsuit as imposed by a judge or other official or *distributive justice* can have an independent influence on support or hostility toward courts and police. They also can be magnified when a person perceives the procedures were unfair (Gibson et al. 2005).

When evaluating the effect of judicial decisions on individuals and groups, some scholars have argued that compliance with the outcome of a judicial decision conforms to a "cost-benefit" or "utility maximization" model. What does this mean? As set forth in their study of school desegregation Harrell Rodgers and Charles Bullock (1976) found that Southern officials resisted judicial desegregation decisions until the costs of resistance became too high. Initially the Southern officials received the benefits of political support from white voters for opposing school desegregation and enforcing racist policies. However, by enacting Title VI of the Civil Rights Act of 1964 the federal

government created costs. The Act allowed the federal government to deny federal funds to segregated school districts and to sue states that allocated federal and state money to segregated districts. Thus, when the federal government started withdrawing money from most segregated districts in the late 1960s, it conveyed the certainty of costly sanctions for the districts. Soon almost all districts desegregated. The lesson of their study is that exercise of political power can create costs and derail resistance to the judicial decisions. Conversely, a lack of enforcement might encourage resistance. Indeed, less aggressive Title VI enforcement during the past three decades has allowed many school districts to neglect efforts to secure quality racially desegregated schools (Halpern 1995).

Sometimes referred to as the *basic deterrence model*, the assumption of Rodgers and Bullock's study is that the severity and certainty of sanctions determines the extent of compliance or resistance to judicial actions. Thus, the existence and application of organized coercion will determine the extent of compliance or resistance. For judicial actions, however, the imposition of coercion poses a problem. American courts often lack direct control over the people or institutions that enforce their decisions. In civil matters judges can issue orders or decrees to enforce money damage judgments or child custody and child support decisions. However, as in the Pittston strike case, a judge's coercive power is limited to situations when a person brings nonenforcement to their attention and they issue a contempt of court citation. Also, this citation has to be enforced by police or sheriffs who are politically independent of the courts. In criminal matters, the enforcement of judicial decisions depends of the cooperation and skills of police and prosecutors. In addition, an ambiguous judicial decision about a complicated social or economic problem can create unwillingness for the detectors of noncompliance or the enforcers of judicial decisions to act. Consequently, the limited authority and competence of judges means that many opportunities for resistance emerge.

This description of resistance is, however, more complicated than the simple statement that ineffective enforcement increases resistance to judicial decisions. With its focus on the nature of detection and coercion, the basic deterrence model fails to include the potential psychological benefits of resistance, the effect of standards of personal morality, and other social influences on the calculation of the costs and benefits of resistance (see Kuperan and Sutinen 1998). It also assumes that persons are fully rational and capable of collecting all necessary information, effectively assessing all costs or benefits of their behavior, and making rational, unemotional decisions that will not endanger their interests (see Casey and Scholz 1991; Gray and Scholz 1993).

What do these qualifications of the basic deterrence model mean for the occurrence of resistance to judicial actions? Beyond ineffective organization of coercion to enforce compliance with judicial decisions, psychological reasons for resistance exist. For example, despite judicially imposed requirements that pedophiles who have served a sentence for their crime stay away from children, the judicial coercion frequently does not work. Pedophiles resist the decision because their entire way of living centers on sexual contact with children. Psychologists have found that no amount of coercion can displace the pathological sexual urge of pedophiles. Therefore, external coercion might not be effective in curtailing resistance to the law when the benefit of resistance for a person's instinctual urges are incapable of being discounted by any form of coercion. As in the case of a pedophile in Western Pennsylvania, his response to a state judge's orders to restrict his contact with children was resisted by his moving to states and then countries outside the authority of the court orders and by adopting seductive tactics beyond those prohibited in the court orders.

Despite the existence of coercion, personal morality also can create resistance to judicial decisions. Persons absolutely dedicated to a moral principle often chose to ignore the real potential for costs in certain contexts because of a belief in the rightness of their principle. For example, despite judicial decisions to allow the Klansmen to exercise First Amendment rights and parade or hold public gatherings in some communities, feelings of moral outrage against racism have aroused individuals to attack Ku Klux Klansmen. Also, persons who are members of a dissident subculture might resist the law because of a shared personal morality. For example, the religious beliefs of some polygamists are so intense and absolute that they have resisted complying with antipolygamy laws and the judicial judgments that have attempted to enforce those laws.

Other social values also encourage persons to resist compliance with the coercive message in judicial decisions. Especially coercive law and judicial decisions have run into resistance when they attack the shared practices of a large community. The risk of detection of misdeeds and the effect of coercion can be offset by the social values of the community. For example, law and judicial actions to enforce the prohibition of the law and consumption of alcoholic beverages during the Prohibition Era (1919 to 1933) met considerable resistance in part because members of ethnic and social communities included the consumption of wine or beer in their way of dining and in their social gatherings. Likewise, until the 1970s, racist values consistently undercut the efforts of judges to desegregate American public life.

A lack of information and knowledge of judicial decisions and the dictates of the law also can create the opportunity for persons to resist judicial decisions. A series of studies provide evidence that Americans do not understand many aspects of the law and judicial proceedings. Many do not know when they have suffered a civil or criminal harm, the difference between criminal and civil proceedings, the adversariness of the judicial process, the need to provide evidence and prove one's own case, and the limits of judicial remedies in civil matters (Conley and O'Barr 1990, 126–49; Merry 1990, 37–63; Williams and Hall 1972). In addition, as described in studies of sexual harassment and offensive speech, personal perceptions of experiences shaped by attitudes toward authority, their assessment of the practicality of action, the meaning they give the legal concept of free speech, and their own sense of personal autonomy influence the choice of different responses (Marshall 2003; Nielsen 2000). Together these studies suggest that choices about legal action and reactions to law and judicial decisions exhibit "bounded rationality." Or, information pertaining to the calculation of the costs and benefits of respecting or resisting the law is incomplete. The result can be that people will chose to resist judicial decisions when they do not understand fully what the decision means, what all of the consequences of resistance might be, and what other options they might have.

Finally, the knowledge people possess about court decisions is subject to manipulation by communicators, such as the media and interest groups. Resistance thus might be encouraged or discouraged by one-sided, incomplete, or hyperbolic communications about the business of courts or the decisions made by the judiciary. For example, it is not uncommon for business interest groups to exaggerate the number and costs of personal injury lawsuits about tobacco, pharmaceutical drugs, and medical malpractice to build public support for legislative measures that limit lawsuits against corporate misbehavior (Haltom and McCann 2004).

Studies of the psychology and utility of compliance with judicial decisions and the origins of resistance offer a complicated picture of individual behavior. The motives for resistance can be psychological or created by judicial action against the economic or political interests or moral and religious beliefs of persons or groups. Clearly procedural unfairness stimulates resistance and the use of coercion does not guarantee a judicial decision will be obeyed. However, the studies indicate that resistance is motivated. It is not just revolt for the hell of it.

THE PRACTICE OF RESISTANCE

If unfairness or ineffective coercion permits persons to resist judicial decisions, *how* do people resist judicial decisions or legal agreements? To simplify a complex set of human behaviors, it is possible to categorize resistance along a continuum from the most legitimate, legal practices of resistance to practices that transgress and deny the legitimacy of the law and judiciary. Along this continuum it is possible to identify four especially different practices of resistance. They are when: (1) a losing party perceives a mistake was made by initial settlement or trial of the case and resists by practicing legal *appeal*; (2) a party resists a loss political power or a preferred policy and engages in various legitimate *political tactics* to reestablish its power and policies through governmental institutions or mass political action; (3) a party resists being put in economic jeopardy or is made to pay money damages and attempts forms of *economic tactics* to retaliate against

the victorious party; and (4) a party resists a judgment, especially about a moral or cultural issue, expresses a different cultural conception of justice, and practices various *cultural expressions* of dissidence through public protest, violence, or an alternative social life. Often responses to specific cases feature more than one of these perceptions or conditions, thereby aggravating and deepening the resistance.

APPEAL: RESISTANCE BECAUSE OF PROCEDURAL ERROR

American law has always recognized the chance of procedural mistakes and unfair treatment. Noting the danger of procedural error, political leaders established a process for appeal of initial judicial judgments in the federal and all state constitutions. Although on occasion appellate courts will adjust the distribution of money damages or criminal sentences, normally appeals address alleged legal errors—mostly procedural errors—when a trial court made the initial judgment. This process permits a review of one dimension of a trial by a participant who finds a judicial action was wrong or prejudiced and wants to resist a judicial action. The appeal allows the loser to assert the rightness of his claim without attacking the legitimacy of judiciary (see Shapiro 1981a, 49–56). For example, in the case of the Pittston strike, union leaders sought review of the procedures by which a trial judge found them in contempt of court for violating his orders to avoid violence and leave the mines open. The judge then imposed massive fines on them. The union leaders and their lawyers were convinced that the trial judge had overstepped his authority. Initially turned down by two state appellate courts in Virginia, they successfully appealed the contempt finding to the Supreme Court of the United States. Thus, a legitimate act of resistance to a judge made the fines disappear. Although the resistance by legal action overcame a procedural legal mistake because the Court's decision came long after the conclusion of the strike, it could correct only a small portion of the distributive inequities the miners suffered at the hands of Pittston and the courts. Instead, success on appeal allowed the Supreme Court to ensure the legitimacy of the judicial process (*United Mine Workers of American v. Bagwell* 1994; Brisbin 2002, 260–99).

POLITICAL RESISTANCE TACTICS

People will also resist judicial decisions when they sense that unfair procedures or legal reasoning has ignored important political values or when they perceive a threat to the existing distribution of political power. In the Boston desegregation case, local leaders saw desegregation as threat to the social structure of local neighborhoods and, potentially, the base of support for their political careers. A study of the effect of the Supreme Court's school prayer decision in *Abington Township v. Schempp* (1963) revealed that the religious and political attitudes of the local school bureaucracy and the interests and preferences of local school board members on religious matters determined whether a public school district accepted or resisted the justice's decision (Dolbeare and Hammond 1971). Other studies have associated resistance to judicial decisions to unhappiness with the distribution of political benefits and costs by a court. For example, President Andrew Jackson and Congress supported the effort of the state of Georgia to seize lands from the Cherokee nation. Although the Supreme Court held that the state had no authority over the Cherokee nation (*Worcester v. Georgia* 1832), the political benefit to federal and state officials of the sale of the lands to whites outweighed any political benefits from supporting the decision favoring the tribe. Thereafter the government assigned the federal military to remove many of the Cherokee to Oklahoma.

Political Resistance from Lower Court Judges

Bradley Canon and Charles Johnson (1999) grouped these and numerous other examples of political resistance to the Supreme Court and other appellate courts into four categories. First, they described studies of resistance to appellate court decisions by lower court judges. From these studies they concluded that lower court judges will tend to resist following appellate courts in three circumstances. One situation is when

the court's outcome is justified by an opinion containing ambiguous or vague statements, multiple opinions, and inconsistent use of precedents. Such conditions raise questions about the procedural fairness of the appellate decision. Another circumstance fostering resistance is the inability of higher courts to communicate authoritatively with lower court judges. Because the appellate court lacks the coercive political authority to enforce its judgments on trial court judges, lower court judges can resist what the appellate court has said. Finally, as shown in studies of Southern school desegregation, local political and social pressures and ideological responses to certain issues can encourage lower court judges to resist the full implementation of an appellate ruling. Normally, these forms of resistance by the lower judiciary are neither exceptionally frequent or of major political significance; however, these forms of resistance by judges suggest that the internal political organization of the judiciary and external politics can affect the justice delivered to the public (see Canon and Johnson 1999, 29–57; Benesh and Reddick 2002).

Political Resistance by Elected Politicians

A second set of studies described political resistance by the federal, state, or local executive and legislative institutions that often must provide for the enforcement of both appellate and trial judges' decisions (Canon and Johnson 1999, 62–89). Controversial appellate court decisions that change social traditions enforced by law, such as the Supreme Court's decision to end racial segregation in public schools (*Brown v. Board of Education* 1954), often encounter resistance from a range of political institutions. Sensitive to the racial values of a majority of their constituents, elected leaders charged with applying or enforcing a judicial decision might balk at performing this responsibility. This refusal to implement is a form of resistance that tends to occur with controversial decisions about personal rights, especially the rights of disadvantaged groups (see also Miller this volume, chapter 19).

In his assessment of the extensive literature about judicial action to desegregate the public schools, Gerald Rosenberg (1991, 39–145) concluded that the Supreme Court and lower federal courts could not bring about desegregation of public schools and facilities on their own in the decade after the *Brown* decision. Congress, federal agencies, and especially state and local officials in the South did not undertake political actions essential for the enforcement of *Brown*. The resistance appeared in state and local legislation that challenged the assumptions of *Brown* about the value of desegregation and to prevent the adoption of remedies. It appeared in the hostility of members of Congress to civil rights legislation. It appeared in the willingness of former Governor George Wallace of Alabama to stand in the doorway of a public university to prevent African American students from entering. It appeared in the reluctance of Presidents Dwight Eisenhower and John Kennedy to use the "bully pulpit" provided by presidential media coverage and behind the scenes pressure to achieve public and legislative support for public school desegregation and attack the "massive resistance" to school and public facility desegregation in the South. Although the passage of the Civil Rights Act of 1964 broke the back of massive resistance by denying federal funds to segregated school districts, a decade later northern school officials, as in Boston, adopted some of the same policies and tactics to resist school desegregation. In these and later cases the courts gradually lost sight of the goal of equal educational opportunity, and the other branches gave lukewarm or little support for the implementation of this goal. Thus, as political and judicial support for *Brown* ebbed, racial segregation often slipped back into the public schools (Halpern 1995).

The practices of political resistance surfaced in a slightly different way in response to the Supreme Court's decision recognizing a right to an abortion, *Roe v. Wade* (1973). Because *Roe* addressed a private act rather than the operation of public facilities, political opponents faced a somewhat different problem. They had to find ways to control or restrict private acts. One way was to prohibit the use of public funds for abortions. These efforts concentrated on banning abortion in public hospitals and preventing the use of public health programs for poor from paying for abortions. The other way was to regulate where, when, and how physicians conducted abortions. Consequently, Presidents Ronald Reagan and the two George Bushes routinely denounced the decision and sought legislation

to stop financial assistance to women seeking abortions both at home and abroad. Congress restricted the use of federal healthcare funds for abortions and related use of fetal tissue. It also considered but did not pass measures to restrict judicial consideration of abortion rights and constitutional amendments to ban abortions. More important, states adopted a series of laws to restrict the use of public funds for abortions, abortion-related healthcare, to require parental notification when minors sought an abortion, to require doctors to discuss alternatives to abortion, to require waiting periods for women seeking abortions, and other measures. Many of the state measures ended in litigation and appeals that sometimes restricted the interpretation of women's rights during pregnancy provided in *Roe* (see Canon and Johnson 1999, 3–16; Epstein and Kobylka 1992, 202–298).

Trial court decisions that change the operation of public institutions also encounter political resistance from numerous public institutions. In their account of litigation brought to curtail the abuse or "cruel and unusual punishment" of prisoners in Arkansas and Texas, Malcolm Feeley and Edward Rubin (1998, 51–95) found state officials used various tactics to delay or frustrate change. After decades of neglect, by 1965 "trusty" prisoners effectively controlled the prisoners in Arkansas's Cummins Prison Farm at night. They and the daytime cadre of guards routinely managed prisoners through violence, including electric torture and beatings. The prisons lacked medical and dental facilities. Prisoners lived in barracks where they commonly suffered sexual assaults, and they labored in fields to produce their own food and food and cotton to be sold to pay for prison operations. Prison officials neglected prison sanitation and overcrowding and prisoner education, clothing, and shoes. Many of the same conditions existed in the Texas prison system.

After intervention on behalf of the prisoners by "cause" lawyers, federal judges issued a creative series of decrees to secure the prisoners' rights against the cruelty and unusually harsh punishment meted out in both prison systems. They had to issue the series of decrees because of resistance within state government. The resistance came from a state legislature that refused to provide adequate funds for prison improvements, especially because the improvements did little for votes in their constituencies. The resistance also came from both states' Departments of Correction. The decrees ran into opposition from these bureaucrats because they challenged the way they had always done business and their attitudes toward convicts. In Arkansas the judge ordered a complete overhaul of prison administration and made the prison bureaucracy respond to his demands as expressed through his "compliance coordinator." This oversight generated additional bureaucratic efforts to frustrate the process of change. In Texas, the Department of Corrections challenged most of the actions of the federal judge in court. Through the delay caused by additional hearings, changes in the virtually every facet of prisoner life came about only as corrections personnel adjusted to practices of modern prison management. Although the resistance of public officials to the judges' actions in the prison cases delayed change, eventually control vanished, medical and educational programs appeared, and living conditions improved.

These examples indicate the potential for political resistance to judicial actions by the legislatures and executives of federal, state, and local governments, and by inferior courts. Legislators, especially through their control of funding for the enforcement of judicial ruling and power to refuse to adjust laws, can significantly frustrate the more controversial rulings of courts about individual rights. Less visibly, but in recent years in response to judicial actions favorable to consumers and injured workers, some state legislatures have rewritten laws insurance company liability and workers compensation laws. The rewritten laws reversed judicial decisions to favor business interests. Executives usually have fewer opportunities to resist, but they can urge legislative action against judicial decisions and ratify such laws that resist judicial decisions.

Of course, these instances of resistance are far from common. Most judicial actions never draw the attention of elected officials. The tendency of judges is to share the same political outlook as the legislative and judicial branches. Judges also prefer to avoid conflict with elected officials (Brisbin 2005, 94–98). As in the three case studies illustrate, when political resistance occurs, it not often successful. Political resistance by elected officials thus is more a threat judges must

consider rather than a real challenge to the legitimacy of their decisions.

Political Resistance by Losing Parties

Adverse decisions can stimulate political resistance by the losing party as well as the political institutions charged with implementing the decision (Canon and Johnson 1999, 106–111). For example, journalists have long contended that the right to a free press prohibits them from having to reveal the sources of information in their stories. After the Supreme Court ruled that journalists had the same duty to testify about the sources of information before grand juries and courts as other persons, news organizations and professional journalism groups sought legislation to protect their sources (*Branzburg v. Hayes* 1972). They were successful in obtaining limited protection of confidential sources in civil and criminal matters in some states, such as New York (NY CLS Civ R § 79–h, 2005). Such resistance by losing parties is not common. However, when the economic or political stakes are high, losing parties can seek to change the law that guides judicial actions.

Political resistance by losing parties need not be so overt. In any American court that adjudicates family disputes, more than a third if not half of the family law hearings involve a divorced parent seeking to change the conditions of a divorce settlement. Often one of the parents–usually the male—has decided to resist further implementation of a divorce decree to which he had previously agreed. The failure of the noncustodial male parent to pay child support to the care-giving mother seems far removed from politics. However, a parent who regards himself as a loser in a divorce settlement is not appealing an error in the interpretation of the law. He is in court because he has either failed to follow the agreement or he has challenged the judicial implementation of policy or legislation. The policy or law requires the judge to protect the best interests of the child by assigning care to the mother and requiring the father to pay to the mother a portion of his income according to a formula set in law.

From these examples it appears that losers can employ almost any legal and illegal political tactic to resist a negative outcome. They can use political pressure to try to have legislators change the law or start the constitutional amendment process. They can raise new issues for litigation. They can, as with "dead beat dads," refuse to follow the law. In the Pittston strike, a few losing miners even turned to acts of intimidation of people and violence against company property to "get even" with the victorious mining company and its management.

Secondary Acts of Political Resistance

Judicial actions have a "radiating" effect. Beyond the courts and implementing officials and parties to the case, but capable of reacting to a judicial decision, are government officials, interest groups and corporations, the media, and the public (Canon and Johnson 1999, 115–48). Usually these "secondary" organizations and individuals remain quiescent. They do not care about judicial actions, or they know little about them. When they do comment or react to decisions, often they rely on inaccurate or misleading information. Or, as with some government officials and interest groups, they pass on information about the judiciary that is misleading to advantage their specific political interests. For example, scholarly studies have shown that American courts are not bedeviled by frivolous lawsuits. Lawyers generally will not waste their time on them, and judges can use their powers to keep them out of court. Yet, a majority of Americans believe there are far too many frivolous lawsuits. Why? As William Haltom and Michael McCann (2004) found, various insurance companies and corporate interests have skillfully induced the media to sell Americans the idea that there are too many frivolous lawsuits. Especially, they provided misinformation about judicial decisions to create the perception of massive frivolous litigation. This perception soon became the "truth" for the public, even though it was a tactic by business interests to encourage legislative measures, and secure the election of judges who would curtail lawsuits against businesses for their misdeeds, such as the harms caused by asbestos, tobacco, pharmaceuticals, and other potentially dangerous products.

In this environment of limited and inaccurate information, what is the nature of resistance to a judicial action by "secondary" publics? For resistance to occur there must be some knowledge of a judicial action. Because public officials, interest group and corporate personnel, and the public usually do not hang out in courtrooms, the electronic and print media communicate the activity of the judiciary in news stories and fictionalized accounts. Their versions of what happens in court can stimulate either support for the judiciary or resistance to its decisions.

However, reporters report on very few cases in American courts. Even the U.S. Supreme Court is covered full-time by a handful of reporters (Canon and Johnson 1999, 138–42; Dreschel 1983; Slotnick and Segal 1998). There are simply not enough reporters to cover the 100 million cases filed in courts and the billions of out-of-court settlements each year. Most reporters know about what goes on in court from press releases or interviews arranged by the parties or stories released by interest groups. The objective of journalists is a good story people will read or view. Because they have little knowledge of legal precedent, procedural rules, and regard judicial interpretations of laws as "technical" and uninteresting for readers or viewers, reporters tend to concentrate on dramatic cases. The dramatic cases include crimes of violence of an unusual nature, crimes that involve children or attractive white women, and civil cases to which their attention is drawn by press releases. In all of these cases the media phrase the case as good against evil or as having produced a counterintuitive judgment that defies "common sense."[3]

Fictional coverage of courts also dwells on the unusual case and often misrepresents reality. For example, during 2005/2006 the most watched prime time television programs about law were the three *CSI* and three *Law and Order* series. They featured homicides—the least common crime of violence in America. Both series had a strong pro-police and pro-prosecution bias. They commonly portrayed defendants in an unflattering light as liars and their counsel as manipulators of the law. Programs that depicted civil litigation, such as *Boston Legal*, overstated the frequency of trials, presented extremely unusual cases, and ignored the massive amount of negotiation and drafting done by attorneys. Indeed, legal procedural rulings by judges often seemed to be contrary to a popular sense of justice. Daytime "reality" court shows such as *Judge Judy* and *Divorce Court* actually gave a more accurate picture of some aspects of trials—the incompetence of *pro se* defendants, the acrimony in postdivorce hearings and neighborhood disputes, and the authority of judges in bench trials. However, they often exaggerated the unusual or adversarial aspects of such proceedings. It is rare to see the out of court settlement or civil trial ever at the center of television or print fiction (see Mather 2005, 242–49).

What do such images of judicial activity mean for resistance to law? The evidence suggest that attentive officials and interest groups, who often provide stories for the media, and writers, who are interested in the unusual and sensational because it creates readers and viewers, secures their jobs, and makes money for their media firm, can create the opportunity for resistance. They also can make choices to not cover or respond to resistance to judicial actions.

For *elected officials*, knowledge about judicial decisions usually comes through the media, press releases and calls from parties to the case, interest groups, and corporations. Studies of legislative and executive behavior indicate that these officials respond to such information in the relatively rare instances when they think their response will encourage support for their reelection or policy agenda from voters and campaign contributors. Their response to a decision is often symbolic. They denounce or support a judicial decision in speeches, media interviews, and press releases. They blast judges (who are usually labeled with the pejorative term "activist") or introduce legislation or propose constitutional amendments that have little chance of passage. Their aim is to create a record on the decision for the voters' consumption (see also Miller this volume, chapter 19).[4]

Executives, especially the president and governors, also can resist judicial actions. As with legislators, such resistance is not common and is usually confined to cases in which the announcement of a response might create a political advantage. Beyond public statements of resistance or support, presidents can try to change some future decisions by nominating their political allies to the federal bench and by directing the Justice Department to undertake certain criminal or civil cases or appearing as a friend of the court to inform appellate judges of the president's views

(Canon and Johnson 1999, 128–31; Kassop 2004). In the states many attorneys general are independent of the governor and can voice their own sentiments on judicial actions and make arguments in future cases that resist previous rulings. Elected county or local prosecutors litigate most criminal cases. They also can express their own sentiments on judicial actions, select cases for prosecution, and make arguments in future cases that resist previous rulings with electoral considerations in mind.

Lurking behind the responses of elected officials to judicial decisions is the vast number of *organized interests and corporations* engaged in efforts to influence policies made implemented by all sorts of elected officials and civil servants. Until the 1970s few groups attempted to influence judicial decisions or encourage resistance to them. However, the success of the NAACP Legal Defense Fund in litigating an end to segregated public schools drew more groups' attention to the judiciary. Today interest groups engage in various proactive and reactive actions in an attempt to effect judicial decision making. Proactive resistance efforts can involve efforts to force change in established patterns of judicial interpretation of law and rights. This is resistance to legitimate legal standards and interpretations of rights. It can involve interest group efforts to search out cases, support litigants, provide them with legal arguments that challenge existing interpretations, or file friend of the court briefs with appellate courts in support of established doctrine. It can involve publicity campaigns and lobbying to mobilize other supporters of its position to support legislation or constitutional amendments that would change a pattern of judicial decisions. It could be support of candidates in judicial elections, support for judicial appointments, or opposition to the retention of some judges to create a judiciary receptive to its attack on existing doctrine (Epstein and Kobylka 1992). Reactive tactics include campaign contributions to elected officials who oppose a judicial action, financial support for a continuation of litigation by a losing party, and the release of negative publicity about a court decision or a judge. The aim is frame the law and support judges who will help the resisters in what is effectively a political campaign to change public policy.

In the politics of resistance, the *public* often seems "outside the loop." Studies of public opinion and the courts have focused on the U.S. Supreme Court. Overall, these and other studies indicate that the public knowledge of court activity is quite limited, there is greater diffuse or nonspecific support for courts than other government institutions, and a small number of people are attentive to courts. The public's knowledge of court decisions is confined to a few famous cases, but the knowledge of the meaning of these cases is commonly vague or mistaken (Caldiera and Gibson 1992; Gibson, Caldiera, and Spence 2003). However, in part because of the efforts of local media, cases that affect a specific community do become better known in that community, especially among better-educated people and those who pay attention to a specific political issue. Despite the wide range of lawful political actions that individuals or groups can undertake once they decide to resist a judicial decision, the pathway to eventual victory is costly and time consuming. Consequently, as in the Boston desegregation case and the Arkansas and Texas prison cases, the voicing of opposition gradually waned. Instead, the opponents either left the field, as when white pupils fled Boston schools, or it accommodated themselves to the change, as with the prison administrators. However, for committed opponents forms of economic and cultural resistance remained viable.

ECONOMIC RESISTANCE TACTICS

Many judicial actions affect the enforcement of contracts to permit the collection of debts, compensation for personal injuries caused during auto accidents or by defective products, and child support and alimony payments. A problem facing the winner in any of these kinds of disputes is collection of a monetary remedy granted by a judge. It is possible for a losing person or firm to resist payment and frustrate the winner.

Unfortunately, legal scholars have not paid a great deal of attention to this practice. Scattered information and discussions with attorneys suggest that collection of money damages is less a problem when the loser is a government, a firm, or an individual in possession of significant assets. Because winners can use a variety of legal measures such a wage garnishment or property seizure orders to attach assets and collect damages, the firm or individual with assets pays the damages to avoid additional legal costs. However, problems exist when the loser is an uninsured individual with few assets or has unaccounted assets from illegal activities. Again the evidence is scattered, but in such instances the collection of a monetary remedy or child support and alimony payments is difficult (see Rosenberg 2005, 284–86).

Also, some people have used the law to frustrate the collection of remedies. Bankruptcy is a way some firms and individuals have used to resist paying winners. Because bankruptcy absolves or "discharges" debts, individuals have used it to resist having to pay off winners. However, recent changes in bankruptcy law have made debts for spousal or child support or alimony, debts for willful and malicious injuries to person or property, debts to governmental units for fines, and debts for personal injury caused by the debtor's operation of a motor vehicle while intoxicated, nondischargeable. Also, by filing appeals and seeking other forms of judicial intervention a resister can drag out the imposition of the remedy, raise legal fees for the winner, and hope that the winner might abandon the pursuit of a remedy. Little is known about the frequency or success of such resistance tactics.

CULTURAL CONFLICT AND RESISTANCE

Finally, when people find that judicial decisions ignore important cultural or moral values, they will resist the decision. This form of resistance often features *discursive breakdown* (Wagner-Pacifici 1994, 143–45). The resisters simply perceive or talk about a dispute in an absolutist, nonlegalistic language or with a logic that is radically different than the language and logic used by the judiciary. For example, many opponents of the Supreme Court's abortion decision, *Roe v. Wade* (1973), expressed a religiously based conception of rights and the ability to exercise rights. The *Roe* opponents perceive a right to life as an absolute moral principles ordained by God. This interpretation of rights is at odds with the notion that Americans have only those rights placed in the Constitution by politicians or interpreted by judges. Judges therefore tend to treat rights as creations of human free will subject to interpretation in various contexts under the guidelines accepted by the legal profession. Their legal conception is so different from the views of the *Roe* opponents that discursive breakdown occurs, thwarts a compromise resolution about the appropriateness of abortion, and buttresses resistance by the *Roe* opponents.[5]

As these cases imply, discursive breakdown can produce what James Scott (1990) called, "public, declared" resistance to the values enshrined in judicial decisions. Such resistance can involve a range of actions. For example, in opposing judicial orders the Pittston strikers employed sit-down demonstrations, blockades of roads by logs and jackrocks, marches and parades, demonstrations and the occupation of Pittston property, camouflage clothes to symbolize they were at war with Pittston and the courts, and even skits that poked fun at the "evil" done by Pittston and the judiciary. They justified these practices of resistance by reliance on drawing on their religious and local cultural roots. They focused the injustices of the "abuse" of the law by greedy Pittston managers and the alleged promanagement use of injunctions by the federal and state judges. They thought that only bad forces could arrest them, abuse them, and penalize them for a transgression or resistance against evil law. This perception drew on aspects of the civic republican and Protestant traditions in American political thought.[6] In addition, culturally based resistance and discursive breakdowns can also result in the alternative practice of a politics of "disguised, low profile, undisclosed resistance." James Scott (1990, 136–201) called this a "hidden transcript" of resistance. These hidden transcripts include efforts to resist the cultural values expressed in judicial decisions through the use of tactics such as foot dragging, grumbling, gossip, folk tales, and the creation of underground economies and alternative social institutions.

Foot dragging is simply delaying compliance with a judicial decision. For example, by inaction in response to the Supreme Court's ban on school prayer, even more than forty years after the Court's decision many school districts have not ended required prayer. Grumbling about frivolous lawsuits in ordinary

conversations is often an expression of a cultural hostility to judicial actions that foster insurance costs and, indirectly, the legal power and economic privileges that personal liability insurance companies possess in the United States. Television fiction and some reality and talk shows convey folk tales about judges letting criminals "get off" on technicalities, which is really quite rare. However, it is also a disguised criticism of the idea of due process of the law by persons who favor a more inquisitorial criminal process and who are culturally or morally invested in retaliation against even suspected criminals.

The underground economy in illegal drugs is an expression of resistance to judicial decisions that penalize a subordinate culture. For some parents enrolling their children in private religious schools or home schooling express resistance to judicial decisions that interpret the No Establishment of Religion Clause of the First Amendment to exclude Bible reading, prayer, religious instruction, "creation science," and religious evangelism in the public schools. After the Supreme Court decision in *Bowers v. Hardwick* (1986) held that the constitutional right to privacy did not encompass homosexual acts, the group Queer Nation organized alternative practices such as the Queer Shopping Network, Queer Nights Out, queer bars, and the like to signal their resistance to the refusal to recognize that their sexual rights were the same as those of heterosexuals (Bower 1994). By adopting these practices, individuals make no public claims and engage in no active or symbolic denunciation of the law. Theirs is a disguised resistance, but it is a form of cultural protest that also creates a boundary on the effectiveness of judicial actions and the law more generally.

The references to the examples of school desegregation, abortion, and the Pittston strike cases in each of the categories of resistance practices points to another significant feature of resistance. Often people opposed to a judicial action will use a combination of practices and targets to change what they find to be an unfair process or unjust outcome. Such a combination of resistance practices is usually not centrally directed. Even in the resistance to court orders during Pittston strike, which the union went to great pains to control, the UMWA leaders lost control of resistance and outbreaks of disorder happened that they did not approve. The often scattershot nature of resistance to court decisions puts some resisters at cross purposes and can undercut the force of their objections. Clearly the practice of resistance is a political action fraught with many pitfalls that might plunge its users into further defeat.

THE EFFECTIVENESS OF RESISTANCE

When is resistance to the judiciary effective? If resistance to judicial decisions to be regarded as effective, it must either prevent the enforcement of a judicial decision or have the decision voided by a higher court, a change in legislation, or constitutional amendment. Thus, the effectiveness of resistance depends on the relative political power of persons, groups, and governmental bodies to *demand* change in judicial actions. Also, it is affected by the willingness of the judiciary to *supply* a favorable response.

The relative power of resisters to demand change and achieve a success with their demands depends on several considerations. First, they must be attentive to judicial decisions that disadvantage their interests. Second, they must have a sense that they should and can oppose the decision. The reason that lower court judges and executive and legislative officials resist decisions is rooted in their attention to judicial actions, often conducted by their staff, and a sense that resistance to the decision will advance their policy goals or reelection. For other people such attention and contrariness often is problematic. Some individuals lack the knowledge and confidence to attend to their disadvantage and the vocabulary to express it to political leaders (Gilliom 2001, 69–92). Other people depend on the creation of a collective organization such as an interest group to attend to judicial decisions that affect them. Indeed, many judicial decisions affect established interest groups with a leadership or staff that monitor judicial actions that might affect their membership and that can readily identify adverse decisions they should oppose on their members' behalf. Resistance thus becomes a by-product of a group mission. For example, the United Mine Workers resistance to the Pittston strike injunctions was a by-product of the union's mission of enhancing the income, employee benefits, and workplace safety of its members. Alternatively, specialized interest groups can organize to resist specific sets of decisions. This has occurred with U.S. Supreme Court decision on abortion. However, the effectiveness of such groups depends on the ability of the leaders to muster a membership, especially for public protests, and have the members commit resources, such as financial donations, that support the group leaders' efforts to conduct mass actions, support the elections of friendly politicians, appeal judgments, support litigants, lobby legislators, and other actions.

Third, resisters must gain access to government to challenge judicial decisions. Fourth, they need the resources to use politics to offset the judicial action they dislike. For lower court judges, elected executives, and legislators, especially those with the resources afforded by leadership positions and majority party membership, access to constitutional or financial means for checking the judiciary is a perquisite of office. Individuals and groups often must seek allies among these officials to effectuate their resistance. When official allies cannot assist individuals or only give their cause symbolic support, as during the Boston desegregation controversy, judicial actions cannot be blocked. Frustrated individuals then can turn to anarchic violence or simply abandon their cause. Groups, especially those representing a bloc of potential voters or with resources they can devote to campaign finance, have the resources to induce officials to use their authority and resist the judiciary. Alternatively, the group can use freedoms of speech, press, and assembly as resources to bring unofficial political pressure on the judiciary and build support for future acts of resistance.

Will the judiciary supply a response to such demands? Effective resistance requires a judiciary that can and will respond to the resisters. With many of the acts of resistance described in this chapter, including those about school desegregation, abortion, and the Pittston injunctions, the response did not come in the form the resisters wished. There was an unwillingness of the judiciary to respond. Indeed, several conditions immunize judges from the demands of resisters. First, the professional norms of the judiciary, such as following precedent and maintaining a stable, reliable body of law, discourage new legal standards or policies. Second, the norm of judicial independence, buttressed by the independence of life-tenure federal judges, is an institutional barrier confronting resisters. Resisters can do an end-run and get other officials to amend the Constitution, enact new legislation, or appoint new judges supportive of their cause, but these are not easily achieved remedies. They demand political organization, resources, and alliances. For the poor, social outcasts, the ill-educated, and people with little political experience or access to attorneys, resistance consequently is a choice that might end in frustration or acts of subterfuge and deception in defiance of the judiciary's actions (see Gilliom 2001). Third, because the constitutive belief in the value of law and courts the public displays, resisters upset with unfavorable judicial rulings must overcome the reservoir of legitimacy that supports any judicial actions. Also, if they protest a decision in ways that turn disorderly and threaten the rule of law, resisters might lose public support.

These conditions minimize the judicial willingness to supply relief and favor the policies demanded by resisters. With the chances of resistance minimized, resisters thus might slip into covert, illegal acts that deny the legitimacy of court rulings. Therefore, when the U.S. Supreme Court upheld a ban on the medical use of marijuana, poor, dying cancer victims illegally toked on a substance illegally supplied to them.

THE CONSEQUENCE OF RESISTANCE

Given the problems in practicing effective resistance to judicial decisions, *what* are the implications of resistance to courts? Three decades ago Marc Galanter (1974) theorized that the legal system works so the "haves"—corporations, governments, and wealthy individuals—come out ahead. The "haves" often possess the advantages of experience and credibility with the judiciary (as "repeat players"), the resources to engage in long-term legal conflicts, afford the best lawyers, and the ability to influence legislatures that define the law, and, hence, the options that judges have in cases. "Have nots," such as working and poor persons, women, and criminal defendants, lack such

assets. Later studies have both refined and provided empirical proof of his assertion (see Glenn 2003; Harris 2003; Kritzer 2003a; Songer, Sheehan, and Haire 2003). If the "haves come out ahead" from the operations of the judicial process, does *resistance* to judicial activity create more advantages for the "haves" than the "haves nots"? To answer this question, the material, social, and political consequences of resistance require attention.

Material Consequences

Resisting judicial decisions can be costly. Appeals require money for legal services—either the money of the appellant, *pro bono* lawyers, interest group allies, charities, or, with some poor appellants, the government. Political, economic, and cultural resistance demand investments of money and time, and can cause a loss of income by appellants, groups, alternative organizations, and the like. However, either directly or because of unanticipated consequences, "have not" resisters end up with fewer resources. Boston's black children won their lawsuit, but unanticipated white flight limited the victory of the children. After more than a year without wages, the Pittston strikers won, but in a few years Pittston closed its union operations to avoid the costs associated with the settlement of the strike.

However, "have" resisters, especially repeat players, tend to win appeals (Songer et al. 2003). Because they already possess political, economic, and cultural advantages or hegemony, the resistance of the "haves" to adverse economic decisions by courts can often be successful. For example, physicians, one of the most highly paid professions, have successfully lobbied for legislation in many states to reduce the ability of judges to impose sizeable money damage remedies against them in medical malpractice cases. Also, to avoid the potential economic costs of litigation and economic uncertainty that it brings, insurance companies, financial institutions, attorneys, and governments have long supported the avoidance of judicial decisions through the adoption of alternatives. Consequently, they have pursued the negotiation of settlements of injuries, contract disputes, the economic aspects of divorce, and the plea bargaining of criminal cases. They also have come to accept court-ordered mediation of a range of civil conflicts, the mandatory arbitration of disputes about credit card charges and other financial conflicts, and similar modes of conflict adjustment to reduce the possible costs of payments to losing "have nots."

Political Consequences

Can resistance to the law shift the distribution of political powers and its benefits? In addition to the general limitations on the effectiveness of resistance described earlier, many scholars find that the isolated nature of most judicial decisions, the success of governments as litigants, and the political and economic resources possessed by political majorities or organized interests limit the success of resistance by "have nots." Abolitionists could not overturn the law of slavery; only a Civil War victory by the North could. Anti-abortion advocates have incrementally chipped away at the availability of abortion, but they have not overturned *Roe*. After court-ordered desegregation, African Americans students often remain in inferior public schools.

Also, successful uses of litigation, such as the success of black litigants to overturn segregation laws in Boston, only begat white's resistance to desegregation of the schools, and the success of Pittston in enjoining (preventing) the miners' union's efforts to close its mines only encouraged new union tactics to stop production. Acts of resistance to judicial decisions therefore might only expand the scope of a political conflict or change the conflict's dimensions, not satisfy the demands of the resisters (see Halpern 1995). Such situations illustrate that winning one battle is, "both the end of a long struggle and the beginning of a new battle for meaning in the courts" (Albiston 1993, 169).

Nonetheless, resistance can affect the political agenda. It affords people the opportunity to offer readings of law and justice that legislators, administrators, and judges have ignored. It challenges the legitimacy of incomplete, symbolic, or biased solutions to disputes offered by the judiciary. Resisters thus can, in effect, propagate new policy alternatives or readings of the meaning of the law. In addition, resistance might strengthen the identity of a group of people, help them recognize their ambitions and the political interests arrayed against them, and induce their articulation

of their version of the law. For example, hostility to Supreme Court decisions on school prayer and Bible reading, "creation science," and abortion caused some evangelical Christians to think the justices discounted the values of people of faith, allege that justices were captured by an ideology of "secular humanism," and then organize politically to influence judicial appointments and to file friend of the court briefs. Therefore, resistance eventually induced their efforts to redefine constitutional doctrine. Because the justices' opinions in these cases did not make sense in light of their vision of a God-centered universe and portended the horror of a nation committed to a law that condemned God's message, their resistance eventually introduced a new series of arguments and new legislation for consideration by the judiciary.

Social Consequences

Does resistance to the law change the social status of the resisters? There is little evidence that resistance to a series of judicial decisions can directly enhance the status of a disadvantaged group by changing the attitudes of the majority. Instead, judicial decisions might have a more subtle influence on the perception of the "have" possessors of social status such as males, whites, and heterosexuals. For example, Michael McCann (1994) found that resistance through litigation can serve as a "catalyst" that raises awareness of an economic and social inequity among "have nots," creates an identity among such people, and forces the "haves" to at least discuss if not justify the inequity. Also, negative judicial decisions, such decisions against gay rights and same-sex marriage, seem to stimulate a group to perceive its "have not" identity (Bower 1994). Therefore, resistance might place the social status of a group on the political agenda, but remedies for their disadvantage probably demand actions elsewhere in the political system.

That acts of resistance and transgressions of the law often benefit the "haves" is no surprise. Yet, sometimes resisters do more than raise attention about an issue. They can succeed in reaching their objectives. Judicial decisions or the economic, political, and social environment in which they occur can change to the benefit of the "have nots," especially through appellate action or continual litigation of aspects of a problem (see Harris 2003; Irons 1990). These changes are important—and not just for the resisters. They keep alive the "myth of rights" or the belief that legal action can foster a more legitimate, democratic, and just America politics (Scheingold 1974, 3–79). They help foster support for the constitutive idea of the rule of law and the American way of governing.

IS RESISTANCE WORTH THE EFFORT?

With the difficulties that losers and "have nots" face in resisting judicial decisions, is it worth their effort? In 1788, James Madison commented that, "Justice is the end of government. It is the end of civil society" (Hamilton, Madison, and Jay 1787–1788, 352). Justice, he added, must be pursued through constitutional government and the weaker individual must be protected against the violence of the stronger. Although resistance to judicial decisions might produce more victories for stronger "haves" than weaker "have nots," many Americans have practiced resistance to unfair judicial procedures and outcomes just as they have resisted injustice elsewhere in their nation's institutions. They are smart enough to recognize that, as with other institutions, the judiciary can do violence to their freedoms and oppress and subject them to often invisible restraints on their liberty. For those who opposed the judicial decisions that upheld the law of slavery, the enforcement of Jim Crow laws, the suppression of opposition to wars, and the subjection of women to male authority, the political legitimacy of resistance will remain more legitimate than judicial decisions. Such resisters would agree with United Mine Workers President Cecil Roberts. During the Pittston strike he remarked that, "There is nothing wrong with going to jail when you are trying to change an unjust system or an unjust law" (Kopple and Davis 1990, 1:27:00).

Notes

1. Indeed, as French legal historian Pierre Legendre (1997, 97) wrote, in American and European thought, "Someone who passes to the other side, who passes above the space humanised by legality, by speech and other signs, is someone who is mad."

2. So, for instance, an instrumental view might investigate how a particular law would bring about a redistribution of property, a constitutive view would question how the very idea of property is "legally constituted" in the first place. As Sarat and Kearns captured this distinction, "[to] acknowledge that law has meaning-making power is to acknowledge, contrary to the instrumentalists' general view, that some social practices are not logically separable from, or intelligible apart from, the laws that shape them" (Sarat and Kearns 1993, 28).

3. For example, on June 23, 2005, the ABC, CBS, CNN, FOX and NBC networks and the Associated Press (the source of stories for most daily newspapers) reported on only two court cases. One was the arrest and interrogation of suspects in the disappearance of Natalee Holloway in Aruba. It was the case of an attractive, blonde, white, teenage woman who vanished in an exotic locale while apparently in the company of several mixed-race males. The other case was the U.S. Supreme Court decision in *Kelo v. City of New London* (2005). This case upheld an interpretation of the "public purpose" language of the Takings Clause of the Fifth Amendment. In the case the justices upheld a decision of the City of New London, Connecticut to take private property—largely homes in an established residential district—and then turn the property over to a developer whose new construction was to serve the public purpose of creating jobs and providing space for businesses and a museum. Although American courts had permitted takings of private property and the conveyance of the property to private firms who constructed railroads

and mill dams in the mid-nineteenth century (Scheiber 1973) and the Supreme Court had supported a broad definition of public purpose in past Takings Clause cases (*Berman v. Parker* 1954; *Hawaii Housing Authority v. Midkiff* 1984), the media—informed by property rights extremists—communicated that the *Kelo* decision was a grave *new* threat to home ownership. The information on this threat was conveyed through a few interviews with homeowners whose property was to be taken. Yet, this "threat" had existed for nearly two centuries.

4. Congressional and state legislative efforts to reverse judicial decisions are uncommon and usually focus on unpopular decisions about individual rights or are actually a result of an invitation by the legislature for a court to consider the constitutionality of a law it previously passed (Lindquist and Yalof 2001; Baum and Hausegger 2004). Congress and many state legislatures can propose constitutional amendments to overturn some court decisions, but this is so rare as to be a virtually meaningless option. However, legislatures can resist judicial by sending implicit messages about their unhappiness with the judiciary. This can occur in legislation that reduces funding for the courts, changes judicial jurisdiction over certain issues, or changes the membership of courts. The U.S. Senate also can use its power to approve presidential nominees to the federal bench to refuse to consent to nominees whose policies or ideology it opposes (Brisbin 2005, 109–11; Canon and Johnson 1999, 116–127).

5. Another example is the case of the medical treatment of Terri Schiavo. After more than a decade in an apparent vegetative state and suffering a brain death of unknown origin, in 2005 Terri Schiavo's husband Michael sought to terminate efforts to feed her. Using religiously grounded arguments about a right to life, her parents and their religious and political allies objected to the decision and initiated legal action. However, a series of Florida state and federal courts ruled that because Terri Schiavo had not provided a living will, medical power of attorney, or other legal documents regarding her care, the law permitted her husband to provide or withdraw her care. Although supported by numerous state and federal political leaders who also employed religious or moral arguments, the judiciary rejected the parents' nonlegal rights claims and allowed her husband to order the removal of her feeding tube. This discursive breakdown engendered further resistance, including protests and some scattered acts of violence. However, additional litigation, proposals of constitutional amendments for the origins of life, and legislation to control abortion and life support indicate that some resisters realized that their success depended on an ability to convert their religious discourse into legal principles that might bind judges (for more details, see Miller this volume, chapter 19).

6. From the civic republican tradition, the strikers adopted a conception of fraternity and community hostile to the materialist ambitions of corporations. The concepts of fraternity and community fit, albeit somewhat uneasily, with Protestant ideas about the need to belong to a community of upright believers often at odds with man's laws. The elements of this discourse did not fit with a legalist perspective. On one hand, if the law rested on civic virtues or the faith of believers, it served moral order. However, if the law permitted the protection of the individual or group rights of corporate moral wrongdoers who threatened the health and security of the community, such as Pittston management, the law was morally offensive or corrupt. If it was not revised, it had to be resisted—even by lawbreaking (Brisbin 2002, 208–18). However, as the various acts of intimidation of Pittston managers and strikebreakers and, allegedly, explosives, assaults, and gunfire during that strike testify, public declared resistance can slip into transgressions of the law and insurrectionary actions.

16

THE SUPREME COURT AND RACE

Barbara A. Perry

Scholars who study judicial politics understand that issues of race have proven themselves to be very difficult in American society. Using a legal model, this chapter discusses how the Supreme Court has handled cases dealing with race. This chapter also examines how the Supreme Court at times has led the nation on issues of race, and how at other times the Court has instead followed the lead of the president and/or the Congress on these issues. Whenever the Supreme Court makes a decision involving issues of race, the media usually give that decision a great deal of attention. One of the most difficult racial issues today deals with the question of affirmative action. On issues of race, the Supreme Court has attempted to balance the principles of equality and justice. Thus, this chapter provides a survey of Supreme Court rulings dealing with race. It is an example of the policy outputs that the Court has created over the years. It is also an example of what happens when legal and political perspectives collide.

Issues of race have plagued American society since the founding of our country. The Founding Fathers thought they had found a compromise on the explosive issue of slavery in the new nation when they wrote the Constitution, but the bloody Civil War proved that the country had not avoided the disasters that slavery created. After the Civil War, the new Reconstruction Congress required the Southern states to ratify the Thirteenth, Fourteenth, and Fifteenth Amendments as their price of readmission to the Union. The Thirteenth Amendment abolished slavery; the Fourteenth Amendment provided various rights to individuals and restricted the rights of the states, while the Fifteenth Amendment provided for voting rights for the former slaves. The modern era of civil rights, however, did not begin until the Supreme Court ruled in *Brown v. Board of Education* (1954) that segregation was unconstitutional in public schools. After *Brown*, the Supreme Court has faced a variety of cases dealing with race issues. These difficult cases include cases on

the issue of affirmative action. The basic question in affirmative action cases is whether declaring discrimination on the basis of race to be illegal is sufficient, or whether our society should take further steps to help groups who faced historical discrimination. Because race discrimination cases have been so difficult for our nation, this chapter will provide a survey of the Supreme Court's decisions on the issue of race.

SLAVERY AND *DRED SCOTT*

The first Africans to trod American soil landed in the Jamestown settlement about a dozen years after its 1607 founding in the British colony of Virginia. The Portuguese had captured and enslaved the Africans in Angola with the intention of transporting them to what is now Mexico. Bound for Veracruz, the Portuguese vessel was set on by two pirate ships—one British, the other Dutch. They each seized twenty to thirty

231

of the black slaves. On landing in Jamestown several days apart, the pirates traded approximately twenty enslaved Africans for supplies. Thus began the sad tale of what would be called America's "peculiar institution" of slavery and its "dilemma" of race.

Almost two centuries later, slavery was so ingrained in the newly independent United States, especially in the agrarian South, that the Founding Fathers, who gathered in Philadelphia to reshape America's governing document, dared not abolish it for fear of irreparably splitting the Union. The nation would hold on to slavery, like a man holding a "wolf by the ear," as Thomas Jefferson (1905, 159) would observe, being able neither to relinquish the beast nor continue to grasp it. Although Article I, Section 9 of the new Constitution made it possible to end the "migration or importation" of "persons," after 1808, if Congress chose to do so, America's founding document also counted a slave as "three fifths" of a person (Article I, Section 2) for purposes of apportioning representatives among the states. The topic was so incendiary that the words "slave" or "slavery" did not appear in the original Constitution (see, e.g., Fisher 2005a).

Seven decades would pass before the United States Supreme Court addressed the constitutional status of black Americans; its decision in the case of *Dred Scott v. Sandford* (1857) was disastrous for all concerned. Scott was a slave who had moved with his master from the slave state of Missouri to Illinois and Wisconsin, a free state and free territory, respectively, before moving back to Missouri. His appeal to the Supreme Court requested that he be declared a free man in light of his sojourn to free soil. Chief Justice Roger B. Taney's decision for the Court rejected Scott's plea, arguing that all blacks, no matter what their status, were not citizens of the United States and could never attain citizenship. Thus, they had no right to bring law suits to court.

According to Taney, the Constitution's framers maintained that blacks "had no rights which the white man was bound to respect; and that the Negro might justly and lawfully be reduced to slavery for his benefit. He was bought and sold and treated as an ordinary article of merchandise and traffic, whenever profit could be made by it" (60 U.S. at 407). The chief justice added that Jefferson's self-evident proposition in the Declaration of Independence that "all men are created equal" did not apply to blacks. "It is too clear for dispute," wrote Taney, "that the enslaved African race were not intended to be included, and formed no part of the people who framed and adopted this declaration" (60 U.S. at 411). His opinion also rendered unconstitutional the 1820 Missouri Compromise, by which one free state would be admitted for every slave state accepted into the Union, to hold the numerical balance between states that permitted slavery and those that did not. The Taney ruling would allow slavery in all of the nation's territories (see also Abraham and Perry 2003).

THE CIVIL WAR AMENDMENTS AND JIM CROW

In the twentieth century, Chief Justice Charles Evans Hughes described the *Dred Scott* decision as the Court's "self-inflicted wound." Indeed, it precipitated the bloody Civil War (1861 to 1865) won by the antislavery Union, whose victory allowed passage of the U.S. Constitution's Thirteenth Amendment, abolishing slavery. The Fourteenth Amendment, ratified in 1868, was to secure (theoretically) civil rights for black Americans. Its Section 1 overturned the *Dred Scott* decision by guaranteeing national and state citizenship to all Americans. It continued, "No state shall make or enforce any law which shall abridge the privileges or immunities of citizens of the United States; nor shall any state deprive any person of life, liberty, or property, without due process of law; nor deny to any person within its jurisdiction the equal protection of the laws."

The Fifteenth Amendment, ratified in 1870, was intended to guarantee the franchise to black men (not until the Nineteenth Amendment, ratified in 1920, would all women have the right to vote; see also Baer this volume, chapter 17). Between 1866 and 1875, Congress passed a handful of civil rights acts to enforce the Thirteen, Fourteenth, and Fifteenth Amendments and to authorize the federal government's imposition of severe penalties for violations of these rights. During Reconstruction, a period of a dozen years after the Civil War when Union troops continued to occupy the states of the defeated Confederacy, blacks experienced a taste of political freedom. Twenty-two blacks were elected to the U.S. House of Representatives, and two black senators represented Mississippi. Yet, when Reconstruction ended, the combination of a recalcitrant South and a Supreme Court unwilling to follow the intentions of those who framed the Civil War Amendments and the civil rights legislation that followed, meant that blacks were still without genuine civil rights as the twentieth century dawned (see Fisher 2005a). By 1910 all of the former Confederate states had effectively disenfranchised blacks via constitutional amendments or statutes implementing "white primaries" or "grandfather clauses" (see, e.g., Klarman 2004).

A cramped and narrow, indeed seemingly contradictory, reading of the Fourteenth Amendment by the Supreme Court in 1873 stunted Section 1's clear purpose. Instead of affirming the rights of national and state citizens, the Court, in a 5 to 4 ruling known as the *Slaughter-House Cases* (1872) determined that "there is a citizenship of the United States, and a citizenship of the state, which are distinct from each other; and which depend upon different characteristics or circumstances in the individual" (83 U.S. at 74). Section 1's privileges or immunities clause did not protect the rights of state citizenship but only of federal citizenship, argued the Court. Under that interpretation, the clause became a meaningless guarantee for newly freed blacks in protecting them from discrimination by state governments.

The Supreme Court's ruling in the *Civil Rights Cases* (1883) narrowed black rights further by invalidating the Civil Rights Act of 1875's prohibition on racial discrimination by private individuals in transportation, inns, and theaters. The Court argued that Congress had no authority under the Thirteenth or Fourteenth Amendments to pass the 1875 Act. The Fourteenth Amendment was confined to *state* action, not *private* behavior, ruled a majority of the justices. Writing in dissent, Justice John Marshall Harlan contended that the Fourteenth Amendment empowered Congress to enact appropriate legislation to protect blacks against deprivation of their civil rights on the basis of race by individuals (see, e.g., Fisher 2005a).

Harlan would find himself in dissent again when the high tribunal addressed the Fourteenth Amendment's

equal protection clause in the case of *Plessy v. Ferguson* (1896). Southern states had implemented so-called Jim Crow laws to separate whites and blacks in public accommodations, from railcars (at issue in *Plessy*) to commercial establishments. In the twentieth century, such segregation laws banned blacks from restaurants, hotels, and pools, and would create racially separate public schools, drinking fountains, restrooms, and seating in movie theaters. An 1890 Louisiana law required separate railway coaches for whites and blacks. Black citizens organized to challenge the law, selecting Homer Plessy, who was only one-eighth black, to ride in the "whites only" rail car. The rail conductor, who knew of Plessy's "octoroon" status, asked him to move to the "colored only" coach. When he refused to do so, a detective arrested him, and he was charged with violating the Jim Crow Car Act of 1890 (see, e.g., Klarman 2004).

In a seven to one vote the U.S. Supreme Court ruled that the Louisiana law did not conflict with the Fourteenth Amendment's equal protection clause because statutes requiring the separation of the races did not imply the inferiority of either race and had been recognized as an exercise of police power (the state's authority to protect the health, safety, welfare, and morals of the people). Such laws did not deprive blacks of equal protection of the laws, the Court asserted, provided they were furnished accommodations equal to those for whites. Justice Henry Brown concluded that if blacks felt inferior as a result of the segregation policy that was a social issue, not a legal one. Thus, the "separate but equal" doctrine became the basic precedent for sustaining and justifying similar legislation.

In his famous lone dissent, Justice John Marshall Harlan stated that Louisiana was regulating the use of a public highway by citizens of the United States solely on the basis of race. This law was in conflict with both the spirit and the letter of the Constitution, which Harlan eloquently noted when he wrote, "In view of the Constitution, in the eye of the law, there is in this country no superior, dominant, ruling class of citizens. There is no caste here. Our Constitution is color-blind, and neither knows nor tolerates classes among citizens. In respect of civil rights, all citizens are equal before the law" (163 U.S. at 559).

As the Library of Congress noted in its study of African American history, black civil rights reached their "nadir" in the period between the end of Reconstruction and World War I (1914 to 1918) because most of the victories achieved under the Civil War Amendments and civil rights legislation had vanished. Even worse, instances of violence against black Americans, including brutal lynchings, soared in the early twentieth century. The establishment of the National Association for the Advancement of Colored People (NAACP) and the National Urban League (NUL), both committed to equal rights for blacks, offered some hope that one day the United States' version of apartheid would end (see also Klarman 2004).

SCHOOL DESEGREGATION

The politically moderate NAACP adopted a policy of carrying their noble fight to the nation's courts. Starting in the 1930s, it successfully began to chip away at the "separate but equal" doctrine from *Plessy* as applied to graduate and professional schools. The NAACP deliberately chose the litigation strategy of starting with graduate and professional schools, before tackling state-imposed segregation in primary and secondary schools, for several reasons. Graduate and professional schools were a much narrower target, their students were adults and their parents were less likely to oppose racial mixing at this level, and it would be harder for states to provide equal facilities in higher education and professional schools (see, e.g., Cushman and Urofsky 2004).

The first litigation to arrive at the Supreme Court's doorstep, *Missouri ex rel. Gaines v. Canada* (1938), pitted Lloyd Gaines, a black Missouri resident, against the law school at his state's flagship university. He was qualified for admission to the University of Missouri Law School on every count except race. S. W. Canada, the school's registrar, rejected Gaines's application on the grounds that the state's law required blacks and whites to be educated "separately but equally." Mr. Canada informed Gaines that the state would pay for his law school education at an adjacent state (Kansas, Nebraska, Iowa, or Illinois) that accepted blacks in their unsegregated institutions. Gaines rejected the

offer, however, noting that he had a right to attend law school and join the legal profession in his home state where he was a taxpaying citizen.

With the NAACP taking his case all the way to the highest court in the land, Gaines's appeal prompted a majority of the Supreme Court to side with his view that Missouri had denied him equal protection of the laws under the Fourteenth Amendment. Explicitly reaffirming the separate but equal doctrine, however, Chief Justice Hughes wrote for the majority that Missouri could have fulfilled the amendment's guarantee "by furnishing equal facilities in separate schools" for blacks (see, e.g., Abraham and Perry 2003).

It took twelve more years, including America's involvement in World War II (1941 to 1945), during which blacks still had to serve their country in segregated military units and were denied opportunities for advancement through the ranks, before the next segregation cases in higher education reached the high court. In neither *Sweatt v. Painter* (1950) nor *McLaurin v. Oklahoma* (1950) did the justices overturn the separate but equal doctrine, but by unanimous votes the Court made it impossible to implement this doctrine at the university level.

Sweatt, a Houston mail carrier, wanted to attend law school at the University of Texas (UT), not the separate law school established by the Lone Star State in the wake of the *Gaines* decision. He argued that the Texas State University for Negroes (TSUN) was "inferior" to Texas's flagship campus, and the Supreme Court agreed. The former's physical facilities, especially size of the library and its number of volumes, could not possibly match UT's offerings. Chief Justice Fred Vinson's majority opinion also observed that the intangible elements of a law school's quality ("reputation of the faculty, experience of the administration, position and influence of the alumni, standing in the community, tradition and prestige") were clearly unequal between UT and TSUN. Still, the Court did not explicitly overturn the separate but equal doctrine.

At the University of Oklahoma, where McLaurin's case originated, the state allowed qualified blacks to attend but only if they were kept segregated from the white students. McLaurin, who was pursuing a doctorate in education, had to sit in separate sections of the classroom, library, and dining hall. Justice Vinson declared such an arrangement unequal and unconstitutional (see, e.g., Klarman 2004).

The nation's high tribunal had actually previewed its approach to the higher education decisions in a series of cases from 1941 to 1950, where it began whittling away at Jim Crow segregation in interstate rail travel. A majority of the justices found that separate railcars for blacks were simply inferior to those for white passengers. Incrementally, the Supreme Court was dismantling the mechanisms of *de jure* (by law) segregation.

The high tribunal's landmark rulings on primary and secondary schools, however, precipitated a sea change in American civil rights history. One constitutional scholar, Professor Alpheus Mason of Princeton, declared, "On May 17, 1954, the Court initiated the greatest social revolution of this generation." Banner headlines on that date announced "School Segregation Banned in Nation" (*The Washington Post*) and "High Court Bans School Segregation" (*The New York Times*). With Thurgood Marshall leading the team of NAACP lawyers in the organization's Legal Defense and Educational Fund, as he had in *Sweatt* and *McLaurin*, the Supreme Court heard appeals in cases from Kansas, South Carolina, Virginia, and Delaware. The combined litigation, known by the parties in the Kansas case (*Brown v. Board of Education of Topeka* 1954), challenged state-mandated segregation in public schools as a violation of the Fourteenth Amendment's equal protection clause, even if the black schools were equal to the white schools in physical facilities, programs, teacher salaries, and other measurable attributes (see, e.g., Wilkinson 1979).

Chief Justice Earl Warren, barely on the high court a year, and never having served as a judge previously, determined that he should write the opinion himself and make it brief and comprehensible enough to be read by Americans in their daily newspapers. The chief had worked mightily to mold a unanimous bench, believing that the nation would be more accepting of a united front on this controversial issue. He began with the premise that education "is the very foundation of good citizenship" (347 U.S. at 492). Warren then answered the constitutional question directly—"segregation of children in public schools solely on the basis of race," even if the schools are equal, "deprive[s] the children

of the minority group of equal educational opportunity" (347 U.S. at 494). Citing social science research findings that segregation produces a "sense of inferiority" in black children, Warren concluded, "[I]n the field of public education the doctrine of 'separate but equal' has no place. Separate educational facilities are inherently unequal....The plaintiffs are...deprived of the equal protection of the laws guaranteed by the Fourteenth Amendment" (347 U.S. at 495).

In light of the profound change the Court would be ordering for southern mores, Warren postponed an enforcement ruling until the next year, after gathering more briefs and hearing another argument in what would become *Brown v. Board II* (1955). In May 1955 the justices released a unanimous ruling requiring districts with schools segregated by law to establish racially nondiscriminatory policies for assignment of students to primary and secondary schools. Federal district courts were to oversee the dismantling of *de jure* school desegregation. Borrowing a timing concept from equity law, included in an Oliver Wendell Holmes 1911 opinion, the Court ordered the transition to take place "with all deliberate speed." The district court judges who had to implement the order literally found their lives on the line as the violent reaction in the South included death threats (see, e.g., Cushman and Urofsky 2004).

"Massive resistance" was the South's response to the U.S. Supreme Court's edicts (see also Brisbin this volume, chapter 15). In the decade following *Brown II*, southern states enacted two hundred segregation statutes. Virginia's Prince Edward County, in the heart of central Virginia, simply closed its public schools, rather than integrate them. Private academies admitted only white students, while Prince Edward's black children were left for years without access to education. (At the dawn of the twenty-first century, the Old Dominion compensated black adults from Prince Edward County by offering them scholarships to further their education.)

BUSING

The goals of *Brown* I and II were still unrealized as the 1970s dawned, and the Supreme Court switched emphasis from desegregation to integration by means of busing, which it ordered in *Swann v. Charlotte-Mecklenburg Board of Education* (1971). It marked one of the last times the Court would reach a unanimous ruling in a race case. The metropolitan Charlotte, North Carolina school system had long operated two sets of schools—one for whites and one for blacks. A ruling by the U.S. District Court for Western North Carolina in 1965, however, ordered the Charlotte school district to dismantle its segregated system. By 1969 about one-third of the black students were attending previously all-white schools. The remaining two-thirds were still in all-black schools. The district court accepted a plan from its expert witness, an education professor, who advocated applying racial percentages, pairing schools, redrawing school districts, and using busing to achieve system-wide integration mandated by the *Brown* decisions (see, e.g., Wilkinson 1979).

The school board thought the plan was too broad. White and black parents opposed to busing argued that the *Brown* rulings actually required color-blind school assignments. They asserted, "We plead the same rights here that the plaintiffs pleaded in *Brown*." The question before the Supreme Court in *Swann* was whether the district court's plan for integrating Charlotte schools violated the Fourteenth Amendment's Equal Protection Clause. Writing for a 9 to 0 Court, Chief Justice Warren Burger, whose opinion Justice William Brennan heavily influenced, upheld all elements of the district court's integration plan—racial quotas, pairing of schools, redrawing school districts, and busing. The goal of such policies was to eliminate "all vestiges of state-imposed segregation....Desegregation plans cannot be limited to the walk-in school" (402 U.S. at 15, 30). The high tribunal extended the potent role of federal trial court judges in school integration by giving them the authority to use racial quotas in pairing schools.

Although the *Swann* ruling applied to southern-style *de jure* segregation (i.e., segregation by law), its use in other parts of the country, where *de facto* segregation (i.e., segregation by fact) existed as a result of socioeconomic/housing patterns, was unclear. Litigation in reaction to court-ordered busing in nonsouthern cities like Denver, Detroit, and Boston arrived at the Supreme Court's doorstep as the 1970s

progressed. In the Denver case, the justices found that intentional racial segregation (whatever its cause) in part of a school district could require the entire district to fall under a busing order. Detroit's situation, which involved a primarily black school district covering the urban area, and a separate white district serving suburban schools, could not sustain a busing edict if the suburban schools were not guilty of unlawful segregation. In Boston the reaction turned violent in when the U.S. district court ordered white children bused from the southern part of the city, made up of working-class Irish, to black neighborhoods. The nation's high court rejected appeals in the Boston case, thus upholding the lower court's orders. Even Senator Edward Kennedy (D.–Mass.), part of the iconic Irish-Catholic clan that South Boston had once revered, was jeered and jostled as he tried to speak in favor of busing at a public rally (see, e.g., Abraham and Perry 2003).

CIVIL RIGHTS AND VOTING RIGHTS

In the realms of employment, public accommodations, and voting, the Supreme Court stamped its approval on the president's and Congress's progressive actions in favor of civil rights for racial and ethnic minorities. In the wake of President John F. Kennedy's November 22, 1963 assassination, the new president, Lyndon Johnson, addressed the Congress with a fervent pledge to pursue the slain chief executive's policies, especially on civil rights. "[N]o memorial or oration or eulogy could more eloquently honor President Kennedy's memory than the earliest possible passage of the civil rights bill for which he fought so long. We have talked long enough about equal rights in this country. We have talked for one hundred years or more. It is time now to write the next chapter and write it in the books of law."

A bill, even more comprehensive than the one the Kennedy administration had proposed, and now supported by the Johnson administration, passed the House of Representatives relatively easily (290 to 130), but an eighty-two day filibuster by southern senators delayed the bill's ultimate passage (73 to 27) through the upper house. A proud Lyndon Johnson, surrounded by the bill's supporters, signed the 1964

Civil Rights Act into law at a White House ceremony on July 2. The act provided for, among other things, the extension of the Civil Rights Commission's tenure; the proscription of employment discrimination on the basis of race, color, sex (a last-minute addition), religion, or national origin; the prohibition of racial discrimination by voting registrars; judicial procedure to desegregate state and local government facilities; the exclusion of federal funding for public or private programs that discriminated on the basis of race, color, or national origin; and the proscription of race, color, or national origin discrimination in public accommodations that are linked to interstate commerce.

As black protests continued, with more brutal reactions from southern law enforcement, President Johnson submitted a bill to Congress that would finally end the unconstitutional effort of those who would deny blacks the right to vote in this country. Congress enacted the Voting Rights Act of 1965 and provided the legal mechanisms for overturning all legal roadblocks to black exercise of the franchise (see, e.g., Fisher 2005a).

Again, the recalcitrant South rejected the federal government's power to change its mores. The segregated Heart of Atlanta Motel brought suit immediately after passage of the 1964 Civil Rights Act, arguing that the law exceeded Congress's interstate commerce power, under which it had passed the landmark legislation. The Court was unpersuaded and voted unanimously to uphold the landmark law, citing the fact that the motel conceded its clientele moved in interstate commerce. Moreover, Justice Tom Clark's opinion for the Court noted that Congress had determined that racial segregation in public accommodations placed a heavy burden on interstate commerce, not to mention those black citizens moving through its channels (*Heart of Atlanta Motel v. U.S.* 1964). When the 1965 Voting Rights Act likewise was challenged in the very year it was enacted, the Supreme Court once again bolstered the other two branches of the federal government by upholding the law 8 to 1 in *South Carolina v. Katzenbach* (1966).

The victories represented by the Civil Rights Act of 1964 and the Voting Rights Act of 1965 were by no means the end of the movement to ensure full participation in American society for minorities and women.

The summers of 1965 and 1966 witnessed more racial violence, especially in the streets of America's large cities with populous black ghettos, where deadly and destructive rioting occurred. Although President Johnson expressed pride at the legislative progress made in establishing the legal framework for equal opportunity in employment, education, and voting, he declared that "freedom is not enough. You do not wipe away the scars of a century by saying":

> "Now you are free to go where you want, and do as you desire."... You do not take a person who for years has been hobbled by chains and liberate him, bring him up to the staring line of a race and then say, "You are free to compete with all the others," and still justly believe you have been completely fair. All our citizens must have the ability to walk through the gates. This is the next and more profound stage of the battle for civil rights (quoted in B. A. Perry 2007, 14).

To reach this next stage, the 1964 Civil Rights Act's Equal Employment Opportunity Commission began to define the kind of additional help minorities should expect from private business in terms of "affirmative action," which would mean "aggressive recruitment" and training of minorities. "We must go out looking for potential employees," the EEOC instructed private businesses, "let them know they are now welcome in places where doors were once closed...and give them special training so that they may qualify." In the wake of a deadly 1965 race riot in the Watts neighborhood of Los Angeles, President Johnson issued Executive Order 11246, which took additional steps to enforce equal opportunity in employment. It established the Office of Federal Contract Compliance (OFCC) and ordered federal contractors to take "reasonable efforts within a reasonable time" to comply with federal requirements of "affirmative action" in recruitment and employment to ensure that applicants and employees were treated, "without regard to their race, creed, color, or national origin" (quoted in B. A. Perry 2007, 15). When such factors became the focus, measurement entered the picture. By what criteria could the government determine that contractors were *not* treating employees equally? An easy statistical measure, advocated by some civil rights leaders, would compare the percentage of minorities on a contractor's payroll with the percentage in the local population. Yet, if employers hired workers on the basis of their race, color, creed, or national origin to meet a population percentage, the company would be in direct violation of Title VII's proscription on the use of such factors in employment. A new dilemma involving race had arrived—how could the United States end its historic racism through color-blind policies that, in effect, prompted color-conscious programs?

In 1967 President Johnson performed a highly symbolic act (with substantive results) for the civil rights movement by nominating the first African American to the nation's highest court. Thurgood Marshall, a veteran leader of successful civil rights litigation, including *Brown v. Board of Education*, which he argued at the Supreme Court, had been appointed by President Kennedy to the U.S. Court of Appeals for the Second Circuit in 1961. When Justice Tom Clark announced his retirement from the Supreme Court after his son Ramsey became attorney general in the Johnson cabinet, LBJ seized the opportunity to make history. On June 13, 1967, Johnson named Marshall to the nation's highest court, declaring, "He is the best qualified by training and by very valuable service to the country. I believe it is the right thing to do, the right time to do it, and the right man and the right place" (quoted in H. W. Perry 1991, 100).

AFFIRMATIVE ACTION

From his new position on the nation's highest court, Justice Marshall would witness the progeny of his civil rights litigation arrive at the tribunal's threshold. The first affirmative action case the U.S. Supreme Court considered began at the University of Washington Law School, which had denied admission to Marco DeFunis, a white male, despite the fact that his entrance exam scores were higher than those of some minorities the law school admitted (*DeFunis v. Odegaard* 1974). DeFunis brought suit in a Washington trial court, arguing that the law school's admission's committee violated his Fourteenth Amendment guarantee of equal protection by using different criteria and procedures for nonminority applicants. The trial court

ruled in his favor and ordered his admittance to the law school. On appeal, the Washington Supreme Court overturned the trial court's judgment, holding that the law school's policy was constitutional. By the time DeFunis's appeal made its way to the nation's highest tribunal for consideration, he was in his third and final year at the University of Washington. Because of that fact, the high court ruled in 1974 that the case was moot and refused to decide the constitutional question posed by DeFunis's appeal. Who could blame the five justices who voted to moot the case for wanting to buy more time to decide one of the twentieth century's most vexatious constitutional questions? They knew that soon enough the issue would again confront them.

Indeed it would. Just four years later the U.S. Supreme Court issued its first substantive ruling on affirmative action, in another case that arrived from academe and also involved a professional school (*Regents of the University of California v. Bakke* 1978). The University of California at Davis Medical School, founded in 1968, did not discriminate against minorities. Yet its first class of fifty students had no blacks, Mexican Americans, or American Indians. Over the next two years, the faculty developed an affirmative action plan that, starting in 1971, doubled the size of the entering class (to 100), and set aside sixteen of the positions for "disadvantaged" applicants to be chosen by a special admissions committee. In practice, "disadvantaged" meant minorities. Students accepted under the special program for the reserved sixteen seats had lower grade-point averages and Medical College Admissions Test (MCAT) scores than those students who competed for the eighty-four remaining positions in the entering class.

Allan Bakke, a white male, applied to the UC-Davis Medical School in 1973 and 1974; each time the school rejected him, as did the other eleven schools to which he applied. Despite having earned an undergraduate degree from the University of Minnesota in mechanical engineering (with just under an A average), serving as a marine captain in Vietnam, receiving a master's degree in engineering from Stanford University, and working as an aerospace engineer at NASA, Bakke decided in mid-career that he really wanted to be a doctor. He took biology and chemistry courses required for medical school admission while he continued to work full time and volunteered in a hospital emergency room. His overall GPA was 3.51, and his MCAT score placed him in the ninetieth percentile. Not only were his statistics significantly higher than the minority students accepted under the special program, he even outscored the average GPA and MCAT rank of the students accepted via the regular admissions process.

Bakke believed that the affirmative action program at UC-Davis had blocked his admittance to the medical school, which was his first choice because of its proximity to his home. Before a California state trial court, his lawyer contended that UCD unlawfully discriminated against him on the basis of his race when it prevented him from competing for the sixteen reserved seats and by operating a two-track admissions system. According to Bakke's position, the medical school's action violated the U.S. Constitution's Fourteenth Amendment's equal protection clause, a similar provision in the California constitution, and the 1964 Civil Rights Act's Title VI, which provides, "No person in the United States shall, on the ground of race, color, or national origin, be excluded from participation in, be denied the benefits of, or be subjected to discrimination under any program or activity receiving Federal financial assistance." The California trial court ruled that the medical school's admissions program violated the U.S. Constitution by giving preference to minority students; the California Supreme Court affirmed and ordered Bakke's admission. Without admitting him, the University of California at Davis, afraid that all of its affirmative action programs would be invalidated, appealed the California Supreme Court's decision to the U.S. Supreme Court. The high tribunal accepted the case, *Regents of the University of California v. Bakke*, and heard a two-hour oral argument on it in October 1977.

After seven months of reviewing the case record and an unprecedented number of *amici curiae* briefs (fifty-eight) submitted by 150 interested parties, the Court finally handed down its decision in late June 1978. Their final product encompassed seven different opinions that covered 154 pages. In effect, the justices were split four to one to four. On each issue raised by the case, the vote was five to four,

with centrist Justice Lewis F. Powell, Jr., casting the swing vote between the liberals in this case (Justices William Brennan, Thurgood Marshall, Byron White, and Harry Blackmun) and the conservatives (Justices Stewart, Rehnquist, and Stevens, and Chief Justice Warren Burger). Justice Powell's controlling opinion applied "strict scrutiny" to the UC-Davis Medical School's program. On a sliding scale of equal protection clause analysis, the Court applies strict scrutiny to a contested government policy when it classifies based on race, ethnicity, or alienage or involves voting or interstate travel. In this highest category of judicial examination, the public entity using the "suspect classifications," or impacting "fundamental rights," must prove a "compelling state interest" and demonstrate a "narrow tailoring" of the policy and an "exact fit" between the classifications and the state interest. Using strict scrutiny, Powell ruled for himself and the four conservatives that U.C. Davis' rigid quota of sixteen seats for minority students was invalid for creating an unconstitutional, broadly tailored, two-track admissions process on the basis of race and ethnicity. The quota resulted in a simple mathematical inequality; minorities could compete for all 100 seats in the entering medical school class, but whites could vie for only the remaining eighty-four, after the sixteen quota seats were filled with minorities.

Nevertheless, Powell, the courtly Virginian, who had led the Richmond school board during desegregation, argued that, "the interest of diversity is compelling in the context of a university's admission programs [at the undergraduate, graduate, and professional levels]" (438 U.S. at 314). Moreover, a narrowly tailored plan for admitting minorities could pass constitutional muster. Powell cited Harvard's admissions plan as a constitutional example in which the university used race and ethnicity as a "plus" (along with other personal attributes like "geographic origin or a life spent on a farm") for its undergraduate admissions decisions but did not segregate a minority applicant from comparison with other applicants or use quotas for admitting minorities. Harvard had provided its plan to the Court in an *amicus* brief, and Powell appended the plan to his opinion.

The U.S. Supreme Court, however, did not sustain Powell's approach to affirmative action—one that eschews strict numerical quotas—in two *employ-ment* cases that came before the tribunal in the two years after *Bakke*. The case of *United Steelworkers of America v. Weber* (1979) arose when yet another white male, Brian Weber, argued that he had been the victim of unconstitutional reverse discrimination. Kaiser Aluminum and Chemical Corporation and the United Steelworkers of America union entered into what they termed a "voluntary" and "temporary" affirmative action plan to try to boost the number of higher-paid black craftsmen at the Kaiser plant in Gramercy, Louisiana. At least half of the thirteen on-the-job training positions were reserved for blacks. Weber, who was passed over for one of the coveted training jobs, filed suit in federal district court, claiming a violation of Title VII of the 1964 Civil Rights Act, which explicitly bans racial discrimination in employment and categorically denies that the title requires racial preferences be used to correct "an imbalance which may exist." Moreover, debates on the Senate floor in 1964 also made crystal clear that Title VII in no way was intended to result in racial preferences or quotas in employment decisions.

Yet neither Weber nor the lower tribunals reckoned on Justice William J. Brennan, Jr.'s, legal interpretation once the case arrived at the nation's highest court. With only seven justices sitting in the case (Powell and Stevens did not participate), Brennan produced a stunning five to two holding for the United Steelworkers' affirmative action plan. Joined by Justices Marshall, White, Stewart, and Blackmun, he conceded that the two courts below had indeed read the *letter* of the law correctly. However, Title VII's *spirit* compelled a different result. If the 1964 Congress's concern had been, as Brennan put it, for "the plight of the Negro in our economy," then it would be "ironic indeed" if Title VII would be used to prohibit, "all voluntary private, race-conscious efforts to abolish traditional patterns" of discrimination.

In 1980 the U.S. Supreme Court faced its third challenge to affirmative action in as many years. A provision of the Public Works Employment Act of 1977 (PWEA) required that 10 percent of the federal funds expended for local public works projects must be used to procure services or supplies from minority business enterprises (MBEs, defined in the statute

as companies in which blacks, Hispanics, Orientals, American Indians, Eskimos, or Aleuts controlled at least a 50 percent interest). In *Fullilove v. Klutznick* (1980), associations of construction contractors and subcontractors challenged the 10 percent set-aside provision as invalid under the equal protection component of the Fifth Amendment's due process clause and Title VI of the 1964 Civil Rights Act, proscribing racial discrimination in any program receiving federal financial assistance. The contractors had to raise their constitutional question under the Fifth Amendment because the *federal* government had established the program at issue; the Fourteenth Amendment only applies to *state* or *local* governments and their entities.

A six-justice majority affirmed the federal court of appeals ruling that the set-aside provision did *not* violate the Fifth Amendment or Title VI of the Civil Rights Act. As in *Bakke*, the Court was badly fractured, producing six opinions. No opinion garnered a majority, but Chief Justice Burger's plurality opinion, joined by Justices White and Powell, announced the Court's judgment. He argued that the PWEA's objective was to ensure that the letting of federal government contracts for public works projects would not result in perpetuating discrimination that had historically impaired or foreclosed access by minority businesses to public funds. The PWEA had appropriated $4 billion for public works projects. Burger declared that such an objective was within the spending power of Congress (Art. I, §8, cl. 1). As to the means Congress employed (the 10 percent set-aside) to meet its objective, the chief justice validated the provision's "narrowly tailored" and "temporary" use of racial and ethnic criteria. (In fact, the policy became permanent in 1987 and added "women" to the list of "minority business enterprises" for which set-asides would apply. See Baer this volume, chapter 17.)

In 1984 the Supreme Court faced a new set of facts in hiring practices. This case, *Firefighters Local Union #1784 v. Stotts* (1984), sprang from a 1980 court-approved affirmative action plan for the firefighters of Memphis, Tennessee. It required that at least 50 percent of all new employees be black until at least 40 percent of the department was African American. Prior to the affirmative action plan, Memphis had increased the number of its black firefighters from

4 percent to 11.5 percent of the department. When a budget crisis occurred in 1981, the city announced that it would follow a traditional "last-hired-first-fired" policy negotiated with the firefighters' union. The policy laid off black firefighters who had less seniority than their white counterparts. A federal district court denied the city's right to fire the new black firefighters, and, as a result, three more senior whites lost their jobs to three recently hired blacks. Both the city of Memphis and the firefighters' union appealed the case to the U.S. Supreme Court. This time the white males won. Coincidentally, it was Justice White who wrote the opinion for the six to three Court, ruling that Title VII of the 1964 Civil Rights Act clearly "protects bona fide seniority systems," unless they are intentionally discriminatory or minorities can prove that they were the victims of individual employment discrimination.

In two more affirmative action cases decided by the Supreme Court in 1986, *Firefighters v. Cleveland* (1986) and *Sheet Metal Workers v. EEOC* (1986), narrow majorities upheld Cleveland's promotion of one minority for every white firefighter promoted and a federal court's order requiring a New York sheet metal workers' union to meet a specific minority goal of 29.23 percent. Led by Justice Brennan, in direct opposition to the Reagan administration's stance, the Court asserted that the 1964 Civil Rights Act's Title VII did not apply remedies solely to actual victims of unlawful discrimination. Rather, quotas could be used to bolster minority-group representation in workforces. Justice Brennan also prevailed during the Supreme Court's next term in the 1987 decision, *United States v. Paradise* (1987), upholding strict racial promotion quotas to overcome "long-term, open and pervasive discrimination."

One month after *Paradise*, yet another affirmative action decision, this one with a gender twist, came down from the high tribunal. *Johnson v. Transportation Agency, Santa Clara County* (1987) validated the California agency's job promotion preferences for women (see also Baer this volume, chapter 17). Paul Johnson, a white male, had worked for the Transportation Agency in Santa Clara thirteen years and had scored two points higher than the successful applicant, Diane Joyce, for the position of road dispatcher—a job no women had ever held. By a vote

of six to three, the Brennan-led majority ruled that, even without any evidence that a particular employer had discriminated against women or minorities, that same employer could use race and *gender* preferences in hiring and promotions to bring its workforce into line with the local population or labor market.

Justice Anthony Kennedy joined the Court in the middle of its 1987 to 1988 term, replacing Justice Powell's swing vote that had been particularly crucial in affirmative action cases. By the tribunal's next session, Kennedy was already making his presence felt in affirmative action cases by voting on the opposite side from his predecessor Justice Powell. In early 1989 Kennedy voted with a six to three majority, led by Justice O'Connor, invalidating in the case *City of Richmond v. J. A. Croson Co.* (1989) a local set-aside law in Virginia's capital that channeled 30 percent of public-works funds to minority-owned construction companies.

At the end of the term in June 1989, a quintet of employment cases also reversed, or chipped away, elements of the Court's previous jurisprudence, with O'Connor in the majority. The *Wards Cove Packing Co. v. Atonio* (1989) decision ruled five to four that a statistical disparity between an employer's workforce and the community's racial composition did not prove discrimination. Overturning a 1971 precedent (*Griggs v. Duke Power Co.* 1971), *Wards Cove* shifted the burden of proving discriminatory effects of employment policies from employers to employees. In another five to four ruling, *Martin v. Wilks* (1989), the Supreme Court determined that white workers, alleging reverse discrimination from court-approved affirmative action settlements (known as consent decrees), could challenge them even if they took no part in the original litigation. A third five-justice majority ruled in *Lorance v. AT&T Technologies* (1989) that lawsuits claiming that seniority systems are discriminatory must be filed within 300 days of their adoption. A five to four judgment by the high Court in *Jett v. Dallas Independent School District* (1989) limited damage suits against state and local government for racial discrimination to the Civil Rights Act of 1871. Finally, Justice Kennedy wrote for a unanimous Supreme Court in *Patterson v. McLean Credit Union* (1989) that the Civil Rights Act of 1866 could not be used for claims of on-the-job discrimination in the private sector, though it could still be used for such claims at the initial hiring stage.

Just when it appeared that the high tribunal had turned firmly, if by narrow majorities, against affirmative action, it approved in the *Metro Broadcasting, Inc. v. Federal Communications Commission* (1990) a two-pronged policy promoting minority ownership of the airwaves. During the Carter administration, the FCC promulgated a policy that favored minority-owned broadcasting companies in bids for new licenses and created a limited category of existing radio and television broadcast stations that could be transferred only to minority-controlled firms. Once more, Justice Brennan, by then eighty-four years of age, proved why he was fond of telling his new law clerks each term that the most important word at the Court was "five," because that many votes could carry the day in any case. He had persuaded Justice White to join the majority. Brennan's five to four majority opinion in *Metro* asserted, "Benign race conscious measures mandated by Congress—even if those measures are not 'remedial' in the sense of being designed to compensate victims of past governmental or societal discrimination—are constitutionally permissible" (497 U.S. at 551).

Congress responded swiftly to the 1989 quintet of employment decisions in which the Supreme Court reached conservative outcomes, including shifting the burden in employment discrimination cases from the employer to the employee. This new statute became know as the Civil Rights Restoration Act of 1991. The legislation amended Title VII of the 1964 Civil Rights Act to allow, in addition to racial and ethnic minorities, religious minorities, the disabled, and women to bring suit against their employers for discrimination or sexual harassment, and to collect back pay and punitive damages if the jury found in their favor. After vigorous debates, particularly over the quota issue, Congress passed the Civil Rights Act of 1991. President George H.W. Bush then signed it into law, when polls clearly showed that businesses continued to support affirmative action goals, if not rigid quotas, for hiring and promotion of minorities and women. The Supreme Court decided eight to one in 1993, however, that the new legislation did not apply to cases pending when Congress passed it (see Fisher 2005a).

With four new justices in place by the 1994–1995 term, including conservative Clarence Thomas in Thurgood Marshall's seat, the high Court once again accepted an affirmative action case on review after a several-year hiatus. In *Adarand v. Peña* (1995), a case challenging federal set-aside programs for minority-business enterprises, Justice O'Connor wrote for the five to four majority that such racial classifications could survive strict scrutiny only if the government (federal, state, or local) could prove a compelling state interest for them and narrowly tailor them to meet a goal of compensating for a specific instance of discrimination. She declared that a general policy of "racial diversity" in this context was not compelling. Her opinion also explicitly overturned the *Metro Broadcasting* precedent and declared *Fullilove* to be no longer controlling. The Court remanded the case to the Tenth U.S. Circuit Court of Appeals to apply the new precedent. Justice O'Connor's majority opinion foreshadowed the key role she would play in the landmark affirmative action cases from the University of Michigan that the U.S. Supreme Court would decide in 2003.

The University of Michigan decisions resulted from litigation brought by two white women, Jennifer Gratz and Barbara Grutter. The University of Michigan undergraduate college had denied Gratz admission, although it accepted certain "underrepresented" minorities (African Americans, Hispanics, and Native Americans), who had lower GPAs and board scores and fewer extracurricular activities. As a result of Gratz's litigation, asserting that the UM policy of evaluating white and some minority applicants under different grids violated the equal protection clause, the university jettisoned the grids and substituted a point system. Underrepresented minorities would now receive an automatic 20-point bonus in the 150-point system. Concurrently, Grutter sued the UM Law School for its affirmative action program that considered race or ethnicity (of the same three underrepresented minorities as the undergraduate college) as a "plus" factor for admissions considerations. Like Gratz, Grutter (with higher grades and test scores than some admitted minorities) had been denied admission under a system that she argued violated the Fourteenth Amendment.

On appeal, the U.S. Supreme Court found six to three in Gratz's favor that the twenty-point bonus for specific minorities was not narrowly tailored to meet the requirements of the tribunal's "strict scrutiny" equal protection analysis (*Gratz v. Bollinger* 2003). Under the same analysis, however, the justices ruled five to four, with Justice O'Connor leading the way, that racial and ethnic diversity is a "compelling state interest" and that the law school plan, following Justice Powell's "plus" factor reasoning in *Bakke*, was constitutional (*Grutter v. Bollinger* 2003). Grutter lost and Gratz won—but the decisions produced a mixed verdict for affirmative action policies in higher education. The Court sanctioned affirmative action won as a means of diversifying student enrollment but only if it was narrowly tailored, via a holistic review of applicants, to meet that compelling state interest. Yet the Michigan Law School's victory was short-lived. Just three years later, in the November 2006 election, 58 percent of voters in the state of Michigan approved a ballot measure to ban state use of affirmative action in employment, education, and contracts. Gratz led the effort, and now her victory was complete. "*Grutter* is history [in Michigan]," declared Ward Connerly, an African American opponent of affirmative action who similarly fostered successful ballot initiatives against the policy in his home state of California and the state of Washington.

DESEGREGATION REVISITED AND GERRYMANDERING

Both Connerly and Gratz were on hand at the High Court just one month after their Michigan ballot-box victory to see the justices argue whether local school districts in Seattle, Washington, and Louisville, Kentucky, could voluntarily use race as a criterion in student assignment to keep public schools integrated (*Parents Involved in Community Schools v. Seattle School District No. 1* (2007)). With O'Connor retired from the bench, and conservative Bush appointee Samuel Alito in her place, the oral argument had a different tone from the one three years earlier in the University of Michigan cases. Only four justices seemed to speak in favor of using race to maintain integration in public schools. In fact, when the Supreme Court released its opinion in this case in June

of 2007, the Court ruled five to four that the Seattle and Louisville voluntary plans for desegregating their schools were unconstitutional. Chief Justice John G. Roberts, Jr.'s, majority opinion concluded that, "the way to stop discrimination on the basis of race is to stop discriminating on the basis of race" (127 S.Ct. at 2768). The Chief Justice's opinion received only four votes for that approach, however. In a much more cautious concurrence, Justice Kennedy stated that while the use of race under the facts in these cases was not appropriate, he would not say that race could never be considered in the future when drawing school district boundaries. The four most liberal justices in dissent would have upheld the constitutionality of the Louisville and Seattle voluntary desegregations plans, stating that the use of race to maintain integration in public schools was necessary.

As in the affirmative action cases, the Supreme Court has required that states' use of race in gerrymandering voting districts also must pass strict scrutiny. In the 1993 case of *Shaw v. Reno* (1993), Justice O'Connor wrote for a five to four Court that "majority–minority" districts, so "bizarre" in their contours, like North Carolina's twelfth congressional district that snaked along Interstate 85, could be challenged by white voters. She warned that such racially motivated gerrymanders could "balkanize" our country. Just two years later, the Court (again narrowly divided five to four) expanded the *Shaw* decision's reach by ruling that two Georgia congressional districts, which the state had created to elect two blacks, ran afoul of the Fourteenth Amendment by having race as their predominant criterion for existence (*Miller v. Georgia* (1995)).

CONCLUSIONS

This survey of the Supreme Court's decisions on race reveals that the justices have sometimes led, and sometimes followed, the other two branches of the federal government, as well as the states, in addressing America's ongoing "dilemma" of race. From contributing to the causes of civil war in *Dred Scott*, to prompting "massive resistance" in the South after *Brown*, to stamping its approval on Congress's landmark 1964

Civil Rights and 1965 Voting Rights Acts, to balancing equal protection of the individual with assertion of group rights in busing, affirmative action, and gerrymandering cases, the Court has often found itself at the vortex of racial controversies. Tocqueville (1969, 270) noted that every political issue in America eventually becomes a judicial one. The corollary to his observation is that ultimately judicial issues may find their way back to the political arena. Thus, litigation on race has come to the high tribunal to be decided and then often returns to the body politic for affirmation or disapproval. The aphorisms over the Supreme Court building's east and west pediments declare- "Equal Justice Under Law" and "Justice the Guardian of Liberty." In historic race cases from the modern era, the justices have tried to find the sometimes illusive jurisprudential line that ensures both equality *and* justice to all Americans, regardless of skin color.

17

WOMEN AND THE LAW

Judith A. Baer

Using a legal approach, this chapter looks at the evolution of laws and court cases affecting the rights of women in the United States. This chapter examines the outputs of the U.S. Supreme Court through a feminist lens in cases dealing with the rights of women and sex discrimination. It is a very good example of how the legal model emphasizes the role of precedent and legal tests. Future courts in the United States depend on the judicial tests and the reasoning articulated in previous U.S. Supreme Court opinions to help them decide the case before them. Judicial tests often guide the lower courts in deciding what level of scrutiny to apply to a given set of facts or to a given class of cases. This chapter also illustrates the importance of both constitutionally based court decisions as well as statutory construction decisions. In theory, the U.S. Congress can only overturn a constitutionally based decision by sending a Constitutional Amendment to the states to be ratified. If the Congress is unhappy with a statutory interpretation decision, however, the legislative branch can simply enact a new statute. This chapter also gives the reader a sense of the historical evolution of women's rights law in our society, and the legal and political aspects of that evolution.

Legal systems were devised by men, for men. Even democracies with universal suffrage, like the United States, inherited a body of law into which women were denied input. Without voting rights, access to higher education and professional training, or control of money, women lacked the resources to challenge their exclusion. The legal system is no longer closed to women. We participate in ever-increasing numbers as lawyers, legislators, and judges; this participation has led to significant progress toward sex equality. However, the law within which we work reflects men's priorities, men's viewpoints, and men's lives.

Law is or has been male-biased in three ways. First, the United States has a long history of overt legal discrimination against women: denying them the vote, barring them from certain occupations, and so forth. Most of these laws have been repealed or invalidated;

they can survive judicial scrutiny today only if they have an important governmental or occupational purpose. Second, a law may be gender neutral on its face but discriminatory in impact; for example, veterans' preference in civil service or minimum height requirements for jobs exclude more women than men. These laws will be sustained unless they lack reasonable justification or there is evidence that their framers intended them to disfavor women. Finally, some laws are gender neutral but nevertheless presume that men's experiences are the societal norm. Criminal law, for instance, limits self-defense to situations where the accused perceives imminent danger. This definition fits the experience of a man in a fight better than that of a domestic violence victim (Baer 1999, 19). Divorce and child custody laws are subject to manipulation by the more affluent party, usually the husband. This kind of male bias is impervious to litigation and resistant to reform. What Catharine MacKinnon wrote about abstract rights is generally true of law: it "authorizes the male experience of the world" (1989, 248).

All three branches of federal, state, and local government have contributed to the radical changes in women's legal status since the mid-nineteenth century. Because this is a book about judicial politics, I concentrate here on appellate courts, especially the United States Supreme Court. The sexual equality cases that come before the Court involve either *statutory construction* or *constitutional interpretation*. In cases involving Title VII of the Civil Rights Act of 1964 or other federal antidiscrimination statutes, the Court must determine what the law means: whether, for example, sex is a "bona fide occupational qualification" for the job of guard in a men's prison. (The answer was yes in *Dothard v. Rawlinson* 1977. Prisons may still hire women guards if they wish.) Constitutional cases ask the Court to decide whether a state or federal law violates one or more federal constitutional provisions: in these cases, usually the due process or equal protection guarantee of the Fifth or Fourteenth Amendment.[1]

The constitutional phrases "due process" and "equal protection" have been given meaning by Supreme Court decisions extending from the 1870s to the present day. The due process clause secures procedural safeguards and invalidates laws that lack a legitimate purpose, are arbitrary or unreasonable, or infringe on guaranteed rights. The equal protection clause, at the very least, protects people from arbitrary discrimination; since the mid-twentieth century, judges have read the provision to demand more exacting scrutiny for some classifications or groups. The constitutional doctrine of gender equality has developed and changed along with these interpretive changes. The Supreme Court's attitude has fluctuated over time, from sympathy with to indifference about to hostility toward individual claims. The content and nature of the recognized rights have also changed over time.

DIRECT DISCRIMINATION

The earliest sex discrimination cases involved constitutional interpretation. By the time the Fourteenth

Amendment was ratified in 1868, the first American feminist movement was strong enough to get women's suffrage on the congressional agenda, though not strong enough to get it into the Constitution. These activists were ready to seek in court what Congress had denied. However, the Supreme Court proved no more willing than Congress had been to extend constitutional equality to women.

Bradwell v. State (1872) was the Court's second Fourteenth Amendment case. Decided the day after the famous *Slaughter-House Cases* (1872), *Bradwell* presented a similar issue: whether a state could restrict the right to engage in an occupation. In *The Slaughter-House Cases*, the city of New Orleans had granted a monopoly on the slaughtering of livestock to one company. In *Bradwell,* the Illinois bar denied admission to Myra Bradwell because of her sex. The Court ruled for the government in both cases: five to four in *Slaughter-House,* eight to one in *Bradwell.* Justice Samuel F. Miller wrote both majority opinions. In *Slaughter-House,* he insisted that the amendment was intended to protect the rights of freed slaves, not the economic interests of butchers. He did not find it necessary to belabor this point in *Bradwell* the next day. *Slaughter-House,* he wrote, established that "the right to control and regulate the granting of license to practice law in the courts of a State is one of those powers which are not transferred for its protection to the Federal government" (83 U.S. at 139; for more discussion of the role of women in the legal profession, see Mather this volume, chapter 4).

The Court was equally cautious in *Minor v. Happersett* (1875). The justices unanimously declined Virginia Minor's invitation to read Section 1 of the Fourteenth Amendment, which conferred federal and state citizenship on all persons born in, naturalized in, or subject to United States jurisdiction, to link citizenship with voting rights. *Minor* made the valid historical argument that the status of citizen had never entailed voting rights. Thus, the justices refused to do what Congress had specifically decided not to do. By citing precedents that separated citizenship from voting, the Court did what it was expected to do in the 1870s. For the Court to overrule a legislature on the basis of an individual's claim to a right would have been unprecedented.

By the time *Muller v. Oregon* (1908) was decided, the statement in the foregoing sentence was no longer true. *Muller* presented the Court with complications partly of the justices' own making. In *Lochner v. New York* (1905) three years earlier, they had ruled five to four that a law limiting the working hours of bakers violated the Fourteenth Amendment. Using the then new, and since repudiated, doctrine of "substantive due process," the majority had found that the law arbitrarily interfered with the freedom of contract of employers and workers. The question presented in *Muller* was whether this rule applied to a maximum hours law for women laundry workers. The law disadvantaged neither sex because only women had this occupation. Occupations were not only divided into men's jobs and women's jobs at this time, but because women had less bargaining power than men, they worked longer hours under worse conditions. The constitutional challenge came not from women workers or rights activists—indeed, many feminists supported "protective" labor legislation—but from employers. The state urged the Court to distinguish *Muller* from *Lochner* and emphasized the differences between men and women workers.

In *Muller*, the Court unanimously upheld the Oregon law. Its short opinion emphasized the physical distinctions between the sexes, especially the childbearing function. "Differentiated by these matters from the other sex," the Court wrote, woman "is properly placed in a class by herself, and legislation for her protection may be sustained, even when such legislation is not necessary for men, and could not be sustained" (208 U.S. at 422). This distinction proved to have remarkable staying power. Only once, in a minimum wage case (*Adkins v. Children's Hospital* 1923), did the Court fail to find an adequate nexus between sex differences and public policy. The Court continued to uphold women-only labor legislation long after it had abandoned substantive due process and reversed *Adkins* (*West Coast Hotel v. Parrish* 1937) and male-dominated labor unions and state legislatures had found restricting women's jobs a useful way of protecting men's jobs (*Goesaert v. Cleary* 1948). *Muller* upheld an hours law because women were different from men; *Goesaert* upheld a law prohibiting most women from working as bartenders because the Court now deferred to states in economic matters.

Muller's impact beyond labor legislation was "a classic example of the misuse of precedent, of later courts being mesmerized by what an earlier court had *said* rather than what it had *done*" (Kanowitz 1969, 154; emphasis in original). Judges read the opinion to establish the principle that sex is a valid basis for classification; therefore, a law discriminating on the basis of sex was sustained unless it was arbitrary and unreasonable. In practice, this doctrine meant that sex discrimination was almost always upheld until the second phase of American feminism began to make its presence felt. Even during Earl Warren's tenure as chief justice (1953 to 1969), a time of extraordinary judicial receptivity to disadvantaged groups, the Court upheld laws excusing women from jury service (*Hoyt v. Florida* 1961) and giving husbands exclusive control of joint marital property (*United States v. Yazell* 1966). The judiciary had basically issued a "blank check" for sex discrimination. The Supreme Court revoked that check in 1971, on both the statutory and constitutional fronts.

SEX DISCRIMINATION AND STATUTORY CONSTRUCTION

By the 1960s, much protective labor legislation for women had either been repealed by legislators or circumvented by employers. The first two federal laws prohibiting sex discrimination in employment predated the modern feminist movement and were not motivated by a desire for equality between the sexes. The Equal Pay Act of 1963 required that men and women receive equal pay for equal work. It was designed to prevent employers from replacing men workers with women who could be paid less (Baer 2002, 69). Its impact was limited because it applied only to men and women in the same jobs.

The 1964 Civil Rights Act prohibited discrimination on the basis of race, religion, national origin, and sex in employment, federally funded programs, and public accommodations. The word "sex" was inserted into Title VII of the Civil Rights Act of 1964 as a "joke" to defeat the provision; after this effort failed, the chair of the commission created to enforce it described it as a "fluke" (Baer 1978, 137, 149).

However, litigants, judges, and, eventually, the Equal Employment Opportunity Commission (EEOC) and Congress took the law seriously.

On its face, Title VII of the Civil Rights Act was incompatible with special labor legislation for women, however protective the legislative intent. There is no way to reconcile a law prohibiting employment discrimination on the basis of sex with a law excluding women from certain occupations or forbidding them to work as many hours as men. This contradiction mattered because the supremacy clause of Article VI makes federal law superior to state law; in a conflict, the state law becomes invalid. However, the statute contained a loophole wide enough to render it almost meaningless. It prohibited employment discrimination on the basis of sex, except where being male or female was a "bona fide occupational qualification" (BFOQ) for a particular enterprise.

Neither Congress nor the Equal Employment Opportunity Commission (EEOC) was eager to decide whether state labor laws could make sex a BFOQ. That task was left to the federal courts, which then took the lead in strengthening Title VII. The emergence of the modern feminist movement in the late 1960s resulted in an increase in Title VII litigation. In 1971, the U.S. Court of Appeals for the Ninth Circuit reached the inevitable conclusion that the statutory phrase, "no employer shall...discriminate on the basis of sex," invalidated labor laws and regulations applying only to women (*Rosenfeld v. Southern Pacific Company* 1971). Laws originally passed to limit employers' ability to exploit women workers had long since become limits on women's ability to compete with men in the workplace. *Rosenfeld* removed these barriers.

Phillips v. Martin-Marietta Corporation (1971) was the Supreme Court's first sex discrimination case that required it to interpret the requirements of Title VII. The company had refused to hire Ida Phillips as an assembly trainee, invoking its rule against hiring women with preschool-age children. This policy, like the airlines' old prohibition against married flight attendants, was an example of "sex plus" discrimination. Ruling unanimously for Phillips, the Court emphasized the absence of any evidence that mothers of young children were less reliable workers than fathers of young children. By 1978, Congress had

gotten ahead of the courts in this area. The Pregnancy Discrimination Act (PDA) reversed the Supreme Court's ruling in *General Electric v. Gilbert* (1976) and prohibited employment discrimination on the basis of pregnancy.

Three decisions between 1987 and 1991 resisted invitations to weaken Title VII and interpreted it far beyond what its authors could have intended. The most controversial of these rulings was *California Federal Savings and Loan Association v. Guerra* (1987). Feminist groups lined up on both sides in *Guerra*. The National Organization for Women (NOW) filed a third-party brief supporting the bank's refusal to reinstate Lillian Garland after a complicated pregnancy and birth had forced her to take four months off from her job. California law required employers to grant up to four months of pregnancy leave, but Cal Fed insisted that this law violated the Pregnancy Discrimination Act by discriminating against workers who took medical leave for other reasons. NOW feared that laws like California's would discourage employers from hiring women of childbearing age. (Any employer who acted on this would, of course, be violating Title VII; NOW's position showed how difficult it was to implement antidiscrimination law.) Other groups like Equal Rights Advocates and California Women Lawyers filed briefs arguing that pregnancy leaves benefited women workers by accommodating real differences between them and male workers.

This sameness-versus-difference debate is an old, tired one that the Supreme Court avoided in deciding this case. It upheld California's law on the grounds that the purpose of the Pregnancy Discrimination Act had been, "to guarantee women the right to participate fully and equally in the workforce without denying them the fundamental right to full participation in family life" (479 U.S. at 288). That may have been what Congress intended, but it was not what the PDA said: The language forbade discrimination on the basis of pregnancy. Three justices dissented, finding statutory text a more reliable guide to construction than legislative history.

Women workers were also victorious in *Price-Waterhouse v. Hopkins* (1989) and *United Auto Workers v. Johnson Controls* (1991). Ann Hopkins challenged her employer's decision not to promote her to partner on the grounds that her superiors' frequent admonitions to look and act "more femininely" constituted sex discrimination. The Supreme Court ruled that Hopkins had shown that gender was a factor in the decision. The case went back to the lower courts, where Price-Waterhouse had a chance to prove that its decision would have been the same even without this factor. (The parties settled out of court.) *Johnson Controls* (1991) was a unanimous decision that the letter of Title VII commanded, "fetal protection policies" that excluded women of childbearing age from jobs requiring exposure to toxic substances were illegal. The Court declared that, "Decisions about the welfare of future children must be left to the parents" (499 U.S. at 206).

THE NEW CONSTITUTIONAL DOCTRINE

Reed v. Reed (1971) was decided eleven months after *Phillips v. Martin-Marietta Corporation* (1971). Because two justices had recently retired and not been replaced; only seven justices decided the case. In a unanimous per curiam opinion, they brought the constitutional doctrine of sexual equality into the modern era. *Reed* invalidated an Idaho law stipulating that in appointing the administrator of a dead person's estate, males would be preferred over equally qualified females. As far as anyone recalled, this situation had never occurred before. The law only applied when someone died intestate (without leaving a will); anyone can choose an administrator in advance by making a will. Failing that, survivors could agree among themselves who would apply for appointment. A potential administrator's qualifications were based on a specific legal order: spouse first, then child, then parent, then sibling. However, Cecil and Sally Reed were the divorced parents of a son who had committed suicide. Both applied to be the administrator of the estate. Cecil was appointed administrator, and Sally sued.

In *Reed*, the state's argument that the preference was justified by "administrative convenience" went nowhere with the Court: "To give a mandatory preference to members of either sex...is to make the very kind of arbitrary legislative choice forbidden by the Equal Protection Clause of the Fourteenth Amendment" (404 U.S. at 76). Idaho's law could not survive even minimal scrutiny. For the first time since *Adkins*, the Supreme Court declared a sex-based classification unconstitutional. Together, *Phillips* and *Reed* gave feminists hope that the Burger Court would be as receptive to women's claims as the Warren Court had been to the claims of ethnic and racial minorities. However, the Idaho law had been so obviously unreasonable that *Reed* provided no clue as what the Court would do when confronted with a more plausible rationale for sex discrimination.

By the 1970s, equal protection doctrine under the Fourteenth Amendment had established two levels of judicial scrutiny. *Ordinary or minimal scrutiny* was used in the majority of cases, in which the classification imposed by the law was innocuous. In these cases, the constitutional test was whether the law had a rational relationship to a legitimate state purpose. If it did, it was constitutional; if it did not, it was arbitrary or capricious or unreasonable and, therefore, unconstitutional. The Court had elevated some classifications, notably race and ethnicity, to the higher tier of suspect classification. Discrimination based on race was presumed unconstitutional and must be subjected to *strict scrutiny*; such a law would be overturned unless there was a compelling justification for it. (Ironically, this doctrine originated in *Korematsu v. U.S.* 1944, in which the Court upheld the internment of Japanese Americans during World War II). Therefore, the Court seemed to have two choices: to continue to use minimal scrutiny in sex discrimination cases, or to declare sex a suspect classification. *Frontiero v. Richardson* (1973) came within one vote of using the same level of scrutiny in both race and sex discrimination cases.

The feminist movement had made significant progress in the two and a half years between *Reed* and *Frontiero*. In 1972, Congress sent the Equal Rights Amendment to the states for ratification. First proposed in 1923, the ERA would have provided that "Equality of rights under the law shall not be denied or abridged by the United States or by any state on account of sex." When the ratification deadline expired in 1982, the ERA was three state legislatures short of the required three-fourths majority. The Supreme Court had established its new sex discrimination doctrine before the

ERA failed, but *Frontiero* revealed that the ERA was very much on the Court's collective mind.

U.S. Air Force Lieutenant Sharron Frontiero sued the Defense Department when she was denied dependents' benefits for her husband, Joseph. Regulations granted these benefits to all married men in the Armed Forces, but women got them only if they provided over half their husbands' support. The Court ruled in Frontiero's favor, with only Justice William Rehnquist (later Chief Justice) dissenting. Writing for a plurality of four, Justice William Brennan compared sex classifications to racial classifications:

> [I]t can hardly be doubted that, in part because of the high visibility of the sex characteristic, women still face pervasive, although at times more subtle, discrimination in our educational institutions, on the job market and, perhaps most conspicuously, in the political arena.
>
> Moreover, since sex, like race and national origin, is an immutable characteristic determined solely by the accident of birth, the imposition of special disabilities upon the members of a particular sex because of their sex would seem to violate "the basic concept of our system that legal burdens should bear some relationship to individual responsibility."
>
> And what differentiates sex from such nonsuspect statutes as intelligence or physical disability, and aligns it with the recognized suspect criteria, is that the sex characteristic frequently bears no relation to ability to perform or contribute to society. As a result, statutory distinctions between the sexes often have the effect of invidiously relegating the entire class of females to inferior legal status without regard to the actual capabilities of its individual members (411 U.S. at 685–87).

Justice Lewis Powell took a more cautious approach:

> In my view, we can and should decide this case on the authority of *Reed* and reserve for the future any expansion of its rationale.
>
> There is another, and I find compelling, reason for deferring a general categorizing of sex classifications as invoking the strictest test of judicial scrutiny. The Equal Rights Amendment, which if adopted will resolve the substance of this precise question,

has been approved by the Congress and submitted for ratification by the States. If this Amendment is duly adopted, it will represent the will of the people accomplished in the manner prescribed by the Constitution. By acting prematurely and unnecessarily, as I view it, the Court has assumed a decisional responsibility at the very time when state legislatures, functioning within the traditional democratic process, are debating the proposed Amendment. It seems to me that this reaching out to pre-empt by judicial action a major political decision which is currently in process of resolution does not reflect appropriate respect for duly prescribed legislative processes (411 U.S. at 692).

Frontiero was the closest the Court ever got to treating sex discrimination like race discrimination. Three years later, the ERA remained unratifed and the spirit of compromise prevailed among the justices. *Craig v. Boren* (1976) was an Oklahoma case challenging a state's law that allowed women to buy 3.2 percent beer three years earlier than men. (Even if the Court had upheld this law, it would have become moot when Oklahoma, like every other state, raised the drinking age to 21 under the threat of losing federal highway funds following the Supreme Court decision in *South Dakota v. Dole* 1987). "To withstand constitutional challenge," wrote Justice Brennan in *Craig v. Boren*, "previous cases establish that classifications by gender must serve important governmental objectives and must be substantially related to achievement of those objectives" (429 U.S. at 197.) A majority of eight found the nexus between end and means too weak to withstand this new *intermediate scrutiny*.

Craig, like *Muller*, put woman in a class by herself. *Craig* also complicated equal protection doctrine. Now there were three tiers instead of two. Unlike race, gender was not a classification presumed to be invalid, but neither was it an innocuous classification. The Court had not given feminist lawyers the doctrine they wanted, but the *Craig* test was a useful tool that increased the likelihood of victory in court.

An abortion case, *Planned Parenthood of Southeastern Pennsylvania v. Casey* (1992), presents a striking, if perhaps inadvertent, parallel to *Craig*. In *Casey*, the plurality opinion of Justices Sandra Day

O'Connor, Anthony Kennedy, and David Souter weakened the holding of *Roe v. Wade* (1973) and demoted abortion from its first-tier status as a right abridgeable only with compelling justification to a second-tier interest subject to any regulation that did not unduly burden its exercise. So both sex equality and the only right belonging exclusively to women occupy the middle tier of scrutiny.

Equal protection doctrine does not distinguish between invidious discrimination, policies that disfavor members of historically disadvantaged groups like African Americans or women, and benign or "reverse" discrimination that gives women or minorities an advantage. *Regents of the University of California v. Bakke* (1978) struck down race-based quotas and ruled that "Racial and ethnic distinctions of any sort are inherently suspect and thus call for the most exacting judicial examination" (438 at 290). In the 1970s and 1980s the Court was less stringent with affirmative action plans, which establish hiring and/or promotion goals for women or minorities, but in 1995 it got tougher. *Adarand Constructors v. Peña* (1995) applied the suspect classification doctrine in a Title VII case involving the Department of Transportation's award of a contract to a minority-owned company. Although Justice Powell's statement in *Bakke* that "the perception of racial classifications as inherently odious stems from a lengthy and tragic history that gender-based classifications do not share" (438 U.S. at 305) did not bode well for affirmative action plans for women, *Johnson v. Santa Clara Transportation Agency* (1987) upheld such a plan despite a Title VII challenge and remains binding precedent almost twenty years later.

INTERMEDIATE SCRUTINY APPLIED

The semi-suspect classification doctrine has produced more wins than losses for sexual equality. The Court's decisions between 1976 and 1996 distinguished clearly between permissible and impermissible sex discrimination. Laws that were based on stereotyped characterizations of the sexes or irrefutable presumptions about gender roles (e.g., that wives are financially dependent on their husbands) were unconstitutional.

Orr v. Orr (1979) struck down a provision that only women could receive alimony after divorce, while *Kirchberg v. Feenstra* (1981) invalidated all marriage laws that differentiated between the rights and duties of husband and wife.

Most laws that withstood the *Craig* test could be linked, however remotely, to sex differences in reproductive function. In *Michael M. v. Superior Court of Sonoma County* (1981), the Court upheld a "statutory rape" law that made it a crime for men to have sex with women under the age of consent but not vice versa on the grounds that treating the sexes differently was substantially related to the state's important purpose of preventing pregnancy. *Miller v. Albright* (1998) and *Nguyen v. Immigration and Naturalization Service* (2001) also relied on biological differences in sustaining a law conferring United States citizenship on the children of single mothers, but not single fathers. *Rostker v. Goldberg* (1981), however, is unique. This decision sustained male-only draft registration, but the opinion had nothing to do with sex role stereotyping, reproduction, or even the merits of the law. Instead, the majority insisted that deference to Congress was necessary in cases involving the Armed Forces. After 1981, however, the Court did not decide a single constitutional sex discrimination case in favor of a woman—and only four in favor of a man—until 1996. Cases on the federal sex discrimination laws were a regular occurrence, but intermediate scrutiny seemed to have outlived its usefulness. Then came *United States v. Virginia* (1996), the constitutional equivalent of *Johnson Controls*.

The facts of the *United States v. Virginia* case are as follows. The state of Virginia, which had not admitted women to its flagship university until 1970, continued to restrict enrollment in the Virginia Military Institute (VMI) to men. The state prided itself on the "adversative training," more stringent than the national military academies, designed to produce military super-heroes. Its loyal alumni, to whom VMI owed the largest endowment of any public institution in the nation and who were well represented in politics and business, supported the college in its argument that such training was impossible in a coeducational setting. The state responded to the efforts of several young women to enter VMI by founding the Virginia

Women's Institute for Leadership (VWIL), a program that evoked memories of the Texas law school set up to keep African Americans out of the University of Texas (*Sweatt v. Painter* 1950), Justice Ruth Bader Ginsburg, who had argued many of the post-1970 sex equality cases, wrote a majority opinion that stated the obvious with eloquence:

> Inherent differences between men and women... are not cause for denigration of the members of either sex or for artificial constraints on an individual's opportunity. Sex classifications... may not be used, as they once were,... to create or perpetuate the legal, social, and economic inferiority of women.

> A purpose genuinely to advance an array of educational options, as the Court of Appeals recognized, is not served by VMI's historic and constant plan—a plan to "afford a unique educational benefit only to males." However "liberally" this plan serves the Commonwealth's sons, it makes no provision whatever for her daughters. That is not *equal* protection.

> The VWIL student does not graduate with the advantage of a VMI degree. Her diploma does not unite her with the legions of VMI "graduates [who] have distinguished themselves" in military and civilian life. "[VMI] alumni are exceptionally close to the school," and that closeness accounts, in part, for VMI's success in attracting applicants. A VWIL graduate cannot assume that the "network of business owners, corporations, VMI graduates and non-graduate employers... interested in hiring VMI graduates," will be equally responsive to her search for employment ("the powerful political and economic ties of the VMI alumni network cannot be expected to open" for graduates of the fledgling VWIL program).

> Valuable as VWIL may prove for students who seek the program offered, Virginia's remedy affords no cure at all for the opportunities and advantages withheld from women who want a VMI education and can make the grade. In sum, Virginia's remedy does not match the constitutional violation; the State has shown no "exceedingly persuasive justification" for withholding from women qualified for the experience premier training of the kind VMI affords (518 U.S. at 533, 539–40, 553–54; Emphasis in original).

This opinion is a perfect example of classical liberalism. It could have been written by John Stuart Mill. The situation fits into his *Essay on Liberty* (1856): Individuals wanted to do something that society forbade them to do. Justice O'Connor's politics were far more conservative than Justice Ginsburg's, but similar liberal rhetoric pervades her plurality opinion in *Casey*. References to "personal dignity and autonomy," "the right to define one's own concept of existence, of meaning, of the universe, and of the mystery of human life," and the woman's "own conception of her spiritual imperatives and her place in society" (505 U.S. at 851), illustrate the influence of liberalism on constitutional doctrine and on the jurisprudence of even conservative judges. However, *Casey* and *Virginia* also illustrate the limits of constitutional liberalism in attaining gender equality under law. Instances of direct discrimination as blatant and dubious as VMI's admissions policy are rare. And, despite its ringing eloquence, *Casey* extended the state's power to limit women's autonomy.

Intermediate scrutiny endures as a weapon against official gender stereotyping.[2] It is an inescapable fact, however, that the majority of constitutional sex discrimination cases have been won by men. Have the post-*Reed* equal protection cases had negative effects on women? Any cost-benefit analysis must factor in *Feenstra* and *Virginia* on the positive side. These rulings vindicate the power of intermediate scrutiny in securing women's rights. Decisions like *Frontiero* benefit both men and women. *Michael M* benefits nobody, and after the Court's decision the California legislature changed the law to make it gender neutral anyway. It is difficult to see any harmful impact on women in some of the men's victories. There is no evidence that *Orr v. Orr* has resulted in fewer or less generous spousal support awards for ex-wives or windfalls for ex-husbands. Decisions that give single fathers greater access to and control over the lives of their children (*Stanley v. Illinois* 1972; *Caban v. Mohammed* 1979) sometimes limit the rights of the mothers. Regardless of results, the new equal protection has enabled more men than women to vindicate their rights. Men bring more cases than women, perhaps because they tend to have greater resources. A gender-neutral doctrine can help reinforce the *status quo*.

INDIRECT DISCRIMINATION

Many laws that are gender neutral on their face can disadvantage more women than men as applied. How are these "disparate impact" policies construed? In *Griggs v. Duke Power Company* (1971), the Court ruled that job requirements that disqualified more African Americans than Caucasians violated Title VII unless the requirements "can be shown to be related to job performance" (401 U.S. at 431). This rule was soon applied to sex discrimination cases (*McDonnell-Douglas Corporation v. Green* 1973). If a plaintiff presented statistical evidence that a facially neutral employment practice tended to discriminate against any race or either sex, the burden of proof shifted to the employer to demonstrate the practice's relationship to job performance. If the employer could prove that such a relationship existed, the requirement was sustained unless the plaintiff could prove that the same goal could be reached equally well by a nondiscriminatory or less discriminatory practices.

Many minimum height and weight requirements for police recruits were struck down under this test. *Dothard v. Rawlinson* (1977) invalidated similar requirements for corrections officers in Alabama prisons. This decision was a Pyrrhic victory for Dianne Rawlinson, a recent college graduate with a degree in correctional psychology. The Supreme Court upheld the requirement that guards be the same sex as inmates under the BFOQ exception.

The test of necessity for job performance prevailed in Title VII disparate impact cases in 1989 and is in force today. However,*Wards Cove Packing Company v. Atonio* (1989) made things harder for plaintiffs. The Court watered down the employer's burden of proof by ruling that an employer need only produce evidence that the practice served legitimate goals of the business. Then Congress stepped in, just as it had after *General Electric v. Gilbert*. The Civil Rights Restoration Act of 1991 restored the *status quo*. The Act stipulated that the employer must, "demonstrate that the challenged practice is job related for the position in question and consistent with business necessity" (Section 105(a)). Even If the employer meets this burden, the employee can still prevail if she/he can

prove that there is an alternative available with a less discriminatory impact that achieves the same business purpose (Baer and Goldstein 2006).

Congress, the courts, and the EEOC have used Title VII to do working women considerable good. Progress has been frustrated by an implicit bias in favor of employers. Current working conditions are accepted as "givens." For example, a minimum height requirement for flight attendants will stand if the airline can show that this height is necessary to reach the overhead cabins. There is no affirmative duty to redesign the interior of the plane. The fact that women were working as guards in all-male prisons, even maximum-security institutions, in other states when Alabama forbade the practice was irrelevant to the outcome in *Dothard v. Rawlinson*. In this business-friendly government, employers' interests are more important than those of workers.

When a facially neutral law faces a constitutional challenge, the Supreme Court has made it much harder for plaintiffs to win. Courts assess the constitutionality of indirect sex discrimination in exactly the same way they treat indirect racial discrimination: leniently. Three Burger Court rulings established the doctrine. *Washington v. Davis* (1976) upheld regulations requiring police recruits in Washington, D.C. to pass a verbal aptitude test even though four times as many blacks failed the test as did whites. *Arlington Heights v. Metropolitan Housing Development Corp.* (1977) rebuffed a claim that the Chicago suburb's zoning policy discouraging multifamily dwellings unconstitutionally kept lower-income black families out. Both cases held that the equal protection clause forbade only arbitrary classification and intentional discrimination. Because both policies furthered legitimate goals, and there was no evidence that either had been adopted to disadvantage African Americans, the Court found that no racial discrimination existed. Therefore, the policies received only lower-tier scrutiny, which they easily survived.

Personnel Administrator v. Feeney (1979) challenged a provision for veterans' preference in civil service jobs. The state of Massachusetts, Helen Feeney's employer for most of her working life, had an "absolute lifetime preference": any veteran who passed the relevant Civil Service test could bump any nonveteran on the eligibility list. Although this rule applied equally to male and female veterans, 98 percent of veterans living in Massachusetts were male. Feeney, the age of many World War II veterans, held several management-level civil service positions until her job was abolished in a reduction in forced in 1975. With fewer civil service jobs available, Feeney was repeatedly bumped by veterans. No managerial state job seemed open to her any longer.

Seven justices found no intentional discrimination. The majority insisted that, "the distinction made by [the law] is, as it seems to be, quite simply between veterans and nonveterans, not between men and women" (462 U.S. at 275). The Court defended the law as a method of rewarding military service and attracting responsible employees to government work. Justices Brennan and Thurgood Marshall, dissenting, found "purposeful gender based discrimination" because "this consequence [the virtual exclusion of women] followed . . . inexorably from the long history of policies severely limiting women's participation in the military." They mentioned a fact the majority had ignored: Until 1971, the regulations had exempted from veterans' preference any job "especially calling for women," namely, low-ranked clerical jobs (462 U.S. at 283–85). They might also, although they did not, have questioned the state's timing; the law dated from World War II, when gender discrimination in employment was widely accepted.

One problem with this reliance on intent that it is impossible to determine, with any degree of certainty, what the intent of a law is. Another is that the Fourteenth Amendment does not protect people from the ill will of those who seek to hurt them; it guarantees due process and equal protection, which are rights, not motives. A third problem is that telling a state that it can do anything as long as it doesn't intend to discriminate on the basis of gender will see to it that no discriminatory purpose is ever again expressed in public. Finally, sexism is so pervasive in American society that it is hardly necessary to formulate sexist ideas to reinforce male supremacy. It reinforces itself. The core beliefs of a society are, after all, the presumptions so entrenched that they need not be articulated.

BEYOND DISCRIMINATION

Feeney provides a good point of transition between sex-based discrimination and the more subtle legal manifestations of male supremacy. Veterans' preference is a practice that rewards people who undertake a dangerous, disagreeable, and difficult task, military service, which is considered necessary to the security of the nation. Does a reward like this bear a substantial relationship to an important purpose? Yes: Although there may be valid arguments against veterans' preferences at certain times and places, it passes the intermediate scrutiny test. Military service is an occupation performed mostly—and once exclusively—by men. Childbearing is a comparable task, similarly risky and necessary, performed only by women—who have never, not once, received any employment preferences for undertaking it. In fact, cases like *Phillips, Gilbert, Guerra*, and *Johnson Controls* suggest that the opposite has been true. Should there be mothers' preference? Who knows? The issue has never gotten on the political agenda to be discussed. The system rewards men, not women. There is no judicial question here. This kind of gender-based disadvantage will never become a constitutional case.

As I wrote earlier, the gender-neutral law of self-defense is based on male experience and fits awkwardly with that of women. A similar example of male bias is found in the workplace. Most full-time jobs presume an "ideal worker" without family responsibilities—in effect, a man (Williams 2000). Ann Hopkins won her case against her employer because she proved that gender was a factor in denying her promotion, but she would have had no case if the company had made this decision because her responsibilities toward her three children caused her to amass fewer billable hours than her male colleagues did. The Uniform Marriage and Divorce Act of 1974, adopted by many states, is carefully written so as not to favor either sex. The male advantages here arise mainly from the fact that husbands typically have greater resources than the women whom they are divorcing.

It is all but impossible to imagine a court decision that ruled a law unconstitutional because it fit men's experience better than women's. Embedded male supremacy is more amenable to new statutes that authorize women's experience. Even these are subject to judicial review. *United States v. Morrison* (2000) and *Brzonkala v. Morrison* (2000), for example, affirmed a circuit court decision invalidating the Violence Against Women Act of 1994 (VAWA) on the grounds that the Act exceeded Congress's power under the interstate commerce clause of Article 1, Section 8 and the Fourteenth Amendment, Section 5 and thus invaded the power of the states.

CONCLUSIONS

The three varieties of legalized male supremacy that I identified early in the chapter have different sources and different solutions. Laws that make gender-based classifications can be traced to cultural beliefs or generalizations about gender roles and gender differences. Beliefs like "woman's place is in the home," "the husband should be the head of the household," or "men need education more than women do," are no longer legitimate bases for public policy. Some generalizations are stereotypes: "women miss more days of work than men," "men and women have different ambitions," and so forth. Some of these are testable, some not; when tested; they often turn out to be false. Other generalizations may be based on fact: for example, insurance plans that limit women's benefits because they live longer than men, or immigration laws that treat mothers differently from fathers. Courts and legislatures have limited the power to base policy on statements that are not necessarily true of individuals.

However, reproductive differences are still often accepted as justifications for laws without much critical analysis of legislative thought processes.

Indirect male bias characterizes laws that are gender neutral on their face but discriminatory as applied. Such laws may be motivated by a desire to disfavor women without running afoul of the law, but they may also by the accidental by-product of reasonable efforts to attain legitimate public goals. In this area, statutory law has forged ahead of constitutional law. Antidiscrimination law has been interpreted to forbid indirect discrimination in which no business necessity exists, but the courts have insisted that the equal protection clause is violated only when the discrimination is intentional. Yet no one has made a convincing argument that the Fourteenth Amendment should apply to intent but not to result.

The last two paragraphs have shown that, although statutory construction and constitutional interpretation have moved American law closer toward gender equality in the last generation, problems remain. The third variety of male-biased law that I described has little to do with discrimination: the embedded male bias that results from the construction of laws to fit men's rather than women's experiences and situations. To the extent that women's lives are similar to men's, the law fits women's interests better and better. Embedded sexism is more amenable to statutory than constitutional change, but women are not yet powerful enough as legislators or activists to restructure law around women's experience. As women gain political power, these changes are a real possibility.

Notes

1. Although the Fifth Amendment contains no reference to equal protection, *Bolling v. Sharpe* (1954) ruled that the Due Process Clause guaranteed it.

2. The words "exceedingly persuasive justification" suggested to some readers of the opinion that Ginsburg was trying to edge the Court closer to adopting the suspect classification doctrine, as she had urged the Court to do as an attorney. Although there is some controversy on this point among scholars, I read *Nguyen v. INS* (2001) as reaffirming the intermediate scrutiny approach used before *U.S. v. Virginia* (1996).

18

THE FEDERAL COURTS AND TERRORISM

Louis Fisher[1]

How do the U.S. Supreme Court and lower courts handle new ideas and changed circumstances in our society? After the terrorist attacks against the United States on September 11, 2001, the country was faced with a brand new legal and political situation. The president of the United States took extraordinary legal actions that he felt would help protect the nation from future terrorist attacks. Facing a new war against unknown terrorists, the president declared that he had the constitutional authority to detain so-called enemy combatants without following the rules set out in the Geneva Convention or in legal precedents describing constitutional practices in the regular U.S. courts. Congress moved to consolidate many executive branch agencies into a new Department of Homeland Security and to enact the Patriot Act. Supporters of the Patriot Act felt that the government needed new tools to fight the terrorist threat. How would the courts respond to the changed political situation? How would the courts use past precedents to help them decide the legal issues surrounding the government's treatment of potential terrorists? Would the courts restrict the power of the president in this area? This chapter explores how the Supreme Court and the lower federal courts used the legal model and legal precedents to help them sort out the wide range of legal issues that arose because of the government's attempt to fight terrorism at home and abroad. One central question was whether the president could act alone in taking actions against potential terrorists. Another central question was whether the courts could review the actions of the executive branch in this area. These issues are at the heart of the question of the proper role of the three branches of government in a separation of powers system similar to the one that we use in the United States. This chapter is another example of the policy-making powers of the U.S. Supreme Court and the lower federal courts.

Initiatives by the Bush administration in response to the terrorist attacks of September 11, 2001 (9/11), tossed a number of novel issues to the federal courts. In some cases, the government relied on civilian courts to indict individuals and prosecute them. However, matters changed fundamentally after President George W. Bush issued a military order on November 13, 2001, authorizing the creation of military tribunals within the executive branch to try non-U.S. citizens who had provided assistance to al Qaeda and to international terrorism. As a next step, and reaching now to American citizens, President Bush claimed the right to designate U.S. citizens as "enemy combatants" and deny them the right to counsel, the right to a trial, constitutional rights, and to hold them incommunicado for as long as the administration considered necessary. All of those issues, initially explored by district and appellate courts, reached the U.S. Supreme Court in 2004 and again in 2006. The first set of Supreme Court rulings pushed issues back to the lower federal courts for clarification, while the ruling in 2006 required congressional action.

"ENEMY COMBATANTS"

Following the September 11, 2001 attacks on the United States, a number of suspected terrorists were not charged in the regular federal courts. Instead, they were designated "enemy combatant" and held incommunicado at a variety of locations without access to an attorney. Some considered this designation to be unique both in U.S. law and in international law. The Justice Department argued that whenever the government or the military decided to place someone in this new category of "enemy combatants," federal judges had no right to interfere with the executive branch judgment. Thus, the president asserted that the courts could not review cases in which he had designated someone "an enemy combatant" because he alone had the power to make such a determination or to delegate that decision to military officials. A government brief argued that courts "may not second-guess the military's determination that an individual is an enemy combatant and should be detained as such.... Going beyond that determination would require the courts to enter an area in which they have no competence, much less institutional expertise, intrude upon the constitutional prerogative of the Commander in Chief (and military authorities acting at his control), and possibly create 'a conflict between judicial and military opinion highly comforting to enemies of the United States'" (Brief for Respondents-Appellants, *Hamdi v. Rumsfeld*, No. 02–6895, 4th Cir., 29–30, 31). (the opinion of the court in this case can be found at 296 F.3d 278 (4th Cir. 2002).

In other briefs, the Justice Department conceded that federal judges may have a review function in determining whether the president has properly designated someone an enemy combatant, but the review function "is limited to confirming based on some evidence the existence of a factual basis supporting the determination" (Respondents' Response to, and Motion to Dismiss, the Amended Petition for a Writ of Habeas Corpus, *Padilla v. Bush*, S.D.N.Y. 2002, 15) (the opinion of the court in this case can be found at *Padilla ex rel. Newman v. Bush*, 233 F.Supp.2d 564 (S.D.N.Y.

2002) . The government urged the judiciary to accept as "some evidence" whatever executive officials submitted without any opportunity for an accused enemy combatant, supported by legal counsel, to challenge the executive assertion. However, courts cannot determine that something is legitimate on its face if they hear only one side of the issue.

Enemy combatant is another term for "unlawful combatant," which the Court used in the Nazi saboteur case (*Ex parte Quirin* 1942). *Lawful combatants* are held as prisoners of war under the Geneva Convention and may not be prosecuted for criminal violations for belligerent acts that do not constitute war crimes. They wear uniforms or display a fixed distinctive emblem, to distinguish them from unlawful combatants, and conduct their operations in accordance with the laws and customs of war. The general counsel of the Defense Department defined, "enemy combatant" as "an individual who, under the laws and customs of war, may be detained for the duration of an armed conflict. In the current conflict...the term includes a member, agent, or associate of al Qaida or the Taliban." The Pentagon considers the definition consistent with this statement by the U.S. Supreme Court in *Quirin*: "Citizens who associate themselves with the military arm of the enemy government, and with its aid, guidance and direction enter this country bent on hostile acts are enemy belligerents within the meaning of the Hague Convention and the law of war."

Enemy combatants who are American citizens can appeal to what is known as the Non-Detention Act: "No citizen shall be imprisoned or otherwise detained by the United States except pursuant to an Act of Congress" (18 U.S.C. § 4001(a) (2000)). The Supreme Court has interpreted the "plain language" of this provision as, "proscribing detention *of any kind* by the United States, absent a congressional grant of authority to detain" (*Howe v. Smith*, 452 U.S. at 479 n.3 1981; emphasis in original). The Bush administration, however, denied that it was limited by this statute because, "Article II alone gives the President the power to detain enemies during wartime, regardless of congressional action." Alternatively, it argued that the Use of Force Act of 2001, authorizing military operations against Afghanistan, represented an act of Congress that satisfied the statutory requirement of the Non-Detention Act (letter of September 23, 2002, from William J. Haynes II, General Counsel of the Department of Defense, to Alfred P. Carlton, Jr., President of the American Bar Association, 2).

The two major "enemy combatants" held by the administration in the United States were Yaser Esam Hamdi and Jose Padilla. Both were U.S. citizens. Hamdi was picked up on the battlefield in Afghanistan. Padilla was apprehended at the O'Hare International Airport in Chicago. This next section will discuss these respective cases in more detail.

Yaser Esam Hamdi

Yaser Esam Hamdi, born in Louisiana and captured in the same Afghan prison rebellion as John Walker Lindh, was first held at Guantánamo Bay but moved to a brig at the Norfolk Naval Station and still later to Charleston, South Carolina. Designated an enemy combatant, he was not charged but instead held incommunicado without access to an attorney. A federal district judge several times rejected the broad arguments put forth by the Justice Department, which relied on an administration affidavit (the "Mobbs Declaration") that Hamdi was legitimately classified as an enemy combatant. The district judge, insisting that Hamdi had a right of access to the public defender and without the presence of military personnel, was repeatedly reversed by the Fourth Circuit (*Hamdi v. Rumsfeld*, 294 F.3d 598 (4th Cir. 2002); *Hamdi v. Rumsfeld*, F.3d 278 (4th Cir. 2002)). In a ruling on January 8, 2003, again overturning the district court, the Fourth Circuit juggled two values—the judiciary's duty to protect constitutional rights of accused criminal defendants versus the judiciary's decision to defer to military decisions by the president—and came down squarely in favor of presidential power.

One of the key questions in the case was the power of the president to designate a U.S. citizen as an "enemy combatant," thus stripping that citizen of the normal constitutional protections found in the regular federal courts. In deciding this issue, the Fourth Circuit offered a strange reading of the principle of the separation of powers. It cited an opinion by the Supreme Court in 1991 that the "ultimate purpose of this separation of powers is to protect the liberty and

security of the governed" (*Hamdi v. Rumsfeld*, 316 F.3d 450 at 463 (4th Cir. 2003), citing *Metro. Wash. Airports Auth. v. Citizens for the Abatement of Aircraft Noise, Inc.*, 501 U.S. at 272 1991). Instead of reading this language as an affirmation of the system of checks and balances that prevent an accumulation of power in a single branch of the federal government, the Fourth Circuit interpreted the Court's sentence as a warning to the federal judiciary not to interfere with powers vested in another branch: "For the judicial branch to trespass upon the exercise of the warmaking powers would be an infringement of the right to self-determination and self-governance at a time when the care of the common defense is most critical." What kind of "self-determination" and "self-governance" exists when power is concentrated in the executive branch?

Although the Fourth Circuit drew attention to the need for independent judicial scrutiny—"The detention of United States citizens must be subject to judicial review" (316 F.3d at 464)—the review scarcely existed. The Fourth Circuit deferred to the president: "The judiciary is not at liberty to eviscerate detention interests directly derived from the war powers of Articles I and II" (316 F.3d at 466). To the Fourth Circuit, it was "undisputed" that Hamdi was captured "in a zone of active combat in a foreign theater of conflict" (316 F.3d at 459). *Undisputed*? The court heard only the government's side. Hamdi, through his attorney, was given no opportunity to challenge assertions by executive officials or their informers in this case.

On July 9, 2003, the full bench of the Fourth Circuit voted eight to four to deny Hamdi's petition requesting a rehearing of the January panel ruling (*Hamdi v. Rumsfeld*, 337 F.3d 335 (4th Cir. 2003)). The dissenters made a variety of arguments in favor of an en banc review of this case. Judge Michael Luttig faulted the panel for calling Hamdi's seizure "undisputed." Hamdi, he said, "has not been permitted to speak for himself or even through counsel as to those circumstances." However, Luttig tilted toward presidential power by criticizing the panel's refusal "to rest decision on the proffer made by the President of the United States...all but eviscerat[ing] the President's Article II power to determine who are and who are not enemies of the United States during times of war" (337 F.3d. at 357). Luttig wanted the full panel to rehear the case and resolve those issues. Unless the judiciary clarified the range of executive power, an "embedded journalist or even the unwitting tourist could be seized and detained in a foreign combat zone," without meaningful judicial review (337 F.3d at 358). However, what kind of judicial review is possible if the court should defer—as Luttig urged—to the president in this type of case?

The designation of Hamdi as an enemy combatant depended on an administration document called the Mobbs Declaration. It was prepared by Michael H. Mobbs, an administration official, who had no direct knowledge of the intelligence information given him. Judge Diana G. Motz of the Fourth Circuit regarded the declaration as a pure hearsay statement by "an unelected, otherwise unknown, government 'advisor'" (337 F.3d at 368). Mobbs did not claim, "*any* personal knowledge of the facts surrounding Hamdi's capture and incarceration" (337 F.3d at 373, emphasis in original). Instead, Mobbs merely reviewed, "undisclosed and unenumerated 'relevant records and reports'" (337 F.3d at 373). Judge Motz further noted, "The panel's decision marks the first time in our history that a federal court has approved the elimination of protections afforded a citizen by the Constitution solely on the basis of the Executive's designation of that citizen as an enemy combatant, without testing the accuracy of the designation. Neither the Constitution nor controlling precedent sanction this holding" (337 F.3d at 369).

With the Hamdi case headed for the U.S. Supreme Court, the Bush administration on December 2, 2003, gave Hamdi access to a lawyer. The Defense Department explained that he could see a lawyer "as a matter of discretion and military policy" rather than as a constitutional right. The government's statement emphasized that there was no obligation to make a lawyer available and that its decision "should not be treated as a precedent" (Markon and Eggen 2003). Pentagon officials stated that the Defense Department had "completed its intelligence collection" with Hamdi and that access to an attorney would not now harm national security (Markon and Eggen 2003). The key point is that the government never acknowledged that U.S. citizens designated as "enemy combatants" had any of the normal constitutional rights available

to accused criminal defendants in the regular federal courts.

On June 28, 2004, eight Justices of the Supreme Court rejected the government's central argument that Hamdi's detention was quintessentially a presidential decision, not to be reevaluated and second-guessed by the courts (*Hamdi v. Rumsfeld*, 542 U.S. 507 2004). This decision clearly placed limits on president powers in this area, and increased the authority of the courts to review executive branch decisions. Only Justice Thomas parted company from the position of the eight Justices that courts have the competence to check and override presidential decisions in the field of national security. However, instead of offering a clean eight to one ruling, the case offered various combinations of the justices. There was a plurality opinion from 4 justices (Justices O'Connor, Kennedy, Breyer, and Chief Justice Rehnquist), joined at times by a concurrence/dissent from Justices Souter and Ginsburg, and at other times by a dissent from Justices Scalia and Stevens. Several of the plurality's judgments and prescriptions were shallow and contradictory. Thus it was very difficult to draw clear principles of law from this fractured Supreme Court decision.

One clear idea that did come from this case was the ability of the courts to review presidential actions in this area. Writing for the plurality in the case, Justice O'Connor supplied language that found ready use in newspaper and media coverage: "we necessarily reject the Government's assertion that separation of powers principles mandate a heavily circumscribed role for the courts in such circumstances. . . . We have long since made clear that a state of war is not a blank check for the President when it comes to the rights of the Nation's citizens. . . . Whatever power the United States Constitution envisions for the Executive in its exchanges with other nations or with enemy organizations in times of conflict, it most assuredly envisions a role for all three branches when individual liberties are at stake" (542 U.S. at 536–37). On such general principles the plurality was joined by Justices Souter, Ginsburg, Scalia, and Stevens. Clearly a majority of the justices did not accept President Bush's assertion that he alone could make decisions about who should be labeled an "enemy combatant."

The Court's opinion placed other limits on the power of the president in this area, by declaring that even enemy combatants had certain rights under our Constitution. The plurality held that an enemy combatant "must receive notice of the factual basis for his classification, and a fair opportunity to rebut the Government's factual assertions before a neutral decisionmaker" (542 U.S. at 533). That position attracted the support of Justices Souter and Ginsburg, but they did so with quite different reasoning. They found Hamdi's detention forbidden by § 4001(a) (the Non-Detention Act) and unauthorized by the Use of Force Act, which Congress enacted to authorize military operations against Afghanistan. Without reaching any questions on the process that would be appropriate for Hamdi, they said that the government had, "failed to justify holding him in the absence of a further Act of Congress, criminal charges, a showing that the detention conforms to the laws of war, or a demonstration that §4001(a) is unconstitutional." Unable to command a majority of the Court for their view, Justices Souter and Ginsburg reluctantly joined with the plurality in ordering the case to be reheard in the trial courts on terms "closest to those I would impose." The terms of the plurality's remand "will allow Hamdi to offer evidence that he is not an enemy combatant, and he should at the least have the benefit of that opportunity." It was on that ground that Justices Souter and Ginsburg agreed that someone in Hamdi's position "is entitled at a minimum to notice of the Government's claimed factual basis for holding him, and to a fair chance to rebut it before a neutral decision maker" (542 U.S. at 553).

Justices Scalia and Stevens, in their dissent, did not express views about the need for notice to Hamdi and an opportunity to present his case before a neutral decision maker. They went to more fundamental grounds, concluding that Hamdi was entitled to a habeas decree requiring his release "unless (1) criminal proceedings are promptly brought, or (2) Congress has suspended the writ of habeas corpus" (542 U.S. at 573).

The plurality held that Hamdi "unquestionably has the right to access to counsel in connection with the proceedings" (542 U.S. at 539). Justices Souter and Ginsburg said they did not disagree with this affirmation of Hamdi's right to counsel (542 U.S. at 553). Justices Scalia and Stevens offered no views on the right to counsel because they objected vehemently to the plurality's effort to prescribe a host of procedural rules to guide a future trial, such as putting the burden of proof on the citizen rather than on the government, and allowing testimony by hearsay rather than live witnesses (542 U.S. at 575). To Scalia and Stevens, the Court had no competence to decide such procedures and should have left those matters to Congress: "If civil rights are to be curtailed during wartime, it must be done openly and democratically, as the Constitution requires, rather than by silent erosion through an opinion of this Court" (542 U.S. at 578).

On several issues the eight Justices differed sharply. The plurality described the World War II precedent of *Quirin* as, "a unanimous opinion. It both postdates and clarifies *Milligan*, providing us with the most apposite precedent that we have on the question of whether citizens may be detained in such circumstances" (542 U.S. at 523). To Justices Scalia and Stevens, the Nazi saboteur case "was not this Court's finest hour" (542 U.S. at 569). They pointed to a number of problems, such as the fundamental difference between the fate of eight saboteurs who were, "admitted enemy invaders" (citing *Quirin*) and Hamdi, who "insists that he is *not* a belligerent" (542 U.S. at 571–72, emphasis in original).

The plurality agreed with the government's assertion that the Use of Force Act constituted, "explicit congressional authorization for the detention of individuals," thus satisfying the Non-Detention Act (542 U.S. at 517). The plurality cited nothing in the text or the legislative history of the Use of Force Act that "explicitly" indicated a willingness by Congress to authorize the detention of U.S. citizens as enemy combatants. In fact, a few paragraphs later the plurality said, "it is of no moment" that the Use of Force Act "does not use specific language of detention" (542 U.S. at 519). Somewhere in the language of the Use of Force Act the plurality found implicit support for the detention of U.S. citizens as enemy combatants, although no member of Congress referred to detention in debating the statute.

Justices Souter and Ginsburg disagreed sharply with the plurality, stating that the government had, "failed to demonstrate that the Force Resolution authorizes the detention complained of here even on the facts the

Government claims. If the Government raises nothing further than the record now shows, the Non-Detention Act entitles Hamdi to be released" (542 U.S. at 541). They pointed out that the Use of Force Act "never so much as uses the word detention" (542 U.S. at 547). They also noted that within a few weeks after passing the Use of Force Act, Congress passed the USA Patriot Act, which authorized the detention of alien terrorists for no more than seven days unless the government pressed criminal charges or instituted deportation proceedings (542 U.S. at 551).

Justices Scalia and Stevens also strongly objected to the plurality's position that Hamdi's imprisonment could be justified on the basis of the Use of Force Act. They said the statute did not authorize the detention of a U.S. citizen "with the clarity necessary to satisfy the interpretive canon that statutes should be construed so as to avoid grave constitutional concerns" (542 U.S. at 574). Thomas's dissent agreed with the plurality that Congress had authorized the president to detain U.S. citizens by passing the Use of Force Act (542 U.S. at 587).

The plurality endorsed Hamdi's right to "a fair opportunity to rebut the Government's factual assertions before a neutral decisionmaker," drawing attention to earlier rulings that due process requires a "neutral and detached judge" (542 U.S. at 533). The plurality later insisted that "an independent tribunal," an "independent review," and an "impartial adjudicator" would not overtax the executive branch or interfere with military operations (542 U.S. at 534–35). However, the plurality appeared to be satisfied by some kind of review panel within the executive branch, perhaps even "an appropriately authorized and properly constituted military tribunal" (542 U.S. at 538).

In my opinion, the plurality seemed to lose sight of how Hamdi became an "enemy combatant." The person who made that designation was President Bush. No review panel within the executive branch, much less within the military, could possibly possess the sought-for qualities of neutrality, detachment, independence, and impartiality. Instead of a military panel reviewing Hamdi's status, the Court's decision prompted the government to release Hamdi rather than try him. Conditions of release included that he renounce his U.S. citizenship, move to Saudi Arabia, and agree not to sue the federal government on the ground that his civil rights had been violated (Markon 2004).

Jose Padilla

Jose Padilla, born in New York, was held by the military as a suspect in a plot to detonate a radiological dispersal device (a "dirty bomb") in the United States. Although the administration designated both Hamdi and Padilla as enemy combatants, their cases are quite different. As explained by Judge Wilkinson of the Fourth Circuit, to compare the battlefield capture of Hamdi "to the domestic arrest in *Padilla v. Rumsfeld* is to compare apples and oranges" (*Hamdi v. Rumsfeld*, 337 F.3d at 344). The FBI arrested Padilla at an airport in Chicago on May 8, 2002 on a material witness warrant to secure his testimony before a grand jury in New York City. On June 9, President Bush designated him an "enemy combatant," and the government moved Padilla to a Navy brig in Charleston, South Carolina. He had access to an attorney, Donna Newman, in New York City, but not after his removal to Charleston, with the exception of brief, monitored visits after the Supreme Court agreed to hear the case.

Unlike Hamdi, initially the government did not claim that Padilla participated in hostilities in Afghanistan or engaged in any way as a "combatant" on a battlefield. However, according to the government, one can be an enemy combatant without ever fighting on a battlefield: "In a time of war, an enemy combatant is subject to capture and detention wherever found, whether on a battlefield or elsewhere abroad or within the United States" (Respondents' Response to, and Motion to Dismiss, the Amended Petition for a Writ of Habeas Corpus, *Padilla v. Bush*, S.D.N.Y. 2002, at 23) (the opinion of the court in this case can be found at *Padilla ex rel. Newman v. Bush*, 233 F.Supp.2d 564 (S.D.N.Y. 2002).

On December 4, 2002, a district judge in New York City ruled that Padilla had a right to consult with counsel under conditions that would minimize the likelihood that he could use his lawyers as, "unwilling intermediaries for the transmission of information to others" (*Padilla ex rel. Newman v. Bush*, 233 F.Supp.2d 564, at 569 (S.D.N.Y. 2002)). Judge Michael B. Mukasey held that Padilla had a right to present facts, and the most convenient way to do that was through an attorney (233 F. Supp.2d at 599). Judge Mukasey insisted on evidence from the government to support Bush's finding that Padilla was an enemy combatant. (Judge Mukasey became attorney general of the United States in November 2007.)

Judge Mukasey did not grant Padilla the right to counsel because of the Sixth Amendment, which applies only to "all criminal prosecutions." With no charges filed against Padilla, there was no criminal proceeding. Instead, Mukasey looked to congressional policy on habeas corpus petitions, entitling an applicant to "deny any of the facts set in the return or allege any other material facts" (28 U.S.C. § 2243). Habeas corpus literally means "produce the body," and this procedure is used by federal courts to ensure that justice in done in any sort of legal proceeding in the state courts (usually for death penalty cases) or in military tribunals. As to the government's concern that Padilla might use his attorney to communicate with the enemy, Judge Mukasey noted that such an argument would even prohibit an indicted member of al Qaeda from consulting with counsel in an Article III proceeding (233 F.Supp.2d at 603–4). The government thought the "some evidence" standard supported the lawfulness of Padilla's detention, but Judge Mukasey replied that no court of which he was aware had applied that standard "to a record that consists solely of the government's evidence, to which the government's adversary has not been permitted to respond" (*Padilla ex rel. Newman v. Rumsfeld*, 243 F.Supp.2d 42 at 54 (S.D.N.Y. 2003)).

The government appealed the case to the U.S. Court of Appeals for the Second Circuit. Like Hamdi, Padilla was designated an enemy combatant on the basis of a Mobbs Declaration. Padilla's attorneys, Donna Newman and Andrew Patel, said that Mobbs's own footnotes "conceded that the government's 'confidential sources' probably were not 'completely candid,' and that one source subsequently recanted and another was being treated with drugs." Attorney Patel remarked: "Someone who's a confirmed liar and someone else who's on drugs, and one of the two has recanted. You really think someone should be locked up for a year in solitary confinement based on *that*?" (quoted in Span 2003, A8, emphasis in original).

On December 18, 2003, the Second Circuit held that the president lacked inherent constitutional authority as commander-in-chief to detain American citizens on American soil outside a zone of combat. To justify such detentions, the president needed specific congressional authorization. As the court noted, the Non-Detention Act specifically prohibited the president from detaining a U.S. citizen on American soil. The court ruled that the Use of Force Act, passed shortly after 9/11 to authorize military action against Afghanistan, did not represent an authorization for the president to employ detentions of U.S. citizens outside of the normal legal system (*Padilla v. Rumsfeld*, 352 F.3d 695 (2d Cir. 2003)).

Another question was whether the Second Circuit could assert jurisdiction in the case, or whether it instead belonged in the more conservative Fourth Circuit that covered the state of South Carolina. The government argued that the petition for a writ of habeas corpus directed to Secretary Donald Rumsfeld should be dismissed or transferred to the district court in South Carolina, where Padilla was being held. The proper custodian of Padilla, said the government, was the commander of the brig in South Carolina. The Second Circuit sitting in New York rejected that analysis as too formalistic. Secretary Rumsfeld was charged by President Bush with detaining Padilla, and Rumsfeld or his designees determined that Padilla would be sent to the brig in South Carolina. The "legal reality of control" was vested with Rumsfeld because only he could inform President Bush that further restraint of Padilla was no longer necessary (352 F.3d at 707). All of the initial actions regarding Padilla's status as an enemy combatant were completed by Rumsfeld or his agents in the Southern District of New York, not in South Carolina (252 F.3d at 710).

With regard to the constitutional issues, the Second Court relied largely on the Steel Seizure Case of 1952, where Justice Black wrote for the Court that presidential power "must stem either from an act of Congress or from the Constitution itself" (252 F.3d at 711, citing *Youngstown Co. v. Sawyer*, 343 U.S. at 585 1952). Justice Black held that President Truman's seizure of steel mills could not be justified as a function of the president's powers as commander-in-chief. A famous concurrence by Justice Jackson in *Youngstown* developed three categories for evaluating the exercise of emergency power by the president. First, when the

president acts pursuant to an express or implied authorization from Congress, "his authority is at its maximum, for it includes all that he possesses in his own
right plus all that Congress can delegate." Second,
when the president acts in the absence of either a
congressional grant or denial of authority, "he can
only rely upon his own independent powers, but there
is a zone of twilight in which he and Congress may
have concurrent authority, or in which its distribution
is uncertain." The third category included situations
where the president takes measures that are incompatible with the express or implied policy of Congress. In
such cases, the president's power "is at its lowest ebb,
for then he can rely only upon his own constitutional
powers minus any constitutional powers of Congress
over the matter" (252 F.3d at 711, citing *Youngstown
Co. v. Sawyer*, 343 U.S. at 637–38).

The Second Circuit ruled that President Bush lacked
inherent constitutional authority as commander-in-
chief to detain American citizens on American soil
outside a zone of combat, and concluded that the
Non-Detention Act served as an explicit congressional
denial of authority within the meaning of Steel Seizure
Case, thus placing Bush's action in the third category.
In other words, the Second Circuit ruled that Congress
had specifically restricted the actions of the president
in this case and that President Bush was acting against
congressional authority when he ordered Padilla to be
detained as an enemy combatant. The Second Circuit
also decided that the Constitution "entrusts the ability to define and punish offenses against the law of
nations to the Congress, not the Executive" (252 F.3d
at 714). Although Congress "may have the power to
authorize the detention of United States citizens under
the circumstances of Padilla's case, the President,
acting alone, may not" (252 F.3d at 715).

The government argued that the Nazi saboteur
case (*Quirin*) "conclusively established the President's
authority to exercise military jurisdiction over
American citizens" (252 F.3d at 715). The Second
Circuit disagreed, stating that the Court's decision
in 1942 "rested on express congressional authorization of the use of military tribunals to try combatants
who violated the laws of war." Second, *Quirin* found
it "unnecessary for present purposes to determine to
what extent the President as Commander in Chief has

constitutional power to create military commissions
without the support of congressional legislation."
Third, when the 1942 decision was issued, the Non-
Detention Act did not exist. Fourth, the German saboteurs "admitted that they were soldiers in the armed
forces of a nation against whom the United States had
formally declared war." Padilla made no such admission. He had clearly disputed his designation as an
enemy combatant (252 F.3d at 716).

Not all the judges on the Second Circuit were in
agreement the president's authority was limited in this
case. Judge Wesley, concurring in part and dissenting
in part, disagreed that the president lacked authority
from Congress or the Constitution to order the detention and interrogation of Padilla. It was his view that
the president, as commander-in-chief, "has the inherent authority to thwart acts of belligerency at home or
abroad that would do harm to United States citizens"
(252 F.3d at 726). He also believed that the Use of Force
Act specifically authorized President Bush's decision
to designate Padilla as an enemy combatant (252 F.3d
at 728–31). Even with those challenges to the majority's decision, Judge Wesley noted that Padilla's right
to pursue a remedy through habeas corpus "would be
meaningless if he had to do so alone. I therefore would
extend to him the right to counsel as Chief Judge
Mukasey did" (252 F.3d at 732).

Following the decision by the Second Circuit and
the government's appeal to the U.S. Supreme Court,
the Bush administration allowed Padilla to consult
with attorney Donna Newman. As with Hamdi, the
government argued that access to an attorney was,
"a matter of discretion and military authority," was
not required by domestic or international law, and
"should not be treated as a precedent" (Ricks and
Powell 2004, A16). On March 3, 2004, Newman and
Padilla talked through a glass security window while
two government officials listened to the conversation
and videotaped the meeting. She said, "this was not an
attorney–client meeting" in the constitutional sense of
that term. She was not allowed to ask, "about the conditions of his confinement." She also wanted to be able
to send Padilla documents without having them first
reviewed by the government, but merely gave Padilla
some newspaper articles about his case (Powell 2004).
The government also consented to a longstanding

request from the International Committee of the Red Cross to meet with Padilla (Sontag 2004).

After the Supreme Court heard oral argument on Padilla's case and the Justices were busy drafting a decision, Deputy Attorney General James Comey made an extraordinary public statement on June 1, 2004 (Fisher 2005b, 234–37). He told reporters that Padilla, supposedly involved in a dirty-bomb plot, also considered a plan to locate high-rise apartment buildings in the United States that had natural gas supplied to all floors. He and his accomplices would rent two apartments in each building, "seal those apartments, turn on the gas, and set timers to detonate and destroy the buildings simultaneously at a later time" (U.S. Department of Justice, 2004). The last line of his statement read: "We now know much of what Jose Padilla knows, and what we have learned confirms that the president of the United States made the right call, and that that call saved lives." The not-so-hidden message: If the justices disposed of the case in a way that put Padilla on the streets, the blood from any terrorist action would belong on their hands.

On June 28, 2004, the U.S. Supreme Court divided five to four in deciding that Padilla's habeas petition had been filed with the wrong court. It should have been filed, said the majority, with a district court in South Carolina, where Padilla was housed in a naval brig, rather than with the southern district in New York. The southern district of New York therefore lacked jurisdiction over the habeas petition, and Padilla's attorney was advised to submit the petition to the "only proper respondent," which is, "the person who has custody over [the petitioner]." That person, said the Court, was the commander at the naval brig in Charleston, South Carolina (*Rumsfeld v. Padilla*, 542 U.S. 426 (2004)).

The issue of the proper custodian was explored with some care during oral argument at the U.S. Supreme Court. Deputy Solicitor General Paul Clement told the Court that the fact that Padilla was in New York "in the first place is a bit of happenstance." Justice Stevens corrected him: "No, but the Government is responsible for him being in New York," referring to the fact that it was the government who initially apprehended Padilla in Chicago and brought him to New York as a material witness (oral argument, April 28, 2004, 18).

Toward the end of the oral argument, Deputy Solicitor General Clement volunteered that on the question of jurisdiction, "it is true that the immediate custodian rule is not a hard and fast rule and it has been—exceptions have been made" (oral argument, April 28, 2004, 56). (For more information about the role of the Office of the Solicitor General in oral arguments at the U.S. Supreme Court, see Ubertaccio this volume, chapter 10).

Chief Justice Rehnquist, joined by Justices O'Connor, Scalia, Kennedy, and Thomas, regarded the commander at the naval brig as the only proper respondent to the habeas petition. He argued that limiting district courts to "their respective jurisdictions" helps prevent forum shopping by habeas petitioners (542 U.S. at 446–47). Justice Stevens, writing for the dissenters, agreed that habeas petitioners should not be allowed to engage in forum shopping. However, he pointed out that if the government had given Newman notice of its intent to ask the district court to vacate the material witness warrant and place Padilla in the custody of the Defense Department, with eventual transfer to South Carolina, she could have properly filed the petition in New York. Had she done so, Stevens said that the government could not then transfer Padilla to another district (542 U.S. at 458–59). The dissenters objected that the government should not have had a tactical advantage in moving unilaterally and informing Padilla's attorney several days later. Padilla's attorney was entitled to fair notice to allow her to present in timely manner a habeas petition (542 U.S. at 459). If anyone engaged in forum shopping to gain an advantage it was the government, not the petitioner.

By the time the Padilla case had been returned to South Carolina, the government had replaced the Mobbs Declaration with the Rapp Declaration, signed by Jeffrey N. Rapp on August 27, 2004. Like Mobbs, Rapp was an administration official. The remarkable fact about the Rapp Declaration is that the original charge against Padilla about the "dirty bomb" does not appear. Evidently the administration discovered that the informers who had provided the information about the dirty bomb were no longer considered reliable. As a substitute charge, Rapp now claimed that Padilla planned to use explosives and natural gas to blow up apartment buildings in the United States.

On February 28, 2005, District Judge Henry F. Floyd in South Carolina granted Padilla's petition for a writ of habeas corpus and directed the government to either bring charges against him in civilian court within forty-five days or to release him. In so deciding, Judge Floyd ruled that the president had no authority to detain a U.S. citizen as an enemy combatant under the circumstances presented in Padilla's case. He found that under the Authorization for Use of Military Force Act (AUMF) it was neither "necessary nor appropriate" for the government to detain Padilla (*Padilla v. Hanft*, 389 F.Supp.2d 678 (D. S.C. 2005)). Nor did he find in Padilla's case the kind of authorization provided by Congress in *Quirin*. He ticked off these differences: (1) the Nazi saboteurs were charged with a crime and tried by a military tribunal, Padilla had not been charged or tried; (2) detention of the German saboteurs was punitive whereas Padilla's detention was "purportedly preventative"; (3) the issue in *Quirin* was whether the Germans should be tried by a military tribunal or a civilian court, the issue with Padilla was whether he would be tried at all; (4) *Quirin* preceded the Non-Detention Act; and (5) *Quirin* involved a war with a definite ending date, the war on terrorism does not (389 F. Supp2d at 714).

The U.S. Court of Appeals for the Fourth Circuit reversed Judge Floyd on September 9, 2005. Writing for the three-judge panel, Judge Luttig held that Padilla's detention was authorized by the AUMF (*Padilla v. Hanft*, 423 F.3d 386 (4th Cir. 2005)). His decision was colored by the procedure used by Padilla's attorneys to seek a "summary judgment" on this legal issue: Did President Bush possess authority to detain Padilla? Under summary judgment, the moving party (Padilla) assumed the facts offered by the nonmoving party (the government). Judge Luttig made it look like Padilla's attorneys *agreed* with the government's assertions, which is not the case. Luttig began his opinion:

> Appellee Jose Padilla, a United States citizen, associated with forces hostile to the United States in Afghanistan and took up arms against United States forces in that country in our war against al Qaeda. Upon his escape to Pakistan from the battlefield in Afghanistan, Padilla was recruited, trained, funded, and equipped by al Qaeda leaders to continue prosecution of the war in the United States by blowing up

apartment buildings in this country. Padilla flew to the United States on May 8, 2002, to begin carrying out his assignment, but was arrested by civilian law enforcement authorities upon his arrival at O'Hare International Airport in Chicago (423 F.3d at 388).

In my opinion, what this does is faithfully repeat the government's *allegations* and *claims* about Padilla, who disputed those allegations when he signed the habeas petition. His attorneys had selected the procedure of summary judgment to get past the factual disputes and go directly to the legal issue. Only on page 7, Note 1, does Judge Luttig mention the procedure being followed, "For purposes of Padilla's summary judgment motion, the parties have stipulated to the facts as set forth by the government. J.A. 30–31. It is only on these facts that we consider whether the President has the authority to detain Padilla." The unwary reader would assume that on pages 30–31 of the Joint Appendix there would be stipulation by the parties to the facts that appear in Luttig's opening paragraph. Instead, J.A. 30–31 merely has David B. Salmons, an attorney in the solicitor general's office, telling the court that Padilla's attorneys "have an argument that they would like to present to the Court initially, that would assume the Government's facts as set forth in our return and the attached declaration [the Rapp Declaration], and that would say even under those facts, the President lacked the authority to detain Mr. Padilla as an enemy combatant."

Judge Luttig proceeded to use the "facts" (not agreed to by Padilla's lawyers) to decide the *law*. For example: "Under the facts as presented here, Padilla unquestionably qualifies as an 'enemy combatant' as that term was defined for purposes of the controlling opinion in *Hamdi*." Again, the Judge wrote that Padilla "entered this country bent on committing hostile acts on American soil," based solely on the Rapp Declaration. Judge Luttig then concluded, "These facts unquestionably establish that Padilla poses the requisite threat of return to battle in the ongoing armed conflict between the United States and al Qaeda in Afghanistan." The "facts" here consist of unproven allegations by the government.

With the Padilla case heading for the U.S. Supreme Court, the government switched courses again on November 17, 2005, when it indicted Padilla in a regular district court in Florida. The charges listed in the indictment had nothing to do with the claims made in the Mobbs and Rapp Declarations. An effort by Padilla's lawyers to appeal the Fourth Circuit's decision and take it to the Supreme Court was turned aside by the Court on April 3, 2006 (*Padilla v. Hanft*, 126 S.Ct. 1649 (2006). On August 21, the district court in Florida threw out one count in Padilla's indictment (carrying a potential life prison sentence). The remaining counts could net a maximum of 20 years (Lichtblau 2006). In October, Padilla's lawyers motioned that the court should dismiss the balance of the indictment because of the government's "outrageous" conduct during his three and a half year detention in the Navy brig in South Carolina.

ANTI-TERRORIST CASES IN THE REGULAR FEDERAL COURTS

The next section of this chapter examines anti-terrorist cases that were heard in the regular federal criminal courts in the United States. Initially after 9/11, the Justice Department went to civilian courts, that is the regular federal courts, to prosecute terrorists charged with assisting the Taliban and al Qaeda. For example, John Walker Lindh, born in California but captured in Afghanistan among Taliban forces, was tried in regular federal court. He pled guilty to assisting the Taliban government in Afghanistan (*United States v. Lindh*, 227 F.Supp.2d 565 (E.D. Va. 2002)). Richard E. Reid, the British "shoe bomber," was also tried and convicted in the regular federal courts (Ferdinand 2003). The Justice Department also prosecuted six Yemenis from Lackawanna, New York. The men admitted to attending an al Qaeda training camp in Afghanistan during the spring of 2001 (Powell 2003; Purdy and Bergman 2003). Indictments were brought against an Algerian and three Moroccans in Detroit for being members of a terror cell (Hakim 2003a). Two were convicted and two acquitted (Hakim 2003b). The outcome was later thrown in doubt when it appeared that prosecutors might have withheld key exonerating evidence (Pierre 2003). In September 2004, a federal judge threw out the two convictions because of prosecutorial abuse (Hakim 2004). Maher Hawash, a software engineer in Portland, Oregon, pled guilty in the

regular federal courts to assisting the Taliban (Harden 2003). Many other terrorist suspects faced charges in the regular federal courts.

The most complicated case in civilian court has been that of Zacarias Moussaoui, a thirty-three-year-old French citizen of Moroccan descent. This next section will provide details about his case and the novel legal issues that his case raised. Moussaoui was arrested on immigration charges in Minneapolis on August 16, 2001, after he had enrolled in a flight school to learn how to fly a Boeing 747 commercial jet. Later he was suspected of being part of the Osama bin Laden conspiracy on 9/11. He seemed to be the type of person the administration had in mind when President Bush authorized military tribunals for suspected terrorists, but the Justice Department chose instead to prosecute him in the regular federal courts.

On December 11, 2001, a federal grand jury indicted Moussaoui for being part of the al Qaeda conspiracy to kill and maim persons and destroy structures in the United States. The indictment included six counts, including conspiracy to commit acts of terrorism, aircraft piracy, destruction of aircraft, and the use of weapons of mass destruction. The indictment listed two supporting conspirators: Ramzi bin al-Shibh and Mustafa Ahmed al-Hawsawi, and stated that bin al-Shibh had wired approximately $14,000 to Moussaoui from Germany (Moussaoui indictment 2001, 6, 17). These allegations would complicate the trial after al-Shibh was apprehended in Pakistan, and Moussaoui insisted he had a right to confront him in court.

Exactly what criminal conduct the government suspected Moussaoui of committing shifted with time. Initially, high-ranking officials in the Bush government, including Vice President Cheney, regarded Moussaoui as the "twentieth hijacker." The three planes that hit the World Trade Center and the Pentagon had five terrorists each. The plane that crashed in a field in Stony Township, Pennsylvania had only four terrorists on board. Federal investigators later suspected that a Yemeni citizen might have been meant to be another hijacker aboard that plane (Van Natta 2001).

Moussaoui learned through court documents that the Justice Department believed he was involved in a potential "fifth plane" that was supposed to be crashed into the White House on September 11, 2001. Moussaoui's attorneys sought access to those statements, made in a secret court hearing, and Judge Leonie M. Brinkema agreed that access was appropriate (Shenon 2003a, 2003b). By August 2003, newspaper reports indicated that the Justice Department had backed away from the "fifth plane" theory, which appeared to be based on information from some al Qaeda prisoners but contradicted by other prisoners (White 2003). With complications mounting in the regular federal courts, the administration again debated the merits of shifting Moussaoui to a military tribunal (Shenon and Schmitt 2002; Graham and Eggen 2002).

The trial stretched from month to month, in part because of Judge Brinkema's decision to let Moussaoui serve as his own lawyer. He used that opportunity to promote al Qaeda goals and create a circus atmosphere in the courtroom. Representing oneself in court is almost always ill-advised, even for seasoned attorneys. For Moussaoui, it was especially harmful. Court-appointed attorneys with security clearances could have been given access to highly classified evidence and witnesses. Moussaoui would never have such rights. After almost two years of the trial, Judge Brinkema decided on November 14, 2003 to remove Moussaoui's right to represent himself and appointed his standby attorneys to provide legal counsel for him (Fisher 2005b, 213–14).

The trial added a new complexity in September 2002 with the capture of Ramzi bin al-Shibh, a young Yemeni apprehended in Pakistan. He was accused of being a key planner of the 9/11 attacks and had been identified in Moussaoui's indictment. Moussaoui insisted that he was entitled under the Sixth Amendment to seek witnesses to prove his innocence and to confront witnesses against him. The rights in the Sixth Amendment apply to any "accused" in a criminal proceeding, not just to a U.S. citizen. Again the government wondered whether it was now time to turn Moussaoui over to the Defense Department to be tried by a military tribunal (Schmidt 2003).

Khalid Sheik Mohammed, an al Qaeda operations chief captured in Pakistan, told U.S. interrogators that Moussaoui was not part of the 9/11 attacks but was in the United States to take part in a planned second wave of attacks. According to press reports, both Mohammed and bin al-Shibh came to distrust

Moussaoui and found him unreliable (Schmidt and Nakashima 2003). It was reported that Moussaoui offered a third explanation, saying he was to take part in another al Qaeda operation outside the United States after the 9/11 attacks (Markon 2003b).

On January 30, 2003, Judge Brinkema ordered the government to allow Moussaoui's lawyers to take a video deposition of bin al-Shibh. The government objected that any questioning by his attorneys would disrupt ongoing interrogations and jeopardize access to crucial intelligence needed in the war against terrorism. Yet the government's indictment charged that bin al-Shibh had wired Moussaoui at least $14,000, making both men part of the conspiracy (Moussaoui indictment, 17; Schmidt and Priest 2003). Moussaoui's attorneys also sought access to Khalid Sheik Mohammed. When the government appealed Brinkema's order, the Fourth Circuit sent the case back to district court, urging the two sides to find a middle ground that would allow Moussaoui some access to bin al-Shibh (Markon 2003a).

Although a civil trial is open for public viewing, much of the Moussaoui trial was conducted in secret. Judge Brinkema's order to give Moussaoui's attorneys access to bin al-Shibh was made in secret, as was the government brief to the Fourth Circuit appealing her ruling, and also a key hearing before the Fourth Circuit on May 6, 2003. Several news organizations went to court to demand access to these secret court documents. Judge Brinkema criticized the "shroud of secrecy" surrounding the Moussaoui case, expressing doubt that the government could prosecute the case in open court. In response to pressure from news organizations and from Judge Brinkema, the government agreed to unseal some of the secret documents they had used in getting the indictment. Also, the Fourth Circuit ruled that part of a hearing scheduled for June 3 had to be open to the public (Fisher 2005b 215–16).

At a hearing before the U.S. Court of Appeals for the Fourth Circuit, Assistant Attorney General Michael Chertoff told the court that Moussaoui's rights were trumped by national security interests. Chief Judge William W. Wilkins, Jr., responded, "National security interests cannot override a defendant's right to a fair trial" (Markon 2003c, A10). The prosecutor Chertoff insisted that, "[t]his is not a Sixth Amendment case,"

(Shenon 2003c, A21) and that what Moussaoui "wants is to expand the Sixth Amendment" (Shenon 2003c, A21). Chertoff denied that the Sixth Amendment could be extended overseas to potential witnesses who are enemy combatants, and that any effort to interrogate bin al-Shibh would, "change the course of a military operation" (Shenon 2003c, A21).

On June 26, 2003, the Fourth Circuit ducked these constitutional issues by holding that Judge Brinkema's order was not yet subject to appeal because it was not technically a "final decision" (*United States v. Moussaoui*, 333 F.3d 509 at 513–14 (4th Cir. 2003)). The order would not become final, in a legal sense, "unless and until the Government refuses to comply and the district court imposes a sanction." The Justice Department had asked the Fourth Circuit to issue a mandamus, reversing the district court's order, but the Fourth Circuit declined to provide that relief.

The government asked the Fourth Circuit to reconsider its ruling, but on July 3 the court refused. Rebuffed, the government asked the entire Fourth Circuit to rehear the case. Losing parties before the three judge panels on the U.S. Courts of Appeals have the right to ask the entire circuit court to rehear the decision *en banc* (see Martinek this volume, chapter 9). Divided seven to five, the appellate court voted against an en banc rehearing (*United States v. Moussaoui*, 336 F.3d 279 (4th Cir. 2003)). The next step was now quite predictable: The government defied Judge Brinkema's order to give Moussaoui access to bin al-Shibh. Instead of taking the case immediately to a military tribunal, the Justice Department hoped to return to the Fourth Circuit and this time secure a more favorable ruling (Markon 2003d; Shenon 2003d). In late August, Judge Brinkema granted Moussaoui access to two al Qaeda operatives: Khalid Sheik Mohammed and Mustafa Ahmed Hawsawi, a Saudi man who reportedly served as paymaster to the 9/11 hijackers and is named in the indictment against Moussaoui. The Justice Department told Judge Brinkema that it would refuse to produce either man for deposition (Markon 2003e, 2003f).

By late September, it appeared that the Justice Department would not object if Brinkema accepted a defense motion to dismiss the indictment. That step would allow the government to have a final order it could appeal to the friendlier Fourth Circuit (Markon 2003g;

Shenon 2003e). Another option, which she selected on October 2, was to prevent prosecutors from seeking the death penalty because there was insufficient evidence linking Moussaoui to 9/11, and he was, "a remote or minor participant" in al Qaeda's actions against the United States (*Moussaoui v. United States*, 282 F.Supp.2d 481, 486 (E.D. Va. 2003)). Judge Brinkema also ruled that it would be fundamentally unfair to require Moussaoui to defend himself against accusations without the opportunity to seek testimony from witnesses held by the government (282 F. Supp.2d at 482). Under her ruling, Moussaoui could still be prosecuted for participating in a broad al Qaeda conspiracy against the United States, leading perhaps to life in prison.

The Fourth Circuit suggested a compromise that would allow Moussaoui access to statements made by three key al Qaeda detainees without letting him or his attorneys interview them in person. These witness statements were called "substitutions." Moussaoui's attorneys objected that the compromise was not comparable to the witnesses' live testimony. One of his attorneys remarked, "It's hard for us to consider substitutions for witnesses that we can't see or talk to" (Markon 2003h, 2003i).

After a lengthy delay, the Fourth Circuit issued a decision on April 22, 2004 that gave a little to each side. It rejected the government's claim that Judge Brinkema exceeded her authority by granting Moussaoui access to the witnesses, and affirmed her conclusion that the witnesses could provide material, favorable testimony on his behalf. It further agreed with Brinkema that the government's proposed substitutions for deposition testimony were inadequate. It remanded the case to her with instructions to craft substitutions that would be acceptable to each side (*United States v. Moussaoui*, 365 F.3d 292 (4th Cir. 2004)).

As to the Sixth Amendment dispute over the right of confrontation, the Fourth Circuit accepted the principle that the writ of habeas corpus did not extend to enemy aliens held abroad, but rejected the assumption that territorial limitations apply to lesser writs. It agreed that Judge Brinkema could reach beyond the boundaries of her district to issue a testimonial writ. Moussaoui's Sixth Amendment right to the testimony of witnesses held by the government would have to be balanced against the government's interest in preventing disruption of its detention of the witnesses.

The Fourth Circuit concluded that several statements by witnesses tended to undermine the theory that Moussaoui was to pilot a fifth plane into the White House. The statements also supported the position that he was relatively unimportant in the conspiracy, and that he was not involved in the 9/11 attacks. On those grounds, Moussaoui had made a sufficient showing that evidence from the witnesses "would be more helpful than hurtful, or at least that we cannot have confidence in the outcome of the trial" without evidence from the witnesses (365 F.3d at 310).

Moussaoui's trial ran into another complication in June 2004 when the 9/11 commission released information to the public, describing how al Qaeda figures differed on Moussaoui's role in the 9/11 attacks. The coordinator of the 9/11 plot (bin al-Shibh) told interrogators that it was his understanding that Moussaoui would be a participant in the 9/11 attacks, but another top al Qaeda detainee (Khalid Sheik Mohammed) expected Moussaoui to be part of a second wave of attacks. An attorney for Moussaoui criticized the 9/11 commission for disclosing the information and the government for declassifying it. Judge Brinkema had agreed to provide classified statements to the 9/11 commission, but only with the understanding that they would not be made public (Fisher 2005b, 220).

On September 13, 2004, the Fourth Circuit denied Moussaoui's argument that he had a right to interview key al Qaeda witnesses. Instead of being able to depose them, he would have to accept written summaries of their statements (*United States v. Moussaoui*, 382 F.3d 453 (4th Cir. 2004)). He took that case to the Supreme Court, but on March 21, 2005, the Court denied his petition for a writ of certiorari (*Moussaoui v. United States*, 544 U.S. 931 (2005). Matters were now supposedly cleared for a trial later in the year, but on April 22 he pleaded guilty to participating in a conspiracy with al Qaeda to fly planes into American buildings (Lewis 2005). His reasons for pleading guilty took some counterterrorist officials by surprise because they were unaware of any evidence that supported his story (Johnston and Lewis 2005). He may have pleaded guilty to bring the matter to a head. The trial to decide whether he would be sentenced to death

was expected to begin in early 2006 (Markon 2005). In May of 2006, Moussaoui was sentenced to life in prison (Markon 2006b).

GUANTÁNAMO DETAINEES

During U.S. military operations in Afghanistan and Pakistan in late 2001 and 2002, the United States and its allies captured thousands of individuals thought to be connected with the Taliban regime and al Qaeda's terrorist network. The military determined that many of the individuals should be detained as enemy combatants, citing two reasons. Detention prevented them from continuing to aid the enemy, and it offered an opportunity to gather intelligence helpful to military operations and the war against terrorism. Some of the detainees were transferred to the American naval base at Guantánamo Bay, Cuba. In time, their number reached about 700. The detainees were not charged with any crimes. None had access to attorneys.

Family members of twelve Kuwaiti nationals held at the base sought a preliminary injunction on their behalf, alleging violations of due process, the Alien Tort Claims Act, and the Administrative Procedure Act. On July 30, 2002, District Judge Colleen Kollar-Kotelly held that the two cases would be considered only as petitions for writs of habeas corpus. On the merits, she ruled that aliens held by the United States outside the sovereign territory of the United States could not use the regular federal courts to pursue petitions for habeas relief (*Rasul v. Bush*, 215 F.Supp.2d 55 (D.D.C. 2002)).

Judge Kollar-Kotelly relied on *Johnson v. Eisentrager* (1950) for the proposition that no court had authority to extend the writ of habeas corpus to aliens held outside the sovereign territory of the United States. The Court in 1950 noted that aliens within the country have a number of rights, including access to federal courts, and those rights expanded as they declare an intent to become a U.S. citizen. She remarked that it was, "undisputed that the individuals held at Guantanamo Bay do not seek to become citizens" (215 F.Supp.2d at 66). Was Guantánamo Bay part of the sovereign territory of the United States? She said that it was "not part of the sovereign territory of the United States" (215 F.Supp.2d at 69). Those who represented the detainees argued that the United States "has de facto sovereignty over the military base at Guantanamo Bay" because the United States exercises control and jurisdiction over the base.

Appealed to the U.S. Court of Appeals for the District of Columbia (commonly known as the D.C. Circuit), Judge Kollar-Kotelly's decision was affirmed on March 11, 2003. The appellate court agreed that *Eisentrager* was correctly cited for the principle that the aliens at Guantánamo could not seek habeas relief in federal court: "the Guantanamo detainees have much in common with the German prisoners in *Eisentrager*. They too are aliens, they too were captured during military operations, they were in a foreign country when captured, they are now abroad, they are in the custody of the American military, and they have never had any presence in the United States" (*Al Odah v. United States*, 321 F.3d 1134 at 1140 (D.C. Cir. 2003)). Left unexplored by the D.C. Circuit were critical differences between the German prisoners in *Eisentrager* and the detainees at Guantánamo. Those differences would be highlighted once the case reached the Supreme Court.

With the Bush administration winning handily in the D.C. Circuit, a different pattern developed in other cases filed in the more liberal U.S. Court of Appeals for the Ninth Circuit. On February 21, 2002, District Judge A. Howard Matz held that a coalition of journalists, lawyers, and clergy, having filed for a writ of habeas corpus on behalf of the detainees at Guantánamo Bay, lacked standing as "next friend," as required by federal law. The district court concluded that it had no jurisdiction to issue the writ (citing *Eisentrager*), and that detainees had no right to a writ of habeas corpus (*Coalition of Clergy v. Bush*, 189 F.Supp.2d 1036 (D.C. Cal. 2002)). The Ninth Circuit agreed that the coalition was not entitled to next-friend standing, but ruled that the district court did not have jurisdiction to decide that neither it nor any other federal court may properly entertain the habeas claims presented in the case (*Coalition of Clergy, Lawyers, & Professors v. Bush*, 310 F.3d 1153, 1164 (9th Cir. 2002)).

A second case also emerged in the Ninth Circuit. On May 13, 2003, Judge Matz held that he had no jurisdiction over a habeas claim from the brother of

Falen Gherebi, who was captured by the United States in Afghanistan and detained at Guantánamo (*Gherebi v. Bush*, 262 F.Supp.2d 1064 (C.D. Cal. 2003)). The Ninth Circuit reversed on December 18, 2003, holding that habeas jurisdiction existed over the petition filed on behalf of "enemy combatants" detained at Guantánamo. It said that for habeas purposes, the naval base was a part of the sovereign territory of the United States (*Gherebi v. Bush*, 352 F.3d 1278 (9th Cir. 2003)). Thus the Ninth Circuit found in favor of granting some constitutional and procedural rights to those detained at Guantánamo Bay.

The Supreme Court did not grant cert. on the case out of the Ninth Circuit (*Gheribi*), but it did agree to hear the consolidated cases out of the D.C. Circuit (*Rasul* and *Al Odah*). When the case was argued before the U.S. Supreme Court on April 20, 2004, matters did not go well for the government. Several Justices expressed discomfort with the scope of power sought by the government in these cases, especially its ability to put individuals at the naval base and claim they were beyond the reach of the judiciary through a habeas petition (Fisher 2005b, 246–47). Toward the end of oral argument, Solicitor General Ted Olson told the Court that the issue of whether Guantánamo was outside the jurisdiction of federal courts was a "political decision" and it would be remarkable for the judiciary to start deciding where the United States is sovereign and where it has control (*Rasul v. Bush*, oral argument, at 51). He did not convince the Court.

On June 28, 2004, in a six to three decision, the U.S. Supreme Court refused to treat *Eisentrager* as an automatic bar to detainee access to a habeas petition (*Rasul v. Bush*, 542 U.S. 466 2004). It ruled that federal courts have jurisdiction to consider challenges to the legality of the detention of foreign nationals captured abroad, in connection with hostilities, and held at Guantánamo. Writing for the majority, Justice Stevens pointed to six critical facts in the *Eisentrager* case: the prisoners were (1) enemy aliens, (2) had never been or resided in the United States, (3) were captured outside of U.S. territory and held there in military custody as a POW, (4) were tried and convicted by a military tribunal sitting outside the United States, (5) were convicted for offenses against laws of war committed outside the United States, and (6) were at all times imprisoned outside the United States. By contrast, the detainees at Guantánamo were not nationals of countries at war with the United States, had denied being engaged in or plotting acts of aggression against the United States, were never afforded access to any tribunal or even charged with or convicted of wrongdoing, and for two years had been detained in a territory over which the United States exercises exclusive jurisdiction and control (542 U.S. at 476).

Justice Scalia wrote a dissenting opinion, joined by Chief Justice Rehnquist and Justice Thomas. For Scalia, the fact that the detainees at the naval base "are not located within the territorial jurisdiction of any federal district court" should "end this case" (542 U.S. at 490). Having warned of the concentration of executive power in *Hamdi*, in this case he worried that the extension of habeas petitions to the detainees will force federal courts "to oversee one aspect of the Executive's conduct of a foreign war," and he warned that the majority's opinion "has a potentially harmful effect upon the Nation's conduct of a war" (542 U.S. at 499, 506).

On July 2, 2004, the administration granted approval to the lawyers for thirteen detainees at Guantánamo to travel to the naval base and meet with their clients (Lewis 2004). Five days later, the Defense Department responded to *Rasul* by establishing a Combatant Status Review Tribunal (CSRT), thus providing detainees with notice to explain the grounds for their detention and an opportunity to contest their designation as enemy combatants. Each detainee would have a "personal representative"—a military officer, not a lawyer—with access to information in DOD files on the detainee's background. The detainee may appear before the tribunal to present evidence and call witnesses if "reasonably available" (U.S. Department of Defense 2004, 1–2).

The lawyers who did meet with detainees at Guantánamo filed a variety of lawsuits on behalf of their new clients. Oral argument in district courts on these cases revealed a number of issues. First, the government embraced a remarkably broad definition of the type of terrorist covered by the Authorization for Use of Military Force Act (AUMF). On December 1, 2004, District Judge Joyce Hens Green asked the government a hypothetical about who would be considered

an enemy combatant or a supporter of the Taliban and al-Qaeda: "A little old lady in Switzerland who writes checks to what she thinks is a charity that helps orphans in Afghanistan but really is a front to finance al-Qaeda activities. Would she be considered an enemy combatant or supporting?" The government replied that the decision would be up to the military, "and great deference would need to be paid to its judgment." Asked if the lady could be taken into custody, the government that she could. Another hypothetical: "How about a resident of Dublin, England who teaches English to the son of a person the CIA knows to be a member of al-Qaeda. Would that teacher be considered an enemy combatant under those circumstances?" The government: "I think he could be" (oral argument, *Rasul v. Bush*, D.D.C., December 1, 2004, 25–27).

At this same oral argument, counsel for Guantánamo detainees objected that the principles established by the Supreme Court in *Hamdi* were not satisfied by the CSRT: minimum due process, the ability to confront the evidence against you, a neutral decision maker, and access to counsel. None of those were provided by the CSRT proceedings (oral argument, *Rasul v. Bush*, D.D.C., December 1, 2004, 73). The CSRT does not exclude evidence obtained by torture (oral argument, *Rasul v. Bush*, D.D.C., December 1, 2004, 85). Detainees had the burden of disproving secret evidence withheld from them, and to do that without the assistance of counsel (oral argument, *Rasul v. Bush*, D.D.C., December 1, 2004, 89). Moreover, some of the detainees had not been picked up in Afghanistan. The attorney for the El-Banna petitioners stated that they "cannot be considered enemy combatants because they were never combatants in the first place. They were not seized in combat, they were not members of enemy forces, they were not armed, and they were never engaged in any violence at the time of their arrest" in Africa. He told the court that "there's no evidence at all in the record, and the factual returns support this, that any of the petitioners was involved in the 9/11 attacks on this country" (oral argument, *Rasul v. Bush*, D.D.C., December 1, 2004, 120–21).

On January 31, 2005, District Judge Green decided eleven coordinated cases filed by detainees held at Guantánamo (*In re Guantanamo Detainee Cases*, 355 F.Supp.2d 443 (D.D.C. 2005)). She ruled that the petitioners had stated valid claims under the Fifth Amendment and that the procedures implemented by the government to confirm that the petitioners are "enemy combatants" violate their rights to due process of law. Among other deficiencies, she found that the CSRTs failed to give detainees access to material evidence used to decide "enemy combatant" status and failed to permit the assistance of counsel to compensate for the government's refusal to disclose classified information directly to the detainee. Furthermore, the CSRTs could not be considered "an impartial decision maker." There was no confidential relationship between the detainee and his personal representative, who was obligated to disclose to the tribunal any relevant incriminating information he obtained from the detainee. The CSRT did not sufficiently consider whether evidence obtained in making an enemy combatant determination had been obtained from the detainee through coercion or torture.

In that same month, another district judge reached the opposite conclusion. Judge Richard J. Leon reviewed habeas petitions from seven foreign nationals detained at Guantánamo: five Algerian-Bosnian citizens, one Algerian citizen, and one French citizen. Six were captured in Bosnia and the seventh in Pakistan. He ruled that no "viable legal theory" existed to justify the issuance of a writ of habeas corpus under the circumstances. Given enactment of the AUMF Act, Judge Leon said it "would be impermissible...under our constitutional system of separation of powers for the judiciary to engage in a substantive evaluation of the conditions of their detention." The framers "allocated the war powers among Congress and the Executive, not the Judiciary" (*Khalid v. Bush*, 355 F.Supp.2d 311, 328–29 (D.D.C. 2005)). During oral argument before Judge Leon, the government acknowledged that if the CSRT determined that evidence produced by torture was reliable, it could use that information to designate someone an enemy combatant (oral argument, *Benchellali v. Bush*, D.D.C., December 2, 2004, 84, 86).

Many other cases were filed on behalf of detainees at Guantánamo. One involved Salim Ahmed Hamdan, captured in Afghanistan in late 2001 and designated by President Bush as eligible for trial by military tribunal. On November 8, 2004, District Court Judge James Robertson ruled that he could be tried only by court-martial convened under the Uniform Code of Military Justice, unless and until a competent tribunal determined that he was not entitled to prisoner of war status. In noting that President Bush had determined that detained al Qaeda members are not prisoners of war under the Geneva Conventions, Judge Robertson observed that "[t]he President is not a 'tribunal'" (*Hamdan v. Rumsfeld*, 344 F.Supp.2d 152 at162 (D.D.C. 2004)). He found the military tribunal "remarkably different" from a court-martial in two respects: "The first has to do with the structure of the reviewing authority after trial; the second, with the power of the appointing authority or the presiding officer to exclude the accused from hearings and deny him access to evidence presented against him" (344 F. Supp.2d. at 166).

The government appealed the case to the D.C. Circuit, which heard oral argument on April 7, 2005. Speaking on behalf of Hamdan, Neal Katyal rejected the government's separation of power analysis: "The government wants to make this case about judicial interference with Executive functions, but what this case is really about is Executive interference with the judicial function. Simply put, the essence of our challenge today is that this is not a system of law. There are no rules written in advance that predictably explain what's going to happen. The procedures can be altered at any time" (oral argument, *Hamdan v. Rumsfeld*, D.C. Cir., April 7, 2005, 30). Also representing Hamdan, Commander Charles Swift objected that two of three members of the military tribunal "have no legal training" and contrasted the tribunal from a court-martial: "Far different from the military court-martial where the Judge is independent. He's independent by statute, he's independent by training, and his decisions—he's free to interpret the rules" (oral argument, *Hamdan v. Rumsfeld*, D.C. Cir., April 7, 2005, 54).

On July 15, 2005, the D.C. Circuit reversed Judge Robertson. It relied heavily on *Ex parte Quirin*, "in which captured German saboteurs challenged the lawfulness of the military commission before which they were to be tried, provid[ing] a compelling historical precedent for the power of civilian courts to entertain challenges that seek to interrupt the processes of military commissions. The Supreme Court ruled against the petitioners in Quirin," (*Hamdan v. Rumsfeld*, 415 F.3d 33 at 35 (D.C. Cir., 2005)). The court held that Hamdan "does not fit the Article 4 definition of a 'prisoner of war' entitled to the protection of the [Geneva] Convention" (415 F.3d at 39). The appropriate court was the military tribunal, not a court-martial (415 F.3d at 43).

On June 29, 2006, the Supreme Court reversed the D.C. Circuit, holding that the military commissions established by President Bush were not expressly authorized by any congressional statute, and that the commissions lacked the power to proceed because their structures and procedures violated both the Uniform Code of Military Justice (UCMJ) and the four Geneva Conventions signed in 1949 (*Hamdan v. Rumsfeld*, 126 S.Ct. 2749 (2006)). The five to three decision required President Bush to seek authorizing language from Congress. Because of that requirement some commentators, including officials in the White House, Justice Department, and the Defense Department, interpreted the Court's decision as merely raising statutory—not constitutional—issues. However, the Court addressed two important constitutional principles. First, it rejected the administration's argument that the president possessed inherent authority under Article II to create military commissions. As Neal Katyal, who argued the case for petitioner Hamdan, has pointed out, "The most important doctrinal lesson of *Hamdan* is its repudiation of the claim that the President is entitled to act alone" (Katyal 2006, 70). Second, the Court concluded that certain statutory provisions were binding on the president because they were enacted under the Article I authority of Congress. Congress responded to the Court's decision by enacting the Military Commissions Act of 2006. Judge James Robertson of he Federal District Court in the District of Columbia ruled in December of 2006 that the Military Commissions Act of 2006 did prevent the detainees at Guantánamo from filing habeas corpus petitions in the regular federal courts.

Thus the judge ruled that the detainees had no rights to seek relief in the regular federal courts (see Lewis 2006). As a result of Democrats taking control of both Houses of Congress in the November 2006 elections, amendments have already been introduced to the Military Commissions Act. It is unclear how the new Congress will approach this issue of the rights of the detainees at Guantánamo Bay.

CONCLUSIONS

Federal courts have offered widely different interpretations of executive and military power, with many judges and justices deferring to the president's determinations as commander-in-chief. Some courts read the separation of power doctrine in such a way as to prohibit any judicial second-guessing of presidential decisions in matters of war. In my opinion, such a constricted view undermines what was intended by an independent judiciary and eliminates a vital constitutional check to executive abuses and violations. Another fundamental check—the legislative branch—has been largely silent since 9/11, other than endorsing such executive initiatives as the two statutes authorizing war against Afghanistan and Iraq, passing the USA Patriot Act, establishing the new Department of Homeland Security, and completing action on the Military Commissions Act when forced to do so by the Supreme Court. Congressional hearings and investigations on a variety of issues surrounding the war on terrorism have been few and far between. With the new Democratic Congress, they are expected to increase in frequency and intensity. In times of emergency, the federal government has a pattern of becoming what the framers feared the most: the concentration of all three powers in the executive branch. An essential check consists of citizens and private organizations remaining active and determined to protect civil liberties by bringing pressure on all three branches.

Note

1. The views expressed by Louis Fisher in this volume are personal and do not reflect the views of the Library of Congress. This chapter discusses court cases through December 2006.

19

THE INTERACTIONS BETWEEN THE FEDERAL COURTS AND THE OTHER BRANCHES

Mark C. Miller

Some scholars argue that the courts should not be studied in isolation, but instead should be seen as part of the broader system of government. The so-called Governance as Dialogue movement among academics in the United States believes that the courts do not have the last word on interpreting the U.S. Constitution and certainly not in their role as interpreters of statutes. Instead, the meaning of the Constitution evolves through a continuous conversation or dialogue among the institutions of government. There is growing literature on the legal and political interactions between the courts and other branches. This chapter examines some of those interactions. The chapter raises questions about whether the independence of the courts is under attack today, especially by conservative politicians associated with the Religious Right in this country. This chapter also illustrates how judicial politics has grown from a field that focused almost exclusively on the U.S. Supreme Court into a field that explores the lower courts as well as the relationships between the courts and other political actors.

Scholars who study judicial issues in the United States have increasingly come to the view that the courts cannot be understood in isolation, but that they must be seen as a part of the larger system of government. As Justice Jackson argued over fifty years ago when expressing his views on the nation's highest court, "No sound assessment of our Supreme Court can treat it as an isolated, self-sustaining, or self-sufficient institution. It is a unit of a complex, interdependent scheme of government from which it cannot be severed" (Jackson 1955, 2). This chapter will use a new institutionalist approach to help us understand the interactions and relationships between the federal courts and the other branches. As I have stated in another work, "As a matter of constitutional design, the United States

simply does not feature a hierarchy of lawmakers or compartmentalized niches for each branch of government. Instead, the U.S. Constitution creates a system of overlapping and diversely representative branches of government, which share and compete for power" (Barnes and Miller 2004a, 202). Or put more simply, as Neustadt argued, in reality in our system of government we have, "separated institutions sharing powers" (Neustadt 1980, 26). Thus this chapter is squarely rooted in the Governance as Dialogue movement, which states that the federal courts do not have the last word on interpreting the U.S. Constitution, but rather that the courts share this responsibility with other institutions of government and with other political actors (see also Comiskey this volume, chapter 14).

Among academics in the United States, Alexander Bickel in his famous book, *The Least Dangerous Branch* (1962), was one of the first voices in what one could label the Governance as Dialogue movement. Bickel said that the courts must engage in a "continuing colloquy" with other branches of government and with various political actors, refuting the judicial supremacy approach then found so often in U.S. law schools and among political scientists and other judicial scholars. In Louis Fisher's *Constitutional Dialogues* (1988) and in his other writings, he argued that the courts, and especially the U.S. Supreme Court, do not have the sole responsibility of interpreting the U.S. Constitution, but that constitutional interpretation involves a very complicated dialogue among various political actors. Others, such as William N. Eskridge (1991a, 1991b) in two highly influential law review articles from the early 1990s, argued that the interactions between the courts, the executive, and the Congress are a highly complex multiple-player game. Baum (2006) argued that judges care deeply about how a variety of audiences will perceive their decisions, including political elites in the other institutions of government. Recently many scholars have begun to examine the interactions among the political institutions, and especially the interactions between the federal courts and other bodies (see, e.g., Fisher 1988; Katzmann 1988; Campbell and Stack 2001; Lovell 2003; Barnes 2004a; Pickerill 2004; Miller and Barnes 2004; Kassop 2004; Melnick 2004; Devins and Whittington 2005). Thus, I do not believe that the federal courts can be understood in isolation, but instead scholars must attempt to understand the relationships between and among the institutions of government.

DIFFERENT INSTITUTIONAL CULTURES AND INSTITUTIONAL WILLS

A clear area in which law and politics can clash is in the relationship between the U.S. Congress and the courts. Lately these interinstitutional interactions have taken on highly ideological and partisan overtones (see, e.g., Mann and Ornstein 2006a, 2006b), as will be discussed in more detail later. The courts and Congress clearly have different institutional cultures, different institutional needs, and different institutional wills (see Miller 2004a, 2004b). As Michael H. Armacost, former president of the Brookings Institution, wrote, "The judiciary seeks an environment respectful of its independence. Congress seeks a judicial system that faithfully construes the laws of the legislative branch and efficiently discharges justice" (quoted in Katzmann 1997, vii). Elaborating on this point, political scientist and now Judge Robert A. Katzmann wrote, "If Congress and the judiciary affect each other in fundamental ways, each also feels that the other needs to better understand its institutional workings. From the judiciary's perspective, Congress seems often unaware of the courts' institutional needs. In this view, the legislative branch consistently adds to the judiciary's burdens without concomitant resources.... From the legislature's vantage point, the judiciary often seems unattuned to the critical nuances of the legislative process." (Katzmann 1995, 1197).

Even though Congress and the courts have different institutional perspectives, it is nonetheless important to note that most of the interactions between these institutions are routine in nature and perhaps even mundane (see Resnik 2000; Resnik, Boggs, and Berman 2004).[1] Thus, many of the regular interactions between the courts and the Congress are positive in nature, but others clearly are more conflictual. Judges see themselves as an independent and co-equal branch of government, but sometimes the Congress views the courts as just one more federal agency begging for money and other resources, as will be discussed in more detail later. Thus the two institutions often just do not understand how and why the other makes decisions. As Davidson and Oleszek noted, "Communications between Congress and the federal courts are less than perfect. Neither branch understands the workings of the other very well" (Davidson and Oleszek 2002, 343). This lack of communication between the branches is clearly a problem for our governmental system. As Katzmann reminded us, "Governance...is premised on each institution's respect for and knowledge of the others and on a continuing dialogue that produces shared understanding and comity" (Katzmann 1997, 1).

These differences in institutional constraints and institutional norms between Congress and the courts are nicely illustrated by the question of whether a single individual would make different choices on the same issue depending on whether they were a legislator or whether they were a judge. In other words, would the different institutional cultures, different institutional norms, and different institutional wills of the courts and the Congress compel different results from the same individual depending on which institution they were serving and on what role they were playing? In *Texas v. Johnson* (1989), the case that declared that burning the American flag is protected political speech under the First Amendment, Justice Kennedy in his concurring opinion wrote about judges in general, "The hard fact is that sometimes we must make decisions we do not like. We make them because they are right, right in the sense that the law and the Constitution, as we see them, compel the result. And so great is our commitment to the process that, except in the rare case, we do not pause to express distaste for the result, perhaps for fear of undermining a valued principle that dictates the decision" (491 U.S. at 420–21). Justice Sandra Day O'Connor addressed this question in her dissent in a case where the majority ruled that the death penalty was unconstitutional for juveniles who committed the crime in question before they were 18 years old (*Roper v. Simmons* (2005)), where she wrote, "Were my office that of a legislator, rather than a judge, then I, too, would be inclined to support legislation setting a minimum age of 18 in this context" (543 U.S. at 607).

Therefore, sometimes judges wish that they could act like legislators, but feel that their reading of the law requires a different result. Take Justice Stewart's dissent in *Griswold v. Connecticut* (1965), where the Court declared the state statutory ban on the use or sale of contraceptives to be unconstitutional. Refusing to follow the liberal judicial activism of his colleagues, Justice Stewart wrote, "I think this is an uncommonly silly law.... As a philosophical matter, I believe the use of contraceptives in the relationship of marriage should be left to personal and private choice, based upon each individual's moral, ethical, and religious beliefs.... But we are not asked in this case to say whether we think this law is unwise, or even asinine. We are asked to hold that it violates the United States Constitution. And that I cannot do" (381 U.S. at 527). Justice Thomas made a similar claim in *Lawrence v. Texas* (2003), a case in which the majority declared

the Texas ban on homosexual sodomy to be unconstitutional. After echoing Justice Stewart's claim in *Griswold* that the statute was "uncommonly silly," Justice Thomas wrote in his dissent in *Lawrence*, "If I were a member of the Texas Legislature, I would vote to repeal it. Punishing someone for expressing his sexual preference through noncommercial consensual conduct with another adult does not appear to be a worthy way to expend valuable law enforcement resources. Notwithstanding this, I recognize that as a member of this Court I am not empowered to help petitioners and others similarly situated. My duty, rather, is to decide cases agreeably to the Constitution and laws of the United States" (539 U.S. at 605).

Justice John Paul Stevens of the U.S. Supreme Court has also said that his decisions on a variety of issues would be different if he were in Congress rather than having to make the decisions from the bench. For example, in 2005 the U.S. Supreme Court handed down two highly controversial decisions. The first said that local governments can use their power of eminent domain to "take" private property to facilitate private economic development (*Kelo v. City of New London* (2005)). The second ruled that the Congress can decide to use federal drug laws to overrule various state decisions that had allowed marijuana use for medical purposes (*Gonzales v. Raich* (2005)). From a policy point of view, Justice Stevens said in a public speech to a bar association meeting in Las Vegas that both outcomes were "unwise," but were required by his reading of the Constitution. Clearly illustrating the differences between decisions made by members of Congress and those made by judges, Justice Stevens concluded that, "in each [decision] I was convinced that the law compelled a result that I would have opposed if I were a legislator" (quoted in Greenhouse 2005b, A1). Thus in areas in which law and politics collide, judges tend to make decisions based on their reading of the law whereas legislators tend to make their decisions based purely on political considerations.

PERIODS OF CONFLICT

The relationships between the federal courts and the other institutions of government are certainly highly complex and sometimes quite strained. The potential for misunderstandings between the courts and the other branches seems to have grown in recent years. In 2004 Justice Sandra Day O'Connor said that the relationship between Congress and the federal courts was, "more tense than at any time in my lifetime" (quoted in Greenhouse 2005a, 10). As reported by Newsweek journalist Debra Rosenberg, in early 2005 Justice O'Connor even invited a variety of federal legislators to the Supreme Court for private meetings to discuss Court–Congress relations among other issues, in part to keep the lines of communication open between members of the different branches (see Rosenberg 2005, 23). The level of understanding between the branches of government reached such a low point that in late 2003 several members of the U.S. House created the bipartisan Congressional Caucus on the Judicial Branch, cochaired by Representatives Adam B. Schiff (D–CA) and Judy Biggert (R–IL). As part of the Caucus's activities, several justices from the U.S. Supreme Court and some chief justices of state supreme courts have met with Members of Congress in roundtable discussions held on Capitol Hill. It is not clear that these meetings lowered the level of tension between the two institutions, especially since the Newsweek article discussing Justice O'Connor's initiatives was entitled, "The War on Judges."

In fact, at the beginning of the twenty-first century we may be experiencing one of the greatest periods of conflicts between Congress and the courts. As Chief Justice Rehnquist stated in his 2004 annual report, "Criticism of judges has dramatically increased in recent years, exacerbating in some respects the strained relationship between the Congress and the federal judiciary" (Rehnquist 2004, 4). And as Lyle Denniston, a journalist who has covered the Supreme Court for many years, said recently, "In 56 years of journalism, most of which has been spent hanging around lawyers and courthouses, I have never experienced the depth of venom that now flows around the relationship between the branches of government, particularly around the judiciary" (quoted in The Courts 2004, 221). Journalist Debra Rosenberg agreed, noting that, "Concern over the rising tide of anti-judge rhetoric has rocked even the Supreme Court. Though judges have been dragged into the culture wars before, lately the animosity—and

a range of new efforts to curb judicial power—have reached fever pitch" (Rosenberg 2005, 23). The current conflicts between the courts and Congress have become both ideological and highly partisan.

Congressional interactions with the federal courts may just be part of a larger partisan culture war being fought in Congress. Mann and Ornstein (2006a and 2006b) argued that Congress has become "the Broken Branch" in large part because everything Congress does now is highly partisan and highly ideological. As these scholars wrote just before the November 2006 elections, "Partisanship [in Congress] particularly increased after the 1994 elections…Now it is tribal warfare. The consequences are deadly serious. Party and ideology routinely trump institutional interests and responsibilities" (Mann and Ornstein 2006b, A17). When I first interviewed Members of Congress in the late 1980s about their attitudes toward the courts, congressmen with law degrees and members of the House Judiciary Committee were the most supportive of the courts, regardless of party and/or ideology (see Miller 1992, 1993, 1995). Today, congressional attitudes toward the courts seem to be driven solely by ideological and partisan concerns.

In interviews with this author conducted during the fall of 2006 before the midterm elections held in that year, various Members of Congress and congressional staff used the following phrases to describe the current relationship between the Congress and the federal courts: "venomous," "hostile," "tense," "deteriorating," "contentious," "animosity," and "strained." As one liberal U.S. Representative lamented, "The relationship between the Congress and the federal courts is at an all time low." Another liberal Representative said that, "There is less respect for the independence of the courts today." A conservative Republican described the relationship as "adversarial." Justice O'Connor even wrote an op-ed piece in *The Wall Street Journal* in September 2006 entitled, "The Threat to Judicial Independence." This piece ran a few days after Justices O'Connor and Breyer appeared on the *Charlie Rose Show* on PBS to defend judicial independence. After outlining many of the current attacks on the judiciary from Congress and the state legislatures, Justice O'Connor concluded in *The Wall Street Journal* op-ed that, "The breadth and intensity of rage currently being leveled at the judiciary may be unmatched in American history. The ubiquitous 'activist judges' who 'legislate from the bench' have become central villains on today's domestic political landscape.... Though these attacks generally emit more heat than light, using judges as punching bags presents a grave threat to the independent judiciary" (O'Connor 2006, A18). In fact, the relationship between Congress and the courts has become so sour that when the House Judiciary Committee in June of 2006 held hearings on a bill to create an inspector general for the judicial branch, no federal judges nor staff from the administrative office of the federal courts were invited to testify on a piece of legislation that would have had enormous impact on the functioning of the federal courts. The House Judiciary Committee eventually approved the bill in September of 2006 on a party line vote (*The Washington Post* 2006, A16), although no final action was taken on this legislation.

Our current era, of course, is not the first time that there have been potential conflicts and misunderstandings between the courts and other branches of government (see, e.g., Nagel 1965; Geyh 2006). President Thomas Jefferson, a member of the Republican–Democratic Party, was very upset with the federal judiciary because it was dominated by Federalist Party judges. Other eras of high tension between Congress and the federal courts have included the 1858 to 1869 period, when Congress was outraged by the decision in *Dred Scott v. Sandford* (1857) and also took efforts to prevent the Court from declaring Reconstruction to be unconstitutional. In fact, following the Civil War, the Radical Republicans in the House of Representatives passed legislation to require a two-thirds majority of the Court before the justices could declare any federal statute unconstitutional (see Fisher 2005a, 1038). In the early part of the 1900s, Progressives were angry at the conservative judicial activism of the Court in reading laissez-faire economics into the Constitution and thus striking down most attempts at governmental regulation of the economy. In fact, at the time Senator Robert M. LaFollette referred to federal judges as, "petty tyrants and arrogant despots" (quoted in McDowell 1988, 1). Progressives in the early part of the twentieth century also proposed requiring a two-thirds vote of the justices of the Supreme Court before

the Court could declare a congressional statute to be unconstitutional, and they proposed that a two-thirds vote in Congress could override Supreme Court constitutional decisions (O'Brien 2003, 357–58). In the 1930s, President Franklin Roosevelt was extremely angry that the New Deal was being declared unconstitutional. This led to FDR's infamous Court Packing Plan (see, e.g., Jackson 1941; Schmidhauser and Berg 1972, 134–42), to be discussed in more detail later. From the late 1950s until the late 1970s, conservatives were quite upset with the liberal activism of the U.S. Supreme Court regarding desegregation, congressional investigations, national security, and other issues (see, e.g., Pritchett 1961; Murphy 1962; Powe 2000). Thus the conflicts between the courts and the other branches are not new, but the current period seems to be accentuating these tensions.

JUDICIAL ACTIVISM AND JUDICIAL RESTRAINT

Part of this recent tension between the courts and Congress may be due to the fact that the Rehnquist Court practiced both liberal judicial activism and conservative judicial activism simultaneously, leading to what Keck (2004) labeled, *The Most Activist Supreme Court in History*. Judicial review is defined as the power of the courts to declare actions of other political actors to be unconstitutional. In fact, from 1995 to 2003 the Court used its power of judicial review and struck down federal statutes as unconstitutional at a rate that is higher than in any period in U.S. history (Keck 2004, 40). Some of the justices on the Rehnquist Court were liberal judicial activists, some were conservative judicial activists, and some practiced both liberal and conservative activism.

When political scientists use the term "judicial activism," they tend to use the term in a descriptive sense and not generally as a pejorative. For political scientists, judicial activism simply means that the courts make public policy when the elected branches cannot or will not, often by declaring the actions of other political actors to be unconstitutional (see Holland 1991, 1). Judicial activism in the U.S. context also means that the judges are willing to interpret the

U.S. Constitution as a living and changing document.[2] Thus, any time that the American courts declare an action of the elected branches to be unconstitutional, they are exercising judicial activism in the political science sense of the term. The ideological direction of the activism leads to the labeling of the action as either liberal judicial activism or conservative judicial activism (see also Keck 2004).

The term "judicial activism," however, often carries a highly negative connotation in its popular use. For example, President George W. Bush often complains about what he sees as activist judges, especially when it comes to issues such as same-sex marriage (see, e.g., Roosevelt 2006, 12). Regarding the use of the term "judicial activism," Lyle Denniston, a long-time journalist who has covered the U.S. Supreme Court for years, stated, "[The use of "judicial activism"] reminds me very much of a time when we used to use the word 'Communist' in order to really demonize something. And now the word 'activist' flows frequently from the mouth...of the President of the United States in reference to judges" (quoted in The Courts 2004, 221). Conservative political analyst Mark Levin wrote that activist judges "have abused their constitutional mandate by imposing their personal prejudices and beliefs on the rest of society" because they "make, rather than interpret the law" (Levin 2005, 10). Religious Right leader Pat Robertson has even written, "The purpose of activists in the courts, as elsewhere in society, is to win cases by judicial overreach that they could never win at the ballot box" (Robertson 2004, 74). Thus in popular language, the term "judicial activism" has become a highly negative political pejorative. As Kermit Roosevelt explained, "In practice 'activist' turns out to be little more than a rhetorically charged shorthand for decisions the speaker disagrees with" (Roosevelt 2006, 3).

Critics of the conservative tilt of the Rehnquist Court say a flexible interpretation of the Constitution is also the approach used by conservative judicial activists like Justices Antonin Scalia and Clarence Thomas (see, e.g., Cohen 2005). In fact, Professor Lori Ringhand found that from 1994 to 2005 conservative justices were far more likely to overturn statutes enacted by Congress than were liberal justices on the U.S. Supreme Court (Ringhand 2007). *The New York Times* even ran an

editorial (2006) entitled, "Activism is in the Eye of the Ideologist," in which the editors argued that conservative judicial activism is on the rise today.[3]

This simultaneous conservative and liberal judicial activism of the Rehnquist Court has increased the distain for the federal courts among many political actors, and it has led to claims that the Supreme Court does not understand the institutional needs of the legislative branch. Following a series of both conservative and liberal activist decisions, in 2000 reporter Tony Mauro concluded, "The Supreme Court has declared constitutional war on Congress" (Mauro 2000, 8). Adding fuel to the fire, Mauro then went on to quote Justice Scalia in a 2000 public speech on this topic, "My Court is fond of saying that acts of Congress come to the Court with the presumption of constitutionality. But if Congress is going to take the attitude that it will do anything it can get away with and let the Supreme Court worry about the Constitution, then perhaps that presumption is unwarranted" (quoted in Mauro 2000, 8). The Supreme Court's decision in *Bush v. Gore* (2000), which had the effect of declaring George W. Bush as the winner of the 2000 presidential election, was a clear case where liberals felt that the Supreme Court was intervening in issues that were better left to other political actors (see, e.g., Bugliosi 2001; Dershowitz 2001; Strauss 2001; Garbus 2002). And as one liberal remarked, "The idea that liberal judges are advocates and partisans while judges like Justice Scalia are not is being touted everywhere these days, and it is pure myth.... The conservative partisans leading the war on activist judges are just as inconsistent: they like judicial activism just fine when it advances their own agendas" (Cohen 2005, 20).

Thus both liberals and conservatives can point to activist decisions of the Supreme Court and other federal courts with which they strongly disagree, but the most serious attacks on the courts today seem to be coming from the conservative wing of the Republican Party (see also Geyh 2006). As one conservative critic of the courts has written, "Judges still routinely usurp power from the other branches of government and act as though they are unconstrained by the Constitution" (Levin 2005, ix). Mark W. Smith even gave the following title to his book, *Disrobed: The New Battle Plan to Break the Left's Stranglehold on the Courts*. Smith wrote, "The Left continues to achieve extraordinary success in the courts even now, despite the sharp right turn the nation has taken over the past quarter century.... Conservatives rightly recognize that what Alexander Hamilton once called the 'least dangerous branch' of government has instead become the *most dangerous branch*" (Smith 2006, 6).

The Religious Right seems to be the most upset in our society about their perception that liberal activist judges are destroying our nation today (see Geyh 2006, 271–75). Professor Doris Marie Provine concluded that, "The most hyperbolic criticism of activist judges comes from the New Right, which uses every available opportunity to express its dismay with decisions that limit the reach of popular Bible-based moral principles" (Provine 2005, 319). One of the leaders of the Religious Right, Pat Robertson, wrote, "Those on the other side, who are socially and politically liberal, want a social revolution. A large number of these men and women want to overthrow Christian values by a majority of nonelected judges who serve for life and answer to no one" (Robertson 2004, xxiii). Phyllis Schlafly, a leader of the far right, wrote, "The unique and brilliant design of our Constitution...has been replaced by the Imperial Judiciary. Judicial supremacists have grabbed unconstitutional powers for the courts, and Congress has filed to retrain their power grab" (Schlafly 2006, 4). In the 2006 congressional elections, a variety of conservative candidates ran ads like one complaining that, "Liberal judges have completely rewritten the Constitution" (quoted in Horrigan 2006, 2755). As Tony Perkins, president of the conservative Family Research Council stated, "Every issue we care deeply about has the fingerprints of judges on it" (quoted in Rosenberg 2005, 24).

FIGHTS OVER CONFIRMATION OF FEDERAL JUDICIAL APPOINTMENTS

The different institutional perspectives and institutional cultures of the Congress, the president, and the federal courts often become most apparent during the confirmation process for federal judges. All so-called Article III federal judges are of course appointed by the president and confirmed by the Senate for life terms (see, e.g., Silverstein 1994; Maltese 1995; Goldman 1997; Comiskey 2004; Epstein and Segal 2005). Federal magistrate judges, federal bankruptcy judges, and a host of other federal judges such as those sitting on specialized courts such as the Tax Court are often called Article I judges and are appointed for limited terms through a completely different appointment process (see, e.g., Tarr 2006, 28).

It is during the confirmation process for the Article III life term federal judges that the tensions between law and politics most often play themselves out (see Bell this volume). Clearly, presidents often see their judicial appointments as a way to shape their future ideological legacy. As David O'Brien argued, "The presidential impulse to pack the Court with politically compatible justices is irresistible" (O'Brien 2003, 55). What sometimes receives less attention, however, is the fact that senators also often use their role in the confirmation process to attempt to shape constitutional interpretation (Gerhardt 2005).

Frustrated with the conservative judicial activism of the Supreme Court in striking down much of his New Deal legislation in the early 1930s, President Franklin D. Roosevelt offered his so-called Court Packing Plan following his landslide reelection in 1936. FDR was furious with the Supreme Court for thwarting the will of the people by declaring the New Deal to be unconstitutional. What FDR proposed was that the size of the Court be increased from nine to fifteen, allowing him to appoint another justice for each current justice then over the age of 70. Thus Roosevelt's court-packing plan would have almost doubled the size of the Supreme Court, giving FDR the ability to appoint a large number of sympathetic new justices. Although the Congress refused to enact this plan, the five to four majority on the Supreme Court that voted to strike down the New Deal as unconstitutional eventually changed to a five to four majority in favor of upholding the constitutionality of the New Deal legislation. This famous "Switch in Time that Saved Nine" prevented FDR and the Democrats in Congress from directly attacking the institutional integrity of the Supreme Court (see O'Brien 2003, 337–38).

Using his appointment power to reshape the Supreme Court and ultimately end the era of conservative judicial activism, Roosevelt clearly appointed justices based on their ideological views and their judicial philosophies. Thus President Roosevelt eventually won his war with the Supreme Court and therefore changed the future relationship between the federal courts and the elected branches. Therefore, Presidents Roosevelt, Truman, and Eisenhower used their judicial appointment powers to usher in the period of liberal judicial activism that epitomized the Warren Court era.

The conservative backlash against the liberal judicial activism of the Warren Court, however, also helped to change the future of the American political landscape. Since the 1950s, conservatives have argued that liberals and activists must be prevented from taking the bench, while liberals have argued the opposite (see, e.g., Comiskey 2004). Presidents Nixon and Reagan campaigned hard against the liberal activism of the federal bench as they saw it. Nixon, the "law and order" presidential candidate, used his opposition to the liberal activism of the Warren Court era as part of his Southern Strategy in 1968 to help convince the formerly solid Democratic South to vote for his Republican presidential candidacy (see Keck 2004, 107–8). Although Nixon was able to appoint four justices to the Supreme Court, the Burger Court did little to dismantle the activist precedents of the prior Warren Court era. The Burger Court was often described in academic circles as, "the counter-revolution that wasn't" (Blasi 1983). President Reagan also used his opposition to liberal judicial activism as a campaign tool in 1980 and in 1984, complaining that the era of liberal judicial activism had not ended despite the fact that Chief Justice Warren had been replaced by Chief Justice Burger (see O'Brien 2003, 55).

Although President Nixon had some trouble reshaping the lower federal courts because he faced a Democratic Senate, President Reagan had no such impediment. Having the luxury of a Republican Senate for much of his presidency, O'Brien argued about President Reagan, "With Reagan's election in 1980, movement conservatives had a White House committed to turning judgeships into not merely political symbols, but instruments of political power" (O'Brien 2001, 72). Before he left office, President Reagan appointed almost half of the lower federal bench (372 out of 736 federal judges), named three justices to the Supreme Court, and elevated William

H. Rehnquist to the Chief Justice's chair (see O'Brien 2003, 69). Alarmed at Reagan's success in reshaping the judiciary, liberals in 1987 eventually blocked the nomination by President Reagan of Judge Robert Bork to the Supreme Court because Bork was perceived as holding extreme judicial restraintist views (see, e.g., Simon 1992; Bronner 1989).[4]

In 2005 and 2006, the confirmation processes for Judge John Roberts to become chief justice and for Samuel Alito to become an associate justice of the Supreme Court nicely illustrate the tensions between the institutional cultures and institutional perspectives of the Congress and the federal courts. Liberals took the opportunity of the Roberts nomination to criticize the Supreme Court's conservative activist decisions in the area of federalism, where the Court restricted congressional power in favor of the states by declaring various federal statutes to be unconstitutional. In a letter to then Judge Roberts, Senate Judiciary Committee Chairman Arlen Specter (R–PA) "blasted the 'judicial activism' of the Supreme Court under Chief Justice William H. Rehnquist" (Perine 2005, 2254). In the letter, Senator Specter stated, "My immediate reaction is to wonder how the Court can possibly assert its superiority in its 'method of reasoning' over the reasoning of Congress" (Perine 2005, 2254). Reacting to Senator Specter's letter, Nan Aron, president of the Alliance for Justice, a liberal interest group, stated, "It's nice to see a Republican senator drawing attention to what every constitutional law scholar in the country has recognized as the real story about the Supreme Court: the aggressive, activist efforts of the court's conservatives" to overturn legislation "that protects ordinary Americans" (quoted in Stolberg 2005a, A16). Objecting to statements in various Supreme Court opinions that he felt denigrated the role of Congress, Senator Specter declared during Judge Roberts' confirmation hearings, "There isn't a method of reasoning which changes when you move across the green from the Senate columns to the Supreme Court columns. And we do our homework, evidenced by what has gone on in this hearing. And we don't like being treated as schoolchildren [by the Supreme Court]" (quoted in Greenhouse 2005c, A23).

Even though Senator Specter eventually voted to confirm now Chief Justice Roberts, this episode makes it clear that both liberals and conservatives in Congress are unhappy with the Supreme Court's judicial activism. At one point, it appeared that the Roberts nomination could become highly ideological and partisan (see, e.g., Stern 2005). In the end, however, the vote to confirm him was seventy-eight to twenty-two, with many liberals eventually voting for him both in committee and on the floor. As two journalists covering the confirmation process reported, "Roberts' swearing-in capped a relatively trouble-free nomination highlighted by three days of polished testimony before the Judiciary Committee that left Democrats grasping for a rationale to oppose his nomination" (Stern and Perine 2005, 2651).

However, the Senate vote on Justice Samuel Alito did become highly ideological and highly partisan. In fact, the confirmation vote for now Justice Alito was the most partisan in history. President Bush nominated Judge Alito only after conservatives had successfully killed his previous nomination of White House Counsel Harriett Miers to fill Justice Sandra Day O'Connor's seat on the Supreme Court. Therefore, Judge Alito was seen as the darling of the right wing of the Republican Party. Liberals voted against Judge Alito on purely ideological grounds, and some even tried to filibuster his nomination. The filibuster failed because all the Republicans and about half of the Democrats voted in favor of cloture to end the filibuster. On January 31, 2006, Justice Alito was confirmed by a vote of fifty-eight to forty-two, with only four Democrats voting in favor of his nomination and one liberal Republican Senator voting against the nomination (Stern and Perine 2006, 340–41). Immediately after his confirmation, Justice Alito attended President Bush's State of the Union address along with three other justices, raising some questions after one of the most partisan confirmation votes in Senate history. The only Justice confirmed to sit on the Supreme Court who received more negative votes than Justice Alito was Justice Clarence Thomas (see Reynolds 2006).[5]

Clearly, the confirmation process for judicial nominees has become highly contentious, partisan, and extremely ideological. Both liberals and conservatives are using the confirmation process for political gains, and both are complaining about judicial activist judges. Both sides are using the confirmation process

for federal judges to raise enormous amounts of money for interest groups and for candidates alike (see, e.g., Bumiller 2005, A13; for more on the role of interest groups in the confirmation process, see Bell this volume, chapter 3). As one reporter explained, "Nothing rallies the bases of both parties like the issue of judges. For conservatives, who have fought for decades to curb what they regard as the liberal activism of the judiciary, the Alito nomination is a sweet reward. For liberals, it is terrifying" (Stolberg 2006, A18).

REVERSING FEDERAL COURT DECISIONS

In addition to using the confirmation process to influence constitutional interpretation, legislators and presidents have other tools at their disposal as well. Of course, individual members of Congress and other politicians have long criticized specific federal court decisions with which they disagree. As former Attorney General Nicholas Katzenbach once observed, throughout history politicians have frequently, "gone after the Supreme Court because it doesn't cost anything" (quoted in O'Brien 2003, 356). Generally members of Congress who are lawyers are thought to be more supportive of the courts than are their nonlawyer colleagues (see Miller 1995), but both lawyer-politicians and nonlawyers feel free to criticize court decisions of which they disapprove. The anti-court rhetoric can be fierce at times, but the real concern of federal judges and other who care about issues of judicial independence is when congressional attacks against the courts go beyond mere verbal criticism.

When Congress is unhappy with the federal courts, it has various weapons at its disposal. Sometimes just the threat of attack will be enough for the federal courts to change their behavior (see Whittington 2005; Epstein, Knight, and Martin 2004; Epstein and Knight 1998). Congress can, of course, overturn court decisions. If the court rulings are statutory interpretations, then Congress can simply enact a new statute when it disagrees with a federal court's rulings. For example, in the Civil Rights Restoration Act of 1991, Congress in effect overturned a series of conservative U.S. Supreme Court statutory interpretation decisions that had made it more difficult for victims of discrimination to sue (see Barnes 2004a, 4, 12–15). Eskridge (1991a) among others has shown us that Congress is quite willing to overturn these statutory interpretation decisions when it disagrees with the rulings of the courts. Congress is more likely to respond to statutory interpretation decisions of the U.S. Supreme Court than it is to the decisions of the U.S. Courts of Appeals (see Lindquist and Yalof 2001). At times, of course, Congress intentionally enacts vague statutes, in part because of the need for compromise in the legislative body and in part because Congress prefers that the courts tackle the tough interpretation questions (see Graber 1993; Lovell 2003). The federal courts, however, view their role in statutory interpretation cases to be discovering the intent of Congress. After examining a variety of instances in which the courts felt compelled to interpret unclear statutory language, Lovell concluded that, "Each time judges settled interpretive controversies about a statutory provision, they justified their choices by claiming that they were following the will of Congress rather than their own personal policy preferences" (Lovell 2003, 252).

When federal courts hand down a constitutionally based decision, in theory Congress should pass a Constitutional Amendment to overturn that decision. The Eleventh, Fourteenth, Sixteenth, and Twenty-Sixty Amendments were all enacted in reaction to U.S. Supreme Court decisions. In reality, however, Congress will express its displeasure with court decisions in any way that it can. Congress often attempts to ignore constitutionally based decisions with which it disagrees such as the decision declaring a one house legislative veto to be unconstitutional (*Immigration and Naturalization Service v. Chadha* 1983). Congress can also enact statutes in an attempt to overturn constitutionally based decisions. Many of these statutes are later declared unconstitutional by the Supreme Court (see, e.g., Bragaw and Miller 2004).[6]

On the other hand, we should not assume that Congress carefully considers constitutional issues during its deliberations on every floor vote. As Pickerill reminded us, "We should not expect members of Congress to routinely or systematically consider, of their own volition, constitutional issues raised by legislation. As congressional scholars have shown, members of Congress are primarily motivated by the 'electoral connection,' notions of representation, and the desire to make good public policy" (Pickerill 2004, 3). Pickerill argued that Congress reacts to constitutional rulings handed down by the courts, but it does not necessarily consider constitutional issues until after courts have raised the issues first.

It is not clear that the Rehnquist Court appreciated the role of Congress in this continuing constitutional dialogue. As evidence of this distain for Congress' role in the constitutional dialogue, Chief Justice Rehnquist himself wrote in *United States v. Morrison* that, "No doubt the political branches have a role in interpreting and applying the Constitution, but ever since *Marbury* this Court has remained the ultimate expositor of the constitutional text" (529 U.S. at 616 n.7). Complaining that Congress was interfering with the responsibilities of the courts by attempting to impose a constitutional interpretation standard through passage of the 1993 Religious Freedom Restoration Act, Justice Kennedy wrote for the majority of the justices in *City of Boerne v. Flores* (1997), "When the Court has interpreted the Constitution, it has acted within the province of the Judicial Branch, which embraces the duty to say what the law is" (521 U.S. at 537). In other words, the Supreme Court decreed that Congress must yield to the pronouncements of the Court on constitutional issues. Thus recent congressional attacks on the federal courts must be understood in this context.[7]

Because some conservative Republicans in Congress became so angry with a host of what they perceive to be improperly liberal activist decisions of the federal courts, and especially the U.S. Supreme Court, in 2003 they created a new House Working Group on Judicial Accountability. According to a press release issued by the new organization, this group would educate members of Congress and the public about judicial abuses, especially the dangers of liberal judicial activism (Smith 2003). Congressman Steve Chabot (R–OH), a founding member of The Working Group, defined judicial activism in the following manner: "Judicial activism occurs when judges exceed the authority given to them under Article III of the Constitution. When judges substitute their own political views for the law, the ramifications can be felt by communities across our nation" (quoted in

Smith 2003). Former Majority Leader of the House Tom DeLay (D–TX) said at the time, "When it comes to judicial abuses, we are going to take no prisoners" (quoted in Administrative Office 2003b, 1). Founding members of the new Working Group later introduced legislation to require that a two-thirds vote in both houses could override any constitutional decisions of the U.S. Supreme Court that struck down a federal statute as unconstitutional (see R. Lewis 2004).

STRIPPING THE COURTS OF JURISDICTION

Congress determines the jurisdiction of the lower federal courts and perhaps of the U.S. Supreme Court, and lately there have been more serious efforts to limit the ability of the federal courts to hear various types of cases. Although few of these measures have been enacted into law (see, e.g., Curry 2005), in the past several years various bills have been enacted or at least have been passed by the U.S. House of Representatives (see, e.g., Bell and Scott 2006). Those who support judicial independence are increasingly worried about these efforts.

In the 1950s through the 1970s, outraged conservatives attempted without success to prevent the courts from hearing cases dealing with school prayer, desegregation, abortion, and other social issues. These proposals are generally called withdrawing jurisdiction from the courts, or more commonly court stripping. Almost all of these efforts failed. For example, in 1979 Senator Jesse Helms (R–NC) bullied the Senate into passing legislation that would have prevented the federal courts from hearing cases dealing with school prayer, but the bill died in the House (see O'Brien 2003, 359–60). Conservatives such as former Attorney General Meese clearly stated their preference that Congress strip the courts of jurisdiction in a variety of cases. Meese stated, "Congress has in the past withdrawn jurisdiction from the lower federal courts when it became dissatisfied with their performance or concluded that state courts were the better forum for certain types of cases" (Meese and Dehart 1997, 181–82).

For scholars who study this issue, the definition of what is and what is not court-stripping legislation has become murky at best. During and after the Civil War, the Radical Republicans enacted various court stripping proposals, but Congress has also enacted some of these measures in the modern era. For example, the 1995 Prison Litigation Reform Act reduced the ability of federal judges to manage state prisons and force the early release of prisoners. Was this court-stripping legislation? Also, the Anti-Terrorism and Effective Death Penalty Act of 1996 limited the ability of the federal courts to hear multiple habeas corpus appeals from death row inmates (see Tarr 2006, 34). The 1996 Immigration Reform Act limited the number of appeals available to immigrants facing possible deportation. The Terrorism Risk Insurance Act of 2002 prohibited the federal courts from reviewing the U.S. Secretary of the Treasury's official designation of particular actions as "terrorist acts" (see Curry 2005). In 2002, then Senate Minority Leader Tom Daschle inserted language into an appropriations bill that stripped all federal courts of jurisdiction over procedures governing timber projects in the Black Hills National Forest in his home state of South Dakota (see Kyl 2004, 7; Hudson 2002, A1; Munn 2002, A16). The Congress included similar provisions in the Healthy Forest Act. In 2005, the U.S. House passed legislation that would prevent the federal courts from hearing any cases arising from the proposed construction of a fence on the U.S.–Mexico border (see, e.g., *The Washington Post* 2005a, A22; Allen 2005a, A4).

Therefore, today court-stripping proposals have begun to receive a great deal more attention in Congress. A September 2004 paper distributed by the Senate Republican Policy Committee was entitled, "Restoring Popular Control of the Constitution: The Case for Jurisdiction-Stripping Legislation." As this report stated, "The American people must have a remedy when they believe that federal courts have overreached and interpreted the Constitution in ways that are fundamentally at odds with the people's common constitutional understandings and expectations" (Kyl 2004, 1). In 2004, the House voted several times to strip the lower federal courts of jurisdiction to hear cases challenging the constitutionality of the Federal Defense of Marriage Act and the constitutionality of the Pledge of Allegiance. Both bills later died in the Senate (see Fisher 2005a, 1040–41). In 2006, the

House again passed the Pledge Protection Act, while the Senate again killed the legislation. The Congress has also enacted legislation designed to prevent the courts from interfering with the enemy combatants held at Guantánamo Bay, as Louis Fisher explains in more detail in chapter 18 of this volume. In fact, Judge James Robertson of the U.S. District Court for the District of Columbia ruled in December of 2006 that the Congress had in fact stripped the courts of the authority to hear challenges from detainees at Guantánamo Bay, including the right of the detainees to seek habeas corpus relief from the regular federal courts (see Lewis 2006, A24).

Louis Fisher and other constitutional scholars argue that court-stripping proposals are probably unconstitutional (see, e.g., Fisher 2005a, 1036–37), but court stripping remains a key strategy for the political right in their fight against liberal judicial activism.[8] Geyh (2006) argued that the courts are protected from the most virulent institutional attacks from Congress because these two institutions over the years have reached a "dynamic equilibrium" that favors judicial independence. Yet Geyh concluded, "Every cycle of court-directed hostility has featured serious and substantial congressional factions intent on curbing the courts in significant ways. It would be a mistake to assume that independence norms have been so deeply entrenched as to render either these episodic challenges inconsequential or the vigilant defense of these norms unnecessary to their preservation" (Geyh 2006, 260).

APPROPRIATIONS, TAXES, AND JUDICIAL SALARIES

There have been many instances in which Congress has used various mechanisms to attack the federal courts for decisions with which a determined legislative majority has disagreed. At times, Congress has used its power of the purse to attempt to influence court decisions. To help ensure judicial independence, the framers gave federal judges life terms so that the judicial branch can be free from potential political considerations. Fearing that the federal courts might still be subject to political pressures from the legislative and executive branches, however, the framers wrote into the Constitution a provision that prevents Congress from reducing the salaries of federal judges.

Even though the Compensation Clause prevents the Congress from reducing any judicial salaries that have already vested (*United States v. Will* 1980), the clause does not require that Congress provide any annual cost of living adjustments for federal judges nor does it prevent Congress from canceling future announced judicial salary increases (449 U.S. at 228). Thus judicial salaries have always been a point of contention, and Congress has sometimes used judicial salaries to send a clear message to the courts. For example, in 1964 Congress increased the salaries for lower federal judges by $7,500 per year, but increased the salaries for Justices of the U.S. Supreme Court by only $4,500 per year. As Schmidhauser and Berg (1972, 9) explained, "The $3,000 differential clearly reflected a direct Congressional reprimand to the Supreme Court. This crude rebuff clearly stemmed from Congressional dissatisfaction with several controversial decisions rendered by the Court."

Clearly, salary issues have added to the tensions between the courts and Congress. Federal judges often feel that Congress does not provide adequate compensation for them. As Professor Paul M. Bator remarked, "federal judges, as a group, complain more about their pay than any other group I have ever encountered" (Bator 1985, 1148). There is probably a great deal of truth to the fact that federal judges feel that they are underpaid. In 2003, Judges Coffin and Katzmann noted that, "Since 1969, federal judicial salaries have lost twenty-four percent of their purchasing power" (Coffin and Katzmann 2003, 377). Various congressional actions regarding annual cost of living adjustments for federal judges have not made federal judges feel better about their financial situations. For example, in 1995, 1996, 1997, and 1999, Congress blocked previously announced "automatic" cost of living increases for various governmental officials, including federal judges, that had been provided for in the Ethics Reform Act of 1989.[9] This concern with judicial salaries and other budgetary resources is not new, of course. Although he was speaking more broadly of his frustration with Congressional budgeting practices, Chief Justice Warren in 1969 stated that,

"It is next to impossible for the courts to get something from Congress" (Warren,1969, A1).

In his annual year-end reports on the State of the Judiciary, Chief Justice Rehnquist often complained about Congress's approach to judicial salary issues. In his 2000 Year-End Report on the Federal Judiciary, Chief Justice Rehnquist focused most of the report on what he termed, "the most pressing issue facing the Judiciary: the need to increase judicial salaries" (Rehnquist 2000, 1).[10] Judicial salary issues remain important to the Supreme Court and to all federal judges. In his first annual report, Chief Justice Roberts also raised the judicial salary issue. The new Chief Justice said, "A more direct threat to judicial independence is the failure to raise judges' pay. If judges' salaries are too low, judges effectively serve for a term dictated by their financial position rather than for life. Figures gathered by the Administrative Office show that judges are leaving the bench in greater numbers now than ever before" (Roberts 2005, 1).

Although Congress cannot reduce the salaries of federal judges, can Congress use the tax code to attack federal judges for decisions the legislators do not like? The Supreme Court of the United States in *United States v. Hatter* (2001) clearly stated that judges should pay nondiscriminatory taxes just like all other citizens (see Entin and Jensen 2006). As Justice Breyer wrote for the Court in *Hatter*, "In practice, the likelihood that a nondiscriminatory tax represents a disguised legislative effort to influence the judicial will is virtually nonexistent" (532 U.S. at 571). The opinion of the Court continued, "In our view, the Clause does not prevent Congress from imposing a 'non-discriminatory tax laid generally' upon judges and other citizens, . . . but it does prohibit taxation that singles out judges for specially unfavorable treatment" (532 U.S. at 561). Although we usually think of the Compensation Clause as preventing Congress from reducing the salaries of federal judges, it is clear from *Hatter* that discriminatory taxes would also violate the Compensation Clause.

More generally, overall appropriations for the judicial branch have long been a source of conflict and concern between Congress and the federal courts (see, e.g., Perry 1999; Rishikof and Perry 1995). In addition to judicial salaries, the federal courts depend on Congress for funds for new judgeships, for courthouses, for staff, for technology, and for a variety of other purposes. As I wrote previously, "The annual appropriations process provides a clear avenue to see the different institutional perspectives of the Supreme Court and of Congress. The courts rightly see themselves as an independent third branch, and many judges seem to resent Congress's interference with their budget requests" (Miller 2004b, 64). Congress, however, often views the federal courts as just one more federal agency begging for funds (see, e.g., Resnik 2000, 1011). When it comes to the annual appropriations process, it seems that Congress does not consider the fact that the courts are a co-equal third branch to be of any significance in their deliberations. As a former chair of the House Appropriations subcommittee with jurisdiction over the budget for the judicial branch explained, "The courts do not have many advocates in Congress. They do not have a constituency. Congress continues to pass more and more laws that require the courts to assume jurisdiction of more cases and add to their workload. Congress is eager to authorize more judges, but when it comes to paying for them, the members of Congress do not think that is a very high priority" (N. Smith 1996, 177).[11]

Concerns over the annual appropriations process led Chief Justice Roberts to also argue that the independence of the courts was under attack. He wrote in his 2005 annual report, "In recent years, the budget for the federal judiciary and the ever-lengthening appropriations process have taken a toll on the operation of the courts" (Roberts 2005, 1). The Chief Justice went on to complain about the overly high rents that the judicial branch pays to the federal General Services Administration for courthouses and other office space. He continued, "Escalating rents combined with across-the-board cuts imposed during fiscal years 2004 and 2005 resulted in a reduction of approximately 1,500 judicial branch employees as of mid-December 2005 when compared to October 2003" (Roberts 2005, 1). At this point, it is worth quoting the new Chief Justice at some length on his views of the intersection of judicial independence and the appropriations process:

The federal judiciary, as one of the three coordinate branches of government, makes only modest requests of the other branches with respect to funding its vital mission of preserving the rule of law under our Constitution. Those of us in the judiciary understand the challenges our country faces and the many competing interests that must be balanced in funding our national priorities. But the courts play an essential role in ensuring that we live in a society governed by the rule of law, including the Constitution's guarantees of individual liberty. In order to preserve the independence of our courts, we must be sure that the judiciary is provided the tools to do its job" (Roberts 2005, 1).

THREATS OF IMPEACHMENT

In addition to using its power of the purse to influence court decisions, some politicians have been calling for the impeachment of federal judges with whom they disagree (see, e.g., Geyh 2006). Technically, articles of impeachment are brought by the House of Representatives, and the Senate votes on whether to remove the judge from the bench. In common language, "impeachment" often refers to both parts of this process. Historically, impeachment has not been used to remove federal judges from the bench merely because a majority of Congress disagrees with a judge's decisions. Impeachment and removal from office for purely political purposes has generally been seen as improper since the Senate refused to remove Justice Samuel Chase from the Court in 1803, even though he was impeached by the House because a majority of the members opposed some of his decisions (see Rehnquist 1992; Volcansek 2001).

Those who oppose various decisions of the federal courts have often called for the impeachment and removal of activist federal judges. Following the Supreme Court's decision in *Brown v. Board of Education*, there were bumper stickers all over the South saying "Impeach Earl Warren." This issue arose again in 1970 when then House Minority Leader Gerald Ford called for the impeachment of Justice William O. Douglas, in part because of the justice's very liberal ideology and his lifestyle. Regarding the proper standards for impeachment of federal judges, Ford argued that a justice or a federal judge can be impeached for "whatever a majority of the House of Representatives

[decides] at a given moment in history" (quoted in O'Brien 2003, 103). In 1996, then presidential candidate Robert Dole called for the impeachment of U.S. District Judge Harold Baer because the judge refused to allow a jury to consider drug evidence seized by New York City police officers. The judge then reversed his prior ruling on the evidence (see Newman 1997; Bright 1997, 166). Conservatives have long been angry about liberal activist judges, but calls for impeachment of federal judges for purely ideological reasons have grown stronger lately. As one Republican member of the House Judiciary Committee told me in an interview in the early fall of 2006, "We need to increase impeachments of federal judges in order to reign in those judges who insist on legislating from the bench."

Following the Terri Schiavo controversy discussed in more detail later, many conservatives called for the impeachment of judges who refused to follow their preferred ideological views. For example, former House Majority Leader Tom DeLay was quoted as saying, "Judicial independence does not equal judicial supremacy" (quoted in Hulse and Kirkpatrick 2005, 21). He did not rule out impeaching judges because the current situation depends on "a judiciary run amok" (quoted in Hulse and Kirkpatrick 2005, 21). He continued, "The failure is to a great degree Congress's. The response of the legislative branch has mostly been to complain. There is another way, ladies and gentlemen, and that is to reassert our constitutional authority over the courts.... This era of constitutional cowardice must end" (quoted in Hulse and Kirkpatrick 2005, 21). Michael Schwartz, then chief of staff to Senator Tom Coburn (R–OK), agreed, saying, "I'm in favor of impeachment," even suggesting that "mass impeachment" of federal judges might be in order (quoted in Hulse and Kirkpatrick 2005, 21).

Various other conservative activists at a conference entitled, "Remedies to Judicial Tyranny," organized by a group called Judeo-Christian Council for Constitutional Restoration, agreed with the impeachment option. Michael P. Farris, chair of the Home School Legal Defense Association, stated at the conference, "If about 40 [federal judges] get impeached, suddenly a lot of these guys would be retiring" (quoted in Milbank 2005, A03). In addition to Congressman

Tom DeLay, Senators Rich Santorum (R–PA) and John Cornyn (R–TX) have not ruled out using impeachment as a tool to influence federal court decisions (see Marcus 2005, A19). Conservative activist Phyllis Schlafly even called for the impeachment of relatively conservative U.S. Supreme Court Justice Anthony M. Kennedy because of his opinion for the Court forbidding the death penalty for juveniles (quoted in Milbank 2005, A03). Others have called for the impeachment of Justice Kennedy because of his habit of citing foreign law sources in his opinions (see DeParle 2005, 1). Although stating that the does not support impeachment of federal judges for ideological reasons, former House Judiciary Committee Chair F. James Sensenbrenner, Jr. (R–Wis) called for an inspector general to oversee the courts and to conduct investigations into the issue of judges overreaching their constitutional powers (see Marcus 2005, A19; Allen 2005b). This legislation was approved by the House Judiciary Committee in September 2006. As a staff member for a conservative Republican member of the Judiciary Committee told me, "The judiciary is not totally independent because Congress has the authority for oversight in order to narrow the focus of decisions where the judges have overreached."

Then there is the case of Chief Judge James M. Rosenbaum of the U.S. District Court for Minnesota, and the aftermath of his testimony before a congressional committee regarding the Federal Sentencing Guidelines. Many federal judges feel that the threats of impeachment against Judge Rosenbaum have had a chilling effect on their work. Judge Rosenbaum testified before a House Judiciary subcommittee against a Republican sponsored bill that would have overturned amendments to the federal sentencing guidelines authorizing shorter sentences for first-time drug defendants. Judge Rosenbaum, a Reagan appointee and former U.S. attorney, simply repeated criticisms of the drug sentencing guidelines that had been made by the U.S. Supreme Court justices, prosecutors, and defense attorneys. Conservatives on the subcommittee were so angry with Judge Rosenbaum's testimony that they tried to subpoena his records, eventually writing a twenty page committee report critical of the judge that hinted that he might have committed perjury in his testimony before the subcommittee. Federal

judges were uniformly outraged at the veiled threats of impeachment against Judge Rosenbaum. As one commentator characterized the situation, "The subcommittee, sensing a political opportunity, went after Judge Rosenbaum with a zeal once reserved for Cold War witch hunts.... This was not criticism of an individual judge's ruling but an attempt by two branches of government to use their official powers to muscle the third" (Wallance 2003, 4).

Impeachment has been threatened against other federal judges as well. For example, the House Judiciary Committee held hearings in September 2006 on the potential impeachment of Federal District Judge Manuel L. Real (Weinstein and Mendoza 2006, B1), while letters were sent from the Judiciary Committee to Chief Judge Boyce F. Martin, Jr., of the Sixth Circuit in 2002 and 2003 investigating his role in panel assignments for certain affirmative actions cases in his circuit. Some members of Congress and congressional staff have told me that they felt that these actions were clearly politically motivated to send a clear message to liberal judges. As one conservative member of the House Judiciary Committee told this author during an interview in the fall of 2006, "We need to increase the threats of impeachment in order to reign in those judges who insist on legislating from the bench." Federal judges seem shocked by these sometimes veiled hints of impeachment. Thus even the threat of impeachment against a single federal judge can have a chilling effect on the behavior of many judges.[12]

In his last two end-of-year reports, Chief Justice Rehnquist (2003, 2004) repeated his belief that federal judges cannot be impeached for political reasons. After expressing concerns about attempts by Congress to gather information on the sentencing practices of individual judges, in his 2003 year-end report Chief Justice Rehnquist concluded, "For side-by-side with the broad authority of Congress to legislate and gather information in this area is the principle that federal judges are not to be removed from office for their judicial acts. The subject matter of the questions Congress may pose about judges' decisions, and whether they target the judicial decisions of individual federal judges, could appear to be an unwarranted and ill-considered effort to intimidate individual judges in the performance of their judicial duties" (Rehnquist 2003).

As one Republican staffer in the House told me, "The judiciary is not totally independent, and they have certainly not been effective in policing themselves. Congress should exercise its authority for more oversight of judicial opinions and judicial ethics."

THE TERRI SCHIAVO CONTROVERSY

One of the clearest illustrations of the differences in institutional culture and institutional will between Congress and the courts revolved around the Terri Schiavo controversy in 2005. Ms. Schiavo was severely injured in a car accident, and she was being kept alive only by a feeding tube. Her husband (and legal guardian) wanted the hospital to remove the feeding tube, thus allowing her to die a natural death. Her parents objected. After the Florida state courts ruled that under Florida law the husband had the right to make the decision regarding whether the feeding tube should be removed, Congress passed legislation allowing the federal courts to take jurisdiction over the Schiavo case. This legislation was strongly supported by President George W. Bush and by Senate Majority Leader Bill Frist (R–TN), a medical doctor (see Stolberg 2005b, A18). All the federal judges who reviewed the case refused to grant a temporary restraining order to stop the removal of the feeding tube, ruling that the state courts had made the proper decision under Florida law (see Klein 2005). During this episode, Congress attempted to force the federal courts to prevent the removal of a feeding tube from Ms. Terri Schiavo even though every court that considered the issue ruled that Ms. Schiavo's husband had the right to request removal of the tube. Thus the legislation passed by Congress and signed by President Bush was attempting to force the federal courts to act as conservative judicial activists. The judges who reviewed this case made their decisions on legal grounds, while the politicians were trying to force them to make politically based rulings.

In addition to illustrating the different institutional perspectives of the courts and Congress, this incident also shows how important the courts have become to interest groups and other ideological political actors on the right. As Canellos wrote regarding this incident,

"The clout of the religious right was put on display when Bush and both houses of Congress rushed back from the Easter recess to allow courts to block the removal of a feeding tube for Terri Schiavo. Large majorities of the public disapproved of the move, however, and Republican approval ratings dropped immediately afterwards" (Canellos 2006a, A3). Despite having public opinion against them,[13] conservatives continued their attacks on the courts in this case.

Some of the attacks on the courts following the Schiavo case were extreme in nature. Representative Steve King (R–IA), a member of the House Judiciary Committee stated, "That kind of judge needs to be worried about what kind of role Congress will play in his future" (quoted in Babington 2005b, A4). Senator Rick Santorum (R–PA) called the courts' actions "unconscionable" (quoted in Egelko 2005, A3). As Newsweek reported, "House Majority Leader Tom DeLay railed against, 'a judiciary run amok' and said judges in the case would have to 'answer for their behavior'" (Rosenberg 2005, 23). James Dobson, founder of the conservative interest group Focus on the Family, "compared black-robed Supreme Court justices to white-robed Ku Klux Klan members" (Rosenberg 2005, 23). Another conservative leader compared activist federal judges to Stalin (*The Economist* 2005, 31). Senator John Cornyn (R–TX) stated that recent examples of violence at courthouses were linked to public anger over activist decisions from the courts (Babington 2005a, A7). As was discussed in more detail earlier, as a result of this incident many conservatives called for the impeachment of judges who refused to follow their preferred ideological views.

Some politicians are quite open about advocating that the Congress use its power of the purse to influence the decisions of the federal courts. Former House Majority Leader Tom DeLay said in the spring of 2005 after the Schaivo controversy, "I have asked the Judiciary Committee to look at the Schaivo case and the actions of the judiciary. The legislative branch has certain responsibilities and obligations given to by the Constitution. We set the jurisdiction of the courts. We set up the courts. We can unset the courts. We have the power of the purse" (quoted in Klein 2005, A9).[14] Before Congressman DeLay resigned from the House in June 2006 because of his indictment for campaign finance law violations, he was a vocal critic of the courts. As the British weekly *The Economist* described his views, "All through his colourful political career, Tom DeLay has never concealed his dislike for judges—especially those who do not rule his way" (*The Economist* 2006a, 26).

The Schiavo case clearly illustrates the institutional differences between courts and Congress. The issue arose again in the confirmation process for Chief Justice John Roberts when Senator Ron Wyden (D–OR) asked the nominee about this case. Senator Wyden reported that the Chief Justice's reaction to the role Congress played in this case was negative. The Senator reported that Chief Justice Roberts said, "I am concerned with judicial independence. Congress can prescribe standards, but when Congress starts to act like a court and prescribe particular remedies in particular cases, Congress has overstepped its bounds" (quoted in Stolberg 2005b, A18).[15] Many have felt that the Republicans suffered in the polls because of their attacks on the judiciary in this case. As one journalist wrote in September of 2006, "If Democrats are successful in [the November elections of 2006], it will be mostly the result of Americans' increasing frustration with the Iraq war and with the perception that Bush and congressional Republicans have bungled everything from Terri Schiavo to Hurricane Katrina" (Bacon 2006, 31).

Thus, it is important for the federal courts to appreciate the potential institutional dangers that can come from an angry Congress, an angry president, or other angry political actors. Again, Louis Fisher wrote that, "Throughout its history, the Supreme Court has understood that its 'independence' relies on an astute appreciation of how dependent the judiciary is on the political system for understanding, supporting, and implementing judicial rulings. The Court has an opportunity to exercise leadership and creativity, but the risk of a political backlash is always around the corner" (Fisher 2004, 153). Katzmann warned that the relationships between the courts and the other branches may always be difficult. He wrote, "No one should harbor any illusions about the ease with which some of the problems in judicial–congressional relations can be resolved. Indeed, some may simply be an inevitable part of the political system" (Katzmann 1995, 1198). It is clear that the federal courts and the other branches of government have radically different institutional cultures and institutional wills. With the Democrats taking control of both houses of Congress after the November 2006 elections, tensions between the courts and Congress will certainly continue due to their different institutional perspectives, but it seems less likely that the Congress will enact legislation that will directly attack the independence of the federal courts.

Notes

1. These routine interactions between the branches do not make the news or usually even get the attention of scholars. As J. Mitchell Pickerill argued, "Those who [always] expect a constitutional revolution, a constitutional moment, or other form of severe confrontation between the Court and Congress simply do not appreciate the more routine and typical type of interaction between Court and Congress in the political process" (Pickerill 2004, 130). And as Lovell wrote, "The appearance of conflict between independent branches frequently masks more cooperative interaction between interdependent branches" (Lovell 2003, xix–xx).

2. This is the approach advocated by liberal judicial activists like Justice Thurgood Marshall and Justice William Brennan (see their speeches reprinted in O'Brien 2004, 178–82, 183–93). In fact, in a 1985 speech, Justice Brennan argued that, "The genius of the Constitution rests not in any static meaning it might have had in a world that is dead and gone, but in the adaptability of its great principles to cope with current problems and current needs" (quoted in O'Brien 2004, 187).

3. The ideological direction of judicial activism has therefore changed from era to era. From the early 1900s until the mid 1930s, the Supreme Court was generally a conservative activist court, focusing mainly on preventing government regulation of the economy and overturning the New Deal. From the late 1940s until the late 1970s, the Supreme Court was a liberal activist court, focusing mainly on the expansion of civil rights and civil liberties in this country. Currently, the Supreme Court uses both ideological activist approaches at the same time. Today, for example, the Supreme Court takes a conservative judicial activist approach to issues of federalism (see, e.g., *United States v. Lopez* 1995 and *United States v. Morrison* 2000), but a liberal activist approach to issues such as prayer at public school functions (*Santa Fe Independent School District v. Doe* 2000; *Lee v. Weisman* 1992), or on such issues as whether sodomy laws are unconstitutional (*Lawrence v. Texas* 2003).

4. Generally, since 1789 over 80 percent of the president's nominations to the Supreme Court have been confirmed (Epstein and Segal 2005, 99). In fact, the period of 1894 to 1968 saw the rejection of only one presidential nominee to the Supreme Court (Comiskey 2004, 9). However, it is the confirmation battles over Supreme Court nominees that have helped shape the political context for all future judicial nominations. For more discussion of the role of interest groups in the confirmation process, see Bell, this volume, chapter 3.

5. The highly partisan confirmation fight over Justice Alito's nomination to the Supreme Court raised a series of institutional concerns. For example, six federal judges who had served on the Third Circuit with Judge Alito testified in his favor at his confirmation hearings, raising questions about whether they had violated institutional norms and ethical dictates in their appearance before the Senate Judiciary Committee. In an editorial on the subject, *The New York Times* argued that, "It is extraordinary for judges to thrust themselves into a controversial Supreme Court nomination in this way, a move that could reasonably be construed as a partisan gesture. The judges will be doing harm to the federal bench" (*The New York Times* 2006a, A34). Other commentators agreed that the testimony of the federal judges in favor of Judge Alito's nomination raised ethical questions. Said Eldie Acheson, a top Justice Department official in the Clinton administration who shepherded nominees Ruth Bader Ginsburg and Stephen Breyer though the confirmation process, "It puts [the judges] in the middle of an executive and congressional branch function. As judges and as a court, this is not their business" (quoted in Mauro 2006a). Their testimony also raised questions about whether Justice Alito in the future would have to recuse himself from any appeals of cases decided by these judges.

6. Some examples of such statutes declared unconstitutional by the Court are parts of the Crime Control and Safe Streets Act of 1968, declared unconstitutional in *Dickerson v. U.S.* (2000); the Flag Protection Act of 1989, declared unconstitutional in *U.S. v. Eichman,* (1990); and the Religious Freedom Restoration Act, declared unconstitutional by *City of Boerne v. Flores* (1997). Even though many of these statutes have been declared unconstitutional by the courts, one should not assume that Congress has no role in interpreting the Constitution.

7. As Devins and Whittington analyzed the situation, "The Rehnquist Court embarked on a sustained assault on congressional power. Although the Rehnquist Court has not matched the Hughes Court that attacked the New Deal in intensity and significance, it has made up for that in endurance. The Court struck down more acts of Congress in the 1990s than in any previous decade, including the 1930s. It has established doctrines that promise to continue to pinch Congress into the future. The justices have accompanied all this with strongly worded opinions

denigrating the authority and capacity of Congress to interpret the Constitution" (Devins and Whittington 2005, 3–4).

8. Bell and Scott (2006) found that court-stripping measures were more likely to be introduced by more senior members of Congress who were ideologically conservative. They concluded that members of Congress introduce these bills for both electoral and policy reasons.

9. Congress was really attempting to prevent the automatic pay raises for its own members from going into effect, but the legislation blocked federal judicial pay increases as well as the pay raises for legislators. When federal judges sued to recover their blocked "automatic" pay increases, the United States Court of Appeals for the Federal Circuit ruled that the proposed "automatic" pay raises had not vested, and thus there was no violation of the Compensation Clause in the legislative actions (*Williams v. U.S.*, 240 F3d 1019 (Fed. Cir. 2001)). Although the Supreme Court refused to grant certiorari in the case, Justice Breyer wrote a strongly worded dissent to the denial of certiorari, which Justices Scalia and Kennedy joined (*Williams v. U.S.*, 535 U.S. 911 (2002)).

10. The Chief Justice went on to say, "But in order to continue to provide the nation a capable and effective judicial system we must be able to attract and retain experienced men and women of quality and diversity to perform a demanding position in the public service. The fact is that those lawyers who are qualified to serve as federal judges have opportunities to earn far more in private law practice or business than as judges. In order to continue to attract highly qualified and diverse federal judges—judges whom we ask and expect to remain for life—we must provide them adequate compensation" (Rehnquist 2000, 1). In a quite lengthy discussion of the subject, the Chief Justice also noted that judicial salary issues had been discussed in thirteen of the last nineteen end-of-year reports on the state of the judiciary. In his 2002 annual report, the Chief Justice stated, "At the risk of beating a dead horse, I will reiterate what I have said many times over the years about the need to compensate judges fairly" (Rehnquist 2002, 1).

11. Frustration with the annual appropriations process for the courts has created some interesting reactions from federal judges. For example, during the fiscal year 2000 budget cycle, the Senate voted to cut $280 million from the $4.3 billion that the federal judiciary has requested that year. In an extraordinary step, Chief Justice Rehnquist sent a letter to the then Senate Majority Leader Trent Lott (R–MS), calling the Senate actions "unjustified and impractical" (quoted in Carelli 1999). Many newspapers around the country ran editorials condemning the proposed budget cuts. Eventually most but not all of the requested funds were approved by the Congress. In some ways, the fiscal year 2004 appropriations process was even more difficult for the federal courts. Congress missed its October 2003 deadline for enacting the judiciary's budget, and when the budget did pass it included some several funding cuts. As Chief Justice Rehnquist described the situation, "the continuing uncertainties and delays in the funding process have necessitated substantial effort on the part of judges and judiciary managers and staff to modify budget systems, develop contingency plans, cancel activities, and attempt to cut costs" (Rehnquist 2003). The fiscal year 2005 appropriation for the judiciary was $5.42 billion, some $300 million below the request from the third branch (Greenhouse 2005a, 10).

12. Such calls for impeachment of federal judges have produced a response from those who worry about threats to the independence of the federal judiciary. *The New York Times* ran an editorial on April 5, 2005 denouncing these attacks on the judiciary. *The Times* editorial stated,

"Through public attacks, proposed legislation, and even the threat of impeachment, ideologues are trying to bully judges into following their political line. Mr. DeLay and his allies have moved beyond ordinary criticism to undermining the separation of powers, not to mention the rule of law" (*The New York Times* 2005, A22). *The Washington Post* ran an editorial on April 1, 2005, condemning among other things calls for impeachment of federal judges for ideological reasons. *The Post* editorial stated that calls of retribution against judges are "a mark of an arrogant and out-of-control federal power—but that power is the legislature, not the judiciary." The editorial concluded, "This country has an independent judiciary precisely to shield judges who make difficult decisions under intense political and time pressure from the bullying of politicians" (*The Washington Post* 2005b, A26). Following the death of Chief Justice Rehnquist, *The New York Times* ran an editorial praising the Chief Justice's efforts to protect the independence of the judiciary from congressional attacks, including the calls for impeachment of judges because of disagreements with their decisions (*The New York Times* 2005b, A28).

13. Geyh reported that 82 percent of the American public disagreed with the congressional actions in the Schiavo case (Geyh 2006, 274). Other polls put that number somewhere between 60 to 80 percent (Babington 2005b, A4). As the *Economist* argued, "The religious right's biggest problem, however, is not scandal; it is the movement's addition to overreach. The most disastrous example of this was the Terri Schiavo affair" (*The Economist* 2006b, 40). Former U.S. Senator John C. Danforth (R–MO), an ordained Episcopal priest, complained after the Schiavo vote that, "Republicans have transformed our party into the political arm of conservative Christians" (quoted in Babington 2005b, A4).

14. Congressman DeLay eventually apologized for saying the federal judges were responsible for the death of Terri Schiavo, although he continued his calls for Congress to investigate the judges as part of a broader attack on liberal judicial activism (Klein 2005, A9). In response to Congressman DeLay's calls for the House Judiciary Committee to investigate the judiciary's role in the Schiavo case, Representative John Conyers (D–Mich), the then ranking Democrat on the Judiciary Committee, stated that DeLay's request, "shows a complete lack of understanding about the principles of separation of powers" (quoted in Klein 2005, A9).

15. Looking back at the Schiavo example, Professor Doris Provine concluded, "The case revealed the readiness of some conservative Christian groups—and their supporters in government at the local, state, and federal levels—to denounce judges in strong, even threatening, terms. The case can also be interpreted as a signal of the vitality of judicial independence in the face of hostile legislative and executive action. Despite these attacks, the state and federal judiciary stood firm in its interpretation of the power of judges to have the final word on matters within their jurisdiction, providing the nation with a lesson in the power of judicial review" (Provine 2005, 319).

20

COMPARATIVE JUDICIAL STUDIES

Nancy Maveety[1]

The field of judicial politics at first focused only on the U.S. Supreme Court. Then judicial scholars reached out and began to study the lower courts in the United States. Fearing that studying the courts in the United States in isolation would limit our knowledge, judicial scholars then began to examine the interactions between the courts and the other institutions of government, as illustrated in chapters 8 and 19 of this volume. Eventually scholars of the courts realized that we could learn a great deal about courts in the United States by comparing them to courts in other countries. Thus the comparative judicial politics field was founded and for the most part continues through the work scholars who first focused on the behavior and decisions of American courts.

This chapter asks whether the approaches used for studying courts in the United States, and specifically studying the Supreme Court of the United States, can apply to the study of courts in other countries. The chapter explores how various models and academic approaches first developed in the United States apply to courts abroad. The chapter also discusses some of the difficulties that scholars encounter when they look at courts outside the United States. Because court structures and functions can be very different in different societies, the chapter focuses mostly on studying constitutional courts in various countries. Unlike in the United States, where our regular courts handle a wide variety of cases including constitutional questions, many countries have chosen to establish special courts whose sole function is to decide constitutional issues. We can learn a great deal about the essence of a thing by understanding how scholars go about studying that thing. Should scholars try to understand each nation's courts in their unique governmental context, or should scholars try to make generalized findings that apply to courts in a variety of societies? This chapter argues that scholars should do both.

Exploring judicial politics requires rethinking U.S. judicial politics as a field of inquiry. The first expansion of the judicial politics field extended the judicial research agenda beyond that most-studied judiciary, the U.S. Supreme Court, to lower courts in the United States. A second expansion of the judicial politics field has extended research to courts outside the United States. A third expansion now looks at the interactions between courts and other institutions of government (see chapters 8 and 19 in this volume). All of these recent scholarly pursuits draw our attention to a central, persistent question about judicial politics studies: To what extent do the models largely developed to explain the decision-making and institutional role of the U.S. Supreme Court help us to understand lower courts in the U.S. as well as non-U.S. judicial behavior and constitutional politics? Because the field of comparative judicial studies in American political science developed out of U.S. judicial process scholarship, most work on non-U.S. courts and courts across jurisdictions engages this question, more or less directly (see, e.g., Shapiro 2004; Widner 2004). Comparative judicial research, as a result, must be evaluated on two dimensions: for its theoretical approach and insights in general concerning courts as political actors, and for its attention to context and the specific legal and political circumstances of the country/regional case(s) under study.

This chapter concentrates its review of the comparative-court studies literature on work that examines judicial policy making by constitutional courts in a political system. Admittedly, this focus on research examining the performance of courts as political institutions necessarily neglects another segment of comparative-courts work: that which examines courts' contribution to social justice; or the role courts can play in bringing about justice in unequal societies and in bridging the breach between formal legality and actual practice. (Kapiszewski and Taylor 2006) Still, the judicial research that focuses on *judicial politics*—on the role of the Supreme Court in the institutional structure or political context of the country under study—addresses the tension between politics and the rule of law, which is an overarching theme of this volume. However, as important, comparative judicial studies with a high court focus also must provide, implicitly or explicitly, a theoretical framework for comparison of judicial behavior and policy making by constitutional courts, thus facilitating our assess to those frameworks. Are they drawn from U.S. court studies? Do they conceptualize high courts as dynamic or constrained policy makers in their respective political systems? What factors affecting judicial decision making do the frameworks isolate and are these factors applicable across national contexts, as well as across levels of the judiciary within national contexts?

A major debate and controversy in comparative-court studies is whether a generalizable theory of judicial behavior must be generated and should be applied in a research design, or whether ethnographic and richly detailed case studies—which highlight courts' unique contextual differences rather than their institutional similarities—remain useful for understanding non-U.S. courts. This methodological debate echoes one in the law and courts subfield of political science generally, which identifies comparative judicial studies of U.S. courts—federal and state, appellate and trial—as a neglected research area due to American judicial scholars' "high court bias." Such bias is both substantive and theoretical: Studies of the U.S. Supreme Court consume the bulk of scholarly attention, and the behavior of this high court is supposed to be representative of the way courts function across the federal court system and within the functional hierarchy of the American judicial process. Yet those court scholars who object to the substantive bias and its erroneously reflexive theoretical presumptions about the factors that influence judicial decision making do not necessarily pursue truly comparative research on American courts. Rather, the tendency has been to address U.S. courts in context: in the context of state politics and state political institutions, or local courthouse culture, or as federal circuits in a case study. Contextual studies normally ask which factors, such as judicial ideology or institutional independence, as powerfully explain lower court behavior as they do that of Supreme Court justices. However, contextual studies, of trial courts, elected state judges, or courts of appeals' panels, also stress the situational factors of difference or uniqueness that render the judges' behavior dissimilar and not comparable to that of Supreme Court justices. Such ethnographic profiling of lower courts aims to broaden scholars' understandings of the U.S. judicial system without necessarily producing a unified, general theory of judicial behavior.

This same methodological debate also asks us to think about the purpose of studying different countries' courts comparatively. Is it to understand more fully courts as courts, including American judicial actors, or is it to comprehend the judicial institutional role in a particular non-U.S. political context? The first stresses the idea of a common judicial process theory that unites all scholars of all courts; the second stresses area studies and regional expertise and admits of either American "exceptionalism" or nonuniversalizability in the judicial realm. By reviewing the comparative-courts literature, we can begin to assess whether one idea seems more persuasive to scholars, and why. The goal is not to choose one approach over another but to evaluate where we are in the field of judicial studies—theory-driven or question-driven, using new empirical objects to resolve old theoretical tensions or employing a geographically broader selection of case studies to broaden scholarly understandings of "courtness." Ultimately, a survey of recent work should cause us to appreciate the value of both approaches, pursued in tandem.

FRAMEWORKS FOR COMPARING COURTS: THREE THEORETICAL PEDIGREES

In the last several decades, the global expansion of judicial power or "judicialization of politics" has meant that courts around the world play an increasingly larger and more significant role in public policy making (Tate and Vallinder 1995). Assessing the impact of this expansion on both "self-assured" majoritarian democracies[2] and new democracies in transition from authoritarianism requires an understanding of what affects judges' decisions. Are entrenched elite interests defended by the judiciary, or is the institution politically independent? What institutional design factors make it so; and how is such independence revealed by judicial decisions? Much comparative-courts literature focuses on the causes and consequences of the expansion of judicial power across political systems, addressing the "why judicialize" question. However, the global trend toward transfer of decision-making prerogatives from the legislature, cabinet, or civil service to the courts also means that theories of judicial behavior are of great moment in evaluating the implications and legitimacy of such transfers. Of vital concern is the degree to which we can generalize about the influences that explain the policy outcomes arrived by courts and, thus, be confident that the decisional patterns we observe are attributable to the influences we think they are.

Various theoretically informed frameworks contend for explanatory preeminence in the comparative judicial-studies literature—or, at least, for preeminence in explaining particular kinds of court situations. Many have been derived from studies of American courts and some specifically from studies of decision making by the U.S. Supreme Court. In general, three theoretical pedigrees from the U.S. law and courts literature (Maveety 2003) inform comparative-court studies. The first, known as the *attitudinal model*, emphasizes the micro environment of judicial decision making and the factors internal to judges that affect their behavior. In a non-U.S. context, the attitudinal approach has come to play the role of foil against which a less ideological approach for understanding court decisions and their political important is measured. The second U.S.-derived theoretical pedigree for comparative judicial studies is *neo-institutionalism*, which emphasizes the institutional structure in which a court operates and the strategic opportunities that structure provides for securing judicial policy preferences as central in understanding and explaining court decision making. Formal dynamics such as the polity's separation of powers design and partisan political conflict are the key factors for analysis of the judicial institution; indeed, the possibility to compare such formal dynamics systematically commits this approach to the pursuit of a unified and generalizable theory of courts. Finally, the third American theoretical pedigree to inform comparative judicial studies is *historical institutionalism* that, adapted to non-U.S. contexts, frequently takes an ethnographic cast, profiling political culture and broadly defining political institutions.[3] This approach concerns itself with describing macro or systemic dynamics that affect court decision making, such as the objectives of the political regime (Orren and Skowronek 1994) or the nature of the social structure and character of social movements.

Although these three pedigrees comprise the theoretical lineage of work in comparative judicial studies, comparative-courts research is "messier" than U.S. judicial studies, in that the three theoretical pedigrees or dominant paradigms of the latter become more fragmented and complicated when applied to the non-U.S. court context. Generally speaking, more dynamics are at work in comparative cases than the attitudinal, neo-institutionalist, and historical institutionalist approaches typically capture for the U.S. case. The result in comparative judicial studies has been a proliferation of frameworks for analysis—some of which are nevertheless informed by or spring from the same theoretical pedigree, but take cognizance of different factors and emphases than their sire or their siblings. Still, the family resemblances that remain allow us to assess which approaches from work on courts in the United States have the most to say about non-U.S. courts, and which comparative-courts research has the most to teach students of judicial process generally—including those committed to U.S.-politics area studies.

"LET 1,000 FLOWERS BLOOM": IDEOLOGY, GAMES, AND STRUCTURES

Promoting a variety of approaches in methodology and subject matter is the official party line in law and courts research, but it is practiced unevenly in reality. Ironically, it was not so long ago that a prominent scholar in the field was lamenting that, "we judicial specialists continue to focus on the U.S. Supreme Court…and continue (with limited exceptions) to ignore courts abroad, despite their increasing prominence" (Epstein 1999, 1). Currently, comparative judicial politics is a burgeoning field of study for judicial specialists, reflecting and responding to the global expansion of judicial power over the last two decades. In the effort to understand what these unfamiliar courts do in reality and how they actually operate, judicial specialists initially drew on those familiar theories of judicial decision making that had been tested against empirical evidence—evidence that was largely U.S. court decisional data. Yet the models of judicial behavior that best fit the U.S. case are not always easily transportable to non-U.S. political and institutional circumstances, and this has diminished their value in generating potential explanations regarding courts abroad. At times, this feature of fit was neglected in favor of theoretical familiarity and methodological parsimony.

This was the case with the first theoretical framework we see used for comparing courts, the *judicial ideology framework* based on the attitudinal model. Attitudinalism has been so dominant in the American political science of American court studies (see Segal and Spaeth 1993) that judicial attitudes or a judge's political ideology was presumed also to explain the decision making of non-U.S. judicial actors. The attitudinal model asserts that judicial ideology (i.e., conservative-liberal attitudes across various political issues) determines judicial voting preferences, and thus accounts for judicial voting differences. Appointment effects determine the ideological make-up of the court— paraphrasing Robert Dahl's (1957) famous notion that the court follows the election returns. The assumption is that judges' behavior is affected by their preferences for certain public policy outcomes, which is also the primary reason for their selection for the bench. Court decisions too are largely explainable in terms of these preferences, and less so in terms of legal factors such as procedural rules or constitutional norms.

Early comparative work, especially during the 1960s and 1970s, applied the attitudinal approach, which was then the unchallenged paradigm of American judicial process studies. Works such as Schubert's (1964) *Judicial Behavior* reader that included a scalogram analysis of civil liberties voting of the Japanese Supreme Court; his later study of the social attributes and voting behavior of the Australian High Court (Schubert 1968); and the empirical research on courts in Korea, India, Canada, and the Philippines in Schubert and Danelski's (1969) *Comparative Judicial Behavior* extended to non-U.S. judicial contexts the argument that ideological factors affected judicial decision making. This empirical, quantitative comparative judicial research did not see the judicial behavior field as divided between courts inside and outside the United States, but rather assumed that courts abroad should be a part of the development of the field's scholarship and that universalizable, generalizable theory building would have to include cross-cultural studies (see Tate and Haynie 2000, 30).

However, attitudinalism's plausibility as a theoretical framework presumes certain facts clearly present in the American case, but not necessarily present abroad. These factors include publicity of judges' political backgrounds or partisanship, an appointment process involving the political branches, signed opinions in which the individual judicial vote is known, common law interpretive freedom of action, and a fairly unconstrained institutional setting, in the case of constitutional courts. The attitudinal approach, a

U.S.-centric model, and individual-judge level explanation of judicial decision making, was fascinated with understanding the cognitive and ideological map of individual justices, but was of limited utility in the cases of courts that deviated from the political and institutional circumstances of the U.S. Supreme Court. It remains doubtful, for example, how suitable or applicable the model is for analyzing judicial behavior in countries such as Canada, Germany, France, or South Africa where the entire system of and basis for judicial appointments is less overtly partisan and less ideological than the U.S. system, and where the judicial selection system is not easily reducible to a simple binary liberal/conservative attitudinal labeling matrix. Because the main source of information about many non-U.S. national high court judges' policy preferences is their judicial decisions, the circularity aspects of the attitudinal model—where judicial vote patterns are used to construct a picture of judicial ideology, which is then used to project judicial votes—are all the more significant in the foreign setting.

For these reasons, comparative judicial scholars from the mid-1980s onward took more account of the institutional setting and legal culture in which courts operated. The *"new" institutionalist models* of judicial decision making that were developed tracked the "institutional turn" of the law and courts field generally (Maveety 2003), and explicitly linked courts' behavior and systemic role to their specific political context. Related to but distinctive from one another, the next several theoretical frameworks share an admission that formal institutional powers matter and that an individual judicial attitude-based approach to comparative-court studies is too reductionist, because it removes from the comparative analysis critically important institutional-structure variables across political systems that demonstrably affect decisional outcomes.

As the law and courts field of political science is currently constituted, neo-institutionalist models dominate contemporary judicial scholarship because they seem to best reflect the objective of generating a unified theory of judicial behavior generalizable across national contexts. That unified theory—a definition of the new institutionalist approach to the study of courts—is that political institutions and the framework of rules, norms, and ideas that constitute

them create an incentive structure for political actors, facilitating some behaviors and discouraging others. Actors are assumed to want to secure their preferred outcomes, which may consist of substantive policy results (including normative constitutional values), institutional power, or a variety of personal goals. A judge's institutional setting, or choice context, is essential to comprehend to understand what kind of preference-seeking explains his/her decisions.

The neo-institutionalist approach, as opposed to attitudinalism, is of relatively recent vintage in judicial scholarship, and so generates new but unevenly embraced frameworks for the comparative explanation of court behavior. Moreover, these neo-institutionalist frameworks for comparative-court studies have developed simultaneously and interdependently with one another. Therefore, their order of discussion here does not imply chronological or foundational sequencing but is instead a rough ranking in terms of the directness of their theoretical linkage to the U.S. court example. Accordingly, the second theoretical framework for comparative judicial studies draws on U.S. Supreme Court as an illustrative but not representative type. It suggests that a formal, separation-of-powers model of judicial interaction with legislative and executive branches is the key to understanding courts comparatively.

The *constrained court framework* is a neo-institutional model-based explanation of judicial decision making that argues that the country's institutional framework in which judges find themselves determines their best strategies to pursue favored decisional outcomes (cf. Langer and Wilhelm this volume, chapter 8). Constraint varies in political structures; the key to comparative study of judicial behavior is to identify those conditions that constrain judicial action, that is that render it conditional on other actors' approval or assent. "Constrained courts" are then presumed to behave differently than "unconstrained" courts that can veto the actions of other political actors within their political system. The framework is somewhat agnostic as to the content of judges' decisional outcomes and whether policy preference or legal values—or some mixture of the two—is more determinative. Its emphasis, rather, is on modeling court decision making as a strategic game by rational instrumentalist, goal-oriented actors who enjoy certain formal powers but are usually constrained by certain formal limits. These actors also benefit from certain information about each other's political objectives, and they wish to maximize their preferred policy goals. Empirically supported by studies of both U.S. courts (Rosenberg 1991; Bosworth 2001) and European constitutional courts (Koopmans 2003; Vanberg 2005; Claes 2006) and transnational courts (Stone Sweet 2004) operating in a separated powers system, the constrained court framework is concerned with policy making and constitutional politics processes. It has been less focused on the individual judge as a decisional actor than the judicial institution as a governmental branch player. Works such as Stone Sweet's (2000) *Governing with Judges*, Epstein, Knight, and Shvetsova's (2001) article on constitutional courts, and Alter's book (2001) on European law therefore link judges' policy and institutional goals.

The explanatory value of the constrained court framework lies in its transportability as a model across country/political contexts and its potential predictive power. Once national institutional constraints are accurately mapped, judicial behavioral outcomes can be predicted with scientifically valid confidence; moreover, cross-country court decision making can be compared along independent (institutional structure) variables that can be operationalized cross-culturally and also reliably measured.

Neo-institutionalist theoretical frameworks like the constrained court model identify key institutional characteristics that define constitutional courts as more like the American system or more like the European system. Table 20.1 denotes the essential differences between the two.

European-type constitutional courts are often conceptualized as the most unconstrained judicial actors, because of the sequence, unilaterality, and finality with which they act in their political systems. In other words, these courts theoretically can act independently without input from other political actors in their systems of government. Yet all constitutional courts, even those in advanced democracies whose independence, legitimacy, and authority are well-established, must be attentive to the preferences of external actors if they wish to advance their goals. This is because justices depend on the cooperation of governing majorities to enforce their decisions. However, constitutional courts in consolidating democracies, whose constitutional systems may lack authority, suffer the constraint of threatened as well as active noncompliance by the governing majorities on whose cooperation they depend. The lack of a culture or tradition of judicial independence jeopardizes the legitimacy and therefore the power of courts that may be institutionally unconstrained. Conversely, the reservoir of public support that courts in advanced democracies enjoy extends the judiciary's range of action and makes it

Table 20.1 Institutional Characteristics of Court Systems

Characteristics	American System	European System
Institutional structure of judicial review	Diffused: Ordinary courts can declare acts unconstitutional	Centralized: Only a single constitutional court can exercise judicial review
Timing of judicial review	Ex post: Only after an act has taken effect	Ex ante and ex post: Constitutional court can have a priori review over treaties, acts
Type of judicial review	Concrete: Courts can resolve only actual cases or controversies	Abstract and concrete: Courts can exercise review in the absence of an actual controversy
Standing of parties	Only litigants with a personal stake in the outcome can bring suit	Litigating parties can include governmental actors, interest groups, and individual citizens
Non-U.S. examples	Canada, India, Australia	Germany, Italy, Argentina, Hungary

Note. Adapted from Epstein, Knight, and Shvetsova (2001).

seem less constrained. The point of the constrained-court framework is to model the way that institutional characteristics, interacting with political context factors, affect court decision making.

The idea of constraint, and whether it operates differently on courts in more dynamic political environments, has lead to the development of theoretical frameworks derived from the assumptions of the constrained-court model, but with a difference in emphasis. These frameworks are interested in incorporating factors of political change or instability into our understandings of judicial politics. Hence, a third theoretical framework for comparing courts focuses explicitly on predicting the behavioral outcomes of *political development* and its resultant institutional design choices or reforms. This neo-institutionalist framework evokes the concept of court constraint while pointedly retaining the explanatory importance of political ideology to judicial decision making. The *insurance model of judicial power* claims that the design and reviewing powers of constitutional courts reflect the interests of the dominant political parties in the government of origin, and that powerful and independent courts are associated with situations of divided or deadlocked politics—or political uncertainty in the future. This framework for comparative studies is a variation on Dahl's (1957) notion that the court follows the election returns which might be termed "court design follows expected election returns," for it is political sentiment and the political setting that configure the judicial decision-making role. When the expected pace of turnover in political leadership is high, according to the beliefs of the leadership in power, the degree of judicial independence in the political system will also be high—by design and in practice. The assumption is that a politically dominant group without fear of loss of power or political competition in the near future will refuse to give courts the power to strike down legislation, because that group in power sees no need to protect itself against imminent opposition status. In other words, the power of courts in a newly designed constitutional system depends on how threatened the constitution writers may predict themselves to be in the future. Power preservation is expected to motivate all political actors, both constitutional designers and constitutional court judges.

Although it is more concerned with tracing the causes and consequences of systemic choices favoring expansive judicial power, the insurance model recognizes that judges' decision making is a product of institutional powers and role orientation as well as their political opportunities and sensibilities. Increasingly important in describing courts and predicting their actions in establishing the rule of law during transitions to democracy, as in Eastern Europe and Latin America, the framework does not discount the explanatory importance of ideological factors on judicial behavior but sees those factors playing themselves out within an institutional context that also has a political story. The relative power of various groups in a society may be just as important as their ideological positions in explaining political support for the exercise of judicial power, as Whittington (2005) demonstrated for the U.S. case of elected officials obstructed from fully implementing their own policy agenda, who then favor the active exercise of constitutional review by a sympathetic judiciary to overcome those obstructions.

Works such as Ginsburg (2003) on constitutional courts' behavior in Asia and Hirschl (2004) on judicial empowerment in constitutional revolutions in Canada, Israel, New Zealand, and South Africa apply this framework to understand courts as part of a political regime and their powers as subject to the preferences of its elites. Chavez (2004) offered a variant of this line of reasoning in her analysis of judicial politics in Argentina, arguing that situations of political party competition foster judicial autonomy; she also suggested the applicability of her argument to the cases of Chile and subnational U.S. politics (specifically the state of Louisiana). Magaloni (2003) and Finkel (2003) make an almost identical argument to explain Mexico's reforms in the 1990s extending the review powers of the Supreme Court: they were enacted once a multiparty system was established and the previously dominant Mexican president no longer had the authority to serve as ultimate arbiter in resolving electoral disputes. Perhaps not surprisingly, the insurance model is somewhat cynical about the transformative or rights-enhancing effect of the judicial review mechanism, for it sees a dependency of constitutional courts on politics, on their political situation. Such a view of contemporary judicializations reminds us of the limited heuristic usefulness, as a template for comparative study, of the optimistic and complacent (and not necessarily historically accurate) American experience of a court-centric rights' revolution.

Lessons from American political development and the history of periodic judicial activism nevertheless inform a fourth theoretical framework that is, like the previous insurance model, also an adaptation of the constrained-court model. The *strategic defection model* is, in theory, generalizable across high courts but of special applicability to courts in one-party or authoritarian regimes, and countries with a history of political instability or conditions of regime transition. Borrowing less from American judicial process literature than from game theoretic conceptualizations of power relations, this approach to comparative-court studies examines how and when judges engage in political resistance—and enjoy political survival. The model suggests that no matter the conception of judicial power "insured" by systemic political design, court opportunities to defy their political masters exist.

Thus far, the model's explanatory utility in understanding the political branch–judicial branch dynamic has been best demonstrated in one particular country context. Drawing on extensive quantitative and qualitative study of the case of the Argentine Supreme Court, Helmke's (2006) central claim is that even courts without institutional independence will rule against the government that appointed them once that government begins to lose power, to avoid sanctions by the likely incoming government. Hers is an explicitly strategic action-based model and explanation of judicial decision making, with ostensibly weak and subservient courts as circumscribed but not utterly feeble "players." Other recent writing on Argentina concurs with its comportment with a strategic defection model (Iaryczower, Spiller, and Tommasi 2002). However, scholars of courts in authoritarian regimes also claim that strategic defection-type behavior by judges is more common in authoritarian states than the usual binary concept of independent–obedient courts would lead one to expect (Moustafa 2005). Even low-level courts, surely not envisioned or designed as "supreme" in a rule of law sense, open

avenues for challenge to the regime's political control. Work on special administrative courts in Suharto's Indonesia suggests that judicial institutions can contribute to regime transition when political dynamics reach a tipping point (Bourchier 1999). Although such judicial action is at best limited "defection" from the political regime, it suggests the complex and nuanced interplay between regime control, regime concessions, and judicial power, even in nondemocratic polities and nonconsolidated democracies.

Although there has been only limited empirical testing of the strategic defection model to date (Sanchez Urribarri and Songer 2006; Helmke 2006), its theoretical reach extends to political contexts in which courts should be expected to be constrained, inactive, and subservient but instead exhibit periodic or even sustained defiance of the government in power. Conditions of transition from authoritarianism or consolidating but still fragile democracy come to mind,[4] as do the recent cases of judicial boldness by high courts in Russia and Romania. Still, not all constitutional courts in these political contexts have been entirely successful in calculating their opportunities for strategic defection or negotiating their constraints in a way that protects the judges from the regime change they anticipate, or durably effectuates their institutional, decisional independence.

A fifth theoretical framework addresses this latter problem, and supplies an account of how newly constituted supreme courts can help establish and further their own institutional legitimacy. In doing so, it departs from neo-institutionalism's fixation on domestic separation-of-powers games and imports an explicitly international dimension to the interbranch contest. By also broadening the conception of an "institutional structure" that conditions judicial decision making, this framework bridges neo-institutionally informed and historical institutionally informed approaches to comparative-court studies. Whereas historical institutionalism as an approach to understanding judicial decision making in the American context focuses on national political regimes' norms, constituitive institutions, and court-society synergies, this historical institutionalist-informed framework for comparative judicial studies does not limit itself to the local deep context.

The *court-as-conduit framework* attends chiefly to the influence of international organizational structure on courts' decisions, and offers a systematic model of how this international dimension of law and justice changes the domestic policy-making setting for national supreme courts. This historical institutionalist-informed framework suggests that under current developments of global "juristocracy" (Hirschl 2004), newly constituted Supreme Courts can serve their own institutional legitimacy by functioning as *translators* of international legal norms into domestic constitutional rights or obligations. Juristocracy describes the circumstance in which the persuasion of parliamentary and public debate has been heavily supplemented—some would say substituted—by the coercion of court orders. The "conduit model" extends this notion and reflects the new reality of the international jurisdiction of rights-claims, as a result of trans-national courts like the European Court of Justice, the European Court of Human Rights, and the International Criminal Court. It also reflects the new judicial hierarchy that incorporates national supreme courts into an international rule of law, which facilitates those courts' successfully enforcing international compacts such as the European Convention of Human Rights against their governments (Alter 2001).

In this environment, "hegemonic preservation" demands the constitutionalization of rights by any threatened elite (whether legal or political), whereby the rhetoric of rights and judicial review is appropriated to bolster that elite's position in the polity (Hirschl 2004, 11–12, 43–44). On this understanding, then, national supreme courts utilize their own national constitutions' rights rhetoric to mollify their political counterparts when they act to enhance their own standing in the transnational judicial hierarchy by enforcing international rules. Case study of the newly created constitutional courts of the newly independent states of the former Soviet Union (Maveety and Grosskopf 2004) suggests that this conduit function is a strategic option for high court judges outside of the constrained–unconstrained dimension of the domestic separation of powers dynamic. Scheppele's study of the Hungarian case (2000) offered another variant of judges constructing a global legal system, with

her analysis of new courts in "posthorror regimes." In such a transition situation, the new court is the guardian of the new constitution's collective repudiation of the past and aspirational goal to be a "normal country"—with the latter judged, by judges, according to international standards. Judicial cooperation, or "legitimacy in numbers," is also a feature of this phenomenon, where the success of aggressively "normalizing" judicial review in one country makes its absence in another a sign of democratic debility (Scheppele 2000, 14).

The globalization of justice is part and parcel of the global expansion of judicial power, and the conduit model argues that any theory of judicial decision making cannot ignore the relevance of international factors. Despite its theoretical appeal, the model remains somewhat imprecise as to the actual workings of the conduit function—both the mechanics and the judicial attitudes that bring it about. For instance, during the struggle to bring former Chilean dictator General Augusto Pinochet to justice for human rights abuses during his military regime, international pressures were prominent. Chilean human rights activists sought an end-run around reluctant Chilean courts (Arceneaux and Pion-Berlin 2005, 133, 135) by appealing to foreign judicial institutions and evoking international rights' guarantees. Ultimately, the Chilean Supreme Court did rule that Pinochet had lost his immunity from prosecution under Chilean law, but this "landmark in jurisprudence" declared by the judges "could be established comfortably within the confines of Chilean statutes, without any need to consult international treaties, norms, or laws" (Arceneaux and Pion-Berlin 2005, 142). The meddling of foreign courts in the lustration matter offended Chilean nationalism, and the Chilean judges shared this prideful stance of the other national political elites. They were clearly less interested in enhancing their own standing in the trans-national judicial hierarchy by enforcing international rules than they were in protecting national sovereignty.

The Chilean case illustrates how constitutional courts can be reluctant conduits of international pressure, to the point of denying the relevance of that pressure as a catalyst for domestic legal policy making. The conduit model is not sufficiently developed to explain why the translation behavior occurs in some contexts but not in others.[5] Although the framework does not neglect the norms of the constitutional situation or the institutional realities of the political process in which a national court finds itself, the idea of a constitutional court as a conduit of international norms focuses on international relations understandings of the importance of international structures and pressures for domestic politics. That some of these structures lack traction cannot disguise the shift in emphasis in this historical institutionalist-informed comparative-courts research. The focus has shifted from a focus on courts' domestic context of political constraints to a setting in which national actors are playing the "game" on an international playing field.

The U.S. Supreme Court is somewhat odd in the transnational human rights approach, because certain of its sitting justices and several American court commentators insist that neither international law nor the decisions of non-U.S. constitutional courts are relevant for U.S. Supreme Court decision making. Posner connects the U.S. Supreme Court's citing of foreign decisions and the nascent judicial cosmopolitanism of Justices such as Kennedy, Breyer, and O'Connor as the "moral vanguardism" (Posner 2005, 84–89) of an "aggressive" approach to judging—suggesting that the behavior, in the U.S. context, has to do with the domestic matter of the current court's grandiose sense of its role. Of course, as Hirschl (2004, 48) reminded us, the latter is not entirely severable from forces of global juristocracy.

The sixth and final theoretical framework currently utilized for comparative-court studies realizes that not only national governmental actors play to an international audience: national political activists do as well. This framework goes the furthest in accepting judges as embedded in and constituted by the social structural relations in which they find themselves. Interestingly, and unlike the aforementioned conduit framework, this last *courts-in-society framework* returns us, in our rethinking U.S. judicial politics, to an American-informed courts literature as theoretical source.

A long tradition in law and society studies has been to see law in action and courts in synergistic feedback loops with social movements and forces. Work on the United States was not always sanguine about the progressive or equalizing effects of law in political society, and saw hierarchies of structural power replicated in groups' litigative success, as in Galanter's seminal study (1974) of the social "haves" coming out ahead in court. Galanter's formula for mapping the fortunes of repeat players versus underdogs in court has been extended beyond the U.S. legal system to non-U.S. court contexts.[6] However, the courts-in-society framework for comparative judicial studies does more than transfer a template about elites and their superior litigational resources from one country case to another. It is also a self-consciously ethnographic, historical institutionalist-informed approach to comparative judicial studies, arguing that courts cannot be understood without reference to their developmental and cultural contexts, and suggesting that the contextual mixture of societal setting, political ideas, and cultural traditions affects courts as institutions and thus court decision making.

Comparison of courts can only occur across admittedly varying and, at times, incommensurable contextual variables, so the courts-in-society framework stresses as foundational the understanding of courts as "situated" institutions. The analytic methodology tends to be the single-case study, or serial-case studies loosely connected by a thematic motif. Yet embracing rather than disparaging this, one scholar recommends building arguments about courts "from the bottom up, formulating hypotheses around the empirical variety [across courts] and designing research with an eye to testing for the effect of variation" (Hilbink 2005, 17). The courts-in-society framework parts company with those theory-driven approaches to comparative judicial studies that analyze behavioral phenomenon removed from their rich and detailed specific context. Instead, comparative work embracing this historical-institutionalist framework depicts those contexts, arguing that their situational factors change the meaning of the behavioral phenomena, of the meaning and significance of judicial decision making.

Although Martin Shapiro's (1981a) *Courts: A Comparative and Political Analysis* is often thought of as the pioneering piece of the historical-institutionalist approach to comparative-court studies in general, it is the more recent work of Epp (1998) that best embodied the social-structural concerns of the courts-in-society framework. In asking how the strength and capacity of civil society affects court behavior and the relative success of rights claims, Epp provided a comparative framework to test the importance of coordinated and systematic litigation from below and finds that the country's judicial support structure is the critical variable. His notion of judicial support structure can be likened to an organizational regime of litigating groups, legal professional associations, and judicial institutions in support of certain ideas. Studies such as Moustafa (2003) and Cichowski (2004) broadened the structural networks of influence to include transnational actors, NGOs as well as courts. However, Widner's *Building the Rule of Law* (2001) stressed the limits of the civil society-courts synergy, observing that ideas are impotent to produce social action and institutional change without structural sponsorship; indeed, she draws on the lessons from U.S. judicial history and political development to suggest that judicialization of politics in Africa depends on leadership and the framing of concrete proposals as acceptable within local discourse (Widner 2004, 42–43). Still, the emphasis of these courts-in-society works on the importance of an organizational support structure should not be mistaken for applying *a priori* a universal and general theory of judicial decision making. Rather, the concern is with producing a sound constitutional ethnography and a political culture-based explanation of court behavior.

The historical institutionalist-informed, courts-in-society framework for comparative judicial studies challenges the institutional design-focused approach to both judicial studies and judicial reform, arguing that scholars must take account of the historical context and national specificities within which understandings of "law," "justice," and "rights" are shaped and that, in turn, affect the development of legal regulation (Sieder 2004). Indeed, some works in this framework stress internal judicial culture as the factor key to the operation of the courts under study, describing how culture within the courts may influence judges' impact on policy making. (Friedman and Perez Perdomo 2003) Although institutions matter, "only by understanding the role of law in long-run processes of state formation and the dynamic, inter-subjective nature of legal interactions can we begin to understand the specificities of socio-legal change" (Gloppen, Gargarella, and Skaar 2004, 4). Yet despite this commitment to specific context and ethnographic detail, both the Widner and the Epp studies explicitly and usefully reference or include the U.S. case as part of their comparative-courts analysis. The courts-in-society approach to comparative judicial studies may be the framework least oriented toward the generation of a unified and scientific model of judicial decision making, and may cast its net the broadest and the deepest in search of factors that influence court behavior, but its works are certainly disposed to consider the American case as one that displays certain universalizable characteristics about courts and, as such, can be treated in a truly comparative fashion with non-U.S. cases.[7]

Reflection on this returns us to the question of what the comparative-courts research has to teach students of the judicial process generally. The six theoretical frameworks profiled above strive to compare courts and their behavior across three different, essential dimensions: judicial ideology, strategic games of domestic politics, and the political broadly defined as institutional and social structures. Table 20.2 offers a summary of each framework, in light of the dimension it stresses and the hypotheses about judging that it generates.

Although their emphases concerning explanatory factors and their conclusions regarding judicial behavior vary, all of the frameworks pay heed in some way to the theoretical claims of the American judicial process literature or lessons of the U.S. judicial case, operationally or developmentally. Collectively, comparative judicial studies instruct us that courts *can* be compared, as political institutions like legislatures routinely are, and that unfamiliar political and legal contexts can be mapped so that their causal implications for judicial decision making can be understood. This is not to say that one unified, general theory of judicial behavior will emerge from this comparative work, or is even its goal. Area studies remains a powerful force in comparative politics, and courts—like any other political entity—are affected by their political background and setting. Acknowledging this does not mean that courts and their behavior cannot be successfully and usefully

Table 20.2 Six Frameworks of Comparative Judicial Studies

Comparative-Courts Framework	Theory of Judicial Behavior	Explanatory Factors Emphasized	Hypothesis About Judging
Judicial ideology framework	Attitudinalist	Political ideology of individual judge	Judicial decisions reflect political attitudes of appointing party/government
Constrained-court framework	Neo-institutionalist	Separation of powers dynamic	Judicial decisions take account of political constraints/veto points in securing policy preferences
Insurance model of judicial power	Neo-institutionalist	Competitive political environment	Enhanced judicial decision-making power reflects interests of dominant political elite
Strategic defection model	Neo-institutionalist	Regime change/ instability	Institutionally weak courts will defy their government given information that it is losing power
Court-as-conduit	Neo/historical institutionalist	International institutions and norms	Newly empowered courts use international association to enhance institutional legitimacy
Courts-in-society	Historical institutionalist	Social structure and social organizations	Social- and cultural-support structures are critical to judicial power

compared; indeed, insight comes from identifying cases that are alike in important ways. One handicap that initially saddled comparative-courts research was that many of its early political science practitioners were area studies specialists who tended to see "their" courts as so special as to be both a universal touchstone and a unique achievement. Those area studies specialists were Americanists, of course, and because their knowledge of courts came principally from one case, the comparative studies they spawned both generalized imperfectly and particularized unnecessarily.

CONCLUSIONS: THE FUTURE OF COMPARATIVE JUDICIAL STUDIES

Will a bifurcated approach to comparative-courts research persist, with unified and universal theory-building and theory-testing animating some scholars and ethnographic poking and soaking delighting others? Or will comparative judicial studies finally come of age, theoretically and substantively, with the study of American courts being just one additional area

studies focus within the search for an understanding of what judges do and why? There are hopeful signs of the latter, as our survey of work done in six theoretical frameworks suggests. The most contemporary work by comparative scholars of courts indicates a desire to balance generalizable and contextual factors in explanation and a realization that there are two distinct audiences for that work: country and region specialists, and judicial specialists.

It is quite clear that the study of the U.S. Supreme Court prompted and informed study of other policy-making courts and other constitutional designs. Quite naturally, the relatively young field of comparative-court studies drew on the mature theory and historical development research coming out of the U.S. case. Some of that theory and some of those lessons from political development bore fruit and some did not, in terms of understanding courts abroad. We will know that the field of comparative judicial studies has truly come of age when *its* findings about courts abroad, theoretical and with respect to political development, prompt and inform new thinking about U.S. judicial politics.

Notes

1. I thank Tamir Moustafa for his helpful comments on an earlier draft of this chapter, and the Woodrow Wilson School of Princeton University for research support provided during the fall of 2005.

2. The phrase "self-assured democracies," to refer to consolidated democracies without a legacy of laws from an authoritarian interlude, is from Erhard Blankenburg, "Institutionalizing the German Constitutional Complaint," cited in Scheppele (2000), p. 12.

3. Political institutions may be formal, like governmental organs, or more informal, like socio-political networks, and may be national entities or international organizations. The neo- and historical institutionalist models differ as to which they stress in explaining actors' political behavior.

4. Pereira's work (2005) on the Brazilian, Argentine, and Chilean cases inquires whether the judiciaries that were most aligned with military governments were, counterintuitively, better able to protect opponents of the regime.

5. Compare Choudhry (1999) and Slaughter's (1994) conceptualizations of cosmopolitan juris-prudes and transjudicial communities with the Brazilian Supreme Federal Tribunal's somewhat nationalistic use of domestic jurisprudence to insulate political legislation from conflicting international obligations. See Dolinger (1993, 1082) and Araujo (2001, 34–35).

6. Interestingly, Galanter's analysis of how litigation provides the occasion to deploy structural advantages was informed by his own work on Indian law. See Galanter (1999). As for the extension of his thesis beyond American courts, Conant's analysis (2002) of industry groups' success before the European Court of Justice is a recent and compelling illustration.

7. Indeed, some adherents of the American Political Development school of U.S. court studies liken their approach to the work of comparativists in political science who chart political directions and the processes of political change across time by evoking distinctive developmental dynamics, such as path dependency or layering, and the interplay of historical traditions, cultural attributes, and currents of ideas. Kahn and Kersch (2006, 12, 15–61). Research on American Political Development and the courts is usually thought of as an historical institutionalist approach.

BIBLIOGRAPHY

Abbe, Owen G., and Paul S. Herrnson. 2002. How judicial campaigns have changed. *Judicature* 85:286–95.

Abel, Richard L. 2005. Legalizing torture. Paper presented at annual retreat of the Baldy Center for Law & Social Policy, University at Buffalo, State University of New York, December 14.

Abel, Richard L., and Philip S. C. Lewis. 1995. Putting law back into the sociology of lawyers. In *Lawyers in society: An overview,* ed. Richard L. Abel and Philip S.C. Lewis, 281–329. Berkeley: University of California Press.

Abelson, A. 2002. All the rage. *Barron's,* January 2002, 8.

Abraham, Henry J. 1975. *The judicial process.* 3rd ed. New York: Oxford University Press.

———. 1999. *Justices, presidents, and senators.* new and rev. ed. Lanham, Md.: Rowman and Littlefield.

Abraham, Henry J., and Barbara A. Perry. 2003. *Freedom and the court: Civil rights and liberties in the United States.* 8th ed. Lawrence: University Press of Kansas.

Abrahamson, Shirley S. 2001. The ballot and the bench. *New York University Law Review* 76:973–1004.

Abramson, Jeffrey. 1994. *We, the jury: The jury system and the ideal of democracy.* New York: Basic Books.

Acheson, Dean. 1957. Recollections of service with the federal Supreme Court. *Alabama Lawyer* 18:355–66.

Adams, Mike. 2005. Merck loses Vioxx lawsuit: Jury awards $253.4 million to widow. *NewsTarget.com* (August 19, 2005), http://www.newstarget.com/z011064.html.

Administrative Office of the United States Courts. 1997. *Judicial business of the United States Courts: Annual report of the director.* Washington, D.C.: U.S. Government Printing Office.

———. 2000. Court, legislature break down walls for better government. *The Third Branch* 8:3 (Winter).

———. 2003a. *Judicial business of the United States Courts: Annual report of the director.* Washington, D.C.: U.S. Government Printing Office.

———. 2003b. Judiciary under attack. *The Third Branch* 35:1.

———. 2004. *Judicial business of the United States Courts: Annual report of the director.* Washington, D.C.: U.S. Government Printing Office.

———. 2005a. *Judicial business of the United States Courts: Annual report of the director.* Washington, D.C.: U.S. Government Printing Office.

———. 2005b. Judicial facts and figures. http://www.uscourts.gov/judicialfactsfigures/contents. html.

Albiston, Catherine. 2003. The rule of law and the litigation process: The paradox of losing by winning. In *Litigation: Do the "haves" still come out ahead?* ed. Herbert M. Kritzer and Susan S. Silbey, 168–211. Stanford, Calif: Stanford University Press.

Alexander, A. Lamar, Jr. 1965. En banc hearings in the federal courts of appeals: Accommodating institutional responsibilities. *New York University Law Review* 40:563–608.

Alfieri, Anthony V. 2005. *Gideon* in white/*Gideon* in black: Race and identity in lawyering. *Yale Law Journal* 114:1459–88.

Alfini, James J., and Terrence J. Brooks. 1989. Ethical constraints on judicial election campaigns: A review and critique of cannon 7. *Kentucky Law Journal* 77:671–722.

Allen, James L. 1977. Attitude change following jury duty. *Justice System Journal* 2:246–59.

Allen, Mike. 2005a. House bill tightens border controls. *The Washington Post*, February 11, A4.

———. 2005b. GOP seeks more curbs on courts; Sensenbrenner proposes an inspector general. *The Washington Post*, May 12, A3.

Almond, Gabriel A. 1990. *A discipline divided: Schools and sects in political science.* Beverly Hills, Calif: Sage.

Alozie, Nicholas O. 1990. Distribution of women and minority judges: The effects of judicial selection methods. *Social Science Quarterly* 69:315–25.

Alschuler, Albert W., and Andrew G. Deiss. 1994. A brief history of the criminal jury in the United States. *University of Chicago Law Review* 61: 86–115.

Alter, Karen J. 2001. *Establishing the supremacy of European law: The making of an international rule of law in Europe.* New York: Oxford University Press.

Amar, Akhil Reed. 1995. Reinventing juries: Ten suggested reforms. *University of California, Davis Law Review* 28:1169–90.

American Bar Association. 1990. *Standards of judicial administration, volume I: Standards relating to court organization.* Chicago: American Bar Association.

———. 1992. *Standards relating to juror use and management.* Chicago: American Bar Association.

———. 1998. *Perceptions of the U. S. justice system.* Chicago: American Bar Association.

———. 2004. January 2005 draft—Model code of judicial conduct (cited June 6, 2005). http://www.abanet.org/cpr/mcjc/toc.html.

American Bar Association Commission on the 21st Century Judiciary. 2003. *Justice in jeopardy.* Chicago: American Bar Association.

American Bar Association Commission on Women in the Profession. 2005. *A current glance at women in the law 2005.* http://www.abanet.org/women/ataglance.pdf.

American Intellectual Property Law Association (AIPLA). 2001. *Report of economic survey.* Arlington, Vir.: American Intellectual Property Law Association.

———. 2003. *Report of economic survey.* Arlington, Vir.: American Intellectual Property Law Association.

American Judicature Society. 1999. *Enhancing the jury system: A guidebook for jury reform.* Chicago: American Judicature Society.

———. 2003a. *Judicial merit selection: Current status.* Chicago: American Judicature Society.

———. 2003b. *Judicial selection in the states: Appellate and general jurisdiction courts initial selection, retention and term length.* Chicago: American Judicature Society.

———. 2003c. *Merit selection: The best way to choose the best judges.* Chicago: American Judicature Society.

——. 2005. *Judicial selection in the states*. Chicago: American Judicature Society. (Available at http://www.ajs.org/js/).

American Law Institute. 1965. *Restatement of the law (2nd) torts*. Eagan, Minn: West.

Anderson, Seth. 2004. Judicial election versus merit selection: Examining the decline in support for merit selection in the states. *Albany Law Review* 67:793–802.

Araujo, Nadia de. 2001. Dispute resolution in Mercosul: The protocol of Las Lenas and the case law of the Brazilian Supreme Court, *University of Miami Inter-American Law Review* 32:25–55.

Arceneaux, Craig, and David Pion-Berlin. 2005. *Transforming Latin America: the international and domestic origins of change*. Pittsburgh, Penn.: University of Pittsburgh Press.

Arizona Supreme Court Committee on More Effective Use of Juries. 1994. *Jurors: The power of twelve*. Phoenix: Arizona Supreme Court, Administrative Office of the Courts.

Armitage, Kelley. 2002. Denial ain't just a river in Egypt: A thorough review of judicial elections, merit selection and the role of state judges in society. *Capital University Law Review* 29:625–56.

Ashman, Alan, and James J. Alfini. 1974. *The key to judicial merit selection: The Nominating process*. Chicago: American Judicature Society.

Associated Press. 2005. Secret Norcross tape may be released to whistleblower. March 11.

Atkins, Burton M., and William Zavoina. 1974. Judicial leadership on the court of appeals: A probability analysis of panel assignment in race relations cases on the fifth circuit. *American Journal of Political Science* 18:701–11.

Atleson, James B. 1989. The legal community and the transformation of disputes: The settlement of injunction actions. *Law and Society Review* 23:41–73.

Babington, Charles. 2005a. Senator links violence to "political" decisions; "unaccountable" judiciary raises ire. *The Washington Post*, April 5, A7.

——. 2005b. Post-Schiavo questions await Congress's GOP leaders. *The Washington Post*, April 5, A4.

——. 2005c. GOP is fracturing over power of judiciary. *The Washington Post*, April 7, A4.

Bacon, Perry Jr. 2006. "Anybody knows not to mess with me": Nancy Pelosi leads the Democrats with a fiery style that could make her the first woman speaker of the house. *Time*, September 4, 31–2.

Bader, Cheryl G. 1996. *Batson* meets the First Amendment: Prohibiting peremptory challenges that violate a prospective juror's speech and association rights. *Hofstra Law Review* 24:567–621.

Baer, Judith A. 1978. *The chains of protection: The judicial response to women's labor legislation*. Westport, Conn: Greenwood

——. 1999. *Our lives before the law: Constructing a feminist jurisprudence*. Princeton, N.J.: Princeton University Press.

——. 2002. *Women in American law: The struggle toward equality from the New Deal to the present*. New York: Holmes & Meier.

Baer, Judith A., and Leslie F. Goldstein. 2006. *The constitutional and legal rights of women: Cases in law and social change*. Los Angeles: Roxbury.

Bailey, Michael, Brian Kamoie, and Forrest Maltzman. 2005. Signals from the tenth justice: The political role of the solicitor general in Supreme Court decision making. *American Journal of Political Science* 49:72–85.

Baird, Vanessa. 2004. The effect of politically salient decisions on the U.S. Supreme Court's agenda. *Journal of Politics* 66:755–72.

——. 2006. *Answering the call: How litigants and justices set the Supreme Court's agenda.* Charlottesville: University of Virginia Press.

Baker, Leonard. 1984. *Brandeis and Frankfurter: A dual biography.* New York: Harper & Row.

Baker, Thomas E. 1994. *Rationing justice on appeal: The problems of the U.S. Courts of Appeals.* St. Paul, Minn.: West.

Balkin, Jack. 1985. Ideology and counterideology from *Lochner* to *Garcia. University of Missouri Kansas City Law Review* 54:175–214.

Ball, Howard. 1978. *Judicial craftsmanship or Fiat?* Westport, Conn.: Greenwood.

Ball, Howard, and Phillip Cooper. 1992. *Of power and right: Hugo Black, William O. Douglas, and America's constitutional revolution.* New York: Oxford University Press.

Banner, Stuart. 1988. Disqualifying elected judges from cases involving campaign contributors. *Stanford Law Review* 40:449–90.

Barnes, Jeb. 2004a. Adversarial legalism, the rise of judicial policymaking, and the separation-of-powers doctrine. In *Making policy, making law: An interbranch perspective,* ed. Mark C. Miller and Jeb Barnes, 35–50. Washington, D.C.: Georgetown University Press.

——. 2004b. *Overruled? Legislative overrides, pluralism, and court-Congress relations in an age of statutes.* Palo Alto, Calif.: Stanford University Press.

——. 2007a. Bringing the courts back in: Interbranch perspectives on the role of courts in American politics and policy making. *Annual Review of Political Science* 10:23–38.

——. 2007b. Rethinking the landscape of tort reform: Legislative inertia and court-based tort reform in the case of asbestos. *Justice Systems Journal,* 28:157–181.

Barnes, Jeb, and Mark C. Miller. 2004a. Governance as dialogue. In *Making policy, making law: An interbranch perspective.* ed. Mark C. Miller and Jeb Barnes, 202–207. Washington, D.C.: Georgetown University Press.

——. 2004b. Putting the pieces together: American lawmaking from an interbranch perspective. In *Making policy, making law: An interbranch perspective,* ed. Mark C. Miller and Jeb Barnes, 3–12. Washington, D.C.: Georgetown University Press.

Barnhizer, David. 2001. On the make: Campaign funding and the corrupting of the American judiciary. *Catholic University Law Review* 50:361–427.

Bartee, Alice Fleetwood. 1984. *Cases lost, causes won.* New York: St. Martin's.

Bator, Paul M. 1985. The judicial universe of Judge Richard Posner. *University of Chicago Law Review* 52:1146–66.

Battle, R. H. 1904. Obituary of Samuel Field Phillips, LL.D. *North Carolina Law Journal* 1:22–7.

Baum, Lawrence. 1977. Judicial impact as a form of policy implementation. In *Public law and public policy.* ed. John A. Gardiner, 127–140. New York: Praeger.

——. 1988. Measuring policy change in the U.S. Supreme Court. *American Political Science Review* 82: 905–12.

——. 1992. Membership change and collective voting change in the United States Supreme Court. *Journal of Politics* 54:3–24.

——. 1997. *The puzzle of judicial behavior.* Ann Arbor: University of Michigan Press.

——. 1999. Recruitment and the motivations of Supreme Court Justices. In *Supreme Court decision-making: New institutionalist approaches.* ed. Cornell W. Clayton and Howard Gillman, 201–213. Chicago: University of Chicago Press.

——. 2001. *American courts process and policy.* 5th ed. Boston: Houghton Mifflin.

——. 2004. *The Supreme Court*. 8th ed. Washington, D.C.: CQ.

——. 2005. The future of the judicial branch: Courts and democracy in the twenty-first century. In *The judicial branch*. ed. Kermit L. Hall and Kevin T. McGuire, 517–542. New York: Oxford University Press.

——. 2006. *Judges and their audiences: A perspective on judicial behavior*. Princeton, N.J.: Princeton University Press.

Baum, Lawrence, and Lori Hausegger. 2004. The Supreme Court and Congress: Reconsidering the relationship. In *Making policy, making law: An interbranch perspective,* ed. Mark C. Miller and Jeb Barnes, 107–139. Washington, D.C.: Georgetown University Press.

Baumgartner, Frank, and Bryan Jones. 1993. *Agendas and instability in American politics*. Chicago: University of Chicago Press.

Beardsley, Elisabeth J. 2004. Lawmakers sue to overturn SJC ruling on gay marriage. *The Boston Herald*, April 29, 14.

Becker, Jo. 2005. Television ad war on Alito begins. *The Washington Post,* November 18, A3.

Belknap, Michael. 2005. *The Supreme Court under Earl Warren, 1953–1969*. Columbia: University of South Carolina Press.

Bell, Lauren Cohen. 2002a. *Warring factions: Interest groups, money and the new politics of Senate confirmation*. Columbus: Ohio State University Press.

——. 2002b. Senatorial discourtesy: The Senate's use of delay to shape the federal judiciary. *Political Research Quarterly* 55:589–608.

Bell, Lauren C., and L. Marvin Overby. 2004. Rational behavior or the norm of cooperation?: Filibustering behavior among retiring Senators. *Journal of Politics* 66:906–24.

Bell, Lauren C., and Kevin M. Scott. 2006. Policy statements or symbolic politics?: Explaining congressional court-limiting attempts. *Judicature* 89:196–201.

Bell, Peter, and Jeffrey O'Connell. 1997. *Accidental justice: The dilemmas of tort law*. New Haven, Conn.: Yale University Press.

Benesh, Sara C. 2002. *The U.S. Courts of Appeals and the law of confession: Perspectives on the hierarchy of justice*. New York: LFB Scholarly.

Benesh, Sara C., and Malia Reddick. 2002. Overruled: An event history analysis of lower court reaction to Supreme Court alteration of precedent. *Journal of Politics* 64:534–50.

Bent, Silas. 1932. *Justice Oliver Wendell Holmes: A biography*. Garden City, N.Y.: Garden City.

Berliner, B. 1994. Wrong message. *Chicago Tribune*, August 31, 18.

Berry, Jeffrey M. 1997. *The interest group society*. 3rd ed. New York: Longman.

Best, Bradley J. 2002. *Law clerks, support personnel, and the decline of consensual norms on the United States Supreme Court, 1935–1995*. New York: LFB Scholarly.

Bickel, Alexander M. 1962. *The least dangerous branch: The Supreme Court at the bar of politics*. Indianapolis, Ind.: Bobbs-Merrill.

——. 1964. *The judiciary and responsible government: 1910–1921*. New York: MacMillan.

——. 1965. *Politics and the Warren Court*. New York: Harper & Row.

Biddle, Francis. 1962. *In brief authority*. Garden City, N.Y.: Doubleday.

Blasi, Vincent. 1983. *The Burger Court: The counter-revolution that wasn't*. New Haven, Conn.: Yale University Press.

Blue Ribbon Commission on Jury System Improvement. 1996. *Final report*. Sacramento Judicial Council of California.

Boatright, Robert G. 1998. *Improving citizen response to jury summonses*. Chicago: American Judicature Society.

Boatright, Robert G., and Beth Murphy. 1999a. Behind closed doors: Assisting jurors with their deliberations. *Judicature* 83:52–8.

——. 1999b. How judges can help deliberating juries: Using the guide for jury deliberations. *Court Review* 36:38–45.

Bogus, Carl T. 2001. *Why lawsuits are good for America: Disciplined democracy, big business, and the common law.* New York: New York University Press.

Bonneau, Chris W. 2005. Electoral verdicts: Incumbent defeats in state supreme court elections. *American Politics Research* 33:818–41.

Bonneau, Chris W., and Melinda Gann Hall. 2006. Does quality matter? Challengers in state supreme court elections. *American Journal of Political Science* 50:20–33.

Bosworth, Matthew H. 2001. *Courts as catalysts: State supreme courts and public school finance equity.* Albany: State University of New York Press.

Bourchier, David. 1999. Magic memos, collusion and judges with attitude: Notes on the politics of law in contemporary Indonesia. In *Law, capitalism and power in Asia: The rule of law and legal institutions. ed.* K. Jayasuriya, 233–252. New York: Routledge.

Bower, Lisa C. 1994. Queer acts and the politics of 'direct address': Rethinking law, culture, and community. *Law and Society Review* 28:1009–33.

Bowles, Roger A. 1980. Juries, incentives, and self-selection. *British Journal of Criminology* 20:368–76.

Brace, Paul, and Melinda Gann Hall. 1995. Studying courts comparatively: The view from the American states. *Political Research Quarterly* 48:5–29.

——. 1997. The interplay of preferences, case facts, context, and rules in the politics of judicial choice. *Journal of Politics* 59:1206–31.

Brady, David, and Joseph Stewart. 1982. Congressional party realignment and transformation of public policy in three realignment eras. *American Journal of Political Science* 26:333–60.

Bragaw, Stephen, and Mark C. Miller. 2004. The City of Boerne: Two tales of one city. In *Making policy, making law: An interbranch perspective,* ed. Mark C. Miller and Jeb Barnes, 140–149. Washington, D.C.: Georgetown University Press.

Brennan, William J. Dean's Day Address, New York University Law School 1979.

Brenner, Saul, and Harold Spaeth. 1995. *Stare indecisis: The alteration of precedent on the Supreme Court 1946–1992.* Cambridge: Cambridge University Press.

Bright, Stephen B. 1997. Political attacks on the judiciary. *Judicature* 80:165–73.

Brisbin, Richard. 1996. Slaying the dragon: Segal, Spaeth and the function of law in Supreme Court decision making. *American Journal of Political Science* 40:1004–17.

——. 2002. *A strike like no other strike: Law and resistance during the Pittston coal strike of 1989–1990.* Baltimore: Johns Hopkins University Press.

——. 2005. The judiciary and the separation of powers. In *The judicial branch. ed.* Kermit L. Hall and Kevin T. McGuire, 89–115. New York: Oxford University Press.

Brodeur, Paul. 1986. *Outrageous misconduct: The asbestos industry on trial.* New York: Pantheon Books.

Brody, David C., and John Neiswander. 2000. Judicial attitudes towards jury reform. *Judicature* 83:298–303.

Bronner, Ethan. 1989. *Battle for justice: How the Bork nomination shook America.* New York: Norton.

Brookings Institution. 1992. *Charting a future for the civil jury system.* Washington, D.C.: Brookings Institution.

Brown, Lucinda. 1998. Court and community partners in Massachusetts. *Judicature* 81:200–5.

Brudney, James J. and Corey Ditslear. 2001. Designated diffidence: District court judges on the courts of appeals. *Law and Society Review* 35:565–606.

Buell, Emmett H., Jr. with Richard A. Brisbin, Jr. 1982. *School desegregation and defended neighborhoods: The Boston controversy.* Lexington, Mass.: Lexington Books.

Bugliosi, Vincent. 2001. None dare call it treason. *The Nation*, February 5.

Bumiller, Elisabeth. 2005. War rooms (and chests) ready for a Supreme Court vacancy. *The New York Times,* June 20, A13.

Bureau of Labor Statistics. 2005. Employed persons by detailed occupation, sex, race, and Hispanic or Latino ethnicity. http://www.bls.gov/cps/cpsaat11.pdf.

Burke, Thomas F. 2002. *Lawyers, lawsuits, and legal rights.* Berkeley: University of California Press.

Burns, James McGregor. 1956. *Roosevelt: The lion and the fox.* New York: Harcourt, Brace.

Bush, George W. 2003. Remarks by the President on the Michigan affirmative action case. January 15, 2003. *www.whitehouse.gov.*

Cain, Maureen. 1979. The general practice lawyer and the client: Towards a radical conception. *International Journal of the Sociology of Law* 7:331–54.

———. 1994. The symbol traders. In *Lawyers in a postmodern world: Translation and transgression*, ed. Maureen Cain and Christine B. Harrington, 15–48. New York: New York University Press.

Caldeira, Gregory A., and James L. Gibson. 1992. The etiology of public support for the Supreme Court, *American Journal of Political Science* 36:635–64.

Caldeira, Gregory A., and John R. Wright. 1988. Organized interests and agenda setting in the U.S. Supreme Court. *American Political Science Review* 82:1109–27.

———. 1990. *Amicus curiae* before the Supreme Court: Who participates, when and how much. *Journal of Politics* 52:782–806.

Caldeira, Gregory A., John R. Wright, and Christopher J.W. Zorn. 1999. Sophisticated voting and gate-keeping in the Supreme Court. *Journal of Law, Economics & Organization* 15:549–72.

Cameron, Charles M., Jeffrey A. Segal, and Donald Songer. 2000. Strategic auditing in a political hierarchy: An informational model of the Supreme Court's certiorari decisions. *American Political Science Review* 94:101–16.

Campbell, Colton C., and John F. Stack, Jr., ed. 2001. *Congress confronts the Court: The struggle for legitimacy and authority in lawmaking.* Landham, Md.: Rowman & Littlefield.

Campbell, David and Philip Thomas, ed. 1998. *The province of jurisprudence determined.* Aldershot: Dartmouth.

Canellos, Peter S. 2006a. The religious right faces its purgatory. *The Boston Globe,* January 10, A3.

———. 2006b. Amid the abortion rifts, a history of court shifts. *The Boston Globe,* February 26, A3.

Canon, Bradley C. 1983. Defining the dimensions of judicial activism. *Judicature* 66:236–47.

Canon, Bradley C., and Charles A. Johnson. 1999. *Judicial policies: Implementation and impact.* 2nd ed. Washington, D.C.: CQ.

Caplan, Lincoln. 1987. *The tenth justice: The solicitor general and the rule of law.* New York: Knopf.

Caplan, Lincoln. 2001. The president's lawyer, and the court's. *New York Times*, May 18, A19.

Cardozo, Benjamin. 1921. *The nature of the judicial process*. New Haven, Conn.: Yale University Press.

Carelli, Richard. 1999. Rehnquist lobbies Congress for money. *The Associated Press Newswire*, August 10, 1999.

Carmines, Edward, and James Stimson. 1989. *Issue evolution: Race and the transformation of American politics*. Princeton, NJ: Princeton University Press.

Carpenter, Charles E., Jr. 1999. Having faced the circuit-splitting conundrum—What about more judges, less staff? *Journal of Law and Policy* 15:531–57.

Carrington, Paul. 1969. Crowded dockets and the courts of appeals: The threat to the function of review and the national law. *Harvard Law Review* 82:542–617.

Carroll, Stephen J. 2002. *Asbestos litigation costs and compensation: An interim report*. Santa Monica, Calif.: RAND Institute for Civil Justice.

———. 2005. *Asbestos litigation*. Santa Monica, Calif.: RAND Institute for Civil Justice.

Carson, Clara N. 2004. *The lawyer statistical report: The U.S. legal profession in 2000*. Chicago: American Bar Foundation.

Carter, Lief. 1991. *An introduction to Constitutional interpretation: Cases in law and religion*. New York: Longman.

Casey, Jeff T., and John T. Scholz. 1991. Beyond deterrence: Behavioral theory and tax compliance. *Law and Society Review* 25:821–43.

Casper, Jonathan D. 1972. *American criminal justice: The defendant's perspective*. Englewood Cliffs, N.J.: Prentice-Hall.

———. 1976. The Supreme Court and national policy making. *American Political Science Review* 70:50–63.

Chamberlain, Ronald S. 1987. Mixing politics and justice: The Office of the Solicitor General. *Journal of Law and Politics* 4:379–428.

Champagne, Anthony. 2001. Television ads in judicial campaigns. *Indiana Law Review* 35:669–89.

Champagne, Anthony, and Judith Haydel. 1993. Introduction. In *Judicial reform in the states, ed.* Anthony Champagne and Judith Haydel, 1–18 Lanham, Md.: University Press of America.

Chase, Harold. 1972. *Federal judges: The appointing process*. Minneapolis: University of Minnesota Press.

Chavez, Rebecca Bill. 2004. *The rule of law in nascent democracies*. Stanford, Calif.: Stanford University Press.

Chawkins, Steve. 2005a. Jackson juror queries stun experts. *Los Angeles Times*, February 3, B3.

———. 2005b. Quick pick: Jackson's jury chosen. *Los Angeles Times*, February 24, B1.

Chayes, Abram. 1976. The role of the judge in public law litigation. *Harvard Law Review* 89:1281–316.

Cheek, Kyle, and Anthony Champagne. 2000. Money in Texas supreme court elections, 1980–1998. *Judicature* 84:20–5.

Chemerinsky, Erwin. 1989. The Supreme Court, 1988 term—Foreword: The vanishing Constitution. *Harvard Law Review* 103:43–104.

Choudhry, Sujit. 1999. Globalization in search of justification: Toward a theory of comparative constitutional interpretation, *Indiana Law Journal* 74: 820–92.

Church, Thomas. 1985. Examining local legal culture. *American Bar Foundation Research Journal* 10:499–518 (Summer,1985).

Cichowski, Rachel. 2004. Women's rights, the European Court and supranational constitutionalism. *Law and Society Review* 38:489–512.

Citizens for Independent Courts. 2000. *Uncertain justice: Politics and America's courts.* New York: Century Foundation.

Claes, Monica. 2006. The national courts' mandate in the European Constitution. Oxford, UK: Hart.

Clayton, Cornell W. 1992. *The politics of justice: The attorney general and the making of legal policy.* Armonk, N.Y.: Sharpe.

———, ed. 1995. *Government lawyers: The federal legal bureaucracy and presidential politics.* Lawrence: University Press of Kansas.

———. 1999. The Supreme Court and political jurisprudence: New and old institutionalisms. In *Supreme Court decision-making: New institutionalist approaches,* ed. Cornell Clayton and Howard Gillman, 15–41. Chicago: University of Chicago Press.

Clayton, Cornell, and Howard Gillman. 1999. Introduction: Beyond judicial decision making. In *The Supreme Court in American politics: New institutionalist interpretations,* ed. Howard Gillman and Cornell Clayton, 1–12. Lawrence: University Press of Kansas.

Clement, Paul. 2005. Statement of the nominee. U.S. Congress. Senate. Committee on the Judiciary. *Confirmation Hearing on the Nomination of Paul Clement to be Solicitor General of the United States.* 109th Cong., 1st sess., April 27, 2005.

Coalition for a Fair Judiciary. 2003. Press release: Grievance filed with Virginia bar against NAACP official. http://fairjudiciary.com/cfj_contents/press/120403.shtml. December 4, 2003.

Coenen, Dan T. 1993. Review of *Deciding to Decide: Agenda Setting in the United States Supreme Court. Constitutional Commentary* 10:180–93.

Coffin, Frank M., and Robert A. Katzmann. 2003. Steps towards optimal judicial workways: Perspectives from the federal bench. *N.Y.U. Annual Survey of American Law* 59:377–91.

Cohen, Adam. 2005. Psst Justice Scalia, you know, you're an activist judge too. *The New York Times*, April 19, 20.

Cohen, Jonathan Matthew. 2002. *Inside appellate courts: The impact of court organization on judicial decision making in the United States Courts of Appeals.* Ann Arbor: University of Michigan Press.

Cohen, Thomas. H. 2006. Appeals from general civil trials in 46 large counties, 2001–2005. *Bureau of Justice Statistics Bulletin*, July 2006. Washington, D.C.: U.S. Department of Justice.

Colker, Ruth. 2005. *The disability pendulum: The first decade of the Americans with Disabilities Act.* New York: New York University Press.

Colorado Supreme Court Committee on the Effective and Efficient Use of Juries. 1997. *With respect to the jury: a proposal for jury reform.* Denver: Colorado Supreme Court.

Comiskey, Michael. 2004. *Seeking justices: The judging of Supreme Court nominees.* Lawrence: University Press of Kansas.

Common Cause. 1977. *The Senate rubber stamp machine.* Washington D.C.: Common Cause.

Conant, Lisa. 2002. *Justice contained: Law and politics in the European Union.* Ithaca, N.Y.: Cornell University Press.

Conley, John M., and William M. O'Barr. 1990. *Rules versus relationships: The ethnology of legal discourse.* Chicago: University of Chicago Press.

Cord, Robert. 1982. *Separation of church and state.* New York: Lambeth.

Cortner, Richard. 1981. *The Supreme Court and the second bill of rights*. Madison: University of Wisconsin Press.

Council for Court Excellence. 1998. *Juries for the year 2000 and beyond: Proposals to improve the jury system in Washington, D.C.* Washington, D.C.: Council for Court Excellence.

Court Statistics Project. 2005. *State court caseload statistics, 2004*. Williamsburg, Vir.: National Center for State Courts. Available at http://www.ncsconline.org/D_Research/csp/2004_Files/SCCSFront%20.pdf.

Cox, Paul N. 2003. An interpretation and (partial) defense of legal realism. *Indiana Law Review* 36:57–100.

Coyle, Anne. 2004. A modest reform: The new Rule 32.1 permitting citation to unpublished opinions in the federal courts of appeals. *Fordham Law Review* 72:2471–505.

Coyle, Marcia. 1988. The judiciary: A great right hope. *The National Law Journal* April, 22.

Crenson, Matthew. 1971. *The unpolitics of air pollution*. Baltimore: Johns Hopkins University Press.

Croley, Steven P. 1995. The majoritarian difficulty: Elective judiciaries and the rule of law. *University of Chicago Law Review* 62:689–791.

Cross, Frank B. 1996. The role of lawyers in positive theories of doctrinal evolution. *Emory Law Journal* 45:524–89.

Crump, David. 1986. Law clerks: Their roles and relationships with their judges. *Judicature* 69:236–40.

Culver, John H., and John T. Wold. 1986. Rose bird and the politics of judicial accountability in California. *Judicature* 70:80–9.

Cunningham, Clark D. 1989. The tale of two clients: Thinking about law as language. *Michigan Law Review* 87:2459–94.

Curry, Brett. 2005. The courts, Congress, and the politics of federal jurisdiction. PhD diss., Ohio State University.

Curry, Ken, and M. Beth Krugler. 1999. The sound of silence: Are silent juries the best juries? *Texas Bar Journal* 62:441–7.

Cushman, Clare, and Melvin I. Urofsky. 2004. *Black, White, and Brown: The landmark school desegregation case in retrospect*. Washington, D.C.: Supreme Court Historical Society and CQ Press.

Dahl, Robert. 1957. Decision-making in a democracy: The Supreme Court as a national policy-maker. *Journal of Public Law* 6:279–95.

——. 1961. *Who governs? Democracy and power in an American city*. New Haven, Conn.: Yale University Press.

Dann, B. Michael. 1993. Learning lessons and speaking rights: Creating educated and democratic juries. *Indiana Law Journal* 68:1229–79.

Dann, B. Michael, and George Logan III. 1996. Jury reform: The Arizona experience. *Judicature* 79:280–86.

Davidson, Roger H., and Walter J. Oleszek. 2002. *Congress and its members,* 8th ed. Washington, D.C.: CQ.

——. 2004. *Congress and its members*, 9th ed. Washington, D.C.: CQ.

Davis, Sue, and Donald R. Songer. 1989. The changing role of the United States Court of Appeals: The flow of litigation revisited. *Justice System Journal* 12:323–30.

DeBow, Michael. 2002. The case for partisan judicial elections. *Judicial Selection White Papers*. Washington, D.C.: Federalist Society.

DeParle, Jason. 2005. In battle to pick next justice, right says avoid a Kennedy. *The New York Times,* June 27, 1.

Dershowitz, Alan M. 2001. *Supreme injustice: How the high court hijacked election 2000.* Oxford: Oxford University Press.

Derthick, Martha A. 2002. *Up in smoke: From legislation to litigation in tobacco politics.* Washington, D.C.: CQ.

———. 2005. *Up in smoke: From legislation to litigation in tobacco politics,* 2nd ed. Washington, D.C.: CQ.

Devins, Neal. 1994. Unitariness and independence: Solicitor general control over independent agency litigation. *California Law Review* 82:255–327.

Devins, Neal, and Louis Fisher. 2004. *The democratic constitution.* Oxford: Oxford University Press.

Devins, Neal, and Keith E. Whittington, ed. 2005. *Congress and the Constitution.* Durham, N.C.: Duke University Press.

Diamond, Shari Seidman. 1993. What jurors think: Expectations and reactions of citizens who serve as jurors. In *Verdict: Assessing the civil jury system, ed.* Robert E. Litan, 282–305. Washington, D.C.: Brookings Institution.

Dionne, E. J., Jr. 2005. Will Republicans go nuclear? *Washington Post,* March 22, A17.

Dinovitzer, Ronit and Bryant G. Garth. 2007. Lawyer satisfaction in the process of structuring legal careers. *Law & Society Review* 41:1–50.

Dodge, Heather, and Kenneth Pankey. 2003. *Case processing time standards in state courts, 2002–03.* Williamsburg, VA: National Center for State Courts. Available at: http://www.ncsconline.org/WC/Publications/KIS_CasManCPTSPub.pdf.

Dolbeare, Kenneth M., and Phillip E. Hammond. 1971. *The school prayer decisions: From court policy to local practice.* Chicago: University of Chicago Press.

Dolinger, Jacob. 1993. Brazilian Supreme Court solutions for conflicts between domestic and international law. *Capital University Law Review* 22:1041–93.

Donahue, Sean. 1995. Behind the pillars of justice: Remarks on law clerks. *The Long Term View* 3:77–84.

Donahue, William. 1985. *The politics of the American Civil Liberties Union.* New Brunswick, N.J.: Transaction.

Douglas, James W., and Roger E. Hartley. 2003. The politics of court budgeting in the states: Is judicial independence threatened by the budgetary process? *Public Administration Review* 63:441–54.

Douglas, William O. 1980. *The court years.* New York: Random House.

Downs, Anthony. 1973. Up and down with ecology—The "issue attention cycle." *The Public Interest* 32:38–50.

Dragich, Martha. 1996. Once a century: Time for a structural overhaul of the federal courts. *Wisconsin Law Review* 1996:11–73.

Dreschel, Robert E. 1983. *News making in the trial courts.* New York: Longman.

Dubois, Phillip L. 1980. *From ballot to bench: Judicial elections and the quest for account-ability.* Austin: University of Texas Press.

Durbin Staff Memo. 2002. Memorandum to Senator Richard Durbin, "Meeting with civil rights leaders yesterday to discuss judges." June 2, 2002. Available online via the Center for Individual Freedom at http://www.cfif.org/htdocs/legislative_issues/federal_issues/hot_issues_in_congress/confirmation_watch/judiciary_memos.pdf.

Durbin Staff Memo. 2001. Memorandum to Senator Richard Durbin, "Meeting with civil rights leaders yesterday to discuss judges." November 7, 2001. Available online via the Center for Individual Freedom at http://www.cfif.org/htdocs/legislative_issues/federal_issues/ hot_issues_in_congress/confirmation_watch/judiciary_memos.pdf.

Dye, Thomas R., and Harmon L. Zeigler. 1975. *The irony of democracy: An uncommon introduction to American politics*, 3rd ed. North Scituate, Mass.: Duxbury.

Easterbrook, Frank. 1983. Statutes' domains. *University of Chicago Law Review* 50:533–52.

——. 1984. Foreword: The Court and the economic system. *Harvard Law Review* 98:4–60.

The Economist. 1999. The gavel and the robe. August 7, 43.

The Economist. 2005. Judge yourself: Conservatives v. the judiciary. April 23, 31–2.

The Economist. 2006a. Tom DeLay: Sweet justice. August 12. 26.

The Economist. 2006b. Inner demons. November 11, 40.

Edwards, Harry T. 1981. A judge's view on justice, bureaucracy, and legal method. *Michigan Law Review* 80:259–69.

Egelko, Bob. 2005. Schiavo case widens divide between Congress and courts. *San Francisco Chronicle*, April 2, A3.

Eggen, Dan. 2005. Padillla is indicted on terrorism charges. *The Washington Post*, November 11, A1.

Eggen, Dan, and Josh White. 2006. U.S. seeks to avoid detainee ruling. *The Washington Post*, January 13, A7.

Eisenstein, James, Roy B. Flemming, and Peter F. Nardulli. 1988. *The contours of justice: Communities and their courts.* Boston: Little, Brown.

Eisenstein, James, and Herbert Jacob. 1977. *Felony justice: An organizational analysis of criminal courts.* Boston: Little, Brown.

Eisler, Kim. 1993. *A justice for all: William J. Brennan, Jr. and the decisions that transformed America.* New York: Simon & Schuster.

Elaine Jones resigns from NAACP legal defense; receives farewell tribute. 2004. *Jet* 105:21.

Ely, John Hart. 1980. *Democracy and distrust: A theory of judicial review.* Cambridge, Mass.: Harvard University Press.

Entin, Jonathan L., and Erik M. Jensen. 2006. Taxation, compensation, and judicial independence. *Case Western Reserve Law Review* 56:965–1015.

Epp, Charles. 1998. *The rights revolution: Lawyers, activists, and supreme courts in comparative perspective.* Chicago: University of Chicago Press.

Epstein, Lee. 1985. *Conservatives in court.* Knoxville: University of Tennessee Press.

——. 1999. The comparative advantage. *Law and Courts Newsletter* 3:1–6.

Epstein, Lee, Valerie Hoekstra, Jeffrey Segal, and Harold Spaeth. 1998. Do political preferences change? A longitudinal study of U.S. Supreme Court justices. *Journal of Politics* 60:801–18.

Epstein, Lee, and Jack Knight. 1998. *The choices justices make.* Washington, D.C.: CQ.

——. 2000. Toward a strategic revolution in judicial politics: A look back, a look forward. *Political Research Quarterly* 53:625–61.

Epstein, Lee, Jack Knight, and Andrew D. Martin. 2004. Constitutional interpretation from a strategic perspective. In *Making policy, making law: An interbranch perspective, ed. Mark C.* Miller and Jeb Barnes, 170–188. Washington, D.C.: Georgetown University Press.

Epstein, Lee, Jack Knight, and Olga Shvetsova. 2001. The role of constitutional courts in the establishment and maintenance of democratic systems of government. *Law and Society Review* 35:117–63.

———. 2002. Selecting selection systems. In *Judicial independence at the crossroads: An inter-disciplinary approach, ed.* Stephen B. Burbank and Barry Friedman, 191–226. Beverly Hills, Calif.: Sage.

Epstein, Lee, and Joseph F. Kobylka. 1992. *The Supreme Court and the legal change: Abortion and the death penalty.* Chapel Hill: University of North Carolina Press.

Epstein, Lee, and Jeffrey A. Segal. 2005. *Advice and consent: The politics of judicial appointments.* New York: Oxford University Press.

Epstein, Lee, Jeffrey A. Segal, Harold J. Spaeth, and Thomas G. Walker. 2003. *Supreme Court compendium*, 3rd ed. Washington, D.C.: CQ.

Epstein, Lee, Thomas Walker, and William Dixon. 1989. The Supreme Court and criminal justice disputes: A neo-institutional perspective. *American Journal of Political Science* 33:825–41.

Erikson, Robert, Michael MacKuen, and James Stimson. 2002. *The macro polity.* Cambridge: Cambridge University Press.

Erlanger, Howard S., Elizabeth Chambliss, and Marygold S. Melli. 1987. Participation and flexibility in informal processes: Cautions from the divorce context. *Law and Society Review* 21:585–604.

Eskridge, William. 1991a. Overriding Supreme Court statutory interpretation decisions. *Yale Law Journal* 101:331–417.

———. 1991b. Reneging on history? Playing the court/Congress/president civil rights game. *California Law Review* 79:613–84.

———. 1994. *Dynamic statutory interpretation.* Cambridge, Mass.: Harvard University Press.

Espeland, Wendy. 1994. Legally mediated identity: The National Environmental Policy Act and the bureaucratic construction of interests. *Law and Society Review* 28:1149–79.

Evans, Peter B., Dietrich Rueschemeyer, and Theda Skocpol, ed. 1985. *Bringing the state back in.* New York: Cambridge University Press.

Ewick, Patricia, and Susan S. Silbey. 1998. *The common place of the law: Stories from everyday life.* Chicago: University of Chicago Press.

Fallahay, John, and David Schneider. 1997. July nullification: An example right before our cameras. *Judges' Journal* 36:30–1.

Fedderson, Timothy, and Wolfgang Pesendorfer. 1998. Convicting the innocent: The inferiority of unanimous jury verdicts under strategic voting. *American Political Science Review* 92:23–35.

Federal Judicial Vacancies. Report of the Administrative Office of the U.S. Courts. 2005. http://www.uscourts.gov/cfapps/webnovada/CF_FB_301/index.cfm?fuseaction=Reports. ViewConfirmations.

Federalist Society. 2002. Judicial selection white papers: The case for judicial appointments. *Toledo Law Review* 33:353–92.

Feeley, Malcolm M. 1979. *The process is the punishment.* New York: Russell Sage Foundation.

Feeley, Malcolm M., and Edward L. Rubin. 1998. *Judicial policy making and the modern state: How the courts reformed America's prisons.* Cambridge: Cambridge University Press.

Feinberg, Wilfred. 1990. Senior judges: A national resource. *Brooklyn Law Review* 56:409–18.

Felstiner, William L.F., Richard L. Abel, and Austin Sarat, 1980–81. The emergence and transformation of disputes: Naming, blaming, and claiming. *Law and Society Review* 15:631–54.

Ferdinand, Pamela. 2003. Would-be shoe bomber gets life terms. *Washington Post,* January 31, A1.

Ferraro, Thomas. 2002. Bush sustains second defeat of judicial nominee. *Reuters,* September 5.

Fine, Sidney. 1984. *Frank Murphy: The Washington years.* Ann Arbor: University of Michigan Press.

Finister, Ada W., ed. 1983. *Political science: The state of the discipline.* Washington, D.C.: The American Political Science Association.

——. 1993. *Political science: The state of the discipline II.* Washington, D.C.: The American Political Science Association.

Finkel, Jodi. 2003. Supreme Court decisions on electoral rules after Mexico's 1994 judicial reform: An empowered court. *Journal of Latin American Studies* 35:777–99.

Fiorina, Morris. 1996. *Divided government,* 2nd ed. New York: Macmillan.

Fisher, Louis. 1988. *Constitutional dialogues: Interpretation as political process.* Princeton, N.J.: Princeton University Press.

——. 2002. Congressional access to information: Using legislative will and leverage. *Duke Law Journal* 52:323–402.

——. 2004. Judicial finality or an ongoing colloquy? In *Making policy, making law: An interbranch perspective,* ed. Mark C. Miller and Jeb Barnes, 153–169. Washington, D.C.: Georgetown University Press.

——. 2005a. *American constitutional law,* 6th ed. Durham, N.C.: Carolina Academic Press.

——. 2005b. *Military tribunals and presidential power.* Lawrence: University Press of Kansas.

Fisher, Louis, and Neal Devins. 1996. *Political dynamics of constitutional law,* 2nd ed. St. Paul, Minn.: West.

——. 2006. *Political dynamics of constitutional law,* 4th ed. St. Paul, Minn.: West.

Flemming, Roy B., Peter F. Nardulli, and James Eisenstein. 1992. *The craft of justice: Politics and work in criminal court communities.* Philadelphia: University of Pennsylvania Press.

Flemming, Roy B., Michael C. MacLeod, and Jeffrey Talbert. 1998. Witnesses at the confirmations? The appearance of organized interests at Senate hearings of federal judicial appointments, 1945–1992. *Political Research Quarterly* 51:617–31.

Florida Jury Innovations Committee. 2001. *Draft recommendations and status.* Tallahassee: Florida Judicial Council.

Formisano, Ronald P. 1991. *Boston against busing: Race, class, and ethnicity in the 1960s and 1970s.* Chapel Hill: University of North Carolina Press.

Franklin, Charles, and Liane Kosaki. 1989. Republican schoolmaster: The U.S. Supreme Court, public opinion, and abortion. *American Political Science Review* 83:751–71.

Fried, Charles. 1991. *Order and law.* New York: Simon and Shuster.

Friedman, Barry. 2002. The birth of an academic obsession: The history of the countermajoritarian difficulty. *Yale Law Journal* 112:153–259.

Friedman, Lawrence, and Rogelio Perez Perdomo, eds. 2003. *Legal culture in the age of globalization: Latin America and Latin Europe.* Stanford, Calif.: Stanford University Press.

Frymer, Paul. 2003. Acting when elected officials won't: Federal courts and civil rights enforcement in U.S. Labor relations, 1935–1985. *American Political Science Review* 97:483–99.

Fukurai, Hiroshi, and Edgar W. Butler. 1991. Organization, labor force, and jury representation: Economic excuses and jury participation. *Jurimetrics Journal* 32:49–69.

Fukurai, Hiroshi, and Richard Krooth. 2003. *Race in the jury box: Affirmative action in jury selection.* Albany: State University of New York Press.

Fukurai, Hiroshi, Edgar W. Butler, and Richard Krooth. 1991. Where did black jurors go? A theoretical synthesis of racial disenfranchisement in the jury system and jury selection. *Journal of Black Studies* 22:196–215.

Fuller, Lon. 1978. The forms and limits of adjudication. *Harvard Law Review* 92:353–409.

Galanter, Marc. 1974. Why the "haves" come out ahead: Speculations on the limits of legal change. *Law and Society Review* 9:95–160.

———. 1993. The regulatory function of the civil jury. In *Verdict: Assessing the civil jury system*, ed. Robert E. Litan, 61–102. Washington, D.C.: Brookings Institution.

———. 1999. Farther along. *Law and Society Review* 33:1113–23.

———. 2004. The vanishing trial: An examination of trials and related matters in federal and state courts. *Journal of Empirical Legal Studies* 1:459–570.

———. 2005. *Lowering the bar: Lawyer jokes and legal culture.* Madison: University of Wisconsin Press.

Gamarekian, Barbara. 1989. O'Connor's agonizing search for law clerks. *The New York Times*, November 3, B7.

Garbus, Martin. 2002. *Courting disaster: The Supreme Court and the unmaking of American law.* New York: Times Books.

Garrow, David J. 2006. Acolytes in arms. *Green Bag*, 2nd Series, 9: 411–21.

George, Tracey E. 1999. The dynamics and determinants of the decision to grant en banc review. *Washington Law Review* 74:213–74.

George, Tracey, and Lee Epstein. 1992. On the nature of Supreme Court decision making. *American Political Science Review* 86:323–37.

Gerhardt, Michael J. 2005. The federal appointments process as constitutional interpretation. In *Congress and the Constitution, ed.* Neal Devins and Keith E. Whittington, 110–130. Durham, N.C.: Duke University Press.

Geyh, Charles G. 2006. *When courts and Congress collide: The struggle for control of America's judicial system.* Ann Arbor: University of Michigan Press.

Gibson, James. 1978. Judges' role orientations, attitudes, and decisions: an interactive model. *American Political Science Review* 72:911–24.

———. 1983. From simplicity to complexity: The development of theory in the study of judicial behavior. *Political Behavior* 5:7–49.

Gibson, James L., Gregory A. Caldiera, and Lester Kenyatta Spence. 2003. Measuring attitudes toward the United States Supreme Court. *American Journal of Political Science* 47:354–67.

———. 2005. Why do people accept public policies? Testing legitimacy theory with a survey-based experiment. *Political Research Quarterly* 58:187–201.

Giles, Michael W., Thomas G. Walker, and Christopher Zorn. 2006. Setting a judicial agenda: The decision to grant en banc review in the U.S. Courts of Appeals. *Journal of Politics* 68:852–66.

Gilliom, John. 2001. *Overseers of the poor: Surveillance, resistance, and the limits of privacy.* Chicago: University of Chicago Press.

Gillman, Howard. 1999. Reconnecting the modern Supreme Court to the historical evolution of American capitalism. In *The Supreme Court in American politics: New institutional interpretations, ed.* Howard Gillman and Cornell Clayton, 235–256. Lawrence: University Press of Kansas.

———. 2002. How political parties can use the courts to advance their agendas: Federal courts in the United States, 1875–1891. *American Political Science Review* 96:511–24.

Gillman, Howard. 2003. Symposium: The Supreme Court and the attitudinal model revisited: Author meets critic: Separating the wheat from the chaff. *Law & Courts* 13:12–8.

Gillman, Howard, and Cornell Clayton. 1999. Beyond judicial attitudes: Institutional approaches to Supreme Court decision-making. In *Supreme Court decision-making: New institutionalist approaches, ed.* Cornell Clayton and Howard Gillman, 1–12. Chicago: University of Chicago Press.

Gilson, Ronald J., and Robert H. Mnookin. 1994. Disputing through agents: Cooperation and conflict between lawyers in litigation. *Columbia Law Review* 94:509–66.

Ginsburg, Ruth Bader. 1988. Confirming Supreme Court justices: Thoughts on the second opinion rendered by the Senate. *University of Illinois Law Review* 1988:101–17.

Ginsburg, Tom. 2003. *Judicial review in new democracies: Constitutional courts in Asian cases.* Cambridge: Cambridge University Press.

Glendon, Mary Ann. 1991. *Rights talk: The impoverishment of political discourse.* New York: Free Press.

Glenn, Brian. 2003. The varied and abundant progeny. In *In litigation: Do the "haves" still come out ahead?* ed. Herbert M. Kritzer and Susan S. Silbey, 371–419. Stanford, Calif.: Stanford University Press.

Glick, Henry R. 1978. The promise and performance of the Missouri plan: Judicial selection in the fifty states. *Miami Law Review* 32:510–41.

——. 1991. Policy making and state supreme courts. In *The American courts*, ed. John B. Gates and Charles A. Johnson, 87–118. Washington, D.C.: CQ.

Glick, Henry Robert, and Kenneth N. Vines. 1973. *State court systems.* Englewood Cliffs, N.J.: Prentice-Hall.

Gloppen, Siri, Roberto Gargarella, and Elin Skaar. 2004. Introduction: The accountability function of the courts in new democracies. In *Democratization and the judiciary: The accountability function of courts in new democracies*, ed. Siri Gloppen, Roberto Gargarella, and Elin Skaar, 1–6. London:Cass.

Goldberg, Deborah, Sarah Samis, Edwin Bender, Rachel Weiss, and Jesse Rutledge. 2005. *The new politics of judicial elections 2004.* Washington, D.C.: Justice at Stake.

Goldman, Sheldon. 1967. Judicial appointments to the United States Courts of Appeals. *Wisconsin Law Review* 86:186–214.

——. 1997. *Picking federal judges.* New Haven, Conn.: Yale University Press.

Gooding, Susan Staiger. 1994. Place, race, and names: Layered identities in *United States v. Oregon*, confederated tribes of the Colville Reservation, plaintiff-intervener. *Law and Society Review* 28:1181–229.

Gould, Stephen Jay. 1983. *Hen's teeth and horse's toes.* New York: Norton.

——. 1985. *The flamingo's smile.* New York: Norton.

Graber, Mark. 1991. *Transforming free speech: The ambiguous legacy of civil libertarianism.* Berkley: University of California Press.

——. 1993. The non-majoritarian difficulty: Legislative deference to the judiciary. *Studies in American Political Development* 7:35–72.

Graham, Barbara Luck. 1990. Do judicial selection systems matter? A study of black representation on state courts. *American Politics Quarterly* 18:316–36.

Graham, Bradley, and Dan Eggen. 2002. Moussaoui case may be moved to military tribunal. *Washington Post*, November 11, B7.

Graham, Duffy. 2005. *The consciousness of the litigator.* Ann Arbor: University of Michigan Press.

Gray, Wayne B., and John T. Scholz. 1993. Does regulatory enforcement work? A panel analysis of OSHA enforcement. *Law and Society Review* 27:177–213.

Green, Justin J., and Burton M. Atkins. 1978. Designated judges: How well do they perform? *Judicature* 61:358–370.

Greenhouse, Carole. J. 1986. *Praying for justice: Faith, order, and community in an American town.* Ithaca, N.Y.: Cornell University Press.

Greenhouse, Linda. 1996. How Congress curtailed the courts' jurisdiction. *The New York Times*, October 27, 5.

———. 2005a. Rehnquist resumes his call for judicial independence. *The New York Times*, January 1, 10.

———. 2005b. Justice weighs desire v. duty (duty prevails). *The New York Times*, August 25, A1.

———. 2005c. The court v. Congress: Specter's questioning reflects recent battle as justices move to curb lawmakers' powers. *The New York Times,* September 15, A1, A23.

———. 2005d. Justices to rule on a challenge to U.S. tribunals. *The New York Times*, November 8, A1.

———. 2006. Supreme Court memo; women suddenly scarce among justices' clerks. *The New York Times*, August 30, A1.

Griffin, Stephen M. 1989. What is constitutional theory? The newer theory and the decline of the learned tradition. *Southern California Law Review* 62: 493–538.

———. 1996. American constitutionalism: From theory to politics. Princeton, N.J.: Princeton University Press.

Guinier, Lani. 1994. *The tyranny of the majority: Fundamental fairness in representative democracy.* New York: Free Press.

Gulati, Mitu, and C.M.A. McCauliff. 1998. On not making law. *Law & Contemporary Problems* 61:157–227.

Hacker, Jacob S. 1997. *The road to nowhere: The genesis of President Clinton's plan for health security.* Princeton, NJ: Princeton University Press.

Haiman, Franklyn. 1981. *Speech and law in a free society.* Chicago: University of Chicago Press.

Haire, Susan Brodie, Stephanie A. Lindquist, and Roger Hartley. 1999. Attorney expertise, litigant success, and judicial decisionmaking in the U.S. courts of appeals. *Law and Society Review* 33:667–85.

Hakim, Danny. 2003a. Trial set to begin for four men accused of being in terror cell, *The New York Times*, March 17, A14.

———. 2003b. 2 Arabs convicted and 2 cleared of terrorist plot against the U.S. *The New York Times*, June 4, A1.

———. 2004. Judge reverses convictions in Detroit terrorism case. *The New York Times*, September 3, A10.

Hall, Kermit L. 1983. The judiciary on trial: State constitutional reform and the rise of an elected judiciary 1846–1860. *The Historian* 45:337–54.

Hall, Melinda Gann. 1992. Electoral politics and strategic voting in state supreme courts. *Journal of Politics* 54:427–46.

———. 2001. State supreme courts in American democracy: Probing the myths of judicial reform. *American Political Science Review* 95:315–30.

Hall, Melinda Gann, and Paul Brace. 1989. Order in the courts: A neo-institutional approach to judicial consensus. *Western Political Quarterly* 42:391–407.

Hall, Peter A., and Rosemary C.R. Taylor. 1996. Political science and the three new institutionalisms. *Political Studies* 94:936–57.

Halpern, Stephen C. 1995. *On the limits of the law: The ironic legacy of Title VI of the 1964 Civil Rights Act.* Baltimore: Johns Hopkins University Press.

Haltom, William, and Michael McCann. 2004. *Distorting the law: Politics, the media, and the litigation crisis.* Chicago: University of Chicago Press.

Hamilton, Alexander, James Madison, and John Jay. 1787–1788. *The federalist papers.* Edited by Jacob E. Cooke. Middletown, Conn.: Wesleyan University Press, 1961.

Hammond, Thomas H., Chris W. Bonneau, and Reginald S. Sheehan. 2005. *Strategioc behavior and policy choice on the U.S. Supreme Court.* Stanford, Calif.: Stanford University Press.

Hanes, Stephanie. 2003. Baltimore County judges get aggressive in election: But some lawyers call their fund-raising tactics extreme for bench seats. *The Baltimore Sun,* April 13, 1B.

Hannaford, Paula L., Valerie P. Hans, and G. Thomas Munsterman. 1999. Permitting jury discussions during trial: Impact of the Arizona reform. *Law and Human Behavior* 24:359–81.

Hannaford-Agor, Paula L., Nicole L. Waters, and Monica L. Wait. 2007. *Jury innovation in practice: The experience in state and local courts.* Williamsburg, Vir.: National Center for State Courts.

Hans, Valerie P, and Alayna Jehle. 2003. Avoid bald men and people with green socks? Other ways to improve the voir dire process in jury selection. *Chicago-Kent Law Review* 78:1779–1201.

Hans, Valerie P., Paula L. Hannaford, and G. Thomas Munsterman. 2000. The Arizona jury reform permitting civil jury trial discussions: The views of trial participations, judges, and jurors. *University of Michigan Journal of Law Reform* 32:349–77.

Hansford, Thomas, and Spriggs, James. 2006. *The politics of precedent on the U.S. Supreme Court.* Princeton, N.J.: Princeton University Press.

Hanssen, F. Andrew. 2004. Learning about judicial independence: Institutional change in the state courts. *Journal of Legal Studies* 33:431–73.

Harden, Blaine. 2003. Ore. man pleads guilty to helping Taliban. *Washington Post*, August 7, A8.

Hartley, Roger E., and Lisa Holmes. 1997. Increasing Senate scrutiny of lower federal court nominees. *Judicature* 80:274–8.

Harrington, Christine B. 1994. Outlining a theory of legal practice. In *Lawyers in a postmodern world: Translation and transgression*, ed. Maureen Cain and Christine B. Harrington, 206–226. New York: New York University Press.

Harrington, Christine B., and Daniel S. Ward. 1995. Patterns of appellate litigation, 1945–1990. In *Contemplating courts, ed.* Lee Epstein, 206–226. Washington, D.C.: CQ.

Harris, Beth. 2003. Representing homeless families: Repeat player implementation strategies. In *In litigation: Do the "haves" still come out ahead?* ed. Herbert M. Kritzer and Susan S. Silbey, 108–136. Stanford, Calif.: Stanford University Press.

Hartley, Roger E. and Lisa Holmes. 2002. The increasing Senate scrutiny of lower federal court nominees. *Political Science Quarterly* 117:259–78.

Hastie, Reid, Steven Penrod, and Nancy Pennington. 1983. *Inside the jury.* Cambridge, Mass.: Harvard University Press.

Hatch, Senator Orrin G. 1997. Letter to colleagues on the Senate judiciary committee, U.S. Senate. Feb. 24.

Haynes, William J. II. 2002a. Letter from William J. Haynes II, general counsel of the Department of Defense, to U.S. Senator Carl Levin. November 26.

——. 2002b. Letter from William J. Haynes II, general counsel of the Department of Defense, to Alfred P. Carlton, Jr., President of the American Bar Association, September 23.

Haynie, Stacia. 2004. The Court's protection against self-incrimination: *Miranda v. Arizona* (1966). In *Creating constitutional change, ed.* Gregg Ivers and Kevin McGuire, 265–280. Charlottesville: University Press of Virginia.

Heinz, John, and Edward Laumann. 1982. *Chicago lawyers: The social structure of the bar.* New York: Russell Sage Foundation and American Bar Foundation.

Heinz, John P., Robert L. Nelson, Rebecca L. Sandefur, and Edward O. Laumann. 2005. *Urban lawyers: The new social structure of the bar.* Chicago: University of Chicago Press.

Hellman, Arthur D. 1980. Central staff in appellate courts: The experience of the Ninth Circuit. *California Law Review* 68:937–1003.

——. 1983. Error correction, lawmaking, and the Supreme Court's exercise of discretionary review. *University of Pittsburgh Law Review* 44:795–877.

——. 1985. Case selection in the Burger court: A preliminary inquiry. *Notre Dame Law Review* 60:947–1055.

——. 2000. Getting it right: Panel error and the en banc process in the ninth circuit court of appeals. *University of California-Davis Law Review* 34:425–69.

Helmke, Gretchen. 2006. Explaining institutional instability in Latin America: A crisis bargaining approach. Paper presented at the annual meeting of the American Political Science Association, August 31–September 3, Philadelphia.

Henschen, Beth, Robert Moog, and Steven Davis. 1990. Judicial nominating commissioners: A national profile. *Judicature* 73:328–34.

Hensler, Deborah R., Bonita Dombey-Moore, Beth Giddens, and Jennifer Gross. 1985. *Asbestos in the courts: The challenge of mass toxic torts.* Santa Monica, Calif.: RAND Institute for Civil Justice.

——. 1991. *Compensation for accidental injuries in the United States.* Santa Monica, Calif.: RAND Institute for Civil Justice.

——. 2000. *Class action dilemmas; pursuing public goals through private gain.* Santa Monica, Calif.: RAND Institute for Civil Justice.

——. 2001. *Asbestos litigation in the U.S.: A new look at an old issue.* Santa Monica, Calif.: RAND Institute for Civil Justice.

Hettinger, Virginia A., Stefanie A. Lindquist, and Wendy L. Martinek. 2003a. The role and impact of chief judges on the United States Courts of Appeals. *Justice System Journal* 24:91–117.

——. 2003b. Separate opinion writing on the United States Courts of Appeals. *American Politics Research,* 31:215–250.

——. 2006. *Judging on a collegial court: Influences on federal appellate decision making.* Charlottesville: University of Virginia Press.

Heuer, Larry, and Steven Penrod. 1994. Juror note-taking and question-asking during trials: A national field experiment. *Law and Human Behavior* 18:121–50.

——. 1996. Increasing juror participation in trial through note-taking and question-asking. *Judicature* 79:256–63.

Heumann, Milton. 1978. *Plea bargaining: The experiences of prosecutors, judges, and defense attorneys.* Chicago: University of Chicago Press.

Hilbink, Lisa. 2005. Beyond Manicheanism: Assessing the new constitutionalism. Paper presented to the annual meeting of the American Political Science Association, September 1–4, Washington, D.C.

Hirschl, Ran. 2004. *Towards juristocracy: The origins and consequences of the new constitutionalism.* Cambridge, Mass.: Harvard University Press.

Hoekstra, Valerie J. 2003. *Public reaction to Supreme Court decisions.* Cambridge: Cambridge University Press.

Hoff, Joan. 1991. *Law, gender, and injustice: A legal history of U.S. women.* New York: New York University Press.

Hoffman, Jan. 1997. A prominent judge retires objecting to the governor's litmus test. *The New York Times,* December 17, 49.

Hoffman, Morris. 1997. Peremptory challenges should be abolished: A trial judge's perspective. *University of Chicago Law Review* 64:809–71.

Holland, Kenneth M, ed. 1991. *Judicial activism in comparative perspective.* New York: St. Martin's.

Horowitz, Donald L. 1977. *The jurocracy: Government lawyers, agency programs, and judicial decisions.* Lexington, Mass.: Lexington Books.

Horrigan, Marie. 2006. Midterm meanness. *Congressional Quarterly Weekly Report,* October 16, 2006, 2755–60.

House Republican Policy Committee. 1996. Policy statement on the judicial selection process. September 13, 1.

Houser, Mark. 2002. A jury of peers? *Pittsburgh Tribune-Review,* July 21, A1, A10.

Howard, J. Woodford, Jr. 1981. *Courts of appeals in the federal judicial system: A study of the Second, Fifth, and District of Columbia Circuits.* Princeton, N.J.: Princeton University Press.

Huber, Gregory A., and Sanford C. Gordon. 2004. Accountability and coercion: Is justice blind when it runs for office? *American Journal of Political Science* 48: 247–63.

Hudson, Audrey. 2002. Daschle seeks to exempt his state; wants logging to prevent fires. *The Washington Times,* July 24, A1.

Hulse, Carl, and David D. Kirkpatrick. 2005. DeLay says federal judiciary has "run amok", adding congress is partly to blame. *The New York Times,* April 8, 21.

Hurwitz, Mark, and Drew Noble Lanier. 2001. Women and minorities on state and federal appellate benches, 1985 and 1999. *Judicature* 85:84–92.

Hutchinson, Dennis J., and David Garrow, eds. 2002. *The forgotten memoir of John Knox: A year in the life of a Supreme Court clerk in FDR's Washington.* Chicago: University of Chicago Press.

Iaryczower, Matias, Pablo T. Spiller, and Mariano Tommasi. 2002. Judicial independence in unstable environments, Argentina 1935–1998. *American Journal of Political Science* 46:699–716.

Ignagni, Joseph. 1993. U.S. States Supreme Court decision-making and the free exercise clause. *Review of Politics* 55:511–29.

Irons, Peter. 1990. *The courage of their convictions: Sixteen American who fought their way to the Supreme Court.* New York: Penguin Books.

Irwin, Jim. 2000. Republicans retain majority on Michigan Supreme Court. *Associated Press,* October 28.

Ivers, Gregg. 1991. *Lowering the wall: Religion and the Supreme Court in the 1980's.* New York: Anti-Defamation League Publication.

Jackson, Robert. H. 1941. *The struggle for judicial supremacy: A study of a crisis in American power politics.* New York: Knopf.

——. 1955. *The Supreme Court in the American system of government.* Cambridge, Mass.: Harvard University Press.

Jacob, Herbert. 1992. The elusive shadow of the law. *Law & Society Review* 26:565–90.

——. 1996. Courts and politics in the United States. In *Courts, law, and politics in a comparative perspective, ed.* Herbert Jacob, Erhard Blankenburg, Herbert M. Kritzer, Doris Marie Provine, and Joseph Sanders, 16–80. New Haven, Conn.: Yale University Press.

Jacob, Herbert, Erhard Blankenburg, Herbert M. Kritzer, Doris Marie Provine, and Joseph Sanders, eds. 1996. *Courts, law, and politics in a comparative perspective.* New Haven, Conn.: Yale University Press.

Jefferson, Thomas. 1905. Letter from Jefferson to John Holmes, April 22, 1820. In *The works of Thomas Jefferson, vol 12.* Ed. Paul Leicester Ford, 159. New York: G.P. Putnam's and Sons.

Jenckes, Thomas. 1870. Letter from John C. Underwood, 27 April 1870. *The papers of Thomas A. Jenckes.* Library of Congress Manuscript Division, Washington, D.C.

Jenkins, Chris L. 2005. Republicans reject two N.Va. judges; assembly Democrats allege cronyism. *The Washington Post*, January 19, B1.

Jenks, Thomas. 1870. Remarks of Representative Thomas Jenks on the floor of the House of Representatives. *Congressional Globe,* April 27, 90:3036.

Johnson, Charles A., and Bradley C. Canon. 1984. *Judicial policies: Implementation and impact.* Washington, DC: CQ.

——. 1999. *Judicial policies: Implementation and impact,* rev. ed. Washington, D.C.: Congressional Quarterly.

Johnson, Timothy R. 2004. The solicitor general, oral arguments, and Supreme Court decision making. Unpublished manuscript.

Johnston, David, and Neil A. Lewis. 2005. Officials say there is no evidence to back Moussaoui's story, *The New York Times*, April 27, A12.

Jones, Leigh. 2007. Starting pay at top firms falls farther behind partners'. *The National Law Journal.* February 8.

Journal of Empirical Legal Studies. 2004. Special issue on the vanishing trial. *Journal of Empirical Legal Studies,* volume 1, Theodore Eisenberg, Michael Heise, Jeffrey J. Rachlinski, Stewart J. Schwab, and Martin T. Wells, ed.

Judge the judges. 1997. Fundraising video for the judicial selection monitoring project. September.

Jury project. 1996. *Jury reform in New York State: A progress report on a continuing initiative.* New York: New York State Unified Court System.

Jury project. 2001. *Continuing jury reform in New York State.* New York: New York State Unified Court System.

Justice at Stake Campaign. 2001. Survey of 1000 respondents from October 30– November 7, 2001. Washington, D.C. Available at http://faircourts.org/files/JASNationalSurveyResults.pdf.

Kagan, Robert A. 2001. *Adversarial legalism: The American way of law.* Cambridge, Mass.: Harvard University Press.

——. 2004. American courts and the policy dialogue: The role of adversarial legalism. In *Making policy, making law: An interbranch perspective, ed. Mark C.* Miller and Jeb Barnes, 13–34. Washington, D.C.: Georgetown University Press.

Kahn, Ronald. 1994. *The Supreme Court and constitutional theory, 1953–1993*. Lawrence: University Press of Kansas.

Kahn, Ronald, and Kersch, Ken I., eds. 2006. *The Supreme Court and American political development*. Lawrence: University of Kansas Press.

Kahneman, Daniel, David A. Schkade, and Cass R. Sunstein. 2002. Shared outrage, erratic awards. In *Punitive damages: How juries decide, ed.* Cass Sunstein, Reid Hastie, John W. Payne, David A. Schkade, and W. Kip Viscusi, 31–42. Chicago: University of Chicago Press.

Kakalik, James S., Patricia Ebener, William L. F. Felstiner, and Michael G. Shanley. 1983. *Costs of asbestos litigation*. Santa Monica, Calif.: RAND Institute for Civil Justice.

Kalven, Harry, and Hans Zeisel. 1966. *The American jury*. Boston: Little and Brown.

Kanowitz. Leo. 1969. *Women and the law: The unfinished revolution*. Albuquerque:University of New Mexico Press.

Kapiszewski, Diana, and Matthew M.Taylor. 2006. Doing courts justice? Studying judicial politics in Latin America. Paper presented at the annual meeting of the American Political Science Association, August 31–September 3, in Philadelphia.

Kaplan, Sheila, and Zoe Davidson. 1998. The buying of the bench. *The Nation,* January 26, 11–7.

Kasindorf, Martin. 2003. The court conservatives love to hate. *USA Today,* February 7, 3A.

Kassop, Nancy. 2004. The view from the President. In *Making policy, making law: An interbranch perspective, ed.* Mark C. Miller and Jeb Barnes, 72–88. Washington, D.C.: Georgetown University Press.

Katzmann, Robert A., ed. 1988. *Judges and legislators: Toward institutional comity.* Washington, D.C.: Brookings Institution.

——. 1995. Judiciary and Congress. In *The encyclopedia of the United States Congress, ed.* Donald C. Bacon, Roger H. Davidson, and Morton Keller, 1191–1198. New York: Simon and Schuster.

——. 1997. *Courts and Congress.* Washington D.C.: Brookings Institution Press.

Katznelson, Ira, and Helen V. Milner. 2002. American political science: The discipline's state and the state of the discipline. In *Political science: State of the discipline, ed.* Ira Katznelson and Helen V. Milner, 1–26. New York: Norton.

Katyal, Neal Kumar. 2006. *Hamdan v. Rumsfeld*: The legal academy goes to practice. *Harvard Law Review* 120:65–122.

Keck. Thomas. 2004. *The most activist Supreme Court in history: The road to modern judicial conservatism*. Chicago: University of Chicago Press.

Keith, Linda Camp. 2005. The United States Supreme Court and judicial review of Congress 1803–2001. Paper presented at the annual meeting of the American Political Science Association. Washington, D.C. September 1–3.

Kelley, Stanley, Jr. 1983. *Interpreting elections*. Princeton, N.J.: Princeton University Press.

Kelly, Michael J. 1994. *Lives of lawyers*. Ann Arbor: University of Michigan Press.

Kennedy Staff Memo. 2002. Memorandum to Senator Ted Kennedy, "Call from Elaine Jones re scheduling of 6th Circuit nominees". April 17, 2002. 2002. Available online via the Center for Individual Freedom at http://www.cfif.org/htdocs/legislative_issues/federal_issues/hot_issues_in_congress/confirmation_watch/judiciary_memos.pdf.

Kenney, Sally J. 2000. Beyond principals and agents: Seeing courts as organizations by comparing *referendaires* at the European court of justice and law clerks at the U.S. Supreme Court. *Comparative Political Studies* 33:593–625.

Kernell, Samuel. 1993. *Going public: New strategies of presidential leadership,* 2nd ed. Washington, D.C.: CQ.

Kerr, Norbert L., and Robert J. McCoun. 1987. The effects of jury size and polling method on the process and product of jury deliberations. In *In the jury box: Controversies in the courtroom*, ed. Lawrence S. Wrightsman, Saul M. Kassin, and Cynthia E. Willis, 209–234. Beverly Hills, Calif.: Sage.

Kiely, Kathy, and Mark Memmott. 2006. Rival factions begin serious push on Alito. *USA Today,* January 3, 7A.

King, Nancy, and G. Thomas Munsterman. 1996. Stratified juror selection: Cross section by design. *Judicature* 79:273–9.

Kingdon, John. 1995. *Agendas, alternatives and public policies*, 2nd ed. Boston: Little, Brown.

Kistler, Thomas King, and Terrence R. Nealon. 2002. Juror note-taking in civil trials: An idea whose time has come. *Pennsylvania Bar Association Civil Litigation Update* 5:1, 11–8.

Klarman, Michael J. 1996. Rethinking the civil rights and civil liberties revolutions. *Virginia Law Review* 82:1–67.

——. 2004. *From Jim Crow to civil rights: The Supreme Court and the struggle for racial equality.* New York: Oxford University Press.

Klein, David E. 2002. *Making law in the United States Courts of Appeals.* New York: Cambridge University Press.

Klein, David, and Lawrence Baum. 2001. Ballot information and voting decisions in judicial elections. *Political Research Quarterly* 54:709–28.

Klein, Rick. 2005. DeLay apologized for blaming federal judges in Schiavo case, but house leader calls for probe of "judicial activism." *The Boston Globe*, April 14, A9.

Knott, Jack H., and Gary J. Miller. 1989. *Reforming bureaucracy: The politics of institutional choice.* Englewood Cliffs, N.J.: Prentice Hall.

Kobylka, Joseph. 1987. A court-related context for group litigation: Libertarian groups and obscenity. *Journal of Politics* 49:1061–79.

——. 1995. The mysterious case of establishment clause litigation: How organized litigants foiled legal change. In *Contemplating courts*, ed. Lee Epstein, 93–128. Washington, D.C.: Congressional Quarterly.

Kolata, Gina. 1995. Will the lawyers kill off Norplant? *The New York Times,* May 28, C1, C5.

Komesar, Neil. 1994. *Imperfect alternatives.* Chicago: University of Chicago Press.

Kommers, Donald P. 2005. American courts and democracy: A comparative perspective. In *The judicial branch,* ed. Kermit L. Hall and Kevin T. McGuire, 200–230. New York: Oxford University Press.

Konvitz, Milton. 1966. *Expanding liberties.* New York: Viking.

Koopmans, Tim. 2003. *Courts and political institutions: A comparative view.* Cambridge: Cambridge University Press.

Kopple, Barbara and Bill Davis, Directors. 1990. Out of the Darkness: The Mineworkers' Story. Washington, D.C.: Labor History and Cultural Trust. (video)

Kort, Fred. 1957. Predicting Supreme Court decisions mathematically: A quantitative analysis of right to counsel cases. *American Political Science Review* 51:1–12.

Kozinski, Alex. 1995. Making the case for law clerks. *The Long Term View* 3:55–9.

Kramer, Larry D. 2004. Popular constitutionalism, circa 2004. *California Law Review* 92:959–1011.

Krehbiel, Keith 1998. *Pivotal politics: A theory of U.S. lawmaking.* Chicago: University of Chicago Press.

Kressel, Kenneth. 1985. *The process of divorce: How professionals and couples negotiate settlements.* New York: Basic Books.

Kritzer, Herbert M. 1990. *The justice broker: Lawyers and ordinary litigation.* New York: Oxford University Press.

———. 1996. Courts, justice, and politics in England. In *Courts, law, and politics in a comparative perspective,* ed. Herbert Jacob, Erhard Blankenburg, Herbert M. Kritzer, Doris Marie Provine, and Joseph Sanders, 81–176. New Haven, Conn.: Yale University Press.

———. 1998. *Legal advocacy: Lawyers and nonlawyers at work.* Ann Arbor: University of Michigan Press.

———. 2003a. The government gorilla: Why does government come out ahead in appellate courts? In *In litigation: Do the "haves" still come out ahead?* ed. Herbert M. Kritzer and Susan S. Silbey, 342–370. Stanford, Calif.: Stanford University Press.

———. 2003b. Symposium: The Supreme Court and the attitudinal model revisited: Author meets critic: Have Segal and Spaeth finally driven a stake through the heart of the legal model? *Law & Courts* 13:19–22.

———. 2004. *Risks, reputations, and rewards: Contingency fee legal practice in the United States.* Stanford, Calif.: Stanford University Press.

Kritzer, Herbert M, and Mark J. Richards. 2003. Jurisprudential regimes and Supreme Court decisionmaking: The *Lemon* regime and establishment clause cases. *Law & Society Review* 37:827–40.

Kritzer, Herbert M., and Frances Kahn Zemans. 1993. Local legal culture and the control of litigation. *Law and Society Review* 27:535–57.

Krivosha, Norman. 1990. In celebration of the 50th anniversary of merit selection. *Judicature* 74:128–32.

Kuperan, K., and Jon G. Sutinen. 1998. Blue water crime: Deterrence, legitimacy, and compliance in fisheries. *Law and Society Review* 32:309–37.

Kyl, Jon. 2004. *Restoring popular control of the Constitution: The case for jurisdiction-stripping legislation.* Report from the U.S. Senate Republican Policy Committee, September 28.

Lambert, Wade. 1995. Costs of settlements reach records in suits against directors, officers. *Wall Street Journal,* March 10, B16.

Landon, Donald D. 1990. *Country lawyers: The impact of context on professional practice.* New York: Praeger.

Landsman, Stephan. 2005. In defense of the jury of 12 and the unanimous decision rule. *Judicature* 88:301–3.

Langer, Laura. 2002. *Judicial review in state supreme courts: A comparative study.* Albany: State University of New York Press.

Langbein, John. 1985. The German advantage in civil procedure. *University of Chicago Law Review* 52:823–65.

———. 1994. Will contests. *Yale Law Journal* 103:2039–48.

Langhauser, Derek P. 2006. An essay: Nominations to the Supreme Court of the United States: Historical lessons for today's debate. *West's Education Law Reporter* March 9.

Larkin, Elizabeth A. 2001. Judicial selection methods: Judicial independence and popular democracy. *Denver University Law Review* 79:65–89.

Lazarus, Edward. 1998. *Closed chambers*: *The first eyewitness account of the epic struggles inside the Supreme Court*. New York: Times Books.

Leahy, Senator Patrick. 1998. Statement on the nomination of Margaret Morrow. *Congressional Record*, February 11.

Lee, Rex E. 1986. Lawyering for the government: Politics, polemics & principle. *Ohio State Law Journal* 47:595–601.

Legendre, Pierre.1997. *Law and the unconscious: A Legendre reader*. Peter Goodrich with Alain Pottage and Anton Schütz, eds and trans. New York: St. Martin's.

Leitsinger, Miranda, and Ben Fox. 2006. US releases IDs of detainees. *The Boston Globe*, March 4, A1.

Levi, Edward H. 1949. *An introduction to legal reasoning*. Chicago: University of Chicago Press.

Levin, Mark. 2005. *Men in black: How the Supreme Court is destroying America*. Washington, D.C.: Regnery.

Lewis, Neil A. 2004. U.S. allows lawyers to meet detainees. *The New York Times*, July 3, A14.

———. 2005. Moussaoui tells court he's guilty of a terror plot. *The New York Times*, April 23, A1.

———. 2006. Judge sets back Guantanamo detainees. *The New York Times*, December 14, A24.

Lewis, Congressman Ron (R–KY). 2004. Press Release: The Congressional Accountability for Judicial Activism Act (H.R. 3920). U.S. House of Representatives, March 9.

Lichtblau, Eric. 2006. Judge throws out overlapping charges in Padilla case. *The New York Times*, August 22, A15.

Light, Paul. 1982. *The President's agenda*. Baltimore: Johns Hopkins University.

Lindblom, Charles E. 1959. The science of muddling through. *Public Administrative Review* 19:79–88.

———. 1979. Still muddling, not yet through. *Public Administrative Review* 39:517–26.

Lindquist, Stefanie A., and David A. Yalof. 2001. Congressional responses to federal circuit court decisions, *Judicature* 85:60–8.

Lipset, Seymour Martin. 1995. Malaise and resiliency in America. *Journal of Democracy* 6:4–18.

Loftus, Elizabeth L., and Douglas Leber. 1986. Do jurors talk? *Trial* 22:59–65.

Long, Alex. B. 2002. An historical perspective on judicial selection methods in Virginia and West Virginia. *Journal of Law and Politics* 18:691–772.

Long, Carolyn. 2000. *Religious freedom and Indian rights: The case of Oregon v. Smith*. Lawrence: University Press of Kansas.

Long, J. Scott. 1997. *Regression models for categorical and limited dependent variables*. London: Sage.

Loomis, Burdett. 2001. The Senate and executive branch appointments: An obstacle course on Capitol Hill? *The Brookings Review* 19:32–6.

Lovell, George I. 2003. *Legislative deferrals: Statutory ambiguity, judicial power, and American democracy*. Cambridge: Cambridge University Press.

Lovrich, Nicholas P., Jr., and Charles H. Sheldon. 1983. Voters in contested, nonpartisan judicial elections; a responsible electorate or a problematic public? *Western Political Quarterly* 41:807–16.

Lowi, Theodore J. 1972. Four systems of policy, politics, and choice. *Public Administrative Review* 32:298–310.

Lumbard, J. Edward. 1968. Current problems of the federal courts of appeals. *Cornell Law Review* 54: 29–44.

Lusky, Louis. 1982. 'Footnote redux' a *Carolene products* reminiscence, *Columbia Law Review* 82:1093–109.

———. 1993. *Our nine tribunes: The Supreme Court in modern America.* Westport, Conn.: Praeger.

Macaulay, Donald A. 2004. Letters to the editor: Redefining marriage; SJC has written and enacted radical law. *The Boston Globe,* February 18, D12.

MacClean, Pamela A. 2006. Race an issue in judicial nomination. *The Legal Intelligencer,* July 5.

MacKinnon, Catharine A. 1979. *The sexual harassment of working women.* New Haven, Conn.: Yale University Press.

———. 1989. *Toward a feminist theory of the state.* Cambridge, Mass.: Harvard University Press.

Madison, James. 1788. Federalist paper No. 10. *The Federalist Papers.* New York: Penguin Books. (reprinted 1987).

Magaloni, Beatriz. 2003. Authoritarianism, democracy and the Supreme Court: Horizontal exchange and the role of law in Mexico. In *Democratic accountability in Latin America,* ed. Scott Mainwaring and Christoper Welna, 266–308. New York: Oxford University Press.

Maltese, John Anthony. 1995. *The selling of Supreme Court nominees.* Baltimore: Johns Hopkins University Press.

Maltzman, Forrest, James Spriggs, and Paul Wahlbeck. 2000. *Creating law on the Supreme Court: The collegial game.* New York: Cambridge University Press.

Mann, Thomas E., and Norman J. Ornstein. 2006a. *The broken branch: How Congress is failing America and how to get it back on track.* New York: Oxford University Press.

———. 2006b. Congress as "the broken branch". *The Washington Post,* October 11, A17.

Mansfield, Edward D., and Richard Sisson, ed. 2004. *The evolution of political knowledge: Theory and inquiry in American politics.* Columbus: The Ohio State University Press.

March, James G., and Johan P. Olsen. 1989. *Rediscovering institutions: The organizational basis of politics.* New York: Free Press.

Marcus, Ruth. 2005. Boot the bench: There's new ferocity in talk of firing activist judges. *The Washington Post,* April 11, A19.

Markon, Jerry. 2003a. Moussaoui says he was to aid later attack. *The Washington Post,* May 14, A2.

———. 2003b. Court seeks deal on terror witness access. *The Washington Post,* April 16, A12.

———. 2003c. Appeals panel hears arguments on deposition sought by Moussaoui. *The Washington Post,* June 4, A10.

———. 2003d. Moussaoui prosecutors defy judge. *The Washington Post,* July15, A1.

———. 2003e. Moussaoui granted access to witnesses. *The Washington Post,* August 30, A12.

———. 2003f. U.S. refuses to produce Al Qaeda officials as witnesses. *The Washington Post,* September 11, A7.

———. 2003g. Defense calls for dismissal of Sept. 11 case. *The Washington Post,* September 25, A15.

———. 2003h. Compromise hinted in Moussaoui case. *The Washington Post,* December 4, A10.

———. 2003i. U.S. might compromise in Moussaoui dispute. *The Washington Post,* December 15, A14.

———. 2004. U.S. to free Hamdi, send him home. *The Washington Post,* September 23, A1.

———. 2005. 2 sides seek trial next year on sentence for Moussaoui. *The Washington Post,* May 6, A4.

———. 2006a. Questioning of jurors begins in Moussaoui penalty trial. *The Washington Post,* February 16, A7.

———. 2006b. Federal court posts online nearly all evidence from Moussaoui trial. *The Washington Post*, August 1, A7.

Markon, Jerry, and Dan Eggen. 2003. U.S. allows lawyer for citizen held as 'enemy combatant.' *The Washington Post,* December 3, A1.

Marshall, Anna-Marie. 2003. Injustice frames, legality, and the everyday construction of sexual harassment. *Law and Social Inquiry* 28:659–89.

———. 2005. *Confronting sexual harassment: The law and politics of everyday life.* Burlington, V.t.: Ashgate.

Marshall, Thomas. 1989. *Public opinion and the Supreme Court.* New York: Unwin/Hyman.

Martin, Andrew D. 2001. Congressional decision making and the separation of powers. *The American Political Science Review* 95:361–78.

Martinek, Wendy L., Mark Kemper, and Steven R. Van Winkle. 2002. To advise and consent: The Senate and lower federal court nominations, 1977–1998. *Journal of Politics* 64:337–62.

Mather, Lynn. 1979. *Plea bargaining or trial? The process of criminal case disposition.* Lexington, Mass.: Lexington.

———. 1991. Policy making in the state trial courts. In *The American courts; A critical assessment,* ed. John B. Gates and Charles A. Johnson, 119–157. Washington, D.C.: CQ.

———. 1995. The fired football coach (or, how trial courts make policy). In *Contemplating courts,* ed. Lee Epstein, 170–202. Washington D.C.: CQ.

———. 1998. Theorizing about trial courts: Lawyers, policymaking, and tobacco litigation. *Law & Social Inquiry* 23:897–940.

———. 2003a. Changing patterns of legal representation in divorce: From lawyers to *pro se. Journal of Law and Society* 30:137–55.

———. 2003b. What do clients want? What do lawyers do? *Emory Law Journal* 52:1065–86.

———. 2005. Courts in American popular culture. In *The judicial branch,* ed. Kermit L. Hall and Kevin T. McGuire, 233–261. New York: Oxford University Press.

Mather, Lynn, Craig A. McEwen, and Richard J. Maiman. 2001. *Divorce lawyers at work: Variety of professionalism in practice.* New York: Oxford University Press.

Mather, Lynn, and Barbara Yngvesson. 1981. Language, audience, and the transformation of disputes. *Law and Society Review* 15: 775–822.

Mathias, Sara. 1990. *Electing justice: A handbook of judicial election reforms.* Chicago: American Judicature Society.

Mauro, Tony. 1998. For lawyers, clerkship is ultimate job. *USA Today*, June 5, 13A.

———. 2000. Little deference to Congress as the Court curbs federal power. *Legal Times*, May 22, 8.

———. 2005. More than one justice among nine. *Legal Times*, September 12, 10.

———. 2006a. Judges turn witnesses for Alito: Unusual endorsement sparks worries about politicization of bench, possible recusals. *Legal Times,* January 16.

———. 2006b. High court clerks: Still white, still male. *Legal Times*, May 25.

Maute, Judith. 2000. Selecting justice in state courts: The ballot box or the backroom? *South Texas Law Review* 41:1197–246.

Maveety, Nancy. 2003. The study of judicial behavior and the discipline of political science. In *The pioneers of judicial behavior,* ed. Nancy Maveety, 1–51. Ann Arbor: University of Michigan Press.

Maveety, Nancy, and Grosskopf, Anke. 2004. "Constrained" constitutional courts as conduits for democratic consolidation. *Law and Society Review* 38:463–88.

McCall, Madhavi. 2001. Buying justice in Texas: The influence of campaign contributions on the voting behavior of Texas supreme court justices. *American Review of Politics* 22:349–73.

———. 2003. The politics of judicial elections: The influence of campaign contributions on the voting patterns of Texas supreme court justices, 1994–1997. *Politics and Policy* 31:31–47.

McCann, Michael. 1994. *Rights at work: Pay equity reform and the politics of legal mobilization.* Chicago: University of Chicago Press.

McCloskey, Robert. 1960. *The American Supreme Court.* Chicago: University of Chicago Press.

McCord, David. 2005. Juries should not be required to have 12 members or to render unanimous verdicts. *Judicature* 88:301–5.

McCubbins, Matthew, and Thomas Schwartz. 1984. Congressional oversight overlooked: Police patrols versus fire alarms. *American Journal of Political Science* 28:165–79.

McDowell, Gary L. 1988. *Curbing the Court: The Constitution and the limits of judicial power.* Baton Rouge: Louisiana State University Press.

McEwen, Craig A., Nancy H. Rogers, and Richard J. Maiman. 1995. Bring in the lawyers: Challenging the dominant approaches to ensuring fairness in divorce mediation. *Minnesota Law Review* 79:1317–411.

McFeeley, Neil D. 1987. *Appointment of judges: The Johnson presidency.* Austin: University of Texas Press.

McGinnis, John O. 1992. Principle versus politics: The solicitor general's office in constitutional and bureaucratic theory. *Stanford Law Review* 44:799–814.

McGuire, Kevin. 1993. *The Supreme Court bar: Legal elites in the Washington community.* Charlottesville: University of Virginia Press.

———. 1998. Explaining executive success in the U.S. Supreme Court. *Political Research Quarterly,* 51:505–26.

———. 1999. The Supreme Court and institutional relationships. In *The Supreme Court and American politics: New institutionalist interpretations,* ed. Howard Gillman and Cornell W. Clayton, 115–132 Lawrence: University Press of Kansas.

McGuire, Kevin, and Barbara Palmer. 1995. Issue fluidity on the U.S. Supreme Court. *American Political Science Review* 89:691–702.

McGuire, Kevin, and James Stimson. 2004. The least dangerous branch revisited: New evidence on Supreme Court responsiveness to public preferences. *American Journal of Political Science* 66:1018–35.

McLeod, Aman. 2005. If at first you don't succeed: A critical evaluation of judicial selection reform efforts. *West Virginia University Law Review* 107:499–523.

McMahon, Colleen, and David L. Kornblau. 1995. Chief Judge Judith S. Kaye's program of jury selection reform in New York. *St. John's Journal of Legal Commentary* 10:263–78.

Mealey's Litigation Report: Asbestos Bankruptcy. 2005. "CRMC to stop accepting reports prepared by silica mdl doctors," E-Mail Bulletin, September 14

Meernick, James, and Joseph Ignagni. 1997. Judicial review and coordinate construction of the Constitution. *American Journal of Political Science* 41:447–67.

Meese, Edwin III, and Rhett DeHart. 1997. Reining in the federal judiciary. *Judicature* 80:178–83.

Melilli, K. Joseph. 1996. *Batson* in practice: What we have learned about *Batson* and peremptory challenges. *Notre Dame Law Review* 71:447–503.

Melnick, R. Shep. 1983. *Regulation and the courts: The case of the Clean Air Act.* Washington, D.C.: Brookings.

———. 1994. *Between the lines: Interpreting welfare rights.* Washington, D.C.: Brookings Institution.

———. 2004. Courts and agencies. In *Making policy, making law: An interbranch perspective,* ed. Mark C. Miller and Jeb Barnes, 89–104. Washington, D.C.: Georgetown University Press.

Memmott, Mark. 2005. Group's TV ad uses storm's aftermath to target Roberts. *USA Today,* September 8, 7A.

Merry, Sally Engle. 1990. *Getting justice and getting even: Legal consciousness among working class Americans.* Chicago: University of Chicago Press.

Milbank, Dana. 2005. And the verdict on Justice Kennedy is: Guilty. *The Washington Post,* April 9, A03.

Mill, John Stuart. 1856. *On liberty.* New York: Holt.

Miller, Mark C. 1992. Congressional committees and the federal courts: A neo-institutional perspective. *Western Political Quarterly* 45:949–70.

———. 1993. Courts, agencies, and congressional committees: A neo-institutional perspective. *Review of Politics* 55:525–66.

———. 1995. *The high priests of American politics: The role of lawyers in American political institutions.* Knoxville: University of Tennessee Press.

———. 1999. A comparison of two evolving courts: The Canadian Supreme Court and the European Court of Justice. *University of California-Davis Journal of International Law and Policy* 5:27–58.

———. 2004a. Interactions between legislatures and courts. *Judicature* 87:213–18.

———. 2004b. The view of the courts from the Hill: A neoinstitutional perspective. In *Making policy, making law: An interbranch perspective, ed. Mark C.* Miller and Jeb Barnes, 53–71. Washington, D.C.: Georgetown University Press.

———. 2006. Conflicts between the Massachusetts Supreme Judicial Court and the legislature: Campaign finance reform and same-sex marriage. *Pierce Law Review* 4:279–316.

Miller, Mark C., and Jeb Barnes, ed. 2004. *Making policy, making law: An interbranch perspective.* Washington, D.C.: Georgetown University Press.

Miller, Richard E., and Austin Sarat. 1981. Grievances, claims, and disputes: Assessing the adversary culture. *Law and Society Review* 15:525–66.

Milligan, Joy. 2006. Pluralism in America: Why diversity improves legal decisions about political morality. *New York University Law Review* 81:1206–41.

Mills, C. Wright. 1956. *The power elite* New York: Oxford University Press.

Mishler, William, and Reginald Sheehan. 1993. The Supreme Court as a countermajoritarian institution? The impact of public opinion on Supreme Court decisions. *American Political Science Review* 87:87–101.

———. 1996. Public opinion, the attitudinal model, and Supreme Court decision making: A micro-analytic perspective. *American Journal of Political Science* 58:169–200.

Mnookin, Robert H., and Lewis Kornhauser. 1979. Bargaining in the shadow of the law: The case of divorce. *Yale Law Journal* 88:950–97.

Mondak, Jeffrey J., and Shannon Ishiyama Smithey. 1997. The dynamics of public support for the Supreme Court. *Journal of Politics* 59:1114–32.

Moore, Lloyd. 1973. *The jury: Tool of kings, palladium of liberty.* New York: Anderson Publishing Co.

Morgan, Richard. 1972. *The Supreme Court and religion.* New York: The Free Press.

Moussaoui indictment. 2001. United States of America v. Zacarias Moussaoui, Criminal No. 01–455–A, U.S. District Court for the Eastern District of Virginia, Alexander Division, July 2002 Term, Superseding Indictment.

Moustafa, Tamir. 2003. Law versus the state: The judicialization of politics in Egypt. *Law and Social Inquiry* 28:883–930.

——. 2005. A judicialization of authoritarian politics? Paper presented at the annual meeting of the American Political Science Association, Sept. 1–4, in Washington, D.C.

Munn, Michelle. 2002. Plan to curb forest fires wins support. *Los Angles Times*, August 2, A16.

Munsterman, G. Thomas, and Paula L. Hannaford. 1997. Reshaping the bedrock of democracy: American jury reform during the last 30 years. *Judges' Journal* 36:5–12.

Munsterman, G. Thomas, Paula L. Hannaford, and G. Marc Whitehead. 1997. *Jury trial innovations.* Williamsburg, Vir.: National Center for State Courts.

Munsterman, Janice T., G. Thomas Munsterman, Brian Lynch, and Steven Penrod. 1991. *The relationship of juror fees and terms of service to jury system performance.* Arlington, Vir.: National Center for State Courts.

Murdoch, Joyce, and Deb Price. 2001. *Courting justice: Gay men and lesbians v. the Supreme Court.* New York: Basic Books.

Murphy, Walter. 1962. *Congress and the court.* Chicago: University of Chicago Press.

——. 1964. *Elements of judicial strategy.* Chicago: University of Chicago Press.

Myers, Robert D., and Gordon M. Griller. 1997. Educating jurors means better trials: Jury reform in Arizona. *Judges' Journal* 36:13–17.

Nagel, Stuart S. 1965. Court-curbing periods in American history. *Vanderbilt Law Review* 18:925–44.

Nather, David. 2005. Race against the nuclear clock. *Congressional Quarterly Weekly Report*, May 30, 1440–3.

NALP (National Association for Law Placement). 2006. Press Release: Partnership at large firms elusive for minority women—Overall, women and minorities continue to make small gains. November 8.http://www.nalp.org/press/details.php?id=64.

National Center for State Courts. 1999. *How the public views the state courts.* Williamsburg, Vir.: National Center for State Courts.

——. 2005. The vanishing trial: Implications for the bench and bar. *Civil Action* 4:1–5.

Navasky, Victor S. 1971. *Kennedy justice.* New York: Atheneum.

Nelson, Jr., John R. 1985. *Black lung: A study of disability compensation policy formation.* Chicago: School of Social Service Administration, University of Chicago.

Nelson, Robert L. 1985. Ideology, practice, and professional autonomy: Social values and client relationships in the large law firm. *Stanford Law Review* 37:503–51.

Nelson, Robert L., and David M. Trubek. 1992. Arenas of professionalism: The professional ideologies of lawyers in context. In *Lawyers' ideals/lawyers's practices,* ed. Robert L. Nelson, David M. Trubek and Rayman L. Solomon, 177–214. Ithaca, NY: Cornell University Press.

Nemeth, Charlan. 1987. Interactions between jurors as a function of majority vs. unanimity decision rules. In *In the jury box: Controversies in the courtroom,* ed. Lawrence S. Wrightsman, Saul M. Kassin, and Cynthia E. Willis, 235–255 Beverly Hills, Calif.: Sage.

Nesson, Charles. 1971. Mr. Justice Harlan. *Harvard Law Review* 85:390–1.

Neubauer, David W., and Stephen S. Meinhold. 2004. *Judicial process: Law, courts, and politics in the United States,* 3rd ed. Belmont, Calif.: Wadsworth.

Neustadt, Richard E. 1980. *Presidential power: The politics of leadership from FDR to Carter.* New York: Macmillan.

New Hampshire Superior Court Jury Reform Study Committee. 1997. *Report of the Superior Court Jury Reform Study Committee.* Rye: New Hampshire Superior Court.

The New York Times. 2005a. Editorial: Attacking a Free Judiciary. April 5. A22.

The New York Times. 2005b. Editorial: A defender of independent courts. September 7. A28.

The New York Times. 2006a. Editorial: Fairness in the Alito hearings. January 11. A34.

The New York Times. 2006b. Editorial: Activism is in the eye of the ideologist. September 11. A18.

Newland, Chester A. 1961. Personal assistants to Supreme Court justices: The law clerks. *Oregon Law Review* 40:299–317.

Newman, Jon O. 1997. The Judge Baer controversy. *Judicature* 80:156–64.

Nicholson-Crotty, Sean, and Kenneth J. Meier. 2002. Size doesn't matter: In defense of single-state studies. *State Politics and Policy Quarterly* 2:411–22.

Nielsen, Laura Beth. 2000. Situating legal consciousness: Experiences and attitudes of ordinary citizens about law and street harassment. *Law and Society Review* 34:1055–90.

Nixon, David C., and David L. Goss. 2001. Confirmation delays for vacancies on the Circuit Courts of Appeals. *American Politics Research* 29:246–74.

Oakley, John B. 1995. Defining the limits of delegation. *The Long Term View* 3:85–93.

Oakley, John B., and Robert S. Thompson. 1979. Law clerks in judges' eyes: Tradition and innovation in the use of legal staff by American judges. *California Law Review* 67:1286–317.

———. 1980. *Law clerks and the judicial process.* Berkeley: University of California Press.

O'Brien, David M. 1990. *Storm center: The Supreme Court in American politics,* 2nd ed. New York: Norton.

———. 1993. *Storm center: The Supreme Court in American politics,* 3rd ed. New York: Norton.

———. 1997. The Rehnquist Court's shrinking plenary docket. *Judicature* 81:58–65.

———. 2001. How the Republican war over "judicial activism" has cost Congress. In *Congress confronts the Court: The struggle for legitimacy and authority in lawmaking,* ed. Colton C. Campbell, and John F. Stack, Jr.,69–78. Lanham, MD: Rowman & Littlefield.

———. 2003. *Storm Center: The Supreme Court in American politics,* 6th ed. New York: Norton.

———. 2004. *Judges on judging: Views from the bench,* 2nd ed. Washington, D.C.: CQ.

O'Connor, Karen. 1980. *Women's organizations' use of the courts.* Lexington, Mass.: Lexington Books.

O'Connor, Karen, and Larry J. Sabato. 2006. *Essentials of American government: Continuity and change.* New York: Pearson Longman.

O'Connor, Sandra Day. 2006. The threat to judicial independence. *The Wall Street Journal,* September 27, A18.

Office of the Jury Commissioner, State of Massachusetts. 1997. Public Outreach Project. Boston: Office of the Jury Commissioner, State of Massachusetts.

Office of Workers Compensation Programs (OWCP) annual report. 2001. Washington, D.C.: Government Printing Office.

Oleszek, Walter. 2003. *Congressional procedures and the policy process,* 6th ed. Washington, D.C.: CQ.

Olsen, Mancur. 1971. *The logic of collective action*. Cambridge, Mass.: Harvard University Press.

Olson, Susan M. 1981. The political evolution of interest group litigation. In *Governing through courts*, ed. Richard A. L. Gambitta, Marilyn L. May, and James C. Foster, 225–258. Beverly Hills: Sage.

——. 1984. *Clients and lawyers: Securing the rights of disabled persons*. Westport, Conn.: Greenwood.

Orren, Karen, and Skowronek, Stephen. 1994. Beyond the Iconography of Order: Notes for a 'New' Institutionalism. In *The dynamics of American politics: Approaches and interpretations,* ed. L. Dodd and C. Jillson, 311–3330. Boulder, Colo.: Westview.

Ostrom, Brian J., and Dan J. Hall. 2005. *CourTools*: *Trial court performance measures*. Williamsburg, Vir.: National Center for State Courts. Available at: www.courtools.org.

Ostrom, Brian J., Shauna M. Strickland, and Paula L. Hannaford-Agor. 2004. Examining trial trends in state courts: 1976–2002. *Journal of Empirical Legal Studies* 1:755–82.

Pabst, William R., G. Thomas Munsterman, and Chester H. Mount. 1976. The myth of the unwilling juror. *Judicature* 60:164–71.

——. 1977. The value of jury duty: Serving is believing. *Judicature* 61:38–42.

Pacelle, Richard L., Jr. 1990. The Supreme Court's agenda and the dynamics of policy evolution. Paper presented at American Political Science Association Meetings, San Francisco, August 30–September 2.

——. 1991. *The transformation of the Supreme Court's agenda: From the New Deal to the Reagan administration*. Boulder, Colo.: Westview.

——. 1995. The dynamics and determinants of agenda change in the Rehnquist Court. In *Contemplating courts*, ed. Lee Epstein, 251–274. Washington, D.C.: CQ.

——. 2002. *The role of the Supreme Court in American politics: The least dangerous branch?* Boulder, Colo.: Westview.

——. 2003. *Between law and politics: The solicitor general and the structuring of race, gender, and reproductive rights policy*. College Station: Texas A&M University Press.

——. 2004. A *Mapp* to legal change and policy retreat: *United States v. Leon*. In *Creating constitutional change,* ed. Gregg Ivers and Kevin McGuire, 249–263., Charlottesville: University Press of Virginia.

Page, Benjamin I., and Robert Y. Shapiro. 1992. *The rational public: Fifty years of trends in Americans' policy preferences*. Chicago: University of Chicago Press.

Palmer, Jan, and Saul Brenner. 1988. The time taken to write opinions as a determinant of opinion assignments. *Judicature* 72:179–84.

Parikh, Sara. 2001. Professionalism and its discontents: A study of social networks in the plaintiff's personal injury bar. PhD diss., University of Illinois at Chicago.

Pearson, Drew and Robert S. Allen. 1936. *The nine old men*. Garden City, N.Y.: Doubleday, Doran.

Peppers, Todd C. 2006. *Courtiers of the marble palace: The rise and influence of the Supreme Court law clerk*. Stanford, Calif.: Stanford University Press.

Pereira, Anthony W. 2005. *Political (in)justice: Authoritarianism and the rule of law in Brazil, Chile, and Argentina*. Pittsburgh: University of Pittsburgh Press.

Peretti, Terri Jennings. 1999. *In defense of a political court*. Princeton, N.J.: Princeton University Press.

Perine, Keith. 2005. In letter to nominee Roberts, Specter criticizes Court's federalism decisions. *Congressional Quarterly Weekly Report*, August 15, 2254.

Perry, Barbara A. 1991. *A "representative" Supreme Court? The impact of race, religion, and gender on appointments.* New York: Greenwood.

———. 1999. *The priestly tribe: The Supreme Court's image in the American mind.* Westport, Conn.: Praeger.

———. 2007. *The Michigan affirmative action cases.* Lawrence: University Press of Kansas.

Perry, H. W., Jr. 1991. *Deciding to decide: Agenda setting in the United States Supreme Court.* Cambridge, Mass.: Harvard University Press.

Perry, Steven W. 2006. National survey of prosecutors: Prosecutors in state courts, 2005. Bureau of Justice Statistics. http://www.ojp.usdoj.gov/bjs/pub/pdf/psc05.pdf.

Peters, Shawn Francis. 2000. *Judging Jehovah's Witnesses: Religious persecution and the dawn of the rights revolution.* Lawrence: University Press of Kansas.

Peterson, Mark 1990. *Legislating together: The White House and Capitol Hill from Eisenhower to Reagan.* Cambridge, Mass.: Harvard University Press.

Phillips, The Honorable Tom. 1999. Interview by Bill Moyers. *Frontline.* "Justice for sale," PBS, November 23, 1999.

Pickerill, J. Mitchell. 2004. *Constitutional deliberation in Congress: The Impact of judicial review in a separated system.* Durham, N.C.: Duke University Press.

Pierre, Robert E. 2003. Terrorism case thrown into turmoil. *The Washington Post*, December 31, A5.

Pierson, Paul, and Theda Skocpol. 2001. Historical institutionalism in contemporary political science. In *Political science: State of the discipline,* ed. Ira Katznelson and Helen V. Milner, 693–723. New York: Norton.

Pinello, Daniel R. 1995. *The impact of judicial selection method on state supreme court policy: Innovation, reaction, atrophy.* Westport, Conn.: Greenwood.

Poole, Keith, and Howard Rosenthal. 1997. *Congress: A Political-economic history of roll call voting.* New York: Oxford University.

Posner, Richard A. 1985. *The federal courts: Crisis and reform.* Cambridge, Mass.: Harvard University Press.

———. 1995. *Overcoming law.* Cambridge, Mass.: Harvard University Press.

———. 1996. *The federal courts: Challenge and reform.* Cambridge, Mass.: Harvard University Press.

———. 2005. Foreword: A political court. *Harvard Law Review* 119:31–102.

Powe, Lucas A., Jr. 2000. *The Warren Court and American politics.* Cambridge, Mass.: The Belknap Press of Harvard University Press.

Powell, Michael. 2003. No choice but guilty: Lackawanna case highlights legal tilt. *The Washington Post*, July 29, A1.

———. 2004. Lawyer visits 'dirty bomb' suspect. *The Washington Post*, March 4, A10.

Price, Deb. 1997. Civil rites: Arguments against same-sex marriage mirror those that kept the races apart. *The Detroit News*, April 18, 1E.

Priest, George L. 1993. Justifying the civil jury. In *Verdict: Assessing the civil jury system,* ed. Robert E. Litan, 103–136. Washington, DC: Brookings Institution.

———. 2002. The problem and efforts to understand it. In *Punitive damages: How juries decide,* ed. Cass Sunstein, Reid Hastie, John W. Payne, David A. Schkade, and W. Kip Viscusi, 1–16. Chicago: University of Chicago Press.

Pritchett, C. Herman. 1948. *The Roosevelt Court: A study in judicial politics and values, 1937–1947.* New York: Macmillan.

——. 1954. *Civil liberties and the Vinson Court.* Chicago: University of Chicago Press.

——. 1961. *Congress versus the Supreme Court, 1957–60.* Minneapolis: University of Minnesota Press.

——. 1984. *Constitutional civil liberties.* Englewood Cliffs, N.J.: Prentice-Hall.

Provine, Doris Marie. 1980. *Case selection in the United States Supreme Court.* Chicago: University of Chicago Press.

——. 2005. Judicial activism and American democracy. In *The judicial branch,* ed. Kermit L. Hall and Kevin T. McGuire, 313–340. New York: Oxford University Press.

Purdy, Matthew, and Lowell Bergman. 2003. Unclear danger: Inside the Lackawanna terror case. *The New York Times,* October 12, 1.

Rabin, Robert. 1993. Institutional and historical perspectives on tobacco tort liability. In *Smoking policy: Law, politics, and culture,* ed. Robert Rabin and S. Sugarman, 110–130. New York: Oxford University Press.

Rabkin, Jeremy. 1989. *Judicial compulsions: How public law distorts public policy.* New York: Basic Books.

Rapoport, Nancy B., and Bala G. Dharan. 2004. *Enron: Corporate fiascos and their implications.* New York: Foundation.

Reddick, Anna Malia. 1997. *The applicability of legal and attitudinal models to the treatment of precedent in the Courts of Appeals.* PhD diss., Michigan State University.

Reed, Barbara, and Roy A. Schotland. 2001. Judicial campaign conduct committees. *Indiana Law Review* 35:781–805.

Rehnquist, William H. 1957. Who writes decisions of the Supreme Court. *U.S. News & World Report,* December 13, 74–75.

——. 1992. *Grand inquests: The historic impeachments of Justice Samuel Chase and President Andrew Johnson.* New York: Quill William Morrow.

——. 1996. The future of the federal courts: Keynote address. *American University Law Review* 46:263–324.

——. 2000. *2000 year-end report on the federal judiciary.* Washington, D.C.: Supreme Court of the United States.

——. 2001. *The Supreme Court.* New York: Knopf.

——. 2002. *2002 year-end report on the federal judiciary.* Washington, D.C.: Supreme Court of the United States.

——. 2003. *2003 year-end report on the federal judiciary.* Washington, D.C.: Supreme Court of the United States.

——. 2004. *The year-end report on the judiciary, 2004.* Washington, D.C.: Supreme Court of the United States.

Reid, Traciel V. 1999. The politicization of judicial retention elections: The defeat of Justices Lanphier and White.*Judicature* 83:68–77.

Remini, Robert V. 1988. *The legacy of Andrew Jackson: Essays on democracy, Indian removal, and slavery.* Baton Rouge: Louisiana State University Press.

Resnik, Judith. 2000. Trial as error, jurisdiction as injury: Transforming the meaning of Article III. *Harvard Law Review* 113:924–1037.

Resnik, Judith, Danny J. Boggs, and Howard Berman. 2004. The independence of the federal judiciary. *Bulletin of the American Academy of Arts and Sciences,* winter:17–28.

Revesz, Richard L. 1997. Environmental regulation, ideology, and the D.C. Circuit. *Virginia Law Review* 83:1717–72.

Reynolds, Maura. 2006. A stark division in vote for Alito. *Los Angeles Times*, February 1, A1.

Richards, Mark, and Herbert Kritzer. 2002. Jurisprudential regimes in Supreme Court decision making. *American Political Science Review* 96:305–20.

Richert, John P. 1977a. A new verdict on juror willingness. *Judicature* 60:496–501.

——. 1977b. Jurors' attitudes towards jury service. *Justice System Journal* 2:233–45.

Richland, Justin B. 2005. 'What are you going to do with the village's knowledge?' Talking tradition, talking law in Hopi tribal court. *Law and Society Review* 39:235–483.

Ricks, Thomas E., and Michael Powell. 2004. 2nd suspect can see lawyer. *The Washington Post*, February 12, A16.

Ringhand, Lori A. 2007. The Rehnquist Court: A by the numbers retrospective. *University of Pennsylvania Journal of Constitutional Law* Spring.

Ripley, Randall, and Grace Franklin. 1982. *Bureaucracy and policy implementation.* Homewood, Ill: Dorsey.

——. 1990. *Congress, the bureaucracy, and public policy,* 5th ed. Homewood, Ill.: Dorsey.

Rishikof, Harvey, and Barbara A. Perry. 1995. Separateness but interdependence, autonomy but reciprocity: A first look at federal judges' appearances before legislative committees. *Mercer Law Review* 46:667–76.

Roberts, John G., Jr. 2005. *2005 year-end report on the federal judiciary.* Washington, D.C.: Supreme Court of the United States.

Robertson, Pat. 2004. *Courting disaster: How the Supreme Court is usurping the power of Congress and the people.* Nashville, Tenn.: Integrity.

Rodgers, Harrell R., Jr., and Charles S. Bullock, III. 1976. *Coercion to compliance.* Lexington, Mass.: Lexington Books.

Rohde, David, and Harold Spaeth. 1976. *Supreme Court decision-making.* San Francisco: Freeman.

Roosevelt, Kermit III. 2006. *The myth of activism: Making sense of Supreme Court decisions.* New Haven, Conn.: Yale University Press.

Rose, Mary R. 1999. The peremptory challenge accused of race or gender discrimination? Some data from one county. *Law and Human Behavior* 23:695–702.

Rosenberg, Debra. 2005. The war on judges. *Newsweek* April 25, 23–27.

Rosenberg, Gerald N. 1991. *The hollow hope: Can courts bring about social change?* Chicago: University of Chicago Press.

——. 2005. The impact of courts on American public life. In *The judicial branch*, ed. Kermit L. Hall and Kevin T. McGuire, 280–312. New York: Oxford University Press.

Rosenthal, Douglas E. 1974. *Lawyer and client: Who's in charge?* New York: Russell Sage Foundation.

Rubin, Edward L. 1996. The new legal process, the synthesis of discourse, and the microanalysis of institutions, *Harvard Law Review* 109:1393–438.

Rubin, Edward L, and Malcolm Feeley. 2003. *Velazquez* and beyond: Judicial policy making and litigation against government. *University of Pennsylvania Journal of Constitutional Law* 5:617–64.

Rubin, Eva. 1987. *Abortion, politics, and the courts.* Westport, Conn.: Greenwood.

Rubin, Paul H. and Martin J. Bailey. 1994. The role of lawyers in changing the law. *Journal of Legal Studies* 23:807–31.

Russell, Peter H., and David M. O'Brien, ed. 2001. *Judicial independence in the age of democracy: Critical perspectives from around the world.* Charlottesville: University Press of Virginia.

Sabel, Charles F., and William H. Simon. 1999. Destabilization rights: How public law litigation succeeds. *Harvard Law Review* 113:1–83.

Sager, Lawrence. 1990. The incorrigible constitution. *New York University Law Review* 65: 893–961.

Salokar, Rebecca Mae. 1992. *The solicitor general: The politics of law.* Philadelphia: Temple University Press.

Sanchez, Samantha. 2001. Money in judicial politics. A report for the American Bar Association Standing Committee on Judicial Independence. March 21.

Sanchez Urribarri, Raul A., and Donald R. Songer. 2006. A cross-national examination of the "strategic defection" theory. Paper presented at the annual meeting of the American Political Science Association, August 31–September 3, in Philadelphia.

Sandler, Ross, and David Schoenbrod. 2004. *Government by decree: What happens when courts run government.* New Haven, Conn.: Yale University Press.

Saphire, Richard B., and Michael E. Solimine. 1995. Diluting justice on appeal?: An examination of the use of district court judges sitting by designation on the U.S. courts of appeals. *University of Michigan Journal of Law Reform* 28:351–407.

Sarat, Austin, ed. 2004. *Law in the liberal arts.* Ithaca, N.Y.: Cornell University Press.

Sarat, Austin, and Wiliam L.F. Felstiner. 1995. *Divorce lawyers and their clients: Power and meaning in the legal process.* New York: Oxford University Press.

Sarat, Austin, and Thomas R. Kearns. 1993. Beyond the great divide: Forms of legal scholarship and everyday life. In *Law in everyday life*, ed. Austin Sarat and Thomas R. Kearns, 21–62. Ann Arbor: University of Michigan Press.

Sarat, Austin, and Stuart A. Scheingold, eds. 1998. *Cause lawyering: Political commitments and professional responsibilities.* New York: Oxford University Press.

Savage, David G. 1993. *Turning right: The making of the Rehnquist Supreme Court.* New York: Wiley.

Scalia, Antonin. 1997. *A matter of interpretation: Federal courts and the law.* Princeton, N.J.: Princeton University Press.

Schauffler, Richard., Robert C. LaFountain, Shauna M. Strickland, and William E. Raftery. 2006. *Examining the work of state courts, 2005: A national perspective from the court statistics project.* Williamsburg, Vir.: The National Center for State Courts.

Scheiber, Harry N. 1973. Property law, expropriation, and resource allocation by government: The United States, 1789–1910, *Journal of Economic History* 33:232–51.

Scheingold, Stuart A. 1974. *The politics of rights: Lawyers, public policy, and political change.* New Haven, Conn.: Yale University Press.

Scheingold, Stuart A., and Austin Sarat. 2004. *Something to believe in: Politics, professionalism, and cause lawyering.* Stanford, Calif.: Stanford University Press.

Scheppele, Kim Lane. 2000. Constitutional interpretation after regimes of horror. *University of Pennsylvania Law School Public Law and Legal Theory Research Paper Series* No. 1–5, May 2000.

Scherer, Nancy. 2005. *Scoring points: Politicians, activists and the lower court appointment process.* Palo Alto, Calif.: Stanford University Press.

Schlafly, Phyllis. 2006. *The supremacists: The tyranny of judges and how to stop it,* rev. and expanded ed. Dallas, Tex.: Spence.

Schlozman, Kay Lehman, and John Tierney. 1986. *Organized interests and American democracy*. New York: Harper & Row.

Schmeling, Thomas 2003. Stag hunting with the state AG: Anti-tobacco litigation and the emergence of cooperation among state attorneys general. *Law & Policy* 25:429–54.

Schmidhauser, John R., and Larry L. Berg. 1972. *The Supreme Court and Congress: Conflict and interaction 1945–1968*. New York: Free Press.

Schmidt, Patrick. 2005. *Lawyers and regulation: The politics of the administrative process*. Cambridge: Cambridge University Press.

Schmidt, Susan. 2003. Prosecution of Moussaoui nears a crossroad. *The Washington Post*, January 21, A8.

Schmidt, Susan, and Ellen Nakashima. 2003. Moussaoui said Not to Be Part of 9/11 Plot. *The Washington Post*, March 28, 2003, A4.

Schmidt, Susan, and Dana Priest. 2003. Judge orders access to detainee for Moussaoui's lawyers. *The Washington Post*, February 1, A9.

Schneider, Elizabeth M. 2000. *Battered women and feminist lawmaking*. New Haven, Conn.: Yale University Press.

Schneider, Mark, and Paul Teske. 1992. Toward a theory of the political entrepreneur: Evidence from local government. *American Political Science Review* 86:737–47.

Schubert, Glendon A. 1960. *Constitutional politics: The political behavior of Supreme Court justices and the constitutional policies they make*. New York: Holt, Rinehard, and Winston.

——, ed. 1964. *Judicial behavior: A reader in theory and research*. Chicago: Rand McNally.

——. 1965. *The judicial mind: Attitudes and ideologies of Supreme Court justices 1946–1963*. Evanston, Ill.: Northwestern University Press.

——. 1968. Political ideology on the high court. *Politics* 3:25–34.

——. 1974. *The judicial mind revisited*. New York: Oxford University Press.

Schubert, Glendon A., and David J Danelski, ed. 1969. *Comparative judicial behavior: Cross-cultural studies in political decision making in the east and west*. New York: Oxford University Press.

Schuck, Peter H. 1993. Mapping the debate on jury reform. In *Verdict: Assessing the civil jury system*, ed. Robert E. Litan., 306–340. Washington, D.C.: Brookings Institution.

Schwartz, Bernard. 1996. *Decision: How the Supreme Court decides cases*. New York: Oxford University Press.

Schwartz, Bernard, and Stephan Lesher. 1983. *Inside the Warren Court: 1953–1969*. Garden City, N.Y.: Doubleday.

Schwartz, William W. 1981. Communicating with juries: Problems and remedies. *California Law Review* 69:731–69.

Scigliano, Robert. 1971. *The Supreme Court and the presidency*. New York: Free Press.

Scott, James C. 1990. *Domination and the arts of resistance: Hidden transcripts*. New Haven, Conn.: Yale University Press.

Seager, Susan. 1991. Saving the earth. *California Lawyer* April, 39–43.

Segal, Jeffrey A. 1984. Predicting Supreme Court cases probabilistically: The search and seizure cases, 1962–1981. *American Political Science Review* 78:891–900.

——. 1986. Supreme Court justices as human decision makers: An individual level analysis of search and seizure cases. *Journal of Politics* 48:938–55.

——. 1988. Amicus curiae briefs by the solicitor general during the Warren and Burger Courts: A research note. *Western Political Quarterly* 41:135–44.

——. 1990. Supreme Court support for the solicitor general: The effect of presidential appointments. *Western Political Quarterly* 43:137–52.

——. 1997. Separation-of-powers games in the positive theory of Congress and courts. *American Political Science Review* 91:28–44.

Segal, Jeffrey, and Albert Cover. 1989. Ideological values and the votes of U.S. Supreme Court justices. *American Political Science Review* 83:557–65.

Segal, Jeffrey, Lee Epstein, Charles Cameron, and Harold Spaeth. 1995. Ideological values and the votes of U.S. Supreme Court justices revisited. *Journal of Politics* 57:812–23.

Segal, Jeffrey A., Donald R. Songer, and Charles M. Cameron. 1995. Decision making on the U.S. courts of appeals. In *Contemplating courts*, ed. Lee Epstein, 227–246. Washington, D.C.: CQ.

Segal, Jeffrey, and Harold Spaeth. 1993. *The Supreme Court and the attitudinal model*. New York: Cambridge University Press.

——. 1996. The Influence of *stare decisis* on the votes of United States Supreme Court justices. *American Journal of Political Science* 40:971–1003.

——. 2002. *The Supreme Court and the attitudinal model revisited*. New York: Cambridge University Press.

Selikoff, Irving, J. Chung, and E.C. Hammond. 1965. The occurrence of asbestos among insulation workers in the United States. *Annals of the New York Academy of Science* 132:139–155.

Seron, Carroll. 1996. *The business of practicing law: The work lives of solo and small firm attorneys*. Philadelphia: Temple University Press.

Shapiro, Martin. 1981a. *Courts: A comparative and political analysis*. Chicago: University of Chicago Press.

——. 1981b. On the regrettable decline of law French: Or Shapiro jettet le brickbat. *Yale Law Journal* 90:1198–1204.

——. 1988. *Who guards the guardians: Judicial control of administration*. Athens: University of Georgia Press.

——. 1993. Public law and judicial politics. In *Political science: The state of the discipline II*, ed. Ada Finifter, 365–381. Washington, D.C.: American Political Science Association.

——. 1995. The United States. In *The global expansion of judicial power*, ed. C. Neal Tate and Torbjorn Vallinder, 43–66. New York: New York University Press.

——. 2004. Judicial review in developed democracies. In *Democratization and the judiciary: The accountability function of courts in new democracies*, ed. Siri Gloppen, Roberto Gargarella, and Elin Skaar, 7–26 London: Cass.

Shapiro, Susan P. 2002. *Tangled loyalties: Conflict of interest in legal practice*. Ann Arbor: University of Michigan Press.

Shavell, Steven. 1995. The appeals process as a means of error correction. *Journal of Legal Studies* 24:379–426.

Sheldon, Charles H. 1981. Law clerking with a state supreme court: Views from the perspective of the personal assistants to the judges. *Justice System Journal* 6:346–71.

——. 1988. The evolution of law clerking with the Washington Supreme Court: from "elbow clerks" to "puisine judges." *Gonzaga Law Review* 24:45–84.

Sheldon, Charles H., and Linda S. Maule. 1997. *Choosing justice: The recruitment of state and federal judges*. Pullman: Washington State University Press.

Shenon, Philip. 2003a. Prosecution says Qaeda member was to pilot 5th Sept. 11 jet. *The New York Times*, April 16, B10.

———. 2003b. Moussaoui should get details in "5th plane" theory, judge says. *The New York Times,* April 29, A13.

———. 2003c. Justice dept. warns of risk to prosecution and security. *The New York Times*, June 4, A21.

———. 2003d. U.S. will defy court's order in terror case. *The New York Times*, July 15, A1.

———. 2003e. In maneuver, U.S. will let terror charges drop. *The New York Times*, September 26, A1.

Shenon, Philip, and Eric Schmitt. 2002. White House weighs letting military tribunal try Moussaoui, officials say. *The New York Times*, October 20, 15.

Shipan, Charles R. 1997. *Designing judicial review: Interest groups, Congress, and communications policy.* Ann Arbor: University of Michigan Press.

Shogan, Robert. 1996. The confirmation wars: How politicians, interest groups, and the press shape the presidential appointment process. In *Obstacle course: The report of the twentieth century fund on the presidential appointment process,* ed. G. Calvin MacKenzie and Robert Shogan, 87–168. New York: Twentieth Century Fund Press.

Shuman, Daniel W., and Jean A. Hamilton. 1992. Jury service: It may change your mind: perceptions of fairness of jurors and nonjurors. *Southern Methodist University Law Review* 46: 449–79.

Sieder, Rachel. 2004. Renegotiating "law and order": Judicial reform and citizen responses in post-war Guatemala. In *Democratization and the judiciary: The accountability function of courts in new democracies,* ed. Siri Gloppen, Roberto Gargarella, and Elin Skaar,137–160. London: Cass.

Silverstein, Mark. 1994. *Judicious choices: The new politics of Supreme Court confirmations.* New York: Norton.

Simon, Paul. 1992. *Advise and consent: Clarence Thomas, Robert Bork, and the intriguing history of the Supreme Court's nomination battles.* Bethesda, Md.: National Press Books.

Simon, William H. 1998. The Kaye Scholer affair: The lawyer's duty of candor and the bar's temptations of evasion and apology. *Law and Social Inquiry* 23:243–95.

Sinclair, Barbara. 1989. *The transformation of the U.S. Senate.* Baltimore: Johns Hopkins University Press.

Skowronek, Steven. 1997. *The politics president make: Leadership from John Adams to Bill Clinton.* Cambridge, Mass.: Belknap.

Slaughter, Anne-Marie. 1994. A typology of transjudicial communities. *University of Richmond Law Review* 29:99–134.

Slotnick, Elliot E. 1991. Judicial politics. In *Political science: Looking to the future. Volume 4: American institutions,* ed. William Crotty, 67–97. Evanston, Ill.: Northwestern University Press.

Slotnick, Elliot E., and Jennifer A. Segal. 1998. *Television news and the Supreme Court: All the news that's fit to air?* Cambridge: Cambridge University.

Smith, Christopher. 1993. *Critical judicial nominations and political change.* Westport, Conn.: Praeger.

Smith, Congressman Lamar (R–TX). 2003. Press release: Smith & Chabot form judicial accountability group. U.S. House of Representatives, July 23.

Smith, Mark W. 2006. *Disrobed: The new battle plan to break the left's stranglehold on the courts.* New York: Crown Forum.

Smith, Martin. 1993. *Pressure power & policy: State autonomy and policy networks in Britain and the United States.* Pittsburgh, Penn.: University of Pittsburgh Press.

Smith, Neal. 1996. *Mr. Smith went to Washington: From Eisenhower to Clinton.* Ames: Iowa State University Press.

Smith, Rogers. 1988. Political jurisprudence: The new institutionalism and the future of public law. *American Political Science Review* 82:89–108.

Solimine, Michael E. 1988. Ideology and en banc review. *North Carolina Law Review* 67:29–76.

———. 2006. The en banc court: Due process and en banc decisionmaking. *Arizona Law Review* 48:325–40.

Some facts about the life and public services of Benjamin Helm Bristow of Kentucky. 1876. Benjamin Helm Bristow Papers, Library of Congress.

Songer, Donald R., and Sue Davis. 1990. The impact of party and region on voting decisions in the United States Courts of Appeals, 1955–1986. *Western Political Quarterly* 43:317–34.

Songer, Donald R., and Susan B. Haire. 1992. Integrating alternative approaches to the study of judicial voting: Obscenity cases in the U.S. Courts of Appeals. *American Journal of Political Science* 36:963–82.

Songer, Donald R., and Stefanie A. Lindquist. 1996. Not the whole story: The impact of justices' values on Supreme Court decision making. *American Journal of Political Science* 40:1049–63.

Songer, Donald R., and Susan Reid. 1989. Policy change on the U.S. Courts of Appeals: Exploring the contribution of the legal and democratic subcultures. Presented at the annual meeting of the American Political Science Association, September 1–3.

Songer, Donald R., Jeffrey A. Segal, and Charles M. Cameron. 1994. The hierarchy of justice: Testing a principal-agent model of Supreme Court-circuit court interactions. *American Journal of Political Science* 38:673–96.

Songer, Donald R., Reginald S. Sheehan, and Susan B. Haire. 2000. *Continuity and change on the United States Courts of Appeals.* Ann Arbor: University of Michigan Press.

———. 2003. Do the haves come out ahead over time? Applying Galanter's framework to the decisions of the U.S. Courts of Appeals, 1925–1988. In *In litigation: Do the "haves" still come out ahead?* ed. Herbert M. Kritzer and Susan S. Silbey, 85–107, Stanford, Calif.: Stanford University Press.

Sontag, Deborah. 2004. Terror suspect's path from streets to brig. *The New York Times,* April 25, 1.

Southworth, Ann. 1996. Lawyer-client decisionmaking in civil rights and poverty practice: An empirical study of lawyers' norms," *Georgetown Journal of Legal Ethics* 9:1–55.

Span, Paula. 2003. Enemy combatant vanishes into a "legal black hole." *The Washington Post,* July 30, A8.

Spiller, Pablo T., and Rafael Gely. 1992. Congressional control or judicial independence: The determinants of U.S. Supreme Court labor-relations decisions, 1949–1988. *RAND Journal of Economics* 23:463–92.

St. Petersburg Times (Florida). 2004. Editorial: High court under attack again. March 5. A14.

Starcher, Larry V. 2001. Choosing West Virginia's judges. *Quinnipiac Law Review* 20: 767–78.

Starr, Kenneth W. 1991. The courts of appeals and the future of the federal judiciary. *Wisconsin Law Review* 1991:1–9.

Steelman, David C., J. A. Goerdt, and Jim E. McMillan. 2000. *Caseflow management: The heart of court management in the new millennium.* Williamsburg, Vir.: The National Center for State Courts.

Steigerwalt, Amy. 2004. Holds and private political fights. Paper prepared for the 2004 annual meeting of the American Political Science Association. in Chicago, September 2–5.

Stern, Robert H. 1953. Denial of certiorari despite a conflict. *Harvard Law Review* 66:465–72.

Stern, Robert H., Eugene Gressman, and Stephen M. Shapiro. 1986. *Supreme Court practice,* 6th ed. Washington, D.C.: Bureau of National Affairs.

Stern, Seth. 2005. Hearings unlikely to pin Roberts down. *Congressional Quarterly Weekly Report,* September 5, 2334–35.

Stern, Seth, and Keith Perine. 2005. Beyond the Roberts confirmation. *Congressional Quarterly Weekly Report,* October 3, 2650–2.

———. 2006. Alito confirmed after filibuster fails. *Congressional Quarterly Weekly Report,* February 6, 340–1.

Stewart, Richard B., and Cass Sunstein. 1982. Public programs and private rights, *Harvard Law Review* 95:1193–322.

Stimson, James, Michael MacKuen, and Robert Erickson. 1995. Dynamic representation. *American Political Science Review* 89:543–65.

Stipp, David. 1993. Dogma in doubt: Extent of lead's risks to kids, need to remove paint. *Wall Street Journal,* September 16, A1, A12.

Stolberg, Sheryl Gay. 2005a. Panel chairman to press Roberts on cases. *The New York Times,* August 9, A16.

———. 2005b. Nominee is pressed on end-of-life care. *The New York Times,* August 10, A18.

———. 2006. In Supreme Court confirmation hearings, test for Democrats as well as Alito. *The New York Times,* January 8, A18.

Stone Sweet, Alec. 2000. *Governing with judges: Constitutional politics in Europe.* New York: Oxford University Press.

———. 2004. *The judicial construction of Europe.* New York: Oxford University Press.

Stow, Mary Lou, and Harold J. Spaeth. 1992, Centralized research staff: Is there a monster in the judicial closet? *Judicature* 75:216–21.

Strauss, David A. 2001. Bush v. Gore: What were they thinking? In *The vote: Bush, Gore, and the Supreme Court,* ed. Cass R. Sunstein and Richard A Epstein, 184–204. Chicago: University of Chicago Press.

Sturley, Michael F. 1992. Cert pool. In *The Oxford companion to the Supreme Court of the United States,* ed. Kermit L. Hall, 133. New York: Oxford University Press.

Suchman, Mark C., and Mia L. Cahill. 1996. The hired gun as facilitator: Lawyers and the suppression of business disputes in Silicon Valley. *Law and Social Inquiry* 21:679–712.

Sugarman, Stephen D. 1989. Doing away with personal injury law: New compensation mechanisms for victims, consumers, and business. New York: Quorum.

Sunstein, Cass. 1993. *The partial constitution.* Cambridge, Mass.: Harvard University Press.

———. 1999. *One case at a time: Judicial minimalism on the Supreme Court.* Cambridge, Mass.: Harvard University Press.

Sunstein, Cass, Reid Hastie, John W. Payne, David A. Schkade, and W. Kip Viscusi, eds. 2002. *Punitive damages: How juries decide.* Chicago: University of Chicago Press.

Tarr, G. Alan. 1998a. Models and fashions in state constitutionalism. *Wisconsin Law Review* 1998:729–45.

——. 1998b. *Understanding state constitutions*. Princeton, N.J.: Princeton University Press.

——. 1999. State constitutional politics: An historical perspective. In *Constitutional politics in the states*, ed. G. Alan Tarr, 3–23. London: Greenwood.

——. 2003. Rethinking the selection of state supreme court judges. *Willamette Law Review* 39:1445–70.

——. 2006. *Judicial process and judicial policymaking*, 4th ed. Belmont, Calif.: Thomson Wadsworth.

Tarr, G. Alan, and Mary Corneila Porter. 1988. *State supreme courts in state and nation*. New Haven, Conn.: Yale University Press.

Tate, C. Neal, and Haynie, Stacia L. 2000. Comparative judicial politics in the year 2000 and the role of research collaboration between indigenous and American scholars. Paper presented to the annual meeting of the American Political Science Association, September 1–4, in Washington, D.C.

Tate, C. Neal, and Torbjorn Vallinder, eds. 1995. *The global expansion of judicial power*. New York: New York University Press.

Taylor Stuart, Jr. 1988. When high court's away, clerks' work begins. *The New York Times*, Sept. 23, B7.

Texans for Public Justice. 2001. *Pay to play: How big money buys access to the Texas supreme court*. Austin, TX. Available at (http://www.tpj.org/docs/2001/04/reports/paytoplay).

The courts, the legislature, and the executive, separate and equal? Issues at the federal level. 2004. *Judicature* 87:220–9.

Thibault, John, and Laurens Walker. 1975. *Procedural justice*. Hillsdale, N.J.: Erlbaum.

Tiersma, Peter H. 1993. Reforming the language of jury instructions. *Hofstra Law Review* 22:37–75.

Tobias, Carl. 1996. The new certiorari and a national study of the appeals courts. *Cornell Law Review* 81:1264–89.

Tocqueville, Alexis de. 1969. *Democracy in America*, trans. by George Lawrence and ed. by J. P. Mayer. New York: Harper & Row.

——. 1990. *Democracy in America*, trans. by Phillips Bradley. New York: Vintage Classics.

Toobin, Jeffrey. 1994. Juries on trial. *The New Yorker*, October, 31, 42.

Trubeck, David M.,Austin Sarat, William L. F. Felstiner, Herbert M. Kritzer, and Joel B. Grossman. 1983. The costs of ordinary litigation. *UCLA Law Review* 31: 72–124.

Truman, David. 1951. *The governmental process: Political interest and public opinion*. New York: Knopf.

Tyler , Tom R. 1988. What is procedural justice?: Criteria used by citizens to assess the fairness of legal procedures. *Law and Society Review* 22:103–35.

——. 1990. *Why people obey the law*. New Haven, Conn.: Yale University Press.

Tyler, Tom R., Jonathan D. Casper, and Bonnie Fisher. 1988. Maintaining allegiance toward political authorities: The role of prior attitudes and the use of fair procedures. *American Journal of Political Science* 33:612–28.

Tyler, Tom R., And Yuen J, Huo. 2002. *Trust in the law: Encouraging public cooperation with the police and courts*. New York: Russell Sage Foundation.

Ubertaccio, Peter N., III. 2005. *Learned in the law and politics: The office of the solicitor general*. New York: LFB Scholarly Publishing.

Uebelein, Christina. 1999. Jury innovations in the 21st century. *Hawaii Bar Journal* 3:6–11.

Ulmer, S. Sidney. 1971. *Courts as small and not so small groups*. New York: General Learning Corporation.

——. 1972. The decision to grant certiorari as an indicator to decision "on the merits." *Polity* 4:429–47.

——. 1978. Selecting cases for Supreme Court review: An underdog model. *American Political Science Review* 72:902–10.

——. 1982. Issue fluidity in the United States Supreme Court. In *Supreme Court activism and restraint*, ed. Stephen Halpern and Charles Lamb, 319–359. Lexington, Mass.: Heath.

——. 1984. The Supreme Court's certiorari decisions: Conflict as a predictive variable. *American Political Science Review* 78:901–11.

Urofsky, Melvin. 1991. *The continuity of change: The Supreme Court and individual liberties*. Belmont, Calif.: Wadsworth.

U.S. Department of Justice. 2004. Remarks of Deputy Attorney General James Comey regarding Jose Padilla, June 1, 2004, 4; http://www/justice.gov/dag/speech/2004/day6104.htm.

U.S. Department of Defense. 2004. News transcript, defense department background briefing on the combatant status review tribunals, July 7, 2004.

Vanberg, Georg. 2005. *The politics of constitutional review in Germany*. Cambridge: Cambridge University Press.

Vandevelde, Kenneth J. 1996. *Thinking like a lawyer: An introduction to legal reasoning*. Boulder, Colo.: Westview.

Van Duch, Darryl. 1996. Senior judge ranks close vacancy gap. *National Law Journal* 22 July 1996.

Van Hoy, Jerry. 1995. Selling and processing law; legal work at franchise law firms. *Law & Society Review* 29:703–30.

Van Natta, Don, Jr. 2001. Debate centers on which court will decide fate of Arab man. *The New York Times*, November 22, B6.

Vikoren, Susanne H. 1996. Justice of jurymander? Confronting the underrepresentation of racial groups in the jury pool of New York's eastern district. *Columbia Human Rights Law Review* 27:605–32.

Vining, Joseph. 1981. Justice, bureaucracy, and legal method. *Michigan Law Review* 80:248–58.

Volcansek, Mary L. 2001. Separation of powers and judicial impeachment. In *Congress confronts the Court: The struggle for legitimacy and authority in lawmaking*, ed. Colton C. Campbell and John F. Stack, Jr., 37–48 Lanham, Md.: Rowman & Littlefield.

Wagner-Pacifici, Robin. 1994. *Discourse and destruction: The city of Philadelphia versus MOVE*. Chicago: University of Chicago Press.

Wahlbeck, Paul. 1997. The life of the law: Judicial politics and legal change. *Journal of Politics* 59:778–802.

Walker, Jack L. 1977. Setting the agenda in the U. S. Senate: A theory of problem selection. *British Journal of Political Science* 7:423–45.

——. 1991. *Mobilizing interest groups in America: Patrons, professions, and social movements*. Ann Arbor: University of Michigan Press.

Walker, Samuel 1990. *In defense of American Liberties*. New York: Oxford University Press.

Walker, Thomas G. 1973. Behavioral tendencies in the three-judge district court. *American Journal of Political Science* 17:407–13.

Wallance, Gregory J. 2003. A judiciary in peril. *The Recorder*, November 7, 4.

Waltenburg, Eric, and Charles Lopeman. 2000. Tort decisions and campaign dollars. *Southeastern Political Review* 28:241–63.

Ward, Artemus, and David L. Weiden. 2006. *Sorcerers' apprentices: Law clerks at the U.S. Supreme Court.* New York: New York University Press.

Warren, Earl. 1969. Chief Justice Earl Warren's address to the bar association of the District of Columbia. *The Washington Post*, March 16, A1, A4.

Wasby, Stephen L. 1980. "Extra" judges in a federal appellate court: The Ninth Circuit. *Law & Society Review* 15:369–84.

——. 1984. How planned is "planned litigation"? *American Bar Foundation Research Journal* 32:83"138.

——. 1993. *The Supreme Court in the federal judicial system.* Chicago: Nelson-Hall.

——. 2002. How do courts of appeals en banc decisions fare in the U.S. Supreme Court? *Judicature* 85:182–9.

——. 2003a. The work of a circuit's chief judge. *Justice System Journal* 24:63–90.

——. 2003b. Clerking for an appellate judge: A close look. Paper presented at the Midwest Political Science Association, April 3–6, in Chicago.

——. 2004. Unpublished court of appeals decisions: A hard look at the process. *Southern California Interdisciplinary Law Journal* 14:67–124.

Wasby, Stephen, Anthony D'Amato, and Rosemary Metrailer. 1977. *Desegregation from Brown to Alexander: An exploration of Supreme Court Strategies.* Carbondale: Southern Illinois University Press.

The Washington Post. 2005a. Editorial: Real ID, real problems. February 10. A22.

The Washington Post. 2005b. Editorial: This is not the way. April 1. A26.

The Washington Post. 2006. Editorial: An inspector general? October 9. A16.

Watson, Tom. 1989. Seniors rescue courts in crisis. *Legal Times,* June 19.

Waxman, Seth P. 1998. "Presenting the case of the United States as it should be": The solicitor general in historical context. Address to the Supreme Court Historical Society, June 1, Washington, D.C.

Webster, Peter D. 1995. Selection and retention of judges: Is there one "best" method? *Florida State University Law Review* 23:1–42.

Weiler, Paul C., Howard Hiatt, Joseph P. Newhouse, and William G. Johnson. 1993. *A measure of malpractice: Medical injury, malpractice litigation, and patient compensation.* Cambridge, Mass.: Harvard University Press.

Weinstein, Henry, and Moises Mendoza. 2006. Ethics charges a bid for revenge, U.S. judge says. *The Los Angles Times,* September 22, B1.

Weyrich, Paul M. 1997. Letter soliciting contributions for the Judicial Selection Monitoring Project. August 17.

White, Josh. 2003. FBI intercepts Moussaoui's mail. *The Washington Post*, August 9, B2.

White, Leonard D. 1948. The federalists: A study in administrative history. New York: Macmillan.

——. 1958. The Republican era: 1869–1901, a study in administrative history. New York: Macmillan.

White, Lucie E. 1990. Subordination, rhetorical survival skills, and Sunday shoes: Notes on the hearing of Mrs. G. *Buffalo Law Review* 38:1–58.

White, Michelle J. 2002. Why the asbestos genie won't stay in the bankruptcy bottle. *University of Cincinnati Law Review* 70:1319–40.

Whittington, Keith. 1999. *Constitutional construction: Divided powers and constitutional meaning.* Cambridge, Mass.: Harvard University Press.

——. 2005. "Interpose your friendly hand": Political supports for the exercise of judicial review by the United States Supreme Court. *American Political Science Review* 99:583–96.

Widner, Jennifer. 2001. *Building the rule of law: Francis Nyalai and the road to judicial independence in Africa.* New York: Norton.

——. 2004. How some reflections on the United States' experience may inform African efforts to build court systems and the rule of law. In *Democratization and the judiciary: The accountability function of courts in new democracies*, ed. Siri Gloppen, Roberto Gargarella, and Elin Skaar, 27–45. London: Cass.

Wigmore, J. H. 1937. Roscoe Pound's St. Paul address of 1906. *Journal of American Judicature Society* 20:176.

Wilkinson, J. Harvie III. 1979. *From Brown to Bakke: The Supreme Court and school integration: 1954–1978.* New York: Oxford University Press.

Williams, Joan. 2000. *Unbending gender: Why family and work conflict and what to do about it.* New York: Oxford University Press.

Williams, Martha, and Jay Hall. 1972. Knowledge of the law in Texas: Socioeconomic and ethnic differences. *Law and Society Review* 7:99–118.

Williamson, David. 2002. Leading expert on U.S. Supreme Court practice publishes latest "Bible." *University of North Carolina News Services*, September 2. www.newswire.com.

Williston, Horace Gray, John B. Oakley and Robert S. Thompson. 1979. Law clerks in judges' eyes: Tradition and innovation in the use of legal staff by American judges. *California Law Review* 67:1286–1317.

Wilson, James Q. 1980. The politics of regulation. In *The politics of regulation*, ed. James Q. Wilson, 357–394. New York: Basic Books.

——. 1989. *Bureaucracy: What government agencies do and why they do it.* New York: Basic Books.

Wittes, Benjamin. 2006. *Confirmation wars: Preserving independent courts in angry times.* Lanham, Md.: Rowman & Littlefield.

Wood, B. Dan, and Richard Waterman. 1993. The politics of the U.S. antitrust regulation. *American Journal of Political Science* 37:1–39.

—— 1994. *Bureaucratic dynamics: The role of bureaucracy in a democracy.* Boulder, Colo.: Westview.

Woodward, Bob, and Scott Armstrong. 1979. *The brethren: Inside the Supreme Court.* New York: Simon & Schuster.

Worthen, Kevin J. 1994. Shirt-tales: Clerking for Byron White. *Brigham Young University Law Review* 1994:349–61.

Yakar, Itir. 2006. Unseen staff attorneys anchor state's top court: Institution's system of permanent employees means workers can outlast the justices. *San Francisco Daily Journal*, May 30.

Zeisel, Hans, and Shari Seidman Diamond. 1987. Convincing empirical evidence on the six-member jury. In *In the jury box: Controversies in the courtroom*, ed. Lawrence S. Wrightsman, Saul M. Kassin, and Cynthia E. Willis. Beverly Hills, CA: Sage Publications.

Zeydel, Edwin. 1955**.** *Goethe, the lyrist: 100 poems in new translations facing the originals with a biographical introduction.* Chapel Hill: University of North Carolina Press.

THE PAPERS OF THE JUSTICES

Hugo Black Papers, Manuscript Division, Library of Congress, Washington, D.C.
Harry A. Blackmun Papers, Manuscript Division, Library of Congress, Washington, D.C.
William O. Douglas Papers, Manuscript Division, Library of Congress, Washington, D.C.
John Marshall Harlan Papers, Princeton University Library, Princeton, N.J.
Thurgood Marshall Papers, Manuscript Division, Library of Congress, Washington, D.C.
Lewis F. Powell, Jr., Papers, Washington and Lee University School of Law, Lexington, Vir.
Stanley Forman Reed Oral History Project, Stanley Forman Reed Collection, Modern Political
    Archives, Division of Special Collections and Archives, University of Kentucky Libraries,
    University of Kentucky, Lexington, Kentucky.
Wiley Rutledge Papers, Manuscript Division, Library of Congress, Washington, D.C.
Harlan Fiske Stone Papers, Manuscript Division, Library of Congress, Washington, D.C.
Earl Warren Papers, Manuscript Division, Library of Congress, Washington, D.C.

TABLE OF CASES

Abington Township v. Schempp, 374 U.S. 203 (1963).
Adarand Constructors v. Peña, 515 U.S. 718 (1995).
Adkins v. Children's Hospital, 261 U.S. 525 (1923).
Al Odah v. United States, 321 F.3d 1134 (D.C. Cir. 2003).
Apodaca v. Oregon, 406 U.S. 404 (1972).
Arlington Heights v. Metropolitan Housing Development Corp., 429 U.S. 252 (1977).
Baker v. Carr, 369 U.S. 186 (1962).
Ballard v. United States, 329 U.S. 187 (1946).
Bates v. State Bar, 433 U.S. 350 (1977).
Batson v. Kentucky, 476 U.S. 79 (1986).
Berman v. Parker, 348 U.S. 26 (1954).
Board of Airport Commissioners v. Jews for Jesus, 482 U.S. 569 (1987).
Board of Education v. Allen, 392 U.S. 236 (1968).
Board of Education of Kiryas Joel v. Grumet, 512 U.S. 687 (1994).
Bob Jones University v. United States, 461 U.S. 574 (1983).
Bolling v. Sharpe, 347 U.S. 497 (1954).
Borel v. Fibreboard Paper Products Corporation, 493 F.2d 1076 (5th Cir. 1973).
Bowen v. Kendrick, 487 U.S. 589 (1988).
Bowers v. Hardwick, 478 U.S. 186 (1986).
Bradwell v. State, 83 U.S. 130 (1872).
Branzburg v. Hayes, 408 U.S. 665 (1972).
Braunfeld v. Brown, 366 U.S. 599 (1961).
Brown v. Board of Education, 347 U.S. 483 (1954).
Brown v. Board, 349 U.S. 294 (1955).
Brzonkala v. Morrison, 529 U.S. 598 (2000).
Bush v. Gore, 531 U.S. 98 (2000).
Caban v. Mohammed, 441 U.S. 380 (1979).
California Federal Savings and Loan Association v. Guerra, 479 U.S. 272 (1987).

Cantwell v. Connecticut, 310 U.S. 296 (1940).

Chaplinsky v. New Hampshire, 315 U.S. 568 (1942).

Cheney v. U.S. District Court for the District of Columbia, 542 U.S. 367 (2004).

Chisholm v. Georgia, 2 U.S. 419 (1793).

Church of Lukumi Babalu Aye v. Hialeah, 508 U.S. 520 (1993).

Civil Rights Cases, 109 U.S. 3 (1883).

City of Boerne v. Flores, 521 U.S. 507 (1997).

City of Richmond v. J. A. Croson Co., 448 U.S. 469 (1989).

Coalition of Clergy v. Bush, 189 F.Supp.2d 1036 (D.C. Cal. 2002).

Coalition of Clergy, Lawyers, & Professors v. Bush, 310 F.3d 1153 (9th Cir. 2002).

Craig v. Boren, 429 U.S. 190 (1976).

Danovitz v. United States, 281 U.S. 389 (1930).

DeFunis v. Odegaard, 416 U.S. 312 (1974).

Dickerson v. United States, 530 U.S. 428 (2000).

Dimick v. Republican Party of Minnesota, 126 S.Ct. 1165 (2006).

Dothard v. Rawlinson, 433 U.S. 321 (1977).

Dred Scott v. Sandford, 60 U.S. 393 (1857).

Edmonson v. Leesville Concrete Co., 500 U.S. 614 (1994).

Edwards v. Aguillard, 482 U.S. 578 (1987).

Elk Grove Unified School District v. Newdow, 542 U.S. 1 (2004).

Elkins v. United States, 364 U.S. 206 (1960).

Employment Division, Department of Human Resources of Oregon v. Smith, 494 U.S. 872 (1990).

Engel v. Vitale, 370 U.S. 421 (1962).

Escobedo v. Illinois, 378 U.S. 478 (1964).

Everson v. Board of Education, 330 U.S. 1 (1947).

Ex parte Milligan, 71 U.S. 2 (1866).

Ex parte Quirin, 317 U.S. 1 (1942).

Firefighters v. Cleveland, 478 U.S. 501(1986).

Firefighters Local Union #1784 v. Stotts, 467 U.S. 561 (1984).

Frontiero v. Richardson, 411 U.S. 677 (1973).

Fullilove v. Klutznick, 448 U.S. 448 (1980).

Furman v. Georgia, 408 U.S. 238 (1972).

General Electric v. Gilbert, 429 U.S.125 (1976).

Gherebi v. Bush, 262 F.Supp.2d 1064 (C.D. Cal. 2003).

Gherebi v. Bush, 352 F.3d 1278 (9th Cir. 2003).

Gideon v. Wainwright, 372 U.S. 335 (1963).

Gillette v. United States, 401 U.S 437 (1971).

Gitlow v. New York, 268 U.S. 652 (1925).

Goesaert v. Cleary, 335 U.S. 464 (1948).

Goldberg v. Kelly, 397 U.S. 254 (1970).

Goldman v. Weinberger, 475 U.S 503 (1986).

Gonzales v. Raich, 545 U.S. 1 (2005).

Goodridge v. Department of Public Health, 440 Mass. 309, 798 N.E. 2d 941 (2003).

Gratz v. Bollinger, 539 U.S. 244 (2003).

Greater Boston Television Corp. v. FCC, 444 F.2d 841 (D.C. Cir. 1970).

Gregg v. Georgia, 428 U.S. 153 (1976).

Griggs v. Duke Power Company, 401 U.S. 424 (1971).

Griswold v. Connecticut, 381 U.S. 479 (1965).

Grutter v. Bollinger, 539 U.S. 244 (2003).

Hamdan v. Rumsfeld, 344 F.Supp.2d 152 (D.D.C. 2004).

Hamdan v. Rumsfeld, 415 F.3d 33 (D.C. Cir. 2005).

Hamdan v. Rumsfeld, 126 S.Ct. 2749 (2006).

Hamdi v. Rumsfeld, 294 F.3d 598 (4th Cir. 2002).

Hamdi v. Rumsfeld, 296 F.3d 278 (4th Cir. 2002).

Hamdi v. Rumsfeld, 316 F.3d 450 (4th Cir. 2003).

Hamdi v. Rumsfeld, 337 F.3d 335 (4th Cir. 2003).

Hamdi v. Rumsfeld, 542 U.S. 507 (2004).

Hawaii Housing Authority v. Midkiff, 467 U.S. 229 (1984).

Heart of Atlanta Motel v. U.S., 379 U.S. 241 (1964).

Hernandez v. Texas, 347 U.S. 475 (1954).

Howe v. Smith, 452 U.S. 473 (1981).

Hoyt v. Florida, 368 U.S. 57 (1961).

In re Guantanamo Detainee Cases, 355 F.Supp.2d 443 (D.D.C. 2005).

Immigration and Naturalization Service v. Chadha, 462 U.S. 919 (1983).

J.E.B. v. Alabama ex rel. T.B., 511 U.S. 127 (1994).

Jett v. Dallas Independent School District, 490 U.S. 701 (1989).

Johnson v. Eisentrager, 339 U.S. 763 (1950).

Johnson v. Louisiana, 406 U.S. 356 (1972).

Johnson v.Transportation Agency,Santa Clara County, 480 U.S. 616 (1987).

Jones v. Opelika, 316 U.S. 584 (1942).

Karjala v. Johns-Manville Products Corporation, 523 F.2d 155 (8th Cir. 1975).

Khalid v. Bush, 355 F.Supp.2d 311 (D.D.C. 2005).

Kelo v. City of New London, 545 U.S. 469 (2005).

Kirchberg v. Feenstra, 450 U.S. 455 (1981).

Korematsu v. United States, 323 U.S. 214 (1944).

Lamb's Chapel v. Center Moriches School District, 508 U.S. 384 (1993).

Larkin v. Grendel's Den, 459 U.S. 116 (1982).

Lawrence v. Texas, 539 U.S. 558 (2003).

Lee v. International Society for Krishna Consciousness, 505 U.S. 830 (1992).

Lee v. Weisman, 505 U.S. 577 (1992).

Lemon v. Kurtzman, 403 U.S. 602 (1971).

Lochner v. New York, 198 U.S. 45 (1905).

Lorance v. AT&T Technologies, 490 U.S. 900 (1989).

Mabee v. White Plains Pub. Co., 327 U.S. 178 (1946).

Malloy v. Hogan, 378 U.S. 1 (1964).

Mapp v. Ohio, 367 U.S. 643 (1961).

Marbury v. Madison, 5 U.S. 137 (1803).

Martin v. Wilks, 490 U.S. 755 (1989).

McDonnell-Douglas Corporation v. Green, 411 U.S. 792 (1973).

McGowan v. Maryland, 366 U.S. 420 (1961).

McLaurin v. Oklahoma, 339 U.S. 637 (1950).

Metro Broadcasting, Inc. v. Federal Communications Commission, 497 U.S. 547 (1990).

Metropolitan Washington Airports Authority v. Citizens for the Abatement of Aircraft Noise, Inc., 501 U.S. 252 (1991).

Michael M. v. Superior Court of Sonoma County, 450 U.S. 464 (1981).

Miller v. Albright, 523 U.S. 420 (1998).

Miller v. Georgia, 515 U.S. 900 (1995).

Miller-El v. Dretke, 545 U.S. 231 (2005).

Minersville School District v. Gobitis, 310 U.S. 586 (1940).

Minor v. Happersett, 88 U.S. 162 (1875).

Miranda v. Arizona, 384 U.S. 436 (1966).

Missouri ex rel. Gaines v. Canada, 305 U.S. 337 (1938).

Monroe v. Pape, 365 U.S. 167 (1961).

Moose Lodge v. Irvis, 407 U.S. 163 (1972).

Moran v. Johns-Manville Sales Corporation, 691 F.2d 811 (6th Cir. 1982).

Morrison v. Olson, 487 U.S. 654 (1988).

Moussaoui v. United States, 282 F.Supp.2d 481 (E.D. Va. 2003).

Moussaoui v. United States, 544 U.S. 931 (2005).

Muller v. Oregon, 208 U.S. 412 (1908).

Murdoch v. Pennsylvania, 319 U.S. 105 (1943).

Myers v. United States, 272 U.S. 52 (1926).

NAACP v. Button, 371 U.S. 415 (1963).

Nguyen v. Immigration and Naturalization Service, 533 U.S. 53 (2001).

O'Lone v. Estate of Shabazz, 482 U.S 342 (1987).

Oregon v. Mitchell, 400 U.S. 112 (1970).

Orr v. Orr, 440 U.S. 268 (1979).

Padilla v. Hanft, 389 F. Supp. 2d 678 (2005).

Padilla v. Hanft, 423 F.3d 386 (4th Cir. 2005).

Padilla v. Hanft, 126 S.Ct. 1649 (2006).

Padilla ex rel. Newman v. Bush, 233 F.Supp.2d 564 (S.D.N.Y. 2002).

Padilla ex rel. Newman v. Rumsfeld, 243 F.Supp.2d 42 (S.D.N.Y. 2003).

Padilla v. Rumsfeld, 352 F.3d 695 (2d Cir. 2003).

Parents Involved in Community Schools v. Seattle School District No. 1, 127 S.Ct. 2738 (2007).

Patterson v. McLean Credit Union, 491 U.S. 164 (1989).

Personnel Administrator v. Feeney, 462 U.S, 256 (1979).

Phillips v. Martin-Marietta Corporation, 400 U.S. 502 (1971).

P.J. Carlin Construction Co. et al v. Heaney et. al., 299 U.S. 41 (1936).

Planned Parenthood of Southeastern Pennsylvania v. Casey, 505 U.S. 833 (1992).

Plessy v. Ferguson, 163 U.S. 537 (1896).

Pollock v. Farmers' Loan & Trust, 158 U.S. 601 (1895).

Powers v. Ohio, 499 U.S. 400 (1991).

Price-Waterhouse v. Hopkins, 490 U.S. 228 (1989).

Rasul v. Bush, 215 F.Supp.2d 55 (D.D.C. 2002).

Rasul v. Bush, 542 U.S. 466 (2004).

R.A.V. v. St. Paul, 505 U.S. 377 (1992).

Reed v. Reed, 404 U.S. 71 (1971).

Regents of the University of California v. Bakke, 438 U.S. 265 (1978).

Republican Party of Minnesota v. White, 416 F.3d 738 (8th Cir. 2005).

Reynolds v. Sims, 377 U.S. 533 (1964).

Reynolds v. United States, 98 U.S. 145 (1878).

Roe v. Wade, 410 U.S. 113 (1973).

Roper v. Simmons, 543 U.S. 551 (2005).

Rosenfeld v. Southern Pacific Company, 444 F.2nd 1219 (9th Cir. 1971).

Rostker v. Goldberg, 453 U.S. 57 (1981).

Rumsfeld v. Padilla, 542 U.S. 426 (2004).

Santa Fe Independent School District v. Doe, 530 U.S. 290 (2000).

Shaw v. Reno, 509 U.S. 630 (1993).

Sheet Metal Workers v. EEOC, 478 U.S. 421(1986).

Shelton v. Tucker, 364 U.S. 479 (1960).

Sherbert v. Verner, 374 U.S. 398 (1963).

Slaughter-House Cases, 83 U.S. 36 (1872).

South Carolina v. Katzenbach, 383 U. S. 301 (1966).

South Dakota v. Dole, 483 U.S. 203 (1987).

Stanley v. Illinois, 405 U.S. 645 (1972).

Strauder v. West Virginia, 100 U.S. 303 (1880).

Swain v. Alabama, 380 U.S. 202 (1965).

Swann v. Charlotte-Mecklenburg Board of Education, 401 U.S. 1 (1971).

Sweatt v. Painter, 339 U.S. 629 (1950).

Texas v. Johnson, 491 U.S. 397 (1989).

Thomas v. Review Board, 450 U.S. 707 (1981).

United Auto Workers v. Johnson Controls, 499 U.S. 187 (1991).

United Mine Workers of American v. Bagwell, 512 U.S. 821 (1994).

United States v. Carolene Products Company, 304 U.S. 144 (1938).

United States v. Eichman, 496 U.S. 310 (1990).

United States v. Hatter, 532 U.S. 557 (2001).

United States v. Lee, 455 U.S. 252 (1982).

United States v. Lindh, 227 F.Supp.2d 565, (E.D. Va. 2002).

United States v. Lopez, 514 U.S. 549 (1995).

United States v. Morrison, 529 U.S. 598 (2000).

United States v. Moussaoui, 333 F.3d 509 (4th Cir. 2003).

United States v. Moussaoui, 336 F.3d 279 (4th Cir. 2003).

United States v. Moussaoui, 365 F.3d 292 (4th Cir. 2004).

United States v. Moussaoui, 382 F.3d 453 (4th Cir. 2004).

United States v. Paradise, 480 U.S. 149 (1987).

United States v. Seeger, 380 U.S. 163 (1965).

United States v. Virginia, 518 U.S. 515 (1996).

United States v. Will, 449 U.S. 200 (1980).

United States v. Yazell, 382 U.S. 431 (1966).

United Steelworkers of America v. Weber, 443 U.S. 197 (1979).

Walz v. Tax Commissioners, 397 U.S 664 (1970).

Wards Cove Packing Company v. Atonio, 490 U.S.642 (1989).

Washington v. Davis, 426 U.S. 229 (1976).

Welsh v. United States, 398 U.S. 333 (1970).

Wesberry v. Sanders, 376 U.S. 1 (1964).

West Coast Hotel v. Parrish, 300 U.S. 379 (1937).

West Virginia State Board of Education v. Barnette, 319 U.S. 624 (1943).

Williams v. United States, 240 F3d 1019 (Fed. Cir. 2001).

Williams v. United States, 535 U.S. 911 (2002).

Wisconsin v. Yoder, 406 U.S. 205 (1972).

Wolman v. Walter, 433 U.S. 229 (1977).

Worcester v. Georgia, 31 U.S. 515 (1832).

Wyatt v. Stickney, 344 F.Supp. 373 (M.D. Ala. 1972).

Youngstown Co. v. Sawyer, 343 U.S. 579 (1952).

INDEX